BRITISH
MILITARY
AIRCRAFT
SERIALS 1878-1987

BRITISH
MILITARY
AIRCRAFT
SERIALS 1878-1987

COMPILED BY
BRUCE ROBERTSON

MIDLAND COUNTIES PUBLICATIONS

First published in 1964 by Ian Allan.
Fourth revised edition 1971
Fifth revised edition by Patrick Stephens Ltd, 1979.

This edition published by
Midland Counties Publications,
24 The Hollow, Earl Shilton, Leicester, LE9 7NA

Printed in England by
Oxford University Press Printing House.

Contents

Front Cover photograph:
Four Tornado F.2s (ZD934/AD, ZD904/AE, ZD901/AA and ZD903/AB) of 229 OCU grace a sunny apron at their Coningsby base during the summer of 1986. Note the unit codes and tail markings, also the lateral serials, carried in white on the fin *(Paul Jackson)*.

Back Cover photograph:
Short S.2 flying boat N177 displays larger than usual serials in keeping with the large proportions of this craft. This particular hull was of all-metal construction, fitted with a Porte-Felixstowe F.5 superstructure.

Foreword

This book contains a compilation of all aircraft known to have been ordered, acquired, impressed for, or presented to the British Services from 1878 to the present day. The Services concerned are the Royal Engineers, Royal Navy, Royal Flying Corps, Royal Naval Air Service, Royal Air Force, Fleet Air Arm, Army Air Corps and the Air Training Corps. Included also are service aircraft held on charge by ministries acting as agencies for the Services, such as the Ministry of Munitions, Ministry of Supply, Ministry of Aviation, Ministry of Technology and the Ministry of Aviation Supplies of the past, and the present Procurement Executive of the Ministry of Defence.

The compilation is by the official service serial numbers allotted in numerical sequence, and then by alphabetical and numerical sequence following the introduction of prefix letters. In general the alphabetical/numerical progression is in chronological sequence, but where this is not so, the compilation has still been given in strict alphabetical/numerical sequence for ease of reference, by letter and number.

The compilations have been divided up into appropriate sections, to make special points about the range of numbers in that section. For example the allocations for Lend/Lease aircraft are compartmented for their numbers were in general in sequence, whereas British aircraft from wartime production had numbers issued in blocks, omitting runs of numbers to confuse enemy intelligence in assessing production. Such changes are explained at the appropriate section headings.

This edition is the sixth revision and the first reprint to be completely revised throughout and reset. Not only does it update the earlier editions, and go back in time to include balloons, but it contains much new information throughout the whole serialling range as a result of continuing research.

In order to derive maximum benefit from a full understanding of this book, readers should consult the 'Compilation Notes' which appear opposite, and which contain more detailed explanations of the conventions which have been adopted.

It is hoped that readers will find this publication useful, and any feedback, whether by way of additions or amendments for inclusion in a possible future edition, would be welcomed, via the publishers.

London, 1987   Bruce Robertson

Acknowledgements

Over the years I have had reason to be grateful to many who gave initial help with the compilation and they and others who have contributed to additions in subsequent editions. I give my thanks to (listed alphabetically) R.C.B. Ashworth, M.J.F.Bowyer, J.M.Bruce ISO MA both for personal assistance and by his works, P.H.Butler for information on gliders and Air Min serials, Robert J. Carter, J.M.Cheers, E.F.Cheeseman for assistance on 1914-18 allocations from the outset, W.R.Chorley, Rose Coombs, R.W.Deacon, Dermot Doran, H.J.Fairhead, M.P.Fillmore, A.A.Foster, H.W.Gandy, M.H.Goodhall, Donald M.Hannah, Terry Hobbs, P.A.Jackson, Philip Jarrett, G.A.Jenks, Stuart Leslie for his regular additions from the first edition, Roger Lindsay, Keith Mann, Tim Mason, D.E.Monk, E.B.Morgan, the late Peter Moss for his research on impressed aircraft, James D.Oughton, Arthur Pearcy Jnr, Stephen Ransom, Alex Revell, Douglas Rough, the late H.H.Russell, Ray Sturtivant, W.J.Taylor, Gerard Terry, J.A.Todd, J.D.Thomas, Lt Col J.D. Thompson USAF, Gordon Swanborough, Norbert F. Yaggi and Frank Yeoman. Of those named, H.W.(Wal) Gandy and P.H.Butler in particular have made a valuable and comprehensive contribution to this new edition. The photographs in this edition are from the author's collection unless specifically stated otherwise. The majority of original research for this work was undertaken by the author but it would be quite unfair to let go unrecorded and unthanked the hundreds of enthusiasts who over many years have contributed to other published sources - most notably those of Air-Britain and the British Aviation Research Group. Long may they continue!

Compilation Notes

In the bulk of the compilations, the numbers on the left of the page relate to the range of numbers allotted to a particular order; whether or not they may be taken as consecutive depends on the section. As a general guide numbers up to L7272 were allotted consecutively and from then onwards, with the exception of Lend/Lease and certain other aircraft numbers have been issued in blocks leaving many numbers unused.

The aircraft type is given by the design firm's name, type number where appropriate, official service type name and mark number. This is to fulfil the prime object of the compilation to provide a precise type for any serial number being checked upon.

Mark numbers are given according to the ruling of the period in which they appeared. In 1942 role prefix letters were introduced to mark numbers and from 1948 marks, previously given in Roman numerals, changed to Arabic figures. It should be appreciated that it would not have been appropriate to introduce these changes at a particular point in the listings, for serials are in general allotted at the ordering stage, and while some aircraft evolve in months, others take years to materialize. Mark numbers have therefore been given in the form appropiate to their time of service entry or to their service period.

Aircraft designing firms are not always the manufacturer. In the First World War less than a tenth of the Sopwith Camels built were made by Sopwith Aviation, between the wars Hawker Hart and Hind production was shared around the industry and the sub-contracting of complete aircraft orders was common in the Second World War. In each case, where aircraft orders were built other than by the design firm this information is always given in the Remarks under the title line.

The quantity is given at the right of the page for each order and relates to the number built. Where an order was not completed the total quantity ordered is given in brackets and the actual number built is placed in front, thus a recording '60(80)' would mean that sixty out of an order for eighty were built and a recording (400) would mean that an order placed for 400 aircraft was cancelled before any were built. If the latter case might seem to be rather negative recording, it does fill in gaps in the sequence of allocations and shows what was planned in addition to what materialised. Although some aircraft orders may not have reached fruition, they may well have involved a considerable effort in man hours, in material preparation, planning, costing and even part-building.

In sections with 'black-out' blocks — numbers not used to confuse enemy or potential enemy intelligence — which concerns the bulk of service aircraft from 1937 to the present day, the numbers actually allotted are given in the Remarks column. Also, where aircraft within a particular order were built to different standards, denoted by Mark or Series number, or converted subsequently to a different standard, this information is given as 'Remarks'.

To give the maximum of information in the minimum of space, considerable abbreviation has been necessary. In all cases a hyphen between numbers should read as 'to'; for example 1054-1563 would mean the 510 numbers from 1054 to 1563. A stroke between the numbers should be read as 'and', so that 1054/1563 would mean the two numbers 1054 and 1563.

It has not been possible to give a run-down on each individual aircraft, for that would take hundreds of books. An appendix of books which list particular aircraft types or particular ranges in detail is included on page 229. Consideration has however been given to the inclusion of general relevant information in addition to the basic information, concerning items as given below.

A guide to the Service to which aircraft were delivered is considered pertinent information. In the case of the RFC and RNAS, the range of numbers is the guide to the service for which they were ordered and the headings to these sections will give such notification. In the case of subsequent transfers to another service, such information will be given in the remarks column. From 1918 the vast majority of orders were for the RAF and this may be taken to be so in all cases except where otherwise stated. Offsets from production for service to Commonwealth and other air forces are also recorded as far as space permits.

Constructors numbers have been given in some cases where available and practicable. Fairey numbers have been given in particular since these were marked near the serial number. In the case of prototypes, their official specification numbers have been given together with significant first flight date.

Subsequent civil registration has been given for a number of aircraft, but it was not practical to give this information for Tiger Moth, Auster, Proctor, etc aircraft which would require another book. For details of British 'demobbed' aircraft readers may like to consult the companion Midland Counties book *British Civil Aircraft Registers* by Dave Peel.

Where old aircraft have been preserved a note has been given to this effect, but this has not been extended to postwar aircraft types in deference to space considerations and clashing with other publications.

Aircraft becoming instructional airframes have been noted in the remarks up to 1945. Further information appears in Appendix C.

In all cases, where lists are given with re-numberings or changes of identity, recordings may be taken to read respectively, although that word has not been used to avoid its repetition throughout.

Abbreviations

Letters	Explanation
A	Airborne Forces Aircraft (as role letter)
AA	Anti-aircraft gunfire
AAC	Army Air Corps
AACU	Anti-Aircraft Co-operation Unit
A & AEE	Aircraft and Armament Experimental Establishment
AAU	Anti-Aircraft Unit
AD	Air Department (of Admiralty)
ADGB	Air Defence of Great Britain
Adm	Admiralty
AEW	Airborne Early Warning (role letters)
AF	Air Force
AFC	Australian Flying Corps
AGS	Air Gunners School
AH	Army Helicopter (role letters)
AHQ	Air Headquarters
AL	Army Liaison (role letters)
AMC	Aircraft Manufacturing Company, later known as Airco
AM Spec	Air Ministry Specification
ANS	Air Navigation School
AOP	Air Observation Post (role letters)
ARD	Aircraft Repair Depot
ARS	Aircraft Repair Station
AS	Armstrong Siddeley, Airspeed or Anti-Submarine as role letters
ASR	Air-Sea Rescue (role letters)
ATA	Air Transport Auxiliary
ATAF	Allied Tactical Air Force
ATC	Air Training Corps
AW	Armstrong Whitworth
B	Bomber (role letter)
BAC	British Aircraft Corporation
BAe	British Aerospace
BAT	British Aerial Transport Company
B & C	British & Colonial Aircraft Company (Bristol Aircraft)
BEA	British European Airways
BEF	British Expeditionary Force
BHP	Beardmore-Halford-Pulinger engine
B(I)	Bomber (Intruder/Interdictor) (role letters)
B(K)	Bomber (Tanker) role letters
BOAC	British Overseas Airways Corporation
B & P/BP	Boulton & Paul (which became Boulton Paul)
B(PR)	Bomber (Photo Reconnaissance) (role letters)
BR	Bentley Rotary (engine designation)
C	Transport (role letter)
CAACU	Civilian Anti-aircraft Co-operation Unit
CAF	Canadian Air Force (1918-19)
CC	Transport/Communications (role letters)
CD	Catapult dummy

CFE	Central Fighter Establishment
CFS	Central Flying School
C/n	Constructor's number
COD	Courier/Carrier Onboard Delivery (role letters)
Comm	Communications
conv	Converted
COW	Coventry Ordnance Works
CSE	Central Signals Establishment
CU	Conversion Unit
D	Drone (role letter)
DB	Dive Bomber (role letters)
DC	Dual Control or Douglas Commercial depending on context
DH	de Havilland
DHC	de Havilland of Canada
D of R	Director of Research
DR	Derated (engine designation suffix)
DW	Role letters for mine exploding installation
E	Electronic (role letter)
EATS	Empire Air Training Scheme
ECM	Electronic Counter Measures
EFTS	Elementary Flying Training School
Est	Establishment
F	Fighter (role letter)
FAA	Fleet Air Arm
FAF	French Air Force
F(AW)	Fighter (All Weather) (role letters)
FB	Fighter Bomber (role letters)
FBA	Franco-British Aviation
FE	Far East
ff	First flight
FFAF	Free French Air Force
FG	Fighter Ground Attack (role letters)
FGA	Fighter Ground Attack (role letters)
FGAF	Federal German Air Force
FGR	Fighter Ground attack Reconnaissance (role letters)
FK	Frederick Koolhoven (designer's initials)
Flt	Flight
FP	Full Power (Engine designation suffix) otherwise Floatplane
FR	Fighter Reconnaissance (role letters)
FRS	Fighter Reconnaissance Strike (role letters)
FTS	Flying Training School
GA	Ground Attack (role letters)
GAL	General Aircraft Limited
GHQ	General Headquarters
Gov't	Government
GP	General Purpose
GR	Ground Attack Reconnaissance or General Reconnaissance pre-1950 (role letters)
GT	Glider Tug (role letters)
HAR	Helicopter Air Rescue (role letters)
HAS	Helicopter Anti-Submarine (role letters)
HC	Helicopter Cargo (role letters)
HF	Henry Farman or High Fighter as role letters
HP	Handley Page

hp	horse power
HR	Helicopter Rescue (role letters)
HS	Hawker Siddeley
HT	Helicopter Training (role letters)
HU	Helicopter Utility (role letters)
IAC	Irish Air Corps
IAF	Indian Air Force (later RIAF)
IEAF	Imperial Ethiopian Air Force
K	Tanker (role letter)
KLM	Koninklijke Luchtvaart Maatschappij (Royal Dutch Airlines)
LAP	London Aircraft Production Group
LF	Low Fighter (role letters)
LL	Leigh Light
LR	Long Range
MAAF	Malayan Auxiliary Air Force
MAEE	Marine Aircraft Experimental Establishment
MAP	Ministry of Aircraft Production
MDAP	Mutual Defence Air Pact
MDD	McDonnell-Douglas
ME	Middle East
MEAF	Middle East Air Force
MET	Meteorological (role letters)
MF	Maurice Farman
mg	machine gun
Mk	Mark number
Mintech	Ministry of Technology
MOA	Ministry of Aviation
MOD	Ministry of Defence
MOS	Ministry of Supply
MR	Martime Reconnaissance (role letters)
MRCA	Multi-Role Combat Aircraft
MS	Morane Saulnier
MU	Maintenance Unit
NA	North American Company
NAF	National Aircraft Factory
NATO	North Atlantic Treaty Organisation
NF	Night Fighter
nr	near
NZ	New Zealand
OCU	Operational Conversion Unit
OTU	Operational Training Unit
PE	Procurement Executive (MOD)
PR	Photographic Reconnaissance (role letters)
PV	Port Victoria (1915-18); Private Venture from 1920
R	Reconnaissance (role letter)
RAAF	Royal Australian Air Force
RAE	Royal Aircraft Establishment
RAF	Royal Aircraft Factory pre-1918, Royal Air Force from 1918
RAN	Royal Australian Navy
RATG	Rhodesian Air Training Group
RATO	Rocket-assisted take-off

RCAF	Royal Canadian Air Force
RCeyAF	Royal Ceylon Air Force
RCN	Royal Canadian Navy
REAF	Royal Egyptian Air Force
RFA	Royal Fleet Auxiliary
RFC	Royal Flying Corps
RHAF	Royal Hellenic Air Force
RIAF	Royal Indian Air Force
RIraqiAF	Royal Iraqi Air Force
RJAF	Royal Jordanian Air Force
RMAF	Royal Malaysian Air Force
RN	Royal Navy
RNAS	Royal Naval Air Service
RNethAF	Royal Netherlands Air Force
RNorAF	Royal Norwegian Air Force
RNZAF	Royal New Zealand Air Force
RNZN	Royal New Zealand Navy
RP	Rocket Projectile or Ruston Proctor (context)
RPAF	Royal Pakistan Air Force
R-R	Rolls-Royce
RRAF	Royal Rhodesian Air Force
RRE	Royal Radar Establishment
RS	Reserve Squadron
RSAF	Royal Swedish Air Force
RSJ	Ransome, Sims and Jefferies
S	Strike (role letters)
SAAF	South African Air Force
SBAC	Society of British Aircraft Constructors
SEAC	South East Asia Command
SEDB	Single-engined day bomber
S & H	Short & Harland
Spec	Specification
Sqn	Squadron
SR	Strategic Reconnaissance (role letter)
SRAF	Southern Rhodesian Air Force
Srs	Series
SS	Single-seat
SSVAF	Straits Settlements Volunteer Air Force
ST	Standard Transport (role letters)
STOL	Short Take-off and Landing
T	Trainer (role letter)
TRE	Telecommunications Research Establishment
TDS	Training Depot Station
TF	Torpedo Fighter (role letters)
TM	Two-man (two-seat)
TS	Training Squadron (1914-19)
TSR	Torpedo Spotter Reconnaissance up to 1945 then Tactical Strike Reconnaissance
TR	Tactical Reconnaissance (role letters)
TT	Target Towing (role letters)
TX	Training glider (role letters)
U	Unmanned, drone (role letter)
u/c	undercarriage
UK	United Kingdom
US/USA	United States of America
USAAF	United States Army Air Force
USAF	United States Air Force
USAS	United States Air Service
USMC	United States Marine Corps

USN	United States Navy
USSR	Union of Soviet Socialist Republics
VA	Vickers Armstrong
VIP	Very Important Person
VTOL	Vertical Take-off and Landing
W	Weather (role letter)
WGAF	West German Air Force
WS	Westland/Sikorsky
W/T	Wireless Telegraphy

Balloons 1878-1919

The first military aircraft was a balloon for which the War Office had allotted the sum of £150; it first ascended on 23rd August, 1878. This balloon was appropriately named *Pioneer* and so set the style of names as the nomenclature for balloons and the army's airships which were to follow some thirty years later. A second balloon, funded by Captain J L B Templer of the Royal Engineers, was given the name *Crusader* and demonstrated to army units the following year.

Those early balloons had been built at Woolwich Arsenal in an allotted building known as the Balloon Store. The so-called store moved in 1882 to Chatham as a balloon factory where *Sapper* of 5,600 cubic feet was followed by *Heron* of 10,000 cubic feet. From 1884 there was an intention to standardise on army balloons in three classes of capabilities in cubic feet as given: F (5,000), S (7,000), T (10,000), followed later by A (13,000) and V (11,500). The class letters, it will be seen, were not allotted alphabetically, but applied to the initial letter of the first of each class, with others to the same pattern having a name with the same initial letter. Examples are *Fly*, first of the F Class and *Spy* and *Swallow* of the S Class.

Experiments with elongated balloons led to airships which the army allotted names as tabled in the section following. All lighter-than-air craft were handed over to the Royal Navy in 1913. As a result the British Expeditionary Force on France, 1915-16 had to rely on the RNAS for observation balloons in the field. The navy's balloons were numbered from No.1 by each unit in which they served. The position in late 1915 before the War Office took over control of sections in the field was as follows:

Station, Unit or Ship	Location	Identities
Balloon Training Station	Roehampton	Nos.1-7
No.1 Kite Balloon Section	HMS *Manica* on foreign service	Nos.1 & 2
No.2 Kite Balloon Section	British Expeditionary Force	Nos.1 & 2
No.3 Kite Balloon Section	HMS *Hector* on foreign service	Nos.1 & 2
No.4 Kite Balloon Section	British Expeditionary Force	No.1 only
No.5 Kite Balloon Section	RFA *Menelaus* in home waters	No.1 only
No.6 Kite Balloon Section	British Expeditionary Force	No.1 only
No.7 Kite Balloon Section	RFA *Canning* relieving *Manica*	Nos.1 & 2
No.8 Kite Balloon Section	British Expeditionary Force	No.1 only
No.9 Kite Balloon Section	Mobilising	No.1 only

As a central record the RNAS allotted balloons a serial number at the contract stage, prefixed by significant letters indicative of the manufacturer as follows:

Serial Number	Type, Maker and Remarks
A1-75	Drachen (800m³)
	Airships Ltd, 7 cancelled, 29 to RFC
AC1-14	Streamline
	Airships Ltd. Delivered 1917-18
A Mk II 1-21	M Mk II
	Airships Ltd, Built in 1917
AM1-78	M
	Airships Ltd. 7 transferred to RFC
AM79-164	M
	Airships Ltd. 2 to Allied Navies
AN1-9	Drachen (900m³)
	Airships Ltd. All transferred to RFC
AS1-9	Drachen (1100m³)
	Airships Ltd. 2 transferred to RFC
AW1-24	W
	Airships Ltd. All retained in RNAS
BM1-2	M (930m³)
	Wm Beardmore & Co. Cancelled
BP1-12	Drachen
	Wm Beardmore & Co. Cancelled
BW1-9	M (200m³)
	Wm Beardmore & Co. Cancelled
F1-14	Drachen
	Made in France. 4 transferred to RFC
FM1-2	M
	Made in France. Both deleted in RNAS
MM1-94+	M
	J Mandelberg & Co. 2 to US Navy

MW1-12	W
	J Mandelberg & Co. Delivered from late 1917
S1-46	Drachen (800m³)
	C G Spencer & Sons. 4 cancelled, 29 to RFC
SM1-12	Drachen (200m³)
	C G Spencer & Sons. 1 transferred to RFC
SM13-16	W
	C G Spencer & Sons. All deleted in RNAS
SW1-88	W
	C G Spencer & Sons. Delivered in 1918
V1-26	Drachen (800m³)
	Vickers Ltd. 12 cancelled

The Type W for Weather balloons were of 117m³ capacity of Mk I and II versions, spherical and with pointed nose and tail respectively.

Balloons for the RFC it appears were recorded as items of equipment and not by individual identities, but that like the RNAS, balloons were numbered for each section in the field. As a section normally held one balloon and a reserve, balloons were known by the Section identity which in 1918 under the RAF were Section Nos. 1 to 6, 8-16, 18-25, 28-32, 34-48 in France; 7 & 33 in Italy; 17, 26-27 in Salonika; 49-50, 54 (disbanded May 1918) and 57 Palestine, 51-52 Mesopotamia and 55 & 56 mobilising at Richmond Park for shipment to Egypt and 58 at Larkhill for Artillery School work.

For fleet use as an anti-submarine measure, balloons were numbered by the Balloon Base holding them, the quantity held varying. Where the establishment of balloons to be held is known this is given for the Balloon Bases, also known by number, in 1918:- 1 Malta, 2 Alexandria, 3 Brindisi, 4 Corfu, 5 Gibraltar, 6 Bizerta, 7 Lowestoft, 8 Immingham, 9 Milford Haven, 12 Shotley, 13 Rathmullan (Lough Swilly), 14 Hythe, 15 Tipnor (4), 16 Merifield, 18 North Queensferry (24), 19 Houten Bay (12), 20 Caldale (12), 21 Lerwick (Grimsta), 22 Port Said, 23 Milo, 25 HMS *Canning* (5). Nos.7, 10, 11, 17 believed transferred to US Navy and 24 not opened.

Balloons were also numbered by the training establishments which in 1918 were: Nos.1 & 2 Balloon Training Depots at Roehampton and Richmond, Nos. 1 & 2 Balloon Training Schools at Larkhill and Lydd, No. 1 Balloon Training Base at Sheerness and No.1 Free Balloon School at Hurlingham. A Free Balloon Training Section at Kennington Oval was disbanded 11th May 1918.

Additionally No.7 Balloon Wing with headquarters at the Royal Forest Hotel, Chingford, controlled Nos.1-3 Balloon Squadrons at Longbridge Farm, Barking; Broomhill Way, Woodford and Wood Lodge, Shooters Hill, SE London. But as these were concerned with un-manned barrage balloons numbered according to the barrage apron they supported, they and the barrage balloons of World War Two have not been deemed to be within the scope of this work.

Most balloon units were disbanded in late 1918 and 1919, but Kite Balloon Mine Clearing Units were still active in 1920. The Deputy Directorate of Kite Balloons ceased to exist at the Air Ministry from 1st June 1919 and the few balloons retained were re-numbered under the Kite Balloon Section of the Director of Research and a few remained until 1940.

Airships 1907-1920

The Army acquired its first airship in 1907; this and all subsequent airships were given names. The Navy acquired its first airship in 1911 and adopted a simple numbering system starting at No. 1; but to distinguish rigid airships (i.e. with gas envelopes contained within a metal or wood frame) from the non-rigid airships (i.e. the gas-filled envelope conditioning shape as with a balloon), an 'R' prefix was added to the number allotted to rigid types.

The Naval Wing of the Royal Flying Corps, which in July 1914 became officially the Royal Naval Air Service, took control of all military airships from 1st July 1914 and the former named Army airships were renumbered in the naval series as Nos.17-22 and are thereby out of chronological sequence as regards their date of building.

Balloons & Airships

Type, Name or Number	Remarks on Class, Builder and Power Units
Nulli Secundus	Built at the Balloon Factory, Farnborough, this was the first military airship constructed in Britain. Of 50,000cu ft it first flew on 10.9.07 powered by an Antoinette engine of 40hp driving two metal-bladed propellers. Rebuilt as *Nulli Secundus II*.
Nulli Secundus II	*Nulli Secundus* rebuilt with Lebaudy-type car, first flew 24.7.08.
Baby	Built 1908-1909 at the Balloon Factory of 21,000cu ft powered by two Buchet engines later replaced by an REP engine. First flew 4.5.09.
Clement Bayard	Built by Clement Bayard and delivered from Paris 16.10.10 under *Daily Mail* reader presentation arrangements. Taken over by the Army but owing to 13,000cu ft of gas being necessary daily was deflated and stored at Farnborough.
Lebaudy	Built by Lebaudy Freres of 350,000cu ft under subscription arrangements by *Morning Post* readers. Powered by two 150hp engines was flown to Farnborough 26.10.10, but damaged entering shed which was too small. After repair was wrecked on trial flight 5.11.
Naval Airship No.1 (Mayfly)	First British naval airship. Built by Vickers at Barrow. Of rigid type of 660,000cu ft and powered by two 200hp Wolseley engines. Broke back on initial trials 24.9.11.
Naval Airship No.2 (ex-Willows No.4)	Small non-rigid of 24,000cu ft for training purposes designed by T E Willows and built in France and Spain; powered by 35hp Anzani engine. Envelope used for the blimp SS1.
Naval Airship No.3 (Astra Torres)	Non-rigid of 229,450cu ft, powered by two 210hp Chenu engines, ordered from France in 1912. Delivered 1913 and was equipped with Hotchkiss machine guns. Deleted May 1916 after service at Kingsnorth.
Naval Airship No.4 (Parseval PL18)	Non-rigid of 330,000cu ft ordered from Germany in 1912. Powered by two 170hp Maybach engines. Deleted July 1917 after service at Kingsnorth.
Nos.5-7 (Parseval PL19-21)	Ordered from Germany as same class as No.4, but were held by Germany when war was declared. Substitute airships were ordered from Vickers powered by two 200hp Renault engines, but were relegated for training use only.
No.8 (Astra Torres)	Delivered from France. Deleted May 1916 after use at Kingsnorth.
R9 (Modified Z4)	Built by Vickers at Barrow. Powered by two 180hp and one 250hp Maybach engines. Was first airship to bear the 'R' for rigid prefix marking. Trials from 27.11.16. To station at Howden 4.4.17.
No.10 (Astra Torres)	French-built. Envelope used for blimp C1.
Nos.11-13 (Forlanini)	Ordered July 1913 from Italy, not delivered.
R14-15 (R9 Type)	Order cancelled.
No.16 (Astra Torres)	French-built. Two 240hp Chenu engines. Deleted May 1916.
No.17 *Beta* rebuilt as *Beta II*	Completed in May 1910 at the Balloon Factory for the Army, powered by a 35hp Green engine driving two propellers. First flight 26.5.10. Was of non-rigid type of 35,000cu ft. Rebuilt with 45hp Clerget engine and flew from 12.9.12. Transferred to Navy January 1914. Deleted May 1916.
No.18 *Gamma* rebuilt as *Gamma II*	Designed at Farnborough, but envelope of 75,000cu ft made by Astra of Paris. Car and carrying frame made in England. Delivered to Army powered by an 80hp Green engine driving swivelling propellers for which gearing and shafting made by Rolls-Royce. First flew 10.12.10. In 1911 two 45hp Iris engines substituted. During 1912 re-rigged with envelope of 101,000cu ft as *Gamma II* flying from 10.9.12. Transferred to Navy January 1914. Deleted May 1916.
No.19 *Delta*	Building started at the Balloon Factory in 1911, but due to alterations completion delayed until August 1912. First flight 7.9.12. Was of non-rigid type similar to Parseval, powered by two 100hp White & Poppe engines. Transferred to Navy January 1914. Deleted May 1916.
No.20 *Eta*	Built at the Royal Aircraft Factory for Army flying from 18.8.13, powered by two 80hp Canton Unne engines, it was of 118,000cu ft. Transferred to Navy January 1914. Deleted May 1916.
Nos. 21-22 Epsilon I & II	Ordered for Army. Building when Navy took over airships. Erected at Kingsnorth but found unsatisfactory in view of standardised blimps becoming available.
R23 (R23 Class Ship)	Built by Vickers at Barrow, powered by three Rolls-Royce Eagle IIIs and an Eagle VI. Delivered to Pulham 15.9.17. Used in aeroplane dropping experiments with Sopwith Camels D8250, N6622 & N6814. Deleted September 1919.
R24 (R23 Class)	Built by Beardmore at Inchinnan, powered by four Rolls-Royce Eagle IIIs. Delivered to East Fortune 28.10.17; later to Pulham station.
R25 (R23 Class)	Built by Armstrong Whitworth at Selby, powered as R24. Delivered to Howden 15.10.17, later on Cranwell station. Scrapped September 1919.
R26 (R23 Class)	Built by Vickers at Barrow, powered by four Rolls-Royce Eagles. Stationed at Pulham. Scrapped March 1919.
R27 (R23X Class)	Built by Beardmore at Inchinnan. Powered by four Rolls-Royce Eagle IIs. Commissioned 29.6.18. Deleted 16.8.19.
R28 (R23X Class)	Ordered from Beardmore & Vickers, but cancelled before completion.
R29 (R23X Class)	Built by Armstrong Whitworth in 1918. Powered as R26. Stationed East Fortune 1918-19. Deleted 24.10.19.
R30 (R23X Class)	Ordered from Armstrong Whitworth, but cancelled before completion.
R31 (R31 Class Ship)	Built by Shorts at Bedford on Schutte Lanz principles, powered by Rolls-Royce Eagles. Deleted at Howden July 1919.
R32 (R31 Class)	Built by Shorts at Bedford. Powered as R31. Used in parachute experiments 1919. Scrapped 1921.
R33 (R33 Class Ship)	Built by Armstrong Whitworth at Barlow. Powered by five 270hp Sunbeam Maoris. Stationed at Pulham, East Fortune and Howden. Became G-FAAG. Scrapped 1927.
R34 (R33 Class)	Built by Beardmore at Inchinnan. Powered as R33. Trials from March 1919. Made Atlantic crossings. Scrapped after hitting high ground 28.1.21.
R35 (R33 Class)	Ordered from Armstrong Whitworth at Barlow but cancelled before completion.
R36 (Large R33 Class)	Built by Beardmore at Inchinnan. Powered by four 350hp Sunbeam Cossacks. Became G-FAAF. Scrapped 1926.
R37 (Large R33 Class)	Ordered from Shorts at Bedford. Cancelled before completion.
R38 (Large R33 Class)	Built by Shorts at Bedford. Sold to USA as ZR-2. Crashed in Humber on trials 24.8.21.
R39	Ordered from Armstrong Whitworth at Barlow, but cancelled before completion.
R40-41	Ordered from Beardmore and Vickers, but cancelled before completion.
R80 (Small R33)	Ordered from Vickers at Barrow with four 250hp Wolseley-Maybachs; delivered to Cardington and first flew 19.7.20. Not used.

N.B. The R100 and R101 were purely civil airships.

Naval Blimps 1915-1919

The naval blimps were non-rigid airships of several types. They were numbered in separate series, starting at No.1 for each type, prefixed with significant letters according to that type. Each one built is listed below in alphabetical/numerical sequence. Except for a few retained for coastal mine watching, all were scrapped during 1919 and where individual craft were deleted before the end of the war their fate is given in the Remarks column. Locations given relate to the normal station for the particular craft. Airships rebuilt or replaced were given an 'A' suffix to their number to denote that their craft was not as originally built.

AP Type

The AP Airship-Plane series was planned for aeroplane-lifting airships to conserve fuel for anti-Zeppelin aeroplanes, held in the air and released as required. Initial experiments were with an SS Type envelope and a BE.2c aeroplane.

Number	Remarks
AP1	First flew August 1915 using BE.2c 989. Trials unsuccessful.
AP2	Developed version of AP1 cancelled after failure of AP1 trials.

Coastal Type

These blimps initially fitted with 150hp Sunbeams were variously fitted with different engines so that, where known, the actual power units fitted are given in the remarks. Where engines of different power were fitted in the one craft, the higher-powered engine was normally at the rear and the other at the front of the car which was constructed from joining two Avro 510 fuselages together. C1 was of 190 feet long with an envelope of 140,000cu ft capacity, but all others were 200 feet long with envelopes of 170,000cu ft capacity.

Number	Remarks
C1	2 x 150hp Sunbeams. First flew 9.6.15. Experimental work at Kingsnorth.
C2	110hp Berliet & 220hp Renault. Mullion & Howden. Deleted 1919.
C3	150hp Sunbeam & 220hp Renault. Pembroke & East Fortune
C4	110hp Berliet & 220hp Renault. Howden & Longside. Deleted 1919.
C5	2 x 150hp Sunbeams. Longside. Replaced 30.1.17 as C5A. 160hp Sunbeam & 220hp Renault. Pembroke, Longside & Howden.
C6	2 x 150hp Sunbeams. Lost at sea from Pembroke 24.3.17.
C7	150hp Sunbeam & 220hp Renault. East Fortune & Longside.
C8	2 x 150hp Sunbeams. Crashed into sea from Kingsnorth 9.6.16.
C9	110hp Berliet & 220hp Renault. Mullion and Howden.
C10	2 x 150hp Sunbeams. Mullion. Replaced as C10A 10.10.16. 150hp Sunbeam & 220hp Renault. Longside.
C11	Rebuilt at Kingsnorth after hitting hill flying from Howden 23.4.17. Power units not known.
C12	Presumed utilised for prototype of C*Star series as C*1.
C13	Number apparently not used.
C14	150hp and 160hp Sunbeam. Longside. Replaced as C14A. 110hp Berliet & 220hp Renault. Experiments at Pulham.
C15	Rebuilt at Kingsnorth. Further details not known.
C16	2 x 150hp Sunbeams. East Fortune. Deleted 14.9.16.
C17	2 x 150hp Sunbeams. Shot down in flames off North Foreland 21.4.17.
C18	2 x 150hp Sunbeams. Longside.
C19	100hp Green & 220hp Renault. Howden and Capel.
C20	2 x 150hp Sunbeams presumed. East Fortune. Deleted 22.12.17.
C21	100hp Green & 220hp Renault. Howden.
C22	2 x 150hp Sunbeams. Mullion. Lost at sea 21.3.17.
C23	2 x 150hp Sunbeams presumed. Replaced by C23A. 150hp Sunbeam & 220hp Renault. Mullion.
C24	2 x 150hp Sunbeams. Rebuilding at Kingsnorth 1918.
C25	100hp Green & 240hp Renault. East Fortune, Mullion and Longside
C26	2 x 150hp Sunbeams presumed. Pulham. Blown over Holland and interned 13.12.17.
C27	2 x 150hp Sunbeams presumed. Shot down in flames over North Sea by Brandenburg W.12 floatplane.

In addition Ca, Cb, Cc & Cd were produced for Russia and Ce for France.

Improved Coastal Type — C Star

The improved Coastal blimps, numbered in a separate series with a 'star' between the 'C' prefix letter and the number, were of 210 feet in length and had an envelope of 210,000cu ft. C1 had a 110hp Berliet replaced later by a 240hp Fiat, and a 220hp Renault, but all others had a 110hp Berliet and a 240hp Fiat as standard power units. Since all survived the war and were scrapped 1919-20, and power units were standardised, remarks are confined to stations. These blimps were commissioned from January 1918.

C*1	East Fortune	C*6	Mullion & Howden
C*2	Howden	C*7	East Fortune & Howden
C*3	East Fortune	C*8	Cranwell & East Fortune
C*4	Howden, East Fortune and Longside	C*9	Howden
		C*10	Pulham & Howden
C*5	Longside	C*11-26	Cancelled late 1918

North Sea Type

The North Sea (NS) Type were larger craft of 262 feet in length and with a capacity of 360,000cu ft. Precise allocation of engine types to individual craft is not known, but the policy effected was original powering with two 250hp Rolls-Royce engines which, by the end of the war, were replaced by two Fiats of 240hp up to and including NS11 and of 300hp for NS12-18. K1 a proposed improved North Sea blimp was cancelled before construction was completed.

Number	Remarks
NS1	Trials from 2.2.17. Replaced at Kingsnorth 22.2.18.
NS2	Wrecked at Stonehaven near Stowmarket 27.6.17.
NS3	East Fortune. Wrecked off Dunbar in gale 22.6.18.
NS4	East Fortune and Longside.
NS5	Longside. Force landed at Agton 22.2.18.
NS6	Longside.
NS7	East Fortune. Instructional craft for US Navy 1919.
NS8	East Fortune. Did War Loans flight tour.
NS9	Howden.
NS10	
NS11	Longside. Lost at sea off the north-east coast, 15.7.19.
NS12	Longside.
NS13	Believed number not used.
NS14	Built for US Government; transferred 8.11.18.
NS15	Held in reserve at Kingsnorth.
NS16	Held in reserve at Wormwood Scrubs.
NS17-18	Held in reserve at Kingsnorth.

Submarine Scout Type

The Submarine Scouts (SS) were relatively small airships of 145 feet in length and of 70,000cu ft. SS1-26 BE.2c fuselage type car with 70 or 75hp Renault engines in general but SS23-25 had 75hp Rolls-Royce Hawks; SS27-39 had Maurice Farman nacelle type cars with Hawk engines, but known exceptions are notified in the remarks column; SS40-49 had Armstrong Whitworth FK.3 fuselage type cars with 100hp Green engines.

Number	Remarks
SS1	Used envelope of Airship No.2. First flight 18.3.15. Burnt landing at Capel 7.5.15.
SS2	Unsatisfactory and not accepted from makers. Deleted 5.15.
SS3	Shipped out to Mudros. Presumed deleted in 1918.
SS4-6	Transferred to Italian Government 1917.
SS7-8	Shipped out to Kassandra 1916. Presumed deleted 1918.
SS9	Replaced at Polegate 13.9.16. SS9A used at Polegate for mooring experiments.
SS10	Replaced at Capel after a crash into the Channel 10.9.15 by SS10A which was replaced 2.6.16 by SS10B which was

	transferred to the Italian Government July 1917.
SS11	Transferred to the Italian Government after service at Capel.
SS12	Replaced at Capel 14.3.17.
SS13	Stationed at Capel.
SS14	Rebuilt at Kingsnorth as SS14A with Hawk engine. Pembroke and Pulham. Had black envelope for experimental night work.
SS15	Pembroke. Wrecked off Lundy Island 18.1.17.
SS16	Polegate. Rebuilding at Wormwood Scrubs early 1918 and believed deleted later that year.
SS17	Shipped to Kassandra after service at Luce Bay.
SS18	Anglesey. Lost at sea 9.11.16.
SS19	Shipped to Mudros in 1915 per SS *Joshua Nicholson*.
SS20	Luce Bay and Wormwood Scrubs. Deleted during 1918.
SS21-22	Transferred to French and Italian Governments respectively.
SS23	Luce Bay. Deleted during 1918.
SS24	Anglesey and Wormwood Scrubs. Deleted during 1918.
SS25	Anglesey. Deleted during 1918.
SS26	Transferred to French Government, 1916.
SS27	Deleted at Marquise 5.8.15.
SS28	Rebuilt at Cranwell as SS28A early in 1918.
SS29	Training craft at Cranwell, after service at Capel.
SS30	Wrecked and rebuilt as SS30A. Cranwell
SS31	Known as 'Flying Bedstead' at Kingsnorth. Rebuilt as SS31A as training craft at Cranwell.
SS32	Replaced at Folkestone 10.10.16 as SS32A. When repaired at Barrow early in 1918 was reported to have 75hp Renault.
SS33	Rebuilt early 1918 at Wormwood Scrubbs; deleted same year.
SS34	Experimental fitting of Nieuport seaplane floats. Believed deleted in 1917.
SS35	Luce Bay, then used for experimental work at Pulham.
SS36	Non-standard with 75hp Renault. Pulham.
SS37	Pembroke. Rebuilt as SS37A with 110hp Berliet. Cranwell.
SS38	Luce Bay. Wrecked at sea 25.2.17.
SS39	Used at Cranwell for training. Rebuilt as SS39A with 110hp Berliet.
SS40	Used on the Western Front 1916 painted black. Rebuilt early 1918 at Wormwood Scrubbs and shipped to Kassandra.
SS41	Caldale. Deleted in 1918.
SS42	Pembroke. Crashed 15.9.16. Replaced as SS42A 4.10.16 and crashed in sea 12.9.17.
SS43	Replaced at Pembroke 4.10.16 and shipped to Kassandra. Returned to UK 1917.
SS44-47	Transferred to Italian Government, 1917.
SS48-49	Transferred to French Government, 1917.
SS50	Not completed.

Submarine Scout Experimentals

The experimental batch of Submarine Scout blimps (SSE) built at RNAS Depots were an attempt to increase the power of the SS Type and were powered by two 75hp Rolls-Royce Hawk engines.

Number	Remarks
SSE1	Built at Wormwood Scrubs; to Pulham. Proved unsatisfactory.
SSE2	Known as 'Mullion Twin' at Mullion. Also used at Pulham.
SSE3	Trials at Kingsnorth.

Submarine Scout Twin Type

The twin-engined SS Types were known as SSTs and were in production when the war ended.

Number	Remarks
SST1-12	Sent to service with 2 x 75hp Rolls-Royce Hawk engines: SST1 Capel, SST2 Polegate and Mullion, SST3-5 Howden, SST6 believed deleted in 1918, SST7 Howden, SST8 Capel, SST9-12 Howden.
SST13-29	Under construction at Wormwood Scrubs. 2 x 110hp Berliets originally specified, but changed to 100hp Sunbeam Dyaks. Not completed.
SST30-68	Ordered from Wormwood Scrubs with 2 x 75hp Rolls-Royce Hawks and cancelled.
SST69-90	Under construction at Kingsnorth with 2 x 110hp Berliets when war ended. Not completed.
SST91-115	Ordered from Kingsnorth with 2 x 75hp Rolls-Royce Hawk engines. Order cancelled.

Submarine Scout Patrol Type

The Submarine Scout Patrol (SSP) craft were modified SS Type initially fitted with 100hp Green engines and the three surviving the war of the six built were re-engined with 110hp Berliets.

Number	Remarks
SSP1	Operational at Anglesey, training craft at Cranwell.
SSP2	Cardale. Lost at sea 26.11.17.
SSP3	Wrecked at Faversham 21.3.17.
SSP4	Cardale. Lost at sea 22.12.17.
SSP5	Operational at Anglesey, training craft at Cranwell.
SSP6	Operational at Anglesey, experimental at Pulham, trainer at Cranwell.

Submarine Scout Zero Type

Zero Type was the name given to the Standard version of patrol blimps put into large-scale production, with the short title SSZ. 75hp Rolls-Royce Hawk engines were standard fitting.

Number	Remarks
SSZ1	Built at, and ran trials from, Capel.
SSZ2	No record.
SSZ3	Pulham and East Fortune.
SSZ4-5	Capel including Godmersham Park sub-station.
SSZ6	Polegate including Slindon and Upton sub-stations.
SSZ7	Polegate. Collided with SSZ10 landing at Jevington, 20.12.17, caught fire and bomb exploded wrecking craft.
SSZ8-9	Polegate including Slindon and Upton sub-stations.
SSZ10	Polegate. Burnt at Jevington. See SSZ7.
SSZ11-13	Luce Bay.
SSZ14-15	Mullion. SSZ14 force landed Crasvily 7.9.17; refitted at Brest.
SSZ16	Pembroke including sub-station at Wexford.
SSZ17	Pembroke. Destroyed by fire 22.1.18.
SSZ18-20	Capel, Polegate and Luce Bay respectively.
SSZ21-22	Transferred to French Government.
SSZ23-24	Transferred to United States Government.
SSZ25	Mullion and Wormwood Scrubs.
SSZ26	Capel including Godmersham Park sub-station.
SSZ27	Polegate and Mullion.
SSZ28-30	Polegate, Capel and Polegate respectively.
SSZ31	Anglesey and Howden.
SSZ32	Howden including Lowthorpe and Kirkleatham sub-stations.
SSZ33	Howden and Anglesey.
SSZ34-35	Anglesey. SSZ35 deleted October 1918.
SSZ36-37	Capel and Pembroke respectively.
SSZ38	Howden. Wrecked in gale at Lowthorpe 11.5.18.
SSZ39-45	Polegate (39, 41, 43, 44) and Mullion (40, 42, 45).
SSZ46-49	Capel, Mullion, Polegate and Mullion respectively.
SSZ50-51	Anglesey including Malahide sub-station.
SSZ52-53	Pembroke including Wexford sub-station.
SSZ54	Howden. Wrecked hitting trees Lowthorpe 1918.
SSZ55-56	Howden and Pembroke respectively.
SSZ57-58	Longside including Auldbar sub-station.
SSZ59-60	East Fortune including Chathill sub-station.
SSZ61	Used for training at Cranwell.
SSZ62-64	Howden including sub-stations at Lowthorpe and Kirkleatham.
SSZ65-66	Longside including Auldbar sub-station.
SSZ67	Pembroke including Wexford sub-station.
SSZ68	Shipped from Wormwood Scrubs to Kassandra 24.8.18.
SSZ69	Capel including Godmersham Park sub-station.
SSZ70	Shipped from Wormwood Scrubs to Kassandra 24.8.18.
SSZ71	Used for experimental work at Pulham.
SSZ72-73	Anglesey including Malahide sub-station.
SSZ74-76	Capel, Mullion and Pembroke respectively.
SSZ77	Held in reserve at Kingsnorth.
SSZ78-93	Construction cancelled.

Semi-Rigid SR1

In addition to the blimps and airships numbered in the R series, a semi-rigid M Type was acquired from Italy and was flown to England 28.10.18. Numbered SR1 for Semi-Rigid No.1, it was powered by two 220hp Itala D.2s and a 200hp S.P.A.6a. Delivered initially to Kingsnorth, SR1 was based at Pulham from November 1918 to August 1919 when it was deflated and stored.

Aeroplane Pre-Serialling System 1909-1912

Army Aeroplanes

Before a continuous serialling system was initiated in 1912, the few aeroplanes acquired by the Army were numbered in two series prefixed by 'B' and 'F'; and the Royal Aircraft Factory designations B.E. for Bleriot Experimental and S.E. for Santos Experimental, both being rather misleading as after the initial aircraft in the series they had no real relevance. Since the Factory had no charter for manufacturing aircraft, their nomenclature was based on existing aircraft names as a cover. Aircraft used up to 1912 were identified as follows:

No.	Aircraft Type and Remarks
B1	Voisin rebuilt as B.E.1
	60hp Wolseley. Became numbered BE1
B2	Bleriot Monoplane
	70hp Gnome. Later serialled 251
B3	Breguet Biplane
	60hp Renault.
B4	Nieuport Monoplane
	50hp Gnome. Later serialled 253
B5	Deperdussin
	60hp Anzani. Later serialled 252
B6	Bristol Prier
	50hp Gnome. Later serialled 256
B7	Bristol Boxkite
	60hp Renault. Non-standard, believed scrapped.
F1	Henry Farman Biplane
	50hp Gnome. Scrapped before serialling started.
F2	Paulhan Biplane
	50hp Gnome. Scrapped before serialling started.
F3	Howard Wright Biplane
	60hp ENV. Became numbered BE5
F4-5	Bristol Boxkite
	50hp Gnome. Used at Larkhill.
F6	Bristol Boxkite
	60hp Renault. Delivered to Larkhill.
F7-8	Bristol Boxkite
	Used by CFS, became Nos.408 and 407.
BE1	B.E.1
	60hp Renault. Later serialled 201
BE2	S.E.1 reconstructed to B.E.2
	60hp Renault.
BE3	B.E.3
	70hp Gnome. Later serialled 203.
BE4	B.E.4
	50hp Gnome. Later serialled 204.
BE5	B.E.2
	60hp ENV. Later serialled 205.
BE6	B.E.2
	60hp Renault. Later serialled 206.
FE2	F.E.2
	50hp Gnome. Later serialled 604.
RE1	R.E.1
	70hp Renault. Later serialled 608.
RE2	R.E.2
	70hp Renault. Later serialled 17.
SE1	S.E.1
	60hp ENV. Crashed 18.8.11.

Navy Aeroplanes

The first aeroplanes used by the Navy were two lent by Francis K McClean, their availability being promulgated in General Fleet Orders 6th December 1910. The marking of aeroplanes loaned by Mr McClean was complicated by his own numbering system. Short Nos.27 and 39 were McClean Nos. 11 and 10 respectively. By agreement with the Royal Aero Club a further two aircraft were taken on loan; gradually, by loan, presentation and purchase, the Admiralty obtained further aircraft.

In 1912 a simple identification system was used consisting of a letter and number. Type letters were: 'H' - 'Hydro-aeroplane' (this term was used up to 17th July 1913, when Winston Churchill announced in the Commons that it would be superseded by 'Seaplane'). 'M' - 'Monoplane' and 'T' - 'Tractor' as follows:

No.	Aircraft Type	Remarks
H1	Short S.41 Tractor Biplane	Later serialled 10
H5	Short S.43 Biplane	Later serialled 401
M1	Deperdussin Monoplane	Ex-Army. Later serialled 7
M2	Short S.37 Tractor Monoplane	Later serialled 14
T1	Short S.34 'Long Range' Biplane	Later serialled 1
T2	Short S.38 Tractor Biplane	Later serialled 2
T3	Short S.39 Triple-Twin	Later serialled 3
T4	Short S.47 Triple-Tractor	Later serialled 4
T5	Short S.45 Tractor Biplane	Later serialled 5

Military Trials Aircraft Numbers 1912

To select the most suitable aircraft to meet Army needs a competition was arranged by the War Office. There were prizes to attract competitors and the trials were held in the autumn of 1912. Although the aircraft entered were privately owned, they are listed here as the numbers they were given for the competition, were officially allotted. The allocations were:

No.	Aircraft and Remarks
1-2	Hanriot Monoplane (100hp Gnome). Completed tests.
3	Vickers Monoplane No.6 (70hp Viale). Completed trials.
4	Bleriot Type X1-2 with tandem seating (70hp Gnome). Initially incorrectly numbered No.3. Became RFC No.221.
5	Bleriot Type XI with side-by-side seating (70hp Gnome)
6	Avro Type G cabin biplane (60hp Green).
7	Avro Type G cabin biplane (60hp ABC).
8	Breguet Biplane, British-built (110hp Canton Unne).
9	Breguet Biplane, French built, crashed before competition.
10	COW Biplane (100hp Gnome) did not complete tests.
11	COW Biplane (110hp Chenu) participation abandoned through engine trouble.
12	Bristol GE.2 (Gordon England 2) (100hp Gnome).
13	Bristol GE.2 (70hp Daimler-Mercedes)
14-15	Bristol-Coanda Monoplane (80hp Gnome) Became RFC Nos. 263 and 262.
16	Flanders Monoplane (100hp ABC). Withdrawn during trials.
17	Martin-Handasyde Monoplane (75hp Chenu). Hampered by engine trouble.
18	Aerial Wheel Monoplane (50hp NEC). Did not fly.
19	Mersey pusher monoplane (45hp Isaacson). Crashed during trials.
20-21	British-built Deperdussin Monoplane (100hp Anzani/Gnome).
22	Maurice Farman S.7 (70hp Renault). Completed trials.
23	DFW (Deutsche Flugzeug-Werke) Mars monoplane. Participation forbidden by the German Government.
24	Lohner biplane (120hp Austro-Daimler). Did not arrive from Austria.
25	Harper Monoplane (60hp Green). Did not arrive, possibly not completed.
26-27	French-built Deperdussin Monoplane (100hp Gnome). 26 became 258. 27 did not arrive.
28	Handley Page Type F monoplane (70hp Gnome). Damaged during trials.
29	Piggott biplane (35hp Anzani). Failed at outset of trials.
30	Cody IV monoplane (120hp Austro-Daimler). Wrecked before trial.
31	Cody V biplane (120hp Austro-Daimler). Trials winner taken over as RFC No.301.
32	Borel monoplane (80hp Gnome). Was not ready in time.

A Joint Numbering System Inaugurated 1912

The Air Committee, newly formed as a permanent body under the Committee of Imperial Defence, advocated in mid-1912 a standard marking and identification numbering system for all military aeroplanes; this coincided with a decision already made by the Admiralty and War Office to standardise on numbering. Elements of the Royal Flying Corps and the Naval Wing between them formed the Central Flying School, and in the summer of 1912 Naval aircraft had participated in army manoeuvres inland, from which both Services had encountered difficulties due to their dual numbering systems. A straightforward system embracing both Services was therefore agreed.

In the early days the Services did not have a nomenclature for aircraft types. Manufacturers' names and engine horse-power were often the terms used to identify a particular type, together with descriptive words such as 'tractor biplane'; in consequence a nickname often became an officially accepted abbreviation. These early aircraft were individually identified by their constructors' serial number, but since the Services were but one customer among many, including foreign governments, flying schools and private owners, the constructors numbers on military aircraft were not consecutive.

Royal Navy

1 to 200

The Admiralty, representing the Senior Service, was allotted the first range of numbers, 1 to 200 and these were applied retrospectively to aircraft already in service.

When the numbering system took effect in November 1912 (coinciding with the setting up of an Air Department in the Admiralty), the Naval Wing had on strength sixteen aircraft, consisting of eight biplanes, five monoplanes and three seaplanes. These were re-numbered into the system and the allocation of numbers was taken up in numerical/chronological sequence as aircraft were ordered but, since some orders took longer than others to fulfil, deliveries were not necessarily in the same sequence. The first 200 were as follows:

No.	Aircraft Type and Remarks
1-5	Short Biplanes ex-T1-5.
6	Breguet Biplane (80hp Chenu, later 110hp Canton Unne). Bought from France, August 1912.
7	Deperdussin Monoplane (70hp Gnome) ex-M1 acquired from the Army 24.7.12 and was for a time fitted with floats.
8	Short S.37 Biplane. (50hp later 80hp Gnome).
9	Etrich Monoplane (65hp Austro-Daimler) purchased from Germany.
10	Short S.41 (100hp Gnome later 140hp engine). Ex-H1. At Dardanelles 1915.
11	Henry Farman (70hp). Built by AMC
12	Short S.46 'Tandem Twin' monoplane (2 x 70hp Gnome). Believed never flown.
13	(Not allotted, officially recorded as 'blank number').
14	Short.
15	Bristol T.B.8H. Bristol No.205. Stationed at Calshot, January 1914.
16	Avro 503 seaplane converted to landplane (100hp Gnome).
17	H.R.E.2 (Hydro Reconnaissance Experimental No.2). Originally built as RE2 with 70hp Renault engine; later a seaplane with a 100hp Renault.
18	Donnet-Leveque flying boat (80hp Gnome). Purchased from France. Delivered to Sheerness 20.10.12.
19	Short Biplane S.38 nacelle type; Short No S.54.

No.	Aircraft Type and Remarks
20-21	Short Improved S.41 type (100hp Gnome). No.20 used in Gregory-Riley-White wheel/float experiments.
22	Deperdussin Monoplane (80hp Anzani) stationed at Eastchurch.
23	Maurice Farman S.7 Longhorn (70hp Renault). Built by AMC.
24	Bristol Boxkite (50hp Gnome) Bristol No.99. Stationed at Eastchurch.
25	Astra (100hp Renault).
26	R.E.5 (120hp Austro-Daimler). Built by the Royal Aircraft Factory. Acquired from War Office.
27	Sopwith Tractor Biplane (80hp Gnome). Used for armament training, Eastchurch, 1914.
28	Short Biplane S.38 nacelle type. Short No S.55.
29	Maurice Farman S.11 Shorthorn seaplane (70hp Renault). Allotted to Yarmouth from June 1913 but was rarely flown.
30	Deperdussin Monoplane (80, later 100hp Anzani).
31	Henry Farman biplane (70/80hp Gnome). Built by AMC.
32	Vickers FB.5 'Gunbus' (100hp Gnome Monosoupape). At Eastchurch 1914-15 on 'Zeppelin standby'.
33	Sopwith Tractor Biplane (80hp Gnome). Stationed at Eastchurch.
34	Short S.38 nacelle type (50, later 80hp Gnome). Short No S.56.
35	Bristol Boxkite (70hp Gnome). Bristol No.139.
36	Deperdussin Monoplane (80hp Anzani). Stationed at Eastchurch.
37	Borel floatplane purchased from France. Crashed in River Swale.
38	Sopwith Bat Boat No.1 (100hp Green, later 90hp Austro-Daimler).
39	Bleriot Monoplane Type XI (80hp Le Rhone). Stationed at Eastchurch. Went to France 1914.
40	Caudron G.3 (80hp Gnome). Built by W H Ewen & Co.
41	Avro 500 (50hp Gnome). Stationed at Eastchurch and Hendon.
42	Short Improved S.41 Seaplane (80hp Gnome). Converted to landplane. Wrecked at Morbecque, France, September 1914.
43	Bristol T.B.8. Wrecked at Leigh, Essex. Rebuilt. In service at Eastchurch in 1916.
44	Deperdussin Monoplane (100hp Anzani).
45	Caudron G.3 (50, later 70hp Gnome). To Chingford, May 1915.
46-47	B.E.2b. Built by the Royal Aircraft Factory. No.46 stationed at Eastchurch; No.47 at Chingford in 1916.
48	Borel floatplane. Wrecked by heavy seas aboard HMS *Hermes* during fleet manoeuvres 23.7.13.
49-50	B.E.2c. (70hp Renault). Built by Hewlett & Blondeau for War Office and transferred to RN. No.50 was used in France, Belgium and Gallipoli.
51-53	Avro 500. No.51 written-off at Hendon 11.8.15; No.52 lost at Hendon 1916; No.53 was at Eastchurch in 1916.
54	COW (160hp Gnome). Also reported as Short seaplane.
55-57	Caudron G.2 seaplane (80/100hp Gnome). No.55 was fitted for amphibious use.
58-60	Sopwith Seaplane (100hp Anzani).
61	Sopwith Biplane (120hp Austro-Daimler).
62-65	Short Biplane S.38 nacelle type. Short Nos S.57/58, 60/61; No.65 was converted to take wheel/float undercarriage.
66	Short Seaplane. Eastchurch 'Gun Machine' used for armament experiments.
67	Maurice Farman S.7 Longhorn built by AMC.
68	Royal Aircraft Factory seaplane order for H.R.E.6.
69-73	Maurice Farman S.7 Longhorn (70hp Renault); 69-70 built by AMC as landplanes; remainder French-built floatplanes.
74-80	Short Admiralty Type 74 seaplane (100hp Gnome). Short Nos S.69-74 and 79.
81-82	Short Folder Seaplane (160/100hp Gnome). Short Nos S.63-64.
83-88	Borel Seaplane (80hp Gnome). Built by Delacombe & Marechal.
89-90	Short Folder Seaplane (160hp Gnome). Believed Short Nos S.65-66.
91-92	Maurice Farman ordered from AMC.
93	Sopwith Pusher 'Gunbus' Seaplane (120hp Austro-Daimler).
94	Avro (not delivered).
95-96	Maurice Farman Seaplane (130hp Canton Unne). French built.
97-100	Henry Farman Biplane (80hp Gnome). 97 fitted with sprung floats and 100hp Gnome). 99-100 not delivered
101	B.E.2a (believed temporary allotment).
102	Henry Farman Biplane (70hp Gnome). Built by AMC.
103-104	Sopwith Tractor Biplane (50hp Gnome).
105	Hamble Luke floatplane (150hp NAG, later 160hp Gnome).
106-107	Astra CM (70 or 100hp Renault).
108	Henry Farman

109	Maurice Farman.
110	Henry Farman Seaplane.
111-112	Breguet Biplane known as 'Tin Whistle'.
113	Maurice Farman Seaplane (100hp Renault).
114-116	Henry Farman Seaplane (70 or 100hp Renault).
117	Maurice Farman Seaplane (120hp Renault). Built by AMC.
118	Sopwith Bat Boat (40hp Austro-Daimler).
119-122	Short Folder Seaplane of enlarged type (160hp Gnome). Short Nos S.82-85.
123-124	Sopwith Pusher Biplane seaplane with land chassis.
125	Farman built by AMC.
126	Short Gunbus Seaplane (160hp Gnome). Short No S.81.
127	Sopwith Bat Boat (200hp Canton Unne).
128-129	Wight Navyplane pusher seaplane (200hp Canton Unne). 129 modified in 1914.
130-134	Avro 510 tractor seaplane (150hp Sunbeam).
135-136	Short Admiralty type 135 (135/200hp Canton Unne).
137-138	Sopwith Seaplane (120hp Austro-Daimler/200hp Canton Unne)
139-144	Henry Farman Seaplane (Gnome).
145	Short (65hp Austro-Daimler). Believed Short No S.145.
146	Maurice Farman S.7 Longhorn (70hp Renault). French built.
147-148	Bristol Seaplane (200hp Canton Unne). Order cancelled.
149	Sopwith 'Churchill' (100hp Gnome) with side-by-side seating suggested by Winston Churchill.
150	Avro 500 (50hp Gnome).
151	Sopwith 'Circuit' Seaplane (100hp Green). Built originally for 'Circuit of Britain' competition.
152	Short S.38 type biplane known as 'Short Sociable' (80hp Gnome).
153	Bristol T.B.8 (80hp Gnome). Served in Belgium 1914.
154	DFW Arrow biplane, ex-Beardmore purchase. Grounded for identification reasons in 1914.
155	Wight Navyplane (200hp Canton Unne). First flew 5.5.14.
156	Henry Farman Seaplane (80hp Gnome). Built by AMC.
157-159	Sopwith Type C floatplane (200hp Canton Unne). 157 was torpedo-carrying experimental seaplane.
160	Sopwith biplane (80hp Gnome), DC.
161-166	Short Admiralty Type 166 (200hp Canton Unne). Initially allotted to HMS *Ark Royal*. 163/166 converted to landplanes in Aegean. Short Nos S.90-95.
167-169	Sopwith Tabloid (80hp Gnome). See 394-395, 604.
170	Sopwith Tractor Biplane (100hp Green).
171-176	Wight Type Al improved Navyplane (200hp Canton Unne).
177	Wight Type AII improved Navyplane (200hp Canton Unne, later 225hp Sunbeam).
178	Short Type B (200hp Le Rhone planned). Torpedo carrier. Order cancelled.
179	Avro 504 (80hp Gnome). To France 1914 for Friedrichshafen raid.
180-183	Short Admiralty Type 74 (100hp Gnome).
184-185	Short Admiralty Type 184 prototypes. Short Nos S.106-107.
186	Short Folder Type Seaplane (160hp Gnome).
187	Wight Type Seaplane (160hp Gnome).
188-189	Henry Farman Biplane (70hp Renault).
190-199	Short Type B (200hp Canton Unne). No.190 only delivered.
200	Henry Farman Biplane (50hp Gnome).

Army Aeroplanes

201 to 800

Following on from the Navy's 1-200 allocation of numbers the Army from August 1912 allotted aircraft numbers in the 201-800 number range, sub-dividing the numbers as follows: 201-250 No.2 Squadron, 250-300 No.3 Squadron, 301-350 No.4 Squadron, 351-400 No.5 Squadron, 401-600 Central Flying School, 601-800 Royal Aircraft Factory and later Military Wing aircraft. It should be appreciated that No.1 Squadron, being concerned with lighter-than-air craft, did not at that time operate aeroplanes.

These sub-divisions meant that numbers in the 201-800 range were not allocated in chronological sequence and that there was some re-numbering on transfer between units. For ease of reference they are presented below in numerical sequence.

Nos.	Aircraft Type and Remarks	Quantity
201	B.E.1 (60hp Renault) ex-B1 from Royal Aircraft Factory	1
202	Breguet L.2 biplane (60hp Renault) ex-B3	1
203	B.E.3 (70hp Gnome) ex-No.BE3 from Royal Acft Factory	1
204	B.E.4 (80hp Gnome) ex-No.BE4 from Royal Acft Factory	1
205	B.E.2 (60hp ENV or 70hp Renault) ex-BE5 from Royal Aircraft Factory	1
206	B.E.2 (60hp Renault) ex-BE6 from Royal Aircraft Factory	1
207	Maurice Farman S.7 Longhorn	1
208-209	Henry Farman biplanes (Gnome) re-numbered 412 & 420	2
210-211	Breguet G.3 biplane (100hp Gnome)	2
212-213	Breguet L.2 biplane (70hp Renault). 212 later had a 85hp Canton Unne.	2
214-216	Maurice Farman S.7 Longhorn (70hp Renault)	3
217-218	B.E.2a (70hp Renault). Built by B & C. C/n 114/117	2
219	Bleriot XI (50hp Gnome). Presented by International Correspondence Schools.	1
220	B.E.2 (70hp Renault) from Royal Aircraft Factory	1
221	Bleriot XI-2 ex-Military Trials aircraft No.4.	1
222	B.E.2 Built by Vickers at Erith	1
223-224	Maurice Farman S.7 Longhorn (70hp Renault)	2
225-234	B.E.2a (70hp Renault). Built by B & C. C/n 140, 141, 168-174, 190	10
235	B.E.2a (70hp Renault). Built by COW	1
236	B.E.2a (70hp Renault). Built by Vickers at Erith	1
237-241	B.E.2a (70hp Renault). Built by B & C. C/n 191-195	5
242	B.E.2a (70hp Renault)	1
243	Sopwith RG (80hp). Tested to destruction	1
244	Henry Farman F.20	1
245	B.E.2	1
246-248	Sopwith RG (80hp Gnome)	3
249-250	B.E.2a	2
251	Bleriot XXI (70hp Gnome) ex-B2.	1
252	Deperdussin monoplane (60hp Anzani) ex-B5	1
253	Nieuport monoplane (50hp Gnome) ex-B4	1
254	Nieuport monoplane (70hp Gnome)	1
255	Nieuport monoplane (100hp Gnome)	1
256	Bristol Prier two-seat monoplane. C/n 75, ex-B6.	1
257	Deperdussin monoplane (60hp Anzani)	1
258	Deperdussin monoplane (100hp Gnome). Ex-Trials No.26	1
259	Deperdussin monoplane (100hp Gnome). Ex-Trials No.21	1
260	Deperdussin monoplane (80hp Gnome). Renumbered 419	1
261	Bristol Prier two-seat monoplane. C/n 91	1
262-263	Bristol Coanda monoplane. Ex-Trials Nos.15 & 14	2
264	Nieuport monoplane (28hp Nieuport)	1
265	Flanders F.4 monoplane (70hp Renault)	1
266	Maurice Farman S.7 Longhorn. To CFS as No.472	1
267	B.E.2a (70hp Renault) Replacement for No.222	1
268	Henry Farman F.20	1
269-270	Maurice Farman S.7 Longhorn	2
271	Bleriot XI (80hp Gnome)	1
272-273	B.E.2a (70hp Renault)	2
274-277	Henry Farman F.20	4
278	Martin-Handasyde monoplane (65hp Antoinette)	1
279-280	Deperdussin monoplane (70/100hp Gnome)	2
281	Flanders F.4 monoplane (70hp Renault)	1
282	Nieuport monoplane (70hp Renault)	1
283	Grahame-White Type VII Popular Biplane (35hp Anzani)	1
284	Henry Farman F.20 (80hp Gnome)	1
285	Avro 502 (Type Es) biplane	1
286	Henry Farman F.20 (80hp Gnome)	1
287	Grahame-White Type VIII biplane	1
288-291	Avro 502 (Type Es)	4
292	Bleriot XI-2 (80hp Gnome), C/n 791	1
293	Bleriot XI (50hp Gnome). Tested to destruction	1
294-295	Henry Farman F.20 (80hp Gnome)	2
296	Bleriot XI-2 (80hp Gnome)	1
297-298	Bleriot XI (50hp Gnome)	2
299	B.E.2a (70hp Renault)	1
300	Sopwith RG (80hp Gnome)	1
301	Cody V biplane (120hp Austro-Daimler). Ex-Trials No.31	1
302	Maurice Farman S.7 Longhorn (70hp Renault)	1
303	B.E.4 (50hp Gnome)	1
304	Cody V biplane (120hp Austro-Daimler). Currently	1

	preserved by the Science Museum, London	
305-307	Maurice Farman S.7 Longhorn	3
308	Caudron G.2 (45hp Anzani)	1
309	Grahame-White Boxkite (50hp Gnome)	1
310	Breguet biplane (110hp Canton Unne). British built	1
311	Caudron G.2	1
312	Breguet biplane (85hp). British built	1
313	(reported as a Dunne)	1
314	B.E.2a. Built by Vickers at Erith	1
315	Sopwith RG (80hp Gnome)	1
316-317	B.E.2a. Built by Vickers at Erith	2
318	B.E.2a. Built by COW	1
319	Sopwith RG (80hp Gnome)	1
320	B.E.2a. Built by Vickers at Erith	1
321	B.E.2c. Built by COW	1
322	Maurice Farman S.7 Longhorn	1
323	Bleriot XI (50hp Gnome)	1
324-325	Sopwith RG (80hp Gnome)	2
326	Sopwith Tabloid	1
327-329	B.E.2a (70hp Renault)	3
330	Henry Farman F.20 (80hp Gnome)	1
331-333	B.E.2a (70hp Renault)	3
334-335	R.E.5 (120hp Austro-Daimler)	2
336	B.E.2a (70hp Renault). Built by Vickers at Erith	1
337-338	Maurice Farman S.7 Shorthorn	2
339-341	Henry Farman F.20 (80hp Gnome)	3
342-345	Maurice Farman S.11 Shorthorn. 343 became 464.	4
346	Henry Farman F.20 (80hp Gnome)	1
347-348	B.E.2a (70hp Renault). Built by COW	2
349	B.E.2a (70hp Renault)	1
350-353	Henry Farman F.20	4
354	Grahame-White Type VIIc Popular Passenger Biplane	1
355-360	Maurice Farman S.7 Longhorn (70hp)	6
361	R.E.5 (120hp Austro-Daimler)	1
362	(temporary number of R.E.1 608 in March 1914)	(1)
362	Sopwith Tabloid (80hp Gnome)	1
363-364	Henry Farman F.20 biplane (80hp Gnome)	2
365	R.E.8. Built by B & C. C/n 201	1
366	Dunne D.8 biplane (80hp Gnome)	1
367	Henry Farman F.20 (80hp Gnome)	1
368	B.E.2a (70hp Renault)	1
369-371	Maurice Farman S.11 Shorthorn	3
372	B.E.2a (70hp) Renault). Built by Vickers at Erith	1
373	R.E.8. Built by B & C. C/n 202	1
374-375	Bleriot XI (50 or 70hp Gnome)	2
376	Avro 500 and MF S.7 Longhorn (duplicated nos)	2
377	B.E.8. Built by Vickers	1
378	Sopwith Tabloid	1
379	Maurice Farman S.11 Shorthorn	1
380	R.E.5. Modified with extended top wings and to single-seat for altitude record attempt.	1
381	Sopwith Tabloid	1
382	R.E.8 (120hp Austro-Daimler)	1
383-385	B.E.2a 383, 385 by AW; 384 by COW	3
386-387	Sopwith Tabloid	2
388-389	Bleriot XI-2 (50 or 70hp Gnome)	2
390	Avro 504	1
391	B.E.8	1
392	Sopwith Tabloid	1
393	Henry Farman F.20 (80hp Gnome)	1
394-395	Sopwith Tabloid re-numbered 904, 905; then 167, 168	2
396	B.E.2b. Built by B & C. C/n 212	1
397-398	Avro 504 (80hp Gnome)	2
399	B.E.8	1
400	(No record of allocation, possibly not used)	(1)
401-402	Short School Biplane. 401 ex-H5. C/ns S.43, S.44	2
403	Maurice Farman S.7 Longhorn (70hp)	1
404-406	Avro 500 (Type E)	3
407-408	Bristol Boxkite. Ex-F8 & F7	2
408	B.E.7 (140hp Gnome). Renumbered 438	(1)
409	Nieuport monoplane	1
410-411	Maurice Farman S.7 Longhorn	2
412	Henry Farman biplane ex-No.208	(1)
413	Short Tractor Biplane (70hp Gnome) C/n S.48	1
414	(No record of allotment)	(1)
415	Maurice Farman S.7 Longhorn. Built by AMC	1
416-417	B.E.4 (50hp Gnome) fitted DC	2
418	Maurice Farman S.7 Longhorn (70hp)	1
419	Deperdussin monoplane (80hp Gnome) ex-No.260	(1)
420	Henry Farman biplane ex-No.209	(1)

421	Deperdussin monoplane (60hp Anzani)	1
422	Flanders F.4 monoplane (70hp Renault)	1
423-424	B.E.8 duplicated numbers below	2
423-424	Short Tractor Biplane (70hp Gnome) C/n S.49, S.50. Re-numbered 1268, 1269.	2
425-429	Maurice Farman S.7 Longhorn (70hp)	5
430	Avro 500 (Type E)	1
431	Maurice Farman S.7 Longhorn (70hp)	1
432-433	Avro 500 (Type E)	2
434	Henry Farman. Built by Grahame White. 'Wake-up England' biplane taken on charge. Interchangeable wheels/floats.	1
435	Henry Farman F.20	1
436-437	Deperdussin monoplane	2
438	B.E.7 ex-No.408	1
439	Flanders F.4 monoplane	1
440	Henry Farman F.20	1
441-442	B.E.2a Built by Vickers	2
443	(No record of allotment)	(1)
444-445	Henry Farman F.20 (80hp Gnome)	2
446	Short S.38 type biplane. C/n S.62	1
447	B.E.2a. Built by Vickers	1
448	Avro 500 (Type E)	1
449	B.E.2a (had experimental oleo undercarriage)	1
450-451	Maurice Farman S.7 Longhorn. 451 built by AMC	2
452-454	B.E.2a. Built by Vickers	3
455-456	Henry Farman F.20 (80hp Gnome)	2
457	B.E.2a	1
458-459	Maurice Farman S.7 Longhorn	2
460	B.E.2a. Built by Handley Page	1
461-462	Henry Farman F.20	2
463	Maurice Farman S.7 Longhorn	1
464	Maurice Farman S.11 Shorthorn ex-No.343	(1)
465	Maurice Farman S.11 Shorthorn	1
466	B.E.2a	1
467	Henry Farman F.20 (80hp Gnome)	1
468-471	B.E.2a. Built per 468/471 COW, 469 Saunders and 470 RAF	4
472	Maurice Farman S.7 Longhorn ex-No.266	(1)
473	Bleriot XI-2 (70/80hp Gnome)	1
474-475	B.E.2a 474 by COW, 475 by Vickers	2
476-478	Maurice Farman S.7 Longhorn	3
479	B.E.8	1
480-481	Maurice Farman S.11 Shorthorn	2
482	Morane Saulnier Type G (80hp Gnome)	1
483	B.E.2a	1
484	B.E.2b (70hp Renault)	1
485	Maurice Farman S.7 Longhorn	1
486	Maurice Farman	1
487-488	B.E.2b	2
489	B.E.2	1
490	Maurice Farman S.7 Longhorn	1
491	Avro 500 (Type E)	1
492-493	B.E.2b (70hp Renault)	2
494-496	Maurice Farman S.7 Longhorn	3
497	(No record of allotment)	(1)
498-501	Maurice Farman S.7 Longhorn	4
502-513	Henry Farman F.20	12
514-545	Maurice Farman S.11 Shorthorn (possible two were S.7 Longhorn)	32
546-557	Maurice Farman S.7 Longhorn	12
558-569	Henry Farman F.20 biplane	12
570-574	Bleriot XI (570-572 70/80hp Gnome, 573, 574 50hp Gnome)	5
575-586	Bleriot Parasol (80hp Gnome)	12
587-598	Morane G & H (1 & 2-seat monoplanes)	12
599	Martinsyde S.1	1
600	(No record of allotment)	(1)
601-602	B.E.2c (70hp Renault). 602 re-serialled 1807.	2
603	(No record of allotment)	(1)
604	Sopwith Tabloid renumbered 169	(1)
604	F.E.2 Ex-No.FE2	(1)
605	F.E.3 (75hp Chenu)	1
606	Bleriot Parasol (70/80hp Gnome)	1
607-608	R.E.1 (608 ex-RE1, temporarily numbered 362)	2
609	S.E.2 numbered after reconstruction by Royal Aircraft Factory.	1
610	Bristol G.B.75 was incorrectly numbered. C/n 223	1
611	Sopwith Tabloid	1
612	B.E.2a	1
613	R.E.5	1
614-615	Bristol T.B.8. 614 to RNAS as 948	2

616	Bristol Parasol	1
617	R.E.5	1
618	Bleriot	1
619	Bleriot XI (80hp) impressed	1
620	Bristol T.B.8. To RNAS as No.917	1
621	Bleriot XI (50hp Gnome) impressed	1
622	*(No record of allotment)*	*(1)*
623	Morane H. Built by GW. Impressed	1
624-625	B.E.8. Built by Vickers for India but impressed	2
626	Bleriot XI (80hp Gnome). Impressed ex-Mme Salmet	1
627	Morane H. Built by GW, impressed	1
628	S.E.4	1
629	Morane G/H. Built by GW, impressed	1
630	Bleriot XI (50hp Gnome) of B C Hucks impressed	1
631	R.E.5	1
632	B.E.8 (80hp Gnome)	1
633	Maurice Farman S.11 Shorthorn	1
634	Bristol T.B.8. Impressed from R P Creagh but condemned as unsafe	1
635	B.E.2a	1
636	B.E.8	1
637-638	Avro 504	2
639	Vickers Boxkite. Impressed ex-Vickers School	1
640-641	Bristol Boxkite. Impressed	2
642	Vickers Boxkite. Impressed ex-Vickers School	1
643	B.E.8. Later operated by the RNAS	1
644	Bristol Scout B (80hp Gnome). Built by B & C	1
645	B.E.8	1
646	B.E.2b	1
647	Bleriot XI (80hp Gnome)	1
648	Bristol Scout B. Built by B & C. C/n 230	1
649	Vickers FB.4	1
650	B.E.2b	1
651	R.E.5	1
652	Avro 504	1
653	Henry Farman biplane	1
654	Sopwith Tabloid (80hp Gnome)	1
655	Maurice Farman (type not ascertained)	1
656	B.E.8	1
657	Bristol Boxkite	1
658	B.E.8 (100hp Gnome early in 1915)	1
659-660	R.E.5	2
661	Maurice Farman S.7 Longhorn	1
662	Bleriot XI (70/80hp Gnome)	1
663	B.E.8	1
664	Vickers FB.4 Gunbus	1
665	Avro 504	1
666	B.E.2b (70hp Renault)	1
667-668	B.E.2a	2
669	Henry Farman F.20	1
670	B.E.8	1
671	Bleriot XI (28hp Anzani)	1
672	Bleriot (type unknown with 45hp Anzani)	1
673	Bleriot XI (50hp Gnome)	1
674	R.E.5 (120hp Beardmore)	1
675	*(No record of allotment)*	*(1)*
676	B.E.2b	1
677-678	R.E.5	2
679	Maurice Farman S.7 Longhorn	1
680	Henry Farman F.20	1
681	Bleriot XI (70/80hp Gnome)	1
682	Vickers FB Gunbus	1
683	Avro 504	1
684	*(No record of allotment)*	*(1)*
685	Henry Farman F.20 biplane	1
686	Vickers FB.4 Gunbus	1
687	B.E.2b	1
688	R.E.5	1
689	Henry Farman F.20	1
691-702	Bristol T.B.8. Transferred to RNAS and renumbered 1216-1227 and RFC numbers re-allotted, but 3 only traced	(12)
692	Avro 504	1
693	B.E.8	1
694	Bleriot XI (80hp Le Rhone)	1
696	Martinsyde S.1. Impressed at Brooklands	1
699	Henry Farman F.20	1
702	Martinsyde S.1	1
703	B.E.2b	1
704	Vickers FB.6	1
705	B.E.2b (70hp Renault)	1

706	Bleriot XI (70/80hp Gnome)	1
707	Maurice Farman S.11 Shorthorn	1
708	Henry Farman F.20	1
709	B.E.2b	1
710	Martinsyde S.1 (had non-standard undercarriage)	1
711	Bleriot XI	1
712-713	Maurice Farman S.7 Longhorn. Built by AMC. Shipped to Egypt	2
714	Bleriot XI	1
715-716	Avro 504	2
717	Martinsyde S.1	1
718	Bristol Boxkite	1
719-720	Henry Farman F.20	2
721	Bleriot XI	1
722	B.E.2b	1
723	Bleriot XI	1
724	Martinsyde S.1	1
725	B.E.8	1
726	Bleriot XI	1
727	B.E.8	1
728	Henry Farman F.20	1
729	B.E.8 (80hp Gnome)	1
730	Martinsyde S.1	1
731	Maurice Farman (type unknown)	1
732	Bleriot XI	1
733	B.E.2b (70hp Renault)	1
734	Martinsyde S.1	1
735	Maurice Farman S.7 Longhorn	1
736	B.E.8	1
737	R.E.5	1
738	Henry Farman F.20	1
739	Maurice Farman S.7 Longhorn	1
740	B.E.8 (80hp Gnome)	1
741	Martinsyde S.1	1
742	Maurice Farman S.11 Shorthorn	1
743	Martinsyde S.1	1
744	Maurice Farman S.11 Shorthorn	1
745	R.E.8	1
746	B.E.2b (70hp Renault)	1
747	Vickers Gunbus. Transferred to RNAS as 862 in exchange for an Avro 504	1
748-749	Martinsyde S.1	2
750-793	Avro 504 (80hp Gnome except 769 80hp Le Rhone and 777 80hp Clerget)	44
794-799	Avro 504D	6

Second Naval Allocation

801 to 1600

By mid-1914 the Royal Navy had used its initial allocation of numbers 1 to 200 and with the Army being allotted 201 to 800 the Navy followed on at No.801, restricted to 1600 to allow a further allocation of numbers to the Army. At this time the Air Department of the Admiralty designated some aircraft types by the serial number of the prototype or production model which was decreed the pattern for the series.

Impressed aircraft numbered from No.881 mark the beginning of the Great War and up to No.1226 was subscribed during 1914, so that numbers from No.1267 onwards are on contracts placed from January 1915.

Nos	Aircraft Type and Remarks	Quantity
801-806	**Sopwith Greek Type Gunbus**	6
	Admiralty Type 806. Also known as Sopwith Gunbus No.2	
807-810	**Sopwith Folder Seaplane**	4
	Admiralty Type 807. First two allotted to HMS *Ark Royal*, remainder to Calshot.	
811-818	**Short Folder Seaplane**	8
	Admiralty Type 74. 811, 816-818 had Rouzet W/T apparatus. C/ns S.96-S.103.	

819-821	**Short Seaplane**	3
	Admiralty Type 830. Allotted to seaplane carriers.	
	C/ns S.108-S.110.	
822-827	**Short Seaplane**	6
	All initially fitted with W/T. C/ns S.111-S.116	
828-830	**Short Seaplane**	3
	Admiralty Type 830. 829 interned in Holland 11.11.14.	
831-834	**Wight AII Imperial Navyplane**	4
	Admiralty Type 177. Built by J.Samuel Wight & Co.	
835-840	**Wight Admiralty Type 840**	6
	Low chassis. Built by J.Samuel White & Co.	
	835 undertook torpedo trials.	
841-850	**Short 184 Seaplane**	10
	225hp Sunbeam. 842 fitted for torpedo-carrying.	
851-860	**Sopwith 860 Seaplane**	10
	225hp Sunbeam. Also known as Sopwith 157 type.	
861-872	**Vickers FB.5 Gunbus**	12
	Admiralty Type 32. 865-872 transferred to RFC	
	as 2340-2347. 862 ex-747.	
873-878	**Avro 504**	6
	80hp Gnome. 873-875 with 179 formed Friedrichafen	
	raid force 1914.	
879	**Sopwith Batboat**	1
	225hp Sunbeam.	
880	**Sopwith Seaplane**	1
	100hp Gnome.	
881	**Avro 510**	1
	150hp Sunbeam. Impressed civil aircraft.	
882-883	**White & Thompson No.2 (Curtiss Batboat)**	2
	Known as Small America Type. Austro-Daimler engines.	
884	**Wight No.2 1913 Navyplane**	1
	Rebuilt and impressed seaplane by J.White & Co.	
885	**Deperdussin monoplane**	1
	100hp Anzani. Impressed civil aircraft.	
886-887	**Henry Farman floatplane**	2
	886 built by AMC. 887 French-built.	
888	**Maurice Farman floatplane**	1
	120hp Sunbeam.	
889	**Avro 503**	1
	80hp Gnome. Impressed civil aircraft.	
890	**Albatros B.II biplane**	1
	100hp Mercedes. Bought privately from Germany	
	pre-war and impressed.	
891	**DFW biplane**	1
	100hp Mercedes. Bought by Beardmore from Germany	
	and impressed.	
892	**Handley Page HP.7 (Type G/100)**	1
	Impressed with its 100hp Anzani.	
893-895	**Wight 1914 Navyplane**	3
	Built by J.Samuel Wight & Co for Germany,	
	but were impressed.	
896-901	**Sopwith Admiralty Type 880**	6
	896, 900, 901 landplanes, 897-899 floatplanes,	
	ex-Greek order.	
902-903	**Bleriot Parasol**	2
	50/70hp Gnome. 903 presented by Miss Trehawke Davies	
904	**Short School Biplane**	1
	70hp. Rebuilt Short S.32 presented by F.McClean,	
	being his No.8.	
904-905	**Sopwith Tabloid**	(2)
	Re-numbered 167-168 to avoid duplication.	
905	**Short Nile Seaplane**	1
	140hp Gnome. Short S.80 presented by F.McClean.	
906	**Sopwith 3-seat tractor biplane**	1
	80hp Gnome. Served in England, France and Belgium.	
907-908	**Bleriot Parasol**	2
	80hp. French-built.	
909-914	**Maurice Farman S.7 Longhorn**	6
	70hp Renault. 909 to RNAS Hendon, the rest to RFC.	
915	**Henry Farman floatplane**	1
	80hp. Built by AMC.	
916-917	**Bristol T.B.8**	1(2)
	917 was ex-RFC 620.	
918	**Flanders B.2 biplane**	1
	70hp Gnome. Civil aircraft impressed for RNAS Yarmouth.	
919-926	**Sopwith 807 Seaplane**	8
	100hp Gnome. 920, 921 to Middle East. 924-926 to	
	Campania. 922 to *Ark Royal*.	
927-938	**Sopwith 860 Seaplane**	10(12)
	225hp Sunbeam. 936, 937 cancelled.	
929	**Avro 500**	1
	50hp Gnome. Impressed. Used at Hendon and Chingford.	
940	**Henry Farman**	1
	80hp Gnome. Built by AMC.	
941	**Morane G**	1
	80hp Le Rhone. French-built.	
942-947	**Bristol Boxkite**	6
	50hp Gnome. B & C-built. C/ns 394-399.	
948	**Bristol T.B.8**	(1)
	Ex-RFC 614.	
949	**Maurice Farman**	1
	100hp Renault. Built by AMC.	
950-951	**Curtiss H.4 Small America**	2
	From USA. 950 with two 125hp Anzani was modified	
	at Felixstowe to Porte-Curtiss H.4. 951 had two	
	100hp Anzani.	
952-963	**B.E.2c**	12
	70hp Renault. Built by Vickers. All transferred to RFC.	
964-975	**B.E.2c**	12
	70hp Renault. Built by Blackburn. 968, 969 were	
	shipped to South Africa.	
976-987	**B.E.2c**	12
	70hp Renault. Built by Hewlitt & Blondeau at Clapham.	
988-999	**B.E.2c**	12
	70hp Renault. Built by Martinsyde.	
1000	**Wight AD Type 1 Seaplane**	1
	Admiralty Type 1000. Built by J.Samuel White & Co.	
	Not completed until 1917.	
1001-1050	**Avro 504B**	50
	80hp Gnome. 1005-1008, 1020-1025 to RFC as 2857-	
	2860, 4221-4225, 4255. 1027 DC. 1014 to USA for	
	exhibition. 1019 and 1035 with 80hp Le Rhone.	
1051-1074	**Sopwith 2-seat Scout**	24
	80hp Gnome. Known as 'Spinning Jenny'. 1052, 1053,	
	1056-1058 fitted with floats for use at RNAS Yarmouth.	
1075-1098	**B.E.2c**	24
	70hp Renault. Vickers-built. All transferred to RFC.	
1099-1122	**B.E.2c**	24
	70hp Renault. Built by Beardmore. 1110, 1111 were	
	shipped to Aegean area.	
1123-1146	**B.E.2c/Maurice Farman S.11**	24
	70hp Renault. Built by Blackburn. 1127 was exchanged	
	with Belgians for a steel-framed Belgian-built MF.	
1147-1170	**B.E.2c**	24
	70hp Renault. Built by Grahame-White Aviation.	
1171-1182	**White & Thompson 'Bognor Bloater'**	9(12)
	70hp Renault. 1180-1182 built for spares only and	
	were not assembled.	
1183-1188	**B.E.2c**	6
	75hp Renault. Built by Eastbourne Aviation Co.	
1189-1194	**B.E.2c**	6
	75hp Renault. Built by Hewlett & Blondeau at Clapham	
1195-1200	**White & Thompson No.3 Flying Boat**	6
	120hp Austro-Daimler. 1199 interned by the	
	Dutch 10.2.15 as their G1.	
1201-1213	**Sopwith Tabloid**	13
	80hp Gnome. 1201-1204 allotted to *Ark Royal*.	
1214-1215	**Sopwith Gordon Bennett**	2
	Racing models acquired by Admiralty.	
1216-1227	**Bristol T.B.8**	12
	Ex-RFC 691-702. C/ns 331-342. 1227 had wings	
	modified by F.Koolhoven.	
1228-1231	**Curtiss H.4 Small America**	4
	Built by AMC and Saunders. All used at Felixstowe.	
	1228-1229 had two 90hp Curtiss, 1230 modified by	
	Porte. 1231 had two 100hp Anzani.	
1232-1239	**Curtiss H.4 Small America**	8
	Curtiss-built. 1232-1235 had two 90hp Curtiss	
	supplied but two 100hp substituted, 1236-1237 had	
	two 90hp Curtiss, 1238 had two 100hp Curtiss, later	
	two 150hp Sunbeam. 1239 two 100hp Curtiss, later	
	two 100hp Anzani.	
1240	**Maurice Farman S.11 Shorthorn**	1
	100hp Renault. AMC-built. Interned Holland 15.12.14.	
1241	**Maurice Farman F.27**	1
	135hp Canton Unne. Origin unknown, possibly impressed.	
1242	**Morane Saulnier Type G**	1
	80hp Gnome. Built by Grahame-White Aviation.	
1243-1266	**Bristol Scout C**	24
	80hp Gnome. B & C built. C/ns 462-485. 1247	

	presented to the French Government.	
1267	**Pemberton Billing (possibly Type IX)**	1
	80hp Gnome. Built by Supermarine.	
1268	**Short Tractor Biplane**	(1)
	100hp Clerget. Ex-RFC 423 re-engined in RNAS.	
1269-1278	*(Cancelled order)*	*(10)*
1279	**Short Tractor Biplane**	(1)
	100hp Clerget. Ex-RFC 424 re-engined in RNAS.	
1280-1299	**White & Thompson**	(20)
	Flying boat order cancelled.	
1300-1319	**Wight Admiralty Type 840**	20
	Low chassis. Built by J.Samuel White & Co.	
1320	**Caudron G.2 or 3**	1
	60hp Anzani. Built by British Caudron.	
1321	**Grahame White XV**	1
	70hp Gnome.	
1322	**Perry Beadle Tractor Biplane**	1
	45hp Anzani. Impressed.	
1323-1334	**Curtiss B.2**	(12)
	160hp Curtiss. Order cancelled.	
1335-1346	**Short Admiralty Type 830**	12
	135hp Canton Unne.	
1347-1350	*(Cancelled order)*	*(4)*
1351-1354	**Wight Admiralty Type 840**	4
	High chassis. Built by J.Samuel White & Co. 1352 used for W/T experiments.	
1355-1361	**Wight AD Type 1 Seaplane**	1(7)
	Admiralty Type 1000. Ordered from J.Samuel White & Co. 1355-1357, 1360, 1361 not completed. 1359 almost completed but not assembled.	
1362-1367	**Curtiss JN-3**	6
	90hp Curtiss. Delivered from USA from March 1915.	
1368	**Henry Farman Seaplane**	1
	80hp Gnome. Built by AMC. Served at RNAS Yarmouth.	
1369-1371	**Maurice Farman S.11 Shorthorn**	3
	100hp Renault. Tested at Buc although reported as AMC-built.	
1372	**Caudron G.3**	1
	50hp Gnome. Built by British Caudron, delivered to Hendon.	
1373	**Wright Biplane**	1
	35hp Wright. Purchased for use at Eastchurch.	
1374	**Pemberton Billing Boxkite**	1
	50hp Gnome.	
1375	*(Cancelled purchase)*	*(1)*
1376-1379	**Deperdussin Monoplane**	4
	100hp Gnome Monosoupape. French-built.	
1380-1387	**Maurice Farman Biplane**	8
	110hp Renault. French built and shipped to the RNAS in the Aegean.	
1388-1389	**Supermarine Night Hawk**	1(2)
	Two 125hp Anzani. Pemberton Billing Type 29. 1389 cancelled.	
1390-1394	**Breguet de Chasse**	5
	1390 135hp Canton Unne, 1391, 1393 200hp Canton Unne, 1392 225hp Sunbeam, 1394 220hp Renault.	
1395-1397	**Nieuport Twin**	(3)
	Two 110hp Clerget. Cancelled	
1398-1399	**Breguet Concours**	2
	225hp Sunbeam. 1398 later with 250hp Rolls-Royce.	
1400-1411	**Wight Admiralty Type 840**	12
	High chassis. Built by Beardmore.	
1412-1413	**AD Flying Boat**	2
	200hp Hispano. Built by Supermarine. 1412 later had a 200hp Arab engine.	
1414	*(Cancelled order)*	*(1)*
1415-1416	**Blackburn GP (General Purpose) Seaplane**	2
	Also called Blackburn Twin. 1415 had two Sunbeam Nubian; 1416 two Rolls-Royce Falcon.	
1417-1423	*(Not allotted)*	—
1424-1435	**B.E.2c**	(12)
	Order to South Coast Aviation cancelled.	
1436-1447	**Sopwith Schneider**	12
	100hp Gnome Monosoupape.	
1448-1449	*(Not allotted)*	—
1450-1451	**Wight Twin Seaplane**	2
	Two 200hp Canton Unne. Built by J.Samuel White. Limited use at Felixstowe only.	
1452-1453	**AD Scout**	2
	100hp Gnome. Built by Hewlett & Blondeau. Stored	

1454	**Henry Farman**	1
	80hp Gnome. Built by AMC.	
1455-1466	**Handley Page O/100**	12
	Rolls-Royce Eagle. 1463 force-landed on delivery to France into German hands.	
1467-1496	**Avro 504C (known as Avro Scout)**	30
	Built by Brush Electrical Engineering. 1491 to French.	
1497-1508	**White & Thompson Flying Boat**	(12)
	Order cancelled.	
1509-1517	**Blackburn TB (known as Twin Blackburn)**	9
	Two 150hp Smith planned, but two 100hp Gnome Monosoupape fitted except for 1517 which had two 100hp Gnome.	
1518-1533	**Henry Farman F.22**	16
	80hp Gnome. French-built. 1531-1533 delivered as spares, later assembled.	
1534-1535	**Vickers Gunbus Admiralty Type 32**	2
	140hp Smith.	
1536-1537	**AD Scout**	2
	100hp Gnome Monosoupape. Built by Blackburn.	
1538-1549	**Bleriot Parasol**	12
	80hp Gnome. French-built.	
1550-1555	**Henry Farman**	(6)
	135hp Canton Unne. Steel-framed version ordered from Brush, but cancelled.	
1556-1579	**Sopwith Schneider**	24
	100hp Gnome Monosoupape.	
1580-1591	**Short S.38 Type**	(12)
	Ordered from Supermarine. No record of delivery.	
1592-1597	**Caudron G.3**	6
	100hp Anzani. French-built; 1595 had 80hp Gnome.	
1598	**Dyott Monoplane**	1
	50hp Gnome. Built by Hewlett & Blondeau.	
1599	**Henry Farman Biplane**	1
	80hp Gnome. Built by South Coast Aviation Works.	
1600	**Grahame-White XV**	1
	Admiralty Type 1600. Prototype RNAS trainer.	

Second Allocation to the Army

1601 to 3000

Having completed their 201-800 allocation, the Army allotted numbers from 1601 to 3000 in November 1914 as follows:

Serial Nos.	Aircraft Type and Remarks	Quantity
1601	**Martinsyde S.1**	1
	80hp Gnome.	
1602-1613	**Bristol Scout C**	12
	80hp Gnome or Le Rhone. Built by B & C. C/ns 451-462.	
1614-1615	**Avro 519A**	2
	150hp Sunbeam Nubian. Prototypes known as 'Big Avros'	
1616-1651	**Vickers FB.5 Gunbus**	36
	1636 stored for preservation but later destroyed. Nos. 1648-1651 were originally issued for B.E.2c order from B & C C/n 343-346 that was not completed.	
1652-1747	**B.E.2c**	96
	70hp Renault or 90hp RAF.1a. Built by B & C, c/ns 348-393, 400-449. From around 1686 RAF.1a engines fitted and some earlier aircraft re-engined.	
1748-1779	**B.E.2c**	32
	70hp Renault or 90hp RAF.1a. Built by Vickers, 1760-1779 at Weybridge.	
1780-1800	**B.E.2c**	21
	70hp Renault or 90hp RAF.1a. Built by Armstrong Whitworth.	

1801-1900	(Allotted for purchases in France by General Headquarters, Royal Flying Corps, British Expeditionary Force in France)	77(100)

Nos.1801-1823 were current squadron aircraft renumbered in France. 1801-1805 HF F.20; 1806 HF F.27; 1807 B.E.2c ex-602; 1808-1812 Bleriot XI; 1813, 1814 HF F.20; 1815, 1816 Bleriot XI; 1817, 1818 HF F.20; 1819, 1820 Bleriot XI; 1821-1823 HF20. Following were those received from French industry: 1824 HF F.20, 1825 Bleriot XI, 1826 HF F.20, 1827 MF S.7 or S.11, 1828 Bleriot XI (70/80hp Gnome), 1829 Morane L, 1830 MF S.7, 1831 Morane L also reported as Bleriot XI, 1832-1834 Bleriot XI, 1835 HF F.20, 1836-1838 Bleriot XI (70/80hp Gnome), 1839-1841 MF S.11, 1842 Bleriot XI, 1843 Morane L, 1844 MF S.11, 1845 Morane L, 1846 MF S.11, 1847 Bleriot XI, 1848, 1849 Morane L, 1850 Bleriot XI, 1851-1854 MF S.11, 1855 Morane.L, 1856 Voisin LA, 1857 MF S.11, 1858 Voisin LA, 1859 Morane L, 1860 Voisin LA, 1861-1863 Morane L, 1864, 1865 Voisin LA, 1866 Morane L, 1867, 1868 Voisin LA, 1869 MF S.11, 1870-1876 Morane L, 1877 Voisin LA, 1878 Morane L, 1879 Voisin LA, 1880-1882 Morane L, 1883 Voisin LA, 1884-1887 Caudron G.3, 1888 Morane L, 1889-1890 Voisin LA, 1891 Caudron G.1, 1892 Morane L, 1893 MF S.11, 1894 Morane L, 1895 Caudron G.3, 1896-1897 Morane L also reported as Caudron, 1898, 1899 Voisin LA, 1900 Caudron G.3.

1901-2000	*(Numbers not allotted)*	–
2001-2029	**B.E.2c**	29

90hp RAF.1a. Built by Armstrong Whitworth. 2023 had oleo u/c. 2028 was armoured, 2029 became B.E.2e and was used for experimental work.

2030-2129	**B.E.2c**	100

90hp RAF.1a. Built by Daimler. 2072 had 70hp Renault. 2122 was armoured.

2130-2132	**B.E.8**	3

2130 Vickers-built, 2131, 2132 COW built.

2133-2174	**B.E.8a**	42

2133-2153 (21) built by Vickers. 2154-2174 (21) built by COW.

2175-2180	**B.E.2b**	6

Built by Jonques.

2181-2184	**B.E.8**	(4)

Ordered from B & C, but cancelled.

2185-2336	**R.E.7**	133(152)

140hp or 120hp Beardmore. 2185-2234 (50) built by COW, 2235, 2236 builder not known, 2237-2266 (30) built by Austin, 2267-2286 only 2267 confirmed, 2287-2336 (50) built by Napier. Transfers to RNAS: 2201, 2241, 2242 and 2260 fitted with 200hp Sunbeam. 2299 modified to 3-seater with R.R. Falcon.

2337	**Kennedy Giant**	1

Components by Fairey Aviation and The Gramophone Co. Erected at Northolt.

2338	**Bleriot XI**	1

80hp Gnome. French-built.

2339	**Curtiss JN-3**	1

Presumed ex-RNAS. Used at CFS.

2340-2347	**Vickers FB.5/FB.5A Gunbus**	(8)

Ex-RNAS 865-872.

2348-2447	**R.E.7**	100

Built by Siddeley-Deasy Motors. 2348 modified to 3-seat. 2362 to RNAS.

2448-2455	**Martinsyde S.1**	8
2456-2459	**R.E.5**	4

Built by Royal Aircraft Factory.

2460	**Maurice Farman**	1

For Indian Government.

2461	**R.E.5**	1

Built by Royal Aircraft Factory.

2462-2464	**Vickers FB.5 Gunbus**	(3)

No delivery record.

2465-2468	**Maurice Farman S.11 Shorthorn**	4

Delivered from Paris to UK without engines.

2469	*(Number not allotted)*	–
2470-2569	**B.E.2c/d/e/f**	100

Built by Wolseley Motors. 2564 to RNAS less engine was later fitted with 150hp Hispano.

2570-2669	**B.E.2c**	100

90hp RAF. Built by Daimler. 2578, 2590, 2636 long distance conversions. 2599 fitted with 150hp Hispano. 2607 armoured, 2661 home defence experimental.

2670-2769	**B.E.2c/d/g**	100

90hp RAF. Built by Ruston Proctor. 2735, 2737 to RNAS. 2692, 2695, 2696, 2698, 2701, 2704 to Belgian forces. 2713-2716 armoured. 2728, 2759 long distance conversion. 2702 conv to single-seat in Mesopotamia.

2770-2819	**B.E.2b/c/e/g**	50

Built by Jonques, ordered as B.E.2b but mainly delivered as B.E.2c.

2820-2831	**Martinsyde S.1**	12

80hp Gnome

2832-2851	**Henry Farman F.20/22**	20
2852-2854	**Bleriot Monoplane**	3

50hp Gnome. French built.

2855-2856	**Maurice Farman S.7 Longhorn**	2

From New Zealand.

2857-2860	**Avro 504**	(4)

80hp Gnome. Ex-RNAS 1005-1008.

2861-2862	**Bleriot Parasol**	2
2863	**Caudron G.3**	1

C/n C109 from French industry.

2864	**F.E.2a**	1

No.3 built by Royal Aircraft Factory.

2865-2868	**Vickers FB.5 Gunbus**	4
2869	**Bleriot XI**	1

70/80hp Gnome

2870-2883	**Vickers FB.5/5A Gunbus**	14

100hp Gnome Monosoupape. Vickers-built at Bexley and Crayford.

2884-2889	**B.E.2b**	6

Initial order to Whitehead Aircraft.

2890-2939	**Avro 504A**	50

Built by Saunders. 2929, 2930, 2933, 2934 to RNAS.

2940-2959	**Maurice Farman S.11 Shorthorn**	20

Maker not known.

2960-3000	**Maurice Farman S.7 Longhorn**	41

Built by AMC. 2973, 2983, 2984 to RNAS.

Third Naval Allocation

3001 to 4000

With orders mounting in 1915 and Admiralty Purchasing Commissions set up in France and America a further 1,000 numbers were allocated to the Royal Navy.

Serial Nos.	Aircraft Type and Remarks	Quantity
3001-3012	**Maurice Farman S.11 Shorthorn**	12
	Built by Brush Electrical Engineering.	
3013-3062	**Bristol Scout C**	50
	80hp Gnome in main. Built by B & C. C/ns 524-560, 771-783. 3013 transferred to Greek service. 3028 used in Porte Composite experiments.	
3063-3072	**Short Admiralty Type 827**	10
	150hp Sunbeam. C/n S.163-S.172.	
3073-3092	**Curtiss Triplane**	1(20)
	Wanamaker-Curtiss. 3073 only built with four 240hp Renault. Rest planned to have four 250hp Curtiss, but cancelled.	
3093-3112	**Short Admiralty Type 827**	20
	C/n S.143-S.162. 3093-3095 to Belgian forces in Congo.	
3113-3114	**FBA Flying Boat**	2
	100hp Gnome. French-built. 3113 interned in Holland and scrapped.	
3115-3142	**Handley Page O/100**	28
	Rolls-Royce Eagle. 3117 tested with Sunbeam and Hispano engines. 3138 became prototype O/400. 3142 powered by Fiat A12bis engines.	

3143-3148	Short S.38 Type	(6)

Ordered from White & Thompson, but no delivery record.

3149	Nieuport Scout	1

100hp Gnome. French-built.

3150	Henry Farman	1

100hp Anzani. Bought from France. Erected at Eastchurch in October 1915.

3151-3162	Grahame White XV	12

Admiralty Type 1600. Early production had 50hp Gnome and late production 60hp Le Rhone engines.

3163-3186	Nieuport 10/12 (Two-seat)	24

French-built. 80hp Le Rhone fitted in general.

3187-3198	Nieuport Seaplane	12

French-built.

3199-3208	FBA Flying Boat	10

100hp Gnome. French-built. 3206 re-constructed by Norman Thompson.

3209-3213	Breguet de Chasse	5

Purchased in France and delivered to RNAS Dunkirk.

3214-3238	Bleriot XI Series II	25

80hp Gnome. French-built for RNAS flying training in the UK.

3239-3263	Morane-Saulnier Type L Parasol	25

80hp Le Rhone. French-built. 3257-3262 to Mudros.

3264-3288	Caudron G.3	25

80hp Gnome. French-built.

3289-3300	Caudron G.4 (known as Caudron Twin)	12

Two 100hp Anzani. French-built for No.1 Wing.

3301-3320	Avro 504C	20

Built by Brush Electrical Engineering.

3321-3332	Short Admiralty Type 827	12

Built by Brush Electrical Engineering.

3333-3344	Caudron G.4 (known as Caudron Twin)	4(12)

Built by British Caudron. 3335, 3336 to French. 3337-3344 no record of delivery.

3345-3423	Curtiss JN-3	79

90/100hp Curtiss. American-built. 3345 to French Government. 3384, 3386, 3393 rebuilt by Fairey.

3424-3444	Curtiss JN-4	21

90hp Curtiss OX-2. American-built. 3425, 3427, 3432, 3434, 3436, 3438, 3440, 3442, 3444 DC fitted.

3445-3544	Curtiss R-2	84(100)

160hp Curtiss as supplied. American-built. 200hp Sunbeam in UK in lieu of Curtiss engines. 3479-3508 stored at Cranwell. 3528 and 3530-3544 not delivered.

3545-3594	Curtiss H-4 Small America	50

American-built assembled at Felixstowe. Supplied with two 100hp Curtiss but most re-engined with two 100hp Anzani. 3580 with re-designed hull and two 150hp Hispano became F1 (Porte 1).

3595-3606	Vickers FB.5 Gunbus	12

Admiralty Type 32. Built by Darracq. 3599, 3600, 3602, 3603, 3605 to RFC less engines.

3607-3616	Grahame-White XV	10

Admiralty Type 1600. Engine types fitted according to availability.

3617-3636	Henry Farman F27	20

140hp Canton Unne. French-built. 3628-3635 shipped to the Aegean.

3637-3656	FBA Flying Boat	20

French built.

3657-3681	Burgess Gunbus	25

140hp Sturtevant. American-built. 3657, 3658 erected at Hendon for trials. Remainder placed in store.

3682	Henry Farman	1

Purchased in France.

3683	Morane Saulnier BB	1

Purchased in France.

3684-3685	Armstrong Whitworth Triplane	(2)

Rolls-Royce Eagle planned. Project cancelled.

3686	Sopwith A1	1

Admiralty Type 9400. Prototype of Sopwith 1½ Strutter.

3687-3688	Dyott Fighter	2

Two 120hp Austro-Daimler. Built by Hewlett & Blondeau.

3689-3690	F.E.8	(2)

100hp Gnome. Allocation cancelled.

3691	Sopwith Pup	1

Admiralty Type 9901. Prototype, later exhibited in USA.

3692-3693	Bristol S.2A	(2)

110hp Clerget. Ordered from B & C, but not delivered.

RFC took over order which materialised as Nos.7836 and 7837.

3694-3695	Avro 529/529A (known as Avro Fighter)	2

Both wrecked at Martlesham Heath on trials during November 1917.

3696-3697	Airco DH.4	2

Prototypes. Re-numbering of 3697 as B394 for RFC was cancelled.

3698-3699	(Numbers not allotted)	–
3700	Curtiss Twin Canada	1

Two 160hp Curtiss. Accepted at Hendon 11.11.16.

3701	Sloane-Day H1 Biplane	1

American-built. Scrapped under repair at Fairey Works 1917.

3702-3703	Fairey AD Tractor	(2)

Two 200hp Brotherhood. Cancelled.

3704-3705	Fairey AD Pusher	1(2)

Two Rolls-Royce Falcon. 3704 only completed but as AD Tractor. 3705 wings only built.

3706	Short Bomber (Type 184 Landplane Bomber)	1

Prototype. 225hp Sunbeam. C/n S.248. Wing span extended after test.

3707-3806	Sopwith Schneider	100

100hp Gnome Monosoupape. Airframes of 3707, 3709, 3765 and 3806 transferred to Canadian Government. 3742 became PV1. 3772 fitted with W/T. 3796 had 110hp Clerget.

3807-3808	White & Thompson No.3 Flying Boat	2

3808 fitted with DC.

3809-3820	Thomas T-2	12

90hp Curtiss. American-built. Did not enter service. Record of 3809-3812, 3814 only being assembled.

3821-3832	Voisin	12

140hp Canton Unne. French-built. 3827-3832 shipped to Aegean. 3825 to the RFC.

3833-3862	Sopwith Admiralty Type 806	17(30)

150hp Sunbeam. Built by Robey & Co. 3850-3862 delivered as spares only.

3863-3998	Allotted for purchases in France as below:	115(136)

3863-3882 (20) Caudron G.3 (80hp Gnome); 3883-3887 Breguet de Chasse; 3888 Breguet de Bomb; 3889 type not delivered; 3890-3893 Bleriot; 3894-3899 Caudron G.4 of which 3896 went to French Government; 3900-3919 (20) HF for overseas service with 150hp Canton Unne engines; 3920-3931 (12) Nieuport 10; 3932 Maurice Farman S.7 Longhorn (70hp Renault); 3933-3939 cancelled order for Maurice Farman; 3940-3945 cancelled order for Nieuport Twin with two 110hp engines; 3946 Breguet Concours; 3947-3952 Bleriot Tractor aircraft; 3953 further cancelled order for Nieuport Twin; 3954, 3955 Maurice Farman S.7 Longhorn; 3956-3958 Nieuport Scout (80hp Le Rhone); 3959-3961 reservation; 3962-3973 (12) Nieuport 10 (80hp Le Rhone) of which some were converted to single-seat; 3974 Nieuport 11; 3975-3994 (20) Nieuport Scout of which 3975, 3978 were transferred to Romanian forces; 3995-3997 further cancelled order for Nieuport Twin; 3998 HF (140hp Canton Unne).

3999	B.E.2c	1

80hp Renault. Built by Blackburn. Used for W/T tests.

4000	Sloane Tractor	1

160hp Sloane-Day. American-built.

Third Allocation to the Army

4001 to 8000

With up to 4000 allotted to the RNAS, the Army was given a further range of numbers, 4001 to 8000.

Serial Nos.	Aircraft Type and Remarks	Quantity
4001-4019	**Maurice Farman S.7 Longhorn** Presumed AMC-built. Extension of 2960-3000 order.	19
4020-4069	**Avro 504A** 4043, 4044 to RNAS.	50
4070-4219	**B.E.2c** 90hp RAF. Built by B & C. C/ns 621-770. 4099, 4201, 4203, 4205 were armoured. 4102 to Belgian Flying Corps. 4111, 4120 and possibly others produced as B.E.2e and 4140 as B.E.2d.	150
4220	**DH.1** Prototype built by AMC.	1
4221-4225	**Avro 504** 80hp Gnome. Ex-RNAS 1020-1024.	(5)
4226	**Caudron G.3** French-built.	1
4227-4228	**F.E.2a** Nos.1 & 2 built by Royal Aircraft Factory.	2
4229-4252	**Martinsyde S.1** 4243, 4244 given identities as MH5, MH6 in Mesopotamia	24
4253	**F.E.2a** Built by Royal Aircraft Factory.	1
4254	**Caudron G.3** French-built.	1
4255	**Avro 504** Ex-RNAS 1025.	(1)
4256-4292	**F.E.2b** 120hp Beardmore. Built by G & J Weir. 4270 had a 140hp RAF engine.	37
4293	**Caudron G.3** C567 purchased in France.	1
4294	**Maurice Farman S.11** To RFC from overseas source.	1
4295	**F.E.2a** Built by Royal Aircraft Factory.	1
4296	**Bleriot Monoplane** French-built.	1
4297-4298	**Maurice Farman** French-built.	2
4299	**Caudron G.3** C1887 from French works.	1
4300-4599	**B.E.2c/d/e** 90hp RAF. Group-built by G & J Weir and other manufacturers including Alex Stephens and North British. Transfers to RNAS of airframes re-engined as follows: 4336, 4337, 4426 DC, 4524, 4570, 4572 90hp Curtiss; 4525, 4526, 4571 70/80hp Renault. Of those in RFC service, 70hp Renaults were fitted in those used for training. 4445, 4541, 4599 were armoured for a period. 4363, 4369, 4460, 4461, 4466, 4467, 4519, 4565, 4567 to Belgian Flying Corps.	300
4600-4648	**Airco DH.1/1A** 80hp Renault. Built by Savages Ltd.	49
4649	**Nieuport Biplane** Built by Nieuport & General.	1
4650-4661	**Bleriot XI** 50hp Gnome. French-built.	12
4662-4699	**Bristol Scout** 80hp Gnome or Le Rhone. B & C. C/ns 480-485, and 492-523.	38
4700-4709	**B.E.2c** B & C. C/n 561-570. Ordered as single-seat version but delivered as standard. 4708 fitted for rocket firing.	10
4710-4725	**B.E.2c** Built by Vickers at Crayford. 4721 fitted with floats.	16
4726-4731	**Maurice Farman S.11** French-built.	6
4732	**DH.2** 100hp Gnome Monosoupape. Prototype by AMC.	1
4733-4734	**Caudron G.3** C910 and C902 purchased in France.	2
4735	**Martinsyde G.100 Elephant** Prototype.	1
4736	**Vickers FB.5 Gunbus** Built at Crayford.	1
4737-4786	**Avro 504A**	50
4787-4836	**Voisin LA** Built by Savages of Kings Lynn.	50
4837	**Caudron G.3** C577 purchased in France.	1
4838-5000	**F.E.2b** Beardmore or RAF.5a engines. Built by G & J Weir. 4861, 4864, 4868, 4869, 4947, 4948 to Russian Government. 4928 had experimental small searchlight fitted.	163
5001-5200	Allotted for purchases from French industry by GHQ, BEF, as follows: 5001 Voisin LA; 5002 Morane L; 5003 Caudron; 5004 Maurice Farman S.11 (80hp Renault); 5005-5007 Morane L; 5008, 5009 Maurice Farman S.11 (80hp Renault); 5010, 5011 Voisin LA; 5012 Morane L; 5013, 5014 Voisin LA; 5015 Maurice Farman S.11; 5016 Caudron; 5017 Voisin LA; 5018, 5019 Maurice Farman S.11; 5020 Caudron G.3 (80hp Gnome); 5021-5023 Morane L; 5024 Caudron G.3 (80hp Gnome); 5025, 5026 Voisin LA.S/LA; 5027 Maurice Farman S.11; 5028 Voisin LA.S; 5029 Morane L; 5030 Maurice Farman S.11; 5031, 5032 Caudron G.3; 5033, 5034 Morane L; 5035 Caudron G; 5036 Maurice Farman S.11; 5037, 5038 Caudron G.3; 5039 Caudron G.3 C902 (80hp Gnome); 5041 Morane L; 5042, 5043 Caudron G.3 C907, C922 (80hp Gnome); 5044-5048 Morane L; 5049, 5050 Caudron G.3; 5051, 5052 Morane L; 5053 Caudron G.3 C597; 5054 Maurice Farman S.11 (80hp Renault); 5055-5058 Morane L; 5059 Maurice Farman S.11 (80hp Renault); 5060, 5061 Morane L; 5062, 5063 Caudron G.3 C612, C516; 5064 Caudron G.3 C592 duplicated following number; 5064, 5065 Morane LA; 5066 Voisin LA; 5067 Caudron G.3 C594 duplicated following number; 5067 Morane N; 5068, 5069 Morane N; 5070 Morane LA; 5071 Maurice Farman S.11 (80hp Renault); 5072, 5073 Morane L; 5074, 5075 Vickers FB.5; 5076, 5077 Morane LA; 5078, 5079 Vickers FB.5; 5080-5082 Morane L; 5083, 5084 Vickers FB.5; 5085-5094 Morane LA; 5095 Maurice Farman S.11; 5096 Morane LA; 5097 Voisin LA; 5098 Morane LA; 5099-5103 Morane LA; 5104 Morane BB; 5105 Morane LA; 5106-5121 Morane LA; 5122 Morane BB; 5123-5125 Morane LA; 5126 Morane BB; 5127 Vickers FB.5; 5128, 5129 Morane LA; 5130 Morane BB; 5131, 5132 Morane LA; 5133 Morane BB; 5134, 5135 Morane LA; 5136, 5137 Morane BB; 5138-5141 Morane LA; 5142 Morane BB; 5143-5148 Morane LA; 5149 Morane BB; 5150-5155 Morane LA; 5156-5170 Morane BB; 5171-5173 Nieuport 16; 5174, 5175 Morane LA; 5176, 5177 Morane BB; 5178, 5179 Morane LA; 5180 Morane N; 5181-5185 Morane LA; 5186-5190 Morane LA; 5191 Morane N; 5192, 5193 Morane BB; 5194-5197 Morane N; 5198, 5199 Morane LA; 5200 Morane BB.	200
5201-5250	**F.E.2b** Built by Boulton & Paul. 5201 was BP's first aircraft and first flew on 2.10.15.	50
5251-5270	**Caudron G.2** Purchased in France.	20
5271-5290	**Vickers FB.9** Built by Vickers at Crayford.	20
5291-5327	**Bristol Scout C** B & C. C/n 784-820.	37
5328-5334	**Armstrong Whitworth F K.2** 5332 tested with oleo undercarriage.	7
5335-5383	**DH.2** Order with AMC cancelled.	(49)
5384-5403	**B.E.2c** 70hp Renault. Built by Wolseley Motors.	20
5404-5412	**Curtiss JN-3** Transferred from RNAS.	9
5413-5441	**B.E.2c/e** Built by Vickers.	29
5442-5453	**Martinsyde S.1**	12
5454-5503	**Vickers FB.5 Gunbus** 100hp Gnome Monosoupape. Built in France by Darracq.	50
5504-5553	**Armstrong Whitworth F K.3** Armstrong-Whitworth-built.	50
5554-5603	**Bristol Scout D** B & C. C/n 1044-1093. Delivered without engines. 110hp Clerget and 80hp Gnome engines fitted. 5564, 5565 to RNAS. 5570 became G-EAGR.	50

5604-5605	Bleriot monoplanes.	2
	Found in an aircraft park and impressed.	
5606-5608	Curtiss JN-3	3
	Presumed ex-RNAS.	
5609-5612	S.E.4a	4
	Built by Royal Aircraft Factory.	
5613	Caudron G.3	1
	C921 French-built.	
5614	Armstrong Whitworth FK.3	1
5615	Caudron G.3	1
	French-built.	
5616	B.E.2c	1
	Believed built up from salvage.	
5617	Maurice Farman S.7 Longhorn	1
	Built at 9 RS from parts of 2976 and 2980.	
5618-5623	Vickers FB.5 Gunbus	6
5624-5641	Curtiss JN-3	18
	Ex-RNAS order.	
5642-5648	F.E.2a	7
	Built by Royal Aircraft Factory.	
5649-5692	Vickers FB.5 Gunbus	44
	100hp Gnome Monosoupape.	
5693-5716	Morane H Monoplane	24
	Built by Grahame-White Aviation.	
5717-5728	Vickers FB.7/7A	1(12)
	5717 only built as FB.7 modified to FB.7a. Nos. 5718-5728 re-allotted.	
5718	Maurice Farman S.11 Shorthorn	1
	Built from spares at 2 RS.	
5719-5721	Sopwith 1½ Strutter	(3)
	Ex-RNAS 9386, 9387, 9389 for No. 70 Squadron, RFC.	
5722-5727	Curtiss JN-3	6
	90hp Curtiss. Ex-Admiralty contract	
5728	Curtiss Twin Canada	1
5729	Vickers FB.5 Gunbus	1
	110hp Clerget. Special armoured version.	
5730-5879	B.E.2c/d/e	150
	90hp RAF. B & C. C/n 894-1043. 5832 DC. 5844 B.E.2e single-seat conversion for home defence.	
5880-5909	Maurice Farman S.11 Shorthorn	30
	Built by AMC.	
5910-5912	Curtiss JN-3	3
	Ex-RNAS.	
5913-5915	Caudron G.3	3
	C544, C473, C598 French-built.	
5916-6015	Airco DH.2	100
	100hp Gnome Monosoupape. AMC-built. 5994 had a 110hp Clerget.	
6016-6115	R.E.7	(100)
	Ordered from Austin Motors. Cancelled.	
6116-6135	Curtiss JN-3	20
	Ex-RNAS.	
6136-6185	B.E.12	50
	Built by Standard Motors.	
6186-6227	Armstrong Whitworth FK.3	42
6228-6327	B.E.2d/e	100
	Built by Ruston Proctor up to 6258 as B.E.2d and then mainly as B.E.2e. 6259 transferred to RNAS less engine and later tested with Rolls-Royce Hawk and 150hp Hispano. 6324-6327 to RNAS and 75hp Rolls-Royce Hawk fitted. 6267 long distance version.	
6328-6377	F.E.2b	50
	Built by Royal Aircraft Factory. 6370, 6371 became F.E.2c.	
6378-6477	F.E.8	100
	Built by Darracq Motor Engineering.	
6478-6677	B.E.12	200
	Built by Daimler. Several conversions to BE.12a.	
6678-6727	Maurice Farman S.7 Longhorn	50
	Presumed AMC-built.	
6728-6827	B.E.2d/e	100
	Built by Vulcan Motor & Engineering. Initial production B.E.2d, then B.E.2e. 6782, 6786, 6787, 6791-6801 to Russian Government on repayment.	
6828-6927	R.E.7	(100)
	Cancelled order placed with G & J Weir.	
6928-7027	F.E.2b	100
	Built by Boulton & Paul.	
7028-7057	Bristol Scout D	30
	B & C. C/n 1094-1123.	

7058-7257	B.E.2d/e/g	200
	B & C. C/n 1174-1373. 7109-7122, 7219 to Russian Government.	
7258-7307	Martinsyde G.100 Elephant	50
7308-7311	Curtiss JN-3	4
	Ex-RNAS contract.	
7312-7320	Caudron G.3	9
	From France	
7321-7345	B.E.2c/d	25
	Built by Vickers	
7346-7395	Maurice Farman S.11 Shorthorn	50
	80hp Renault. Built by AMC. 7385 to RNAS and returned to RFC.	
7396-7445	Henry Farman F.20	50
	Constructor not known.	
7446-7455	Avro 504A	10
	Possibly ex-RNAS.	
7456-7457	F.E.8	2
	Prototypes. Built by Royal Aircraft Factory.	
7458	Voisin LA	1
	V562 from French Industry.	
7459-7508	Martinsyde G.100 Elephant	50
7509	Vickers ES.1	1
	Experimental Scout No. 1 known as the 'Barnwell Bullet'.	
7510-7519	Vickers FB.5 Gunbus	10
	Built by Darracq Motor Engineering.	
7520-7544	Avro 521	?(25)
	A number built but type proved unsatisfactory and none entered service.	
7545-7594	R.E.7	(50)
	Cancelled order with Napier.	
7595-7644	F.E.8	50
	Built by Vickers at Weybridge.	
7645-7664	Bleriot XI	20
	80hp Gnome. Deliveries from mid-May 1916, but maker not traced.	
7665	Vickers FB.9 prototype	1
	100hp Gnome Monosoupape.	
7666-7715	F.E.2b	50
	Built by Boulton & Paul.	
7716-7740	Avro 504A	25
7741-7743	Caudron G.3	3
	French-built.	
7744-7745	Airco DH.3/3A	1(2)
	7744 DH.3 modified to DH.3A. No record of 7745 being completed.	
7746-7749	Henry Farman F.27	4
	From French industry to AMC for engine fitting.	
7750-7751	Bristol TTA (Type 6)	2
	(TT=Twin Tractor). B & C. C/n 1375-1376.	
7752-7755	Henry Farman F.27	4
	From French industry to AMC for engine fitting.	
7756-7760	Vickers ES.1	5
	7756-7759 ES.1 Mk.1, 7760 ES.1 Mk.II.	
7761	Caudron G.4	1
	C500 French-built.	
7762-7811	Sopwith 1½ Strutter	50
	110hp or 130hp Clerget. Built by Ruston Proctor.	
7812-7835	Vickers FB.9	24
	Built by Darracq Motor Engineering.	
7836-7837	Bristol S.2A	2
	B & C. C/n 1377-1378.	
7838-7841	Armstrong Whitworth FK.12	1(4)
	7838 only built.	
7842-7941	Airco DH.2	100
	100hp Gnome Monosoupape. Built by AMC. 7862 rocket-armed.	
7942	Sopwith 1½ Strutter	(1)
	Ex-RNAS 9381.	
7943-7992	Avro 504A	50
	Some deliveries to Egypt.	
7993-7994	F.E.4	2
	Prototype built by Royal Aircraft Factory.	
7995	F.E.2d	1
	Built by Royal Aircraft Factory.	
7996-7997	R.E.8	2
	Prototypes built by Royal Aircraft Factory.	
7998-8000	Sopwith 1½ Strutter	3
	Ex-Admiralty contract.	

Fourth Naval Allocation

8001 to 10000

Following on from the 4000 numbers allotted to the RFC, the RNAS took up the numbers 8001-10000 in 1916.

Serial Nos	Aircraft Type and Remarks	Quantity
8001-8030	**Short 184**	30
	225/240hp Sunbeam Maori. Built by S. E. Saunders.	
8031-8105	**Short 184**	75
	225hp Sunbeam. Short Nos S.173-247. Some re-engined with 240hp Sunbeams in service and 8076 with 260hp Sunbeam Maori III. 8053 DC. Transfers to foreign governments: 8083, 8084 France, 8057 Japan.	
8106-8117	**Maurice Farman S.11 Shorthorn**	12
	70hp Renault. French-built. 8112-8117 to RFC.	
8118-8217	**Sopwith Baby**	100
	Various engines fitted, the first five and last three having 100hp Gnome Monosoupape and the others 110hp Clergets replaced later by 130hp Clergets. Transfers to other governments: 8125, 8197, 8204, 8209 to Canada less engines, 8128, 8129 with 110hp Clergets and 8185 less engine to France, 8214, 8215 to Italy, 8201 to Japan.	
8218-8229	**Short Admiralty Type 827**	12
	150hp Sunbeam. Built by Parnall. 8226-8229 DC. 8219 to Belgian Government for African service.	
8230-8237	**Short Admiralty Type 827**	8
	150hp Sunbeam. Built by Brush Electrical Engineering.	
8238-8249	**Henry Farman F.27**	12
	140hp Canton Unne. French-built. 8238-8242 to South African Aviation Force, 8243 to RFC.	
8250-8257	**Short Admiralty Type 827**	8
	150hp Sunbeam. Built by Parnall.	
8258-8268	**Burgess Gunbus**	11
	Purchased in the USA. Not used and presumed stored.	
8269-8280	**Thomas T2**	12
	Purchased in the USA. Not used and presumed stored.	
8281-8292	**Wight 840**	4(12)
	Built by J. S. White & Co. 8285-8292 delivered as spares to White City, London.	
8293-8304	**B.E.2c**	12
	90hp RAF. Built by Grahame-White Aviation. Several fitted for night flying.	
8305-8316	**Grahame White XV**	12
	Admiralty Type 1600. Service use limited to UK.	
8317-8318	**Short Type 310(A)**	2
	C/n S.299, S.300. Prototype torpedo-carriers.	
8319-8320	**Short Type 320(B) North Sea**	2
	C/n S.311, S.312. Prototype reconnaissance and Zeppelin attack aircraft. 8320 became N1480.	
8321-8322	**Wight Trainer Seaplane**	2
	Built by J. S. White & Co. 8321 100hp Anzani, 8322 Gnome Monosoupape B2.	
8323-8325	*(Not allotted)*	–
8326-8337	**B.E.2c**	12
	90hp RAF. Built by Beardmore. 8335 fitted for night flying.	
8338-8343	**Norman Thompson NT.4 Small America**	6
	Two 150hp Hispano. 8338 had Davis gun in nose.	
8344-8355	**Short Admiralty Type 184**	12
	Torpedo version. Built by Mann Egerton and fitted for carrying 14-inch torpedoes. 225hp Sunbeam Mohawk engine initially installed.	
8356-8367	**Short Admiralty Type 184**	12
	Various engines fitted. Built by Westland. 8359 was only seaplane used in Battle of Jutland and is currently preserved. 8364 had Davis gun fitted in rear cockpit.	
8368-8379	**Short Admiralty Type 184**	12
	Built by Phoenix Dynamo Co for home stations use.	
8380-8391	**Short Admiralty Type 184**	12
	Built by Sage & Co.	
8392-8403	**Curtiss JN-3(CAN)**	12
	Built by Canadian Curtiss. 8403 to French Government.	
8404-8409	**B.E.2c**	6
	90hp RAF. Built by. Eastbourne Aviation. C/n 118-123. 8406 fitted for Le Prieur rocket firing. Home use only.	
8410-8433	**B.E.2c**	24
	90hp RAF. Built by Hewlett & Blondeau. 8414 to Greek service. 8415, 8416 90hp Curtiss OX-2, 8424, 8425, 8427, 8428 to Royal Flying Corps.	
8434-8439	**Short S.38 Type**	6
	Built by Norman Thompson Flight Co.	
8440-8441	**Avro 519 Bomber**	2
	Two 200hp Sunbeam. Experimental aircraft by A. V. Roe for evaluation.	
8442-8453	**Bristol Boxkite**	12
	B & C. C/n 870-881.	
8454-8465	**REP Parasol**	12
	110hp Le Rhone. French (Robert Esnault-Pelterie)-built. 8460 interned in Holland 3.10.15 becoming LA-23 and REP-3 in Dutch service.	
8466-8473	**Maurice Farman S.11 Shorthorn**	8
	75hp Renault. French-built.	
8474	**Maurice Farman S.7 Longhorn**	1
	French-built.	
8475-8486	**Nieuport Twin**	(12)
	Two 110hp. Order cancelled.	
8487	**Pemberton-Billing School**	1
	80hp Le Rhone. Built by Supermarine. PB Type 23E.	
8488-8500	**B.E.2c**	13
	90hp RAF. Built by Beardmore.	
8501-8509	**Voisin**	9
	140/150hp Canton Unne. French-built. 8501-8504 140hp, 8505-8509 150hp initially.	
8510-8515	**Nieuport 12**	6
	110hp Clerget. French-built. 8513, 8514 to Romania.	
8516-8517	**Nieuport**	2
	80hp Le Rhone. French-built. 8516 reported as single-seat, 8517 as two-seat.	
8518-8523	**Voisin LA**	6
	150hp Canton Unne. French-built. 8518, 8523 to Royal Flying Corps Force D.	
8524-8529	**Nieuport 12**	6
	110hp Clerget. French-built. 8524 and 8525 to Romanian forces.	
8530-8541	**Short S.38 Type**	(12)
	80hp Gnome. Ordered from Norman Thompson Flight Co. No delivery record.	
8542-8549	**Wight Admiralty Type 840**	(8)
	Built by Portholme Aerodrome Ltd but delivered unassembled as spares.	
8550-8561	**Short Admiralty Type 827**	12
	150hp Sunbeam. Fairey c/n F4-F15. 8560 to Royal Flying Corps as A9920.	
8562-8573	**Bristol Boxkite**	12
	B & C c/n 882-893.	
8574-8603	**Avro 504C**	30
	80hp Gnome. Known as Avro Scout. 8603 became 504F.	
8604-8605	**Maurice Farman S.7 Longhorn**	2
	Built by AMC. Delivered to Chingford and Cranwell during mid-1916.	
8606-8629	**B.E.2c**	24
	90hp RAF. Built by Blackburn. 8624 modified to single-seat.	
8630-8649	**Short Admiralty Type 827**	20
	150hp Sunbeam. Built by Sunbeam.	
8650-8699	**Curtiss H-12 Large America**	50
	Built in USA. 8650 reported as H-8 type. 8651, 8656, 8657, 8661, 8677, 8690 became H-12 Convert. 8691 had telescopic W/T mast fitted.	
8700-8707	**Voisin**	8
	150hp Canton Unne. French-built. Known as New Type in Royal Naval Air Service.	
8708-8713	**Nieuport 12**	6
	110hp Clerget. French-built.	
8714-8724	**B.E.2c**	11
	90hp RAF. Built by Beardmore.	
8725	**Airco DH.2**	(1)
	Built by AMC, ex-RFC.	
8726-8744	**Nieuport 12**	19
	110hp Clerget. French-built. 8741 130hp Clerget. Some converted to single-seat. 8731 to Romanian forces.	

8745-8751	**Nieuport Scout**	7
	80hp Le Rhone. French-built.	
8752-8801	**Grahame White XV**	50
	Admiralty Type 1600. 8752, 8753 to Australia became CFS11, CFS12 at Point Cook.	
8802-8901	**Curtiss JN-4**	80(100)
	90hp Curtiss OX-2. USA-built. Even numbers fitted with DC. 8881-8900 not delivered. 8901 to RFC. 8852, 8856, 8858 to French Government. 8805, 8814, 8824, 8828-8830, 8834, 8838, 8861, 8874, 8876, 8878, 8879 to US Forces, mainly ex-RNAS Vendome.	
8902-8920	**Nieuport 12**	19
	110hp Clerget. French-built. 8918 fitted with W/T.	
8921-8940	**Maurice Farman S.7 Longhorn**	20
	Built by Brush Electrical Engineering.	
8941-8950	**Caudron G.3**	10
	Known as Caudron School. Built by British Caudron.	
8951-9000	**Bristol Scout D**	50
	100hp Gnome Monosoupape. B & C. C/n 1124-1173. 8976 to Australia as their CFS10, later CFS4.	
9001-9020	**Pemberton-Billing P-25 Scout**	20
	Built by Supermarine. 9001-9004 flown, the rest built and delivered but probably scrapped before erection.	
9021-9040	**Wight Admiralty Type 840**	8(20)
	Built by Beardmore. 9029-9040 delivered as spare parts.	
9041-9060	**Short Admiralty Type 184**	20
	Built by Robey & Co. First five 225hp Sunbeam Mohawk engines, the rest with 240hp Sunbeam Gurkha.	
9061-9064	**Norman Thompson NT4A Small America**	4
	160hp Green planned, but 140hp Hispano fitted.	
9065-9084	**Short Admiralty Type 184**	20
	225/240hp Sunbeam. Built by Sage & Co.	
9085-9094	**Short Admiralty Type 184 modified**	10
	Built by Mann Egerton as their Type B.	
9095-9096	**Admiralty AD Navyplane**	1(2)
	9095 built by Supermarine. 9096 cancelled.	
9097-9098	**Wight Baby Seaplane**	2
	100hp Gnome Monosoupape. Built by J.S. White & Co.	
9099	**Henry Farman**	1
	160hp Canton Unne. French-built. To RFC as A8974.	
9100	**Wight Baby Seaplane**	1
	100hp Gnome Monosoupape. Prototype by J.S. White & Co.	
9101-9131	**Caudron G.4**	31
	Known as Caudron Twin. French-built. 9101, 9104-9106 to French Government.	
9132	*(Cancelled order)*	(1)
9133	**Maurice Farman F.37**	1
	110hp Renault. French-built.	
9134-9153	**Henry Farman F.27**	20
	160hp Canton Unne. French-built and shipped to the Aegean. 9134-9136, 9142-9144, 9146-9149, 9151, 9153 tropical version. 9135, 9151 to Greek service. 9152 to Royal Flying Corps as A8975.	
9154	**Voisin Canon**	1
	150hp Canton Unne. French-built.	
9155-9174	**Farman F.56**	20
	150hp Renault. French-built.	
9175-9200	**Breguet Concours**	26
	225hp Renault. French-built. Limited use.	
9201-9250	**Nieuport 12**	50
	110/130hp Clerget. Built by Beardmore. 9213-9232 to RFC as A3281, A3270-A3275, A3282-A3294. 9241 was built as a single-seater.	
9251-9260	**Henry Farman Astral**	1(10)
	Ordered from Brush Electrical Engineering but only 9251 was built.	
9261-9275	**Henry Farman Astral**	(15)
	Order cancelled.	
9276-9285	**Avro 504E**	10
	100hp Gnome Monosoupape. A.V. Roe-built with DC.	
9286-9305	**Caudron G.4**	(20)
	Known as Caudron Twin. Order cancelled. Two 100hp Anzani engines proposed.	
9306-9355	**Short Bomber**	35(50)
	250hp Rolls-Royce. C/n S.249-S.298 issued but 9341-9355 were cancelled. 9311 to French Government. Transfers to RFC: 9315, 9316, 9319, 9320, 9325 and renumbered 9152 A5203, A5157, A5155, A5214, A4005.	
9356-9375	**Short Bomber**	15(20)

	Built by Sunbeam Motors. 9371-9375 cancelled.	
9376-9425	**Sopwith 1½ Strutter**	50
	Admiralty Type 9400. Initial batch of type by Sopwith, 110 or 130hp Clerget engines fitted. 9376, 9396, 9420 interned in Holland to become LA34 (later S412), LA33 and LA38 (later S24) in Dutch service. 9381, 9386, 9387, 9389 to RFC as Nos. 7942, 5719-5721.	
9426-9455	**Breguet Concours**	10(30)
	250hp Rolls-Royce. Built by Grahame-White as their Type XIX. 9436-9455 (20) cancelled.	
9456-9475	**B.E.2c**	20
	Various engines fitted. Transferred from RFC without engines. Re-engined as follows: 9456, 9457 90hp Curtiss, 9458 75hp Hawk, 9459-9461 90hp RAF, 9462-9469 90hp Curtiss, 9470 90hp RAF, 9471-9475 90hp Curtiss.	
9476-9495	**Short Bomber**	20
	250hp Rolls-Royce. Built by Mann Egerton. 9476-9485, 9487, 9488 transferred to RFC as A5182, A5180, A5170, A5489, A5158, A5159, A5179, A5154, A5153, A5173, A5490, A5181.	
9496-9497	**Sopwith Pup**	2
	Admiralty Type 9901. 80hp Clerget. Sopwith prototypes.	
9498-9499	**Robey-Peters Davis gun machine**	1(2)
	Prototype built by Robey & Co. 9499 not completed.	
9500-9600	**Curtiss Twin Canada**	(101)
	Order cancelled.	
9601-9610	**FBA Flying Boat**	10
	100hp Gnome Monosoupape. French-built.	
9611	**Spad S.7**	1
	French-built pattern aircraft ex-Mann Egerton works to RFC as B388.	
9612-9635	**FBA Flying Boat**	24
	100hp Gnome Monosoupape. French-built. 9615, 9622, 9623 to RFC as B3984-B3986.	
9636-9650	**Reserved for French aircraft**	—
9651-9750	**Sopwith 1½ Strutter**	100
	Admiralty Type 9400/9700. 110hp Clergets standard but 130hp Clergets fitted in some cases. Type 9400 (two-seat fighter) except for Type 9700 (single-seat bomber) as follows: 9651, 9652, 9655, 9657, 9660, 9661, 9664, 9666, 9673, 9700, 9706, 9709, 9711, 9714, 9715, 9718, 9720, 9723, 9724, 9727, 9729, 9732, 9733, 9736, 9738, 9741, 9742, 9745, 9747. Transfers: 9655, 9657, 9661, 9664, 9665, 9669, 9673, 9714, 9720, 9729, 9736, 9738, 9742, 9745 to French Government; 9668, 9675, 9676, 9678, 9679, 9681, 9682, 9684, 9685, 9687, 9688, 9690-9697, 9702, 9703, 9705, 9707, 9710, 9713, 9716, 9719, 9721, 9725, 9728, 9731, 9737, 9740, 9743, 9746, 9749 (36) to RFC as A882, A888, A889, A890, A896, A891, A2432, A2983, A897, A2988, A2985, A2986, A2984, A2989, A2987, A2431, A2983, A1904, A1907, A1911, A1908, A1909, A1910, A1913, A1912, A1914-A1919, A1921-A1925.	
9751-9770	**Short Admiralty Type 166**	20
	200hp Canton Unne. Built by Westland.	
9771-9780	**Short Bomber**	6(10)
	250hp Rolls-Royce. Built by Parnall & Sons except 9777-9780 which were cancelled. 9772 transferred to Royal Flying Corps as A5171.	
9781-9790	**Short Admiralty Type 830**	10
	140hp Canton Unne.	
9791-9799	*(Not allotted)*	—
9800-9820	**Porte Baby**	12(21)
	Three Rolls-Royce Eagle. Hulls built by May, Harden and May. 9800-9811 only erected at Felixstowe, rest of hulls stored.	
9821-9830	**Avro 504B**	10
9831-9840	**Short Bomber**	6(10)
	250hp Rolls-Royce. Built by Phoenix Dynamo but 9837-9840 were cancelled. 9832, 9833 to the RFC as A6300 and A3932.	
9841-9860	**Wight Landplane Bomber/converted Seaplane**	20
	9841-9845 built as Wight 1916 Landplane Bomber. 9841 crashed on second flight and 9842-9845 were converted to seaplanes and the rest were built as seaplanes.	
9861-9890	**Avro 504B**	30
	80hp Gnome. Built by Parnall & Sons fitted for bombing training. 9890 fitted with gun interrupter gear.	

9891	**Sopwith 1½ Strutter**	1
	80hp Gnome. Prototype known as Sopwith School.	
9892-9897	**Sopwith 1½ Strutter**	6
	Admiralty Type 9400. Sopwith pre-production. 110hp Clerget engines fitted. 9892 to the RFC.	
9898-9900	**Sopwith Pup**	3
	Admiralty Type 9901. Sopwith pre-production. 80hp Clerget engines fitted.	
9901-9950	**Sopwith Pup**	50
	Admiralty Type 9901/9901A. Built by Beardmore. 80hp Clerget or Le Rhone engines fitted. From 9909 aircraft fitted alternatively with gun/rocket armament. 9950 converted to Beardmore W.B.III (SB3D).	
9951-10000	**B.E.2c**	50
	Built by Blackburn. 9969 to French Government and still preserved by the Musee de l'Air, Paris.	

Letter Prefixes Introduced

A1 to A9999

From 1916 the character of serialling changed. Without exception numbers allotted in a 1 to 9999 range were given a letter prefix in an alphabetical sequence that continues today. The RNAS having been allotted Nos.8001-10,000, the RFC took up the letter/number series starting at A1.

Serial Nos.	Aircraft Type and Remarks	Quantity
A1-A40	**F.E.2d**	40
	Royal Aircraft Factory built. A40 tested to destruction.	
A41-A65	**F.E.8**	(25)
	Ordered from Darracq Motor Engineering. Not built.	
A66-A115	**R.E.8**	50
	Royal Aircraft Factory built. A95 converted to R.E.8a.	
A116-A315	Various types purchased by GHQ, BEF	200
	A116-A118 Nieuport 16; A119 Morane BB; A120 Morane P; A121 Nieuport 16 fitted for rocket firing; A122 Morane N; A123, A124 Morane LA; A125, A126 Nieuport 16; A127, A128 Morane N; A130, A131 Nieuport 16; A132 Morane BB; A133-A136 Nieuport 16; A137-A139 Morane BB; A140-A146 Morane LA; A147 Morane BB; A148 Morane N; A149-A151 Morane BB; A152, A153 Morane LA; A154 Nieuport 20; A155 Morane BB; A156 Nieuport 20; A157-A159 Morane LA; A160 Morane V; A161-A163 Morane BB; A164, A165 Nieuport 16; A166, A167 Morane N; A168-A170 Morane LA; A171-A174 Morane N; A175-A179 Morane N; A180-A182 Morane LA; A183 Morane BB; A184 Nieuport 16; A185 Nieuport 20; A186 Morane N; A187 Nieuport 16; A188 Nieuport 20; A189-A191 Morane BB; A192 Morane LA for experimental work in the UK; A193 Morane P; A194 Morane LA; A195 Morane BB; A196 Morane N; A197 Morane P; A198, A199 Morane LA; A200, A201 Nieuport 17; A202 Morane I; A203 Nieuport 17; A204 Morane V; A205 Morane P; A206 Morane I; A207 Morane V; A208 Nieuport 16; A209 Morane V; A210-A212 Nieuport 16; A213 Nieuport 17; A214 Nieuport 16; A215 Nieuport 17; A216 Nieuport 16; A217, A218 Morane BB; A219 Morane V; A220 Morane BB; A221 Morane P; A222 Morane BB; A223-A225 Nieuport 16; A226, A227 Morane BB; A228, A229 Nieuport 20; A230-A233 Morane BB; A234, A235 Morane V; A236-A238 Morane V; A239-A241 Morane P; A242-A244 Morane BB; A245, A246 Morane V; A247-A250 Morane P; A251 Morane BB; A252 Morane V; A253 Spad 7; A254 Morane V; A255 Morane P; A256, A257 Morane BB; A258, A259 Nieuport 20; A260, A261 Morane P; A262, A263 Spad 7; A264-A270 Morane P; A271-A276 Nieuport 17;	

	A277 Morane P; A278, A279 Nieuport 17; A280 Morane P; A281 Nieuport 17; A282-A284 Morane BB; A285 Nieuport 20; A286-A290 Morane BB; A291, A292 Nieuport 20; A293-A296 Morane BB; A297, A298 Morane P; A299-A304 Morane BB; A305-A307 Nieuport 17; A308 Morane P; A309 Nieuport 20; A310 Spad 7; A311 Nieuport 17; A312 Spad 7; A313 Nieuport 17; A314 Nieuport 20; A315 Morane P.	
A316-A317	**Avro**	(2)
	Was allotted for two prototypes.	
A318-A323	**Martinsyde Trainer**	(6)
	Projected prototypes.	
A324-A373	**Maurice Farman S.11 Shorthorn**	50
	80hp Renault. AMC-built.	
A374-A375	**Albatros**	2
	Captured German aircraft.	
A376	**B.E.2b**	1
	Built up from spares.	
A377-A386	**Sopwith 1½ Strutter**	10
	Type 9400. Ex-RNAS order.	
A387-A410	**Henry Farman F.27**	24
	All-steel version for overseas service.	
A411	**Armstrong Whitworth F.K.7.**	1
	Prototype built by Armstrong Whitworth at Newcastle.	
A412-A461	**Avro 504A**	50
	Built by S. E. Saunders.	
A462-A511	**Avro 504A**	50
	80hp Gnome. Built by Bleriot & Spad.	
A512-A561	**Avro 504A**	50
A562-A611	**B.E.12A**	50
	Built by COW.	
A612-A613	**Bristol F.3A**	2
	Prototypes c/n 1485, 1486.	
A614-A625	**Curtiss JN-3**	12
	Ex-Admiralty contract.	
A626-A675	**Sopwith Pup**	50
	Built by Standard Motors.	
A676-A727	**Vickers FB.14**	52
	Built by Vickers at Weybridge. Mainly delivered as airframes to store at Islington and later scrapped.	
A728	**Maurice Farman S.11 Shorthorn**	1
	Built from salvage by No.2 RS.	
A729-A777	**Armstrong Whitworth**	(49)
	Biplane type cancelled.	
A778-A877	**F.E.2b**	100
	Built by G. & J. Weir. A778 to Australia as their CFS14. A826 to RNAS, A838 fitted with searchlight.	
A878-A897	**Sopwith 1½ Strutter**	20
	Type 9400. Ex-RNAS contract. A882, A888-A891, A896, A897, ex-9668, 9675, 9676, 9678, 9681, 9679, 9685.	
A898-A903	**Curtiss JN-3**	6
	Transferred from RNAS.	
A904-A953	**Maurice Farman S.11 Shorthorn**	50
	80hp Renault. AMC-built. A942 to CFS Australia.	
A954-A1053	**Sopwith 1½ Strutter**	100
	Type 9400. Built by Fairey Aviation. C/n F.27-F.126. Offsets to foreign governments: A966, A969, A983-A985 Russia, A986-A990 France, A998, A999 Romania, A1034-A1036, A1046 Belgium.	
A1054-A1153	**Sopwith 1½ Strutter**	100
	Type 9400. Built by Vickers at Crayford. A1090 DC. A1100 converted to single-seater. A1118-A1126, A1131, A1133, A1135, A1136, A1147 to Russian and A1127-A1130, A1137-A1146 to French Government.	
A1154-A1253	**Henry Farman F.20**	100
	AMC contract sub-let to Grahame-White.	
A1254-A1260	**Curtiss JN-3 (CAN)**	7
	Ex-RNAS contract for Canadian-built JN-3s.	
A1261-A1310	**B.E.2c/e**	50
	Built by Barclay, Curle & Co. A1284-A1287 to RNAS. A1280-A1283 to Norwegian Government. A1298 became G-EAJA.	
A1311-A1360	**B.E.2c/e**	50
	Built by Napier & Miller. A1326-A1329 to RNAS less engines. A1325 to Norwegian and A1327 to the Greek Governments.	
A1361-A1410	**B.E.2c/d**	50
	Built by Denny. A1382-A1385 to RNAS less engines of which the last two went to the Greek Government.	

A1378-A1381 to Norwegian Government.
A1404, A1410 became G-EAJN and G-EAJV.

A1411-A1460	Vickers FB.9	50
	Vickers-built at Weybridge. A1424, A1428 fitted with Scarff gun rings.	
A1461-A1510	Armstrong Whitworth FK.3	50
	Built by Hewlett & Blondeau.	
A1511-A1560	Sopwith 1½ Strutter	50
	Type 9400. Built by Hooper. All but A1512-A1515 to the Russian Government on repayment terms. A1527 subsequently captured by Lithuania.	
A1561-A1610	Martinsyde G.102 Elephant	50
	Martinsyde-built.	
A1611-A1660	Airco DH.1/1A	50
	AMC contract sub-let to Savages. A1631, A1635 DH.1As.	
A1661-A1710	Grahame-White Type XV	50
A1711	Maurice Farman S.11 Shorthorn	1
	Constructed from spares by No.2 RS.	
A1712-A1741	Henry Farman F.20	30
	AMC-built.	
A1742-A1791	Bristol Scout D	50
	Built by British and Colonial. A1769-A1772 and A1790, A1791 to the RNAS.	
A1792-A1891	B.E.2c/d/e	100
	90hp RAF. Built by Vulcan Motor & Engineering. A1819 B.E.2g. A1829, A1833, A1835 to RNAS less engines, A1826, A1830-A1832, A1836, A1839 also to the RNAS.	
A1892-A1901	Caudron G.3	10
	British Caudron built.	
A1902-A1931	Sopwith 1½ Strutter	(30)
	Type 9400. Transferred from RNAS. Known previous identities: A1903, A1904 ex-9695, 9696; A1907-A1919 ex-9697, 9703, 9705, 9707, 9702, 9713, 9710, 9716, 9719, 9721, 9725, 9728, 9731; A1921-A1925 ex-9737, 9740, 9743, 9746, 9749.	
A1932-A1966	F.E.2d	35
	Royal Aircraft Factory built.	
A1967	Armstrong Whitworth FK.3	1
	70hp Renault. Origin not known.	
A1968-A1969	Vickers FB.19 Mk.1	2
	Prototypes. A1968 to Russian Government.	
A1970-A2019	Avro 504A	50
	Built by Bleriot & Spad.	
A2020-A2119	F.E.4	(100)
	Order cancelled.	
A2120-A2121	Vickers FB.15	(2)
	Prototypes ordered from Vickers (Bexley) but later cancelled.	
A2122	Vickers FB.19	1
	Built by Vickers at Weybridge.	
A2123-A2124	Caudron G.3	2
	Built by British Caudron at Cricklewood.	
A2125-A2174	Airco DH.4	50
	Eagle or BHP engines fitted. AMC-built. A2168 had an RAF.3a engine and A2148 was experimentally fitted with a Renault 12F3. A2168 had COW gun fitted for the anti-Zeppelin role.	
A2175	Maurice Farman S.11 Shorthorn	1
	Erected at Brooklands from spare parts in July 1916.	
A2176-A2275	Maurice Farman S.11 Shorthorn	100
	Built by Whitehead at Richmond.	
A2276-A2375	Henry Farman F.20	(100)
	Ordered from Grahame-White. No delivery record.	
A2376-A2380	Bristol Scout D	(5)
	Ex-RNAS 8981-8985 allotment not effected.	
A2381-A2430	Sopwith 1½ Strutter	50
	Type 9400. Built by Ruston Proctor. A2421-A2423, A2425, A2427-A2430 to the Russian Government.	
A2431-A2432	Sopwith 1½ Strutter	(2)
	Type 9400. Ex-RNAS 9694 and 9682. See A3431.	
A2433-A2532	Maurice Farman S.11 Shorthorn	100
	70hp Renault. AMC-built. A2494 with 80hp Renault.	
A2533-A2632	Airco DH.2	100
	AMC-built. A2538, A2594 fitted with 110hp Le Rhone. A2562 to RNAS with 90hp RAF.	
A2633-A2682	Avro 504A	50
	A.V.Roe-built at Manchester. Deliveries suggest that the last 25 aircraft were shipped to Egypt.	
A2683-A2732	Armstrong Whitworth FK.8	50

	Armstrong Whitworth-built. A2696 fitted with 150hp Lorraine Dietrich and A2725 a 140hp RAF.	
A2733-A2982	B.E.2e/g	250
	Built by British & Colonial Aeroplane Co.	
A2983-A2991	Sopwith 1½ Strutter	(9)
	Type 9400. Ex-RNAS. A2983-A2989 ex-9684, 9691, 9688, 9690, 9693, 9687, 9692.	
A2992	Vickers FB.19 Mk.1	1
	Prototype, later to service in No.50 Squadron.	
A2993-A3005	Caudron G.3	13
	British Caudron-built. A3005 became K-121 (G-EACK).	
A3006-A3020	Bristol Scout D	(15)
	Allotted for 8986-9000 from RNAS but transfer not effected.	
A3021-A3023	Various types used at CFS	3
	A3201 Fokker captured; A3022 Curtiss JN-3; A3023 HF.	
A3024-A3048	Caudron G.3	25
	British Caudron-built. A3030, A3032 became G-EAOO and G-EALV respectively.	
A3049-A3168	B.E.2e/f	120
	Built by Wolseley Motors. Over half bore presentation names. A3109, A3110 presented to South Africa.	
A3169-A3268	R.E.8	100
	Built by Austin Motors.	
A3269	B.E.2c	1
	No.2076 rebuilt with spares by the 19th Wing.	
A3270-A3275	Nieuport 12	(6)
	Ex-RNAS 9214-9219 issued to equip No.46 Squadron.	
A3276-A3280	Curtiss JN-3	5
	Ex-RNAS order.	
A3281-A3294	Nieuport 12	(14)
	Ex-RNAS 9213, 9220-9232 for No.46 Squadron, RFC.	
A3295-A3302	Maurice Farman S.11 Shorthorn floatplanes	8
	Ordered from AMC for School of Aerial Gunnery, Loch Doon.	
A3303-A3354	Bristol F.2A Fighter	52
	Rolls-Royce Falcon engines. Built by British & Colonial Aeroplane Co. A3303, A3304 prototypes (c/ns 1379, 1380) the latter with 150hp Hispano fitted. A3305-A3354 had c/ns 1431-1480.	
A3355-A3404	Avro 504A	50
	Built by S.E.Saunders.	
A3405-A3504	R.E.8	100
	RAF.4a engines. Built by Siddeley-Deasy Motors. A3406 had 200hp RAF.4d engine.	
A3431	Sopwith 1½ Strutter	(1)
	Number incorrectly given to A2431.	
A3505	Vickers FB.14	1
	Experimental aircraft.	
A3506-A3530	R.E.8	(25)
	Ordered from Royal Aircraft Factory but not built.	
A3531-A3680	R.E.8	150
	Built by Daimler. A3542, A3561 converted to R.E.9.	
A3681-A3830	R.E.8	150
	Built by Siddeley-Deasy Motors.	
A3831	Curtiss JN-3	(1)
	Ex-RNAS.	
A3832-A3931	R.E.8	100
	Built by Napier. A3902 had increased fin area. A3909-A3912 converted to R.E.9.	
A3932	Short Bomber	(1)
	Ex-RNAS 9833.	
A3933-A3934	Martinsyde F.1	2
	Prototype contract.	
A3935-A4004	Martinsyde G.102 Elephant	70
A4005	Short Bomber	(1)
	Ex-RNAS 9325.	
A4006-A4055	B.E.12a	50
	Built by Daimler.	
A4056-A4060	Curtiss JN-3	5
	Ex-RNAS contract. Curtiss Nos.147, 157, 163, 169, 172.	
A4061-A4160	Maurice Farman S.11 Shorthorn	100
	AMC-built. A4144-A4146 to RNAS less engines.	
A4161-A4260	R.E.8	100
	Built by Daimler. A4179 to Belgian Flying Corps.	
A4261-A4410	R.E.8	150
	Built by Austin Motors. A4322, A4323, A4358-A4361 to Belgian Flying Corps. A4397 to Australian Government.	
A4411-A4560	R.E.8	150
	Built by Standard Motors.	

A4561-A4563	**S.E.5**	3
	Royal Aircraft Factory prototypes. A4562 broke up in the air on trial.	
A4564-A4663	**R.E.8**	100
	Built by Standard Motors. A4600, A4609 conv to R.E.9	
A4664-A4763	**R.E.8**	100
	Built by COW. A4695-A4700 and 4719 to the Belgian Flying Corps.	
A4764-A4813	**D.H.2**	50
	AMC-built.	
A4814-A4815	**Vickers FB.11**	2
	Experimental escort fighter built by Vickers at Bexley.	
A4816-A4817	**B.E.2c**	2
	Built from spares at Nos.2 and 18 RS.	
A4818-A4844	**F.E.9**	8(27)
	Royal Aircraft Factory order. Only 8 built and 3 flown.	
A4845-A4868	**S.E.5**	24
	Royal Aircraft Factory built. Some converted to S.E.5a.	
A4869-A4987	**F.E.8**	119
	Built by Darracq Motor Engineering.	
A4988-A5087	**Airco DH.2**	100
	AMC-built. A5041 sold and A5084 free issue to USA.	
A5088-A5137	**Airco DH.3**	(50)
	Ordered from AMC but cancelled.	
A5138-A5142	**Bristol Monoplane**	5
	B & C. C/n 1373, 1481-1484. A5138 Type M.1A, the rest being M.1B with various engines for trials.	
A5143-A5152	**F.E.2d**	10
	Royal Aircraft Factory built.	
A5153-A5155	**Short Bomber**	(3)
	Ex-RNAS 9484, 9483, 9319.	
A5156	**R.E.7**	1
	Built up from spares.	
A5157-A5159	**Short Bomber**	(3)
	Ex-RNAS 9316, 9480, 9481.	
A5160-A5168	**Curtiss JN-3/4**	9
	Ex-RNAS contract.	
A5169	**Voisin LA**	1
	Original pattern aircraft from France.	
A5170-A5171	**Short Bomber**	(2)
	Ex-RNAS 9478, 9772.	
A5172	**Airco DH.5**	1
	Prototype by AMC.	
A5173	**Short Bomber**	(1)
	Ex-RNAS 9485.	
A5174	**Vickers FB.19 Mk.II**	1
	Prototype	
A5175-A5176	**Airco DH.6**	2
	Prototypes by AMC.	
A5177-A5178	**Bristol MR.1**	2
	Experimental all-metal aircraft. B & C. C/ns 2067, 2068. A5177 delivered with wooden wings and bore the unexplained number A58623.	
A5179-A5182	**Short Bomber**	(4)
	Ex-RNAS 9482, 9477, 9488, 9476.	
A5183-A5202	**Nieuport 12**	(20)
	Ex-Beardmore built, from the RNAS.	
A5203	**Short Bomber**	(1)
	Ex-RNAS 9315.	
A5204	**Martinsyde G.102 Elephant**	1
	Built from spares at Farnborough.	
A5205-A5206	**Curtiss JN-3**	(2)
	Ex-RNAS.	
A5207-A5208	**B.E.2c**	2
	Built from salvage by 18 RS.	
A5209	**Bristol Scout**	1
	Built from salvage by 18 RS.	
A5210	**Vickers FB.12A**	1
	Prototype	
A5211	**Airco DH.2**	1
	Built from salvage at 19 RS, Northolt.	
A5212-A5213	**Armstrong Whitworth F.K.10 Quadruplane**	2
	Armstrong Whitworth experimental aircraft.	
A5214	**Short Bomber**	(1)
	Ex-RNAS 9320	
A5215-A5224	**Curtiss Twin**	10
	Curtiss c/n C2, C4-C12.	
A5225-A5236	**Vickers FB.19 Mk.II**	12
	Vickers-built at Weybridge. At least seven aircraft shipped to minor theatres.	
A5237	*(Reservation)*	(1)
A5238-A5337	**Sopwith 1½ Strutter**	60(100)
	Built by Wells but nearly half cancelled. A5280 was single-seat. To allies: A5243 Belgian Flying Corps; A5246-A5251, A5256 to Russia; A5254 to Japan, but also reported delivered to Latvia.	
A5338-A5437	**F.E.2b**	(100)
	Order from Wells Aviation, but cancelled.	
A5438-A5487	**F.E.2b**	50
	Built by Boulton & Paul.	
A5488	**B.E.2c**	1
	Built up from spares by 18 RS.	
A5489-A5490	**Short Bomber**	(2)
	Ex-RNAS 9479, 9487.	
A5491	**F.E.8**	1
	Built by Darracq Motor Engineering.	
A5492-A5496	**Curtiss JN-3**	5
	Ex-RNAS. Curtiss c/n 127, 152, 61, 33, 10.	
A5497-A5499	**B.E.2c**	3
	Built from spares at 18 RS.	
A5500-A5649	**F.E.2b**	150
	Built by G. & J.Weir. A5607 re-numbered H7230.	
A5650-A5799	**F.E.2b**	150
	Group-built in Scotland. A5658, A5783, A5789 were re-numbered F5852, H7145, H7233. A5744 was F.E.2c. A5650, A5671, A5692 to the US Government.	
A5800-A5899	**Avro 504A**	(100)
	Cancelled order.	
A5900-A5949	**Avro 504A**	50
	A. V. Roe built at Manchester.	
A5950-A6149	**Sopwith Pup**	71(200)
	Types 9400 and 9700. Built by Morgan up to A6020 at least. A5951, A5952, A5982-A6000, A6006, A6010, A6014, A6019 converted to Ship Strutter. Bomber 9700 version to foreign governments: A5973-A5976, A6011, A6015, A6017 to Russia; A5977-A5981, A6001, A6002, A6012, A6013, A6018, A6020 to Japan.	
A6150-A6249	**Sopwith Pup**	100
	Built by Whitehead Aircraft.	
A6250-A6299	**Martinsyde G.102 Elephant**	50
	Martinsyde-built.	
A6300	**Short Bomber**	(1)
	Ex-RNAS 9832.	
A6301-A6350	**B.E.12**	50
	Built by Daimler, many converted to B.E.12a.	
A6351-A6600	**F.E.2b/d**	250
	Nacelles by Garrett, rest and erection by Boulton & Paul. Planned as 220 F.E.2d and 30 F.E.2b but the shortage of Rolls-Royce engines increased number of F.E.2bs. A6545, A6580 became F.E.2h. A6501-A6503 renumbered E3151-E3153 and A6504, A6565, A6600 renumbered H7228, H7176, H7178.	
A6601-A6800	Purchases of French aircraft by GHQ, BEF.	200
	A6601 Morane P; A6602 Nieuport 20; A6603-A6605 Nieuport 17; A6606-A6608 Morane P; A6609-A6611 Nieuport 17; A6612 Morane P; A6613-A6624 Nieuport 17; A6625 Nieuport 20; A6626 Morane P; A6627 Spad 7; A6628 Morane; A6629-A6632 Morane P; A6633, A6634 Spad 7; A6635-A6638 Morane P (110hp); A6639 Morane P (80hp); A6640-A6642 Spad 7; A6643 Morane P; A6644-A6647 Nieuport 17; A6648 Morane P; A6649 Spad 7; A6650-A6653 Morane P; A6654 Spad 7; A6655, A6656 Morane P (110hp/80hp); A6657, A6658 Nieuport 17; A6659, A6660 Morane P; A6661-A6663 Spad 7; A6664, A6665 Nieuport 17; A6666 Morane P (80hp); A6667-A6680 Nieuport 17; A6681-A6683 Spad 7; A6684 Nieuport 17; A6685 Spad 7; A6686 Nieuport Triplane; A6687, A6688 Spad 7; A6689 Nieuport 17; A6690 Spad 7; A6691-A6694 Nieuport 17; A6695-A6697 Spad 7; A6698-A6700 Morane P; A6701 Nieuport 20; A6708 Morane P; A6709-A6714 Spad 7; A6715-A6717 Morane P; A6718 Nieuport 17; A6719 Morane P; A6720, A6721 Nieuport 17; A6722-A6725 Morane P (110hp); A6726 Nieuport 17 or 23; A6727-A6730 Morane P; A6731, A6732 Nieuport 20; A6733, A6734 Nieuport 17 or 23; A6735-A6737 Nieuport 20; A6738, A6739 Nieuport 17 or 23; A6740-A6743 Nieuport 20; A6744, A6745 Nieuport 17 or 23; A6746-A6749 Spad 7; A6750 Morane P; A6751, A6752 Nieuport 17; A6753	

Spad 7; A6754-A6756 Nieuport 17; A6757, A6758 Morane P; A6759 Spad 7; A6760 Morane P; A6761-A6772 Nieuport 23; A6773 Nieuport 17; A6774-A6798 Nieuport 23; A6799-A6800 Morane P.

A6801-A7000	R.E.8	(200)
	Ordered from B & C. Cancelled and numbers reallotted.	
A6801-A6900	Maurice Farman S.11 Shorthorn	100
	AMC-built.	
A6901-A7000	Sopwith 1½ Strutter	100

Type 9700. Built by Hooper. A6905, A6911, A6913, A6919-A6922, A6952, A6966-A6968, A6971, A6972, A6980, A6985-A6990 converted to Ship Strutter; A6906, A6907 single-seat night fighters. A6910, A6918, A6969 also to RNAS but no evidence of conversion. To foreign governments: A6924-A6926, A6929-A6942, A6949-A6951, A6953-A6955, A6957, A6958, A6960, A6973-A6978 to Russia, A6927, A6956, A6959, A6961-A6965, A6979 to Japan and A6987 reported as sent both to Japan and Latvia.

A7001-A7100	Maurice Farman S.11 Shorthorn	100

70hp Renault. A7043-A7050 to RNAS Vendome of which A7046 eventually went to USA.

A7101-A7300	Bristol F.2B Fighter	200

Rolls-Royce Falcon. British & Colonial. C/ns 2069-2268. A7101-A7176 and A7178-A7250 Series I with Falcon I engines and A7177 and A7251-A7300 Series II with Falcon II. A7260 had RAF.4d engine. A7256 was re-numbered as H7171.

A7301-A7350	Sopwith Pup	50
	Built by Standard Motors.	
A7351-A7400	Vickers FB.12C	18(50)
	Ordered from Vickers, Weybridge. 18 built by Wells.	
A7401-A8090	Airco DH.4	690

AMC-built. A7559 DH.9 prototype. A7507, A7626, A7713, A7820, A7964, A8016, A8021, A8028, A8029, A8034, A8047, A8088 re-numbered F6214, F6215, F6212, H6881, H6858, F6222, F6002, F6207, H7125, F6001, F6003, H6882. A7457, A7459, A7620, A7629, A7632, A7644, A7647, A7663, A7684, A7726, A7742, A7744, A7751, A7760, A7764, A7768, A7772, A7773, A7829, A7830, A7845, A7846, A7848, A7849, A7863, A7867, A7868, A7870, A7878, A7902, A8006, A8013, A8022, A8025, A8032, A8044, A8066 to RNAS, plus A8059, A8063, A8065-A8067, A8079 replaced on contract by D9231-D9236. Mainly Eagle engines fitted but some had RAF.3a or BHP and A7532 had a 250hp Fiat. A7726, A7751 to RNAS without engines and were fitted with 190hp Renaults and A8083 with a Sunbeam Matabele. A7964 had experimental fitting of RAF.4d. A7893, A7929, A7993 to New Zealand, A7531 to US Government. A7988 became G-EAXH.

A8091-A8140	Armstrong Whitworth FK.3	50
	Built by Hewlett & Blondeau.	
A8141-A8340	Sopwith 1½ Strutter	200

Type 9400. Built by Ruston Proctor mainly for allies as follows: A8162-A8171 Belgium, A8146-A8153, A8156 France, A8194-A8197, A8199, A8202, A8205, A8206, A8208 Romania, A8141, A8143-A8145, A8154, A8155, A8157-A8161, A8175-A8182, A8185-A8192, A8264-A8266, A8309-A8313, A8316, A8318-A8324, A8327-A8331 to Russia.

A8341-A8490	Vickers FB.14	51(150)

Ordered from Vickers at Weybridge but only 51 believed delivered and those as airframes mainly to store. A8391 converted to FB.14F.

A8491-A8500	(Cancelled order/reservation)	(10)
A8501-A8600	Avro 504A	100

A.V. Roe built at Manchester. A8591 pattern aircraft for group building in Scotland, refurbished and renumbered F9572.

A8601-A8625	Vickers FB.9	25
	Vickers-built at Weybridge.	
A8626-A8725	B.E.2e	100

British & Colonial built. C/n 1737-1836. A8710 B.E.2c.

A8726-A8731	(Cancelled order/reservation)	(6)
A8732-A8737	Sopwith Pup	(6)

RNAS N5193, N5194, N5190, N5183, N5182, N5192 transfer to RFC cancelled.

A8738-A8743	(Cancelled order/reservation)	(6)

A8744-A8793	Sopwith 1½ Strutter	50

Built by Vickers at Crayford mainly for allies: A8744-A8746, A8748, A8749, A8751-A8758, A8769, A8770, A8772-A8776, A8791 to Russia; A8759, A8761-A8765 to Romania; A8779 to the RNAS.

A8794-A8893	Spad 7	100
	Built by Air Navigation Co.	
A8894-A8897	Various Royal Aircraft Factory types.	4

Built from salvage and spares by No. 1 (Southern) Aircraft Repair Depot, Farnborough, as their Nos.005-008; A8894 F.E.8b, A8895 F.E.2b, A8896, A8897 B.E.2c.

A8898-A8947	S.E.5	50

Royal Aircraft Factory built. A8898, A8900, A8908, A8918, A8923-A8927, A8934, A8935, A8938, A8939, A8941-A8943 became S.E.5a; A8947 S.E.5b.

A8948-A8949	B.E.2c	2
	Built from salvage at No.18 RS, Montrose.	
A8950-A8999	Armstrong Whitworth FK.10 Quadruplane	(50)

Ordered December 1916, cancelled March 1917 and numbers reallotted. See B3996-B4000.

A8950	F.E.2b	1
	Built by the Royal Aircraft Factory.	
A8951-A8956	T.E.1	(6)
	R.E.8 replacement. Cancelled.	
A8957-A8962	Radio-controlled experimental aircraft	?(6)
A8963	Vickers FB.16A/D	1
	Vickers-built FB.16A at Bexley, modified to FB.16D.	
A8964	Grahame-White M.1	(1)
	Twin airscrew experimental project not built.	
A8965	Spad 7	1
	French S1321 pattern aircraft.	
A8966	Avro 504	1
	Built from spares by 21st Wing.	
A8967	Nieuport 12	1
	French Government sample for Beardmore, for the RFC.	
A8968-A8969	Henry Farman	(2)
	Ex-RNAS N3035 and N3029.	
A8970-A8973	Sopwith Sparrow	4
	Sopwith 'run-about aircraft' allotted numbers.	
A8974-A8998	Henry Farman	(25)

Ex-RNAS 9099, 9152, N3025-N3028, N3030-N3034, N3036-N3049.

A8999	Aviatik	1
	200hp Benz. Ex-German.	
A9000-A9099	Sopwith Triplane	(100)
	Re-numbered in RNAS service.	
A9100-A9161	Spad 7	62
	Mann Egerton-built. Transferred from RNAS.	
A9162	Maurice Farman	1
	Built from spares by 4 RS, Northolt.	
A9163-A9362	Airco DH.5	(199)200
	AMC-built. A9362 cancelled as A5172 prototype was included in the contract.	
A9363-A9562	Airco DH.5	200
	Built by Darracq Motor Engineering.	
A9563-A9762	Airco DH.6	200
	Built by Grahame-White.	
A9763-A9812	Avro 504A/J	50
	Built by S.E.Saunders. A9785 night fighter modification. A9812 converted to 504K.	
A9813-A9918	Sopwith Triplane	(106)
	Clayton & Shuttleworth contract transferred to RNAS.	
A9919	Airco DH.1	1
	Built from spares.	
A9920	Short 827	(1)
	120hp Sunbeam. Ex-RNAS 8560.	
A9921	Maurice Farman S.11 Shorthorn	1
	Built from spares at 2 RS, Brooklands.	
A9922-A9971	Avro 504A	(50)
	Ordered from Bleriot & Spad. Cancelled.	
A9972	Armstrong Whitworth FK.3	1
	90hp RAF. Used by 58 Sqn, probably built from spares.	
A9973-A9974	B.E.2c	2
	Built from spares at Montrose.	
A9975-A9977	Avro 504B	(3)
	Ex-RNAS Parnall-built N6015-N6017.	
A9978-A9979	Maurice Farman S.7 Longhorn	(2)
	Ex-RNAS N5010, N5011 Robey-built.	
A9980-A9999	Armstrong Whitworth FK.8	20
	Armstrong Whitworth-built at Gosforth.	

British Production, French Purchases, and Rebuilds

B1 to B9999

This range of numbers allotted to the RFC, following on from A9999 in late 1916, included large numbers of aircraft re-built from salvaged remains and issued with a new number. Different ranges of numbers were reserved for each Aircraft Repair Depot. The final local purchases by GHQ, BEF of French aircraft appear in this issue of numbers.

Serial Nos.	Aircraft Type and Remarks	Quantity
B1-B200	**S.E.5a**	200
	Built by Air Navigation Co. B18 converted to 2-seater.	
B201-B330	**Armstrong Whitworth FK.8**	130
	Armstrong Whitworth-built. B214, B215 fitted with RAF.4d, RAF4a engines.	
B331-B380	**DH.5**	50
	Built by British Caudron.	
B381	**Sopwith Camel**	(1)
	Ex-RNAS.	
B382-B385	**Avro 504B**	(4)
	Ex-RNAS N6018-N6021.	
B386-B387	**B.E.2c**	2
	Built by 18 RS, Montrose, from salvage.	
B388	**Spad 7**	(1)
	Ex-RNAS 9611 French-built sample aircraft.	
B389-B392	**Avro 504B**	(4)
	Ex-RNAS N6022-N6025.	
B393	**Maurice Farman S.7 Longhorn**	(1)
	Ex-RNAS N5012.	
B394	**Airco DH.4**	(1)
	RNAS 3696 DH.4 prototype temporarily re-numbered.	
B395-B396	**Avro 504B**	(2)
	Ex-RNAS N6026, N6027.	
B397-B400	**Maurice Farman S.7 Longhorn**	(4)
	Ex-RNAS N5016, N5014, N5013, N5015.	
B401-B500	**F.E.2b/c**	100
	Built by Ransomes, Sims & Jeffries. B434, B442, B445, B447, B449, B450 F.E.2c, remainder F.E.2b.	
B501-B700	**S.E.5a**	200
	Built by Vickers (Weybridge). B609 had Sunbeam Arab engine fitted. B670 converted to two-seater.	
B701-B900	**Various types rebuilt from salvage by No.**	200
	No.1 (Southern) ARD, Farnborough. B701 B.E.12; B702 B.E.2e; B704 F.E.2b; B705 B.E.2c; B706 B.E.2e; B707, B708 B.E.2c; B709, B710 B.E.2c; B711 Sopwith 1½ Strutter; B712 B.E.2e; B714, B715 Sopwith 1½ Strutter; B718 B.E.2b; B719 B.E.2e; B720, B721 B.E.12; B722-B725, B728 B.E.2e; B729 Sopwith 1½ Strutter; B730, B732 R.E.8; B733 S.E.5a; B734 R.E.8; B735 Sopwith Pup; B736-B739, B741, B742 R.E.8; B744 Sopwith Ship Strutter; B745 Sopwith 1½ Strutter; B746 Bristol Scout (also reported as B.E.2e); B748 B.E.2e; B749 B.E.12; B750 R.E.8; B752 B.E.2e; B753, B755-B760 R.E.8; B762 Sopwith 1½ Strutter single-seat home defence conversion; B763 Bristol Scout D; B764, B765 R.E.8; B770 B.E.2e; B771 B.E.2c; B772 B.E.2e; B774-B776 DH.4; B778 Sopwith Camel; B780 R.E.8; B781 B.E.12 or R.E.8; B782, B783, B786, B787 R.E.8; B790 B.E.2e; B791-B793 R.E.8; B797 B.E.2e; B798 R.E.8; B799 Sopwith 1½ Strutter; B802 Sopwith Camel; B803-B805 Sopwith Pup; B810, B811 R.E.8; B812 Sopwith 1½ Strutter; B813 Bristol Scout D; B814 R.E.8; B816 Sopwith 1½ Strutter; B817 Bristol F.2B; B820-B825 R.E.8; B827 Sopwith 1½ Strutter; B828 Nieuport 17; B830, B832-B837, B840-B846 R.E.8; B847 Sopwith Camel; B848 S.E.5a; B849 Sopwith Pup; B851, B852 Martinsyde Elephant; B853, B854 R.E.8; B856 Armstrong Whitworth FK.8; B860 Martinsyde Elephant; B861	

Spad 7; B862 Sopwith 1½ Strutter; B864-B866 Martinsyde Elephant; B870, B871 Armstrong Whitworth FK.8; B872, B873 Martinsyde Elephant; B875 S.E.5a; B876 R.E.8; B879-B881 Spad 7; B882 DH.4; B883 Bristol F.2B; B884 DH.4 (rebuilt as F6070); B885 Camel; B887 Spad 7; B891 S.E.5a; B893, B895, B898, B900 Camel.

B901-B1000	**Avro 504A/J**	100
	100hp Gnome Monosoupape.	
B1001-B1100	**S.E.5a**	(100)
	Ordered from Whitehead but cancelled.	
B1101-B1350	**Bristol F.2B Fighter**	250
	Falcon III engines. Built by B & C. C/ns 2269-2518. B1209, B1234, B1307 re-numbered H7069, H7070, H7172. B1124 interned became BR401 in Dutch service.	
B1351-B1388	**Spad 7**	38
	Built by Mann Egerton. B1352-B1363, B1372, B1374-B1376, B1384, B1386 to the US Government.	
B1389	**Airco DH.4**	1
	Presumed built from spares.	
B1390-B1394	**Avro 504B**	(5)
	Ex-RNAS N6028, N6029, N6650-N6652.	
B1395-B1396	**Morane Monocoque AC**	2
	Received via Paris.	
B1397-B1400	**Avro 504B**	(4)
	Ex-RNAS N6653-N6656.	
B1401-B1481	**Henry Farman**	(81)
	Ordered from AMC, but cancelled.	
B1482	**Airco DH.4**	1
	Built by AMC.	
B1483	**Maurice Farman S.11 Shorthorn**	1
	Built from spares by 2 RS.	
B1484-B1489	**Vickers FB.26 Vampire I/II**	3(6)
	Prototypes: B1484, B1486 Mk.I and B1485 Mk.II, the rest being cancelled.	
B1490-B1495	**Martinsyde F.3**	5(6)
	Prototypes. B1493 cancelled.	
B1496	**Sopwith B2**	1
	Experimental bomber prototype.	
B1497	**Armstrong Whitworth FK.8**	1
	Built by 18th Wing ARS from spares.	
B1498	**R.E.8**	1
	Built from spares by 21st Wing ARS.	
B1499	**Sopwith Pup**	1
	Built from spares by 7th Wing ARS.	
B1500	**B.E.12**	1
	Built by No.37 Squadron from spares.	
B1501-B1700	**Purchases by GHQ, BEF**	200
	B1501-B1511 Nieuport 17; B1512 Nieuport 23; B1513 Nieuport 17; B1514 Nieuport 23; B1515-B1517 Nieuport 17; B1518 Nieuport 23; B1519, B1520 Nieuport 17; B1521 Morane P; B1522, B1523 Nieuport 17; B1524-B1538 Spad 7; B1539-B1556 Nieuport 17; B1557 Nieuport 23; B1558 Nieuport 17; B1559 Nieuport 23; B1560-B1565 Spad 7; B1566 Nieuport 17; B1567 Nieuport 23; B1568 Nieuport 17; B1569 Nieuport 23; B1570 Nieuport 17; B1571, B1572 Nieuport 23; B1573 Spad 7; B1574-B1576 Nieuport 23; B1577 Nieuport 17; B1578, B1579 Nieuport 23; B1580, B1581 Spad 7; B1582 Nieuport 17; B1583 Nieuport 23; B1584, B1585 Nieuport 17; B1586-B1589 Spad 7; B1590 Nieuport 17; B1591-B1593 Spad 7; B1594 Morane P; B1595 Nieuport 17; B1596 Morane P; B1597, B1598 Nieuport 17; B1599 Morane P; B1600-B1602 Nieuport 17; B1603 Nieuport 23; B1604 Morane P; B1605, B1606 Nieuport 17; B1607-B1610 Nieuport 23; B1611, B1612 Morane P; B1613 Nieuport 23; B1614, B1615 Nieuport 17; B1616-B1618 Nieuport 17; B1619 Nieuport 23; B1620 Spad 7; B1621 Nieuport 17; B1622, B1623 Spad 7; B1624-B1626 Nieuport 23; B1627, B1628 Spad 7; B1629 Nieuport 23; B1630-B1643 Nieuport 17; B1644 Nieuport 23; B1645-B1651 Nieuport 17; B1652 Nieuport 23; B1653 Spad 7; B1654, B1655 Nieuport 23; B1656-B1659 Nieuport 17; B1660, B1661 Spad 7; B1662 Nieuport 23; B1663, B1664 Spad 7; B1665, B1666 Nieuport 17; B1667 Spad 7; B1668, Morane P; B1669 Spad 7; B1670-B1672 Nieuport 17; B1673 Morane P; B1674 Nieuport 17; B1675 Nieuport 23; B1676-B1678 Nieuport 17; B1679 Nieuport 23; B1680-B1691 Nieuport 17; B1692 Nieuport 23; B1693 Nieuport 17; B1694 Nieuport 27; B1695-B1698 Spad 7; B1699, B1700 Nieuport 17.	

B1701-B1850	Sopwith Pup	150
	Built by Standard Motors. B1816-B1825 to the RNAS. B1807 became G-EAVX.	
B1851-B1900	F.E.2d/b	50
	Built by Boulton & Paul. B1873, B1877 (F.E.2b) to US Government.	
B1901-B1950	Curtiss JN-4/4A	50
	Ex-Admiralty contract.	
B1951-B2050	Maurice Farman S.11 Shorthorn	100
	Built by AMC. B2011, B2012 shipped to Australia.	
B2051-B2150	Airco DH.4	100
	BHP engines. Built by Berwick. B2060 had RAF engine.	
B2151-B2250	Sopwith Pup	100
	Built by Whitehead.	
B2251-B2300	R.E.8	50
	Built by Napier.	
B2301-B2550	Sopwith 1F1 Camel	250
	Built by Ruston Proctor. First Camel sub-contract. B2438, B2504 converted to 2-seat. B2402 special night fighter conversion. B2301 to French and B2543 to Greek Governments. B2371 re-built as F6303.	
B2551-B2600	Sopwith 1½ Strutter	50
	Two-seat Type 9400. Built by Ruston Proctor. B2551 to RNAS less engine. B2555 single-seat. B2566 converted to Ship Strutter. B2568, B2575, B2580, B2584 to the Belgian Flying Corps.	
B2601-B3100	Airco DH.6	500
	90hp RAF. AMC-built. B2639 had a 90hp Renault, B2903, B2929 90hp Curtiss. B2840 special experimental rigging. B2801-B2804 shipped to Australia. B2661 to Greek Government. B2689, B2791, B2861, B2868, B2917, B2934, B2943, B3003, B3061, B3065, B3067, B3068, B3082, B3094 became G-EAMS, 'EBWG, 'EANJ, 'AARN, 'EAHE, 'EAHD, 'EAFT, 'EARL, 'EARJ, 'EARK, 'EARR, 'EARM, 'EAQY, 'EALT.	
B3101-B3250	Avro 504J	150
	A.V. Roe-built at Hamble. B3104, B3106, B3157 and B3196 converted to 504K.	
B3251-B3300	Avro 504A	50
	80hp Gnome. Built by Humber. B3255, B3276, B3277, B3294-B3300 only to RFC, rest to the RNAS.	
B3301-B3400	Armstrong Whitworth FK.8	100
	Armstrong Whitworth-built. B3316 used in doping and camouflage experiments. B3317 re-built as F6160.	
B3401-B3450	R.E.8	50
	Built by Daimler.	
B3451-B3650	Purchases by GHQ, BEF.	200
	B3451 Morane P; B3452 Nieuport 17; B3453 Nieuport 23; B3454, B3455 Nieuport 17; B3456 Nieuport 23; B3457 Spad 7; B3458, B3459 Nieuport 17; B3460 Spad 7; B3461, B3462 Nieuport 17; B3463 Nieuport 23, B3464 Spad 7; B3465-B3469 Nieuport 17; B3470 Nieuport 23; B3471, B3472 Spad 7; B3473 Nieuport 17; B3474 Nieuport 23; B3475 Spad 7; B3476, B3477 Morane P; B3478 Nieuport 17; B3479 first Spad 13 for the RFC; B3480 Morane P; B3481 Nieuport 17; B3482 Nieuport 23; B3483, B3484 Nieuport 17; B3485, B3486 Nieuport 23, B3487 Nieuport 17; B3488-B3493 Spad 7; B3494-B3497 Nieuport 17, B3498, B3499 Spad 7; B3500 Nieuport 17; B3501-B3510, B3515, B3516 Spad 7; B3517 Morane P; B3519, B3520 Spad 7; B3521 Morane P; B3523, B3524 Spad 7; B3525, B3527 Morane P; B3528-B3535, B3537-B3539 Spad 7; B3540, B3541 Nieuport 17/23; B3545, B3547-B3549 Morane P; B3550-B3553 Spad 7; B3554, B3555 Nieuport 17/23; B3556, B3557 Spad 7; B3558 Nieuport 17; B3559, B3560 Spad 7; B3561 Nieuport 17; B3562-B3576 Spad 7; B3577, B3578, B3581 Nieuport 17; B3582 Nieuport 24; B3583-B3589 Nieuport 17; B3591, B3592 Nieuport 24bis; B3593, B3595, B3597, B3598 Nieuport 17; B3600 Nieuport 27; B3601 Nieuport 24; B3602, B3603 Nieuport 24bis; B3604 Nieuport 24; B3605 Nieuport 24bis; B3606, B3607 Nieuport 24; B3608 Nieuport 24bis; B3609, B3610 Nieuport 24; B3611 Nieuport 24bis; B3612-B3614 Nieuport 24; B3615, B3616 Spad 7; B3617 Nieuport 24; B3618-B3620 Spad 7; B3621-B3635 Nieuport 27; B3636, B3637 Nieuport 17/27; B3638-B3642 Spad 7; B3643, B3644 Nieuport 17; B3645, B3546 Spad 7; B3647-B3650 Nieuport 27.	
B3651-B3750	B.E.2c/e	100
	90hp RAF. Built by Vulcan Motor & Engineering. From B3701 practically all to RNAS stations. B3708 fitted with Curtiss OX-2 engine.	
B3751-B3950	Sopwith 1F1 Camel	200
	130hp Clerget. Sopwith-built. B3773, B3781, B3782, B3785, B3786, B3794, B3795, B3798, B3808-B3810, B3817, B3835, B3841, B3853, B3855-B3858, B3865, B3866, B3879, B3880, B3883, B3888, B3895, B3926, B3935-B3937, B3939, B3940 had Bentley B.R.2 engine, B3801 converted to 2-seat and B3829 had 110hp Le Rhone engine; B3811 had a 100hp Monosoupape and B3891 to French Government had Clerget, Le Rhone and 150hp Gnome Monosoupape engines successively fitted. B3786 re-numbered H7234. B3769 to Greek Government. B3772 to RAF (Canada) via USA.	
B3951	B.E.2c	1
	Built from spares by 18 RS.	
B3952-B3953	Avro 530	2
	Experimental prototypes.	
B3954	B.E.2d	1
	Built from spares by 25th Wing ARS.	
B3955-B3968	Airco DH.4	(14)
	Ex-RNAS N5970, N5980, N5986, N5987, N5990, N5991, N5994, N5995, N5998, N5999, N6002, N6003, N6006, N6007.	
B3969	Airco DH.1	1
	Built from spares by 19 TS.	
B3970	B.E.2c	(1)
	Built at Netheravon with main parts salvaged from 7189.	
B3971-B3976	N.E.1 (Night Experimental No.1)	6
	Royal Aircraft Factory experimental aircraft.	
B3977	Sopwith 1F1 Camel	(1)
	RNAS N6338 to RFC from Sopwith factory.	
B3978-B3979	B.E.2c	2
	Built from spares by 20th Wing ARS.	
B3980	Sopwith 1F1 Camel	1
	Repaired and taken on RFC charge.	
B3981	Maurice Farman S.11 Shorthorn	1
	Built from spares by 5 TS.	
B3982	Maurice Farman S.7 Longhorn	1
	Built from spares by 5 TS.	
B3983	B.E.2e	1
	Built from spares at Montrose.	
B3984-B3986	Franco-British Aviation Flying Boat	(3)
	100hp Monosoupape. Ex-RNAS 9615, 9622, 9623.	
B3987	Airco DH.4	(1)
	RAF.3a engine. Ex-RNAS N6380.	
B3988	Maurice Farman S.11 Shorthorn	1
	Built from spares by 4 TS.	
B3989-B3994	Bristol F/F1 (retrospectively Types 21/21A)	3(6)
	B & C. C/ns 2845-2850. B3989, B3990, B3991 F converted to F1, 3992 not completed, 3993, 3994 not built.	
B3995	B.E.2c	1
	Built from spares by 18 TS.	
B3996-B4000	Armstrong Whitworth FK.10 Quadruplane	(5)
	Numbers re-allotted from airframes built to A8950-A8999 contract and used as targets.	
B4001-B4200	Aircraft built from salvage and spares by No.2 (Northern) ARD. B4004 B.E.2e; B4005 F.E.2b; B4006 B.E.2e; B4009 B.E.2c; B4014 Armstrong Whitworth FK.8; B4016 Sopwith 1½ Strutter; B4017, B4018, Armstrong Whitworth FK.8; B4020 B.E.2c; B4021 R.E.8; B4022, B4023, B4026 B.E.2e; B4028-B4030, B4032-B4034, B4038, B4040 R.E.8; B4044 Sopwith Ship Strutter; B4045, B4046, B4048 R.E.8; B4049 Armstrong Whitworth FK.8; B4050, B4051, B4054-B4057, B4059, B4060 R.E.8; B4061 Armstrong Whitworth FK.8; B4062, B4065, B4067, B4069, B4075 R.E.8; B4080 Armstrong Whitworth FK.8; B4082 Sopwith Pup; B4086, B4089-B4091, B4093, B4094, B4097, B4098 R.E.8; B4100 Sopwith Pup; B4101, B4103-B4106 R.E.8; B4108 Armstrong Whitworth FK.8; B4109, B4118 R.E.8; B4120 Armstrong Whitworth FK.8; B4124, B4128, B4131 Sopwith Pup; B4134, B4135 R.E.8, B4140, B4141 Sopwith Pup; B4145-B4150, B4154, B4156 Armstrong Whitworth FK.8; B4158 Sopwith Pup; B4160, B4161, B4163, B4164-B4167, B4169, B4170, B4172, B4174-B4177, B4179, B4185, B4187, B4188, B4190, B4194, B4195, B4198, B4200 Armstrong Whitworth FK.8.	200

B4201-B4400	Avro 504J/A	200

A.V.Roe-built. B4201-B4300 504J (100hp Monosoupape) B4301-B4400 504A (80hp Gnome). B4221, B4242, B4266 converted to 504K. B4222 had single bay wings of reduced area. To RNAS: B4309, B4310, B4338, B4339 without engines, B4311-B4317 with engines. B4305, B4306 to Norwegian Army.

B4401-B4600	B.E.2e	200

Built by British & Colonial Aeroplane Co at Filton, c/ns 2519-2718. B4562 converted to B.E.2c standard. Several night fighter conversions. B4574 free gift to the French.

B4601-B4650	Sopwith 1F1 Camel	50

Built by Portholme. B4614 converted to 2-seater, B4622 to Belgian Flying Corps.

B4651-B4850	Maurice Farman S.11 Shorthorn	200

80hp Renault. AMC-built. Twenty-five aircraft to the RNAS. B4674 to G-EAAZ.

B4851-B4900	S.E.5a	50

Royal Aircraft Factory-built. B4885 interned became SE214 in Dutch service.

B4901-B5000	Airco DH.5	38(100)

Built by March, Jones & Cribb up to B4938 at least.

B5001-B5150	R.E.8	150

Built by Daimler.

B5151-B5250	Sopwith 1F1 Camel	100

Built by Boulton & Paul. B5228, B5242, B5248 to the Belgian Flying Corps.

B5251-B5400	Sopwith Pup	150

Built by Whitehead.

B5401-B5450	Sopwith 1F1 Camel	50

Built by Hooper. B5428 to 17th Aero Sqn USAS.

B5451-B5550	Airco DH.4	100

Built by Vulcan Motor & Engineering Co.

B5551-B5650	Sopwith 1F1 Camel	100

130hp Clerget. Built by Ruston Proctor. B5556 rebuilt as F9548 but reverted to B5556. B5644 re-numbered F6220. B5605, B5607 to the Belgian Flying Corps. B5581 fitted for W/T. B5630 had 110hp Le Rhone.

B5651-B5750	Sopwith 1F1 Camel	100

130hp Clerget. Built by Clayton & Shuttleworth. All deliveries to RNAS. B5713 converted to 2-seat. B5710, B5711, B5745, B5747, B5748 to Belgian Flying Corps, and B5747 is preserved at Brussels. B5657, B5682, B5726 to Greek Government. B5679, B5680, B5727 to White Russian Forces.

B5751-B5850	Armstrong Whitworth FK.8	100

AW-built at Gosforth. B5751, B5783, B5836 re-built as F5803, F5801, F6137. B5795 W/T experiments.

B5851-B5900	R.E.8	50

Built by Austin Motors.

B5901-B6150	Sopwith Pup	250

Built by Standard Motors. At least 64 delivered to RNAS.

B6151-B6200	Sopwith 2F1 Camel	(50)

Re-allotted Nos N6600-N6649 and B6151-B6200 used as below.

B6151-B6200	B.E.2c/e	50

Built by British Caudron at Alloa. B6183 became CFS18 in Australia.

B6201-B6450	Sopwith 1F1 Camel	250

130hp Clerget. Sopwith-built. B6242 rebuilt as F6027. B6241-B6243, B6257, B6276, B6300, B6351, B6357-B6359, B6389, B6397-B6399, B6400, B6408, B6409, B6411, B6422, B6430 fitted with Bentley B.R.1 engines. B6322, B6326, B6333, B6395 had Le Rhone engines and B6329 a 150hp Gnome Monosoupape. B6255, B6338, B6360, B6367 to Greek Government.

B6451-B6630	R.E.8/R.T.1	180

Built by Siddeley-Deasy. Last six completed as R.T.1s.

B6631-B6730	R.E.8	100

Built by COW. B6631 rebuilt as F6204.

B6731-B7130	French aircraft purchased by GHQ, BEF	141(400)

B6731-B6739 Spad 7; B6751-B6756 Nieuport 27; B6757 Morane P; B6758 Spad 7; B6759, B6760 Morane P; B6761, B6762 Spad 7; B6763, B6764 Morane P; B6765-B6770 Nieuport 27; B6771 Morane P; B6772, B6773 Spad 7; B6774 Nieuport 27; B6775-B6777 Spad 7; B6778, B6779 Nieuport 27; B6780 Spad 7; B6781-B6783 Morane P; B6784-B6786 Nieuport 27; B6787 Spad 7; B6788-B6793 Nieuport 27; B6794-B6796 Spad 7; B6797, B6798 Nieuport 27; B6799 Nieuport 23bis; B6800 Nieuport 27; B6801 Morane P; B6802 Spad 7; B6803, B6804 Nieuport 27; B6805 Spad 7; B6806 Morane P; B6807 Nieuport 27; B6808 Spad 7; B6809, B6810 Nieuport 27; B6811 Nieuport 27; B6812-B6815 Nieuport 27; B6816, B6817 Spad 7; B6818-B6832 Nieuport 27; B6835 Spad 13; B6836, B6837 Nieuport 27; B6838-B6862, B6864-B6867 Spad 13; B6868-B6871 Spad 7; B6872-B6875 Spad 13; B6877 Spad 12; B6878-B6886 Spad 13.

B7131-B7180	Sopwith 1F1 Camel	50

Built by Portholme. B7147 to Belgian Flying Corps. B7150 to the USA.

B7181-B7280	Sopwith 1F1 Camel	100

Mainly 130hp Clerget and Bentley B.R.1 engines fitted. Built by Clayton and Shuttleworth. B7219, B7244 converted to 2-seat. Majority delivered to RNAS. B7235-B7237 to Belgian Flying Corps. B7182, B7207, B7209, B7211, B7270 to Greek Government. B7181 to White Russians.

B7281-B7480	Sopwith 1F1 Camel	200

Built by Ruston Proctor, B7289, B7323, B7371, B7464 converted to 2-seat. B7329 to 148th Aero Sqn USAS.

B7481-B7580	Sopwith Pup	100

Built by Whitehead. Some delivered as spares.

B7581-B7680	Airco DH.9	100

Built by Westland. Fiat engines initially fitted, B.H.P. engines later. 27 delivered to RNAS. B7664 converted to DH.9A. B7620, B7623 interned became deH433/8 in Dutch service.

B7681-B7730	R.E.8	50

Built by Siddeley-Deasy.

B7731-B8230	Built from salvage by No.1 (Southern) ARD	500

B7732 Sopwith Camel; B7733 S.E.5a; B7734 R.E.8; B7735, B7737 S.E.5a; B7738-B7740 R.E.8; B7742 DH.9; B7743-B7746 Camel; B7747 DH.4; B7749 DH.9; B7752 Pup; B7754 R.E.8; B7755, B7756, B7760 Camel; B7761 R.E.8; B7763 Bristol F.2B; B7764 DH.4; B7765 S.E.5a; B7769 Camel; B7770, B7771 S.E.5a; B7772 Camel; B7775 DH.5; B7776, B7777 Camel; B7779 F.E.2b; B7781 Bristol F.2B; B7782 F.E.2b; B7783-B7785 Camel; B7786, B7787 S.E.5a, B7788 F.E.2b; B7789-B7791, B7793 Camel; B7794, B7795 F.E.2b; B7796 S.E.5a; B7797 Camel; B7800 F.E.2b; B7802-B7805 R.E.8; B7806, B7807 Camel; B7808, B7809 F.E.2b; B7812 DH.4; B7813-B7816 F.E.2b; B7817, B7820-B7822 Camel; B7824 S.E.5a; B7827 R.E.8; B7829 Camel; B7830-B7833 S.E.5a of which B7832 became D7017; B7834 R.E.8; B7835 Camel; B7836-B7841, B7843, B7847, B7848 F.E.2b; B7849 Dolphin; B7850 S.E.5a; B7851 Dolphin; B7853 R.E.8; B7855 Dolphin; B7856, B7858 F.E.2b; B7859, B7860 Camel; B7861 Dolphin; B7862-B7864 Camel; B7865, B7866 DH.4; B7867-B7869 Camel; B7870 S.E.5a; B7872 F.E.2b; B7874, B7875 Camel; B7876, B7877 Dolphin; B7881, B7882 S.E.5a, B7883 Camel; B7884 Dolphin; B7886 DH.9; B7887 R.E.8; B7889 Camel; B7890 S.E.5a; B7891 DH.4; B7893 R.E.8; B7896 Camel; B7899, B7901 S.E.5a; B7903 Sopwith 1½ Strutter; B7905, B7906 Camel; B7910, B7911 DH.4; B7917 R.E.8; B7920 S.E.5; B7925 DH.4; B7927, B7928 Dolphin; B7932 Camel; B7933 DH.4; B7935, B7937 Dolphin; B7938-B7942 DH.4; B7945 DH.9; B7946 1½ Strutter; B7947 Bristol F.2B; B7949 S.E.5a; B7950, B7951 DH.4 (Eagle); B7953, B7955 Dolphin; B7963 DH.4 (Eagle); B7964-B7967 DH.4; B7968 Camel; B7969, B7976 DH.4; B7978 Dolphin; B7979 DH.4 (Eagle) to SAAF; B7982, B7986, B7987 DH.4; B7991-B7993 DH.4 (Eagle) to SAAF; B8005, B8013, B8016 DH.4 (Eagle); B8025 Camel; B8064 Pup; B8068 Armstrong Whitworth FK.8; B8097 R.E.8; B8108, B8155, B8187 Camel; B8189 Dolphin; B8201, B8205, B8212, B8217, B8220 Camel.

B8231-B8580	S.E.5a	350

Built by Austin Motors. B8305, B8309 to White Russian forces. B8567 to Australian Government.

B8581-B8770	Avro 504A/J/K	200

Built by Parnall. Most early deliveries direct to RNAS including B8622-B8636 for Vendome. B8758, B8774 became G-EABH, G-EAEB.

B8781-B8830	**Avro 504J**	(50)

Cancelled and numbers re-allotted.

B8781-B8783 **A.E.3 Ram** 3
Royal Aircraft Factory prototypes. B8781, B8782 had Arab engines; B8783 had Bentley B.R.2.

B8784-B8801 Various types built from spares and salvage. 18
B8784-B8786 Sopwith Pups by 6th Wing ARS; B8787 B.E.2c by 6th Wing ARS; B8788 Maurice Farman S.11 Shorthorn by 27th Wing ARS; B8789, B8790 DH.6 by 35th & 27th Wings; B8791 S.E.5a by 18th Wing ARS; B8792 Avro 504 (Mono) by 23rd Wing ARS; B8793 Maurice Farman S.11 Shorthorn by 47 Training Squadron; B8794 B.E.2e by Sopwith Pup; B8796, B8797 Avro 504 (Mono) and B8798 R.E.8 by 26th Wing ARS; B8799, B8800 DH.6 by 1 TDS; B8801 Sopwith Pup by 7th Wing ARS.

B8802-B8813 **Handley Page O/400** 12
Rolls-Royce Eagle engines. Royal Aircraft Factory-built. B8806 fitted for mail carrying.

B8814-B8821 Various types built up from spares and salvage 8
B8814 Avro 504 (Mono) by 23rd Wing; B8815 Maurice Farman S.11 Shorthorn by 2 TS; B8816, B8817 B.E.2e by 19th Wing; B8818, B8819 Avro 504 (Mono) by 18th Wing and 6 TDS; B8820 B.E.2e by 18th Wing ARS; B8821 Sopwith Pup (Gnome) by 26th Wing ARS.

B8822-B8823 **Caudron R.11** 2
French-built ex-C4962, C4964 in French service.

B8824-B8836 Various types built up from spares and salvage 13
B8824 DH.2 by Fighting School at Ayr; B8825 B.E.2d by 6th Wing; B8826 B.E.12 by 19th Wing at Catterick; B8827 Armstrong Whitworth FK.3; B8828 B.E.2e and B8829 Sopwith Pup by 7th Wing at Norwich; B8830 Sopwith Camel by 6th Wing at Dover; B8831-B8836 B.E.2e.

B8837-B8840 **Blackburn Kangaroo** 4
Blackburn-built. B8837, B8839, B8840 became G-EBMD, 'EBOM, 'EBPK.

B8841-B9030 Various types 120(190)
Rebuilt from spares and salvage at No.3 (Western) Aircraft Repair Depot, Yate. B8849-B8854, B8863 B.E.2e by B8864 B.E.2c by B8872, B8874, B8877, B8878, B8880-B8891, B8893-B8899, B8900, B8902-B8907, B8909 R.E.8; B8914, B8915, B8919 Bristol F.2B; B8921 Sopwith Camel; B8923, B8925, B8928 Bristol F.2B; B8932 S.E.5a; B8937, B8941 Bristol F.2B; B8942 S.E.5a; B8943, B8947, B8948 Bristol F.2B; B8962 RAF Aerial Target; B8997 Avro 504.

B9031-B9130 **Airco DH.6** ?(100)
AMC order reported cancelled but first few may have been built.

B9131-B9330 **Sopwith 1F1 Camel** 200
Built by Boulton & Paul. B9149 re-numbered H7212. Conversions: B9140 to 2-seat, B9276 to Scooter later Swallow, B9278 to TF1 Camel.

B9331-B9430 **Airco DH.4** 100
Built by Vulcan Motor & Engineering. B9388, B9393 to White Russian forces.

B9431-B9432 **Avro 530 prototypes** 2
B9433 **Maurice Farman S.11 Shorthorn** 1
Built up from salvage at ARS Turnhouse.

B9434-B9439 **Airco DH.4** (6)
RAF.3a engines. Ex-RNAS N6382-N6387.

B9440-B9444 Various types built from salvage and spares 5
B9440 Sopwith Pup by 63 TS; B9441-B9443 Maurice Farman S.11 Shorthorn by 25 TS at Thetford, 26th Wing ARS and 2 TS; B9444 B.E.2c by 26th Wing.

B9445 **Spad 7** 1
French-built. Ex-pattern aircraft for Air Navigation Co.

B9446-B9451 **Handley Page O/400** 6
Two 320hp Sunbeam Cossacks. Handley Page-built. B9446 fitted with W/T.

B9452-B9455 Various types built from salvage and spares 4
B9452 Avro 504A by 19th Wing; B9453, B9454 B.E.2e by 18 TS at Montrose; B9455 Sopwith Pup by 6th Wing.

B9456 **Airco DH.4** (1)
B.H.P. engine. Ex-RNAS N6393.

B9457 **B.E.2e** 1
Built up from salvage.

B9458 **Airco DH.4** (1)
Ex-RNAS N6397 fitted with high compression B.H.P.

B9459 **B.E.2c** 1
Built up from spares at 30th Wing ARS.

B9460-B9461 **Airco DH.4** (2)
Ex-RNAS N6401, N6405.

B9462 **B.E.12** 1
Built up from salvage by No.75 (HD) Squadron.

B9463-B9465 **Handley Page V/1500** 3
Prototypes. B9463 crashed before acceptance. B9464, B9465 built by Handley Page from components supplied by Harland & Wolff, becoming J1935, J1936.

B9466 **Maurice Farman S.11 Shorthorn** 1
Built from spares by 27th Wing.

B9467 **Beardmore Competition Bomb-dropper** (1)
Prototype not completed.

B9468 **Airco DH.5** 1
Built from spares at Dover.

B9469 **B.E.2e** 1
Built from salvage by 19 TS.

B9470 **Airco DH.4** (1)
B.H.P. engine. Ex-RNAS N6409.

B9471-B9475 Various types built from salvage and spares 5
B9471 DH.4 (B.H.P) by 7th Wing ARS; B9472 DH.6; B9473 R.E.8 and B9474 B.E.2e by 26th Wing ARS; B9475 MF S.11 Shorthorn by 27th Wing ARS.

B9476-B9500 **Airco DH.4** 25
B.H.P. engine. Westland-built mainly for RNAS. B9488 fitted with 190hp Renault. B9477, B9492 and B9500 fitted with W/T. B9477 to Greek Government.

B9501-B9800 **Armstrong Whitworth FK.8** 175(300)
Built by Hewlett & Blondeau up to about B9675. B9518, B9603, B9612, B9629 became G-EABZ, 'EALK, 'EAEU, 'EABY.

B9801-B9900 Cancelled order (100)
B9901 **Avro 504** 1
Re-built and re-numbered.

B9902-B9908 **Morane Type P Parasol** 7
80hp. French-built.

B9909 **Austin Ball AFB.1** 1
Prototype by Austin Motors to Captain Albert Ball's specification.

B9910 **Sopwith 1½ Strutter** 1
Type 9700. Built from salvage by 6th Wing.

B9911-B9930 **Spad S.7** 20
Built by Mann Egerton. Ex-RNAS N6580-N6599. B9911, B9913-B9917, B9920, B9922-B9924, B9928 to USA.

B9931 **Sopwith Pup** 1
Built from salvage by 6th Wing.

B9932 **Avro 504** 1
Presumed built from spares.

B9933-B9937 **Morane Type P Parasol** 5
80hp. Taken on charge 14 Oct 1917 probably ex-BEF.

B9938-B9943 Various types built from salvage and spares 6
B9938 B.E.2e; B9939 Avro 504; B9940, B9941 B.E.2e; B9942 not known; B9943 B.E.2e by 42 TS.

B9944-B9949 **BAT FK.22 & 22/1 & 2 Bat & Bantam** 4(6)
Prototypes. B9944 FK.22 Bat (120hp Mosquito), B9945 FK.22/2 (100hp Gnome Monosoupape & 110hp Le Rhone), B9946 FK.22/2 not flown, B9947 FK.22/1 (170hp Wasp), B9948, B9949 FK.22/1 not flown.

B9950 **B.E.12** 1
Rebuilt from salvage and spares.

B9951 **Airco DH.4** 1
Origin unknown. Served at 9 TS.

B9952-B9954 **Vickers FB.27 Vimy** 3
Vickers prototypes built at Bexley. Hispano, Sunbeam and Fiat engines respectively. B9952 became G-EAAR, B9953, B9954 crashed on test.

B9955-B9961 Reservation probably for rebuilds 3(7)
B9955 not known; B9956 Maurice Farman S.11 Shorthorn; B9957 B.E.2e; B9958 not known; B9959 rebuilt Avro 504; B9960, B9961 not known.

B9962-B9967 **Sopwith 7F1 Snipe** 6
Prototypes. B9962 not flown or crashed at an early stage. B9964 believed strength-tested to destruction. B9967 fitted with 320hp Dragonfly.

B9968 **Armstrong Whitworth FK.3** 1
Presumed built up from spares.

B9969 **Spad 7** 1
Built from salvage by 27th Wing ARS.

B9970-B9989	**Blackburn Kangaroo**	20
	RNAS N1720-N1739 renumbered. B9970, B9972,	
	B9973, B9977, B9978, B9981, B9982, B9985 became	
	G-EAOW, 'EAKQ, 'EAIU, 'EAMJ, 'EAIT, 'EADE-	
	'EADG.	
B9990	**Sopwith 1F1 Camel**	(1)
	Ex-RNAS N6344 sample aircraft from Boulton & Paul.	
B9991-B9999	**Various types built from salvage and spares.**	9
	B9991 Maurice Farman S.11 Shorthorn; B9992 DH.6	
	by 7th Wing; B9993 B.E.2c by 19 TS; B9994 DH.4 by	
	6th Wing; B9995 Avro 504 by 7th Wing; B9996 Maurice	
	Farman S.11 Shorthorn by 2 TS; B9997 R.E.8 by 26th	
	Wing; B9998 B.E.2c by 53 TS; B9999 Maurice Farman	
	S.11 Shorthorn at Beverley.	

British Production Mid-War

C1 to C9999

The 'C' series allocations reflect the increasing size in orders placed by the Air Board in 1917, including a contract to Daimler for 850 R.E.8s which was the largest single order for aircraft placed that year. This series is practically uncomplicated, being straight-forward production aircraft for the Royal Flying Corps, except for small batches reserved for experimental aircraft. This allocation was fully subscribed by August 1917.

Serial Nos.	Aircraft Type and Remarks	Quantity
C1-C200	**Sopwith 1F1 Camel**	200
	130/140hp Clerget. Built by Nieuport & General Aircraft. C19 and C57 converted to 2-seaters. C145-C148, C151, C153, C155-C157, C159-C165 transferred to Belgian Flying Corps; C41 and C51 shipped to White Russian Forces; C49 transferred to Greek Government.	
C201-C550	**Sopwith Pup**	350
	Built by Standard Motor Company. C481-C499, C503-C509, C533-C538 shipped to Japan. C521-C528 and C530-C532 became A4-1 to 11 of RAAF. C242, C312, C438, C440, C476, C540 became G-EBFJ, 'EAVW, 'EAVY, 'EAVV, 'AUCK, 'EAVZ.	
C551-C750	**Sopwith 1F1 Camel**	(200)
	Ordered from British Caudron. Cancelled and numbers re-allotted.	
C551-C750	**Avro 504A/J/K**	200
	Built by The Humber Motor Company. C691, C723, C724, C746-C749 became G-EBEO, 'EABN, 'EAAY, 'EAGJ, 'EABW, 'EABF, 'EABG.	
C751-C1050	**Bristol F.2B Fighter**	300
	Rolls-Royce Falcon III. Built by the British & Colonial Aeroplane Company. C1025 fitted with Sunbeam Arab engine. C842, C868, C983 re-built as H7173, H7196, H7197. C949 bought by the USA.	
C1051-C1150	**Airco DH.4**	(100)
	Ordered from Vulcan Motor & Engineering. Cancelled and numbers re-allotted.	
C1051-C1150	**S.E.5a**	100
	Built by the Royal Aircraft Factory. C1115, C1119-C1121 to British Aviation Mission, Washington, for USAS	
C1151-C1450	**Airco DH.9**	300
	Original order stated DH.4. Built by G & J Weir. C1211 and C1294 interned in Holland as deH434 and deH441. C1296 to Australian Government. C1313, C1391, C1392 part of Imperial Gift to India.	
C1451-C1550	**Sopwith Pup**	100
	Built by Whitehead Aircraft. C1502, C1503, C1508, C1516-C1518, C1523, C1532, C1533, C1535, C1537, C1541 allotted for Fleet use with 80hp Le Rhones. C1496 shipped to Japan. C1524 became G-EBAZ.	
C1551-C1600	**Sopwith 1F1 Camel**	50
	Clerget or Le Rhones. Built by Hooper. C1588 fitted with Bentley B.R.1 engine.	

C1601-C1700	**Sopwith 1F1 Camel**	100
	Built by Boulton & Paul. C1616, C1620, C1622, C1624, C1626, C1632, C1634 transferred to Belgian Flying Corps.	
C1701-C1750	**B.E.2e**	(50)
	Ordered from B & C. Cancelled.	
C1751-C1950	**S.E.5a**	200
	Built by Air Navigation Co. C1916, C1917 to Australia.	
C1951-C2150	**Airco DH.6**	200
	Built by Grahame-White Aviation. C1972, C2101, C2136 became G-AUDO, 'EAGG, 'EAQQ.	
C2151-C2230	**Airco DH.9**	80
	Original order stated DH.4. Built by F. W. Berwick & Co. C2207 had a boosted Puma engine. C2208, C2218, C2219 part of Imperial Gift to India.	
C2231-C3080	**R.E.8**	800 (850)
	Built by Daimler. Last 50 cancelled. C2878 to USAS in France.	
C3081-C3280	**B.E.12/12a/12b**	200
	Built by Daimler. Believed mainly B.E.12b.	
C3281-C3385	**Sopwith Triplane**	(105)
	Order cancelled and numbers re-allotted.	
C3281-C3380	**Sopwith 1F1 Camel**	100
	Built by Boulton & Paul. C3302, C3351, C3353, C3355, rebuilt as H6889, H6904, H6867, H7217. C3281, C3283, C3285, C3287, C3289, C3291, C3295, C3297, C3301, C3303, C3305, C3307, C3309, C3311, C3315, C3317, C3319, C3321, C3329, C3331, C3333, C3335, C3339, C3341, C3345, C3346, C3350, C3352, C3354, C3358, C3366, C3376 to USAS. C3326, C3328, C3330, C3332, C3334 shipped to White Russian forces.	
C3381-C3480	**Handley Page O/400**	(100)
	Various engines specified. Ordered from Handley Page but cancelled.	
C3481-C3530	**R.E.8**	(50)
	Ordered from Napier. Cancelled and numbers re-allotted.	
C3481-C3483	**Grahame-White E.IV Ganymede**	1(3)
	C3481 only built which became G-EAMW.	
C3484-C3486	**Nieuport BN.1**	3
	British Nieuport built. C3484 crashed on test. C3485 static tested to destruction. C3486 not completed.	
C3487-C3498	**Handley Page O/400**	12
	R-R Eagle engines. Built by Royal Aircraft Factory.	
C3499	**Maurice Farman S.11 Shorthorn**	1
	Built from spares by No.2 Training Squadron.	
C3500-C3503	**Sopwith Pup**	4
	Built from spares by 6th Wing early in 1918.	
C3504	*(Not known)*	—
C3505	**Avro 504**	1
	Built from spares by 6th Wing.	
C3506	**Airco DH.6**	1
	Built from spares at No.2 TDS.	
C3507-C3706	**Armstrong Whitworth FK.8**	200
	Built by Angus Sanderson. 5 re-built in F-series.	
C3707-C3776	**Sopwith Pup**	70
	Ordered from Whitehead Aircraft as spares.	
C3777-C4276	**Sopwith 5F1 Dolphin**	500
	Sopwith-built, their largest order to date.	
C4277	**Curtiss JN-3**	1
	Presumed ex-RNAS or built from spares.	
C4278	**Maurice Farman S.11 Shorthorn**	1
	Built from spares by No.12 Training Squadron.	
C4279	**Maurice Farman S.7 Longhorn**	1
	90hp Curtiss. Built from spares by Brush Ltd.	
C4280	**Reserved for captured German aircraft**	(1)
C4281	**Airco DH.6**	1
	Built from spares by No.1 TDS.	
C4282	**R.E.8**	1
	Built from spares by 7th Wing.	
C4283	**Airco DH.10**	1
	200hp B.H.P. Prototype. Modified to DH.10C with Liberty engines.	
C4284-C4289	**Sopwith 8F1 Snail**	6
	Experimental. C4285, C4289 Mk.I, remainder Mk.II.	
C4290	**Avro 504A/J**	1
	Built from spares by 7th Wing.	
C4291-C4293	**Westland Wagtail**	3
	Originally named Hornet. Experimental aircraft.	
C4294	**R.E.8**	1
	Built from spares by 26th Wing.	
C4295	**Sopwith Pup**	1
	Built from spares by 30th Wing.	

C4296-C4298	Bristol Types 24/25/26 Braemar/Pullman	3
	British & Colonial built. C4296 Braemar I, ff 10.8.18, C4297 Braemar II, C4298 Pullman became G-EASP.	
C4299	Avro 504A/J	1
	Built from spares by 7th Wing.	
C4300	Sopwith 1½ Strutter	1
	Bomber version built from spares by 26th Wing.	
C4301-C4500	Avro 504J	200
	Avro-built. C4312 to USAS, became P-25 at Wright Field.	
C4501-C4540	Airco DH.4	40
	260hp Fiat A12. Airco-built.	
C4541-C4546	Siddeley SR.2 Siskin	3(6)
	Siddeley-Deasy built. C4544-C4546 cancelled.	
C4547	Vickers FB.14D	1
	Experimental version of FB.14 with 250hp Rolls-Royce Mk.IV.	
C4548	Bristol F.2B Fighter	1
	Built from spares by 18th Wing.	
C4549	Avro 504	1
	Built from spares by 18th Wing.	
C4550	Armstrong Whitworth F.K.8	1
	Built from spares by 18th Wing.	
C4551-C4600	R.E.8	50
	Built by Napier.	
C4601-C4900	Bristol F.2B Fighter	300
	R-R Falcon engines. British & Colonial built. C4746, C4817 rebuilt as H7174, H7175. C4654, C4655 fitted with Pumas. C4729 to British Aviation Mission, Washington, for USAS.	
C4901-C5025	Bristol M.1C Monoplane (retrospectively Type 20)	125
	British & Colonial built. C4929, C4982-C4989, C4991-C4993 supplied to Chile. C4964, C5001 became G-EAER and VH-UCH.	
C5026-C5125	R.E.8	100
	Built by COW.	
C5126-C5275	Airco DH.6	150
	Built by Kingsbury Aviation. C5220, C5224, C5230 became G-EAGF, 'EAGE, 'EANU.	
C5276-C5300	Caudron G.3	25
	Built in France for use at RNAS Vendome.	
C5301-C5450	S.E.5a	150
	Built by Vickers at Crayford.	
C5451-C5750	Airco DH.6	300
	Built by Harland & Wolff. C5527, C5533, C5547 became G-EARA-'EARC.	
C5751-C6050	Avro 504J	300
	Built by Harland & Wolff. Some converted to 504K. C5752-C5754, C5886-C5889, C5965 to USAS.	
C6051-C6350	Airco DH.9	300
	B.H.P. engine. AMC-built. C6122, C6350 modified by Westland to DH.9A prototypes and replaced by E5436 and E5435. C6052 fitted with Fiat A-12 and C6078 with Napier Lion. C6128, C6145 part of Imperial Gift to India. C6241, C6246, C6323 to Australian Government. C6070 to French Government. C6058 to USAS. C6225 to Greek Government. C6237, C6337 handed to White Russian forces. C6054 became G-EAAA.	
C6351-C6500	S.E.5a	150
	Built by Wolseley Motors. C6362-C6365, C6369, C6371, C6372, C6374, C6381 to White Russian forces. C6376, C6378 became G-EBID, 'EBIE.	
C6501-C6700	Airco DH.6	200
	Built by Morgan & Co. C6503 became G-EAPW.	
C6701-C6800	Sopwith 1F1 Camel	100
	Built by British Caudron at Alloa. C6723 rebuilt as H6869.	
C6801-C6900	Airco DH.6	100
	Built by Savages Ltd. C6889 became G-EAHI.	
C6901-C7000	B.E.2e	100
	Built by Wm Denny. C6981, C6983 to Estonia and C6954-C6956 to US Government. C6980 was experimentally fitted with metal mainplanes in 1919. C6953, C6964, C6968, C6986 became G-EARW, 'EATW, 'EATT and G-AUBF.	
C7001-C7100	B.E.2e	100
	Built by Barclay Curle. C7089-C7095 to US Government.	
C7101-C7200	B.E.2e	100
	Built by Napier & Miller. C7176, C7177 to US Government. C7101, C7175, C7178, C7179, C7185, C7198 to G-EAGH, 'EACY, 'EAVA, 'EAVS, 'EANW and G-AUBD.	
C7201-C7600	Airco DH.6	250(400)
	Built by Ransome, Sims and Jeffries up to C7450. C7320, C7390, C7430, C7434, C7436 became G-EAFZ, 'EAFY, 'EAPG, 'EAOT, 'EAQC.	
C7601-C7900	Airco DH.6	300
	Built by Grahame-White Aviation. C7736, C7741, C7745, C7747, C7753, C7754, C7756, C7757, C7759, C7760 transferred to US Navy. C7620, C7739, C7763, C7768, C7797 became G-EALS, 'EAPH, 'EAUS, 'EARD and 'EAVR.	
C7901-C8000	Sopwith T1 Cuckoo	(100)
	Ordered from Fairfield Engineering. Re-numbered as N7000-N7099.	
C8001-C8200	Sopwith 5F1 Dolphin	200
	Built by Darracq Motor Engineering. C8022 converted to 2-seater. C8194 converted to Mk.III.	
C8201-C8300	Sopwith 1F1 Camel	100
	Clerget engines fitted. Built by Ruston Proctor.	
C8301-C8400	Sopwith 1F1 Camel	100
	Built by March, Jones & Cribb. C8382 rebuilt as H6899. C8307, C8308 to Belgian Flying Corps.	
C8401-C8651	Armstrong Whitworth F.K.8	251
	Armstrong Whitworth-built. 4 re-built in F-series.	
C8652-C8654	Boulton & Paul P.5 Hawk	(3)
	Aircraft not built and numbers re-allotted.	
C8652	Avro 504	1
	Built from spares by 18th Wing.	
C8653-C8654	Sopwith Pup	2
	Built from spares by 7th Wing.	
C8655-C8657	Boulton & Paul P.3 Bobolink	1(3)
	C8655 only delivered.	
C8658-C8660	Airco DH.10 Amiens	3
	AMC-built. C8658-C8660 Mks.I-III respectively.	
C8661-C9310	S.E.5a	650
	Built by Austin Motors. C8738-C8757, C9073-C9090 to USAS on repayment. C9182-C9184 and C9204 free issue to Chile, C8994-C8996 part of Imperial Gift to Australia. C8674, C8675, C8702, C9020, C9029, C9208 became G-EBGJ, 'EBDW, 'EBDZ, 'EBGK, 'EBDY, 'EBCE.	
C9311-C9335	Maurice Farman S.7 Longhorn	25
	Built by Brush Electrical Engineering from spares held by Phoenix and Robey and delivered to RNAS stations.	
C9336-C9485	Airco DH.6	150
	Built by Gloucestershire Aircraft. C9372-C9374 to CFS Point Cook, Australia. C9374, C9432, C9436, C9448, C9449 became G-AUBW, 'EAHJ, 'EAUT, 'EAMK and 'EAML.	
C9486-C9635	S.E.5a	150
	Built by Vickers at Weybridge. C9491 rebuilt as H7161.	
C9636-C9785	Handley Page O/400	150
	Handley Page-built. C9648 became Dutch HP-703, C9670 sold to US Government. C9699, C9704, C9713, C9731 became G-EASL, 'EAGN, 'EAPJ, 'EASM.	
C9786-C9835	F.E.2b	50
	Built by Ransome, Sims & Jeffries. C9829 rebuilt as H6888. C9802, C9821 to US Government.	
C9836-C9985	Bristol F.2B Fighter	150
	Gloucestershire Aircraft-built. C9896 rebuilt as H6893.	
C9986	Avro 504	1
	Built from spares at No.7 TDS, Feltwell.	
C9987	B.E.2e	1
	Built from spares at No.7 TDS, Feltwell.	
C9988-C9989	B.E.2d	2
	Built from spares at 6th Wing ARS, Dover.	
C9990-C9991	Sopwith Pup	2
	Built from spares at No.7 TDS, Feltwell, March 1918.	
C9992	B.E.12b	1
	Built from spares by No.50 Squadron.	
C9993	Sopwith Pup	1
	Built from spares by 26th Wing ARS, Thetford.	
C9994	Airco DH.6	1
	Built from spares by 27th Wing ARD, Waddington.	
C9995	B.E.2d	1
	Built from spares by 7th Wing ARS.	
C9996	B.E.2e	1
	Built from spares by 18th Wing ARS.	
C9997	Armstrong Whitworth F.K.8	1
	Built from spares by 24th Wing ARS.	
C9998-C9999	Avro 504	2
	Built from spares at 39th Wing ARS, Feltwell.	

RFC/RAF Canada

C101 to C2500

In early 1917 an RFC Training Brigade was organised in Canada with the Curtiss JN-4 adopted as the standard trainer to be locally produced by Canadian Aeroplanes Ltd. They were numbered in RFC (Canada) service from C101, the 'C' for Canada. One DH.6 was built for the service (number unknown) and a change-over to locally-built Avro 504As was being made when the Armistice came. Overall output of JN-4(CAN) aircraft was at least 2,900 of which 680 were purchased by the American Government, including RFC (Canada) aircraft switched to Texas, USA, for training during the Winter 1917-18; but on the other hand 150 JN-4As were bought from the USA early in 1917.

The table below has been based on the compiler's logging records.

Serial Nos.	Aircraft Type and Remarks	Quantity
C101-C1380	Curtiss JN-4(CAN)/JN-4/4A	1280
	Canadian-built JN-4(CAN) except as follows built at Curtiss US plant at Buffalo as JN-4 and JN-4A: C171, C502-C512, C518-C520, C522-C528, C530-C538, C540, C543, C546, C550-C553, C556-C559, C561, C567, C570, C571, C577, C578, C580, C581, C583-C587, C590, C593-C595, C597, C599, C603, C605-C608, C611, C615, C618, C620-C623, C625-C630, C634-C636, C638, C640, C642, C647, C1015, C1023-C1030, C1034, C1037, C1038 recorded. C343-C366, C377-C412, C440-C466, C470-C472, C486-C499, C501, C648-C655, C657, C658, C685, C687, C688, C690-C825 to Texas as RFC Canada aircraft and handed over to USAS. C830-C931, C936-C998, C1052-C1288 direct to USAS.	
C1381-C1450	Possible reservation for DH.6 considered for production of which only one was built.	1(70)
C1451-C1500	Curtiss JN-4(CAN)	7(50)
	Production halted by change to Avro 504s. First six built as air ambulances.	
C1501-C2000	Avro 504(CAN)	4(500)
	130hp Clerget. First four only completed.	

Shipped from UK to RAF (Canada): Avro 504K D8281 and D8842 and Sopwith Camel B3772.

Final RFC Allocations

D1 to D9999

Like the preceding C1-C9999 series, the 'D' series, resulting from orders placed in late 1917/early 1918, was a straight-forward allocation of numbers mainly for production aircraft.

Serial Nos.	Aircraft Type and Remarks	Quantity
D1-D200	Avro 504J/K	200
	D49, D53-D55 to French Government. D4, D7, D9 became G-AUBJ, 'AUGZ, 'AUDR.	
D201-D300	S.E.5a	100
	Built by Vickers at Weybridge. D203 non-standard with Dolphin type rudder and narrow chord ailerons.	
D301-D450	S.E.5a	150
	Built by Vickers at Crayford. D340-D343 to USA. D369-D371 to Australian Government.	
D451-D950	Airco DH.9	276(500)
	Built by Cubitt. Delivery up to D727 only confirmed. D629, D640, D646, D654, D658, D664, D666, D667, D671, D674, D678, D684, D697, D704 to Greek Government. D543, D561, D618, D620, D622, D649, D652, D686 to White Russian forces. D503 to US Government on repayment. D514, D524, D585, D611, D612, D645, D650, D661 part of Imperial Gift to India. D638, D657, D659, D663, D665, D668, D670, D675, D677, D680, D681, D683, D687, D688, D690, D695, D698, D703, D705 part of Imperial Gift to South Africa. D651, D660, D693 to Estonian Government. D516 became G-EAXG.	
D951-D1000	Airco DH.6	(50)
	Ordered from Grahame-White. No delivery record.	
D1001-D1500	Airco DH.9	384(500)
	Ordered from No.2 NAF, Heaton Chapel. Official history gives 326 built, but serials extend to D1384. D1115, D1119, D1127, D1129, D1187 D1257 to Australian Government. D1053, D1248, D1282 part of Imperial Gift to India. D1081, D1258, D1273, D1275, D1278 free issue to Polish Purchasing Commission. D1142 to White Russian forces. D1152 to Greek Government. D1246 to Estonian Government. D1295, D1296, D1307, D1308, D1326, D1327 free issue to Chilean Government. D1347 became G-EBEG.	
D1501-D1600	R.E.8	100
	Built by Standard Motors. All delivered by May 1918.	
D1601-D1650	Avro 504A	50
	Built by Eastbourne Aviation. C/ns 201-250.	
D1651-D1750	Airco DH.9	100
	Built by Mann Egerton. D1733 became deH443 in Dutch service after being interned.	
D1751-D1775	Airco DH.9	25
	200hp B.H.P. Built by Westland Aircraft. From D1769 had higher undercarriage. D1760, D1771 to Greek Government.	
D1776-D1975	Sopwith 1F1 Camel	200
	Built by Ruston Proctor. D1851, D1887, D1942 re-numbered H7223, H7111, H6903.	
D1976-D2125	Avro 504K	150
	Built by Sage & Co. D2035 became G-EAWJ.	
D2126-D2625	Bristol F.2B Fighter	120(500)
	Built by NAF No.3 Aintree. Up to D2245 delivered. D2128, D2132 fitted with Arabs.	
D2626-D2775	Bristol F.2B Fighter	83(150)
	Sunbeam Arab. Built by Marshall & Sons. Up to D2708 confirmed as delivered.	
D2776-D2875	Airco DH.9	100
	Fiat engines specified, B.H.P. fitted. Built by Short Bros. D2776 part of Imperial Gift to India. D2781 interned in Holland. D2840-D2842, D2844, D2847, D2853 to White Russian forces.	
D2876-D3275	Airco DH.9	400
	Airco-built. D2886, D2888, D2892-D2896, D2912, D2940, D2942-D2944, D2948, D2953, D2958, D3120, D3121, D3123, D3124, D3126-D3134, D3137, D3147, D3149, D3150, D3152-D3154 to White Russian forces. D2978, D2983, D2997, D3018, D3180, D3185, D3188, D3190, D3192, D3193, D3197, D3200, D3201, D3204, D3208 part of Imperial Gift to India. D3017, D3187, D3189, D3191, D3207, D3220 became A6-11, A6-14, A6-9, A6-16, A6-20, A6-21 of RAAF and D3186, D3195, D3196, D3203 also supplied. D3136, D3139 supplied to New Zealand, became G-NZAH, 'NZAM. D3194, D3199, D3205, D3206 to Greek Government. D3242 acquired by Polish Purchasing Commission. D3107, D3251, D3271 interned in Holland, the last two becoming deH444, deH446 in Dutch service. D2884 became G-EALJ.	
D3276-D3325	Sopwith T1 Cuckoo	(50)
	Renumbered N6900-N6949.	
D3326-D3425	Sopwith 1F1 Camel	100
	Bentley B.R.1 engines. Built by Clayton & Shuttleworth	
D3426-D3575	S.E.5a	150
	Built by Vickers at Weybridge. D3544, D3546, D3548, D3550-D3552 to White Russian forces. D3554 converted to 2-seat.	
D3576-D3775	Sopwith 5F1 Dolphin	200
	Sopwith-built. D3615 Mk.II to French Government.	
D3776-D3835	F.E.2b	60
	Built by Garrett & Sons. D3781, D3782, D3785 and D3821 to US Government. D3832 became G-EAHC.	
D3836-D3910	R.E.8	(75)

D3911-D4010	Ordered from Napier, but cancelled. **S.E.5a**	100
D4011-D4210	Built by Martinsyde. **DH.9**	(200)
D4011-D4210	Ordered from Weir. Cancelled, numbers re-allotted. **Sopwith Pup**	200
D4211-D4360	Ordered from Whitehead. Bulk delivered as spares. D4144-D4152, D4155, D4156, D4160, D4161, D4163, D4165, D4168, D4169 assembled for Japanese Government. **Sopwith Pup**	(150)
D4211-D4360	Ordered from Beardmore. Cancelled 26 November 1917 and numbers re-allotted. **Martinsyde F.4 Buzzard**	150
D4361-D4560	Martinsyde-built. First 45 (except D4214 to French Government) held in store awaiting engines. D4274, D4281, D4285, D4298 became 4, 2, 1, 3 of Irish Air Corps. D4326 became MA-24 of Finnish Air Force. D4267, D4275, D4279, D4295, D4352 became G-EATD, 'EAYP, 'EAXB, 'EBMI, 'EAUR. **Avro 504J/K**	118(200)
D4561-D4660	Built by Sunbeam Motors up to D4478 at least. D4365 to the British Air Mission, Washington. **Handley Page O/400**	100
D4661-D4810	Eagle or Liberty engines specified. Built by Metropolitan Wagon Co. D4609, D4611, D4614, D4618, D4623, D4624, D4631, D4633 became G-EATM, 'EASN, 'EASY, 'EATG, 'EAMB, 'EAMC, 'EATH, 'EAMD. **R.E.8**	150
D4811-D4960	Built by Standard Motors. **R.E.8**	150
D4961-D5000	Built by Napier. D4946 re-numbered H7181. **R.E.8**	40
D5001-D5200	Rebuilt aircraft by No.3 (Western) Aircraft Repair Depot. **Armstrong Whitworth FK.8**	·200
D5201-D5400	Built by Angus Sanderson. D5150 became G-EAET. **Sopwith 5F1 Dolphin**	200
D5401-D5450	Built by Hooper. D5369 became G-EATC. **Handley Page O/400**	50
D5451-D5550	Built by Birmingham Carriage Co. D5444 became G-EASO. **Avro 504J/K**	100
D5551-D5850	Delivered as spares for erection in Egypt. D5499 became G-EAGD, and later G-EALE. **DH.9**	300
D5851-D5950	Built by Waring & Gillow. D5649, D5686, D5689, D5709, D5756, D5765, D5774, D5793, D5814, D5818, D5846 part of Imperial Gift to India. D5717 became deH437 in Dutch service after internment. D5622, D5777, D5799 became G-EAMX, 'EBEH, 'EBEP. **Avro 504J/K**	100
D5951-D6200	Built by the Henderson Scottish Aviation Factory. D5858 became G-EASF. **S.E.5a**	250
D6201-D6250	Built by Vickers at Weybridge. D6101-D6112 to USAS. D6194 re-numbered H7242. **Avro 504A/J/K**	50
D6251-D6400	Built by Humber Motors. D6243 to RNZAF. D6201, D6202, D6205, D6217, D6229, D6239, D6245 became G-EABT, 'EABO, 'EAAX, 'EAGT, 'EABV, 'EADX, 'EADR. **Avro 504A/J/K**	150
D6401-D6700	Built by Brush Electrical Engineering. D6400 to US Forces, Issoudun. D6382 became 504N. D6330, D6387, D6396 became G-EBSL, 'EATV and VH-UBL. **Sopwith 1F1 Camel**	300
D6701-D6850	Built by Boulton & Paul. D6442, D6446, D6596, D6615, D6627, D6638, D6644 re-numbered H6862, H7239, H7214, H6847, H6856, H7237, H7110. **R.E.8**	150
D6851-D7000	Built by Coventry Ordnance Works. **S.E.5a**	150
D7001-D7050	Built by Wolseley Motors. **S.E.5a**	50
D7051-D7200	Built by Royal Aircraft Factory. D7017 built from B7832. D7016, D7020, D7022 became G-EBPA, G-EBQM, G-EBPD. **Avro 504J/K**	150
	Built by Hewlett & Blondeau. D7185 part of Imperial Gift to India.	

D7201-D7300	**Airco DH.9**	48(100)
	Built by Westland Aircraft except D7215, D7216 and D7251-D7300 cancelled. D7204 became deH439 in Dutch service after internment. D7211 to Greek Gov't.	
D7301-D7400	**Airco DH.9**	100
	Built by F.W.Berwick & Co and mainly delivered as spares to No.3 Stores Depot, Milton. D7336 became deH442 in Dutch service after being interned. D7368 part of Imperial Gift to India.	
D7401-D7500	**Avro 504A/J**	(100)
	Cancelled plan to build aircraft at 'X' Aircraft Depot, RFC, Egypt.	
D7501-D7800	**Avro 504J/K**	300
	A.V. Roe-built. D7588, D7619, D7648 became G-EADQ, 'EAJK, 'EAFE.	
D7801-D8100	**Bristol F.2B Fighter**	300
	Falcon and Arab engines fitted. Built by B & C. D7860 had RAF.4d engine. D8065 re-numbered H7198. D7879 (Arab engine) to British Aviation Mission, Washington. D7865, D7882, D7885, D7886 became V, VII, VIII, VI of Irish Air Corps. D7842 became G-EBBD for delivery to Belgian air arm. D8096 became G-AEPH and is currently with the Shuttleworth Trust.	
D8101-D8250	**Sopwith 1F1 Camel**	150
	140hp Clerget. Built by Ruston Proctor. D8162, D8171, D8196 re-numbered H7215, H6878, H6848. D8137, D8155 to Greek Government.	
D8251-D8300	**Avro 504K**	50
	Built by Humber Motors. D8281 to RAF (Canada), D8282 to British Aviation Mission, Washington. D8287 became G-EABK.	
D8301-D8350	**Handley Page O/400**	50
	Built by British Caudron and Harris Lebus. D8350 became G-EAAE and was to be replaced by J6578.	
D8351-D8430	**Airco DH.4**	80
	Mainly Eagle IV engines fitted. Airco-built. D8377, D8378, D8382, D8383, D8427 re-numbered H7147, H6885, H7148, H7124, H6859.	
D8431-D8580	**S.E.5a**	70(150)
	Built by Vickers at Crayford up to D8500 at least. D8471, D8473-D8477, D8480, D8482, D8486, D8488, D8490, D8491, D8495 part of Imperial Gift to Australia where D8476, D8490 became A2-13, A2-19 of RAAF. D8472, D8479, D8487, D8489 became G-CYBJ, 'CYBE, 'CYBQ, 'CYBY as part of Imperial Gift to Canada. D8500 part of Imperial Gift for SAAF.	
D8581-D8780	**Airco DH.6**	(200)
	Ordered from Airco. No delivery record.	
D8781-D9080	**Avro 504K**	300
	Built by Grahame-White. D9026-D9057, D9060-D9063, D9066, D9067, D9069-D9075 to US Government. D9059, D9064, D9065 part of Imperial Gift to India. D8842 to RAF (Canada). D8984, D9018, D9058 became G-EAGZ, 'EAEN, 'EAXY.	
D9081-D9230	**F.E.2b**	100(150)
	Built by Alex Stephens & Sons and G.& J.Weir. Last 50 to Barclay Curle for erection, but no delivery record. D9117 to US Forces.	
D9231-D9380	**Sopwith 1F1 Camel**	(150)
	Ordered from Boulton & Paul. Cancelled and numbers re-allotted.	
D9231-D9280	**Airco DH.4**	50
	R-R Eagle. Airco-built. D9231-D9236 replaced A8059, A8063, A8065-A8067, A8079, with Eagle engines. D9263 re-numbered F6209.	
D9281-D9380	**Avro 504K**	100
	Built by Parnall. D9313-D9318, D9320 to the US Government. D9298, D9303, D9304, D9329, D9340, D9341, D9343 became G-EACL, 'EAIB, 'EAEA, 'EADU, 'EAFS, 'EACS, 'EAGO.	
D9381-D9530	**Sopwith 1F1 Camel.**	150
	Clerget and Le Rhone. Built by Boulton & Paul. D9402, D9427, D9486, D9492 re-numbered H7235, H6844, H6872, H6861. D9400 and even numbers from D9518 to US Government.	
D9531-D9580	**Sopwith 1F1 Camel**	50
	Built by Portholme. D9567 re-numbered H7114. D9552, D9553, D9557 to White Russian forces.	
D9581-D9680	**Sopwith 1F1 Camel**	100
	Built by Clayton & Shuttleworth. D9588, D9598,	

D9599, D9634, D9653, D9669 re-numbered as H7115, H7206, H7210, H7224, H6890, H6898.

D9681-D9730	Handley Page O/400	46(50)

R-R Eagle. Built by Clayton & Shuttleworth, except the last four which were cancelled.

D9731-D9736	BAT FK.24 Baboon	1(6)

British Aerial Transport experimental trainer. D9731 only built and later became K-124/G-EACO.

D9737-D9739	R.E.8	3

Built from spares by No.3 (Western) Aircraft Repair Depot.

D9740-D9789	F.E.2b	50

Built from spares. D9757, D9759, D9776 re-numbered H7229, H7179, H7180. D9764, D9765 to US Gov't.

D9790-D9799	R.E.8	10

Built from spares by No.3 (Western) Aircraft Repair Depot.

D9800-D9899	Airco DH.9	100

Built by G. & J.Weir. D9838 to Greek Government.

D9900-D9999	F.E.2b	100

Built by Ransome, Sims & Jeffries. D9908, D9910, D9912, D9915, D9916, D9927, D9942, D9959 to the US Government.

The First Royal Air Force Orders

E1 to E9999

When the RNAS and RFC merged on 1 April 1918 no change in serialling resulted, since the function of the Ministry of Munitions remained unchanged and that Ministry was the agency for aircraft procurement for the Services. The 'E' series was subscribed in early to mid-1918 and, on the day of the merger of the two former air arms, allocations for the RFC had reached E1600.

Serial Nos.	Aircraft Type and Remarks	Quantity
E1-E300	R.E.8	300

Built by Siddeley-Deasy Motors. E187, E188, E190, E192-E195, E199, E201, E202, E204, E206-E220, E222, E277-E300 to White Russian forces. E189, E191, E198, E200, E203, E205 to General Gough's Russian Corps at Reval.

E301-E600	Avro 504K	205(300)

Built by Harland & Wolff but delivery beyond E505 not confirmed. E361-E363, part of Imperial Gift to Canada, became G-CYEE, 'CYAC, 'CYAI. E444 converted to 504N. E446 became A15 of Brazilian Navy. E448 became G-EBNU and E449 the first Avro 548 as G-EBKN.

E601-E700	Airco DH.9	100

Built by Whitehead Aircraft.

E701-E1100	Airco DH.9A	400

Liberty engines except where given. Built by Whitehead Aircraft. E715, E761, E764-E767, E808, E817, E818 to White Russian forces. E736-E741 allotted to USMC Northern Bombing Group in Europe. E857, E859, E861, E960 re-built as J7012, J7016, J7009, J7017. E793-E795, E900, E901, E903-E910, E916 to Australia as part of Imperial Gift. E992-E1002 to Canada as part of Imperial Gift becoming G-CYBI, 'CYBN, 'CYAK, 'CYBF, 'CYAN, 'CYAZ, 'CYAJ, 'CYDO, 'CYAD, 'CYCG, 'CYAO. E750, E752-E754, E756, E757 became G-EAOF-'EAOK. E746, E748-E750, E752-E757, E775 had Napier Lion engines.

E1101-E1150	R.E.8	50

Built by D. Napier & Sons. E1119-E1132 to White Russian forces.

E1151-E1250	R.E.8	100

Built by Siddeley-Deasy Motors. E1178, E1180-E1193, E1195-E1206 to White Russian forces.

E1251-E1400	S.E.5A	150

Built by Vickers.

E1401-E1600	Sopwith 1F1 Camel	200

130/140hp Clerget. Built by Ruston Proctor. E1483, E1547 renumbered H7238, H6877. E1431, E1451-E1454, E1475, E1476 to US Government. E1466 to White Russian forces. E1537 became S-226 in Dutch service after internment.

E1601-E1900	Avro 504J/K	300

E1757 to White Russian forces. E1772 rebuilt as ER1772. E1611, E1640, E1644, E1660, E1663, E1665, E1671, E1675, E1707, E1728, E1826, E1843, E1850, E1860, became G-EAHU, 'EALA, 'EAVI, 'EAFC, 'EACW, 'EADD, 'EACB, 'EAIG, 'EAHM, 'EAJP, 'EBII, 'EBBF, 'EBFW, 'EAZX.

E1901-E2150	Bristol F.2B Fighter	250

Arab engines fitted. Built by Armstrong Whitworth. E1901 became IV of IAC. E2058 became G-EBCU.

E2151-E2650	Bristol F.2B Fighter	500

R-R Falcon. B & C built. C/ns 3754-4253. E2400 fitted with 300hp Hispano. E2354 became G-EBFD.

E2651-E2900	Bristol F.2B Fighter	250

Built by Angus Sanderson. Mainly delivered to store.

E2901-E3050	Avro 504K	150

Built by Morgan. E3046 part of Imperial Gift to India. E2969, E3021, E3022, E3043, E3045 became G-EBKB, 'EAQU, 'EATZ, 'EBAJ, 'EATU.

E3051-E3150	Avro 504K	100

Built by Savages. E3137, E3142 part of Imperial Gift to New Zealand. E3145 to Estonian Government.

E3151-E3153	F.E.2h	(3)

F.E.2ds A6501-A6503 modified by Ransome, Sims & Jeffries.

E3154-E3253	S.E.5a	58(100)

Built by Martinsyde up to E3211 at least. E3167 to the SAAF. E3169-E3171 to Australia and E3172, E3173 to Canada (becoming G-CYAB, 'CYBY) as part of the Imperial Gift to these countries. E3182 renumbered H7072.

E3254-E3403	Avro 504K	150

Built by Parnall. E3273, E3278, E3364 night fighter version. E3323, E3333 converted to 504N. E3269 slot and aileron control experiments at RAE, 1925. E3390-E3397 fitted with 100hp Monosoupapes and allotted for Grand Fleet use. E3289, E3291-E3293, E3297, E3358, E3359, E3363, E3364, E3366, E3379, E3382, E3386, E3387, E3399 became G-EAAM, 'EBEL, 'EADI, 'EADN, 'EAKZ, 'EANT, 'EAIO, 'EAFP, 'EAHW, 'EAHX, 'EBCK, 'EBKR, 'EBKX, 'EBPO, 'EAMI.

E3404-E3903	Avro 504K	500

Conversions: E3460 504N, and E3797 504L. ER3426 was re-built in service. Imperial Gifts: E3741-E3750 to Australia with 110hp Le Rhones, E3742-E3746, E3749, E3750 became A3-27 to A3-33 of RAAF. E3700-E3703. E3706 to India with 100hp Monosoupape engines. To other governments: E3415, E3417-E3420 to French with Le Rhone engines, E3525 to US with 150hp Monosoupape. E3408, E3480, E3481, E3501, E3502, E3505, E3671, E3672, E3724, E3794 became G-EADY, 'EABA, 'EADP, 'EAEC, 'EADH, 'EACB, 'EAWK, 'EAWI, 'EAMZ and 'EBHM.

E3904-E4103	S.E.5a	200

Built at Vickers at Weybridge. E3962, E3981 renumbered H7074, H7073.

E4104-E4303	Avro 504K	200

Built by Humber Motors. E4149 night fighter version. E4136 became A13 of Brazilian Navy. E4153, E4237, E4242 bought by Canterbury Aviation, NZ. E4118, E4137, E4143, E4144, E4154, E4164, E4170, E4180, E4221, E4222, E4224, E4225, E4230, E4233, E4234, E4246 became G-EAHL, 'EABE, 'EAIP, 'EAIQ, 'EAAL, 'EAIR, 'EAIS, 'EAFQ, 'EADA, 'EAAK, 'EACD, 'EAAN, 'EABX, 'EACV, 'EAGI, 'EAKR.

E4304-E4323	Handley Page V/1500	20

Built by Harland & Wolff. E4304-E4306 assembled by Handley Page at Cricklewood. E4307-E4311 delivered by air from Aldergrove. E4312-E4323 delivered as spares.

E4324-E4373	Avro 504K	50

Built by Eastbourne Aviation. C/ns 324-373. E4324, E4329, E4336, E4340, E4343, E4348, E4359, E4360,

E4362 became G-EABL, 'EAFD, 'EADM, 'EAHK, 'EADW, 'EADL, 'EABJ, 'EABM, 'EAEO. E4348 had Cosmos Lucifer fitted.

E4374-E4423	**Sopwith 1F1 Camel**	50

Bentley B.R.1. Built by Clayton & Shuttleworth. E4400 and E4403 renumbered H6864, H6884. E4412-E4417 allotted to the Grand Fleet.

E4424-E4623	**Sopwith 5F1 Dolphin**	200

Sopwith-built. E4505 converted to Mk.III.

E4624-E4628	**Airco DH.4**	5

Airco-built.

E4629-E5128	**Sopwith 5F1 Dolphin**	200(500)

Sopwith-built but not all delivered. To foreign governments: E4641, E4644 to France, E4642, E4643, E4645-E4650 to USA, E4722, E4815 Polish Purchasing Commission.

E5129-E5178	**Sopwith 1F1 Camel**	50

Built by Portholme. E5156, E5173, E5178 renumbered H7218, H7208, H6851. E5165 converted to 2-seat.

E5179-E5428	**Bristol F.2B Fighter**	130(250)

Ordered from Standard Motors. E5179-E5252 (74) Standard-built with Arab engines. E5253-E5258 (6) Standard-built but transferred to Bristol for fitting of Puma engines. E5259-E5308 (50) built at Bristol on transfer of contract to B & C. E5309-E5428 (120) cancelled. E5219 became G-EBDB.

E5429-E5434	**Sopwith TF2 Salamander**	6

Sopwith-built prototype order.

E5435-E5436	**Airco DH.9**	2

Airco-built to replace C6350, C6122.

E5437-E5636	**Airco DH.10**	200

Airco-built but not all entered service. E5488 became G-EAJO.

E5637-E5936	**S.E.5a**	300

Built at Austin Motors. E5692, E5693, E5703-E5705 re-numbered H7166, H7163, H7162, H7165. E5923 had non-standard tail surfaces 1919-20. E5696 had modified fuselage for parachute. E5814 issued free to Chilean Government.

E5937-E6036	**S.E.5a**	100

Built by Air Navigation Co. E5958, E5959 on repayment and E5962 free issue to Chile. E5956, E6013 became G-EBCA, 'EAZT.

E6037-E6136	**Airco DH.10**	60(100)

Built by Birmingham Carriage Co, but only some 60 delivered. E6042 had experimental twin fins.

E6137-E6536	**Sopwith 7F1 Snipe**	400

Built by Boulton & Paul. Not all entered service.

E6537-E6686	**Sopwith 7F1 Snipe**	150

Built by COW. E6570, E6611 fitted with arrester hooks for deck-landing trials.

E6687-E6736	**F.E.2b**	(50)

Ordered from Garrett. Cancelled.

E6737-E6786	**Avro 504K**	50

Built by Morgan. E6757, E6765 became G-EAVD and 'EACA.

E6787-E6936	**Sopwith 7F1 Snipe**	150

Built by Napier. E6862 converted to 2-seat.

E6937-E7036	**Sopwith 7F1 Snipe**	40(100)

Built by Nieuport & General. Record of first 40 only delivered. E6938 extant in Canada. E6949 used in USA films in the 'thirties as 'E8100'.

E7037-E7136	**F.E.2b**	100

Built by Ransome, Sims & Jeffries. E7112, E7113 modified to F.E.2c. E7072, E7075, E7076, E7090, E7095, E7100, E7102, E7108, E7110 to US Gov't.

E7137-E7336	**Sopwith 1F1 Camel**	200

Built by Ruston Proctor. E7173, E7182 re-numbered. H7151, H7225. E7290 to US Government. E7306-E7310, E7316-E7324, E7331, E7332 to Belgian Flying Corps.

E7337-E7836	**Sopwith 7F1 Snipe**	500

Built by Ruston Proctor except E7798, E7802-E7832, E7834 completed by Portholme.

E7837-E7986	**Airco DH.10**	18(150)

Built by Siddeley Deasy but delivery beyond E7854 not confirmed.

E7987-E8286	**Sopwith 1F1 Camel**	300

Sopwith-built. E8024, E8032, E8049, E8060, E8075, E8107, E8109, E8130 re-numbered H6880, H6894,

H7152, H6895, H7149, H7150, H7227, H7153. E7990 converted to Dragon. E8137 modified to carry parachute. E8076 night fighter experimental. E8213 part of Imperial Gift to Canada.

E8287-E8306	**Handley Page V/1500**	20

R-R Eagle. Built by Beardmore. E8287-E8295 delivered by air, remainder as spares.

E8307-E8406	**Sopwith 7F1 Snipe**	100

Built by Portholme. E8406 fitted with dropping chassis and floatation bags for fleet use.

E8407-E8806	**Airco DH.9A**	400

E8699, E8700, E8702, E8710 re-numbered J7308, J7307, J7309, J7306 and E8522 to J6585. Rebuilds: E R8599, E R8637, E R8649. DC conversions: E8722, E8742. Modified for floatation tests: E8444, E8456, E8457. Delivered to White Russian forces: E8429, E8555. E8590, E8597, E8616 part of Imperial Gift to Australia. E8463, E8465-E8467, E8469, E8470, E8472, E8475-E8478, E8480, E8501-E8507, E8538-E8545, E8565-E8568, E8570, E8571, E8632-E8634 to US Government for USMC Northern Bombing Group and E8449 to US as pattern. E8781, E8788, E8791 became G-EBLC, 'EBAC, 'EAXC.

E8807-E8856	**Armstrong Whitworth FK.8**	50

Armstrong Whitworth-built.

E8857-E9056	**Airco DH.9**	200

Airco-built. E8932, E8938, E8983 re-numbered H7201-H7203. E8882, E8894, E8909, E8915 part of Imperial Gift to India. To foreign forces: E8910 to Belgium; E8916, E8917, E8991 to Greece; E8924-E8928, E8942, E8944, E8945, E8947-E8952, E8986-E8988, E8992-E8994 to White Russians; E9022, E9031 free issue to Polish purchasing commission.

E9057-E9206	**Airco DH.10**	48(150)

Built by Daimler up to E9104 at least.

E9207-E9506	**Avro 504K**	300

Built by Grahame-White. E9261, E9265, E9266, E9268 converted to 504N. Imperial Gift issues: E9382, E9400-E9405 to India; E9424, E9427, E9429, E9432 to NZ. Foreign issues: E9463 became A11 of Brazilian Navy, E9469, E9474, E9481, E9488, E9493-E9495 to Estonia with 130hp Clergets. E9227, E9245, E9337, E9341, E9358, E9443 became G-EBCL, 'EAWM, 'EBPJ, 'EAWL, 'EBGV, 'EAQV.

E9507-E9656	**Bristol F.2B Fighter**	150

Arab engines fitted. Built by Gloucestershire Aircraft.

E9657-E9756	**Airco DH.9A**	100

Built by Mann Egerton. E9689 used in floatation tests. E9692, E9694 allotted to Australia as part of Imperial Gift. E9747, E9749-E9752 to White Russian forces.

E9757-E9856	**Vickers FB.27 Vimy**	(100)

Ordered from Metropolitan Carriage Co. Cancelled.

E9857-E9956	**Airco DH.9A**	100

Built by Vulcan Motor & Engineering. E9857 fitted with flotation gear. E9868-E9876 to USMC for Northern Bombing Group.

E9957-E9963	**R.E.8**	7

Built by No.3 (Western) Aircraft Repair Depot from salvage.

E9964-E9983	**Sopwith 1F1 Camel**	20

Built by No.3 ARD from spares. E9968 conv to 2-seat.

E9984	**Avro 504J**	1

Monosoupape. Built by 23rd Wing from spares.

E9985	**B.E.2e**	1

Built at ARS, Hounslow, from spares.

E9986-E9988	**Maurice Farman S.11 Shorthorn**	3

Built by 29th Wing from spares.

E9989-E9994	**Avro 504**	6

Monosoupape. E9989, E9990 built by 6th Wing ARS. Origin of rest not known.

E9995	**Avro 504K**	1

Built from spares.

E9996	**Sopwith Pup**	1

Gnome. Built from spares by 7th Wing, April 1918.

E9997	**Sopwith 5F1 Dolphin**	1

Sopwith-built.

E9998	**Maurice Farman**	1

Built from spares by 2 TS.

E9999	**Avro 504**	1

Monosoupape. Built by 23rd Wing ARS from spares.

Royal Air Force Requirements 1918

F1 to F9999

Contracts placed in 1918 allotted numbers in the 'F' series were production aircraft intended for the battles envisaged in 1919 and experimental aircraft for production in 1919. In the event, the Armistice came in November 1918 and many aircraft went straight into store and other contracts were cancelled. Some of the experimental aircraft, freed from the urgency of war, were not completed until 1920.

Serial Nos.	Aircraft Type and Remarks	Quantity
F1-F300	**Airco DH.9** 142(300) Ordered from NAF No.1, Waddon. 142 only built.	
F301-F320	**Handley Page O/400** 20 R-R Eagle. Built by Birmingham Carriage Co. F307, F308, F310, F312 to G-EATJ, 'EASX, 'EASZ, 'EATL.	
F321-F350	Reservation for No.2 (Northern) ARD (30)	
F351-F550	**Airco DH.10** 5(200) Ordered from NAF No.2, Heaton Chapel. Only five confirmed as completed.	
F551-F615	**S.E.5a** 65 Built by Vickers at Crayford.	
F616-F700	**Nos allotted to No.2 (Northern) ARD** 85 Confirmed allotment as follows: F616-F618, F622, F623, F625-F628, F631-F634, F638, F642, F644, F646, F647, F649, F650, F651 Armstrong Whitworth FK.8; F662, F663, F666, F669, F672, F675-F677, F681-F685, F687, F689, F690, F694, F699, F700 R.E.8.	
F701-F850	**Vickers Vimy** 12(150) Fiat or B.H.P. engines specified. Ordered from Vickers. 14 only completed at Crayford.	
F851-F950	**S.E.5a** 100 Built by Wolseley Motors. F896, F904, F932, F935, F937, F938 became G-EBFF, 'EBIA, 'EBFG, 'EBFH, 'EBIB, 'EBIC. G-EBIB now in Science Museum charge.	
F951-F1100	**Airco DH.9A** 150 Built by Westland Aircraft. F963 re-numbered F9515. F1086-F1092, F1094, F1095 to White Russian forces.	
F1101-F1300	**Airco DH.9** 200 Built by Waring & Gillow. F1238, F1295 became A6-6, A6-8 or RAAF. F1104, F1125, F1152, F1184, F1246, F1247 part of Imperial Gift to India. F1252 part of Imperial Gift to NZ. To foreign governments: F1140, F1141, F1201, F1204, F1221-F1229, F1275, F1293 to Belgium; F1258 to France and is extant in Paris; F1300 to Greece; F1137, F1138, F1217 free issue to Polish Purchasing Mission; F1111, F1147, F1151, F1164, F1193, F1202, F1232, F1233 to White Russian forces.	
F1301-F1550	**Sopwith 1F1 Camel** 250 Various engines fitted. Built by Boulton & Paul. F1312, F1413, F1415, F1538 re-numbered H7207, H7113, H7205, H6850. To US Government: F1301, F1302, F1304, F1306, F1308, F1316, F1318, F1322, F1338, F1340-F1342, F1344, F1348, F1350, F1354, F1356, F1360, F1364, F1366, F1368, F1370, F1372, F1374, F1376, F1378, F1380, F1382, F1384, F1425, F1427-F1432, F1434, F1435, F1437, F1440, F1444-F1446, F1449-F1452, F1455, F1461, F1463, F1464, F1466, F1469, F1471, F1473, F1475-F1477, F1484, F1485, F1488, F1490, F1491, F1493-F1499, F1500-F1503, F1505-F1507, F1509, F1511, F1514, F1515, F1517, F1521, F1523, F1527, F1531, F1535, F1541, F1543, F1545, F1547, F1549.	
F1551-F1552	**Airco DH.4** 2 AMC-built to replace D8408, D9231.	
F1553-F1602	**R.E.8** 50 Built by Siddeley Deasy Motors.	
F1603-F1652	**DH.9A** 50 Built by Westland Aircraft. F1632 re-built as J6914. F1626 to White Russian forces.	
F1653-F1664	**BAT FK.23 Bantam** 9(12) F1662-F1664 not completed. F1653, F1654 re-numbered J6579, J6580. F1655-F1659, F1661 became G-EAFM, 'EACP, 'EAFN, 'EAJW, 'EAMM, 'EAYA.	
F1665-E1764	**R.E.8** 100 Built by Standard Motors.	
F1765-F1766	**Tarrant Tabor** 1(2) Built by W.G.Tarrant Ltd, Byfleet. F1765 crashed on first flight. F1766 not completed.	
F1767-F1866	**Airco DH.9** 25(100) Puma engines fitted. Ordered from Westland Aircraft. Up to F1793 delivered.	
F1867-F1882	**Airco DH.10/10A** 16 Built by AMC.	
F1883-F1957	**Sopwith 1F1 Camel** 75 130hp Clerget. Built by Boulton & Paul. F1899, F1917 re-numbered H6871, H6886. F1952, F1953 to Greek service. F1950, F1951, F1954-F1957 to White Russian forces.	
F1958-F2007	**Sopwith 1F1 Camel** 50 110hp Le Rhone. Built by Portholme Aerodrome Ltd. F1962 re-numbered H7117. F1967, F1968 to Greek service. F1966, F1971 to White Russian forces.	
F2008-F2082	**Sopwith 1F1 Camel** 75 130hp Clerget. Built by Ruston Proctor.	
F2083-F2182	**Sopwith 1F1 Camel** 100 Built by Hooper & Co. F2129, F2139, F2144, F2154 re-numbered H7209, H6897, H7222, H6854. F2090 2-seat version with 110hp Le Rhone.	
F2183-F2188	**Aircraft built from spares and salvage** 6 F2183-F2185 Maurice Farman built at 29th Wing ARS, F2186, F2187 details not known, F2188 Avro 504A/J (Gnome Monosoupape).	
F2189-F2208	**Sopwith 1F1 Camel** 20 Built from spares at No.3 (Western) ARD. F2195 to Australian Government.	
F2209	**Avro 504A/J** 1 80hp Le Rhone. Erected from salvage at 23rd Wing ARS.	
F2210-F2229	**Sopwith Ship Strutter** 20 130hp Clerget. Ex-French. C/ns 7034, 7083, 7084, 7096, 7100, 7107-7112, 7119-7121, 7124, 7126, 7098, 7099, 7103, 7104 built as landplanes and converted for fleet use in 1918.	
F2230	**Maurice Farman S.11 Shorthorn** 1 Built from salvage by No.132 Squadron.	
F2231-F2232	**Avro 504** 2 Built from salvage at ARS Hounslow and Dover.	
F2233-F2332	**Avro 504K** 100 Built by Brush Electrical Engineering. F2269, F2286 converted to 504N. F2284 became G-EBDP. F2309, F2310 to Fleet bases with 100hp Gnome Monosoupape.	
F2333-F2532	**Sopwith 7F1 Snipe** 200 Bentley B.R.2. Sopwith-built. F2340 had 200hp Clerget. F2408 converted to 2-seat.	
F2533-F2632	**Avro 504K** 100 Built by Sunbeam Motors. F2575 converted to 504N. F2533 rebuilt to FR2533.	
F2633-F2732	**Airco DH.4** 100 Except for mainplanes and ailerons, built by Glendower. F2663-F2665, F2681, F2694, F2699, F2702, F2704 converted to DH.4A. F2670, F2671, F2686, F2694, F2699, F2702, F2704 became G-EANK, 'EANL, 'EAXD, 'EAHG, 'EAHF, 'EAJC, 'EAJD. F2675, F2677, F2678, F2680, F2684, F2689, F2693, F2697, F2698 registered G-EAYE, 'EAYJ, 'EAXN, 'EAXO, 'EAYH, 'EAYR, 'EAYI, 'EAXE, 'EAXI temporarily before export for Belgian Air Force. F2682, F2691 became G-AUBZ, 'AUCM as part of Imperial Gift to Australia. F2672, F2673, F2705-F2714 became G-CYBW, 'CYDB, 'CYBO, 'CYDM, 'CYEM, 'CYDO, 'CYBU, 'CYBV, 'CYDK, 'CYDL, 'CYCW, 'CYEC as part of Imperial Gift to Canada.	
F2733-F2902	**Airco DH.9A** 170 Built by Berwick. F2747, F2828 re-numbered H7204, J7304. F2867, F2868, F2872 became G-EBAN, 'EBCG, 'EBGX. F2776, F2779 became RAAF A1-16 and A1-17.	
F2903-F2905	**Boulton & Paul Bourges I/IA/II** 3 B & P Type P.7. F2903 Mk.I became K-129/G-EACE. F2904 Mk.IA became P.8 Atlantic project. F2905 Mk.II became G-EAWS.	

F2906-F2908	**BAT FK.25 Basilisk**	3
	Prototypes. F2906 first flew 10.1.19.	
F2909-F2911	**Nieuport Nighthawk**	3
	Built by Nieuport & General. Prototypes.	
F2912-F2914	**Westland Weasel**	3
	Prototypes. Engines as follows: F2912 Dragonfly, F2913 Jupiter, F2914 Jaguar.	
F2915-F2944	**Vickers FB.27 Vimy**	30
	Fiat engines specified. Built by Royal Aircraft Establishment 1918. F2916, F2919, F2920 completed as H651, H656, H657. 7 more re-numbered in H651-H660 batch.	
F2945-F2994	**F.E.2b**	(50)
	Ordered from Barclay Curle to erect with material from Alex Stephens, but order cancelled.	
F2995	**Beardmore WBII experimental**	1
F2996-F3095	**Vickers Vimy**	3(100)
	B.H.P. and Fiat specified. Ordered from Clayton and Shuttleworth but only 3 delivered.	
F3096-F3145	**Sopwith 1F1 Camel**	50
	Bentley B.R.1 mainly fitted. Built by Clayton and Shuttleworth. F3108 re-numbered H7241.	
F3146-F3195	**Vickers FB.27 Vimy**	41(50)
	Built by Morgan & Co. Up to F3186 delivered.	
F3196-F3245	**Sopwith 1F1 Camel**	50
	Bentley B.R.1 mainly fitted. Built by Nieuport & General.	
F3246-F3345	**R.E.8**	100
	Built by Siddeley Deasy.	
F3346-F3441	**Airco DH.6**	96
	RAF/Curtiss engines. AMC-built. F3435, F3437, F3439 and F3440 became G-EAHH, 'EAWT, 'EAWU, 'EAWV.	
F3442-F3491	**Armstrong Whitworth FK.8**	50
	Built by Angus Sanderson.	
F3492-F3494	**Avro 533 Manchester I/II/III**	3
	F3492 Mk.II, F3493 Mk.III, F3494 planned as Mk.III but completed as Mk.I.	
F3495-F3497	**Bristol Type 23 Badger**	3
	Dragonfly. B & C-built. C/ns 4254-4256. F3495 first flew 4.2.19. F3496 initially had a Jupiter engine first flew on 24.4.19, but a Dragonfly was substituted. F3497 was cancelled, but re-instated.	
F3498-F3547	**F.E.2b**	(50)
	Cancelled order with Barclay Curle.	
F3548-F3747	**R.E.8**	200
	Built by Daimler. F3663, F3680-F3682, F3684, F3685 to White Russian forces.	
F3748-F3767	**Handley Page O/400**	11(20)
	11 of order built by HP at Cricklewood.	
F3768-F3917	**F.E.2b**	(150)
	Cancelled order with RSJ.	
F3918-F3967	**Sopwith 1F1 Camel**	50
	Bentley B.R.1 mainly fitted. Built by Nieuport & General. F3938 re-numbered H7219.	
F3968-F4067	**Sopwith 1F1 Camel**	100
	Built by Ruston Proctor. F4019 converted to 2-seat.	
F4068-F4070	**Sopwith Snark**	3
	Sopwith prototypes to RAF Spec 1.	
F4071-F4170	**F.E.2b**	(100)
	Cancelled order with Alex Stephens.	
F4171-F4220	Various types built up from salvage	50
	F4171-F4174 Avro 504 by ARS Dover, Chattis Hill, Hounslow and Dover; F4175 Camel by 112 Squadron; F4176 built in Salonika; F4177-F4216 (40) Sopwith 1F1 Camel by No.3 (Western) ARD; F4217 Avro 504 by 207 TDS, Chingford; F4218 B.E.2d by 191 Squadron; F4219 Armstrong Whitworth FK.3 by 26 TS; F4220 Pup by ARS Salisbury.	
F4221-F4270	**Armstrong Whitworth FK.8**	50
	Armstrong Whitworth-built. F4231 became G-AUDE.	
F4271-F4970	**Bristol F.2B Fighter**	700
	R-R Falcon III in general. Built by B & C. C/ns 4257-4956. F4630 experimental single bay wings and F4728 3-bay wings. F4631 200hp Sunbeam Arab. F4336 only F.2B of Imperial Gift to Canada, as G-CYBC. Rebuilds: FR4582, FR4600, FR4640, FR4925. Seven to British Civil Register.	
F4971-F4973	**Armstrong Whitworth Ara**	3
	Dragonfly engine. Experimental. Final aircraft built by Armstrong Whitworth at Gosforth.	
F4974-F5073	**Sopwith 1F1 Camel**	52(100)

	Bentley B.R.1 mainly fitted. Built by Clayton & Shuttleworth up to F5025.	
F5074-F5173	**Bristol F.2B Fighter**	100
	Built by Harris & Sheldon.	
F5174-F5248	**Sopwith 1F1 Camel**	75
	Built by Marsh, Jones & Cribb. F5177 re-numbered as H6855. F5234 to Polish Air Force.	
F5249-F5348	**S.E.5a**	100
	Built by Martinsyde. F5249, F5253, F5257-F5259, F5285 became G-EAXQ, 'EAXV, 'EAXX, 'EAXT, 'EAXW, 'EAXS, F5300, F5303, F5333 became G-EAYL, 'EAXR, 'EAXU.	
F5349-F5448	**Handley Page O/400**	70(100)
	Two Liberty 12N. Built by NAF No.1. F5349 erected at Ford Junction, next 69 by Handley Page. 30 cancelled. F5414, F5417, F5418 became G-EAAF, 'EAAW, 'EAAG.	
F5449-F5698	**S.E.5a**	250
	Built by Vickers at Weybridge. F5696 parachute development aircraft.	
F5699-F5798	**Airco DH.4**	100
	Built by Palladium Autocars. F5764 converted to DH.4A. F5764, F5779, F5797 became G-EAWH, 'EAYF, 'EAYV.	
F5799-F5800	**Avro 504J**	2
	Built from spares at 23rd Wing.	
F5801-F6300	Nos allotted for rebuilds at depots in France.	500
	Known allocations as follows: F5801-F5808 Armstrong Whitworth FK.8 (ex-B5783, C3627, B5758, (?), C3650, C3641, C3508, C8433); F5809-F5815, F5817, F5819-F5824 Bristol F.2B Fighter; F5825, F5826 (re-numbered H6873); F5827, F5828 DH.4; F5832 Camel; F5833, F5837, F5840 DH.4; F5844, F5845 DH.9; F5846-F5849 DH.4; F5850 DH.9; F5852 F.E.2b (ex-A5658); F5856, F5858, F5859, F5861, F5862 F.E.2b; F5864 DH.9; F5871, F5872, F5874, F5876, F5877, F5879-F5883, F5885, F5891, F5895-F5899, F5900-F5909 R.E.8; F5910, F5912 S.E.5a; F5914-F5921, F5923 Camel; F5924 S.E.5a; F5925-F5928, F5930, F5931 (re-numbered H6875), F5932, F5936 (re-numbered H7220), F5938-F5948, F5950, F5951, F5953-F5960 Camel; F5961, F5962 Dolphin; F5964-F5968 Camel; F5969 S.E.5a; F5970, F5972 Camel; F5973, F5974, F5976-F5980 R.E.8; F5981 (re-numbered H7116), F5982, F5983, F5985, F5987 (re-numbered H6863), F5989-F5994 Camel; F5995-F5999 Bristol F.2B; F6001-F6003 DH.4 (ex-A8034, A8021, A8047); F6005-F6019 R.E.8; F6020 Dolphin; F6022-F6039 Camel; F6040-F6043 Bristol F.2B; F6044-F6050 R.E.8; F6052, F6053 (became H7240) Camel; F6055, F6057 DH.9; F6058 Camel; F6060 S.E.5a; F6061, F6063, F6064 Camel; F6066 DH.9; F6067, F6069 Camel; F6070 (ex-B884) DH.4; F6071 F.E.2b; F6072, F6073 DH.9; F6075 F.E.2b; F6076 Camel; F6077, F6080, F6081 F.E.2b; F6082-F6084 Camel; F6085 R.E.8; F6086-F6090 Camel; F6091, F6092 R.E.8; F6093, F6094 Bristol F.2B; F6096 DH.4; F6097 R.E.8; F6098 DH.9; F6099 DH.4; F6100 Camel; F6101 Bristol F.2B; F6102 Camel; F6103, F6104 DH.4; F6105-F6107, F6109 Camel; F6110 Camel; F6111 Camel; F6112, F6113 DH.9; F6114, F6115 DH.4; F6116 Bristol F.2B; F6117 Camel; F6119, F6120, F6121 Bristol F.2B; F6122, F6123 Camel; F6124 Armstrong Whitworth FK.8 (ex-C8601); F6125 DH.9; F6126, F6127 Camel; F6128 F.E.2b; F6129 Camel; F6131 Bristol F.2B; F6132 Camel; F6133 DH.4; F6134 R.E.8; F6135 Camel; F6137 Armstrong Whitworth FK.8 (ex-B5836); F6138 Camel; F6139 DH.4; F6140 Camel; F6141 DH.9; F6142 Bristol F.2B; F6143 R.E.8; F6144-F6146 Dolphin; F6147, F6149-F6153, F6155-F6157 Camel; F6158 Bristol F.2B; F6159-F6163 Armstrong Whitworth FK.8 (ex-C3646, B3317, C8503, C8436, D5003); F6164-F6168 DH.4; F6169 Camel; F6172 DH.9; F6173, F6174 F.E.2b; F6175-F6177 Camel; F6178 R.E.8; F6180, F6182 Camel; F6183 DH.9 or Camel; F6184 (re-numbered H6860); F6185 Camel; F6187 DH.4; F6188-F6194 Camel; F6195 Bristol F.2B; F6196 DH.9; F6197-F6201 Camel; F6203, F6204 (ex-B6631) R.E.8; F6205 DH.9; F6206 Bristol F.2B; F6207 DH.4 (ex-A8028); F6208 Bristol F.2B; F6209 DH.4 (ex-D9263); F6210 Camel (re-numbered H6891); F6211 Camel; F6212	

DH.4 (ex-A7713); F6213 DH.9; F6214, F6215 DH.4
(ex-A7507, A7626); F6216 Camel; F6217 Bristol F.2B;
F6218 R.E.8; F6219, F6220 (ex-B5644), F6221 Camel;
F6222 DH.4 (ex-A8016); F6223 Camel; F6224 DH.4;
F6225, F6226 Camel; F6227 DH.4; F6228-F6230 Camel;
F6234 DH.4; F6235 Bristol F.2B; F6238, F6240,
F6244, F6245, F6249-F6252 Camel; F6253 DH.4;
F6254 Camel or R.E.8; F6257-F6259, F6261, F6264,
F6268, F6269 Camel; F6270 R.E.8; F6271 Camel;
F6273 R.E.8; F6276 S.E.5a; F6277, F6279 R.E.8;
F6281, F6282, F6285, F6292, F6294, F6295 Camel;
F6299, R.E.8; F6300 Camel.

F6301-F6308 Sopwith 1F1 Camel   8
Numbers allotted by depots in France overlapped the
allocation to F6300 by F6301-F6308 for Camels ex-
D8617, D1808, B2371, D6628, B6635, D8511, C1584,
D8385.

F6301-F6500 Sopwith 1F1 Camel   200
130hp Clerget. Built by Boulton & Paul. F6337 re-
numbered H7255. F6317, F6319 to Belgian Flying
Corps. F6310, F6473, F6481 to RCAF. F6302 became
G-EBER. F6394, F6398 180hp Le Rhone. F6314 is
extant in UK. Owing to an official allocation mistake
full re-numbering cannot be assessed.

F6501-F7000 Sopwith TF2 Salamander   160(500)
Sopwith built at Ham up to F6660. F6533 to USA.

F7001-F7030 Sopwith 7F1 Snipe/Dragon   30
Snipes ordered from Ham factory with Dragon engines.

F7031-F7033 Sopwith Snapper   3
Kingston-built prototypes. F7031 later K-149/G-EAFJ.

F7034-F7133 Sopwith 5F1 Dolphin   100
Built by Darracq at Fulham. Transfers: F7046 to French
Government, F7128 free issue to Polish Purchasing
Mission, F7076, F7078, F7085, F7091 to CAF in UK.

F7134-F7143 Handley Page V/1500   10
Ordered from Alliance, completed by Handley Page.

F7144-F7146 Sopwith 1F1 Camel   (3)
Special experimental order; later cancelled.

F7147-F7346 Airco DH.10   (200)
Ordered from Alliance but no delivery record.

F7347-F7546 Armstrong Whitworth FK.8   200
Built by Angus Sanderson. F7384, F7484 became
G-EATO, 'EALW.

F7547-F7596 Sopwith Ship Strutter   50
130hp Clerget. French-built airframes acquired for
conversion to shipborne use. F7590 reported both as
transferred to Japan and Latvia.

F7597-F7598 Airco DH.4   2
Replacement order.

F7599-F7600 Allotted officially to 'odd Aircraft'   2

F7601-F7750 Sopwith TF2 Salamander   (150)
Cancelled order placed with Wolseley Motors.

F7751-F7800 S.E.5a   50
Built by Wolseley Motors. F7773-F7779, F7781-
F7785, F7787, F7792, F7793, F7796, F7797, F7799
and F7800 were part of Imperial Gift for SAAF.

F7801-F7950 Sopwith TF2 Salamander   107(150)
Ordered from Air Navigation Co but not all delivered.

F7951-F8200 S.E.5a   250
Built by Austin Motors. From F8001 (200) delivered to
the USAS. F7960, F7976, F7978, F7991, F7997 became
G-EBGL, 'EBGM, 'EBFI, 'EBDX, 'EBDV.

F8201-F8230 Handley Page V/1500   10(30)
Ordered from Beardmore. 10 reported completed.

F8231-F8280 Sopwith T1 Cuckoo   (50)
Ordered from Blackburn. Cancelled.

F8281-F8320 Handley Page V/1500   10(40)
Ordered from HP but only 10 reported delivered.

F8321-F8420 S.E.5a   (100)
Ordered from Martinsyde, but cancelled.

F8421-F8495 Airco DH.10A   21(75)
Ordered from Mann Egerton but only up to F8441,
built as a 10C, delivered.

F8496-F8595 Sopwith 1F1 Camel   58(100)
Bentley B.R.1. Ordered from Nieuport & General but
only up to F8553 confirmed delivered.

F8596-F8645 Vickers FB.27 Vimy   50
Built by Vickers at Weybridge. 10 with Fiat engines and
rest B.H.P.s when ordered, but R-R Eagles fitted in
general. F8625, F8630 became G-EAOL, 'EAOU.

F8646-F8695 Sopwith 1F1 Camel   50
Bentley B.R.1. Built by Portholme Aerodrome Co.

F8696-F8845 Avro 504K   150
Built by Parnall & Sons. F8713, F8812, F8834 con-
verted to 504N. F8824, F8826, F8829, F8831 with
100hp Gnome Monosoupape part of Imperial Gift to
India. F8841 with Lucifer engine exported to Argentina.
F8706, F8717 became G-EADO, 'EAIA.

F8846-F8945 Avro 504K   100
Built by Sage. F8940 at RAE had enlarged tail surfaces
and modified undercarriage. F8864, F8865, F8902
became G-EBNR, 'EBOB, 'EATB.

F8946-F9145 S.E.5a   200
Built by Vickers. F9106, F9107, F9110, F9113, F9119,
F9122, F9131, F9143-F9145 part of Imperial Gift to
Australia and F9016, F9114, F9117, F9128, F9136,
F9139 became G-CYBP, 'CYAY, 'CYCE, 'CYCC, 'CYCQ,
'CYCV as part of Imperial Gift exported to Canada. F9022,
F9130 became G-EATE, 'EBQK.

F9146-F9295 Vickers FB.27 Vimy   50(150)
Vickers-built. Only 50 completed. F9186 did ditching
trials in 1920.

F9296-F9395 F.E.2h   (100)
Cancelled order with Richard Garrett & Sons.

F9396-F9445 Reservation for 45th Wing rebuilds   50
Known allocations: F9406 Bristol Scout; F9407, F9410
Camel; F9413 Avro 504; F9417 Camel.

F9446-F9495 Cancelled order placed with British Caudron   (50)

F9496-F9695 Sopwith 1F1 Camel   (200)
Cancelled order placed with Boulton & Paul. Numbers
reallotted.

F9496-F9545 Rebuilds by No.5 (Eastern) ARD   ?(50)
Known allocations: F9502 Bristol F.2B; F9504-F9506
Avro 504; F9509 Camel; F9511 DH.4; F9515 DH.9A
ex-F963; F9616 Bristol F.2B ex-E2460.

F9546-F9568 Re-builds from spares and salvage   23
F9546, F9547 Avro 504K (130hp Clerget); F9548
Camel ex-B5556 which reverted to its original number;
F9549 Bristol F.2B (Arab) by Marshall & Sons additional
to contract; F9550 F.E.2b (160hp Beardmore); F9551-
F9565 not known; F9566 F.E.2b by 4th Wing; F9567
B.E.2e by 5 TDS; F9568 S.E.5a by 30 TDS.

F9569-F9570 Vickers FB.27 Vimy   2
Replacements for B9953, B9954.

F9571 B.E.2d   1
Built from salvage by 16 TDS.

F9572 Avro 504A   (1)
A8591 taken on charge ex-pattern aircraft to Scottish
factory.

F9573-F9622 Rebuilds by No.3 (Western) ARD   ?(50)
F9575, F9579, F9591 Camel; F9598 Bristol F.2B;
F9599 Camel; F9606, F9616 Bristol F.2B Fighter.

F9623-F9695 Rebuilds from salvage and spares   ?(73)
F9623, F9624 Camel and F9625 Avro 504 by 6th Wing;
F9626 Bristol Scout by 2 School of Aerial Navigation;
F9627 B.E.2c engine unknown; F9628-F9630 Camel by
3 TDS; F9631, F9632 Camel by 43 TDS; F9633 Avro
504 (Le Rhone) origin unknown; F9634, F9635 Camel
by 29 TDS and CFS; F9636 Avro 504 by 58th Wing;
F9637 Camel by 42 TS; F9638 Bristol F.2B; F9639-
F9694 reservation for No.2 ARD; F9695 Camel by
Upavon.

F9696-F9745 Avro 504K   50
Built by Eastbourne Aviation. F9723 became J8029,
F9705 converted to 504N, F9745 (100hp Gnome
Monosoupape) part of NZ Imperial Gift.

F9746-F9845 Avro 504K   100
Built by Hewlett & Blondeau. F9783, F9802, F9809,
F9810 became G-EBAV, 'EABP, 'EASA, 'EASB.

F9846-F9995 Sopwith 7F1 Snipe   (150)
Ordered from COW but cancelled.

F9996-F9999 Reservation for No.2 (Northern) ARD   (4)

Captured Enemy Aircraft

'G' series

'G' did not follow 'F' as a prefix letter in the general numbering series, because it could easily be confused with 'C', but it was used as a prefix in a special series for the identification of enemy aircraft falling into British hands on the Western Front as it was an appropriately significant letter for 'German'. The numbers were not allocated for aircraft taken on charge by units as in the general series, but as a reference number, chiefly for intelligence purposes. In fact, in a number of cases, the 'G' number denoted merely a heap of wreckage.

Strewn wreckage or wreckage under fire was not always salvaged, but in most cases it was taken to a depot for examination by intelligence officers in France. Usually the engine was in one piece and it was normal to despatch this to England where it was stored at the Agricultural Hall, Islington, for technical survey or awaiting allocation.

Ex-enemy aircraft that were airworthy, were flown to England on the normal ferry route to Lympne from where they were collected for store at Islington or held pending allocation to experimental establishments or Fighting Schools. Other aircraft, reasonably intact but not flyable, were shipped and transported to Islington. It was these two classes of relatively intact machines that actually bore their 'G' numbers in a manner similar to normal British service aircraft. The majority were scrapped after a survey in February 1919. G1 to G9 were apparently all allotted retrospectively to earlier aircraft.

Serial No.	Aircraft Type and Number (if known)	Date acquired	Remarks on circumstances of acquisition.
G10	Albatros DIII D1990/16	13.02.17	Shot down nr Saily-Saillisel.
G11	Albatros	15.02.17	Fell in lines nr Vlamertinge.
G12	Halberstadt DV	15.03.17	Hit by AA fire. Sent to UK.
G13	DFW		Wreckage found.
G14	Albatros Scout	04.03.17	Shot down by No.29 Sqn.
G15	Albatros Scout	25.03.17	Shot down by Lt Binnie of No.60 Squadron.
G16	Albatros Scout	25.03.17	Shot down by Lt Binnie of No.60 Squadron.
G17	Albatros DI D410/16	21.03.17	Prince Charles Frederick of Prussia forced down by S.E.5a of No.32 Squadron.
G18	Albatros DIII D2012/16	01.04.17	Shot down.
G19	Albatros CVII C2217/16	02.04.17	Brought down by AA. Crew captured.
G20	Albatros Scout DIII D1942/16	05.04.17	Forced down nr Neuve Eglise.
G21	Albatros Scout DIII D2234/16	08.04.17	Shot down in British lines by French fighter.
G22	Albatros	21.04.17	Shot down by RNAS pilots.
G23	Gotha GIV G610/16	23.04.17	Shot down by RNAS pilot near Vron.
G24	DFW CV C5927/16	24.04.17	Forced down nr Havrincourt.
G25	Aviatik	24.04.17	Shot down.
G26	Albatros Scout	25.04.17	Wreck under shell fire not salvaged.
G27	DFW	30.04.17	Completely wrecked.
G28	Albatros 2-seater	30.04.17	Brought down by ground fire. Crew captured.
G29	DFW CV C5909/16	01.05.17	Brought down by AA fire nr Arras.
G30	Albatros Scout DIII D771/17	01.05.17	Shot down by No.1 Squadron near Elverdinghe.
G31	DFW	02.05.17	Brought down by fire from trenches.
G32	Albatros D473/16	03.05.17	Landed undamaged. Flown to the UK.
G33	Albatros	05.05.17	Conflicting reports of salvage.
G34	Albatros	05.05.17	Wreckage completely burned.
G35	Albatros Scout	06.05.17	Shot down by F.E.s. Aircraft not salvaged.
G36	(Unidentified)	07.05.17	Not salvaged.
G37	Albatros CV C1394/17	12.05.17	Shot down by AA fire near Armentieres.
G38	DFW	18.05.17	Shot down by machine-gun fire from trenches.
G39	Albatros Scout DIII D796/16	19.05.17	By S.E.5a near St Pol. Pilot captured.
G40	DFW CV C5872/16	20.05.17	By No.3 Squadron over Havrincourt Wood.
G41	(Unidentified)	21.05.17	AA fire. Found to have fallen in German lines when investigated.
G42	Albatros DIII D2015/16	04.06.17	Forced down by No.29 Sqn. Flown in England with engine from G39.
G43	Albatros DIII	05.06.17	By No.60 Squadron. Crashed near the front.
G44	DFW C.V C9045/16	12.06.17	By No.8(N) Sqn nr Arras.
G45	DFW	13.06.17	Wrecked.
G46	(Unidentified)	—	False report of wreckage in lines.
G47	DFW CV C5046/16	16.06.17	By 2 pilots of No.8(N) Sqn.
G48	Rumpler	23.06.17	By AA fire at Steenwich.
G49	Albatros	23.06.17	By AA fire near Ypres.
G50	Albatros	02.07.17	By fire from No.12 Kite Balloon Section.
G51	Albatros CX C9289/16	12.07.17	By No.70 Sqn over Bellevue.
G52	DFW	12.07.17	Shot down by Mannock south of Lens.
G53	DFW CV C799/17	12.07.17	By No.56 Sqn nr Armentieres
G54	(See remarks)	—	False report.
G55	DFW CV	13.07.17	By AA fire south east of Arras
G56	Albatros DV D2129/17	15.07.17	Forced down intact. To UK.
G57	Ago CIV C8964/16	29.07.17	By No.32 Squadron. Crashed later in the UK.
G58	DFW CV C776/17	05.08.17	By No.5 Squadron. 1 survivor.
G59	DFW	10.08.17	Shot down. Nothing salvaged.
G60	Albatros DIII	12.08.17	By Mannock over Farbus.
G61	Albatros DIII	12.08.17	By No.7 Squadron.
G62	Rumpler CIV	19.08.17	By AA fire north-west of Ypres.
G63	Rumpler CIV	20.08.17	By No.66 Sqn near Ypres.
G64	(Unidentified)	21.08.17	Found to be in enemy lines.
G65	(Unidentified)	22.08.17	Found to be in enemy lines.
G66	Rumpler CIII C1898/16	31.08.17	Landed near Elverdinghe.
G67	AEG GIV G166/16	3/4.09.17	By AA fire. 2 prisoners.
G68	(Unidentified)	04.09.17	Completely burned.
G69	Rumpler CIV C8483/16	03.09.17	Believed forced landed.
G70	(Unidentified)	14.09.17	No.48 Squadron. Salvaged by the Belgians.
G71	(Unidentified)	16.09.17	Landed in No Man's Land.
G72	Fokker Dr.I F103/17	23.09.17	Voss shot down nr St. Julien.
G73	(Unidentified)	27.09.17	Wreck. Shot down in flames.
G74	Gotha GIV G1064/16	25.09.17	By AA fire at Oost Dunkerke.
G75	Albatros DV D2284/17	27.09.17	Forced down jointly by the RFC/RNAS.
G76	(Unidentified)	28.09.17	Completely destroyed.
G77	(Unidentified)	28.09.17	Wreckage not salvaged.
G78	(Unidentified)	01.10.17	Wreckage at Hooge.
G79	(Unidentified)	14.10.17	Wreckage at Poelcapelle.
G80	(Unidentified)	17.10.17	By No.22 Sqn east of Ypres.
G81	LVG	17.10.17	By Capt McCudden near Dickebusch.
G82	(Unidentified)	17.10.17	Wreckage in Polygon Wood.
G83	(Unidentified)	18.10.17	Wreckage in Polygon Wood.
G84	Rumpler CIV C8431	21.10.17	Shot down by Capt McCudden.
G85	Rumpler	22.10.17	Shot down by No.11 Sqn.
G86	(Unidentified)	05.11.17	Shot down by infantry.
G87	(Unidentified)	05.11.17	Shot down by infantry.
G88	(Unidentified)	08.11.17	Nothing salvaged.
G89	Albatros DIII	13.11.17	Shot down by No.24 Sqn.
G90	Albatros DVa D5253/17	14.11.17	By AA in Third Army area.
G91	DFW CV C4977/16	22.11.17	Forced down intact by Capt Childs, No.84 Squadron near Bourlon Wood.
G92	(Unidentified)	29.11.17	Nothing salvaged. Near Passchendaele.
G93	Pfalz DIIIa D1116/17	30.11.17	Shot down by Capt G.E. Thompson, No.46 Squadron near Flesquieres.
G94	LVG CV C4958/17	30.11.17	Wreckage at Havrincourt, by AA fire.
G95	Rumpler	05.12.17	Wreckage near Hermies.
G96	(Unidentified)	05.12.17	Wreckage near Hermies.

G97	Albatros DV D4545/17	05.12.17	Down near Bethune. To UK.
G98	Albatros DV	07.12.17	Total wreck. Second Army area.
G99	(Unidentified)	12.12.17	By AA of Second Army.
G100	Albatros DV D2356	17.12.17	Shot down north of Ypres.
G101	Albatros DVa D5390/17	17.12.17	Forced down by No.3 Sqn AFC. Flown to UK. Shipped to Australia.
G102	(Unidentified)	10.12.17	Presumed false report of wreck.
G103	(Unidentified)	18.12.17	Wreckage reported but not located.
G104	DFW	22.12.17	Shot down by Capt J.B. McCudden.
G105	AEG GIV G1125/16	23.12.17	AA at Achiet-le-Grand. Intact.
G106	Rumpler	23.12.17	Shot down by Capt McCudden.
G107	Rumpler	23.12.17	By Capt McCudden near Gontescourt.
G108	LVG	23.12.17	By Capt McCudden near Metz.
G109	(Unidentified)	23.12.17	Found to be in enemy lines.
G110	Pfalz DIII D1370/17	27.12.17	Landed intact. No.35 Sqn took over.
G111	Rumpler	28.12.17	By Capt McCudden near Velu Wood.
G112	Rumpler	28.12.17	By Capt McCudden nr Flers.
G113	LVG	28.12.17	By Capt McCudden, wreckage spread in Havrincourt Wood.
G114	(Unidentified)	28.12.17	By 46 Sqn over Gouzeacourt.
G115	(Unidentified)	28.12.17	By AA fire at Saillisel.
G116	Pfalz DIII	28.12.17	By AA fire near Le Transloy.
G117	Rumpler CIV C8500/16	28.12.17	Forced down by AA fire at Monchy. Flown to the UK, but crashed at Grain on trials.
G118	LVG	29.12.17	By Capt McCudden near Havrincourt.
G119	LVG	29.12.17	By Capt McCudden nr Ephey.
G120	Rumpler CIV	01.01.18	By AA fire near Peronne.
G121	(Unidentified)	01.01.18	By Capt Mannock over Fampoux.
G122	(Unidentified 2-seater)	03.01.18	Wreckage found to be in the German lines.
G123	Albatros Scout	06.01.18	By No.13 Sqn. Nothing was salvaged as wreckage could only be viewed at distance on enemy's trench wire.
G124	(Unidentified 2-seater)	13.01.18	Wreckage.
G125	Fokker DrI DR144/17	13.01.18	Lt Stapenhorst after shooting down British balloon was brought down by AA fire. Shipped to the UK.
G126	AEG	26.12.17	Brought down in Italy.
G127	–	–	False report of wreckage.
G128	DFW	26.12.17	Brought down in Italy.
G129	(Unidentified)	29.01.18	Brought down in French lines.
G130	LVG CV C9725/17	02.02.18	Brought down by Capain McCudden.
G131	Albatros Scout	04.02.18	Shot down by No.60 Sqn pilots.
G132	LVG CV C9658/17	18.01.18	By AA fire near Lens.
G133	Friedrichshafen GIII/ G283/17	15.02.18	Landed in Third Army area.
G134	Albatros DV D4422/17	16.02.18	Intact, but turned over in ploughed field when forced down by No.1 Squadron.
G135	LVG CV	16.02.18	Landed near Catigny.
G136	Friedrichshafen G111 G326/17	16.02.18	Forced down by AA fire near Isbergues. Crew of 4 prisoners.
G137	Rumpler CIV	16.02.18	By Capt McCudden near Lagnicourt.
G138	Albatros Scout DV D4495/17	19.02.18	By No.60 Sqn nr Hollebeke.
G139	Halberstadt	–	Crashed in British lines.
G140	(Unidentified 2-seater)	21.02.18	By No.29 Sqn. Crashed in front line.
G141	Pfalz DIII 4184/17	26.02.18	By No.24 Sqn. Landed intact on RFC aerodrome. Flown to the UK on 06.03.18.
G142	Rumpler	–	Wreckage found.
G143	DFW CV	01.03.18	Believed by naval pilots.

G144	Albatros DV D2359/17	06.03.18	By No.13 Sqn near Arras. Flown to the UK.
G145	Albatros	06.03.18	Wrecked.
G146	(Unidentified)	06.03.18	Fell in front line trenches.
G147	Friedrichshafen GIII G199/17	11.03.18	Landed and destroyed by crew.
G148	(Unidentified)	12.03.18	By No.56 Sqn over Ribecourt.
G149	Albatros two-seater	12.03.18	By No.11 Sqn near Doignies.
G150	(Unidentified)	15.03.18	By No.84 Sqn S of Villeret.
G151	Albatros DV	18.03.18	Forced down near Essigny-le-Grand.
G152	(Unidentified)	22.03.18	Down in flames. Not salvaged.
G153	Albatros Scout	22.03.18	Brought down by infantry fire.
G154	Albatros Scout	22.03.18	Brought down by infantry fire.
G155	Albatros Scout	22.03.18	Brought down by infantry fire.
G156	Hannover CLII	29.03.18	Brought down by AA fire and flown to the UK 26.04.18.
G157	Pfalz DIIIa D8078/17	–	Engine and guns to the UK.
G158	Fokker DrI	22.03.18	Shipped to the UK.
G159	Albatros DVa D5734/17	01.04.18	Flown to the UK 21.04.18.
G160	DFW	01.04.18	Shot down by No.3 Sqn AFC
G161	(Unidentified 2-seater)	10.04.18	Not salvaged.
G162	(Unidentified 2-seater)	10.04.18	Not salvaged.
G163	(Unidentified)	10.04.18	Not salvaged.
G164	–	10.04.18	Report not substantiated.
G165	Hannover CLII 13135/17	09.04.18	Engine only salvaged.
G166	LVG	09.04.18	Engine only salvaged.
G167	LVG	11.04.18	Engine only salvaged.

'XG' series

The 'G' series had been started early in 1917, and once functioning as the standard register for captured aircraft, it was appreciated that earlier enemy aircraft captured had not been similarly registered. A register of these was therefore compiled in retrospect in a numbered series starting at No.1 prefixed by 'XG' to denote the 'Extra G-series'.

Serial No.	Aircraft Type and Number (if known)	Remarks on acquisition and disposal
XG1	Albatros A375	Believed arrived in UK 20.04.16.
XG2	Albatros A374	Farnborough 22.09.15. Given to Cambridge University.
XG3	LVG C2234	From France 25.05.16. To London University.
XG4	Fokker EIII E210/16	To Science Museum.
XG5	Fokker	Was A3021. To USA 11.12.17.
XG6	Albatros DI 391/16	Captured 01.12.16.
XG7	LVG CII	Farnborough from 14.06.17.
XG8	Albatros 2-seater	Arrived at Farnborough 05.07.18.
XG9	Halberstadt	Wreckage held at Islington.
XG10	Albatros CVI C1788/16	Exhibited February 1917.
XG11	LVG C4238	Allotted to HQ Honourable Artillery Coy.
XG12	Friedrichshafen GIII	Wreckage salvaged from sea by French after machine hit cliffs at Cape Blanchey 4/5.11.17.
XG13	DFW CV C4686/17	RNAS capture. Believed sent to Canada.
XG14		Wreckage held at Islington.

'AB' series

During 1917 the Germans intensified raids over Britain by aeroplanes and the occasional one was shot down. In the same way that HQ, RFC in the Field allotted serials in the 'G' series, so at Home, the RFC registered the wrecks in this country in a series prefixed by the letters 'AB'.

Serial No.	Aircraft Type and Number (if known)	Date captured	Remarks on location and how acquired
AB1	–	–	No details known.
AB2	Gotha	5/6.12.17	Hit by AA over Canvey Island was forced to land at Rochford. Burnt out after landing.
AB3	Gotha	5/6.12.17	Brought down near Canterbury. Crew set it on fire before capture.
AB4	Gotha	22.12.17	Landed in field at Margate and set on fire by crew before capture.

AB5	Gotha GV 938/16	28.12.17	Brought down in flames at Wichford.
AB6	Gotha GV 978/16	19.05.18	Shot down by Bristol Fighter. Wreckage fell at East Ham, London.
AB7	Gotha GV 925/16	19.05.18	Shot down by coastal AA at St Osyth.
AB8	Gotha GV 979/16	19.05.18	After aerial combat crashed at Frinstead.
AB9	Gotha	19.05.18	Shot down by Sopwith Camel at Shellness, Isle of Sheppey.

'AG' series

In November 1917 two RFC Wings were sent to assist Italian Forces. Initially their intelligence reports were submitted through GHQ in France and the first wreckage recordings were in the 'G' series. From December 1917 RFC, HQ, Italy (VIIth Brigade RFC) compiled its own register of enemy aircraft or their remains examined in a numbered series prefixed 'AG' to denote Austro-Hungarian and German series.

Serial	Aircraft Type	Remarks
AG1	DFW	Totally wrecked at Povegliano, December 1917.
AG2	AEG G(?)	Brought down by AA fire at Biadenne.
AG3	Albatros Dv D4879/17	Shot down December 1917.
AG4	AEG G.IV	Brought down by AA fire at Castelfranco.
AG5	Albatros DIII	Brought down February 1918.
AG6	Aviatik-Berg D.I 138.27	Crashed in British lines.
AG7	AEG G.IV G.180	Landed with engine trouble, night of 18/19.02.18.
AG8	AEG	Shot down in flames during night of 20/21.02.18.

'G/HQ' & 'G/Bde' series

The general 'G' series lapsed in March 1918 in favour of General Headquarters and each RFC Brigade in the Field (which became RAF Brigades on 1st April 1918) with responsibility for sectors of the Front reporting enemy aircraft down in their area and reporting them separately. The approved form was in the styling G/1Bde/1 for the first registered by 1 Brigade, but the actual marking varied from G-1-1 to G/1BDE/1; for presentation here the approved form is used.

Serial No.	Aircraft Type and Number (if known)	Date captured	Remarks on acquisition, condition and disposal
G/HQ/1	Rumpler CVII 6460/17	16.05.18	Landed fuel shortage at Cappelle.
G/HQ/2	Friedrichshafen GIII 402/17	19.05.18	By AA fire near Calotteries.
G/HQ/3	Gotha GV	22.05.18	Crew burnt aircraft before capture.
G/HQ/4	DFW C287/16	31.05.18	Forced down. To UK 5.6.18.
G/HQ/5	(2-seater)	01.07.18	Wreckage found on dump.
G/HQ/6	Pfalz DXII 2486/18	15.09.18	By Nos.1 and 62 Sqns.
G/1Bde/1	DFW CV 7823/17	29.04.18	Shot down by No.40 Sqn.
G/1Bde/2	Pfalz DIIIa 8151/17	03.05.18	Landed Gonnelieu with engine trouble.
G/1Bde/3	DFW CV	03.05.18	Brought down by AA fire.
G/1Bde/4	DFW CV 938/18	08.05.18	Brought down by small arms fire.
G/1Bde/5	DFW	07.05.18	Shot down by No.46 Sqn.
G/1Bde/6	Rumpler CIV 1469/17	16.05.18	Forced down.
G/1Bde/7	AEG JI 209/17	16.05.18	Brought down near Hianges by R.E.8 B6568. To UK.
G/1Bde/8	(Twin-engined)	01.06.18	Wrecked.
G/1Bde/9	LVG	07.07.18	Shot down by No.40 Sqn.
G/1Bde/10	Albatros DIII	09.07.18	Total wreck near Steenwerck
G/1Bde/11	DFW	03.08.18	Wreck not salvaged.
G/1Bde/12	Gotha G.Vb	10.08.18	Forced down near Caucourt.
G/1Bde/13	Friedrichshafen	21.08.18	By No.151 Sqn near Arras.
G/1Bde/14	Gotha G.Vb	24.08.18	By No.151 Sqn near Haute-Avesnes.
G/1Bde/15	Halbaerstadt (2-seat)	—	Wreckage found. Salvaged on 31.08.18.

G/1Bde/16	Fokker DVII	15.09.18	Details not known.
G/1Bde/17	Fokker DVII	—	Flown to UK 06.11.18.
G/2Bde/1	DFW CV 7877/17	21.04.18	Brought down by AA fire at Westoutre. To Islington on 06.05.18.
G/2Bde/2	Albatros DV	21.04.18	Not salvaged.
G/2Bde/3	Rumpler	23.04.18	Salvaged by French.
G/2Bde/4	Albatros DV	22.04.18	Salvaged by French.
G/2Bde/5	Halberstadt	26.04.18	Not salvaged.
G/2Bde/6	Halberstadt	30.04.18	Destroyed on ground by shells.
G/2Bde/7	LVG	03.05.18	By No.32 Sqn.
G/2Bde/8	Albatros	14.05.18	Completely wrecked. Unsalvageable.
G/2Bde/9	Albatros DIII	14.05.18	Details not known.
G/2Bde/10	Fokker DrI	19.05.18	Engine only salvaged.
G/2Bde/11	Halberstadt CL11	22.05.18	Hit by machine-gun fire, Poperinghe.
G/2Bde/12	Albatros Scout	29.05.18	Wreckage.
G/2Bde/13	Albatros Scout	31.05.18	Unsalvageable.
G/2Bde/14	Fokker DVII D368/18	06.06.18	Shot down near Hazebrouck by S.E.5a D5969. Shipped to the UK.
G/2Bde/15	Fokker DrI 588/17	09.06.18	Shot down near Dickenbusch. Engine and parachute to UK.
G/2Bde/16	Pfalz DIII	19.06.18	Shot down near Bailleul.
G/2Bde/17	Rumpler	30.06.18	Shot down by No.74 Sqn.
G/2Bde/18	Friedrichshafen GIII 507/18	1/2.07.18	Forced down.
G/2Bde/19	Friedrichshafen GIII 555/17	1/2.07.18	Brought down by AA fire at Fanquernbergues. Fired by crew.
G/2Bde/20	LVG	27.07.18	Shot down and burned.
G/2Bde/21	LVG CVI	02.08.18	By S.E.5as C6468 and D3438 near Proven.
G/2Bde/22	Fokker DVII	17.09.18	Shot down.
G/2Bde/23	DFW	17.09.18	Complete wreck sent for scrap.
G/2Bde/24	Albatros	—	Engine salvaged from wreck.
G/2Bde/25	Rumpler	—	Engine sent to Islington, November 1918.
G/2Bde/26	—	—	No record.
G/2Bde/27	Fokker DVII	28.10.18	Shot down.
G/2Bde/28	Fokker DVII	28.10.18	Engine salvaged.
G/2Bde/29	Friedrichshafen	—	Believed by AA fire.
G/2Bde/30	LVG	—	Shipped to the UK.
G/2Bde/31	—	—	No record.
G/2Bde/32	—	—	No record.
G/2Bde/33	Fokker DVII	—	No further details.
G/3Bde/1	(Unidentified)	11.04.18	Not salvaged.
G/3Bde/2	Hannover CLII 13103/17	16.04.18	Force-landed. Flown to UK.
G/3Bde/3	DFW CV 7787/17	22.04.18	By AA fire. To UK 13.05.18.
G/3Bde/4	Pfalz DIIIa 8282/17	24.04.18	By small arms fire. To UK.
G/3Bde/5	LVG CV 9746/17	29.04.18	Forced down. Sent to UK.
G/3Bde/6	Gotha GV 969/16	21.05.18	Shot down by AA. To UK.
G/3Bde/7	Albatros DVa 7221/17	25.05.18	Engine salvaged for UK.
G/3Bde/8	Halberstadt CLII 1231/18	29.06.18	Crashed near Fillieres.
G/3Bde/9	Friedrichshafen	17.07.18	Completely burnt. Engines to the UK.
G/3Bde/10	Staaken RXIV R43/16	10.08.18	By Camel of No.151 Sqn, near Amiens.
G/3Bde/11	Gotha GV 922/16	22.08.18	Shot down by Camel of No.151 Sqn.
G/3Bde/12	Fokker DVII	21.08.18	Shot down by No.3 Sqn pilot.
G/3Bde/13	Fokker DVII	23.08.18	By No.12 Sqn R.E.8 crew.
G/3Bde/14	Pfalz DIII	27.08.18	Details not known.
G/3Bde/15	LVG	29.08.18	Found during an advance.
G/3Bde/16	Halberstadt	03.09.18	Located on ground at Biefvillers le Bapaume. Sent to UK.
G/3Bde/17	Fokker DVII	05.09.18	Date is day of location.
G/3Bde/18	Albatros	05.09.18	Date is day of location.
G/3Bde/19	Fokker DVII	04.09.18	Shot down by Camel F1972.
G/3Bde/20	(Unidentified)	03.09.18	Not salvaged.
G/3Bde/21	Friedrichshafen or Gotha	13.09.18	Shot down by No.151 Sqn Camel. An engine sent to Wolseley Motors.
G/3Bde/22	Friedrichshafen	17.09.18	By No.151 Sqn Camel. Parts to the UK.
G/3Bde/23	Friedrichshafen	17.09.18	By No.151 Sqn Camel.

G/3Bde/24	Staaken RVI	15.09.18	Badly burnt.
G/3Bde/25	(Twin-engined)	21.09.18	Badly burnt.
G/3Bde/26	LVG	27.09.18	Date is day of location.
G/3Bde/27	Friedrichshafen	28.09.18	Date is day of location.
G/3Bde/28	Hannover	26.10.18	Engine to UK.
G/3Bde/29	Hannover	26.10.18	Engine to UK.
G/3Bde/30	—	—	No details.
G/3Bde/31	Junkers JI J181/17	.11.18	Salvaged near La Vacquerie.
G/3Bde/32	LVG	. .18	No further details known.
G/3Bde/33	—	. .18	Presume wreck found during an advance.
G/3Bde/34	—	. .18	Presume wreck found.
G/3Bde/35	—	. .18	Presume wreck found.
G/3Bde/36	—	. .18	Presume wreck found.
G/3Bde/37	Halberstadt CLII	01.11.18	Wreck found.
G/5Bde/1	Rumpler	12.04.18	Complete wreck but engine sent to the UK.
G/5Bde/2	Fokker DrI 425/17	21.04.18	von Richthofen brought down near Corbie.
G/5Bde/3	(Two-seater)	22.04.18	Shot down near Somme-Aure.
G/5Bde/4	Albatros	25.04.18	Shot down near Villers-Bretonneux.
G/5Bde/5	(Unidentified)	25.04.18	Believed shot down by AA fire.
G/5Bde/6	Hannover CLII 13282/17	03.05.18	Brought down by joint efforts of AA and aircraft.
G/5Bde/7	LVG	04.05.18	Brought down by AA nr Arras.
G/5Bde/8	Fokker DrI	16.05.18	Shot down by Camel B7199.
G/5Bde/9	AEG GIV 588/17	16.05.18	Hit by AA. Landed near Villers-Bretonneux.
G/5Bde/10	Albatros Scout	17.05.18	Unsalvageable.
G/5Bde/11	LVG	27.05.18	Completely burnt.
G/5Bde/12	Pfalz DIIIa 8284/17	30.05.18	Landed short of fuel. Flown to UK 21.06.18.
G/5Bde/14	Rumpler	31.05.18	Total wreck.
G/5Bde/15	Rumpler	01.06.18	Badly burnt.
G/5Bde/16	Halberstadt CLII	09.06.18	Brought down by R.E.8 crew nr Villers Bocage. Flown to UK.
G/5Bde/17	Fokker DVII	17.06.18	Shot down by S.E.5as.
G/5Bde/18	LVG CV	17.06.18	Shot down nr Ailly sur Noye.
G/5Bde/19	DFW CV C342/18	26.07.18	Shot down.
G/5Bde/20	Fokker DVII	12.08.18	By Camel. Sent to UK.
G/5Bde/21	AEG GIV 875/17	15.08.18	Brought down by AA fire.
G/5Bde/22	Halberstadt CLIV	23.08.18	Landed at Chipilly.
G/5Bde/23	AEG JII 202/18	24.08.18	Found near Morcourt.
G/5Bde/24	Fokker DVII	12.08.18	Shot down.
G/5Bde/25	Friedrichshafen	07.09.18	Believed forced landed.
G/5Bde/26	Fokker DVII	10.09.18	Salvage sent to the UK.
G/5Bde/27	AEG GV	17.09.18	Shot down by Camel.
G/5Bde/28	(Twin-engined)	13.09.18	Believed not salvaged.
G/5Bde/29	Hannover	24.09.18	Brought down nr St.Quentin.
G/5Bde/30	Albatros JII 1566/1830	30.10.18	Found crashed near Montbrehain.
G/5Bde/31	AEG	—	Two engines sent to the UK.
G/10Bde/1	Friedrichshafen GIVa	24.07.18	Engines sent to the UK.
G/10Bde/2	DFW CV 2238/18	10.08.18	Wrecked near Hinges.
G/10Bde/3	AEG	.08.18	Wreck found. Parts to UK.
G/10Bde/4	—	05.09.18	Wreckage found.
G/10Bde/5	Fokker DVII	16.09.18	Shot down. Engine salvaged.
G/10Bde/6	DFW	16.09.18	Date of location of wreck.
G/10Bde/7	Pfalz	17.09.18	Complete wreck found.
G/10Bde/8	Pfalz DXII 2600/18	09.10.18	Driven down by Camels E7190 and E7241. Flown to the UK. Shipped to Australia.

End of World War I Orders

H1 to H9999

The 'H' series followed directly on from the 'F' series in late 1918 and so consists largely of reduced or incomplete orders due to the end of hostilities.

Serial Nos.	Aircraft Type and Remarks	Quantity
H1-H200	**Airco DH.9A** Airco-built. H93 rebuilt as HR93 and H111, H126, H128 as J7013-J7015. H5 to Australia. H52 went to Russia and probably remained with White Russian forces.	**200**
H201-H350	**Avro 504K** Built by Scottish Aviation, ordered 9.8.18. H244 rebuilt as HR244. H221, H257 became G-EBCB, 'EBSG.	**150**
H351-H650	**Sopwith 7F1 Snipe** 100 approx (300) Partly built by Ruston Proctor except H408-H418 completed by Portholme. H365-H375, H378-H380, H385, H404, H407 delivered direct to Waddon store without engines. H376, H377, H381-H384, H386-H403, H405, H406, H419-H450 not completed. Remainder presumed cancelled.	
H651-H670	**Vickers FB.27 Vimy** 10 re-numbered from RAE F2915-F2944 batch. 10 cancelled.	**(20)**
H671-H673	**Sopwith Cobham** H671 Mk.II, H672 Mk.I. Work on H673 stopped in July 1919.	**2(3)**
H674-H733	**S.E.5a** Built by Air Navigation Co.	**60**
H734-H833	**Sopwith 1F1 Camel** Night fighter version. Built by Hooper.	**100**
H834-H1083	**Bristol F.2B Fighter** Ordered from Gloucestershire Aircraft. H834-H925 and H1061-H1083 cancelled. H926, H927 registered as G-EBEE, 'EBDN prior to export for Belgian Air Service. H951 became G-EAWA.	**135(250)**
H1084-H1239	**Martinsyde F.4 Buzzard** Cancelled order with parent firm. Duplicated D4211-D4360 (150) and B1490-B1495 (6).	**(156)**
H1240-H1739	**Bristol F.2B Fighter (Engines as specified)** **468(500)** B & C-built. C/n 4957-5456 but H1708-H1739 cancelled. H1240-H1289 Arab, H1290-H1298 Falcon, H1299-H1389 Arab, H1390-H1398 Falcon, H1399, H1400 Arab, H1401-H1406 Falcon, H1407 Arab, H1408-H1689 Falcon, H1690-H1707 Puma. H1240, H1242, H1244, H1245, H1258, H1281, H1291, H1292, H1389 became G-EBAM, 'EBAT, 'EBAU, 'EBCW, 'EBBO, 'EBCV, 'EBAK, 'EBAL and 'EAYQ for export to Belgian Air Service. H1279 to Irish Air Force as 20.48. H1251, H1485 became II, III of Irish Air Corps. H1420 prototype Mk.III, H1436 and H1559 used for parachute development, H1460 converted to Coupe (Bristol Type 27), H1642 DC 'Cranwell Special'. H1688 converted to Tourer (Bristol Type 29). H1557, H1558 part of Imperial Gift to New Zealand. H1254, H1282, H1376, H1638, H1639 became G-EBIO, 'EAWZ, 'EASH, 'EASV, 'EASU and H1248 became VH-UEB.	
H1740-H1745	**Nieuport London** Built by Nieuport & General. H1740 first flew 13.4.20 and H1741 7.20. Remainder cancelled.	**2(6)**
H1746-H1895	**Bristol F.2B Fighter** Cancelled. Duplicated D2626-D2775 allocation.	**(150)**
H1896-H2145	**Avro 504K** Built by Sunbeam Motors up to H2075 at least. Imperial Gift offsets: H1934, H1936 India; H1952, H1958, H1964-H1968, H1970 New Zealand; H1917, H2041-H2049 Canada as G-CYAL, 'CYAX, 'CYHA, 'CYAP, 'CYAS, 'CYDA, 'CYCY, 'CYFI, 'CYAQ, 'CYCX. H2021 became 104 of Danish Navy. H2024, H2026 became A2, A3 of Brazilian Navy. H2073, H2075 became II, III of	**180(250)**

Irish Air Corps. H2052, H2060, H2062, H2065, H2071 became G-EBDJ, 'EBDC, 'EBCS, 'EBCF, 'EBCT on export for Belgian Air Services. H1925, H1956, H1959, H2025, H2053, H2067 became G-EALD, 'EAJG, 'EAHO, 'EBAG, 'EBFL, 'EBHL, and H1909, H1960, H1973, H2030 became VH-UBR, 'UEC, 'UCI, 'UBA.

H2146-H2645 Avro 504K 500
Conversions: H2308, H2581, H2582, H2590 504L, H2432, H2618 504N. Imperial Gift offsets: H2146, H2153, H2155, H2546-H2548, H2621-H2625 (Gnome Monosoupape) India; H2171-H2180 (Le Rhone) became A3-1 to A3-9 of RAAF plus one spare. H2160, H2161, H2235-H2244, H2296 to fleet bases for naval use. H2509, H2516, H2553, H2558, H2565, H2595 became G-EAZU, 'EAZQ, 'EAZR, 'EAZS, 'EAZV, 'EAIH for export for Belgian Air Service. H2212, H2234, H2262, H2295, H2297, H2318, H2322, H2323, H2365, H2411, H2416, H2507, H2514, H2518, H2560, H2561, H2581, H2582, H2585-H2590, H2592-H2594, H2600 became G-EBBC, 'EBSE, 'EBZB, 'EAZW, 'EAHV, 'EANC, 'EAPQ, 'EAPR, 'EBSJ, 'EAHZ, 'EBGI, 'EADS, 'EANN, 'EBFB, 'EAEY, 'EAEZ, 'EADJ, 'EADK, 'EAGU, 'EAEV, 'EAJQ, 'EAKB, 'EALB, 'EAKA, 'EAJU, 'EAKW, 'EAJZ, 'EAII, 'EAIJ, 'EAJB, 'EAKY, 'EAKX. H2402 rebuilt as HR2402 modified with large rudder. H2545 to Iceland. H2549, H2556 became Avro 1 and 2 of the Danish Army. H2566, H2568 became A16 and A7 of the Brazilian Navy. H2583, H2584, H2591 became G-EAFU-'EAFW prior to going to South Africa.

H2646-H2745 Sopwith 1F1 Camel 100
Built by Boulton & Paul. H2668 to US government. H2700 became G-EAWN.

H2746-H2945 Airco DH.10 (200)
Ordered from parent firm. Believed not built.

H2946-H3195 Avro 504K 200(250)
Built by Brush Electrical Engineering up to about H3145. Conversions: H2986, H2988-H2990, H3034, H3042 504L; H2962, H2972, H2995, H3105 504N; H2968 504R. Imperial Gift offsets: H2986-H2990 New Zealand; H3033, H3034, H3036-H3038, H3040-H3043 which became A3-16, A3-46, A3-17-A3-19, A3-21, A3-22, A3-47, A3-23 of RAAF; H3078-H3080 (Gnome Monosoupape) India. H3048, H3049, H3052-H3055 to Greek government. Parts of H2976 used to construct J6896.

H3196-H3395 Airco DH.9 (200)
Cancelled order with NAF No.1.

H3396-H3545 Airco DH.9A 150
Built by Westland Aircraft. H3459-H3465, H3502 allotted to Australian government. H3511-H3513, H3515, H3518, H3529, H3530, H3534, H3536, H3539, H3540, H3543 converted to 3-seat for naval duties. Rebuilds: HR3545; 2 rebuilt as J7010, J9011.

H3546-H3795 Airco DH.9 114(250)
Built by Vulcan Motor & Engineering up to H3659 at least. H3581, H3595, H3617 rebuilt as J7303, J7305, J7302. H3657 oleo undercarriage tests 1922.

H3796-H3995 Bristol F.2B Fighter (200)
Cancelled order with Armstrong Whitworth.

H3996-H4045 Sopwith 1F1 Camel (50)
Cancelled order with British Caudron.

H4046-H4195 Vickers FB.27a Vimy (150)
Ordered from Boulton & Paul 30.8.18. Cancelled.

H4196-H4215 Vickers FB.27a Vimy (20)
Ordered from Kingsbury Aviation 13.8.18. Cancelled.

H4216-H4315 Airco DH.9 100
Airco-built. H4259, H4260, H4262, H4279, H4315 free issue to the Polish Purchasing Commission. Imperial Gift offsets: H4291 Australia, H4307 India, H4313 South Africa.

H4316 DH.9 (1)
Replacement order cancelled.

H4317-H4319 Austin Greyhound 3
Prototypes by Austin Motors.

H4320-H4369 DH.9 (50)
Cancelled order with Berwick & Co.

H4370-H4419 Handley Page O/400 (50)
D8301-D8350 already allotted.

H4420-H4421 Sopwith 3F2 Hippo (2)
X11 and X18 re-numbered.

H4422-H4423 Sopwith 2FR2 Bulldog (2)
X3 and X4 re-numbered.

H4424 Sunbeam Bomber (1)
Presumed ex-N515.

H4425-H4724 Armstrong Whitworth FK.8 188(300)
Built by Angus Sanderson up to H4612. H4473, H4573, H4585, H4600, H4612 became G-EAIC, 'EAVT, 'EAVQ, 'EATP, 'EAJS and H4561 VH-UCF.

H4725-H4824 Vickers FB.27a Vimy (100)
Ordered from Metropolitan Wagon Co, 19.8.19. Cancelled.

H4825-H4864 Handley Page V/1500 (40)
Cancelled order placed with Grahame-White Aviation.

H4865-H5064 Sopwith 7F1 Snipe 38(200)
Sopwith-built up to H4902.

H5065-H5139 Vickers FB.27a Vimy 25(75)
Westland Aircraft order. H5090-H5139 cancelled. Liberty engines planned but Rolls-Royce Eagles fitted. H5089 rebuilt as HR5089.

H5140-H5239 Avro 504K 100
Built by London Aircraft Co. H5185, H5196, H5199 converted 504N. H5172, H5173, H5199 became G-EAGC, 'EAGB and G-ADEV. (See BK892).

H5240-H5289 Avro 504K 9(50)
Built by Eastbourne Aviation. Up to H5248 only confirmed. H5240, H5241 became G-NZAB, 'NZAO.

H5290 Airco DH.4 1
Built by Glendower.

H5291-H5540 S.E.5a (250)
Ordered from Austin Motors. Cancelled.

H5541-H5890 Airco DH.9 350
Built by Alliance Aeroplane Co. Imperial Gift offsets: H5544, H5545, H5562, H5563, H5570, H5581, H5583, H5586, H5593, H5601, H5608, H5611, H5631, H5639, H5644, H5647-H5649, H5651, H5657, H5665, H5667, H5669, H5670, H5685, H5687, H5689, H5692 SAAF; H5546, H5609, H5627, H5636, H5637, H5641, H5672 New Zealand; H5592, H5679, H5697 Australia. Other offsets: H5552, H5558, H5569, H5587, H5588, H5602, H5622, H5642, H5660, H5661, H5664, H5673, H5683, H5695, H5800 Greek government; H5638, H5710, H5715, H5722, H5725, H5726, H5730 free issue to Chile; H5702, H5721, H5733 free issue to Polish Purchasing Mission; H5607, H5619, H5621, H5629, H5662, H5666, H5668, H5705-H5707, H5709, H5711, H5712, H5716, H5719, H5735, H5736, H5741, H5742, H5747, H5753, H5757, H5783, H5820, H5836, H5845, H5851, H5865, H5868 were under temporary British civil registrations prior to export to Belgian Air Service; H5774, H5797, H5823, H5830, H5862, H5869 became III, I, V, II, VIII, IV of Irish Air Corps. H5833, H5839, H5848, H5860 registered G-EAYY, 'EAZH, 'EAYZ, 'EAZI and re-registered CH-82, CH-81, CH-83, CH-84 in Switzerland. H5873 became H-101 in Netherlands East Indies service. H5579, H5632, H5652, H5678, H5688, H5747, H5775, H5844, H5858, H5886 became G-EAOP, 'EBGQ, 'EBDF, 'EBDL, 'EBEN, 'EBAR, 'EBEF, 'EBHV, 'EAZD, 'EBIG. H5889, H5890 became G-EAOZ, 'EAPL for export to Holland.

H5891-H5893 Airco DH.11 Oxford 1(3)
H5891 prototype built by Airco. Rest cancelled.

H5892-H5893 Sopwith Buffalo 2
Experimental aircraft. Compromised numbers above.

H5894-H5939 Airco DH.4 46
Built by Palladium Autocars. H5894, H5895, H5905, H5928, H5929, H5934, H5939 converted to DH.4A. H5896, H5898 became G-EAYX, 'EAYS for export to Belgium and H5915, H5925, H5929, H5931, H5936 went into service with SABENA. H5902, H5905, H5934, H5939 became G-EAYG, 'EAVL, 'EAXF, 'EAMU.

H5940-H6539 Bristol F.2B Fighter 2(600)
Siddeley Puma engine. Ordered from Austin 25.9.18. H6055, H6058 only confirmed as delivered.

H6540-H6542 Martinsyde F.4 Buzzard 1A 3
Prototype long range version.

H6543-H6842 Avro 504K 114(300)
Ordered from Humber Motors. Up to H6656 confirmed delivered. H6593, H6596 rebuilt as J6896 and HR6596. H6601, H6605, H6611, H6653, H6656 became G-EAZL, 'EAZG, 'EAZK, 'EBBP, 'EBCC for export for Belgian Air Service. H6543, H6547, H6551, H6598, H6599,

H6602, H6608, H6609 became G-EASG, 'EBCQ, 'EARZ,
'EAGV-'EAGW, 'EBGH, 'EAYB, 'EAYC.

H6843-H6992   **Allocation for aircraft rebuilt in France**   61(150)
H6843 R.E.8; H6844 Camel ex-D9427; H6845 R.E.8;
H6847, H6848 Camel ex-D6615, D8196; H6849 R.E.8;
H6850-H6856 Camel ex-F1538, E5178, F5947, D3415,
F2154, F5177, D6627; H6857 R.E.8; H6858, H6859
DH.4 ex-A7964, D8427; H6860-H6864 Camel ex-F6184,
D9492, D6442, F5987, E4400; H6865 R.E.8; H6866
Dolphin ex-D3632; H6867-H6869 Camel ex-C3353,
F6197, C6723; H6870 R.E.8; H6871, H6872 Camel ex-
F1899, D9486; H6873 DH.4 ex-F5826; H6874-H6878
Camel ex-F5946, F5931, B7896, E1547, D8171; H6879
R.E.8; H6880 Snipe ex-E8024; H6881, H6882 DH.4 ex-
A7820, A8088, H6883 R.E.8; H6884 Camel ex-E4403;
H6885 DH.4 ex-D8378; H6886 Camel ex-F1917; H6887
DH.4 ex-B7911; H6888 F.E.2b ex-C9829; H6889-H6892
Camel ex-C3302, D9653, F6210, F6147; H6893 Bristol
F.2B ex-C9896; H6894, H6895 Snipe ex-E8032, E8060;
H6896 R.E.8; H6897-H6899 Camel ex-F2139, D9669,
C8382; H6900 R.E.8; H6901-H6904 Camel ex-H7276,
F6216, D1942, C3351; H6934 Dolphin.

H6993-H7016   **Sopwith 1F1 Camel**   (24)
Re-numbering of previously wrongly numbered rebuilds.

H7017-H7076   **Allocation for aircraft rebuilt in France**   57(60)
H7017-H7038, H7040-H7057 R.E.8; H7060-H7065
Bristol F.2B; H7069 Bristol F.2B ex-B1209; H7070
Bristol F.2B ex-B1234; H7072-H7074 S.E.5a ex-E3182,
E3981, E3962; H7075 DH.9.

H7077-H7092   **Sopwith 1F1 Camel**   (16)
Re-numbering of previously wrongly numbered rebuilds.

H7093-H7342   **Allocation for aircraft rebuilt in France**   ?(250)
Known allotments: H7097, H7098, H7104 Camel;
H7107 DH.9A; H7110-H7117 Camel ex-D6644, D1887,
B7769, F1413, D9567, D9588, F5981, F1962; H7118-
H7120 DH.4 wrongly numbered F6511-F6513; H7123
DH.4; H7124, H7125 DH.4 ex-D8383, A8029; H7136-
H7143 R.E.8; H7145 F.E.2a ex-A5783; H7147, H7148
DH.4 ex-D8377, D8382; H7149, H7150 Snipe ex-
E8075, E8107; H7151 Camel ex-E7173; H7152-H7154
Snipe ex-E8049, E8130, E7341; H7156, H7157 Arm-
strong Whitworth FK.8; H7160 Camel; H7161-H7166
S.E.5a ex-C9491, E5703, E5693, E5704, E5705, E5692;
H7171-H7175 Bristol F.2B ex-A7256, B1307, C842,
C4746, C4817; H7176, H7178-H7180 F.E.2b ex-A6565,
A6600, D9759, D9776; H7181 R.E.8 ex-D4946;
H7182-H7193 R.E.8; H7196-H7198 Bristol F.2B ex-
C868, C983, D8065; H7201-H7203 DH.9 ex-E8932,
E8938, E8983; H7204 DH.9A ex-F2747; H7205-
H7226 Camel ex-F1415, D9598, F1312, E5173, F2129,
D9599, F6328 (previously wrongly numbered), B9149,
D6442, D6596, D8162, F5955, C3355, E5156, F3938,
F5936, F1928, F2144, D1851, D9634, E7182, D9438;
H7227 Snipe ex-D9857; H7228-H7231 F.E.2b ex-A6504,
D9757, A5607, B460; H7232 Camel ex-B7817; H7233
F.E.2b ex-A5789; H7234-H7241 Camel ex-B3786,
D9402, B895, D6638, E1483, D6446, F6053, F3108;
H7242 S.E.5a ex-D6194; H7243-H7246 Dolphin;
H7247-H7254 S.E.5a previously numbered F6420-F6427
in error; H7255 Camel previously falsely numbered
F6337; H7256-H7261 S.E.5a previously numbered
F6428-F6433 in error; H7262, H7263, H7265-H7268
R.E.8; H7269-H7289 renumbering of previously wrongly
numbered rebuilt Camels; H7291-H7293 Bristol F.2B
ex-F6405, F6407, F6408.

H7343-H7412   **Sopwith 1F1 Camel**   70
Built by Hooper. H7367 presented to Canada.

H7413-H7562   **Avro 504K**   150
Built by Hewlett & Blondeau. H7524, H7534 converted
to 504N. Imperial Gift offsets: H7461, H7462 to Canada
as G-CYAR, 'CYFE; H7495, H7496 (Gnome Mono-
soupape) to India. Other offsets: H7426, H7467, H7474,
H7482, H7487 became G-EAZF, 'EBAF, 'EBCR,
'EBCO, 'EBCD prior to export to Belgian Air Service;
H7473, H7479 became A9 and A4 of the Brazilian Navy.
H7428, H7488, H7513 became G-EAYD, 'EBHK, 'EAHY
and H7499 became G-AUGY.

H7563-H7612   **Airco DH.9**   (50)
Cancelled order with G & J Weir for materials only.

H7613-H7912   **Martinsyde F.4 Buzzard**   174(300)
Ordered from parent firm 25.9.18. Deliveries to about
H7786 which was converted to F.4A (two-seat). H7688,
H7692, H7780, H7786 became G-EBFA, 'EBDM, 'EAWE,
'EAUX.

H7913-H8112   **Airco DH.9**   (200)
Ordered from No.4 NAF (Crossley Motors) 25.9.18 but
cancelled.

H8113-H8252   **Allocation of rebuilds by No.2 (Northern) ARD**   ?(140)
Reported numbers taken up: H8141 R.E.8; H8174
DH.9; H8200-H8202 type not known.

H8253-H8264   **Allocation for aircraft built from salvage**   12
H8253 Camel by 42 TS; H8254, H8255 Avro 504
(Clerget) by 58th Wing; H8256 B.E.2d by 77 Sqn at
Penston; H8257 Avro 504 (Clerget) by 42 TS; H8258,
H8259 Camel (two-seater) and H8260-H8262 standard
Camel by 43 TDS; H8263 DH.4 by Palladium Autocars
original sample conv to DH.4A; H8264 Camel by CFS.

H8265-H8288   **Caudron**   24
Type and origin not known.

H8289-H8292   **Allocation for aircraft built from salvage**   4
H8289, H8290 Avro 504 by 7 TDS; H8291, H8292
Camel by CFS.

H8293-H8412   **Allocations not known. Presumed cancelled**   (120)
H8413-H8512   **Martinsyde F.4 Buzzard**   (100)
Cancelled order.

H8513-H8662   **Nieuport Nighthawk**   41(150)
Originally ordered as Sopwith Snipes from Nieuport &
General this order was changed to their own design. Up
to H8553 confirmed built. Conversions: H8535, H8536,
H8538-H8540 Nightjar (Mars X), H8534, H8544 Gloster
Mars VI.

H8663-H8762   **Sopwith 7F1 Snipe**   (100)
Ordered from Portholme Aerodrome Co 26.9.18 but
cancelled.

H8763-H9112   **Martinsyde F.4 Buzzard**   (350)
Ordered from Boulton & Paul 26.9.18. Cancelled.

H9113-H9412   **Airco DH.9**   300
Siddeley Puma engines. Airco-built. H9115 part of the
Imperial Gift to India. Other offsets: H9117, H9118,
H9209, H9216, H9228, H9261, H9263 free issue to
Chile; H9133, H9135, H9157 to Estonia; H9212 to
Belgium; H9247 became VII of Irish Air Corps. H9125,
H9128, H9147, H9176, H9187, H9196, H9197, H9203,
H9205, H9243, H9255, H9258, H9271, H9273, H9276,
H9277, H9282, H9289, H9319, H9324, H9333, H9337,
H9340, H9369, H9370 became G-EAUQ, 'EAUN, 'EBJX,
'EAUP, 'EAUO, 'EAUH, 'EAUI, 'EBHP, 'EBQD, 'EAVM,
'EAGX, 'EAGY, 'EATA, 'EAAD, 'EBXR, 'EAAC,
'EAUC, 'EBJR, 'EBKO, 'AACR, 'EBJW, 'EBKV, 'AUFS,
'EBTR, 'EBUM. H9140 converted to HP.17 as J6906.

H9413-H9512   **Vickers FB.27a Vimy**   (100)
Ordered from RSJ. Cancelled.

H9513-H9812   **Avro 504K**   300
Mainly 130hp Clerget. Built by Grahame-White Aviation.
Imperial Gifts offsets: H9552-H9558, H9621-H9633,
H9665, H9666, H9668-H9672, H9690, H9714, H9715,
H9717, H9722, H9727, H9729, H9732, H9735-H9745
Canada; H9679-H9686, H9688, H9689, H9691-H9699,
H9700-H9703, H9706-H9712 SAAF; H9704, H9705
(100hp Gnome Monosoupape) India. Other aircraft
offsets: H9591, H9608, H9618, H9660 became A17,
A6, A12, A8 of Brazilian Navy; H9673-H9678, H9747-
H9758 White Russian forces; H9687, H9716, H9725,
H9730, H9734, H9746 Greek Government.

H9813-H9912   **Avro 504K**   58(100)
Built by Sage & Co up to H9870 at least. H9816, H9821,
H9826, H9866, H9870 converted to 504N. H9828,
H9832-H9844 allotted to Australia of which H9835-
H9840 became A3-36 to A3-41 of RAAF. H9833,
H9859 became G-AAYH and G-EBSM.

H9913-H9962   **F.E.2b/c**   1?(50)
Ordered from RSJ. H9913-H9924 F.E.2c, H9925-H9962
F.E.2b of which H9939 is confirmed delivered.

H9963   **Vickers FB.27a Vimy**   1
Replacement order.

H9964-H9966   **Sopwith 7F1 Snipe 1A**   (3)
Cancelled, numbers already allotted.

H9967-H9999   **Reservation, not used.**

Final World War I Allocations

J1 to J6576

'J' followed directly on from the 'H' allocations because 'I' was not used to avoid confusion with No.1. Only a few of the aircraft ordered in this series from October to November materialised.

Serial Nos.	Aircraft Type and Remarks	Quantity
J1-J150	Sopwith 5F1 Dolphin	39(150)
	Ordered from Hooper. Only up to J39, which went to Polish Military Purchasing Mission, confirmed built. Most of those delivered went to CAF squadrons forming in the UK.	
J151-J250	Sopwith 5F1 Dolphin	31(100)
	Ordered from Darracq Motor Engineering, but only up to J181 confirmed built. J151, J153, J162, J169, J178, J181 issued free to Polish Military Purchasing Mission.	
J251-J300	Vickers FB.27a Vimy	(50)
	Ordered from Clayton & Shuttleworth 7.10.18. Cancelled	
J301-J400	Sopwith 7F1 Snipe	?(100)
	Ordered from Marsh, Jones & Cribb. Number built not ascertained.	
J401-J450	Airco DH.9A	(50)
	Ordered from Westland. Cancelled.	
J451-J550	Sopwith 7F1 Snipe	20(100)
	Ordered from Boulton & Paul but only up to J470 confirmed built. J453, J455, J459, J461, J465 became G-EAUV, 'EAUW, 'EAUU, 'EBBE, 'EATF.	
J551-J600	Airco DH.9A	50
	Built by Mann Egerton.	
J601-J650	F.E.2b	(50)
	Cancelled order with Barclay Curle.	
J651-J680	Sopwith 7F1 Snipe	(30)
	British Caudron cancelled order.	
J681-J730	Sopwith 7F1 Snipe	(50)
	Marsh, Jones & Cribb cancelled order.	
J731-J1230	Avro 504K	145(500)
	A. V. Roe-built up to J875 at least. J731, J733, J735, J738, J750 converted to 504N. J754, J757-J763 became G-EANP, 'EANX-'EANZ, 'EAOA-'EAOD for export to Imperial Japanese Navy. Other exports: J749, J753 to Belgian Air Service as G-EAND, 'EANG; J746 to Chile as G-EAMO; J803 to Switzerland as G-EAKV. J743, J745 J747, J748, J752, J755, J756 became G-EALF, 'EAMP, 'EAMN, 'EAMQ, 'EANF, 'EANQ, 'EANO.	
J1231-J1730	Bristol F.2B Fighter	(500)
	Siddeley Puma engines planned. Cancelled B & C order.	
J1731-J1930	Bristol F.2B Fighter	(200)
	Cancelled order with Standard Motors.	
J1931-J1933	Bristol Badger I	(3)
	Cancelled order with B & C.	
J1934	Handley Page O/400	1
	Rolls-Royce Eagle engines. Replacement order placed with Harland & Wolff for aircraft sent as pattern to Standard Aircraft Corp, USA. Components sent to HP for erection.	
J1935-J1936	Handley Page V/1500	(2)
	Ex-B9464, B9465. B9465 became HMA Old Carthusian.	
J1936-J1937	DH.15 Gazelle	1(2)
	One only built, given identity of J1937 as J1936 compromised number above.	
J1938-J1940	DH.14/14A Okapi	3
	DH c/n E44-E46. J1938, J1939 DH.14; J1940 DH.14A became G-EAPY.	
J1941-J1990	Vickers FB.27a Vimy	(50)
	Cancelled order with Morgan.	
J1991	Bristol SSF3	(1)
	Prototype, cancelled.	
J1992-J2141	Martinsyde F.4 Buzzard	(150)
	Cancelled order placed with Boulton & Paul.	
J2142-J2241	Avro 504K	(100)
	Cancelled order with Scottish Aviation.	
J2242-J2291	Handley Page O/400	34(50)
	Built by Birmingham Carriage Co. J2276-J2291 cancelled J2243, J2247-J2252, J2261, J2262 became G-EALZ, 'EALY, 'EAMA, 'EAKF, 'EAKG, 'EALX, 'EAKE, 'EATN, 'EATK and converted to various Handley Page types.	
J2292-J2391	Bristol F.2B Fighter	(100)
	Cancelled order with Marshall.	
J2392-J3341	Sopwith 7F1 Snipe	(950)
	Cancelled orders: J2392-J2541 British Caudron, J2542-J3041 British Caudron, J3042-J3341 Gloucester Aircraft.	
J2403-J2417	Nieuport Nighthawk	15
	Re-allotted numbers. J2416 became Gloster Mars VI.	
J3342-J3541	Martinsyde F.4 Buzzard	(200)
	Hooper order cancelled.	
J3542-J3616	Handley Page O/400	(75)
	Cancelled order placed with Metropolitan Wagon Co.	
J3617-J3916	Sopwith Snipe/Dragon	4(300)
	Snipe order to Sopwith changed to Dragon. Delivery record for J3628 (to US Government), J3704, J3726 and J3809 only.	
J3917-J3991	Sopwith 7F1 Snipe	(75)
	Barclay Curle order cancelled.	
J3992-J4091	Avro 504K	(100)
	Hewlett & Blondeau order cancelled.	
J4092-J4591	Sopwith 7F1 Snipe	(500)
	NAF No.3 order cancelled.	
J4592-J5091	Reservation for aircraft rebuilt in France	(500)
J5092-J5191	Avro 504K	100
	Built by Sage & Co. J5185, J5187 became 504N.	
J5192-J5491	DH.9A	(300)
	Cancelled order with Airco.	
J5492-J5591	Avro 504K	21(100)
	Built by Savages Ltd up to J5512 at least.	
J5592-J5891	Martinsyde F.4 Buzzard	(300)
	Cancelled order placed with Standard Motors 1.11.18.	
J5892-J6491	Sopwith TF2 Salamander	22(600)
	Orders placed 1.11.18 as follows: J5892-J5991 (100) Glendower of which up to J5913 were built, J5992-J6091 Palladium Autocars (100 all cancelled), J6092-J6491 NAF No.1 (400 all cancelled).	
J6492	Bristol Badger II	1
	B & C c/n 5657 4th prototype, 3rd built.	
J6493-J6522	Sopwith 7F1 Snipe	30
	Built by Kingsbury Aviation.	
J6523-J6572	Handley Page V/1500	(50)
	Handley Page order cancelled.	
J6573	Handley Page V/1500	1
	Napier Lion engines. Ordered from HP to replace F7140.	
J6574-J6576	Handley Page O/400	(3)
	Rolls-Royce Eagle. Ordered from Handley Page to replace F5414, F5417, F5418. Cancelled.	

First Post World War I Orders

J6577 to J9999

At this point the character of serialling changes. The immediate change is apparent, small quantities and even single orders from 1919 onwards, differing vastly from the orders of the previous year; but more important is the change in the system itself. Hitherto the range of numbers had been from No. 1 to 9999, but when J9999 was reached the following 'K' series started at K1000. Thus all serials then had a 5 letter/digit combination. The alphabetical series continued, and for the next twenty years 'J' to 'Z' were allotted in sequence (with certain exceptions, as explained later) to a 1000-9999 range of numbers. Apart from this the end of the war made no immediate change to the system of allocation, but the rate of allocation was greatly affected: whereas J1 to J6846 had been taken up in a matter of two months, it was several years, from 1919 to 1928 in fact, before J9999 was reached. Aircraft can be assumed to have been built by their design firm unless otherwise stated.

Serial Nos.	Aircraft Type and Remarks	Quantity
J6577	**Westland Weasel**	1
	Jupiter and Jaguar engines. Experimental aircraft ordered 29.8.19.	
J6578	**Handley Page O/400**	(1)
	Intended to replace D8350, but cancelled.	
J6579-J6580	**BAT FK.23 Bantam**	(2)
	F1653, F1654 bought back.	
J6581-J6582	**Westland Wagtail**	2
	Experimental models. J6581 trials with Dragonfly and Wasp, J6582 with Dragonfly and Lynx engines.	
J6583	**Armstrong Siddeley Siskin III**	1
	First steel Siskin ordered 31.5.20. AW c/n 12.	
J6584	**Boulton & Paul P.15 Bolton**	1
	Development of Bourges to Spec 4/20 with all-metal construction.	
J6585	**Armstrong Whitworth Tadpole**	1
	Prototype built from DH.9A E8522 at Farnborough.	
J6586-J6800	**Bristol F.2B Fighter Mk.II**	215
	C/n 5893-6107. J6586, J6589, J6600, J6602, J6622, J6632, J6658, J6659, J6661-J6664, J6676, J6677, J6685, J6689, J6697, J6702, J6708, J6734, J6738, J6788-J6792 fitted DC in service. Rebuilds: JR6635, JR6767, JR6785, JR6788, JR6789; J6766 converted to Mk.III DC. J6790 became G-ACCG. J6800 long range trials aircraft.	
J6801-J6848	**Nieuport Nighthawk**	(48)
	Ordered from British Caudron Co and RAE but cancelled.	
J6849-J6850	**DH.29 Doncaster**	2
	C/ns 7, 8 to Spec 10/20. J6850 became G-EAYO.	
J6851	**Westland Limousine III**	1
	G-EAWF taken over for Air Council 11.11.20.	
J6852-J6853	**Avro 549 Aldershot I/II**	2
	To Spec 2/20. J6852 Avro 549 (Mk.I) modified to 549A (Mk.II) then 549C (Mk.IV). J6853 Mk.I.	
J6854	**Short Silver Streak**	1
	C/n S.543 acquired 23.12.20 for evaluation. G-EARQ reserved.	
J6855	**Vickers Vernon**	1
	Ambulance version to Spec 6/20.	
J6856-J6857	**Vickers Virginia I/III**	2
	Prototypes to Spec 1/21. J6856 converted to Mk.VII with 'fighting top nacelles', then Mk.VIII and rebuilt as Mk.X. J6857 later Mks.VII and X.	
J6858-J6859	**Armstrong Siddeley Sinai**	1(2)
	Ex-X21, X22. J6858 Mk.I ff 25.6.21, grounded 10.21. J6859 not completed.	
J6860-J6861	**Vickers Victoria I/II**	2
	Prototypes to Spec 5/20. J6860 Mk.I ff 22.8.22; J6861 Mk.II (note J6897 was initially incorrectly numbered as J6860).	
J6862-J6863	**Parnall Possum**	2
	Prototypes to Specs 9 & 11/20.	
J6864-J6893	**Vickers Vernon I**	30
	Ordered as Vickers Commercial. J6864, J6867, J6883 converted to Mk.II.	
J6894-J6895	**DH.27 Derby**	2
	C/ns 9, 10. Folding wing experimental bombers to Spec 2/20.	
J6896	**Avro 504K**	1
	Built at Halton from parts of H2976 and H6593.	
J6897-J6898	**Armstrong Whitworth Awana**	2
	C/ns 13, 14. Experimental troop transport to Spec 5/20. J6897 initially incorrectly numbered J6860.	
J6899-J6900	**DH.18B**	2
	G-EAWW, 'EAWX purchased by Air Council 9.7.21.	
J6901-J6903	**Bristol Bullfinch**	3
	C/ns 6125-6127. J6901, J6902 Type 52 monoplane, J6903 Type 53 converted to biplane.	
J6904-J6905	**Vickers Vernon**	2
	Ambulance version. J6904 rebuilt as JR6904.	
J6906	**DH.9A/Handley Page HP.17**	1
	H9140 rebuilt with variable incidence wing to HP.17 design.	
J6907-J6909	**Fairey Fawn I/II/III**	3
	C/ns F.403-F.405. Prototypes to Spec 5/21. J6907 Mk.I converted to Mk.III, J6908, J6909 Mk.II.	
J6910-J6911	**Boulton & Paul P.12 Bodmin**	2
	Postal biplane to Specs 9 & 11/20.	
J6912-J6913	**Bristol Type 37 Tramp**	2
	C/ns 5871, 5872 to Spec 1/20 not flown. Used as ground test rigs at Farnborough.	
J6914	**Handley Page HP.20/X4B**	1
	Cantilever monoplane using fuselage of F1632. First flew 24.2.21.	
J6915-J6917	**DH.30 Denbigh**	(3)
	Project to D of R Type 3A not completed.	
J6918-J6920	**Hawker Duiker**	1(3)
	J6918 trials to Spec 7/22, J6919, J6920 cancelled.	
J6921-J6923	**Armstrong Whitworth Wolf**	3
	C/ns 15-17. D of R Type 3A project. J6921 ff 19.1.23.	
J6924	**Vickers Type 62 Vanguard**	1
	Troop carrier experimental. Became G-EBCP.	
J6925-J6941	**Nieuport Nighthawk/Nightjar**	17
	Built by Gloucester Aircraft except for J6928, J6929 at RAE. J6925-J6929 Nighthawk, J6930-J6941 Nightjar.	
J6942-J6956	**Avro Type 549B Aldershot III**	15
	Production version to equip No.99 Squadron.	
J6957-J6968	**DH.9A**	12
	Lion/Liberty engines. J6957-J6962 built by Westland, J6963-J6968 by Handley Page.	
J6969-J6972	**Nieuport Nighthawk/Nightjar**	4
	Built by Gloucester Aircraft. J6969-J6971 ordered as thick-winged Nighthawk of which J6969 became Grebe prototype. J6972 ordered as Nightjar.	
J6973	**English Electric Wren**	1
	Ultra-light powered glider.	
J6974-J6975	**Short Springbok I**	2
	C/ns S.586, S.587. Spec 19/21 for Bristol F.2B replacement. J6974 first flew 19.4.23.	
J6976-J6980	**Vickers Vernon**	5
	Built for Middle East service.	
J6981-J6983	**Armstrong Whitworth Siskin III**	3
	C/ns 19-21. J6981, J6982 became G-EBJQ, 'EBJS. J6983 crashed on test.	
J6984-J6985	**Boulton & Paul P.25 Bugle I**	2
	Bomber to Spec 30/22.	
J6986	**Westland Dreadnought Postal Monoplane**	1
	Crashed on first flight 3.5.25.	
J6987-J6988	**Hawker Woodcock I/II**	2
	Prototype to Spec 25/22. J6987 Mk.I, J6988 Mk.II.	
J6989	**Hawker Heron**	1
	Ordered as a Woodcock. First Hawker metal aircraft, became G-EBYC.	
J6990-J6991	**Fairey Fawn II**	2
	C/ns F.415, F.416. 4th & 5th prototypes ordered 13.1.23.	
J6992-J6993	**Vickers Virginia IIIDC**	2
	Both converted to Mk.VII, then J6992 to Mk.X and J6993 to Mk.IX.	
J6994	**Handley Page HP.24 Hyderabad**	1
	Bomber prototype to Spec 31/22, first flew Oct 1923.	
J6995-J6996	**Hawker Duiker**	(2)
	Not completed.	
J6997	**Bristol Type 79 Brandon**	1
	C/n 6146. Prototype ambulance.	
J6998-J7003	**Armstrong Whitworth Siskin III**	6
	C/ns 22-27. J7000 DC prototype, J7002, J7003 converted to DC.	
J7004	**Bristol Type 36 Seely Puma**	1
	C/n 5870 ex-G-EAUE modified to Type 85 for RAF.	
J7005	**DH.42 Dormouse**	1
	C/n 84. Experimental aircraft to Spec 22/22.	
J7006-J7007	**DH.42A/B Dingo I/II**	2
	C/ns 85 and 115. J7006 DH.42A Mk.I; J7007 DH.42B Mk.II metal version.	
J7008-J7017	**DH.9A**	10
	Liberty engines. Ex-E848, E861, H3496, H3397, E857, H111, H126, H128, E859, E960 from store re-conditioned by de Havilland.	
J7018-J7032	**DH.9A**	15
	Liberty engines. Built by Handley Page. J7028 had Jupiter engine. J7024 rebuilt as JR7024.	
J7033-J7072	**DH.9A**	40
	Liberty engines. Built by Westland. J7063 converted DC	

J7073-J7087	**DH.9A** Liberty engines. Built by Gloucester Aircraft.	15
J7088-J7102	**DH.9A** Liberty engines. Built by Hawker.	15
J7103-J7127	**DH.9A** Liberty engines. Erected from spares and stores at RAF Ascot. J7107 rebuilt as JR7107 with DC.	25
J7128	**Peyret Tandem Glider** Built by Morane-Saulnier at Puteaux; purchased 1.5.23.	1
J7129-J7132	**Vickers Virginia III** All converted to Mk.VII. J7129 to Mk.X. J7130-J7132 to Mk.IX then Mk.X.	4
J7133-J7144	**Vickers Vernon II/III** J7133-J7142 Mk.II, J7143, J7144 converted to Mk.III ambulance and rebuilt as JR7143, JR7144. Named aircraft J7134, J7135, J7137, J7138, J7141 as *Valkyrie*, *Vagabond*, *Vesuvius*, *Morpheus*, *Aurora*.	12
J7145-J7181	**Armstrong Whitworth Siskin III** C/ns 29-65. Conversions: J7176-J7179 to IIIA, J7146, J7149, J7150, J7152-J7154, J7156-J7158, J7160, J7162, J7164, J7165, J7167, J7170, J7173, J7180, J7181 to III DC. J7148, J7161 used for experimental work.	37
J7182-J7231	**Fairey Fawn I/II** C/n F.481-F.483, F.486-F.532. J7182, J7183 Mk.I, rest Mk.II except J7215 Mk.IV prototype.	50
J7232	**Junkers F.13** Acquired for evaluation.	1
J7233	**Handley Page HP.22** 2-seat sailplane, project only.	(1)
J7234	**Gloster Bamel I** G-EAXZ to RAF December 1923. Later became float-plane for Schneider Trophy team training.	1
J7235	**Boulton & Paul P.25 Bugle I** Prototype, re-engined and modified.	1
J7236-J7237	**Bristol Types 84A & 84B Bloodhound** C/ns 6710, 6711, wooden wings.	2
J7238-J7247	**Vickers FB.27a Vimy IV** Interim replacement order.	10
J7248	**Bristol Type 84 Bloodhound** Prototype to Spec 8/24. Metal construction.	1
J7249-J7258	**DH.9A** Liberty engines. Built by Gloucester Aircraft.	10
J7259-J7260	**Boulton & Paul P.25 Bugle** Ordered 21.1.24.	2
J7261-J7264	**Avro Type 561 Andover** J7264 leased to Imperial Airways as G-EBKW.	4
J7265	**Handley Page HP.23** Glider purchased but condemned as unsafe.	1
J7266-J7267	**Boulton & Paul P.25A Bugle II** Improved version.	2
J7268-J7273	**DH.53 Humming Bird** C/ns 107-112. Became G-EBRW, 'EBRJ, 'EBRA, 'EBXN, 'EBTT, 'EBRK.	6
J7274-J7275	**Vickers Virginia IV** Both converted to Mk.VIII. J7274 became Mk.IX, J7275 used in flight refuelling trials.	2
J7276	**Dornier Komet** Acquired by Air Ministry, via HP for evaluation.	1
J7277-J7282	**Vickers Type 94 Venture** C/ns 1-6. To Spec 45/23.	6
J7283-J7294	**Gloster Grebe II** First Grebe production, all initially to No.25 Sqn.	12
J7295-J7300	**Short S.3a Springbok II** C/ns S.665-S.670. J7298-J7300 cancelled. J7295 ff 25.3.25, later modified to S.3b Chamois.	3(6)
J7301	**Avro 504N** Fitted with arrester gear.	1
J7302-J7309	**DH.9A** Reconnaissance version. Rebuilt as c/n 119-126 ex-H3617, H3581, F2828, H3595, E8710, E8700, E8699, E8702.	(8)
J7310-J7321	**DH.9A** Standard version. Built by Hawker. J7317 converted to trainer.	12
J7322	**Avro Type 560** Light monoplane evaluated as trainer.	1
J7323-J7324	**Parnall Pixie II/III** Ex-1923 Lympne trials. J7323 became G-EBKM.	2
J7325-J7326	**DH.53 Humming Bird**	2
	C/n 113, 114. J7325 used for launching trials from R33. Became G-EBXN, 'EBQP.	
J7327-J7356	**DH.9A** Rebuilt. J7327-J7346 by Westland, rest by Gloucester Aircraft.	30
J7357-J7402	**Gloster Grebe II** J7381, J7394, J7400 to RNZAF as NZ501-NZ503. J7400 used in launching experiments from R33 and was converted to 2-seat.	46
J7403-J7405	**Bristol Type 90 Berkeley** C/n 6718-6720. J7403 ff 5.3.25.	3
J7406-J7417	**Gloster Grebe** J7413 converted to two-seat DC.	12
J7418-J7439	**Vickers Virginia V (Type 100)** Conversions to various Mks: J7418 VI, J7419-J7421 VII-X, J7422 VI-VII-X, J7423 VI-IX, J7424 VII-X, J7425-J7426 VII, J7427 VII-X, J7428 VII-IX-X, J7429-J7430 VII-X, J7431-J7432 VII, J7433-J7434 VII-X, J7435 VII-IX, J7436 VII-IX-X, J7437 VI-IX-X, J7438 VI-VII-IX-X, J7439 VI-VII-X.	22
J7440-J7454	**Vickers Vimy IV** Ordered in June 1924. Rebuilds: JR7444, JR7454.	15
J7455-J7496	**Fairey Flycatcher** Re-numbered N9854-N9895.	(42)
J7497	**Gloster Gamecock** Prototype. Grebe development to Spec 37/23.	1
J7498-J7500	**Handley Page HP.28 Handcross** Experimental night bomber to Spec 26/23.	3
J7501-J7503	**Gloster G.16/16A Gorcock** Napier Lion engines. J7501 Lion IV (wooden wings), J7502 Lion VIII (metal wings) modified to Guan, J7503 Lion IV (all metal).	3
J7504-J7505	**Gloster II** Prototypes to Spec 37/23.	2
J7506	**ANEC 1** Air Navigation & Engineering Co. Light aircraft for evaluation, became G-EBIL.	1
J7507	**Breguet 19** Acquired for RAE evaluation. Wrecked on trials.	1
J7508-J7510	**Westland Yeovil I/II** Day bomber to Spec 26/23. J7508, J7509 Mk.I composite construction, J7510 Mk.II all-metal.	3
J7511	**Hawker Horsley** Originally known as Kingston. Bomber to Spec 26/23.	1
J7512-J7517	**Hawker Woodcock II** J7515 as G-EBMA entered in 1925 King's Cup Air Race.	6
J7518	**Raynham Monoplane** Purchased from owner for evaluation.	1
J7519-J7538	**Gloster Grebe III** J7519 won 1929 King's Cup.	20
J7539-J7548	**Vickers Vernon III** Ordered November 1924.	10
J7549-J7554	**Armstrong Whitworth Siskin III** C/ns 133-138. J7549, J7551, J7552, J7554 cnvtd to DC.	6
J7555-J7556	**Avro 504K** Built in USA by Sperry & Co. J7555 not used. J7556 used for auto-control experiments.	2
J7557	**Beardmore Inflexible** Constructed as G-EBNG, first flew 5.3.28.	1
J7558-J7567	**Vickers Virginia VI** Converted to Mks given: J7558 IX, J7559 VII-X, J7560 VII-X, J7561-J7563 IX-X, J7564 IX, J7565-J7566 VII-X, J7567 IX-X.	10
J7570	**Bristol F.2B Fighter Mk.II** Probably built from spares. Number duplicated.	1
J7568-J7603	**Gloster Grebe** Bristol Fighter number above compromised Grebe J7570.	36
J7592-J7595	**Hawker Woodcock II** J8313-J8316 incorrectly numbered.	(4)
J7604-J7615	**DH.9A** Liberty engines. Reconditioned airframes by Hawker Aircraft.	12
J7616-J7699	**Bristol F.2B Fighter Mk.II** C/ns 6721-6804. Conversions: J7636, J7652, J7659, J7670, J7689, J7692 Mk.III DC.	84
J7700	**DH.9A** Probably built from spares.	1
J7701-J7705	**Vickers Vimy II** Final Vimy order. All but J7703 re-engined with Jupiters. J7704, J7705 DC.	5

J7706-J7720	**Vickers Virginia VI**	15
	Converted to Mks as given: J7706 VII-X, J7707 IX, J7708 IX-X, J7709 VII-IX, J7710 VII-X, J7711 VII-IX-X, J7712-J7713 VII, J7715 IX-X, J7716 IX, J7717 X, J7718-J7719 IX-X, J7720 IX.	
J7721	**Hawker Horsley**	1
	Second prototype.	
J7722-J7723	**Gloster Guan**	2
	Napier Lion engines. J7722 450hp geared, J7723 525hp direct drive.	
J7724-J7737	**Hawker Woodcock II**	14
	Ordered March 1925.	
J7738-J7752	**Handley Page HP.24 Hyderabad**	15
	To Spec 31/22. J7745 prototype Hinaidi. J7741 converted to Hinaidi.	
J7753-J7755	**Armstrong Whitworth Ape**	3
	C/ns 144-146. J7753 Jaguar III later had lengthened fuselage. J7754, J7755 Lynx III.	
J7756-J7757	**Gloster Gamecock**	2
	J7756 Jupiter IV, J7757 Jupiter VI.	
J7758-J7764	**Armstrong Whitworth Siskin III**	7
	C/ns 147-153. J7760-J7764 converted to III DC. J7758-J7759 to RCAF.	
J7765-J7766	**Westland Westbury**	2
	To Spec 4/24. J7765 wooden wings, J7766 composite wood/metal wings.	
J7767	**Bristol Type 95 Bagshot (originally Bludgeon)**	1
	C/n 7018. First flew 15.7.27.	
J7768-J7779	**Fairey Fawn III**	12
	Napier Lion supercharged. C/n F.783-F.794. Production to Spec 1/25. J7768 Mk.IV prototype.	
J7780-J7781	**DH.56 Hyena**	2
	C/ns 182, 195. Spec 33/26.	
J7782	**Hawker Hornbill**	1
	Variously modified. Flew 1080 hours	
J7783	**Hawker Woodcock**	1
	Presumed replacement order.	
J7784-J7786	**Gloster Grebe**	3
	Ordered during 1924 as replacement aircraft.	
J7787-J7798	**DH.9A**	12
	C/ns 202-213.	
J7799-J7819	**DH.9A**	21
	Built by Westland.	
J7820-J7822	**Armstrong Whitworth Siskin III**	3
	C/ns 157-159. Replacement order. J7820, J7821 converted to DC.	
J7823-J7890	**DH.9A**	68
	Builders: J7823-J7834 (12) Short Bros, J7835-J7854 (20) Hawker, J7855-J7866 (12) Westland, J7867-J7876 (10) Hawker, J7877-J7883 (7) de Havilland, J7884-J7890 (7) Short Bros; J7832, J7872 converted to DC.	
J7891-J7920	**Gloster Gamecock I**	30
	Production to Spec 18/25. Conversions: J7900 DC and J7910 to Mk.II.	
J7921-J7935	**Vickers Victoria III**	15
	Conversions: J7921 Mk.IV and to Valentia. J7934 Mk.IV. J7935 Mk.IV & Mk.VI. Rebuilds: JR7931-JR7933.	
J7936-J7937	**Boulton & Paul P.31 Bittern I/II**	2
	Twin-engined fighter to Spec 27/24. J7936 Mk.I to II, J7937 Mk.II.	
J7938-J7939	**Boulton & Paul P.29 Sidestrand I**	2
	Medium bomber to Spec 9/24. J7938 Jupiter VI & VIII, J7939 Jupiter VI and VIF.	
J7940	**Gloster G.23 Goldfinch**	1
	Metal version of Gamecock to Spec 16/25.	
J7941-J7958	**Fairey Fox I/IA**	18
	C/n F.847 to F.864 to Spec 21/25 for 12 Sqn. J7947-J7949 Mk.IA with Kestrel engines, rest initially Mk.I with Curtiss engines. J7942, J7943, J7945, J7958 later became Mk.IA. J7950 became G-ACXO.	
J7959	**Gloster Gamecock**	(1)
	All-metal Gamecock ordered from Boulton & Paul but cancelled.	
J7960-J7977	**Hawker Woodcock**	18
	Order included six rebuilt aircraft possibly renumbered.	
J7978-J7985	**Fairey Fawn III**	8
	C/ns F.865-F.872.	
J7986	**Fokker F.VIIA/3m**	1
	Evaluated at RAE. Monospar ST2 wing fitted.	
J7987-J8026	**Hawker Horsley I**	40

	Condor IIA engines. J7999, J8000, J8002 converted for TT. J8003 fitted with Condor IIIB. J8006 prototype torpedo-bomber version.	
J8027-J8028	**Armstrong Whitworth 14 Starling I/II**	2
	C/n 276 & 455. To Spec 28/24 & 9/26. J8027 became G-AAHC.	
J8029	**Avro 504K**	(1)
	F9723 rebuilt.	
J8030-J8032	**DH.60 Moth**	3
	C/ns 223, 247, 248. J8030 Cirrus Moth. J8031 became G-EBVD.	
J8033-J8047	**Gloster Gamecock I**	15
	J8047, rebuilt with lengthened fuselage, became G-ADIN.	
J8048-J8060	**Armstrong Whitworth Siskin IIIA**	13
	C/n 161-173. J8048 modified by Vickers, J8058-J8060 reconditioned by Bristol.	
J8061-J8066	**Vickers Victoria IIIA**	6
	J8062, J8063, J8065 became Valentia.	
J8067	**Westland Pterodactyl IA**	1
	34hp Cherub engine. Experimental, first flew 3.12.25.	
J8068	**Avro Type 574/Cierva C.6C**	1
	Air Ministry design sponsored project built by Avro incorporating Cierva design.	
J8069-J8095	**Gloster Gamecock I**	27
	J8074, J8075 converted to Mk.II and used in variable pitch airscrew experiments.	
J8096-J8225	**DH.9A**	130
	Rebuilt airframes by constructors: J8096-J8128 (33) Westland, J8129-J8153 (25) de Havilland, J8154-J8171 (18) Short Bros, J8172-J8189 (18) Parnall of which J8183 had rear gun mounting removed for passenger use, J8190-J8207 (18) by Saunders, J8208-J8225 (18) by Blackburn.	
J8226-J8235	**Vickers Victoria VII**	10
	J8230-J8232 to later marks and to Valentia. J8231, J8232 were rebuilt and sold to IAF.	
J8236-J8241	**Vickers Virginia VII**	6
	Conversions: J8236 Mk.IX and temporarily fitted with French-built Jupiter engines, J8237, J8238, J8240, J8241 Mk.X.	
J8242-J8291	**Bristol F.2B Fighter Mk.IIIA**	50
	Bristol Type 96 fitted for Army Co-operation. Conversions: J8244, J8246-J8249, J8252, J8253, J8255, J8258, J8260, J8262, J8265, J8267, J8269-J8277, J8279-J8281, J8284, J8286-J8291 to Mk.IV; J8243, J8245, J8250, J8254, J8256, J8257, J8259, J8261, J8278, J8282, J8285 fitted DC. J8245, J8258, J8285 became G-ABZG, 'ABXA, 'ACFK.	
J8292-J8316	**Hawker Woodcock II**	25
	J8313-J8316 were incorrectly numbered J7592-J7595.	
J8317-J8324	**Handley Page HP.24 Hyderabad**	8
J8325	**Hawker Harrier**	1
	To Specs 23 & 24/25. Various engines tested.	
J8326-J8330	**Vickers Virginia VIII (Type 112)**	5
	J8326, J8328-J8330 converted to Mk.X.	
J8331-J8380	**Avro 504K**	50
	J8333, J8342, J8343, J8347, J8348, J8351, J8353, J8365, J8370-J8373, J8375, J8379 became G-ABLL, 'ABHI, 'ABHJ, 'ABAW, 'ABAV, 'ABHK, 'ABAU, 'ABUK, 'AAYM, 'ABHP, 'ABVH, 'AADY, 'AAFJ, 'AAFT.	
J8381-J8404	**Armstrong Whitworth Siskin IIIA**	24
	C/n 174-197. J8390 catapult trials. J8381, J8382 reconditioned and J8396 modified by Vickers. J8383 and J8386 rebuilt by Bristol.	
J8405-J8422	**Gloster Gamecock I (standard)**	18
J8423-J8427	**Fairey Fox**	5
	C/ns F.875-F.879. J8424 became G-ACXX. J8427 had experimental TT gear.	
J8428	**Armstrong Whitworth Siskin IIIA**	1
	Experimental wing fitted for RAE evaluation.	
J8429-J8458	**Bristol F.2B Fighter III (DC)**	30
	C/ns 6988-7017. Bristol Type 96 trainers. J8429, J8434, J8437, J8444, J8446, J8448, J8455 converted to Mk.IV, became G-ABYF, 'ABYT, 'ACAC, 'ABYL, 'ABYD, 'ACPE, 'ADJR. Final Bristol Fighter production.	
J8459	**Boulton & Paul P.33 Partridge**	1
	To Spec F9/26. Designed for Mercury but Jupiter fitted.	
J8460-J8494	**DH.9A (DC)**	35
	J8460-J8482 (23) built by Westland, J8483-J8494 (12) by Parnall.	

J8495	**Westland Wapiti**	**1**
	Prototype, first flew June 1928.	
J8496-J8595	**Avro 504N**	**100**
	J8571 rebuilt as JR8571. J8507, J8533, J8548, J8573 became G-AEIJ, 'ADET, 'AECS, 'ACLV of which G-ADET later became AX875.	
J8596	**Westland Witch I-II**	**1**
	To Spec 23/25. Later used for parachute training.	
J8597-J8621	**Hawker Horsley III**	**25**
	J8607, J8608 special long range versions. Engine test beds: J8611 Merlin, J8620 Leopard and Jumo.	
J8622	**Handley Page HP.34 Hare**	**1**
	Spec 23/25 contender. First flew 24.2.28. To G-ACEL.	
J8623-J8672	**Armstrong Whitworth Siskin IIIA**	**50**
	J8627 converted to IIIB and used in armament and J8628 in wireless experiments. J8626, J8629, J8632, J8633, J8649 rebuilt by Vickers and J8631, J8646, J8660 rebuilt by Bristol.	
J8673	**Gloster G.22 Goral**	**1**
	Experimental design to utilise DH.9A mainplanes. First flew 8.2.27.	
J8674	**Gloster G.25 Goring**	**1**
	To Spec 23/25, first flew March 1927. Modified to a floatplane in 1931 with Jupiter VIII in place of earlier VI.	
J8675	**Armstrong Whitworth Atlas**	**1**
	Prototype, ex-G-EBLK, first flew 10.5.25. Fitted with horn-balanced ailerons, 1932.	
J8676-J8775	**Avro 504N**	**100**
	Standard trainers.	
J8776	**Hawker Hawfinch**	**1**
	G-AAKH with increased camber for RAE tests.	
J8777-J8801	**Armstrong Whitworth Atlas 1**	**25**
	Production to Spec 33/26. J8777 2nd prototype, J8792 trainer version with DC, J8799 FP version. J8798 became RCAF 406.	
J8802-J8803	**Armstrong Whitworth Ajax**	**2**
	C/ns 273 and 274.	
J8804	**Gloster Gamecock II**	**1**
J8805-J8815	**Handley Page HP.24 Hyderabad**	**11**
	J8809 converted to Hinaidi.	
J8816-J8821	**DH.60 Cirrus Moth**	**6**
	Acquired for CFS. J8818 used by Director of Civil Aviation as G-EDCA.	
J8822-J8905	**Armstrong Whitworth Siskin IIIA**	**84**
	J8822-J8863 (42) built by Bristol, c/ns 7179-7220. J8864-J8905 built by Blackburn.	
J8906	**Vickers 134 Vellore I**	**1**
	To Spec 34/24 first flew 17.5.28, became G-EBYX Type 166 Vellore II.	
J8907-J8914	**Vickers Virginia IX**	**8**
	J8907, J8908, J8910, J8912-J8914 converted to Mk.X.	
J8915-J8929	**Vickers Victoria III**	**15**
	Conversions to Mks V & VI. J8916, J8919, J8921 converted to Valentia. Rebuilds: JR8920, JR8926.	
J8930-J8931	**Cierva C.8/C.9**	**2**
	Built by Avro. J8930 C.8, J8931 C.9.	
J8932	**Hawker Horsley**	**1**
	All-metal version prototype.	
J8933-J8974	**Armstrong Whitworth Siskin IIIA**	**42**
	Built by Gloster.	
J8975-J9024	**Avro 504N**	**50**
	Rebuilds: JR8976, JR8983, JR8991. J9017 became G-AEMP and was impressed as BV208.	
J9025-J9028	**Fairey Fox I/IA**	**4**
	C/n F.952-F.955. Ordered as Mk.I, built as Mk.IA.	
J9029	**Wibault 12c2 (Vickers 127)**	**1**
	Bought from Vickers for evaluation.	
J9030-J9036	**Handley Page HP.33 Hinaidi**	**7**
	J9030 Hinaidi prototype. J9031-J9036 ordered as Hyderabad but converted to Hinaidi.	
J9037	**Armstrong Whitworth 17 Aries**	**1**
	Prototype to Spec 20/25.	
J9038	**Cierva C.10/Parnall Gyroplane**	**1**
	Autogiro of Cierva design to Spec 4/26 built by Parnall, crashed on first flight.	
J9039-J9050	**Armstrong Whitworth Atlas 1**	**12**
	Production.	
J9051	**Bristol Bullpup**	**1**
	C/n 7178. Jupiter VIA, Mercury IIA and Aquila engines in succession.	

J9052	**Hawker Hart**	**1**
	Prototype to Spec 12/26 for high performance bomber.	
J9053-J9077	**Fairey IIIF Mk.IVc/m**	**25**
	C/n F.969-F.975, F.980-F.997. Composite wood/metal fuselage, wooden mainplanes. J9061 communications version, J9062, J9067, J9073 rebuilt as Gordons. J9062, J9073 became 1584M and 693M.	
J9078-J9102	**Westland Wapiti I**	**25**
	First production Wapitis. J9082, J9083 fitted DC and latter was first Wapiti to fly in India 13.7.28. J9094 used as floatplane. J9095 Mk.IA with special rear cockpit, less gun ring, for Prince of Wales.	
J9103-J9121	**DH.60X Moth**	**19**
	C/n 510-528. J9107, rebuilt as DH.60G, became G-ABID. J9115, J9119 became G-ADIL, 'ACMB and J9116 to 596M.	
J9122	**Vickers 151 Jockey**	**1**
	To Spec F20/27. Delivered 11.3.29. Conv to Type 171.	
J9123	**Hawker Interceptor**	**1**
	Bristol Jupiter VII. To Spec F20/27. Fitted later with Bristol Mercury II.	
J9124	**Westland F20/27**	**1**
	Trials with Mercury IIA & Jupiter VII.	
J9125	**Gloster SS.18/19/19B**	**1**
	To Specs F9/26 & F10/27. Designation changes due to engine changes: Mercury II, Jupiter III, Mercury IV. Became 2458M.	
J9126	**Handley Page HP.35 Clive I/III**	**1**
	To Spec 30/27, originally named Chitral, became G-ABYX.	
J9127	**DH.65 Hound**	**1**
	C/n 250 G-EBNJ transferred to RAF January 1928.	
J9128	**Armstrong Whitworth Ajax II**	**1**
	C/n 141. To Spec 20/25 for easily maintained army co-op aircraft. First flight 24.1.25 as G-EBLM.	
J9129	**Armstrong Whitworth Atlas**	**1**
	G-EBNI general purpose version of Atlas.	
J9130	**Handley Page HP.38 Heyford**	**1**
	Prototype to Spec B19/27. First flew June 1930.	
J9131	**Vickers 150 Vannock I**	**1**
	To Spec B19/27. Rebuilt as Vickers Vannock II, re-constructed as Vickers 255 Vanox.	
J9132-J9174	**Fairey IIIF Mk.IV (GP)**	**43**
	C/n F.998-F.1040. J9132-J9154 Mk.IVc/m with wooden wings, J9155-J9174 Mk.IVm with metal wings. Rebuilds: JR9140, JR9151, JR9160-JR9162. Reconstruction as Gordon: J9136 prototype conversion, J9138, J9154, J9156, J9161, J9167, J9171, J9172. Special engine installations: J9150 Jupiter VIII, J9154 Jaguar VI, J9173, J9174 Kestrel II. J9138, J9167, J9170 became 1007M, 1533M, 565M.	
J9175	**Avro 504R Gosport**	**1**
	Mongoose. Ex-G-EBUY acquired January 1929.	
J9176-J9181	**Boulton & Paul P.29 Sidestrand II/III**	**6**
	Built as Mk.II, converted to Mk.III. For 101 Sqn.	
J9182	**Avro 594 Avian IIIA**	**1**
	C/n 125.	
J9183	**Avro 604 Antelope**	**1**
	To Spec 12/26 for high performance bomber. Became RAE test-bed.	
J9184	**DH.72 Canberra**	**1**
	C/n 392. Experimental night bomber, first flew 28.7.31.	
J9185-J9189	**Boulton & Paul P.29 Sidestrand III**	**5**
	J9185, J9186 converted to Overstrand.	
J9190-J9236	**Armstrong Whitworth Siskin IIIA (DC)**	**47**
	C/n 299-345 ordered April 1928.	
J9237-J9247	**Westland Wapiti II/IIA**	**11**
	J9247 built as Mk.IIA, rest Mk.II.	
J9248	**Gloster Gamecock**	**(1)**
	Project for evaluation of G-EBOE with Bristol Orion.	
J9249	**Avro 613**	**(1)**
	Spec B19/27 project for experimental light bomber.	
J9250	**Vickers 145 Victoria IV**	**1**
	Tropical trials in Iraq. Converted to Mk.VI.	
J9251	**Westland Pterodactyl Mk.IA/B/C**	**1**
	Successively modified Mk.IA to C.	
J9252	**Westland Wizard I/II**	**1**
	Aircraft crashed; rebuilt as Mk.I; modified to Mk.II.	
J9253-J9292	**Avro 504N**	**40**
	Standard trainers.	

J9293-J9303	**Handley Page HP.24 Hyderabad**	11
	J9298-J9303 completed as Hinaidi.	
J9304-J9379	**Armstrong Whitworth Siskin IIIA**	76
	J9304-J9330 (27) built by Bristol with c/ns 7274-7300, J9331-J9352 (22) by Gloster and J9353-J9379 (27) by Vickers.	
J9380-J9414	**Westland Wapiti IIA**	35
	Standard production.	
J9415-J9434	**Avro 504N**	20
	Trainers mainly to No.5 FTS.	
J9435-J9477	**Armstrong Whitworth Atlas (DC)**	43
	C/n 347-359, 365-394.	
J9478	**Handley Page HP.36 Hinaidi II**	1
	First all-metal Hinaidi. First flew February 1929.	
J9479	**Fairey Long Range Monoplane**	1
	C/n F.1131. F/f November 1928. Crashed in Tunisia.	
J9480	**Bristol Bulldog II**	1
	Prototype Mk.II C/n 7235. First flew 21.1.28.	
J9481-J9514	**Westland Wapiti IIA**	34
	Produced for squadrons in India. J9487, J9488, J9497, J9498 used as floatplanes. J9503 DC.	
J9515	**Fairey Fox**	1
	Rolls-Royce FXIB. Steam cooling experiments, ff 3.1.25.	
J9516-J9564	**Armstrong Whitworth Atlas I**	49
	C/n 401-425, 429-452. J9564 became RCAF 407.	
J9565	**Westland COW Gun Fighter**	1
	To Spec F29/27. Became 738M.	
J9566	**Vickers 161**	1
	To Spec F29/27 with 37mm COW gun.	
J9567-J9590	**Bristol Bulldog II**	24
	C/ns 7322-7330, 7332-7340, 7342-7347. Production to Spec F17/28.	
J9591	**Bristol Bulldog II**	1
	G-AATR to RAF December 1930. Mercury IV test-bed.	
J9592-J9636	**Westland Wapiti IIA**	45
	Subsequent identities: J9605 to Wallace K3677, J9612, J9617 to RCAF 539, 540; J9598, J9614 to 576M, 572M.	
J9637-J9681	**Fairey IIIF Mk.IVM/A**	45
	C/n F.1139-F.1183. Mainly delivered for overseas service. J9642, J9643, J9647, J9648, J9651, J9655, J9656, J9660, J9663, J9670, J9674, J9681 converted to Gordon of which J9651 was sold to Egypt. Rebuilds other than Gordon conversions: JR9640, JR9653, JR9654, JR9657. J9673, J9674 became 750M, 870M.	
J9682	**Hawker Hornet (Fury)**	1
	Prototype to Spec F20/27. Name Hornet changed to Fury.	
J9683-J9707	**Avro 504N**	25
	J9689, J9702 became G-ADGC, 'AEGW.	
J9708-J9759	**Westland Wapiti IIA/V**	52
	J9708-J9724 Mk.IIA, J9725-J9759 Mk.V. All but J9734 shipped to India.	
J9760-J9766	**Vickers Victoria V**	7
	Conversions: J9760, J9762, J9763, J9765 Mk.VI, then a II but J9761 to Valentia.	
J9767-J9770	**Boulton & Paul P.29 Sidestrand III**	4
	J9770 converted to Mk.V and renamed Overstrand, later used as tanker trials.	
J9771	**DH.77 Interceptor**	1
	C/n 391 to Spec F20/27. Completed by Gloster. First flew December 1929.	
J9772-J9782	**Hawker Tomtit**	11
	C/n HT1-HT8, HT10, HT11, HT13. J9781, J9782 became G-AEXC, 'AEVP.	
J9783	**Avro Avian IVM**	1
	G-AACV for evaluation and comparison with Tomtit.	
J9784-J9831	**Fairey IIIF Mk.IV (GP)**	48
	C/n F.1184-F.1231. J9784-J9788, J9790, J9794, J9795, J9798, J9799, J9801, J9803-J9806, J9808, J9811, J9813, J9819, J9821, J9822, J9829 were converted to Gordon. Aircraft rebuilds, other than conversions: JR9793, JR9827. J9784 sold to Egypt. J9787, J9795, J9799, J9804, J9822 became 1534M, 967M, 698M, 1525M, 697M.	
J9832	**Gloster G.33 Goshawk**	1
	Prototype troop-transport bomber, first flew 23.2.32.	
J9833	**Handley Page HP.43/51**	1
	Prototype to Specs C10/28 & C26/31. Later used as a tanker.	
J9834	**Fairey Fox IIM**	1
	C/n F.1138 to Spec 12/26. F/f 25.10.29. To G-ABFG.	

J9835-J9871	**Westland Wapiti IIA**	37
	J9838 used as floatplane. J9854 to RIAF. J9868-J9871 became RCAF 541-544. J9864 rebuilt as Wallace K3676. J9857, J9861 became 592M, 625M.	
J9872-J9921	**Armstrong Whitworth Siskin IIIA/B**	50
	J9872-J9896 (25) IIIA built by Vickers, J9897-J9911 (15) IIIB built by Bristol c/ns 7404-7418; J9912-J9921 (10) IIIA built by Gloster.	
J9922-J9932	**DH.60G Gipsy Moth**	11
	Later identities: J9922 to G-ABNE, J9925, J9932 to 1308M and 1645M.	
J9933-J9947	**Hawker Hart**	15
	To Spec 9/29 for No.33 Sqn. Conversions: J9933 to Demon, J9934, J9946 fitted with DC. J9933, J9936, J9942, J9945, J9946 to 1120M, 606M, 610M, 607M, 616M.	
J9948-J9949	**Handley Page HP.35 Clive II**	2
	Metal version of Chitral J9126.	
J9950	**Boulton & Paul P.32**	1
	Prototype to B22/27.	
J9951-J9999	**Armstrong Whitworth Atlas I**	49
	J9951 sold to Egypt. Rebuilds: JR9958, JR9959, JR9964, JR9969, JR9971, JR9975. J9974 fitted DC at RAF Depot Aboukir. J9998 used as floatplane for 1931 Schneider Trophy team training.	

Between the Wars

K1000 to K9999

For the first time numbers started at No.1000 instead of No.1 so that all serial allocations would consist of five characters - and they still do in the 'eighties. Also for the first time a single order bridged the two separate series for the order, for eighty-seven Atlas I aircraft, was numbered J9951-J9999 and K1000-K1037. During the British aircraft industry's lean years in the early 'thirties, work was shared to keep firms alive and where a builder is other than the designing firm this information is given. With the Rearmament Programme bringing industrial expansion a further qualification becomes necessary, in some cases, to show in which plant of a firm the aircraft were built. The period of 'K' series allocations was August 1929 to July 1936.

Serial Nos	Aircraft Type and Remarks	Quantity
K1000-K1037	**Armstrong Whitworth Atlas I**	38
	Continuation of J9951-J9999 order. K1018, K1035 became 642M, 828M.	
K1038-K1062	**Avro 504N**	25
	K1055 became G-ADBM and was impressed as AX871. K1061 became G-ADFW.	
K1063-K1078	**Handley Page Hinaidi (HP Type 36)**	16
	Delivered to equip No.99 Squadron.	
K1079-K1101	**Bristol Bulldog II**	23
	C/ns 7364-7386. Deliveries to 9 to 17 Sqn and 14 to 54 Sqn.	
K1102	**Hawker Hart I**	1
	Non-standard. Acquired to test experimental Rolls-Royce Kestrel V with steam cooling. Cockpit enclosed.	
K1103-K1112	**DH.60M Moth**	10
	C/n 1450-1459. K1111 became 792M.	
K1113-K1114	**Armstrong Whitworth Atlas**	2
	Replacement aircraft.	
K1115-K1121	**Fairey IIIF Mk.IVM/A**	7
	K1120 converted to Gordon. K1115, K1117, K1120 became 689M, 690M, 1514M.	
K1122-K1157	**Westland Wapiti IIA**	36
	K1139, K1143, K1146, K1148, K1149, K1152 became RCAF 527-529, 508, 530, 509. K1136, K1140 became 752M, 753M.	
K1158-K1170	**Fairey IIIF Mk.IVM/A (GP)**	13
	C/n F.1302-F.1314. K1159-K1170 converted to Gordon	

	of which K1161 went to RNZAF and K1160, K1166-K1169 became 1583M, 1318M, 869M, 1319M, 1582M.	
K1171	Isacco Heliogyre	1
	Evaluated at RAE January 1930 to December 1931.	
K1172-K1197	Armstrong Whitworth Atlas (DC)	26
	K1175 converted to single-seat. K1196 became 724M.	
K1198-K1227	DH.60 Gipsy Moth	30
	Gipsy I. C/n 1510-1529, 1500-1509. K1213-K1217 specially rigged for CFS aerobatic team. K1205, K1208, K1213-K1215, K1218, K1224 became 1072M, 1304M, 757M, 895M, 1288M, 886M, 691M. K1202 became G-ADLJ and K1227 G-AFKM later impressed as MA931.	
K1228-K1229	Parnall Parasol	2
	Experimental aircraft for wing pressure and aileron tests and operation from submarines. K1229 modified as Avro Type 661.	
K1230-K1240	Avro 621 Tutor	11
	Uncowled Mongoose IIIC. K1230, K1231, K1233, K1237 became 666M, G-ADYW, 679M, 667M.	
K1241	DH.60G Gipsy Moth	1
	Used by Cambridge University Air Squadron.	
K1242-K1253	Avro 504N	12
	K1243, K1249-K1251 became 1060M, 1217M, G-ACPV, G-ADBS. G-ACPV impressed as BV209, became 2447M.	
K1254-K1309	Westland Wapiti IIA	56
	Built for army co-operation squadrons in India.	
K1310-K1315	Vickers Victoria V	6
	K1311, K1312, K1315 converted to Mk.VI. K1311-K1314 converted to Valentia.	
K1316-K1415	Westland Wapiti II	100
	Conversions/transfers: K1316 to 593M; K1318, K1322, K1324-K1326, K1328-K1330 became RCAF 510, 531, 532, 511-513, 533, 534. K1331-K1334 became Wallace K3567, K3564, K3565, K4012; K1336 became RCAF 535; K1339, K1341 became Wallace K4013, K4014. K1342 became RCAF 538; K1344-K1360, K1362-K1365 became Wallace K4015, K3563, K3562, K3566, K3569-K3571, K3568, K3572, K3573, K3664-K3670, K3672-K3675. K1366 became RCAF 537; K1370, K1372-K1375 became Wallace K4016-K4020. K1378 became RCAF 536. K1338, K1386, K1405 became 615M, 617M, 619M. K1412, K1413 became Wallace K5081, K5082.	
K1416-K1447	Hawker Hart I	32
	K1438 became Audax prototype. K1420 went to SAAF. K1416, K1419, K1422, K1426, K1427, K1430, K1433, K1434, K1436, K1437, K1439, K1443-K1446 became 1369M, 1031M, 705M, 2310M, 608M, 609M, 712M, 877M, 1367M, 595M, 917M, 611M, 918M, 1040M, 2267M.	
K1448-K1453	Hawker Tomtit I	6
	For 3 FTS except K1453 for RAE. K1451 to G-AEVO.	
K1454-K1602	Armstrong Whitworth Atlas (TM/AC)	149
	K1454-K1506 (53) built as TM trainers, remainder built as AC. K1529, K1531, K1540, K1545, K1550, K1556, K1561, K1566 became RCAF 408-415. K1464, K1471, K1472, K1477, K1479, K1501, K1513, K1514, K1516, K1528, K1534, K1541, K1547, K1553, K1557, K1558, K1564, K1568, K1570, K1591-K1594, K1596-K1598, became 730M, 802M, 818M, 722M, 819M, 678M, 855M, 641M, 847M, 725M, 848M, 640M, 741M, 735M, 586M, 736M, 742M, 793M, 796M, 668M-672M, 862M, 863M.	
K1603-K1694	Bristol Bulldog IIM	92
	C/n 7459-7550. K1603, K1606, K1616, K1617, K1627, K1633, K1648, K1665, K1667, K1684, K1687, K1692 became 597M, 905M-907M, 701M, 700M, 1112M, 1129M, 655M, 920M, 951M, 972M.	
K1695	Fairey Hendon	1
	Prototype to Spec B19/27 modified to 20/34. Fitted with Rolls-Royce Kestrel III, then VI and later Bristol Pegasus engines.	
K1696	Cierva C.19/III (Avro 620)	1
	G-AAYO built by A.V. Roe purchased for evaluation 1930	
K1697-K1728	Fairey IIIF Mk.IVB (GP)	32
	C/n F.1396-F.1427. K1697, K1721-K1728 converted on production line and K1699, K1700, K1702, K1710, K1715 during service to Gordon I. K1726 had trial installation of Junkers Jumo V (205C) engine. K1698, K1700 became 776M, 1100M; K1715 to RNZAF after conversion.	

K1729-K1748	Fairey Gordon	20
	C/n F.1428-F.1447. K1729 rebuilt as KR1729. K1731 long range experimental aircraft and K1740 fitted with floats at Felixstowe. K1731, K1733-K1735, K1737, K1744-K1748 became 827M, 612M, 613M, 602M, 603M, 850M, 851M, 1374M, 1375M, 1377M.	
K1749-K1778	Fairey IIIF Mk.IVB	30
	C/n F.1448-F.1477. K1756-K1758, K1762-K1778 converted to Gordon. K1757, K1765, K1767, K1770, K1772, K1775 to RNZAF and K1771 to REAF. K1749, K1756, K1762, K1764, K1766, K1768, K1769, K1773, K1774, K1777 became 751M, 711M, 1511M, 1537M, 755M, 699M, 1536M, 1316M, 1317M, 694M.	
K1779-K1786	Hawker Tomtit	8
	K1781-K1786 became G-AFIB, 'AEES, 'AGEF, 'AFVV, 'AFKB, 'AFTA, but last aircraft restored at Old Warden in original K1786 markings.	
K1787-K1797	Avro Tutor	11
	Mongoose III. K1797 had Lynx IV setting style for further Tutors. K1790, K1792-K1796 became 680M-685M and K1791 G-ACOV.	
K1798-K1823	Avro 504N	26
	K1799, K1806, K1811, K1813, K1822 became 1061M, 1004M, 807M, 1247M, 826M and K1802, K1808, K1810, K1819, K1823 became G-ACRS, 'ACNV, 'ADDA, 'ADBR, 'AEDD.	
K1824	DH.80A Puss Moth	1
	C/n 2044 used by Air Officer Commanding, Inland Area.	
K1825-K1907	DH.60M Moth	83
	5 as trainers, 78 for communications. C/ns 1658-1662, 1580-1599, 1624-1633, 1600-1623, 1634-1657. K1826, K1830, K1832, K1833, K1835, K1839, K1840, K1843, K1847, K1849-K1853, K1856, K1859, K1862, K1878, K1881, K1884, K1886-K1888, K1892, K1894, K1896, K1897, K1899, K1900-K1902, K1905 became 618M, 1194M, 842M, 1392M, 1305M, 930M, 744M, 868M, 1298M, 706M, 772M, 1297M, 1314M, 815M, 1393M, 1390M, 1002M, 707M, 817M, 1240M, 1295M, 1391M, 1299M, 1253M, 1306M, 1208M, 1307M, 1287M, 1310M, 1593M, 1296M, 1289M. K1828, K1845, K1860 became G-ADLK, 'AFZB, 'AFWJ.	
K1908	Handley Page HP.39 'Gugnunc'	1
	G-AACN purchased December 1930 for evaluation.	
K1909-K1925	Handley Page HP.36 Hinaidi	17
	Delivered 1931 mainly to No.10 Squadron.	
K1926-K1946	Hawker Fury I	21
	K1926 prototype Mk.I, K1935 prototype Mk.II, K1927 propeller trials. K1926-K1928, K1930, K1932, K1935, K1942-K1944, K1946 became 928M, 1068M, 1739M, 2196M, 987M, 1949M, 749M, 974M, 853M, 1045M. K1929 to SAAF.	
K1947	Westland Pterodactyl IV	1
	Inverted Gipsy III. Third of experimental tail-less aircraft series built.	
K1948	Cierva C.19 Mk.III (Avro 620)	1
	Built by A.V. Roe at Hamble, c/n 5142 as G-ABCM, acquired by RAF early 1931.	
K1949	Saro F20/27	1
	Experimental fighter.	
K1950-K1955	Hawker Hart (F)	6
	Kestrel IIS. Forerunners of Hawker Demon. All served in No.23 Squadron. K1954, K1955 became 916M, 626M.	
K1956-K1990	Avro 504N	35
	K1963, K1968, K1969, K1971, K1972, K1974, K1980, K1985, K1988, K1989 became 781M, 1082M, 1058M, 1053M, 1054M, 1248M, 1064M, 813M, 1085M, 881M. K1962, K1964 became G-ADGM, 'AFRM.	
K1991	Fairey Long Range Monoplane	1
	Lion XIA. C/n F.1671. Used by the RAE.	
K1992-K1994	Boulton & Paul P.29 Sidestrand III	3
	Replacement aircraft for No.101 Squadron.	
K1995-K2034	Hawker Audax	40
	K1996 completed as Hart Trainer. K1999 and K2020 converted to Hart (Special). K1996, K1999, K2002, K2012, K2013, K2015, K2016, K2033, K2034 became 1141M, 1769M, 973M, 936M, 2623M, 937M, 1047M, 929M, 900M. K2000, K2018, K2029 to SAAF in 1940.	
K2035-K2082	Hawker Fury I	48
	K2037, K2041-K2043, K2046, K2048, K2051, K2052, K2055, K2060, K2062, K2063, K2066, K2069, K2070,	

K2075, K2078, K2081 became 849M, 947M, 925M, 1019M, 1131M, 1018M, 1017M, 2018M, 1044M, 1026M, 1465M, 976M, 992M, 946M, 1122M, 998M, 948M, 1048M. K2050, K2071 shipped for SAAF.

K2083-K2132   **Hawker Hart (India)**   **50**
K2105 fitted DC and K2114 converted to Demon in India

K2133   **Vickers Vellore IV (Type 173)**   **1**
G-ABKC mail carrier for evaluation eventually used as ferry.

K2134   **Short S.8/8 Rangoon**   **1**
C/n S.764. Trials aircraft used 1932-1936.

K2135-K2234   **Bristol Bulldog IIA (Type 105)**   **100**
C/n 7590-7689. K2188 Bristol Type 124 trainer prototype. K2135-K2137, K2139, K2144, K2145, K2152, K2153, K2165, K2168, K2170, K2172, K2175, K2179, K2186, K2188, K2195, K2197, K2198 became 954M, 1148M, 1075M, 986M, 952M, 909M, 921M, 1010M, 955M, 941M, 1076M, 1077M, 1150M, 1012M, 1078M, 1923M, 778M, 956M, 1011M and K2205-K2207, K2209, K2213, K2223, K2224, K2227, K2229 became 1079M, 640M, 899M, 1159M, 953M, 1151M, 977M, 978M, 1152M.

K2235   **DH.60M Moth**   **1**
Built from standard parts at RAE. Used in float trials. Became 1652M.

K2236-K2320   **Westland Wapiti IIA/VI**   **81(85)**
K2236-K2247 (12) Mk.VI of which K2239, K2242, K2243, K2246, K2247 became 830M, 995M, 996M, 660M, 661M and K2245 was converted to Wallace K4010. K2248-K2251 not delivered. K2252-K2320 (69) Mk.IIA of which K2256, K2258, K2278, K2281, K2282, K2285, K2288, K2299, K2300 became 598M, 1135M, 1588M, 844M-846M, 1591M, 1590M, 1589M and K2252, K2254, K2260, K2264, K2266, K2279, K2280, K2306-K2320 were converted to Wallace K5076-K5080, K5074, K5075, K4337-K4348, K5071-K5073. K2257, K2262, K2265, K2268, K2286, K2287 to RAAF.

K2321-K2339   **Vickers Virginia X**   **19**
K2327, K2329 modified for parachute dropping training.

K2340-K2345   **Vickers Victoria V (Type 241)**   **6**
K2343 converted to Mk.VI. All others to Valentia.

K2346-K2423   **Avro 504N**   **78**
Final production of 504 series. K2346-K2349, K2364, K2368, K2372, K2373, K2376, K2381, K2386, K2387 became 782M, 811M, 814M, 1249M, 1145M, 803M, 780M, 881M, 1303M, 821M, 1250M, 1144M; K2400-K2402, K2408, K2409, K2411-K2415, K2419, K2420, K2423 became 1220M, 1225M, 1251M, 1223M, 1055M, 1219M, 1059M, 1086M-1088M, 1224M, 1221M, 1218M. K2353, K2354 became G-ADBP, 'ADBO.

K2424-K2475   **Hawker Hart I**   **52**
K2434 Napier Dagger I/II test bed, K2455 fitted for communications work and K2459 converted to trainer. K2474, K2475 produced as Hart Trainer (Interim). K2426, K2427, K2429, K2431, K2434, K2437, K2438, K2440-K2445, K2450, K2454, K2456, K2458, K2459, K2461, K2464, K2467, K2468, K2470 became 993M, 1032M, 889M, 888M, 1745M, 599M, 652M, 878M, 887M, 932M, 651M, 2188M, 879M, 880M, 709M, 775M, 2195M, 2186M, 1502M, 695M, 1607M, 653M, 1497M. K2439, K2446, K2462, K2463, K2465, K2469, K2471-K2473 sold to SAAF.

K2476-K2495   **Bristol Bulldog IIA**   **20**
C/n 7691-7710. K2476, K2481 became 714M, 900M.

K2496-K2513   **Avro 621 Tutor I**   **18**
Lynx IV uncowled. All to 3 FTS. K2497, K2499, K2500, K2502-K2504 became 805M, 771M, 740M, 654M, 806M, 747M.

K2514-K2566   **Armstrong Whitworth Atlas I (Trainers)**   **53**
K2516, K2523, K2527, K2535, K2549, K2553-K2556 became 798M, 723M, 721M, 875M, 703M, 731M-734M.

K2567-K2601   **DH.60T Tiger Moth I**   **35**
Gipsy III. C/n 1739-1773. To Spec 23/31. K2586, K2587 rigged for inverted flying, K2588-K2592 built as floatplanes for Far East. K2567, K2568, K2575, K2576, K2578, K2582, K2583, K2585-K2587 and K2600 became 2049M, 1008M, 897M, 896M, 898M, 1134M, 1118M, 1157M, 1156M, 5983M, 1942M.

K2602   **Gloster AS.31 Survey**   **1**
First Gloster twin-engined aircraft, ex-G-AADO.

K2603-K2649   **Fairey Gordon I**   **47**
C/n F.1584-F.1630. All except a few shipped to the Middle East. K2603, K2613, K2615, K2637, K2641 rebuilt in service. K2605, K2610, K2614, K2619, K2628, K2641 became 1101M, 1102M, 1516M, 1508M, 1517M, 1523M. K2620, K2633, K2636 to RNZAF.

K2650-K2680   **Vickers Virginia X**   **31**
Final Virginia production.

K2681   **Saro A.19 Cloud**   **1**
Flying boat trainer to Spec 15/32.

K2682   **Avro 618 Ten**   **1**
Delivered 24.7.36 for evaluation.

K2683-K2769   **Fairey Gordon I**   **87**
K2711 used for Panther development. K2683-K2691, K2693, K2696, K2697, K2703, K2710, K2713, K2714, K2721, K2729, K2732, K2748, K2751, K2754, K2761, K2766, K2768, K2769 became 872M, 1535M, 871M, 994M, 716M, 1103M, 1104M, 715M, 1376M, 1515M, 1512M, 1105M, 1006M, 2452M, 1509M, 1518M, 1521M, 2445M, 2446M, 1522M, 1519M, 1513M, 1520M, 1495M, 1320M, 1510M. K2694, K2706, K2709, K2715-K2717, K2723, K2726, K2727, K2731, K2742, K2759, K2763, K2767 to RNZAF. K2705, K2712, K2738 to REAF.

K2770   **Westland Pterodactyl V**   **1**
4th and final Westland-Hill Pterodactyl built.

K2771   **Vickers Type 253**   **1**
Prototype to Spec G4/31. Became 2574M.

K2772   **Parnall G4/31**   **1**
Prototype to Spec G4/31 for general purpose aircraft.

K2773   **Handley Page HP.47**   **1**
Prototype to Spec G4/31.

K2774-K2790   **Hawker Osprey I**   **17**
Convertible wheel/float u/c. K2774 became 646M.

K2791-K2808   **Vickers Victoria V/Valentia**   **18**
All but K2791, K2794 converted to Valentia. K2796, K2800-K2802, K2804, K2805 to SAAF, in 1940.

K2809   **Short 8/8 Rangoon**   **1**
C/n S.765 delivered late 1932, sold mid-1936.

K2810-K2822   **Vickers Vildebeest I (Type 244)**   **13**
K2816 modified to long range floatplane. K2818 to Mk.II and K2821 to Mk.III. K2819 used in engine and propeller experiments. K2810, K2813, K2814, K2817, K2819, K2822 became 1750M, 1381M, 901M, 969M, 2461M, 1753M. K2821 became NZ135 of RNZAF.

K2823-K2841   **Hawker Nimrod I**   **19**
K2823 Mk.II prototype and K2840 converted to Mk.II. K2823, K2826, K2827, K2831, K2833 became 1146M, 1046M, 1190M, 894M, 622M.

K2842-K2858   **Hawker Demon I**   **17**
Kestrel IIS initially. K2842, K2846-K2848, K2850, K2853-K2855, K2857 became 1896M, 1399M, 1398M, 1123M, 1400M, 1109M, 1403M, 1003M, 1853M.

K2859-K2872   **Bristol Bulldog IIA**   **14**
C/n 7713-7726. Replacement order.

K2873   **Bristol Type 118A**   **1**
Pegasus test-bed ex-G-ABEZ and R-3.

K2874-K2883   **Hawker Fury I**   **10**
Replacement order. K2874, K2876, K2879, K2881, K2882 became 2239M, 1719M, 1911M, 1049M, 2241M. K2875, K2877 to SAAF in 1940.

K2884-K2887   **Blackburn Ripon IIc/Baffin I (Types T5B/T8)**   **4**
Built as Ripon IIc, converted to Baffin I. All destroyed in storm at Hal Far in November 1936.

K2888-K2889   **Supermarine Southampton II**   **1(2)**
K2888 was ex-N253.

K2890   **Supermarine Type 224**   **1**
To Spec F7/30. Prototype known as Supermarine day and night fighter.

K2891   **Westland PV4**   **1**
To Spec F7/30. Delivered 1935 and dismantled same year.

K2892   **Blackburn F3**   **1**
To Spec F7/30. Not flown, became 874M.

K2893   **Avro 646 Sea Tutor**   **1**
Ex-G-ABGH for trials and service.

K2894-K2898   **Saro A.19 Cloud**   **5**
Flying boat trainers for B Flight, Calshot. K2894, K2897, K2898 became 1255M, 938M, 1203M.

K2899-K2904   **Hawker Fury**   **6**
Replacement order. K2899, K2903 to SAAF in 1940.

K2905-K2908	Hawker Demon I	4

Kestrel IIB/S later VDR. Replacement order. K2906, K2908 became 1394M, 933M.

K2909-K2914	Hawker Nimrod II	6

K2909-K2911 built of stainless steel. K2910 became 1183M.

K2915	Hawker Hart/Hind	1

Kestrel IIS to V. Hart converted to Hind to Spec G7/34; to SAAF, 1940.

K2916-K2945	Vickers Vildebeest II	30

Vickers Type 258. K2916 did floatplane trials for the Latvian version and K2945 became Vincent prototype, later becoming 1178M and 1093M. K2940 modified to Mk.III. Remainder shipped to Far East where K2929, K2934, K2936 were converted to TT.

K2946-K2963	Bristol Bulldog IIA	18

C/n 7746-7763. K2946, K2948, K2952, K2955, K2957, K2958 became 884M, 1161M-1163M, 1149M, 1164M.

K2964-K2965	Supermarine Southampton II/III	2

K2964 Mk.III, K2965 Mk.II.

K2966-K3030	Hawker Hart	65

Built by Vickers. K3011 Pegasus test-bed, K3012 loaned to Canada, K3013 converted to Hardy prototype, K3014 flight refuelling trials, K3020 Pegasus and Mercury engine trials. K2967, K2969, K2971, K2973, K2977, K2979, K2980, K2982, K2985, K2988, K2990, K2991, K2994, K2995, K2998, K2999 became 1128M, 1073M, 924M, 960M, 2331M, 2390M, 2276M, 2262M, 773M, 2384M, 621M, 2300M, 2283M, 1498M, 1138M, 1346M and K3000-K3002, K3010, K3012, K3013, K3018, K3020, K3027 became 1642M, 1481M, 1447M, 1503M, 2026M, 1448M, 1349M, 1169M, 2274M. K2966, K2970, K2975, K2976, K2978, K2987, K2993, K2997, K3004, K3008, K3011, K3014-K3016, K3019, K3021, K3026, K3029 to SAAF during 1938-40. K2986, K3028 to SRAF in 1937.

K3031-K3054	Hawker Hart I	24

Built by Armstrong Whitworth. K3031 converted to Hart Trainer (Intermediate), K3033 Youngman dinghy fitment experiments, K3036 Merlin C & E test-bed. K3033, K3036-K3038, K3040, K3043, K3050, K3051 became 2265M, 1435M, 2104M, 2187M, 2277M, 2194M, 1348M, 2391M. K3041, K3053 to SAAF, during 1938-39.

K3055-K3145	Hawker Audax I	91

K3072, K3128-K3138, K3140-K3144 converted to Hart (Special). K3057, K3061, K3063, K3067, K3087, K3100, K3139, K3141 became 989M, 1052M, 729M, 2004M, 1907M, 748M, 2025M, 1170M. K3060, K3068, K3073, K3079, K3085, K3096, K3101, K3104, K3114, K3134, K3137 to SAAF 1940-42. K3108, K3117 to SRAF, K3100 went temporarily to RCAF.

K3146-K3158	Hawker Hart (T)	13

First Harts produced as trainers. K3148, K3150, K3155, K3156, K3158 became 843M, 883M, 743M, 1767M, 1766M. K3147, K3149 to SAAF 1941, K3154 to REAF.

K3159-K3169	Vickers Victoria VI/Valentia	11

All converted to Valentia. K3169 sold to IAF.

K3170-K3186	Bristol Bulldog (TM)	17

Type 124. C/n 7727-7743. K3183 test-bed for various engines. K3172, K3173, K3175, K3185 became 910M, 791M, 911M, 829M.

K3187-K3188	(Numbers not used)	–
K3189-K3476	Avro Tutor	288

Avro Type 621. K3308 research aircraft with modified wings. K3372-K3380, K3475, K3476 produced as Avro Type 646 Sea Tutor floatplanes. K3190, K3192-K3198 became 833M, 831M, 832M, 834M-838M, K3200, K3204, K3205, K3207, K3208, K3210, K3213, K3218, K3222, K3225, K3226, K3230, K3232, K3242, K3243, K3245, K3248, K3263, K3271, K3272, K3282, K3291 became 839M, 1848M, 840M, 1849M, 841M, 2705M, 1063M, 639M, 1097M, 891M, 892M, 1130M, 988M, 2009M, 1629M, 2271M, 2005M, 1850M, 1344M, 2046M, 675M, 2540M. K3302, K3316, K3327, K3329-K3331, K3342, K3349, K3358, K3365, K3367, K3382, K3388, K3391, K3392, K3399 became 2006M, 1600M, 2272M, 2047M, 2281M, 2048M, 1446M, 2273M, 649M, 2709M, 1630M, 2707M, 2138M, 2567M, 1089M, 2179M; K3409, K3442, K3453, K3455, K3467, K3474 became 1230M, 2706M, 1480M, 2995M, 1921M, 2708M. K3215 became

G-AHSA and was refurbished as K3215 for the Shuttleworth Collection. K3237, K3363 became G-AFZW and 'AIYM. K3317, K3420 to SAAF in 1942.

K3477-K3487	Fairey Seal	11

C/n F.1843-F.1853. K3485 converted to trainer.

K3488	Westland PV-6	1

Ex-Wapiti V G-AAWA became G-ACBR. Prototype Wallace.

K3489-K3503	Handley Page HP.50 Heyford I	15

K3489 non-standard, K3492 prototype Mk.II, K3503 prototype Mk.III. K3499 became 1009M.

K3504-K3513	Bristol Bulldog IIA	10

Bristol Type 105. C/n 7764-7773. K3512 developed aircraft with enlarged fin. K3504, K3508-K3511 became 885M, 1014M-1016M, 1013M.

K3514-K3545	Fairey Seal I	32

C/n F.1854-F.1874, F.1897-F.1907. K3519 trainer version to Spec 24/32. K3521 became 657M.

K3546-K3559	Blackburn Ripon/Baffin (T8 Type)	14

Ordered as Ripon, converted on line to Baffin. All shipped to Malta. K3558 became NZ175 of RNZAF.

K3560	Saro London	1

Pegasus IIM3. Prototype flying boat to Spec R24/31. Converted to Mk.II.

K3561	Vought V-66E Corsair	1

Purchased from USA for evaluation.

K3562-K3573	Westland Wallace I	12

Rebuilt Wapiti airframes K1346, K1345, K1332, K1333, K1347, K1331, K1351, K1348-K1350, K1352, K1353. K3564, K3569 became 1810M, 1809M.

K3574	Short R24/31 'Knuckleduster'	1

C/n S.767. Prototype. Became 1154M.

K3575-K3579	Fairey Seal	5

C/n F.1908-F.1912. Wheel or float u/c. K3577 became 1098M.

K3580-K3582	Blackburn Perth I	3

Type RB3A. All discarded by January 1936.

K3583	Bristol Bombay	1

Type 130. C/n 7809. Troop carrier prototype to Spec C26/31.

K3584	DH.82B Queen Bee	1

C/n 5027 radio controlled prototype. Converted from Tiger Moth.

K3585	Armstrong Whitworth AW.23	1

C/n 1251. Prototype to Spec S26/31, became G-AFRX. of Flight Refuelling.

K3586	Hawker Fury II (Hawker F14/32)	1

High Speed Fury; became Merlin test bed and 1436M.

K3587	Bristol Type 120	1

C/n 7562. Experimental GP aircraft ex-R-6.

K3588	Vickers Vespa VI/VII	1

Types 210 & 250. Ex-G-EBLD, G-ABIL and O-5. Became 1051M.

K3589-K3590	Blackburn Baffin	2

Type T8 with Pegasus IM3. First production as Baffin.

K3591	Blackburn B.3	1

Buzzard IIIMS. Prototype to Spec M1/30A.

K3592-K3595	Short Singapore III	4

Short type S.19. c/n S.770-S.773. All withdrawn by April 1938.

K3596	Heinkel He 64C	1

Ex-D-2305 and G-ACBS for flap research. Became VP-YBI

K3597-K3598	DH.82B Queen Bee	2

C/n 5038, 5039 ex-DH.60G III converted for radio control.

K3599-K3614	Vickers Valentia	16

Type 264. K3601, K3603 equipped as flying classrooms for home service, rest served overseas as troop carriers.

K3615-K3653	Hawker Osprey III	39

K3615 trials aircraft only, K3616-K3619 equipped for communications duties and later converted for TT; rest fleet duties. K3631, K3634, K3640, K3648 became 1953M, 1000M, 922M, 1228M.

K3654-K3662	Hawker Nimrod II	9

Initially to 802 Squadron and No.1 FTS.

K3663	Cierva C.29	1

Panther II. Acquired for evaluation by RAE.

K3664-K3677	Westland Wallace I	14

Ex-Wapiti airframes K1354-K1360, 1 built from spares, K1362-K1365, J9864, J9605. K3664, K3665, K3673, K3674, K3677 later 605M, 604M, 1084M, 601M, 2118M.

K3678	**Short Rangoon**	1
	Short Type S.8/8. C/n S.780 delivered May 1934, sold August 1936.	
K3679-K3721	**Hawker Audax I**	43
	K3719 became Hector prototype, later 1062M. K3688, K3692, K3695, K3696, K3701, K3711 became 1020M, 1133M, 1661M, 2017M, 1177M, 2698M. K3720 direct to SSVAF. K3679, K3680, K3682, K3685, K3690, K3697, K3702, K3705, K3721 to SAAF, 1940-42.	
K3722-K3729	**Saro Cloud**	8
	Saro Type A.19P. Delivered 1933-34. Withdrawn in mid-1939.	
K3730-K3742	**Hawker Fury I**	13
	All delivered to 43 Squadron K3736 became 1464M. K3731, K3733, K3735, K3739-K3741 to SAAF 1940.	
K3743-K3763	**Hawker Hart (T)**	21
	K3752 equipped for night flying. K3748, K3749, K3751, K3753, K3761 became 770M, 970M, 1581M, 1258M, 1765M. K3743, K3745, K3754, K3756, K3758-K3760 to SAAF from 1940.	
K3764-K3807	**Hawker Demon I**	44
	Kestrel II later VDR. K3764 armament trials. K3764, K3766, K3767, K3773, K3775-K3777, K3780, K3782-K3784, K3787, K3788, K3790-K3792, K3794, K3795, K3799, K3800, K3802, K3805-K3807 became 2510M, 997M, 1406M, 1404M, 949M, 958M, 1412M, 1022M, 980M, 950M, 1401M, 957M, 934M, 935M, 2206M, 1408M, 979M, 1687M, 1414M, 1532M, 1005M, 961M, 926M, 1686M.	
K3808-K3854	**Hawker Hart**	47
	Built by Vickers. K3844 converted to Trainer (Intermediate). K3810, K3811, K3814, K3819, K3838, K3841, K3844, K3849 became 1504M, 1499M, 1501M, 1335M, 2284M, 1500M, 2202M, 1476M. K3809, K3813, K3815, K3820-K3829, K3832-K3836, K3839, K3842, K3845, K3851 to SAAF 1938-39. K3831, K3847, K3852, K3853 to REAF 1940.	
K3855-K3904	**Hawker Hart (SEDB)**	50
	Built by Armstrong Whitworth. K3873, K3874 produced as Hart (Comm), K3881 converted to Hart (Intermediate); K3855-K3858, K3862, K3870, K3872-K3874, K3881, K3891, K3893, K3896, K3898, K3899, K3903 became 2023M, 2024M, 1347M, 2321M, 1351M, 1153M, 789M, 1469M, 2572M, 2275M, 1350M, 696M, 1586M, 2389M, 816M, 1185M. K3863, K3867, K3868, K3876, K3883-K3886, K3890 to SAAF 1937-42. K3877, K3888 to SRAF 1937.	
K3905	**Fairey G4/31 Mk.II (ex Mk.I)**	1
	C/n F.1926. Became Tiger test bed.	
K3906-K3913	**Westland Wallace I**	8
	K3907, K3908, K3910 became 1813M, 2501M, 2529M.	
K3914-K3920	**Hawker Osprey IIIL**	7
	Wheeled u/c on delivery. K3914, K3915, K3918 became 965M, 873M, 971M.	
K3921-K3922	**Hawker Hart (India)**	2
	Delivered May 1934.	
K3923-K3953	**Bristol Bulldog (TM)**	31
	C/n 7777-7807. K3923, K3932, K3934 became 912M, 1168M, 1167M.	
K3954	**Hawker Osprey IIIL**	1
	Converted to Mk.IV.	
K3955-K3972	**Hawker Hart I**	18
	K3960, K3961, K3965, K3968 became 1608M, 1696M, 944M, 737M. K3956, K3958, K3962, K3963, K3966, K3969 from 1938. K3972 to REAF 1940.	
K3973	**Supermarine Stranraer**	1
	Pegasus IIM later X. Prototype to Spec R24/31.	
K3974-K3985	**Hawker Demon I**	12
	Kestrel II. K3975-K3977, K3979, K3980, K3982, K3984 became 1413M, 1405M, 1683M, 1655M, 2244M, 2242M, 713M.	
K3986-K4009	**Fairey Gordon I**	24
	C/n F.1941-F.1964. K3987, K3993, K3995, K3999-K4009 to RNZAF 1939.	
K4010	**Westland Wallace**	1
	Ex Wapiti airframe K2245.	
K4011	**Blackburn Perth I**	1
	Final Perth with modified fuel system.	
K4012-K4020	**Westland Wallace I**	9
	Ex-Wapiti airframes K1334, K1339, K1341, K1344,	

	K1370, K1372-K1375. K4012, K4014, K4017 became 1541M, 1559M, 2530M.	
K4021-K4043	**Handley Page HP.50 Heyford IA**	23
	K4021 non-standard converted to Mk.III, K4029 was intermediate Mks.IA/II.	
K4044-K4046	**DH.82B Queen Bee**	3
	C/n 5044-5046. Delivered to RAE February 1934.	
K4047	**Airspeed AS.5 Courier**	1
	Used at RAE for experimental work, then for communications.	
K4048	**Westland PV.3**	1
	C/n WA2419 ex P-3 and G-ACAZ. Used in Everest expedition.	
K4049	**Vickers Wellington**	1
	Type 271. Prototype to Spec B9/32. First flight 15.6.36.	
K4050-K4070	**Hawker Hardy**	21
	Kestrel IB. Built by Gloster, shipped to Middle East for No.30 Squadron. K4050, K4065 to SRAF 1940.	
K4071-K4080	**Blackburn Baffin**	10
	Type T8 with Pegasus IM3. Delivered to No.810 Sqn. K4071, K4078 became NZ176, NZ177 of RNZAF.	
K4081-K4104	**Gloster Gauntlet I**	24
	Mercury VIS2. Production to Spec 24/33. K4094 Browning gun installation trials. K4082, K4086, K4090, K4098, K4102, K4103 became 867M, 1290M, 2126M, 1137M, 2127M, 2216M. K4089, K4100 to SAAF 1940.	
K4105-K4155	**Vickers Vincent**	51
	K4105 became 2285M. K4110, K4122, K4124, K4125 K4151 to RNZAF 1939. K4152, K4153 to Iraqi AF 1939.	
K4156-K4188	**Vickers Vildebeest III**	33
	Vickers Type 267. K4164 Mk.IV prototype. K4157 modified to Vincent. K4187 became NZ117 of RNZAF.	
K4189	**Bristol Bulldog IIA**	1
	Stainless steel construction to Spec 11/31 for static test.	
K4190	**Fairey Swordfish**	1
	Originally known as TSRII. C/n F.2038. Prototype to Spec S15/33.	
K4191-K4200	**Supermarine Scapa**	10
	Kestrel III.	
K4201-K4225	**Fairey Seal**	25
	Panther IIA. C/n F.1971-F.1995. K4212 DC. K4202-K4204, K4214, K4218, K4224 became 1175M, 1186M, 1176M, 1070M, 1169M, 1091M.	
K4226-K4229	**DH.82B Queen Bee**	4
	C/n 5048-5051. K4229 fitted with towing winch.	
K4230-K4239	**Avro Rota I**	10
	Avro Type 671. Cierva C.30A built for School of Army Co-operation. K4237 became 1142M.	
K4240	**Handley Page HP.52 Hampden**	1
	Prototype to Spec B9/32. F/f 21.6.36. Became 1490M.	
K4241	**Blackburn CA.15C Monoplane**	1
	C/n 2780, 2781 G-ABKV for trials to Spec 6/29.	
K4242-K4291	**DH.82A Tiger Moth II**	50
	C/n 3238-3287. K4242, K4243, K4245, K4264, K4274, K4275, K4282 became 1858M, 1452M, 1820M, 4698M, 1821M, 1859M, 5284M. K4259, K4260 became G-ANMO and 'ALMV.	
K4292	**Bristol Bulldog IV**	1
	Bristol Type 105. C/n 7745 ex-Mk.IIIA R-7 and G-ABZW. Became 1180M.	
K4293-K4294	**DH.82B Queen Bee**	2
	C/n 5088, 5089. Floatplane versions.	
K4295	**Blackburn Shark I**	1
	Blackburn TSR. Ex-B.6 prototype to Spec S15/33, converted to Mk.II, became 931M.	
K4296	**Avro Rota**	1
	Avro Type 671 floatplane version.	
K4297-K4298	**Hawker Hart (Comm)**	2
	Kestrel IB4. Built by Armstrong Whitworth for No.24 Squadron. K4298 became 1563M.	
K4299	**Armstrong Whitworth Type 29**	1
	C/n 1168. Prototype to Spec P27/32.	
K4300-K4302	**Saro Cloud**	3
	Saro Type 19P. K4302 became 939M.	
K4303	**Fairey Battle**	1
	C/n F.2121. Prototype to Spec P27/32. First flew 10.3.36. Became 1475M.	
K4304-K4305	**Fairey Seafox**	2
	C/n F.2122, F.2123. Prototypes to Spec 11/32. K4304 floatplane became 1463M. K4305 landplane version.	

K4306-K4321	**Hawker Hardy I**	**16**
	Kestrel 1B. Built by Gloster, delivered to No.30 Squadron and transferred to No.6 Squadron.	
K4322-K4336	**Hawker Osprey III**	**14(15)**
	K4336 cancelled.	
K4337-K4348	**Westland Wallace I/II**	**12**
	Ex-Wapiti airframes K2306-K2317. K4346-K4348 built as Mk.II. K4344 converted to experimental tanker. K4340, K4348 became 1812M, 2531M.	
K4349-K4364	**Blackburn Shark I**	**16**
	Blackburn T.9. All to No.820 Squadron except K4360 to RAE. K4357 became 990M.	
K4365-K4436	**Hawker Audax/Hart (Special)**	**72**
	Built by Gloster and ordered as Audax, but K4365-K4369, K4371-K4379, K4407-K4436 completed as Hart (Special). K4370, K4386, K4390, K4407, K4409, K4410, K4412, K4414, K4416, K4420, K4421, K4426, K4432, K4436 became 902M, 963M, 2034M, 2302M, 2702M, 1763M, 1387M, 2102M, 1445M, 2101M, 2263M, 2264M, 2301M, 2703M. K4369, K4374, K4375, K4378, K4379, K4382, K4383, K4388, K4392, K4399, K4428 to SAAF from 1940.	
K4437-K4495	**Hawker Hart**	**59**
	Built by Armstrong Whitworth. K4439, K4442 converted to Hart (Intermediate). K4437, K4438, K4446, K4459, K4487 became 2309M, 1631M, 1231M, 1214M, 2020M. K4440, K4442, K4443, K4481, K4483 to REAF 1939-40. K4444, K4447-K4451, K4453-K4458, K4460-K4465, K4467-K4472, K4474-K4477, K4479, K4480, K4484-K4486, K4488-K4493, K4495 to SAAF 1938-39.	
K4496-K4544	**Hawker Demon**	**49**
	Kestrel V. K4496 fitted with Frazer Nash turret. K4498, K4499, K4500, K4501, K4503-K4505, K4507-K4511, K4513, K4520, K4521, K4525, K4527, K4530-K4532, K4534, K4537, K4538, K4540, K4542, K4544 became 1243M, 1759M, 2298M, 2029M, 1397M, 1682M, 1760M, 1761M, 1407M, 1409M, 1684M, 1416M, 2028M, 1484M, 1395M, 1694M, 1396M, 1212M, 1410M, 1693M, 975M, 1001M, 1038M, 1415M, 1402M, 1067M.	
K4545	**DH.82B Queen Bee**	**1**
	C/n 5099 delivered December 1934, crashed April 1936.	
K4546-K4564	**Boulton & Paul Overstrand**	**19**
	BP Type P.75. Built for No.101 Squadron. K4552, K4558, K4563 became 1822M, 2146M, 2174M.	
K4565	**Supermarine Scapa**	**1**
	Served November 1935 to October 1939.	
K4566-K4576	**Bristol Bulldog (TM)**	**11**
	Sold before entering service.	
K4577-K4585	**Short Singapore III**	**9**
	Type S.19. C/n S.781-S.784, S.798-S.802.	
K4586-K4587	**Armstrong Whitworth Whitley**	**2**
	AW Type 38. Prototypes to Spec B3/34. K4586 first flew 17.3.36, became 4070M.	
K4588-K4614	**Vickers Vildebeest III**	**27**
	Vickers Type 267. K4599 DC. K4610 became 1599M. K4589, K4591-K4593, K4595-K4598, K4612 to RNZAF during 1940-41.	
K4615-K4619	**Vickers Vincent**	**5**
	All to Middle East. K4617 became NZ321 of RNZAF.	
K4620-K4629	**Hawker Nimrod II**	**10**
K4630-K4635	**Vickers Valentia I**	**6**
	Type 263. K4632 Type 282 fitted with loud-hailer; K4633 type 283 with cabin gun; K4631 to SAAF.	
K4636-K4655	**Hawker Hind**	**20**
	K4636, K4638, K4639, K4641, K4644, K4645, K4647, K4649, K4650 converted to trainers by General Aircraft, 1938. K4640, K4643 to Kenya; K4638, K4645, K4647, K4649, K4653 to SAAF 1940-41; K4642, K4650 to RNZAF. K4637 became 945M.	
K4656-K4750	**Vickers Vincent**	**95**
	K4659-K4662, K4676, K4680, K4710, K4717-K4722, K4729, K4734, K4739, K4740, K4742-K4750 to the RNZAF 1939. K4730, K4735, K4737 to R Iraqi AF.	
K4751-K4770	**Hawker Hart (T)**	**20**
	Kestrel 1B. K4770 initially to SSVAF fitted for TT. K4753, K4763 became 2228M, 2312M. K4756, K4761, K4764, K4767 to SAAF 1941-42.	
K4771	**Avro Anson**	**1**
	Avro Type 652A. Prototype to Spec G18/35 first flew 24.3.35. Became 2562M.	

K4772	**DH.89M Dragon Rapide**	**1**
	Prototype to Spec G18/35, eventually used by ATA.	
K4773	**Saro A.33**	**1**
	Prototype to Spec R2/33. Crashed on test.	
K4774	**Short Sunderland**	**1**
	Short Type S.25. C/n S.803. Prototype to Spec R2/23, first flew 16.10.37.	
K4775	**Avro Rota**	**1**
	Avro Type 671. Rota with Civet Major engine for trials.	
K4776-K4778	**Blackburn Baffin**	**3**
	Type T8A with Pegasus IIM3. K4776, K4778 destroyed in storm 1936. K4777 to RNZAF 1937.	
K4779-K4796	**Fairey Seal**	**17(18)**
	Panther IIA. C/n F.2093-F.2110. K4796 not built. K4786, K4792-K4794 became 1090M, 1069M, 1096M, 1568M.	
K4797	**Supermarine Seagull V/Walrus I**	**1**
	Prototype Seagull V re-named Walrus in 1935.	
K4798-K4837	**Avro Tutor**	**40**
	K4799, K4798, K4807, K4813, K4829, K4830 became 799M, 2568M, 1851M, 2996M, 2710M, 1699M.	
K4838-K4862	**Hawker Audax (India)**	**25**
	Kestrel 1B. Built by Gloster. All for service in India.	
K4863-K4878	**Handley Page HP.50 Heyford II**	**16**
	Kestrel VI engines fitted.	
K4879	**Bristol 138A**	**1**
	Pegasus IV on delivery. C/n 7840. High altitude research aircraft to Spec 2/34, became 1951M or 2393M.	
K4880-K4882	**Blackburn Shark II**	**3**
	Blackburn T.9A. K4882 became prototype Mk.III.	
K4883-K4885	**Vickers Vincent**	**3**
	K4885 became NZ314 of RNZAF.	
K4886-K5052	**Hawker Hart (T)**	**167**
	Kestrel X. Built by Armstrong Whitworth for FTSs. K4887, K4893, K4935, K4961, K4969, K4972, K4990, K4991, K5003, K5011, K5016, K5024, K5025, K5045 became 2020M, 2051M, 1209M, 2345M, 2313M, 1764M, 1526M, 2011M, 2314M, 1862M, 1771M, 2055M, 2279M, 2237M. K4889, K4891, K4936, K4940-K4943, K4946, K4962, K4968, K4974, K4975, K4981, K4995, K4999, K5001, K5004, K5009, K5018, K5022, K5028, K5033-K5035, K5039, K5042, K5047 to SAAF from 1940. K4954, K5020, K5032 to REAF 1940. K4929 to FAA.	
K5053	**Northrop 2E**	**1**
	Bought from USA for evaluation, 1934.	
K5054	**Supermarine Spitfire**	**1**
	Type 300. Prototype to Spec F37/34, first flew 5.3.36, crashed 1939.	
K5055	**DH.82B Queen Bee**	**1**
	C/n 5116 Tiger Moth conversion for service in India.	
K5056-K5058	**Hawker Nimrod I**	**3**
	Replacement order.	
K5059-K5060	**DH.82B Queen Bee**	**2**
	C/n 5127, 5128. Delivered to RAE 1935.	
K5061-K5062	*(Reserved numbers not used)*	**—**
K5063-K5069	**Avro Prefect**	**7**
	Avro Type 626. Produced to Spec 32/34. K5063, K5065, K5067 became 1594M, 4038M, 4039M. K5066, K5069 became G-AHVO, 'AHRZ.	
K5070	**DH.89 Dragon Rapide**	**1**
	C/n 6267 for Air Council members. To BOAC 1941.	
K5071-K5082	**Westland Wallace I**	**12**
	Ex-Wapiti airframes K2318-K2320, K2279, K2280, K2252, K2254, K2260, K2264, K2266, K1412, K1413. K5071, K5073, K5077, K5081, K5082 became 2462M, 2502M, 1811M, 774M, 2528M.	
K5083	**Hawker Hurricane**	**1**
	Merlin C initially. Prototype to Spec F36/34, first flew 6.11.35. Became 1211M.	
K5084	**DH.88 Comet**	**1**
	C/n 1996 ex-G-ACSS restored as G-ACSS.	
K5085-K5098	**Fairey Hendon**	**14**
	Built at Stockport. C/n F.2124-F.2137. All to 38 Sqn. K5085-K5089, K5092, K5093, K5096-K5098 became 1614M, 1564M, 1565M, 1615M-1617M, 1566M, 1618M, 1619M, 1567M.	
K5099	**Fairey P4/34**	**1**
	Merlin F. C/n F.2231. Prototype. F/f 13.1.37. To 3665M.	
K5100-K5114	**DH.82B Queen Bee**	**15**
	Gipsy Major. C/n 5134-5137, 5153-5163. All expended by August 1938.	

K5115

K5115	Hawker Henley	1

Prototype to Spec P4/34, later Vulture test-bed.

K5116	Westland Wallace	1

Ex-G-ACJU acquired for service June 1935.

K5117	(Reservation)	–
K5118	DH.82B Queen Bee	1

Replacement.

K5119	Bristol Type 146	1

C/n 7841. Prototype to Spec F5/34. First flew 11.2.38.

K5120-K5176	Hawker Audax I	57

Kestrel X. Built by Avro. K5121-K5123, K5125, K5139, K5153 became 864M, 865M, 2085M, 866M, 2016M, 3406M. K5129, K5135, K5136, K5138, K5148, K5162, K5166, K5176 to SAAF 1940. K5141, K5142, K5167 initially to SSVAF.

K5177	Vickers 027/34 project	(1)

Cancelled.

K5178-K5179	Blackburn Skua	2

Type DB1. Prototype to Spec 027/34. K5178 first flew 9.2.37.

K5180-K5199	Handley Page HP.50 Heyford III	20

K5180 originally built as Mk.II, K5184 modified by Flight Refuelling Ltd.

K5200	Gloster Gladiator	1

Gloster Type SS.37. Prototype to Spec F7/30, first flew 12.9.34 with Mercury VIS2, later Mk.IX fitted.

K5201-K5256	Hawker Audax I	56

Kestrel X. Built by Bristol. C/n 7845-7900. K5225, K5238, K5244, K5247 became 904M, 876M, 1528M, 1236M. K5205, K5226, K5252, K5254 to SAAF 1940-41.

K5257-K5263	Saro London I/II	7

Saro Type A.27. Initial deliveries with Pegasus III engines, later all had Pegasus as London Mk.II.

K5264-K5367	Gloster Gauntlet II	104

Mercury VIS2; K5266, K5274, K5275, K5279, K5280, K5282, K5283, K5285, K5287, K5289, K5290, K5291, K5294, K5296, K5297 became 2248M, 1558M, 1956M, 3619M, 3487M, 1845M, 1846M, 2252M, 2336M, 3408M, 1929M, 3318M, 2133M, 2130M, 2340M and K5300, K5301, K5305, K5308, K5309, K5311, K5314, K5315, K5317, K5319, K5321, K5322, K5329, K5336, K5339, K5340, K5342, K5345, K5346, K5350, K5353, K5354, K5356, K5357, K5360, K5362, K5363, K5367 became 2001M, 2115M, 2422M, 1557M, 2131M, 1963M, 1244M, 983M, 1622M, 2132M, 1957M, 2341M, 2640M, 3319M, 1958M, 2249M, 2360M, 1198M, 2342M, 2343M, 1485M, 2234M, 2254M, 1959M, 1538M, 2518M, 2335M. K5267, K5270, K5271, K5288, K5293, K5313, K5324, K5326, K5338, K5341, K5352, K5358, K5364, K5365 sold to Finnair 1939-40. K5276, K5330 to SAAF and K5277, K5347 to SRAF 1939-40.

K5368-K5560	Hawker Hind	193

Kestrel VFP on delivery. Built as light bombers but K5373, K5377, K5379, K5384, K5397, K5408, K5410, K5423, K5427, K5436, K5439, K5440, K5446, K5447, K5449, K5450, K5460, K5465-K5469, K5473, K5485, K5486, K5488, K5495, K5500, K5502-K5509, K5511-K5513, K5515, K5517, K5518, K5521, K5523, K5550, K5553, K5559 converted to trainers by General Aircraft in 1938. K5370, K5377, K5381, K5386, K5394, K5397, K5412, K5414, K5434, K5438, K5442, K5459, K5464, K5480, K5525, K5531, K5538, K5551, K5557 became 982M, 2622M, 1860M, 2624M, 968M, 2621M, 1433M, 1592M, 1378M, 1861M, 1931M, 964M, 927M, 2106M, 1371M, 1863M, 1609M, 1864M, 1864M. K5372, K5374-K5376, K5379, K5393, K5396, K5400, K5407, K5410, K5417, K5435, K5436, K5460, K5467, K5471, K5473, K5475, K5478, K5481, K5485, K5486, K5488, K5490, K5493, K5495-K5497, K5505, K5507-K5509, K5513, K5517, K5519, K5521, K5524, K5527, K5532, K5535, K5539-K5541 to SAAF 1940-42. K5390, K5392, K5402, K5406, K5423, K5431, K5433, K5441, K5449, K5451, K5465, K5476, K5492, K5499, K5500, K5502, K5504, K5523, K5533, K5534, K5536, K5550, K5553, K5560 to RNZAF 1940-41. K5409, K5457, K5554 to R Afghan AF; K5427, K5542 to Kenya, K5462, K5477, K5483 sold to India. K5415, K5446, K5559 became 70, 67, 68 of the Irish Air Corps.

K5561-K5585	Hawker Audax (India)	25

Kestrel IBS. Built by Avro. All shipped to India.

K5586-K5603	Hawker Audax I	18

Kestrel X. Built by Avro ex-Westland contract. K5600 became 2015M. K5586 to SAAF 1940 and K5602 to FAA 1941.

K5604	Gloster F5/34	1

Mercury IX. Gloster monoplane fighter prototype, became 2232M.

K5605	Vickers Valentia	1

Replacement order.

K5606	Armstrong Whitworth AW.19	1

C/n 923. Prototype to Spec G4/31 ex-A-3.

K5607-K5659	Blackburn Shark II	53

Blackburn T.9A. Wheel/float u/c version. K5607, K5617, K5633, K5641 became 1482M, 903M, 1461M, 1460M. K5621, K5646, K5651 converted to TT.

K5660-K5662	Fairey Swordfish	3

C/n F.2142-F.2144. Landplanes except K5662 floatplane.

K5663-K5682	Hawker Fury I	20

Kestrel IIS or VDR. K5664, K5667 became 2246M, 1732M. K5663, K5669, K5670, K5672, K5674-K5676, K5678, K5680 to SAAF 1940.

K5683-K5741	Hawker Demon	59

Kestrel VDR. Built by Boulton & Paul. K5694, K5695, K5698, K5699, K5700, K5705, K5706, K5710-K5712, K5718, K5719, K5725-K5727, K5729-K5741 fitted with Frazer Nash turrets. K5683, K5684, K5686-K5688, K5691-K5696, K5698, K5699, K5700-K5702, K5704, K5706-K5711, K5713-K5721, K5723, K5725-K5729, K5731-K5735, K5737-K5740 became 1411M, 1680M, 2030M, 2198M, 1902M, 1676M, 1762M, 1379M, 2325M, 2329M, 2200M, 2326M, 1444M, 2199M, 1897M, 2507M, 1678M, 2330M, 2245M, 2197M, 1681M, 2324M, 1056M, 1417M, 991M, 1418M, 1419M, 1677M, 1030M, 2311M, 1420M-1422M, 2299M, 2348M, 2008M, 1235M, 2296M, 2328M, 2480M, 2327M, 2288M, 2323M, 2290M, 2287M, 2298M, 2350M.

K5742-K5767	Hawker Osprey IV	26

K5755, K5760 became 1229M, 1172M.

K5768-K5771	Fairey Hendon	(4)

Order cancelled.

K5772-K5783	Supermarine Walrus I	12

Initial production to Spec 2/35.

K5784-K5897	Hawker Hart (T)	114

Kestrel X engines. Built by Vickers. K5796, K5811, K5812, K5820, K5830, K5839, K5875, K5891 became 1770M, 2052M, 2010M, 2086M, 1758M, 2053M, 1527M, 919M. K5784, K5787, K5788, K5790, K5792, K5793, K5804, K5807, K5814, K5821, K5827, K5831, K5835, K5838, K5848, K5850, K5852, K5855, K5857, K5858, K5865, K5867, K5868, K5872, K5873, K5876, K5878, K5879, K5882, K5887, K5889, K5894, K5896, K5897 to SAAF from 1940. K5874, K5895 transferred to Royal Navy. K5880 to REAF 1940.

K5898-K5907	Hawker Demon	10

Kestrel X engines initially. Built by Boulton & Paul. Turreted version except K5906. K5907, K5898, K5899, K5900, K5901, K5904, K5906, K5907 became 2268M, 2293M, 2460M, 1197M, 2347M, 2291M, 2297M.

K5908-K5913	Saro London I/II	6

K5908-K5910 Mk.I converted to Mk.II, K5911-K5913 built as Mk.II.

K5914-K5923	Hawker Hardy	10

Built by Gloster. All but K5919 despatched overseas. K5916, K5917 to SRAF 1930. K5919 became 2247M.

K5924	Miles M.3 Falcon	1

Used by RAE for flap research.

K5925	Miles M.6 Hawcon	1

Acquired for drag research at RAE.

K5926-K6011	Fairey Swordfish	86

C/n F.2145-F.2230. Initial Swordfish production. K5986 became 985M.

K6012-K6086	Westland Wallace II	75

K6012, K6013, K6015, K6018, K6020, K6024, K6027, K6033-K6036, K6038-K6040, K6042, K6048, K6050, K6054-K6056, K6059, K6060, K6065, K6066, K6075, K6076, K6078-K6082 became 943M, 2503M, 2364M, 1561M, 2463M, 2532M, 2382M, 2441M, 1814M, 2361M, 2359M, 2365M, 2533M, 2443M, 2442M, 2504M, 3554M, 3608M, 2439M, 1560M, 2366M, 2362M, 2361M, 1633M, 1562M, 1543M, 2497M-2499M, 1544M, 1542M.

K6087-K6126   **Avro Tutor I**   **40**
Avro Type 621. K6090, K6093, K6098, K6115, K6118,
K6119, K6122 became 1343M, 1819M, 3352M, 4193M,
3572M, 2280M, 2007M. K6105 became G-AKFJ.

K6127-K6128   **Westland Lysander**   **2**
Prototypes to Spec A39/34. K6127 first flew 15.6.36,
later modified to Westland P.12 project with twin
tailfins.

K6129-K6151   **Gloster Gladiator I**   **23**
Mercury XI. Production to Spec F14/35. K6129 did
development trials for Sea Gladiator, later becoming
2645M. K6135 to RHAF in 1940.

K6152-K6325   **Avro Anson I**   **174**
Avro Type 652A. K6212-K6223 direct to RAAF as
A4-1 to A4-12. K6154, K6156, K6157, K6159, K6160,
K6161, K6167, K6168, K6170-K6173, K6182, K6186,
K6188, K6191, K6199, K6204, K6206, K6237, K6243,
K6244, K6261, K6269, K6280, K6285, K6299 became
2205M, 2175M, 2423M, 2399M, 3621M, 2428M, 2527M,
2467M, 2521M, 4485M, 1695M, 2468M, 4508M, 2519M,
2520M, 2523M, 959M, 2509M, 2508M, 4260M, 4422M,
2142M, 2471M, 4424M, 1438M, 2398M, 2125M. K6177,
K6192, K6197, K6225, K6230, K6241, K6251, K6264,
K6265, K6278, K6281, K6293, K6297, K6298, K6300,
K6302, K6303, K6310, K6316, K6324 to Canada 1940-
41. K6178, K6180, K6211, K6229, K6235, K6238,
K6247, K6256, K6266, K6279, K6282, K6284, K6289,
K6311, K6318, K6323 to SAAF 1941.

K6326-K6368   **Vickers Vincent I**   **43**
All shipped to Middle East. K6326, K6327, K6329,
K6330, K6333-K6336, K6338-K6345, K6348, K6351-
K6357, K6360, K6361, K6368 to RNZAF from 1939.

K6369-K6414   **Vickers Vildebeest III/IV**   **46**
Types 267/286. K6369-K6407 Mk.III shipped to Far
East. K6408-K6414 Mk.IV retained for home service.
K6398, K6406 became 2375M, 2420M. K6395-K6397,
K6401, K6409, K6410, K6413, K6414 to RNZAF in
1940-41.

K6415-K6550   **Hawker Hart (T)**   **136**
Kestrel X engine. Built by Armstrong Whitworth. First
12 tropicalised for overseas service; K6426 with SSVAF.
K6430, K6456, K6459, K6475, K6509, K6510, K6514,
K6517, K6529, K6536, K6546 became 1772M, 2054M,
2012M, 2039M, 1779M, 2043M, 1598M, 2189M, 1954M,
1945M, 2019M. K6428, K6435, K6439, K6443, K6448,
K6450, K6453-K6455, K6462, K6463, K6468, K6470-
K6472, K6474, K6483, K6484, K6488, K6491, K6495,
K6498, K6500, K6502, K6504, K6506, K6513, K6516,
K6518, K6520, K6524, K6527, K6530, K6531, K6535,
K6542, K6544, K6545 to SAAF from 1940. K6433 to
Royal Navy 1939. K6473 to REAF 1940.

K6551-K6552   **Bristol 148**   **2**
C/n F.7843, F.7844 prototypes to Spec A39/34. K6551
Type 148, K6552 Type 148B. Used as test-beds. K6551
became 2374M.

K6553-K6554   **Cierva Gyroplane**   **(2)**
Order cancelled.

K6555-K6612   **Fairey Hendon II**   **(58)**
Order cancelled.

K6613-K6856   **Hawker Hind**   **244**
Built as light bombers. K6621, K6640, K6657, K6658,
K6671, K6673, K6683, K6685, K6687, K6688, K6690,
K6703, K6712, K6714-K6716, K6722, K6724, K6729,
K6735, K6736, K6739, K6741, K6743, K6756-K6760,
K6775, K6776, K6793, K6805, K6810, K6811, K6813,
K6818, K6820, K6821, K6823, K6827, K6829, K6831,
K6834-K6837, K6840, K6841 converted to trainers by
General Aircraft. K6627, K6635, K6637, K6641, K6681,
K6686, K6691, K6694, K6713, K6725, K6727, K6772,
K6828, K6847, K6856 became 2107M, 2044M, 2620M,
1865M, 1140M, 1117M, 1434M, 1866M, 2424M, 1943M,
1944M, 2040M, 1427M, 2003M, 1193M. K6668, K6675,
K6832, K6842, K6853, K6855 to Afghanistan in 1939.
K6618, K6696, K6804 to IAF 1939. K6755, K6781
became 71, 72 of Irish Air Corps. K6791 to Kenya 1941.
K6622, K6626, K6649, K6666, K6672, K6679, K6687,
K6692, K6693, K6701-K6703, K6705, K6708, K6710,
K6717, K6720, K6721, K6735, K6749, K6761, K6764,
K6768, K6786, K6787, K6792, K6793, K6800, K6810,
K6820, K6829, K6844, K6849 to RNZAF from 1940.

K6621, K6623-K6625, K6640, K6642, K6648, K6650,
K6654, K6660, K6663, K6664, K6669-K6671, K6673,
K6674, K6676, K6677, K6680, K6683, K6688, K6690,
K6695, K6699, K6704, K6707, K6709, K6711, K6715,
K6718, K6722, K6726, K6729, K6736, K6738, K6739,
K6741, K6743, K6759, K6765, K6767, K6769-K6771,
K6775, K6776, K6783, K6788, K6789, K6798, K6811,
K6813, K6816, K6818, K6823, K6831, K6840, K6841,
K6843, K6846, K6850, K6852 to SAAF from 1940.

K6857-K6906   **Handley Page HP.50 Heyford III**   **50**
Delivered 1936. All withdrawn before 1941.

K6907-K6922   **Short Singapore III**   **16**
Short S.19. C/n S.805-S.809, S.823-S.833. K6912,
K6916-K6918 to RNZAF 1941.

K6923-K6925   **Avro Sea Tutor**   **3**
Avro Type 646. K6924, K6925 converted to landplanes.

K6926   **Hawker IPV-4**   **1**
Private venture aircraft allotted serial for trials.

K6927-K6932   **Saro London I/II**   **6**
Mk.Is all converted to Mk.II.

K6933-K7032   **Handley Page HP.54 Harrow I/II**   **100**
K6933-K6970 built as Mk.I, some later converted to
Mk.II; from K6971 built as Mk.II. K6933 tanker
conversion became G-AFRG and 794 of RCAF. K6934,
K6987, K7032 became 2525M, 5050M, 4943M. K7027,
K7029 to Flight Refuelling became G-AFRL, 'AFRH.

K7033-K7182   **Bristol Blenheim I**   **150**
Type 142M. C/n 7986-8135. K7034-K7036, K7041,
K7042, K7167 fitted DC. K7072 variously modified
and to Canada as Bolingbroke. K7033-K7035, K7038-
K7040, K7042, K7043, K7045, K7046, K7051, K7056,
K7059, K7060, K7062, K7064, K7069-K7071, K7079,
K7085, K7105, K7111, K7115, K7121, K7122, K7124,
K7128, K7141, K7143, K7149, K7151, K7167, K7179
became 2373M, 3241M, 1327M, 1023M, 1024M, 1042M,
1372M, 1025M, 1328M, 1329M, 3014M, 1027M, 2649M,
1043M, 1330M, 3570M, 1333M, 1331M, 1332M, 1245M,
2990M, 4026M, 1345M, 3536M, 1246M, 3348M, 3571M,
1107M, 2182M, 2852M, 1113M, 3483M, 3400M, 2879M.

K7183-K7262   **Armstrong AW.38 Whitley I/II**   **80**
C/n 1171-1250. K7183-K7216 Mk.I, remainder Mk.II.
K7183, K7186, K7191-K7193, K7198, K7201, K7202,
K7205, K7208, K7213-K7215, K7217-K7219, K7223,
K7224, K7233, K7235, K7236, K7245, K7248, K7249,
K7256 became 2181M, 1702M, 2282M, 1780M, 3381M,
3093M, 3382M, 1889M, 1890M, 2600M, 3297M, 3295M,
1928M, 2454M, 4114M, 3334M, 3287M, 3335M, 3407M,
3298M, 3121M, 2474M, 3337M, 3339M, 3336M. K7243
Deerhound test bed.

K7263-K7285   **Hawker Fury II**   **23**
K7263-K7266, K7268-K7272, K7274-K7277, K7280-
K7283, K7285 became 1569M, 1570M, 2033M, 1571M-
1575M, 2027M, 2031M, 2032M, 1065M, 1576M, 1334M,
1577M, 1578M, 2230M, 1579M.

K7286   *(Number not allotted)*   –

K7287-K7303   **Supermarine Stranraer**   **17**
Standard production. K7300 became 2784M.

K7304-K7306   **Supermarine Scapa**   **3**
K7304 became 2191M.

K7307-K7468   **Hawker Audax I**   **162**
Built by Avro. K7324, K7349, K7383, K7400, K7425,
K7429, K7433, K7438, K7464 became 1908M, 1132M,
2218M, 2219M, 2113M, 2035M, 1039M, 2036M, 2037M.
K7387 to IAF 1940. K7315, K7316 initially to SSVAF.
K7314, K7320, K7330, K7339, K7341, K7343, K7348,
K7362, K7365, K7373, K7378, K7396, K7388, K7399,
K7404, K7407, K7409, K7410, K7414, K7417, K7420,
K7428, K7430, K7436, K7437, K7441, K7463 to SAAF
from 1940.

K7469-K7553   **Hawker Audax I**   **85**
Kestrel X. Built by Bristol. C/n 7901-7985. K7485
became 2014M. K7474, K7500, K7533, K7540 to
SAAF 1940-41. K7534, K7546 to SRAF 1940.

K7554   **Hawker Henley**   **1**
Second prototype modified to TT, became 3674M.

K7555   **Fairey P4/34**   **1**
Merlin I. C/n F.2266. Second prototype.

K7556   **Vickers Wellesley**   **1**
Pegasus II, then X engine. Prototype rebuilt from
PV O-9. Became 1852M.

K7557	**Bristol Type 142**	**1**
	C/n 7838. Ex-R-12 and G-ADCZ, became 2211M.	
K7558-K7712	**Fairey Battle**	**155**
	136 with Merlin I and 19 with Merlin II initially. Built at Stockport. C/n F.2316-F.2470. K7560, K7561, K7564, K7566, K7568-K7570, K7576-K7586, K7590, K7592, K7595, K7597 became 1033M, 1034M, 1110M, 1939M, 1035M-1037M, 1955M, 1792M, 1785M, 1021M, 1640M, 1794M, 1924M, 1786M, 1784M, 1787M, 1797M, 1795M, 1774M, 1872M, 1875M and K7601, K7605, K7612, K7616, K7621, K7624, K7625, K7628, K7629, K7635, K7637, K7641, K7644, K7645, K7648, K7650, K7653, K7655-K7657, K7662, K7663, K7665, K7667-K7669, K7674, K7675, K7677-K7680, K7682, K7691-K7694, K7704, K7705, K7709 became 1793M, 1796M, 1938M, 2585M, 1873M, 1871M, 1936M, 1894M, 1925M, 1798M, 1114M, 1937M, 2476M, 2484M, 1831M, 1877M, 1881M, 1870M, 1799M, 1139M, 1933M, 1879M, 1775M, 1934M, 1878M, 1874M, 1880M, 1876M, 1800M, 1801M, 1788M, —?—, 1119M, 1165M, 1782M, 1802M, 1341M, 1613M, 2546M, 3555M. K7559, K7587, K7602, K7606, K7608, K7632-K7634, K7640, K7647, K7652, K7660, K7671, K7695, K7701, K7703, K7710 to RCAF from 1940. Others to RAAF and SAAF 1940-42.	
K7713-K7791	**Vickers Wellesley**	**79**
	Type 287 with Pegasus XX. K7717 became test-bed and long range development aircraft. K7772 Type 289 as test-bed for Hercules. K7746 became 1041M. K7728 temporarily to REAF.	
K7792-K7891	**Gloster Gauntlet II**	**100**
	K7797, K7798, K7801, K7803, K7804, K7806, K7815, K7817, K7819, K7821, K7824, K7827, K7829, K7832, K7841, K7842, K7846, K7848, K7851, K7854, K7855, K7860, K7862, K7864, K7871-K7877, K7880, K7882, K7886-K7888 became 1607M, 2116M, 2344M, 2319M, 2320M, 2224M, 1453M, 1540M, 2117M, 2337M, 2250M, 1961M, 2255M, 1155M, 1962M, 1554M, 2253M, 2251M, 1555M, 2215M, 1604M, 1602M, 2109M, 1603M, 2050M, 1050M, 2128M, 1432M, 1556M, 2129M, 1478M, 1940M, 1830M, 3638M, 1605M, 1964M. K7807, K7813, K7826, K7837, K7839, K7857, K7858, K7865, K7867, K7869, K7878 to Finland 1939-40. K7831, K7833 to SAAF 1940. K7825 to SRAF.	
K7892-K8077	**Gloster Gladiator I**	**164(186)**
	K8056-K8077 cancelled. K7976 crashed on test before delivery. K7981, K7991, K7992 became 1597M, 1783M, 1755M. K7892, K7923, K7971, K7973, K8013, K8017-K8019, K8031, K8047, K8054 to RHAF 1940-41. K7907, K7928, K7989, K8005-K8008 to Iraqi AF. K7922 to SAAF 1939. K7917, K7952, K7979, K8052 to FAA 1942 and K8039 from delivery.	
K8078-K8087	**Vickers Vildebeest IV**	**10**
	Vickers Type 286. K8078-K8081, K8083-K8086 became NZ136, NZ129, NZ124-NZ126, NZ138, NZ139, NZ127 of the RNZAF 1940-41.	
K8088	**Bristol 146**	**(1)**
	To Spec F5/34. Not completed.	
K8089	**Gloster F5/34**	**1**
	Second prototype, became 2231M.	
K8090-K8167	**Hawker Hector**	**78**
	Built by Westland. K8091, K8095, K8101, K8106, K8107, K8109, K8118, K8120, K8128, K8131, K8133, K8138, K8144, K8147, K8149, K8160 became 2407M, 2401M, 2416M, 1336M, 2402M, 1111M, 2403M, 2404M, 1125M, 2167M, 3635M, 1941M, 2400M, 2405M, 2193M, 2575M. K8098, K8102, K8105, K8114, K8115, K8117, K8130, K8148, K8159 became 78-83, 88, 84, 89 of the Irish Air Corps 1942.	
K8168-K8172	**Avro Tutor**	**5**
	Avro Type 621. For University Air Squadrons. K8169 became 3353M.	
K8173-K8177	**Boulton Paul Overstrand I**	**5**
	BP Type P.75. Final production. K8177 became 2147M.	
K8178	**Vickers Warwick**	**1**
	Prototype to Spec B1/35. Became engine test-bed.	
K8179	**Handley Page HP.55**	**(1)**
	To Spec B1/35. Not built.	
K8180	**Armstrong Whitworth B1/35**	**(1)**
	Not built.	
K8181-K8217	**Hawker Demon**	**37**
	Kestrel VDR or VI engines. Built by Boulton & Paul. Majority fitted with Frazer Nash turrets. K8181-K8184, K8187, K8188, K8190, K8193-K8195, K8198, K8203-K8206, K8208, K8210-K8212, K8214, K8215, K8217 became 2352M, 2354M, 2289M, 2353M, 1147M, 2459M, 1679M, 1675M, 2392M, 2295M, 2294M, 2292M, 1673M, 1691M, 1690M, 1692M, 1689M, 1685M, 1688M, 2269M, 1234M, 2349M.	
K8218-K8306	**Hawker Fury II**	**89**
	Kestrel VDR. Built by General Aircraft. K8218, K8225-K8227, K8229-K8233, K8235, K8237-K8240, K8242, K8246-K8250, K8252, K8254-K8256, K8259, K8261, K8262, K8264-K8269 became 1912M, 1731M, 1715M, 1725M, 1730M, 1716M, 1729M, 1726M, 1717M, 1195M, 1733M, 1920M, 1918M, 1910M, 1740M, 1948M, 1546M, 1553M, 1547M, 1734M, 1712M, 1913M, 1737M, 1823M, 1741M, 1710M, 1705M, 1914M, 1707M-1709M, 1742M, 1727M and K8272, K8273, K8275, K8276, K8278-K8281, K8283-K8288, K8290-K8293, K8295-K8299, K8303-K8306 became 1552M, 1644M, 1711M, 1548M, 1714M, 1551M, 1643M, 1549M, 1720M, 1721M, 1915M, 1722M, 1724M, 1718M, 1824M, 1847M, 1919M, 1704M, 1735M, 1550M, 1728M, 1723M, 1713M, 1916M, 1706M, 1909M, 1736M.	
K8307-K8308	**General Aircraft Monospar ST.25 Jubilee**	**2**
	Evaluated at RAE. K8308 became G-AHBK.	
K8309	**Hawker Hotspur**	**1**
	Prototype to Spec F9/35.	
K8310	**Boulton Paul Defiant**	**1**
	BP Type P.82. Prototype to Spec F9/35, became 2783M.	
K8311-K8335	**Hawker Audax I**	**25**
	Westland contract sub-let to Avro. K8323 became 1174M. K8313, K8314, K8316, K8318, K8330, K8333 to the SAAF 1940-42.	
K8336-K8337	**DH.82 Tiger Moth floatplanes**	**2**
	Delivered 1936. K8336, K8337 became 1506M and 1505M in 1939.	
K8338-K8345	**Supermarine Walrus I**	**8**
	Delivered 1936.	
K8346-K8449	**Fairey Swordfish I**	**104**
	C/n F.2528-F.2631. Wheel or float u/c.	
K8450-K8519	**Blackburn Shark II**	**70**
	Blackburn T.9A. K8457, K8459, K8461, K8462, K8502, K8505, K8517 converted to TT. K8450-K8452, K8475, K8479, K8500 became 1457M-1459M, 1127M, 1456M, 1462M.	
K8520-K8536	**Vickers Wellesley**	**17**
	K8534, K8536 became 1092M, 1066M.	
K8537-K8564	**Supermarine Walrus**	**28**
	K8563 became 1071M.	
K8565-K8568	**Short Singapore III**	**4**
	C/n S.852-S.855. K8567 became —?—M.	
K8569-K8617	**Fairey Seafox I**	**49**
	C/n F.2267-F.2315. Delivered for catapult flights.	
K8618-K8619	**DH.91 Albatross**	**2**
	C/n 6800, 6801 ex E2, E5 registered G-AEVV, 'AEVW for temporary evaluation, eventually impressed as AX903, AX904.	
K8620	**Boulton Paul Defiant**	**1**
	BP Type 82. Second prototype.	
K8621	**Hawker Hotspur**	**(1)**
	Second prototype not built.	
K8622-K8623	**Fairey F9/35**	**(2)**
	Prototypes, not built.	
K8624	**Armstrong Whitworth AW.30**	**(1)**
	To Spec F9/35, not built.	
K8625	**Gloster F34/35**	**(1)**
	Project not built.	
K8626	**Miles Hawk Major**	**1**
	For evaluation. Became 1081M.	
K8627-K8631	**Hawker Hart (India)**	**5**
	Kestrel 1B engine. Delivered to No.39 Squadron.	
K8632-K8673	**DH.82B Queen Bee**	**42**
	C/n 5165-5206. K8673 became 1182M.	
K8674-K8702	**Westland Wallace II**	**29**
	K8674-K8677, K8679, K8680, K8698, K8700, K8701 became 1697M, 1698M, 1491M, 1545M, 2440M, 2506M, 2367M, 2112M, 2537M.	

24 From 1917 the large rigid airships known by number, had this marked large in black fore and aft as shown.

Eta Early balloons and airships carried no identity markings, their names or numbers being allotted for accounting purposes. This airship, *Eta*, became No.20.

R27 From No.26 onwards, rigid airships were given their R for Rigid prefix to their numbers. Other standard markings were the nose and amidships roundel and striped tail.

R33 Double identity for the civilianised R33 which also carries the civil registration (barely discernable) G-FAAG in lieu of an amidships roundel.

NS11 North Sea Class blimps bore their numbers large in black on the side of their envelopes, plus further representation under the nose.

R34 Sister to R33, the R34 remained on RAF charge as the nose roundel indicates. R34's number was marked higher on the envelope than on other airships.

BE2 The type designation is also its official identity number in the case of this early Royal Aircraft Factory aeroplane which has RAF marked above its designation. Pilot is Geoffrey de Havilland.

SSZ25 By 1918 it was usual for all blimp cabs to have their identity marked on the side, as in the case of SSZ25 shown.

RE1 Marked RE1, its original identity, this aircraft has its newly allotted serial 607 marked in very small digits beneath the designation.

T.5 An example of pre-joint serialling. This Short tractor biplane later became just 5 under the joint serialling system.

28 What might easily be mistaken for a military serial is the Military Trials Number allotted to this Handley Page monoplane which bears its firm's monogram.

219 With Bleriot Type IX monoplanes in service it will be seen that with such aircraft the rudder alone gave a vertical area suitable for placing its identity.

326 From the early days the Sopwith Aviation Company adopted the styling of placing the official number in black on a white painted rectangle.

993 Variations in marking serials on the rudder are evident in this early WWI shot of aircraft of the Royal Naval Air Service.

424 While serials continued to be displayed on the rudder, size and style varied on aircraft of the RFC.

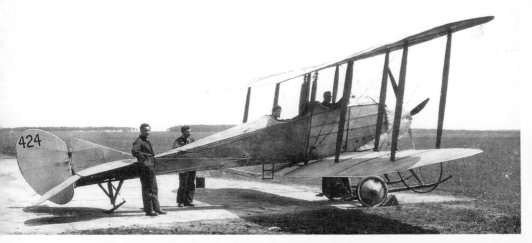

2480 When rudder striping was introduced in March 1915, the fin then became a more appropriate area on which to mark the serial.

4962 For clarity most manufacturers outlined in white the black digits on the red and blue portions of the rudder striping.

5127 When black serials were marked on the fin after PC10 dark green/brown camouflage doping was introduced in 1916, some manufacturers outlined all the characters in white.

4606 AMC producing DH designs marked serials over just two of the three rudder stripes, but in photos black did not contrast with red and so the 06 of 4606 is lost to view.

10000 The only time five figures have ever appeared in a serial was for No.10,000. Blackburn using the fin for their trademark, marked the number on the rear fuselage.

8416 With the introduction of rudder striping Hewlett & Blondeau took to marking the serial mid-fuselage on clear-doped panels.

1724 Anomolies continually occur in serial marking. Henry Farmans bore their numbers on their nacelles, but in this case the A of A1724 has been omitted.

1785 Anomolies abound, no fuselage roundel, serial placed almost mid-fuselage and without its A prefix.

A3064 The serial of this BE.2 has been scratched on to the negative and shows presentation details of the Maharajah who donated the money for the aircraft.

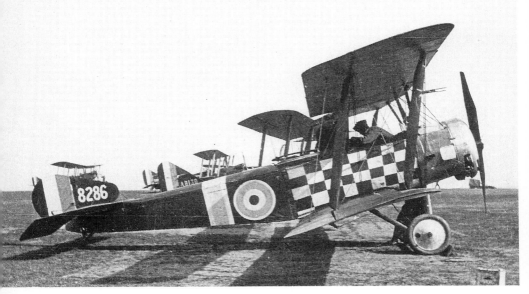

A3433 The small fin of the RE.8 led to a cramped serial presentation with the prefix letter above the number.

A3340 Their number was up - victims of Manfred von Richthofen who attempted to keep tangible evidence of his aerial victories.

C4 etc Here the numbers are rearranged in the Richtofen Room of his residence in Schweidnitz, they show the difference in style variations.

A2725 Armstrong Whitworth made full use of the large fin of their FK.8s to display the serial both large and artistically.

A8286 When aircraft were given fancy finishes in service and serials were re-marked, things could go wrong such as leaving out the prefix letter.

B7775 Another Farnborough rebuild with a most pronounced apostrophe between letter and number.

This famous photograph of No.1 Squadron personnel and craft, taken at Clairmarais near St Omer in France in July 1918, clearly shows the variation in size and style of serial presentation on their SE.5As.

Captions for the four photographs below appear in the nearest column on the opposite page.

B'763 Marked B'763 with an apostrophe because it has been rebuilt at the Royal Aircraft Factory, Farnborough, this Bristol Scout also bears the McCook Field number P32 in the USA.

A/6901 The Sopwith rectangular box for serial marking applied only to Sopwith factory products, not to the many more Sopwith aircraft built by other manufacturers.

C-4823 Like Armstrong Whitworth, the British & Colonial Aeroplane Company marked serials large and clear on the ample area provided by the fins of Bristol Fighters.

C4288 Classic Sopwith factory styling on a white box. The small CD marked on the fin and rudder relate to the finish of the aircraft to Cellon D-scheme doping.

This Dolphin prototype, at Brooklands for trials, clearly displays the 'Sopwith Box' which awaits the application of the serial number.

C5194 Mid-fuselage serial presentation on this DH.6 produced by the Kingsbury Aviation Company.

C5464 Another anomoly with serial presentation on DH.6s, in this case a small white band over the rudder stripping.

C.6908 A full stop between letter and number was often applied but never decreed. Fuselage inscription reads 'HOFOOK - HONG KONG'.

C.9636 Strangely large aircraft like Handley Page O/400s usually had serials applied smaller than on other aircraft and at the extreme end of the fuselage, C.9636 in this case.

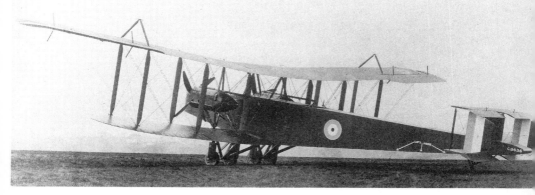

D5816 D5816 presented in cramped form on a DH.9 built by Waring & Gillow in light blue-grey panelling and khaki/brown doping finish. Number 5816 also applied with a 'V/2' prefix below the Scarff Ring.

D4170 The Australian Flying Corps were allotted aircraft from RFC and later, RAF sources, so normal British serial markings were applied to their aircraft.

D16 A quirk of serial presentation on aircraft built by A.V. Roe was the presentation of the prefix letter smaller than the digits.

E8015 Although built in the Sopwith works, this Snipe has its serial marked on the fin.

E2627 Late in 1918 it became usual to double-bank serials by placing them both over the rudder striping and at the rear of the fuselage.

E8553 Later in Airco's DH.9A production batch, serials also appeared on the rear fuselage.

E43 A Siddeley-Deasy built RE8 with its black serial outlined in white on the dark finish.

E8407 Right to the last AMC, known in its later stages as Airco, marked serials over the last two stripes on the rudder instead of a centralised presentation used by other manufacturers.

ER8728 Many of the older DH.9As built to wartime contracts were rebuilt in the Middle East in the '20s for which an R was added to the prefix letter.

F-2699 Military serials were retained as civil identities in 1919 prior to the official registration letter scheme when this DH.4A became G-EAHF.

E.9665 Yet another variation in serial presentation with the prefix letter off-centre and stops after the letter.

F.1946 From 1st October 1918 all Avro 504K trainers were to have serials marked under their wings, which was extended to all aircraft at training units including this Australian Flying Corps Camel.

F5417 A Handley Page O/400 well labelled with its military serial presented as a provisional civil registration.

F4337 F4337 repaired with the rudder of C9894 giving it seemingly a dual identity.

H2581 Further examples of military serials being used as provisional civil registrations by these two Avro 504Ks modified to 504Ls.

G144 A captured Albatros is given its intelligence record G-number by its newly marked roundel.

H72 DH.9As in service overseas, originally delivered in dark finishes were re-doped 'silver' with some variations in serial styling but were generally consistent in serial sizing.

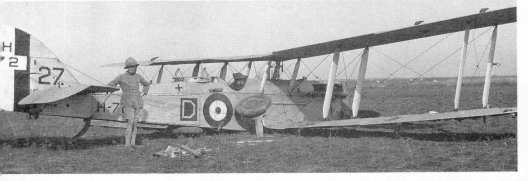

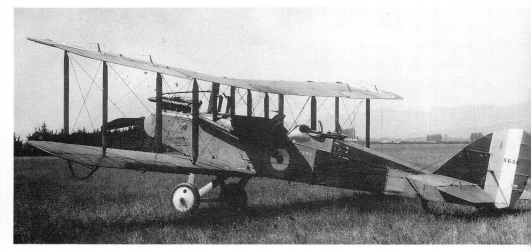

5636 Ex-RAF DH.9s used by the New Zealand Permanent Air Force retained their original number but not the prefix letter, so that just 5636 of H5636 is marked small by the roundel and on the rudder.

H7004 A small serial marking on the night fighter version of the Sopwith Camel in order not to compromise its night camouflage.

JR6904 A larger than usual serial on this Vernon and also longer than usual by the introduction of the R for Re-built.

J7960 Against regulations the zig-zag squadron markings of No.17 Squadron compromised the fuselage serial and the prefix letter is missing from the rudder presentation on this Woodcock.

J1937 Into the J-series and still Airco persist with their off-centre serial presentation on the rudder striping.

J6982 A larger and stylised serial presentation on an early Armstrong Whitworth Siskin.

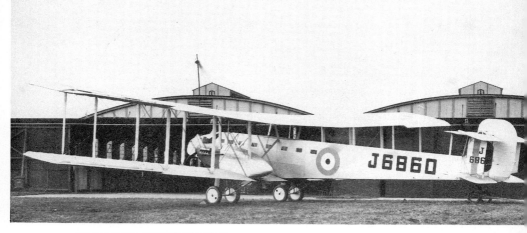

J6860 A good example of a wrongly painted serial. J6860 was actually a Vickers Victoria, but is seen here on an Armstrong Whitworth Awana, which should be either J6897 or J6898. (R.Bonser)

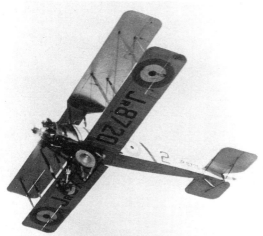

JR-8720 Unusual, but to indicate that the R for Rebuilt was not really part of the serial number, it is marked half-size on this Avro 504N.

J7275 From March 1927 the rule for displaying serials under the wings was extended to all RAF aircraft.

J-8792 By the late '20s markings of serials had been regularised but Armstrong Whitworth still continued to hyphenate fuselage serials.

J9740 Some Wapitis saw service in WWII, and by that time their serials had been repainted several times, but presentation remained constant.

K-1300 In No.27 Squadron the role of the aircraft, according to being fitted for bombing or army co-operation, was denoted by B or AC in small letters by the fuselage serial.

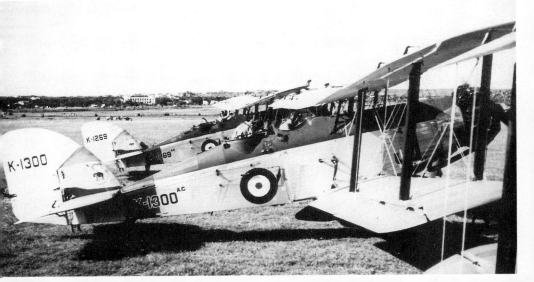

K3908 When the Wallace followed the Wapiti from the Westland works, the company persisted with their stops after the prefix letter and the number.

K3661 Fleet Air Arm aircraft often omitted the serials on their rear fuselages because the fleet fuselage colour band took up too much space.

K3086 On No.2 Squadron aircraft, serials were marked over their red triangle unit marking.

K4712 A Vincent in camouflage post-1938 shows that the serialling position and size remains as before, still in black.

K4303 In addition to its serial number this prototype Fairey Battle bears the New Types Park No.4 for the 1936 RAF Display at Hendon.

K4134 This Vincent conforms to the standard serial presentation of the pre-1938 period.

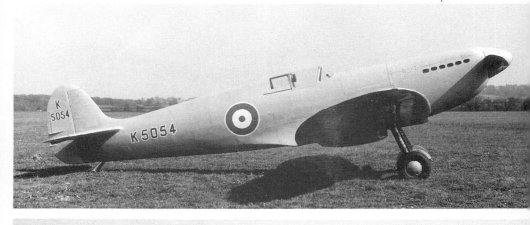

K5054 How the famous prototype Spitfire was marked; serials in black outlined in white on the pale blue finish with the rudder serial marking smaller than standard.

K5737 Biplane fighter underwing serial presentation of the 'thirties shown by Hawker Demon K5737.

K6085 With early camouflage on tails and fuselage decking, the rudder serial was sometimes marked in white to contrast.

K6159 Someone got it wrong about serial markings on the wings and marked the number on the wing uppersurfaces of some Ansons.

K6409 Resplendent uniformity in the marking of serials on these Vildebeests of No.42 Squadron.

K7279 In No.25 Squadron their black fuselage marking phased in neatly with the aircraft's serial number.

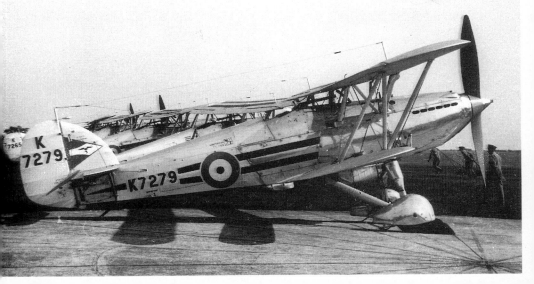

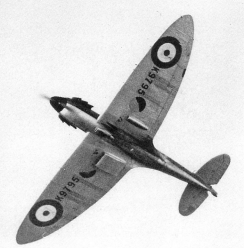

K7557 Bristol 142 'Britain First', a presentation aircraft taken on charge and serialled, seen here as New Types Park No.5 at the 1936 Hendon Display.

K9795 The underwing display of serials on early Spitfires was inordinately small, as seen here.

K9755 As with their Audax, so with their Hectors, the serial number marked over the red triangle marking of No.2 Squadron.

L1732 A patch behind the serial to contrast was not unusual, but in this case it is to 'deaden' the presentation of L1732.

L2052 Since unit code letters (501 Sqn in this case) were placed before the roundel it often meant that on the starboard side code letters and serial clashed.

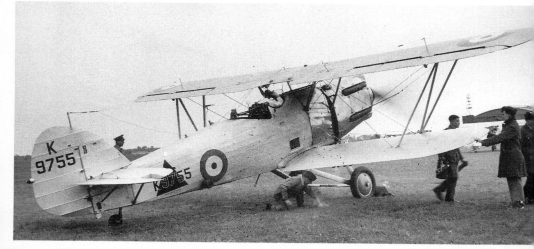

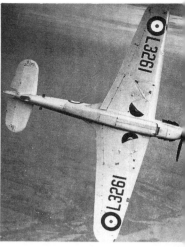

L2101 Unlike early Spitfires, underwing presentation of serials on Hurricanes was relatively large.

L3261 A neat full-view shot of underwing serial presentation on a Hawker Henley with its retracting wheels conditioning the markings to well outboard.

L7233 A Hawker Hind in trainer yellow with top surfaces camouflages goes into ATC service for ground instruction with No.1051 (Dartford Borough) Squadron, ATC.

N59 A characteristic of the flying boats built for the Services by Supermarine was the large presentation of the serial on the rear hull.

N129 In this case the rudder presentation of the serial has the prefix letter in line. Fairey c/n can be seen adjacent to the fuselage serial.

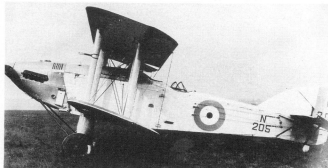

N220 On the racing floatplanes of the RAF serials were displayed only on the rudder to leave the fuselage clear for their allotted contest numbers.

N205 Unusual is the presentation of the fuselage serial with the prefix letter above the number as in the normal rudder marking.

N2233 N2233 retains its British identity number and Fairey c/n in Red Air Force service indicated by the red star in a white circle replacing the roundel.

N9730 Anomalies abound in FAA serial presentation. Here N9730 (left) has just a fuselage serial marked while N9632 has this conventionally on fuselage and the rudder.

N9926 All five Flycatchers of this flight have serials marked on their rudders, but only N9926 displays it on the fuselage.

N1030 RAF serial N1030 is retained by this Beaufort of No.149 (TB) Sqn, RCAF seen 18th June 1943 at Patricia Bay, British Colombia. (Public Archives of Canada).

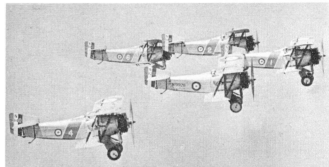

P2277 So small you could hardly see, let alone read, the serial P2277 on the rear fuselage of this Fairey Battle trainer.

N3117 Even the serial number is in light paint on this white photographic reconnaissance Spitfire based in France 1939-40.

P7110 When the fighter band was introduced around the rear fuselage the placing of serial numbers on Whirlwinds was moved forward to clear it.

K8703-K8845	**Avro 652A Anson I**	**143**

Diverted from contract: K8738-K8740 became AN101-AN103 of Finnish AF; K8741 became 158 of Estonian AF; K8792-K8812, K8840-K8844 became A4-13 to A4-38 of the RAAF. K8705, K8715, K8716, K8758, K8765, K8771, K8776, K8822, K8838 became 1291M, 4429M, 2851M, 2522M, 4427M, 2634M, 4421M, 2317M, 4426M. K8706, K8709, K8713, K8714, K8724, K8726, K8727, K8729, K8730, K8734, K8743, K8745, K8748, K8751-K8753, K8756, K8760, K8761, K8770, K8774, K8775, K8777, K8782, K8786, K8814, K8818, K8820, K8824, K8830 to RCAF 1940-41. K8725, K8737, K8742, K8747, K8762, K8768, K8787, K8815, K8821, K8832, K8839 to SAAF 1940-41.

K8846-K8847	**Airspeed AS.27 Irving**	**(2)**

Biplanes, not built.

K8848-K8852	**Vickers Valentia**	**5**

K8850 radio trainer at Cranwell, rest went overseas, K8851 to the SAAF 1940.

K8853	**Hendy Heck IIC**	**1**

Built by Parnall, ex-G-AEGL. Became 3125M.

K8854-K8855	**Supermarine Sea Otter**	**2**

Prototype to Spec S7/38. K8855 destroyed in works during 1940.

K8856-K8859	**Short S.19 Singapore III**	**4**

C/n S.856-S.859. Delivered 1937, all disposed of by February 1941.

K8860-K8886	**Fairey Swordfish I**	**27**

C/n F.2632-F.2658.

K8887-K8888	**Airspeed AS.30 Queen Wasp**	**2**

Prototype to Q32/35.

K8889-K8890	**Percival P.8**	**(2)**

Prototypes to Spec Q32/35. Cancelled.

K8891-K8935	**Blackburn Shark III**	**45**

Blackburn T.9B. K8896, K8898, K8899, K8901-K8903, K8909, K8910, K8923, K8926, K8927, K8929, K8931, K8933 converted for TT. K8895, K8906, K8929 became 1451M, 1867M, 3490M.

K8936-K9175	**Armstrong Whitworth AW.38 Whitley III/IV**	**120(240)**

C/n 1389-1508. K8936-K9015 (80) Mk.III, K9016-K9055 (40) Mk.IV. K9056-K9175 cancelled. K8939, K8949, K8951, K8953-K8955, K8959, K8962, K8971, K8979, K8980, K8983, K8992, K9009, K9011, K9023, K9049 became 1927M, 3340M, 3293M, 4112M, 3342M, 1926M, 3343M, 3445M, 3120M, 3446M, 4113M, 3142M, 3294M, 3338M, 3341M, 3302M, 3296M. K8985 interned in Belgium in 1939.

K9176-K9675	**Fairey Battle I**	**311(500)**

Merlin II engines. C/n F.2471-F.2515, F.2809-F.3074. K9222 Exe, K9240 Dagger VIII, K9257 Merlin X, K9331 Taurus II, K9370 P24 Prince, K9477 Peregrine test-beds. K9487-K9675 cancelled. K9179, K9196, K9209, K9220, K9234-K9237, K9239-K9241, K9257, K9260, K9261, K9287, K9301, K9305, K9313-K9315, K9334-K9336, K9354, K9360, K9363, K9364, K9373, K9418, K9438, K9482 became 1126M, 1196M, 2553M, 1835M, 1833M, 1834M, 1321M, 1471M, 1836M, 2213M, 1449M, 1437M, 1472M, 1189M, 1326M, 2438M, 1353M, 1837M, 1838M, 1293M, 1354M, 1292M, 2434M, 1869M, 1839M-1842M, 1651M, 2431M, 2432M, 1322M. K9206, K9219, K9227, K9228, K9232, K9262, K9282, K9290, K9291, K9297, K9322-K9324, K9346, K9362, K9368, K9371, K9375, K9380, K9388, K9393, K9411, K9422, K9426, K9429, K9435, K9442-K9444, K9447, K9464, K9468, K9478, K9486 to the RAAF 1940-43. K9178, K9182, K9187, K9190, K9191, K9194, K9203, K9204, K9210-K9215, K9217, K9225, K9229, K9231, K9233, K9244, K9247, K9248, K9250, K9253, K9255, K9258, K9265, K9268, K9272, K9274, K9275, K9281, K9284, K9288, K9292, K9298, K9299, K9300, K9303, K9304, K9307, K9309, K9311, K9312, K9316, K9317, K9321, K9326, K9332, K9341, K9344, K9350, K9351, K9355, K9358, K9365, K9376, K9378, K9379, K9382, K9395, K9399, K9401, K9403, K9405-K9408, K9413, K9414, K9417, K9421, K9423-K9425, K9427, K9431, K9436, K9439, K9449, K9451, K9453-K9459, K9461, K9462, K9465, K9466, K9474-K9476, K9479 to RCAF from 1940. K9246, K9269, K9286, K9296, K9308, K9320, K9385, K9386, K9392, K9394, K9400, K9402, K9410, K9415, K9432, K9446, K9460, K9471 to SAAF 1939-43.

K9676-K9681	**Supermarine Stranraer**	**(6)**

Order cancelled.

K9682-K9686	**Saro A.27 London II**	**5**

Delivered from September 1937.

K9687-K9786	**Hawker Hector**	**100**

Built by Westland. K9688, K9691-K9694, K9700, K9701, K9705, K9709, K9710, K9717, K9720, K9722, K9732, K9739, K9750, K9777, K9786 became 2406M, 2356M, 2418M, 1173M, 2408M, 2414M, 2411M, 2409M, 2410M, 2413M, 2338M, 2412M, 2417M, 2208M, 1612M, 2871M, 2357M, 2415M. K9697, K9715, K9725, K9761 became 85, 87, 86, 90 of the Irish Air Corps.

K9787-K9999	**Supermarine Spitfire I**	**213 of 310**

First production Spitfires, order continues in L series following. First 174 Merlin II engines, remainder Merlin III. Conversions: K9787, K9906 PRI; K9788, K9825, K9830 Mk.II; K9834 PRI & III and N-17 'Special Spitfire' project; K9871 Mk.Vc. K9789, K9795, K9798, K9800, K9806, K9808, K9812, K9820, K9822, K9829, K9831, K9833, K9837, K9839, K9843, K9845, K9855, K9859, K9866, K9872, K9876, K9881, K9895 became 3594M, 2867M, 1494M, 3277M, 1638M, 1238M, 1382M, 1361M, 1357M, 3200M, 1362M, 2573M, 1628M, 2868M, 3229M, 1479M, 1646M, 1825M, 1428M, 1450M, 4384M, 3215M, 4868M and K9913, K9918, K9921, K9934, K9955, K9983, K9998 became 1632M, 2768M, 2457M, 3083M, 3276M, 3275M, 2822M. K9828, K9991 to Portugal 1943. All were used in home service except K9873 shipped via Port Sudan to Egypt. K9942 is currently preserved in the RAF Museum.

Blackout Blocks Introduced

L1000 to L9999

'L' prefixes followed on alphabetically from 'K', and the actual carry-over came in the middle of the initial production order for Spitfires. A major change occurred after L7272. Hitherto, numbers had been allotted in direct numerical sequence, but from there onwards allocations for production orders were broken down into batches of between 10 and 50 numbers in runs, with unused numbers, known as 'blackout blocks', in between. This system continued throughout the war and ever since.

Serial Nos	Aircraft Type and Remarks	Quantity
L1000-L1096	**Supermarine Spitfire I**	**97**

Type 300. Continuation of 310 order allotted from K9787. All home service except for L1000 shipped to the Middle East 1942, L1066 intended for export to Poland and diverted to Turkey, and L1090 in USA 1939-40. Conversions: L1004 to Mk.Va and XIII, L1028, L1031, L1096 to Mk.Va. L1008, L1011, L1012, L1015, L1017, L1030, L1048, L1049, L1057, L1068, L1089, L1090, L1092 became 3242M, 3236M, 3223M, 3253M, 3206M, 2823M, 3248M, 3876M, 2644M, 3259M, 3178M, 3201M, 3230M.

L1097-L1546	**Bristol 142M Blenheim I**	**450**

C/n 8380-8813, 8816-8831. L1431 offset direct to the SAAF, returned as AX683. L1424 became prototype Mk.IF. L1242 tricycle u/c trials. L1066 intended for export to L1489, L1493, L1497 sold to Turkey 1939. L1345, L1347, L1354, L1362 to Finland 1940. L1118, L1121, L1136, L1143, L1144, L1150, L1152, L1159, L1165, L1167, L1182, L1186, L1199 became 2654M, 3782M, 1233M, 1136M, 1227M, 1116M, 3146M, 2638M, 1455M, 3542M, 1184M, 3538M, 1342M; L1206, L1225, L1230, L1231, L1241, L1253, L1255, L1266, L1269, L1273, L1276, L1277, L1281, L1288 became 2974M, 4013M, 3993M, 3786M, 1635M, 4125M, 4314M, 3250M, 3423M,

3208M, 4040M, 3758M, 2727M, 3738M; L1310, L1311,
L1320, L1344, L1361, L1364, L1367, L1372, L1398
became 2642M, 3787M, 3537M, 3540M, 3687M,
1470M, 2650M, 3187M, 1486M; L1400, L1419, L1420,
L1430, L1436, L1447, L1450, L1451, L1455-L1457,
L1460, L1461, L1467, L1473, L1474, L1478, L1480,
L1510, L1511, L1522 became 3424M, 3218M, 1886M,
3785M, 1648M, 1352M, 3169M, 3686M, 1355M, 1360M,
3243M, 1892M, 1483M, 2652M, 3497M, 3231M, 3484M,
2880M, 1637M, 2180M, 3975M.

L1547-L2146   Hawker Hurricane   600
Merlin II/III engines. First Hurricane production batch.
L1652 crashed on initial test. Direct off-sets: L1708,
L1710, L1711, L1874-L1876, L1909 to SAAF; L1751,
L1752, L1837-L1840, L1858-L1863 to Yugoslav AF
nos 205, 206, 291-294, 312-317; L1759-L1763, L1878-
L1888, L2021-L2023 RCAF nos 310-329;
L1918-L1920, L1993-L1997, L2040-L2044, L2105-
L2111 Belgian AF nos. 1-20; L2015-L2017, L2019,
L2024, L2025, L2027-L2033, L2125-L2139 to Turkish
AF; L2077, L2078, L2085, L2093-L2097, L2104,
L2112-L2114 to Romanian AF; L2079 Iran AF no.252.
Development aircraft: L1695 armament; L1702 first
with Merlin III; L1884 (RCAF 321) Hillson FH40 slip-
wing Hurricane; L1980 first with VP airscrew. Conversions:
L1895, L2014, L2039, L2086 to Sea Hurricane; L1562,
L1581, L1596, L1636, L1658, L1684, L1769, L1807,
L1824, L1831, L1836, L1989, L2099, Mk.IIA were
renumbered DR344, BV157, DG618, DG640, DG622,
DR354, DR359, DG628, DG625, DG642, DG636,
DG649, DG637; L1548, L1551-L1554, L1559-L1561,
L1568, L1575, L1597 became 3273M, 2307M, 2643M,
1430M, 1493M, 1359M, 1191M, 1368M, 4534M, 1380M,
1242M; L1600, L1602-L1604, L1621, L1622, L1625,
L1627, L1634, L1643, L1648, L1650, L1651, L1656,
L1657, L1659, L1660, L1663, L1672, L1675, L1677,
L1683, L1691, L1697, L1698 became 4862M, 1703M,
1181M, 1468M, 1431M, 1237M, 1370M, 2524M, 1358M,
1474M, 1364M, 1365M, 1215M, 1232M, 2834M, 3222M,
3587M, 4501M, 1466M, 1426M, 1226M, 3589M, 1373M,
3202M, 3174M; L1701, L1727, L1731, L1735, L1745,
L1750, L1754, L1780, L1783-L1786, L1791, L1795,
L1798 became 3586M, 3368M, 2797M, 1363M, 1439M,
2637M, 1424M, 3441M, 3084M, 3285M, 2141M, 2741M,
2172M, 1388M, 3576M; L1809, L1810, L1814, L1818,
L1867, L1869, L1873 became 1442M, 1454M, 3579M,
2577M, 1843M, 1467M, 3244M, 2984M; L1903, L1910,
L1929, L1952, L1957, L1969, L1999 became 1884M,
4321M, 3086M, 3369'. 3274M, 3672M, 2466M; L2006,
L2010, L2018, L2020, L2046, L2067, L2084, L2098,
L2101, L2102 became 4343M, 1611M, 3194M, 2160M,
3573M, 3581M, 3575M, 3193M, 3582M, 3592M.
L1606 became G-AFKX and L1592 is currently
preserved.

L2147-L2157   Saro A.33   (11)
To Spec 21/36. Cancelled.

L2158-L2168   Short S.25 Sunderland I   11
C/n S.860-S.870. L2160, L2162 became 3372M and
L2162/G.

L2169-L2336   Supermarine Walrus I   168
L2301-L2303 offset to Eire. L2186, L2192, L2203,
L2215, L2270, L2272 became 1241M, 1325M, 1188M,
1340M, 1338M, 1339M. L2318, L2319 to RAN, L2222,
L2236, L2285 to RNZAF.

L2337-L2386   Blackburn Shark III   50
Blackburn T.9B. L2374 became 1752M.

L2387-L2636   DH.93 Don   50(250)
From L2437 cancelled. 50 built of which only 28 were
fully completed and those were grounded in March 1939.
L2391 crashed on trials. L2387-L2390, L2392-L2399,
L2400-L2416, L2426, L2427 became 1259M-1261M,
1284M-1286M, 1276M, 1279M, 1282M, 1262M, 1283M,
1280M, 1278M, 1281M, 1267M, 1277M, 1268M, 1263M,
1269M, 1264M-1266M, 1275M, 1270M, 3356M, 1271M-
1274M, 2563M, 2564M.

L2637-L2716   Vickers Wellesley   80
L2637-L2639, L2680, L2681 modified for the Long
Range Development Unit; rest, apart from L2716,
shipped to Middle East. L2638, L2657 became 1856M,
4723M.

L2717-L2866   Fairey Swordfish I   150
C/n F.2659-F.2808. L2840 fitted for RP testing, L2747
for long range. L2761 became 1356M.

L2867-L3056   Blackburn Skua   190
Type DB1A. Sole production to Spec 25/36. L2888,
L2973-L2986 converted to TT after trials on L3006.
L2869, L2870, L2871 became 1200M, 1201M, 1294M.

L3057-L3192   Blackburn Roc   136
Type B-25. Built by Boulton Paul as landplanes except
L3057, L3059, L3060, L3074 floatplanes. L3071,
L3072, L3075, L3079, L3082, L3083, L3085, L3089,
L3118, L3126, L3127, L3129, L3131, L3132, L3143,
L3146, L3149, L3162, L3172, L3173, L3175, L3179,
L3190 converted to TT. L3057, L3111, L3122 became
2436M, 2559M, 3264M.

L3193-L3242   Hawker Hart   (50)
Cancelled Avro order.

L3243-L3642   Hawker Henley   200(400)
Built by Gloster. First 100 Merlin II, second 100 Merlin
III, remainder cancelled. L3302 Vulture and L3414
Griffon II test-beds. L3441 only tropicalised. Bulk
converted to TT. L3283, L3355, L3392, L3407, L3417,
L3421, L3430 became 4458M, 4441M, 2381M, 4459M,
2158M, 4440M, 4674M.

L3643-L4031   Hawker Hotspur   (389)
Avro order cancelled.

L4032-L4211   Handley Page HP.52 Hampden I   180
First Hampden production order. L4032 experimentally
fitted with Wright Cyclones. L4108, L4141, L4144,
L4145, L4170, L4201 converted to TB1. L4032, L4033,
L4130, L4139, L4153, L4177, L4181, L4206 became
2711M, 2782M, 1647M, 2170M, 1888M, 1883M, 2165M,
2166M. L4157 to RCAF and L4208-L4211 to Canada
as pattern aircraft of which L4210, L4211 returned to
the RAF.

L4212-L4391   Vickers Wellington   175(180)
Type 290. First Wellington production order. L4312-
L4316 not delivered. L4250 prototype Mk.II (Type
298), then fitted with 40mm cannon in dorsal position
and finally modified with twin fins. L4251 prototype
Mk.III (Type 299). L4255 became an ambulance.
L4244 converted to transport for RN. L4212, L4221,
L4227, L4356, L4358, L4374 converted to DW1. L4212,
L4213, L4218, L4221, L4225, L4229, L4234, L4238,
L4242, L4245, L4247, L4249-L4251, L4269, L4271-
L4273, L4277-L4279, L4284, L4287, L4292, L4293,
L4295 became 2937M, 2720M, 3119M, 2451M, 2773M,
3122M, 2721M, 1625M, 2557M, 3420M, 3419M, 3044M,
3477M, 2795M, 2775M, 3048M, 2875M, 3421M, 3040M,
2719M, 2985M, 2718M, 3051M, 2657M, 3105M, 2774M,
and L4307, L4309, L4311, L4317, L4325, L4327,
L4329, L4330, L4332, L4334, L4337, L4341, L4342,
L4351-L4353, L4359, L4365, L4368, L4370, L4373,
L4377, L4386, L4389 became 2772M, 3043M, 3037M,
3047M, 3138M, 3039M, 3038M, 2686M, 3543M, 3305M,
3046M, 3049M, 3041M, 3123M, 2426M, 3045M, 3136M,
3050M, 3306M, 3628M, 2792M, 2771M, 3137M, 3042M.

L4392-L4436   Miles M.16 Mentor I   45
Military communications version of Miles Nighthawk.
L4398, L4425 became 2681M, 2145M.

L4437-L4440   (Numbers not allotted)   —

L4441-L4518   Bristol Beaufort I   78
Type 152. C/n 8302-8379. First five non-standard.
L4444 DC, L4448 to Australia as pattern, L4456
experimental modification. L4441 became 3147M.

L4519-L4533   Fairey Seafox   15
C/n F.3436-F.3450. For Royal Navy.

L4534-L4669   Airspeed AS.10 Oxford I   136
L4556, L4557, L4592, L4593, L4610 offset to RNZAF
to become NZ250-NZ254. L4538 became G-AFFM and
L4539 was fitted with McLaren u/c. L4543, L4545,
L4548, L4551, L4555, L4561-L4563, L4566, L4572,
L4585, L4586 became 3840M, 3827M, 3808M, 3830M,
3828M, 3829M, 1239M, 4812M, 3851M, 3843M, 3814M,
2838M and L4606, L4609, L4615, L4634, L4655
became 3832M, 2122M, 3847M, 3813M, 5485M.

L4670   Dewoitine 510   1
Purchased from France for evaluation.

L4671-L4672   General Aircraft Monospar   2
Purchased for evaluation.

L4673-L4816	**Westland Lysander I/II**	**144**

Mk.I to L4738, remainder Mk.II. L4673 had twin cannon fitted. Several later converted for TT. L4674, L4682, L4691, L4692, L4697, L4701, L4704-L4706, L4708, L4733, L4753, L4757, L4781, L4790, L4792, L4800, L4805 became 3188M, 3175M, 3914M, 3283M, 2651M, 3915M, 3221M, 3220M, 3234M, 1213M, 3887M, 3937M, 1425M, 3989M, 3938M, 3932M, 3974M, 3931M. L4678, L4681, L4703 to Finland 1940. L4687 to 8th USAAF. L4807 to Free French Air Force 1942.

L4817-L4934	**Bristol Blenheim I/IV**	**118**

Types 142M/L. L4823-L4906 (84) Mk.IV, remaining 34 Mk.I. L4821, L4824, L4826, L4828 sold to Turkey 1939. L4858, L4865, L4869, L4874, L4877, L4879, L4882, L4890, L4902, L4931, L4934 became 2207M, 2777M, 2171M, 2543M, 2544M, 2873M, 2874M, 3883M, 3986M, 3535M, 3533M.

L4935-L5797	**Fairey Battle**	**863**

Built by Austin Motors. L4935-L4937 non-standard. Merlin II fitted up to L4993, then Merlin III. L5286 Sabre test-bed. L5598-L5797 produced as TTI. Majority (567) shipped for EATS from 1940 onwards mainly RAAF, RCAF & SAAF, but few to SRAF and India. L4965, L4972, L4983, L4995, L5075; L5127, L5133, L5141, L5275, L5299, L5423, L5559, L5631, L5705, L5707, L5715, L5769 became 2433M, 1441M, 1832M, 3969M, 2204M, 2210M, 2173M, 3560M, 2201M, 3556M, 3558M, 3947M, 3962M, 3961M, 3906M, 2260M, 3907M. L5623 to Turkish AF, 1940.

L5798-L5807	**Short S.25 Sunderland I**	**10**

C/n S.887-S.896.

L5808-L5887	**Bristol Bombay I**	**50(80)**

Type 130. Built by Short & Harland. C/n SH1-SH50. Last 30 of 80 ordered cancelled. L5810, L581J, L5815, L5816, L5825 DC. L5827 to RAAF in Middle East.

L5888-L5911	**DH.82B Queen Bee**	**24**

Delivered to store 1937.

L5912-L6001	**Miles Magister I**	**90**

Miles M.14. L5952, L5961 to Royal Navy 1939. L5916, L5933, L5937, L5946, L5968 became 5362M, 1199M, 6172M, 1074M, 5363M. L5987 to Turkey 1943. L5966, L5978, L5988, L5992 sold to Argentine AF postwar.

L6002-L6101	**Handley Page HP.53 Hereford I**	**100**

Built by Short & Harland c/n 81-180. L6011, L6018-L6020, L6049, L6055, L6069, L6076, L6080, L6085, L6089, L6090, L6096 converted to Hampden of which L6069 went to RCAF. L6002-L6004, L6006, L6007, L6028, L6032, L6034, L6038, L6039, L6042-L6046, L6048, L6050, L6051, L6054, L6060, L6063-L6065, L6068, L6077, L6082, L6091, L6092, L6094, L6095, L6098, L6099-L6101 became 3023M, 2800M, 2712M, 2164M, 2163M, 3024M, 3028M, 2801M, 2716M, 3020M, 3130M, 2968M, 3030M, 3031M, 3018M, 3095M, 2713M, 3029M, 2802M, 3021M, 3025M, 3026M, 2803M, 2715M, 3022M, 2717M, 3032M, 2714M, 2162M, 2969M, 3033M, 2964M, 2831M, 3027M, 2967M, 2914M, 2832M, 2753M, 2963M, 2912M, 2737M.

L6102	**Vickers Viastra X**	**1**

Type 259. G-ACCC for radio and icing tests, ex-King's Flight aircraft.

L6103	**De Bruyne DB.2 Snark**	**1**

Built by Aero Research, Duxford, as G-ADDL.

L6104-L6345	**Blackburn Botha**	**242**

Type B-26. Built at Brough. L6104, L6105 prototypes. L6129 crashed on maker's tests. L6104-L6106, L6110, L6133, L6152, L6159, L6168, L6194, L6198, L6200, L6204, L6206, L6240, L6254, L6260, L6267, L6322 became 2217M, 2479M, 2936M, 3374M, 3379M, 3365M, 3364M, 3794M, 3395M, 3378M, 3799M, 3367M, 3366M, 3376M, 3375M, 3363M, 3380M, 3739M.

L6346	**Miles M.8 Peregrine**	**1**

Acquired for boundary layer control research at RAE.

L6347-L6590	**Blackburn Botha**	**200(244)**

Type B-26. Built at Dumbarton; only L6347-L6546 completed. L6390 crashed on initial test. L6364, L6368, L6431, L6472, L6474, L6476, L6477, L6481, L6483, L6532 became 3660M, 3078M, 2571M, 3801M, 3797M, 3798M, 3796M, 3805M, 3795M, 3394M.

L6591-L6593	*(Numbers not allotted)*	**–**

L6594-L6843	**Bristol Blenheim**	**250**

Type 142M. Built by Avro. Offset from RAF delivery: L6696-L6708, L6713-L6718 to Romania; L6813, L6814, L6817-L6819, L6821-L6834 to Yugoslavia. L6594, L6596, L6619, L6626, L6640, L6644, L6673, L6675, L6711, L6736, L6737, L6749, L6759, L6775, L6778, L6787, L6791, L6797, L6811, L6842 became 1805M, 2178M, 3965M, 3534M, 4014M, 3964M, 3817M, 1701M, 3963M, 3564M, 3783M, 4044M, 3966M, 4042M, 3225M, 4041M, 3271M, 3539M, 4034M, 3170M.

L6844-L6845	**Westland P.9 Whirlwind**	**2**

Prototypes to Spec F37/35. L6844 first flew 11.10.38, became 3063M.

L6846	**Miles M.7 Nighthawk**	**1**

Instrument trainer for evaluation, became 1587M.

L6847-L6888	**Westland Lysander II**	**42**

L6869 to FFAF. L6850, L6866, L6873 became 3928M, 3944M, 3933M.

L6889-L6890	**Supermarine B12/36**	**(2)**

Prototypes destroyed by bombs at Woolston before completion 26.9.40.

L6891-L6893	**Blackburn B.2**	**3**

Ex-G-AEBM, 'AEBN, 'AEBO purchased 1937, became 3158M, 3159M, 3877M.

L6894-L6919	**Miles M.14 Magister I**	**24(26)**

L6914, L6917 not built. L6909-L6913 initially non-standard M.14B with Cirrus Major instead of Gipsy Major engines. L6905 became 5360M.

L6920-L6949	**DH.82 Tiger Moth I**	**30**

Purchased from civil production. L6922, L6930, L6941 became 4464M, 6993M, 2491M.

L6950-L7036	**Boulton Paul Defiant I**	**87**

BP Type P.82. First production batch. Merlin III engines fitted. Some conversions to TT. L6950, L6951, L6956, L6962, L6964, L6976, L6979, L6983, L6984, L6987-L6990, L6993, L6997, L7000, L7008, L7012, L7014, L7019, L7022, L7024, L7030, L7033, L7036 became 2980M, 3210M, 3199M, 3009M, 3182M, 3171M, 3240M, 3198M, 3284M, 3279M, 3251M, 3281M, 3280M, 3196M, 3197M, 3263M, 3282M, 3227M, 3212M, 3181M, 3172M, 3211M, 3262M, 3278M, 3226M.

L7037	**Bristol 138B**	**1**

Rolls-Royce Merlin. To Spec 2/34 but not flown, became 2339M.

L7038-L7043	**Saro A.27 London II**	**6**

L7044	**Fairchild 24**	**1**

Purchased in USA for use of British Air Attache, Washington.

L7045	**Fairey Fantome**	**1**

C/n F.3451 acquired for evaluation 1937.

L7046-L7073	**Avro 652M Anson I**	**28**

Replacement order for offsets from earlier orders. L7050 became 1384M. L7048, L7051, L7053, L7055, L7063, L7073 to SAAF, 1941. L7054, L7056, L7060, L7062, L7070 to RCAF 1940-41.

L7074-L7173	**Fairey Albacore**	**100**

C/n F.3274-F.3373. L7074 prototype landplane, L7075 trials as floatplane. L7166 became 2588M.

L7174-L7243	**Hawker Hind (LB) & (T)**	**70**

Final production of Hart variants for RAF. L7174-L7223 (50) built as light bombers of which a number were converted to trainers by General Aircraft in 1938. L7224-L7243 (20) built as trainers. L7183, L7189, L7201, L7215, L7222, L7237, L7243 became 2869M, 2870M, 2229M, 1389M, 1257M, 1108M, 2699M. L7205 allotted 1383M but reverted. L7178 sold to India in 1939. L7180, L7181, L7191 to Afghan AF 1939. L7175, L7177, L7179, L7186, L7196, L7197, L7203, L7209, L7213, L7229, L7230, L7232, L7234 to SAAF 1940-42. L7184, L7187, L7195, L7210, L7218, L7220, L7221, L7224, L7225 to RNZAF, 1940.

L7244-L7245	**Handley Page HP.56/57 Halifax**	**2**

Prototypes to Spec P13/36 became 3299M, 3474M. L7244 first flew 25.10.39.

L7246-L7247	**Avro 679 Manchester**	**2**

Prototypes to Spec P13/36 became 3422M, 2738M. L7246 first flew 25.7.39.

L7248-L7268	**Saro A.36 Lerwick I**	**21**

Only production batch. To Spec R1/39. L7254 became 3300M.

L7269	*(Number not allotted)*	–
L7270	**Airspeed AS.6J Envoy III**	1
	Ex-G-AEXX c/n 66 of Royal Household. Became SE-ASN June 1946.	
L7271	**Handley Page HP.53 Hereford**	1
	Prototype became 2057M.	
L7272	**Percival P.10C Vega Gull III**	1
	To British Air Attache, Buenos Aires, as G-AFWG.	
L7273-L7275	*(Numbers not used, start of blackout blocks, see section heading)*	
L7276-L7584	**Avro 679/683 Manchester I/Lancaster I**	200

L7276-L7325, L7373-L7402, L7415-L7434, L7453-L7497, L7515-L7526 (157) Manchester I of which L7517 was destroyed before delivery. L7527-L7549, L7565-L7584 (43) completed as Lancaster I. L7283, L7293, L7305, L7307, L7325, L7376, L7378, L7382, L7389, L7393, L7397, L7419, L7425, L7431, L7434, L7455, L7458, L7461, L7464, L7468, L7483, L7484, L7488, L7492 Manchesters became 3743M, 3773M, 4279M, 4118M, 3751M, 3747M, 3752M, 3753M, 3763M, 2600M, 3762M, 3748M, 3741M, 3772M, 4221M, 3742M, 4280M, 4278M, 3624M, 3732M, 3749M, 3776M, 3750M, 3985M. L7535, L7566, L7569, L7577, L7582 Lancasters became 3107M, 5792M, 4166M, 3610M, 5453M.

L7589-L7595	**Cierva C.40 Rota II**	5
	L7589-L7591, L7594, L7595 to Spec 2/36.	
L7596	**DH.86A**	1
	G-ADYJ c/n 2348 purchased for 'flying classroom'. Crashed 28.7.39.	
L7600 & L7605	**Short S.29 Stirling**	2
	C/n 900, 901 to Spec B12/36. L7600 crashed on first flight 14.5.39, L7605 became 3443M.	
L7608-L7623	**Gloster Gladiator**	16
	L7609, L7611, L7620, L7621, L7623 to R Hellenic AF in 1940.	
L7632-L7701	**Fairey Swordfish I**	62
	L7632-L7661, L7670-L7701, c/n F.3374-F.3435. L7698 became 1311M.	
L7706-L7707	**Heston JA3**	1(2)
	Spec T1/37. L7706 became 2371M, L7707 not completed.	
L7714	**Miles M.15**	1
	Prototype to Spec T1/37.	
L7720-L7764	**DH.82B Queen Bee**	30
	L7720-L7729, L7754-L7764, c/n 5231-5260.	
L7770-L7899	**Vickers Wellington I/IA/IC**	100

Vickers (Chester) built. L7770-L7772 Mk.I, L7773-L7789 Mk.IA, L7790-L7819, L7840-L7874, L7885-L7899 Mk.IC. Conversions: L7771 DW1, L7776 Mk.XV. L7772, L7797, L7804, L7806, L7847-L7849, L7862, L7885, L7887, L7889, L7890, L7892 became 3117M, 4056M, 3669M, 4116M, 3561M, 3164M, 2437M, 3216M, 3502M, 3224M, 3358M, 4565M, 3268M.

L7903-L7994	**Avro 652A Anson**	67

L7903-L7932, L7945-L7977, L7991-L7994. L7913-L7922 offset to RAAF 1938. L7910, L7911, L7931, L7946, L7959, L7961, L7962, L7966, L7967, L7970, L7971 to RCAF 1940-41. L7925, L7947, L7948, L7951, L7952, L7954-L7956, L7974, L7975, L7977, L7991, L7992 to SAAF 1940-41. L7923 became 4310M.

L7999 & L8002	**Gloster F9/37**	2
	Prototypes. L7999 Taurus TE1M then III engine, became 2863M. L8002 Peregrine engine, became 2864M.	
L8005-L8032	**Gloster Gladiator I**	28
	L8005, L8012-L8028 to REAF. L8006 used for spares only. L8011 to R Hellenic AF. L8032 currently preserved.	
L8037 & L8040	**DH.86B**	2
	G-ADYC, 'ADYD c/ns 2340, 2341 acquired for W/T training. Transferred to Royal Navy.	
L8051-L8359	**Miles M.14A Magister**	214

L8051-L8095, L8127-L8176, L8200-L8237, L8249-L8295, L8326-L8359. L8132, L8141, L8168, L8205, L8230, L8251, L8253, L8337, L8340 became 4526M, 1099M, 5279M, 1124M, 4497M, 1254M, 5947M, 4770M, 3641M. L8076, L8166, L8270 sold to Turkey 1942-43. L8204 to Royal Navy 1940. Many sold postwar including L8056, L8072, L8127, L8143, L8149, L8170, L8171, L8206, L8219, L8234, L8271, L8274, L8278, L8280, L8283, L8289, L8293, L8295, L8338 to Argentine AF.

L8362-L9044	**Bristol Blenheim I/IV**	380

Types 142M/L. Built by Rootes. L8362-L8407, L8433-

L8482, L8500-L8549, L8597-L8632, L8652-L8701, L8714-L8731 (250) Mk.I; L8732-L8761, L8776-L8800, L8827-L8876, L9020-L9044 (130) Mk.IV. L8372, L8373, L8480, L8512, L8515, L8521, L8548, L8601, L8614, L8659, L8669, L8694, L8700, L8714, L8719, L8724, L8781, L9034, L9036, L9037 became 3195M, 3354M, 4045M, 1885M, 3967M, 3569M, 3476M, 4043M, 4107M, 3425M, 3541M, 3563M, 1893M, 3071M, 3256M, 2576M, 1895M, 2542M, 3436M, 3437M. L8384, L8385 to R Hellenic AF 1941. L8603-L8608, L8619, L8620, L8622, L8624-L8630, L8632, L8652-L8654 to Romanian AF 1939. L9025, L9026, L9028 to Finland 1940.

L9145-L9165	**Avro 652A Anson I**	21
	L9161-L9163 offset to RAAF and L9158-L9160 to RCAF 1940-41.	
L9166	**Avro 642/4m**	1
	VT-AFM c/n 773 'Star of India' to RAF in India.	
L9170-L9482	**Bristol Blenheim I/IV**	220

Types 142M/L. Built by Rootes. L9170-L9218, L9237-L9273 built as Mk.I and modified to Mk.IV. L9294-L9342, L9375-L9422, L9446-L9482 built as Mk.IV. L9195-L9203 offset to Finland 1940; L9309, L9311, L9312, L9376, L9377, L9380, L9384 offset to Canada later that year. L9192 had long range tanks fitted. L9171, L9209, L9306, L9478 became 2161M, 4007M, 3431M, 3981M.

L9485-L9624	**Handley Page HP.54 Halifax I/II**	100

L9485-L9534, L9560-L9584, L9600-L9608 (84) Mk.I, L9609-L9624 (16) Mk.II. L9485, L9486, L9488, L9505, L9514, L9515, L9520, L9523, L9524, L9526, L9528, L9532, L9534, L9563, L9564, L9573, L9580, L9604, L9606, L9607 became 3362M, 3005M, 3678M, 3677M, 3506M, 4185M, 4064M, 3690M, 3489M, 3034M, 3882M, 3953M, 3455M, 3691M, 3850M, 3865M, 3454M, 3161M, 4046M, 3866M.

L9635-L9703	**Airspeed AS.10 Oxford I**	50

L9635-L9650, L9692-L9703 intermediate trainers, L9651-L9660, L9680-L9691 advanced trainers. L9680, L9692, L9683 became 3841M, 4062M, 1747M. L9659 to R Norwegian AF in 1947.

L9704	**Vickers 410/427 Warwick**	1
	Centaurus, later Double Wasp engines. Second prototype to Spec B1/35.	
L9705	**Miles M.3B Falcon Six 'Gillette Falcon'**	1
	Purchased for tests, later fitted with 'knife edge' wings.	
L9706	**Miles M.13 Hobby**	1
	G-AFAW purchased in 1938 for wind tunnel tests, RAE.	
L9714-L9785	**Fairey Swordfish I**	60
	L9714-L9743, L9756-L9785, c/n F.3458-F.3517 for Royal Navy.	
L9786	**Short S.22 Scion Senior**	1
	G-AETH c/n S.836 floatplane for evaluation.	
L9790-L9999	**Bristol 152 Beaufort I**	137

L9790-L9838, L9851-L9897, L9932-L9972 part of larger order continued in 'N'-prefixed serials, second series. L9872, L9892, L9934, L9955 became 3148M, 2387M, 2380M, 3165M. L9940, L9941, L9956-L9958, L9960 to SAAF 1941. L9967, L9968 to RCAF 1941.

'M' As A Suffix

The letter 'M' was not used as a prefix in the alphabetical series because it was already in use for a non-flying series of airframes used for instruction on the ground. Up to 1921 aircraft used in that way retained their original number, but from that year they were renumbered. This renumbering is thought to have retrospectively included all those used in that way as it is only from 592M that documentation is fairly complete. Where aircraft were relegated to an instructional airframe number, this is given throughout in the appropriate batch. To check from an 'M' number to the original series, refer to Appendix X where this is tabled.

Naval Numbers
1916-1925 (First series)

N1 to N9999

When the Admiralty reached No. 10,000 and the RFC adopted letter prefixes from A, the prefix letter N was used for naval aircraft, being a significant letter and also the start of the second half of the alphabet. In using N1 to N9999, the RNAS used blocks of numbers for various classes, so that allocations were not in chronological sequence throughout. Blocks of numbers allocated were:

N1-N499	experimental maritime aircraft
N500-N999	experimental landplanes
N1000-N2999	production N1 and N2 seaplanes
N3000-N3999	French aircraft purchases in general
N4000-N4999	large flying boats of N3 class
N5000-N8999	naval aeroplanes
N9000-N9999	seaplanes

A thin line across the tables denotes the end of allocation in grouping. Within each grouping small ranges of numbers were not used, so that where numbers are 'jumped' it may be taken that these numbers were not used.

Serial Nos	Aircraft Type and Remarks	Quantity
N1	**Port Victoria P.V.2** Built by RNAS using Sopwith Baby fuselage. Modified to P.V.2bis.	1
N2	**Mann Egerton Type F** 130hp Clerget engine. Cancelled.	(1)
N3	*(Number not allotted)*	–
N4	**Sopwith Baby** 130hp Clerget engine.	1
N5	**Sopwith Camel** Prototype	1
N6-N7	*(Numbers not allotted)*	–
N8	**Port Victoria P.V.4** Built by RNAS. Proved unsatisfactory.	1
N9	**Fairey III** Type N2a with 190hp Rolls-Royce engine. C/n F.127. Used in catapult experiments. Became K-103/G-EAAJ.	1
N10	**Fairey III/IIIA** Type N2b. C/n F.128 variously modified. Became G-EALQ.	1
N14-N15	**Wight Type 4 triplane** Type N1b. Not accepted after maker's trial. N15 cancelled, also given as cancelled Nieuport As.14 seaplane.	1(2)
N16-N17	**Westland Scout Seaplane** Type N1b. N16 experimental floats, N17 standard floats.	2
N18-N19	**Norman Thompson Cruiser flying boat** Type N2c. Design delayed and finally cancelled.	(2)
N20-N25	**(Anti-submarine patrol aircraft)** Pusher types ordered from Short (N20, N21), Phoenix (N22, N23) and Supermarine (N24, N25) but all cancelled.	(6)
N26	**Norman Thompson flying boat** 140hp Hispano engine.	1
N27-N32	**Handley Page R/200** Type N2a. N27, N28 floatplanes and N29 wheeled u/c. N30 landplane and N31, N32 floatplanes cancelled.	3(6)
N33-N35	**Robey Seaplane** Type N2a with 200hp Hispano engine. Construction abandoned mid-1917.	(3)
N36	**Short N2a Scout No.1** 200, later 260hp Sunbeam engine. C/n S.313 modified to Scout No.2.	1
N37	**Norman Thompson tandem seater flying boat fighter** 150, later 200hp Hispano engine. Tadpole-like hull.	1
N38-N40	**Beardmore WB.4** Type N1a. N38 tested 20.5.18. N39, N40 not completed.	1(3)
N41-N43	**Beardmore WB.5** Type N1a. N41 wrecked on trial, N43 cancelled.	2(3)
N44-N49	**Mann Egerton H1/2** Type N1a Seaboat Scout. N44 H1, N45 H2, N46-N49 not completed.	2(6)
N50	**Grain Griffin** Ex-Sopwith B1.	1
N51-N52	**Kingsbury-Davis gun machine project** One fuselage only completed.	(2)
N53-N54	**Port Victoria P.V.5a**	2
N55	**Port Victoria P.V.9** RNAS-built at Grain.	1
N56-N58	**Blackburn 'N1b'** Type N1b. Hull of N56 completed as Pellet G-EBHF. N57, N58 cancelled before completion.	1(3)
N59-N61	**Supermarine Baby** Type N1b. N59 200hp Hispano then 200hp Sunbeam. N60 stored as spare, N61 cancelled.	2(3)
N62-N63	**Handley Page Type T** Experimental folding wings for F3 flying boats, cancelled.	(2)
N64	**Felixstowe F3** Two Rolls-Royce Eagle VIII engines. Prototype that was used operationally.	1
N65	**Felixstowe F2c** Two 250hp Sunbeam engines. Experimental F2 that was used operationally.	1
N66-N73	**Short N2b** N66, N67 c/n S.419, S.420. Rest cancelled.	2(8)
N74	**Sopwith T1 Cuckoo** 200hp Hispano engine. Prototype later fitted with Sunbeam Arab engine.	1
N75	**Kingsbury-Davis triplane** Gun machine project cancelled due to firm's commitments.	(1)
N76-N81	**Fairey N2a** Folding tractor biplane project. Cancelled.	(6)
N82-N83	**Norman Thompson N2c** N82 first flew 10.18, N83 built but not erected.	2
N84-N85	**Tellier flying boat** 200hp Hispano engine. Acquired from France for trials at Grain.	2
N86-N87	**Phoenix P5 Cork I/II** N86 Mk.I, N87 Mk.II. Hulls built by May, Harden & May.	2
N88, N89	**Fairey N3** Cancelled.	(2)
N90	**Felixstowe F5** Prototype	1
N91-N96	**Parnall Panther** N91 type tests, N92 fleet trials, N93 flotation trials, N94 proof loading.	6
N97-N98	**Short School Seaplane** Cancelled, numbers reallotted.	(2)
N97-N98	**CE1 (Coastal Experimental No.1)** Built by RAE. N97 RAF3a engine, N98 Sunbeam Maori.	2
N100-N106	**Grain Griffin** RNAS built. N100-N103 Arab later Bentley BR2 engines, N104-N106 Bentley BR2 only.	7
N107-N109	**Norman Thompson School flying boat project** Cancelled.	(3)
N110-N112	**Short Shirl** Rolls-Royce Eagle VIII engine. C/n S.421-S.423. N110 'V' u/c, N111 split u/c, N112 converted to 2-seat.	3
N113-N115	**Blackburn Blackbird** Rolls-Royce Eagle VIII engines.	3
N116-N117	**Sage N4 School** N116 N4a converted to N4b, N117 N4c.	2
N118-N119	**Fairey Atalanta** C/n F.275, F.276. N118 hull only built by Phoenix, N119 built by Dick Kerr Ltd.	1(2)
N120-N122	**Short Cromarty** N120 c/n S.539. N121 partly built. N122 cancelled.	1(3)
N123	**Felixstowe Fury** Crashed on tests and written off.	1
N124-N126	**Vickers Valentia** N124 built at Barrow, except hull at Cowes. N125, N126 cancelled.	1(3)
N127	**Felixstowe F5** Ordered from Vickers and May, Harden & May. Cancelled	(1)
N128	**Felixstowe F5L** Liberty engine. Purchased in America.	1
N129	**Fairey Titania** C/n F.337. Hull by Fyfes, Hamble; erected by Phoenix.	1

N130	**Felixstowe Fury**	(1)
	Construction abandoned in September 1919 following the crash of N123.	
N131-N132	**Vickers Vigilant project**	(2)
	Eight Rolls-Royce Condor planned. Cancelled.	
N133-N135	**Fairey Pintail**	3
	C/n F.339-F.341 to Spec XXI. N133-N135 Mks.I-III.	
N136-N138	**Parnall Puffin**	3
	450hp Napier Lion engine.	
N139	**Blackburn T.1 Swift**	1
	Civil demonstrator G-EAVN purchased January 1921.	
N140-N142	**Blackburn T.2 Dart**	3
N143-N145	**Handley Page HP.19 Hanley**	3
	To Spec 3/20. N141-N143 Mks.I-III. N144 sold to Russia.	
N146	**Supermarine Seal**	1
N147	**Vickers Viking III**	1
	G-EAUK acquired for trials January 1921.	
N148-N149	**English Electric M.3 Ayr**	2
	450hp Lion IIB engine.	
N150-N152	**Blackburn R.1 Blackburn**	3
	To Spec 3/21 for fleet spotter.	
N153-N155	**Avro 555 Bison**	3
	To Spec 3/21.	
N156-N157	**Vickers Viking V**	2
	Type 59. Ordered for trials in Middle East.	
N158	**Supermarine Seagull II**	1
	Revised Mk.Ii for performance trials.	
N159	**Supermarine Seal**	1
N160-N162	**Parnall Plover**	3
	Admiralty Type 6. N160 Jupiter III, N161 Jupiter IV, N162 Jaguar. N161 was amphibious version.	
N163-N165	**Fairey Flycatcher**	3
	Admiralty Type 6. C/n F.406-F.408 to Spec 6/22. N163 landplane with Jaguar later Jupiter IV, N164 shipplane with float of ski u/c fitted with Jaguar engine, N165 amphibian with Jupiter engine.	
N166-N167	**Blackburn T.4 Cubaroo I**	2
	To Spec 16/22.	
N168	**English Electric P.6 Kingston I**	1
N169	**Vickers 83 Viking VII**	1
	Renamed Vanellus.	
N170	**Supermarine Sea Lion II/III**	1
	G-EBAH acquired December 1923.	
N171-N172	**Avro 557 Ava**	2
	N171 Mk.I rounded wingtips, N172 Mk.II all-metal, square tipped wings.	
N173	**Fairey Fremantle**	1
	C/n F.420 G-EBLZ temporarily flown as N173.	
N174-N175	**Supermarine Swan**	2
	To Spec 21/22. N175 became G-EBJY.	
N176	**Dornier Delphin II**	1
	Built by Handley Page.	
N177-N178	**Felixstowe F5**	2
	N177 metal hull by Short. N178 hull by Saunders.	
N179	**Short Singapore I**	1
	Two Condor IIIA. C/n S.677 loaned to Sir Alan Cobham as G-EBUP.	
N180	**Supermarine Sheldrake**	1
	Lion V engine.	
N181-N182	**Parnall Peto**	2
	N181 Mongoose & Lucifer engines, N182 Lucifer IV.	
N183-N184	**Beardmore-Rohrback Inverness**	2
N185	**Blackburn RB.1 Iris I/II/IV**	1
	To Spec R14/24 and variously modified.	
N186	**Saro A.3 Valkyrie**	1
	Three Condor IIIA engines.	
N187	**Hawker Hedgehog**	1
	Ex-G-EBJN civil demonstration aircraft.	
N188-N189	**Blackburn R.2 Airedale**	2
	To Spec 37/22. N189 had auxiliary fins.	
N190-N192	**Fairey Ferret**	3
	C/n F.538-F.540 to Spec 37/22, N190-N192 Mks.I/II/III.	
N193	**Short S.1 Cockle**	1
	C/n S.638 G-EBKA acquired July 1925.	
N194-N195	**Gloster III/IIIA-B**	2
	Schneider Trophy contest aircraft. N194 III to IIIA, N195 IIIB became G-EBLJ.	
N196	**Supermarine S.4**	1
	Schneider Trophy contest aircraft G-EBLP.	

N197	**Saunders A4 Medina**	1
N198	**Fairey IIIF**	1
	C/n F.574 to Spec 19/24 tested as land and floatplane.	
N199-N200	**Short S.6 Sturgeon**	2
	C/n S.710, S.711 to Spec 1/24.	
N201-N202	**Parnall Pike**	2
	To Spec 1/24 convertible wheel/float u/c.	
N203-N204	**Blackburn T.5 Ripon**	2
	Landplane/seaplane versions. To Spec 21/23. N203 Mk.I, N204 Mk.II.	
N205-N206	**Handley Page HP.31 Harrow I**	2
	To Spec 21/23 first flew 24.4.26. N205 conv to Mk.II.	
N207	**Blackburn TR.1 Sprat**	1
	To Spec 5/24 for interchangeable wheel/float advanced trainer.	
N208	**Vickers Vendace I**	1
	Type 120 with Falcon III engine. To Spec 5/24.	
N209-N210	**Avro 584 Avocet**	2
	Lynx IV engine. To Spec 17/25. Interchangeable wheel/float undercarriage.	
N211	**Vickers Vireo**	1
	Type 125 with Lynx IV engine. To Spec 17/25. Interchangeable wheel/float undercarriage	
N212-N213	**Supermarine Seamew**	2
	Scaled-down Southampton to Spec 31/24.	
N214	**Saunders A4 Medina**	1
	Presumed allocation of G-EBMG during trials.	
N215	**Gloster Gnatsnapper I**	1
	To Spec 21/26.	
N216	**Fairey Flycatcher II**	1
	C/n F.873 to Spec 33/26. First flew 4.10.26.	
N217	**Parnall Perch**	1
	To Spec 5/24.	
N218	**Supermarine Southampton II**	1
	Two Lion engines. Metal-hull version.	
N219-N221	**Supermarine S.5**	3
	To Spec 6/26 for Schneider Trophy contest.	
N222-N224	**Gloster-Napier IV**	3
	To Spec 6/26. N222 converted to IVA, N223, N224 to IVB.	
N225	**Fairey IIIF**	1
	C/n F.890. Second prototype.	
N226	**Short-Bristol Crusader**	1
	C/n S.736 to Spec 6/26 for Schneider Trophy contest.	
N227	**Gloster SS.35 Gnatsnapper**	1
	Mks.I-III in succession with Mercury, Jaguar and Kestrel engines.	
N228-N229	**Short S.10 Gurnard**	2
	C/n S.744, S.745. N228 Mk.I with Jupiter X, N229 Mk.II with Kestrel II. Interchangeable wheel/float undercarriage and N229 converted to amphibian.	
N230	**Vickers Vildebeest**	1
	Prototype. Types 132, 192, 194 Series I-III. Became G-ABGE.	
N231	**Blackburn T.5A Ripon IIA**	1
	Lion XI engine fitted.	
N232-N233	**Parnall Pipit**	2
	To Spec 21/26 superseded by 16/30.	
N234	**Blackburn 2F1 Nautilus**	1
	To Spec O22/26.	
N235	**Fairey Fleetwing**	1
	Rolls-Royce Kestrel XIIMS engine. C/n F.1132 to Spec O22/26. Wheel/float undercarriage.	
N236	**Blackburn BT.1 Beagle**	1
	Jupiter VIIIF/XF engines fitted. To Specs 24/25 & 23/25 first flew 18.2.28.	
N237	**Hawker Hoopoe**	1
	Mercury/Jaguar III/Panther III engines. To Spec 21/26. Wheel/float undercarriage.	
N238	**Blackburn RB.1 Iris III**	1
N239	**Avro 572 Buffalo II**	1
	Napier Lion XIA. G-EBNW Type 571 acquired 1928 for conversion to floatplane.	
N240	**Saro A.7 Severn**	1
	Three Jupiter IX engines. Acquired for trials.	
N241	**Blackburn RB.2 Sydney**	1
	Three Rolls-Royce FXIIms. To Spec R5/27. ff 18.7.30.	
N242	**Short S.11 Valetta**	1
	Three Rolls-Royce Jupiter X1F. C/n S.747 to Spec 21/27 ex-G-AAJY.	

N243	Short Singapore II	1
N245	Saro Severn	1
N246	Short S.12 Singapore II	1
	Four Kestrel engines. C/n S.749 to Spec R32/27.	
N247-N248	Supermarine S.6	2
	Built for 1929 Schneider contest. Converted to S.6A.	
N249-N250	Gloster-Napier VI	2
	Built for 1929 Schneider Trophy contest.	
N251-N253	Supermarine Southampton	3
	N253 with Kestrel IV engines. Became K2888.	
N254	Gloster Gnatsnapper	1
	To Spec 16/30.	
N255	Parnall Peto	1
	First of six ordered.	
N300	Sopwith Baby	1
	110hp Clerget engine. Built by Blackburn. Number allotted out of sequence.	
N500	Sopwith Triplane	1
	110hp Clerget engine. Prototype.	
N501	Wight Landplane Bomber	1
	225hp Sunbeam or Rolls-Royce engines.	
N502	Blackburn Triplane	1
	110hp Clerget engine.	
N503	Sopwith Pup	1
	80/110hp Clerget engine. Admiralty Type 9901.	
N504	Sopwith Triplane	1
	130hp Clerget engine. Second prototype.	
N505-N506	Parnall Zepp Strafer	1(2)
	Also known as Night Flyer. N505 had Sunbeam Maori engine. N506 not built.	
N507-N508	Short Day Bomber	(2)
	Two 200hp Sunbeam engines specified. Cancelled.	
N509-N510	Sopwith Triplane	2
	N509, N510 with 150/200hp Hispano engines.	
N511-N514	Armstrong Whitworth FK.10 Quadruplane	4
	N511 fighter and N512 bomber built by Phoenix. N513 built but not accepted. N514 accepted but written off as unsatisfactory.	
N515-N516	Sunbeam Bomber	1(2)
	Admiralty Type 7. 200hp Sunbeam engine. N515 c/n 171, N516 not built.	
N517-N518	Sopwith 1F1 Camel	2
	Prototypes, various engines fitted.	
N519-N520	Handley Page HP.13 Triplane	(2)
	Admiralty Type 320. Cancelled. 320hp Sunbeam Cossack planned.	
N521-N522	Nieuport Triplane	1(2)
	130hp Clerget. N521 transferred to RFC. N522 purchase cancelled.	
N523	Avro Pike	1
	Avro 523. Built at Hamble. Known as Avro Fighter.	
N524	Sopwith Triplane	1
	Loaned to French and returned.	
N525	Beardmore WB1 bomber	1
N526-N531	Caproni Ca.42	6
	Bomber triplanes acquired from Italy and returned to Italian forces in 1918.	
N532	Nieuport Triplane	1
	110hp Clerget. Transferred from RFC.	
N533-N538	Sopwith Triplane	6
	130hp Clerget. Built by Clayton & Shuttleworth. Fitted with two Vickers guns.	
N539-N540	Port Victoria P.V.7 & P.V.8	2
	N539 P.V.7 Grain Kitten, N540 P.V.8 Eastchurch Kitten.	
N541-N543	Sopwith Triplane	3
	130hp Clerget. Loaned to French Government and returned.	
N544-N545	Voisin Gun Machine	2
	200hp Hispano. French-built loaned for gun trials.	
N546	Wight Quadruplane	1
	110hp Clerget engine.	
N1000-N1009	Fairey Campania	10
	C/n F.16-F.25. N1000-N1005 Eagle IV, V or VI engines. N1006 Maori II, N1007-N1009 Eagle VII engines.	

N1010-N1039	Sopwith Baby	30
	110hp Clerget initially. First Blackburn-built batch. Wing modification from N1030.	
N1040-N1059	FBA Flying Boat	20
	100hp Gnome Monosoupape. French-built hulls, erected by Norman Thompson.	
N1060-N1069	Sopwith Baby	10
	110hp Clerget initially. Built by Blackburn. N1068 to Chilean government.	
N1070-N1074	Admiralty AD Naviplane	(5)
	140hp Smith. Ordered from Supermarine. Cancelled.	
N1075-N1078	FBA Flying Boat	4
	160hp Isotta-Fraschini. Presented by Italians to RNAS Otranto.	
N1080-N1099	Short 184	20
	240hp Renault engine. C/n S.314-S.333. N1080-N1089 improved version, N1090-N1099 original version. N1098 later had 260hp Sunbeam.	
N1100-N1129	Sopwith Baby	30
	110hp Clerget originally. Built by Blackburn for anti-submarine work. N1121 presented to French government.	
N1130-N1139	Short 184	10
	240hp Renault engine. Built by Sage & Co. N1130-N1134 improved and N1135-N1139 original type.	
N1140-N1149	Short 184	10
	240hp Renault. Built by Saunders. Improved version.	
N1150-N1159	Short 320	10
	Sunbeam Cossack engine. C/n S.354-S.363 mainly shipped direct to Otranto.	
N1160-N1179	Curtiss H.12	(20)
	Two 250hp Sunbeam engines. Cancelled.	
N1180-N1189	Norman Thompson NT2b	10
	N1180-N1185 120hp Beardmore. N1186-N1189 150hp Hispano.	
N1190-N1219	Fairey Hamble Baby	30
	130hp Clerget. Built by Parnall. N1192, N1211, N1213, N1216 to Greek government.	
N1220-N1239	Short 184	20
	240hp Renault. N1220-N1229 built by Robey, N1230-N1239 built by Sage. N1232 interned in Holland as Dutch K1.	
N1240-N1259	Short 184	20
	Intermediate type. Built by J.S.White. N1240 225hp Sunbeam, N1241-N1249 240hp Sunbeam, N1250-N1254 240hp Renault, N1255 power unit not known, N1256-N1259 260hp Sunbeam.	
N1260-N1279	Short 184	20
	Built by Robey. N1260 260hp Sunbeam, N1261-N1271 225/240hp Sunbeam, N1272-N1279 240hp Renault. N1260-N1269 Intermediate type, N1270, N1271 original type, N1272-N1279 type not known.	
N1280-N1289	Wight Converted Seaplane	10
	260hp Sunbeam Maori. Built by J.S.White. N1281 had Renault fitted for a period.	
N1290-N1299	Admiralty AD flying boat	1(10)
	N1290 only completed by Supermarine. N1295-N1299 delivered as spares. Rest cancelled.	
N1300-N1319	Short 320	20
	300hp Sunbeam Cossack. C/n S.334-S.353. All except N1303 to Mediterranean.	
N1320-N1339	Fairey Hamble Baby	20
	C/n F.129-F.148. N1320-N1329 110hp Clerget, but N1328 later with 130hp Clerget initially fitted to N1330-N1339.	
N1340-N1359	Sopwith 'Daily Mail'	(20)
	Pre-war competition aircraft design. Order cancelled.	
N1360-N1409	Short 320	50
	320hp Sunbeam Cossack. N1360-N1389 built by Sunbeam Motors mainly for home delivery, N1390-N1409 built by Short Bros c/ns S.399-S.418 mainly for Mediterranean stations.	
N1410-N1449	Sopwith Baby	40
	110/130hp Clerget. Built by Blackburn with Rankin Dart containers for anti-Zeppelin duty. N1425 to Greek Navy and N1430, N1431 to French government.	
N1450-N1479	Fairey Hamble Baby	30
	130hp Clerget. C/n F.149-F.178. N1455, N1467, N1468, N1470-N1472 to Greek government.	
N1480-N1504	Short 320	24(25)
	320hp Sunbeam Cossack. C/n S.312, S.365-S.388.	

N1485 to Japanese government. N1480 ex-8320.

N1505-N1519 Large America type flying boat (15)
Cancelled order placed with AMC.

N1520-N1529 Admiralty AD flying boat 10
200hp Hispano. Built by Supermarine. N1525 had Wolseley Viper temporarily fitted. N1527 sand-tested to destruction. N1526, N1528, N1529 became Channel Mk.I G-EAEM, 'EAEL, 'EAED.

N1530-N1579 Maurice Farman floatplane 1(50)
140hp Renault. Order placed with AMC. Record only of N1530 built.

N1580-N1589 Short 184 10
240hp Renault. C/n S.389-S.398. N1586, N1587 DC.

N1590-N1599 Short 184 10
260hp Sunbeam Maori in general. Built by Sage. N1590-N1592 had 240hp Renault.

N1600-N1624 Short 184 25
240hp Renault. Built by Saunders. Last four had Sunbeam Maori engines.

N1630-N1659 Short 184 30
Improved version. 240hp Renault. Built by Phoenix. Last seven had 260hp Sunbeam Maori. N1651-N1655 to Greek government.

N1660-N1689 Short 184 30
260hp Sunbeam Maori. Built by Brush. First twelve fitted with 240hp Renault.

N1690-N1709 Short 320 20
320hp Sunbeam Cossack. Built by Sunbeam Motors. N1697-N1701 to Japanese Navy.

N1710-N1719 Admiralty AD flying boat 10
200hp Hispano engine. Built by Supermarine. N1710, N1711, N1714-N1716 became Channel Mk.Is G-EAEE, 'EAEK, 'EAEJ, 'EAEI, 'EAEH. N1719 was fitted with Wolseley Adder for trials.

N1720-N1739 Blackburn Kangaroo (20)
Renumbered B9970-B9989.

N1740-N1774 Short 184 35
260hp Sunbeam Maori. N1740-N1759 (20) built by Phoenix, N1760-N1774 (15) built by Saunders.

N1780-N1799 Short 184 20
260hp Sunbeam Maori. Built by Sage & Co.

N1820-N1839 Short 184 20
260hp Sunbeam Maori. Built by Robey & Co. First seven had 240hp Renaults fitted. N1824 to Greek government.

N1840-N1959 Fairey Campania 12(120)
N1840-N1889 (50) ordered from Barclay, Curle & Co, but only N1840-N1851 (12) delivered. N1890-N1959 cancelled placed orders with Sunbeam Motors and Sage & Co.

N1960-N2059 Fairey Hamble Baby 85(100)
130hp Clerget engine. Ordered from Parnall. N1960-N1985 built as floatplanes of which N1960, N1961, N1964, N1965, N1978, N1979 went to Greek government. N1986-N2003 built as landplanes as Hamble Baby Converts. N2004-N2044 mainly at Killingholme built without engines. N2045-N2059 no delivery record.

N2060-N2134 Sopwith Baby 75
130hp Clerget. Built by Blackburn. N2103, N2104 to Chilean government, N2121 to USA for exhibition.

N2140-N2159 Norman Thompson NT4A 20
Two 200hp Hispano. Known as Small America type. N2155 became G-EAOY.

N2180-N2229 Wight converted Seaplane 20(50)
Ordered from J. S. Wight. N2180-N2194 (15) completed as trainers, N2195-N2199 delivered as spares, remainder cancelled.

N2230-N2259 Fairey IIIB/C 30
C/n F.277-F.306 IIIB as ordered, from N2255 (which became G-EAPV) built as IIIC.

N2260-N2359 Norman Thompson NT2b 35(100)
Sunbeam Arab engines. Up to N2294 delivered. N2286, N2287 to Estonian government, N2284 to USA and N2290 became G-EAQO.

N2360-N2399 Fairey Campania 40
C/n F.180-F.219 built at Hayes, erected and tested at Hamble. N2360-N2368 Eagle VI, VII or VIII. N2369-N2374 Eagle VIII. N2375-N2399 Maori II engines.

N2400-N2429 Norman Thompson NT2b 30
Sunbeam Arab. Majority stored without engines.

N2450-N2499 Admiralty AD flying boat 6(50)
150/200hp Hispano. N2450-N2455 built by Supermarine rest cancelled. N2451, N2452 became Channels G-EAEG and 'EAEF.

N2500-N2523 Norman Thompson NT2b 15(24)
Sunbeam Arab engine. Fifteen only built by Saunders. N2501 had Hispano fitted.

N2555-N2579 Norman Thompson NT2b 25
150/200hp Hispano. Fifteen to store without engines.

N2600-N2659 Short 184 30(60)
260hp Sunbeam Maori engine. N2600-N2629 cancelled.

N2680-N2739 FBA flying boat 60
100hp Gnome Monosoupape. Built by Gosport Aviation. Main deliveries to Lee. N2685 DC.

N2740-N2759 Norman Thompson NT4A (20)
Two 200hp Hispano. No delivery record, presumed cancelled.

N2760-N2789 Norman Thompson NT2b 19(30)
No delivery record after N2778, rest held in store.

N2790-N2849 Short 184 60
260hp Sunbeam Maori. N2790-N2819 built by Brush, N2820-N2849 by Robey & Co.

N2850-N2899 Fairey IIIA 50
C/n F.220-F.269. N2853-N2862, N2864-N2874 fitted with skid u/c, remainder wheeled u/c. Majority stored at Renfrew and Turnhouse. N2876 became G-EADZ.

N2900-N2999 Short 184 100
260hp Sunbeam Maori. N2900-N2949 built by Robey, N2950-N2999 by J. S. White. N2986, N2996, N2998 became G-EAJT, 'EBGP, EALC.

N3000-N3049 Henry Farman F27 50
160hp Canton Unne engine. Tropical version, French-built. N3000-N3024 shipped to Aegean bases. N3011, N3018 to Greek government. N3025-N3049 to RFC, see A8968-A8998 range for renumbering.

N3050-N3099 Caudron G.3 50
100hp Anzani engine. French-built mainly for RNAS Vendome.

N3100-N3104 Nieuport 17 5
130hp Clerget. French-built.

N3170-N3209 Nieuport types 40
110/130hp Clerget engines; N3170-N3173 Type 12 (110hp), N3174-N3183 Type 12 (130hp), N3184-N3197 Type 17/17bis, N3198 Type 12, N3199-N3209 Type 17/17bis.

N3210-N3239 Farman F.4 30
160hp Renault. French-built.

N3240-N3299 Caudron G.3 50(60)
90hp Anzani. French-built for RNAS Vendome. N3270-N3279 cancelled.

N3300-N3374 Norman Thompson NT2b (75)
Ordered from Supermarine. Cancelled.

N4000-N4049 Felixstowe F3/F5 50
Rolls-Royce Eagle VIII. Built by Shorts, c/n S.588-S.637. N4000-N4036 built as F3, rest as F5. N4018 to the Portuguese Navy. N4019 became G-EAQT. N4009-N4016 part of Canadian Imperial Gift becoming G-CYDH, 'CYDI, 'CYDJ, two unnumbered hulls and G-CYDQ, 'CYEN, 'CYBT.

N4060-N4074 Curtiss H16 15
R-R Eagle VIII; American-built. Engines fitted in UK.

N4080-N4099 Felixstowe F2A 20
Built by Saunders. N4093-N4098 stored less engines.

N4100-N4149 Felixstowe F3/F5 18(50)
R-R Eagle VIII. Ordered from Dick Kerr. N4100-N4117 only built. Remainder ordered as F5s cancelled.

N4160-N4229 Felixstowe F3/F5 39(70)
R-R Eagle VIII when fitted. F3s ordered from Phoenix. N4160-N4176 stored less engines. N4177 became G-EBDQ. N4178, N4179, N4181 part of Imperial Gift to Canada as two hulls and one complete as G-CYEO. From N4184 built as F5 but no delivery record beyond N4198.

N4230-N4279 Felixstowe F3 50
R-R Eagle VIII. Built by Dick Kerr prior to N4100-N4149 batch above. Some to store without engines.

N4280-N4309 Felixstowe F2A 30

	R-R Eagle VIII. Built by Saunders. N4280 had Eagle VII.	
N4310-N4321	Felixstowe F3	12
	R-R Eagle VIII. Built by Malta Dockyard. Deliveries from March 1918.	
N4330-N4353	Curtiss 12B	21(24)
	R-R Eagle VIII. Built in USA, erected in UK. N4351-N4353 cancelled.	
N4360-N4397	Felixstowe F3	11(38)
	R-R Eagle VIII. Order from Malta Dockyard reduced to 28 but record of only up to N4370 delivered.	
N4400-N4429	Felixstowe F3	30
	R-R Eagle VIII. Built by Phoenix prior to N4160-N4229 batch above. N4400 to Portugal.	
N4430-N4479	Felixstowe F2A/F5	50
	R-R Eagle VIII. Built by Saunders. Late production as F5.	
N4480-N4579	Felixstowe F2A/F5	80(100)
	R-R Eagle VIII. Hulls by May, Harden & May, erected by AMC. Late deliveries as F5. N4505-N4509, N4520-N4529, N4555-N4559 cancelled. N4545 F2B. N4567 free issue to Chile.	
N4580-N4629	Felixstowe F5	(50)
	R-R Eagle VIII. Ordered from Saunders. No delivery record.	
N4630-N4679	Felixstowe F5	8(50)
	R-R Eagle VIII. Ordered from Gosport Aviation but bulk cancelled. N4634 became G-EAIK.	
N4680-N4729	Felixstowe F5	(50)
	R-R Eagle VIII. Cancelled order placed with May, Harden & May.	
N4730-N4779	Felixstowe F5L	(50)
	Liberty engines. Cancelled order placed with Dick Kerr.	
N4780-N4829	Felixstowe F5	(50)
	R-R Eagle VIII. Cancelled order placed with Phoenix.	
N4830-N4879	Felixstowe F5	10(50)
	R-R Eagle VIII. Short c/ns S.529-S.537 for N4830-N4839. Rest cancelled.	
N4890-N4950	Curtiss H16	61
	R-R Eagle VIII. Built in USA erected in UK. From N4900 to store as hulls, but N4902, N4905 withdrawn as Canadian Imperial Gift aircraft, the latter becoming G-CYEP.	
N5000-N5029	Maurice Farman S.7 Longhorn	17(30)
	Hawk engines. Built by Robey. N5010-N5016 to RFC becoming A9978, A9979, B393, B398, B400, B397. N5017-N5029 cancelled.	
N5030-N5059	Maurice Farman S.7 Longhorn	30
	80hp Renault. Built by Brush Electrical Engineering.	
N5060-N5079	Maurice Farman S.11 Shorthorn	20
	80hp Renault. Built by Eastbourne Aviation c/ns 124-143	
N5080-N5119	Sopwith 1½ Strutter	40
	110hp Clerget in the main. Type 9700 except N5080-N5087, N5090, N5093, N5096, N5099, N5102, N5105, N5108, N5111, N5114, N5117, N5119 Type 9400. N5088, N5091, N5092, N5094, N5095, N5097, N5098, N5100, N5101, N5104, N5113, N5115, N5116, N5118 to French.	
N5120-N5169	Sopwith 1½ Strutter	50
	Type 9700 bomber. Built by Westland. N5122, N5123, N5125-N5148, N5157, N5158 to French.	
N5170-N5179	Sopwith 1½ Strutter	10
	Type 9400 fighter. N5176 to Greek government.	
N5180-N5199	Sopwith Pup	20
	80hp Le Rhone or Gnome. Note: N5180 applied to a surviving Pup is not this actual aircraft.	
N5200-N5249	Sopwith 1½ Strutter	50
	110/130hp Clerget. Built by Mann Egerton. N5200-N5219 Type 9700 of which N5204, N5213 were converted to Type 9400, remainder Type 9400. N5205, N5213 to Greek, N5219, N5244 to Russian and N5235-N5242 (less engines) to Belgian governments.	
N5250-N5279	Avro 504B	30
	80hp Gnome engine. Built by Sunbeam Motors as bomber trainers. N5256-N5258, N5261, N5262, N5264, N5267-N5270, N5273 converted to 504H.	
N5280-N5309	Sage N3 School	2(30)
	75hp Rolls-Royce Hawk. N5280, N5281 only built.	
N5310-N5329	Avro 504B	20
	80hp Gnome. Built by British Caudron and Regent	

	Carriage Co. N5311, N5312, N5315-N5325, N5329 converted to 504G.	
N5330-N5349	Maurice Farman S.7 Longhorn	20
	Hawk engines. Built by Phoenix Dynamo Co.	
N5350-N5389	Sopwith Triplane	40
	Built by Clayton & Shuttleworth, N5384, N5388 presented to French.	
N5390-N5419	Bristol Scout D	30
	B & C built. C/n 1837-1866. N5390-N5399 100hp Monosoupape, N5400 80hp Le Rhone, N5401 no record, N5402-N5419 80hp Gnome.	
N5420-N5494	Sopwith Triplane	
	130hp Clerget. N5430 to RFC, N5486 to Russia. to	
N5500-N5549	Sopwith 1½ Strutter	38(50)
	Type 9700 bomber. N5506, N5515, N5527 converted to Type 9400. N5502, N5507, N5511, N5514, N5523 to French, N5506, N5515, N5516, N5527, N5529 to Greek governments. N5504 became G-EAVB. N5538-N5549 cancelled.	
N5560-N5599	Nieuport XV	(40)
	230hp Renault. Order cancelled.	
N5600-N5624	Sopwith 1½ Strutter	25
	Built by Westland. N5600-N5604 Type 9700, rest Type 9400. N5611 to Greek government.	
N5630-N5654	Sopwith 1½ Strutter	25
	Type 9400 fighter. Built by Mann Egerton. N5633-N5636, N5638, N5643, N5644 converted to Ship Strutter. N5650 to Greek government.	
N5660-N5709	Curtiss JN-4	?(50)
	Order reported cancelled. but N5670-N5673 recorded.	
N5720-N5749	Maurice Farman S.7 Longhorn	30
	70/80hp Renault. Built by Brush Electrical Engineering.	
N5750-N5759	Maurice Farman S.7 Longhorn	10
	Hawk engine. Built by Phoenix Dynamo Co.	
N5770-N5794	B.E.2c	(25)
	150hp Hispano. Cancelled order with Robey.	
N5800-N5829	Avro 504B	30
	80hp Gnome. Built by Parnall.	
N5860-N5909	Nieuport 24	50
	110/130hp Clerget. Built by British Nieuport. N5884-N5903, N5907-N5909 stored at Hendon less engines. N5906 to USA.	
N5910-N5934	Sopwith Triplane	3(25)
	130hp Clerget. Ordered from Oakley. N5910-N5912 only built. N5912 preserved at Hendon.	
N5940-N5954	Sopwith 1½ Strutter	(15)
	Order cancelled.	
N5960-N6009	Airco DH.4	50
	R-R Eagle engine. Built by Westland. N5995 et seq had higher u/c. N5970, N5980, N5986, N5987, N5990, N5991, N5994, N5995, N5998, N5999, N6002, N6003, N6006, N6007 to RFC as B3955-B3968.	
N6010-N6029	Avro 504B	20
	80hp Gnome. Built by Parnall. N6015-N6029 to RFC as A9975-A9977, B382-B385, B389-B392, B395, B396, B1390, B1391.	
N6030-N6079	Spad S.7/Nieuport	(50)
	130hp Clerget. Cancelled order re-allotted and cancelled again.	
N6100-N6129	Beardmore WB.III	30
	80hp Le Rhone in general. N6100-N6112 SB3F with folding u/c, rest SB3D with dropping u/c. SB3= Shipboard type 3. N6104-N6108, N6110 used for spares. N6125, N6126 80hp Clerget.	
N6130-N6159	Avro 504B	30
	80hp Gnome. Built by Sunbeam Motors as armament trainers.	
N6160-N6209	Sopwith Pup	50
	80hp Gnome or Le Rhone. N6204 to Russian government	
N6210-N6285	Spad S.7	3(76)
	Ordered from Mann Egerton. N6210-N6212 only built.	
N6290-N6309	Sopwith Triplane	20
	Final production batch by Sopwith.	
N6310-N6329	Maurice Farman S.11 Shorthorn	20
	80/170hp Renault. Built by Eastbourne Aviation, c/ns 144-163.	
N6330-N6379	Sopwith 1F1 Camel	50
	130hp Clerget. First production Camels. N6344 pattern to Ruston Proctor and BP became B9990. N6338 to RFC as B3977. From N6336 some fitted with BR1 engines.	

N6380-N6429 Airco DH.4   50
RAF.3a or BHP engine. Built by Westland. N6380,
N6382-N6387, N6393, N6397, N6401, N6405, N6409
to RFC as B3987, B9434-B9439, B9456, B9458, B9460,
B9461, B9470. N6399, N6411 to Greek government.

N6430-N6459 Sopwith Ships Pup   30
Admiralty Type 9901A. Built by Beardmore with skid
u/c but some later converted to wheeled u/c. N6432,
N6433 to Greek government.

N6460-N6529 Sopwith Pup   20(70)
Admiralty Type 9901. N6460-N6479 only built. N6470,
N6471 to Greek government.

N6530-N6579 Nieuport Scout   (50)
British Nieuport order cancelled.

N6580-N6599 Spad S.7   (20)
Ordered from Mann Egerton, renumbered B9911-B9930.

N6600-N6649 Sopwith 2F1 Camel   50
Bentley BR1 engines in general. Was originally allotted
to Scout D under B6151-B6200. N6605 interned in
Denmark. N6616 to Estonian Government.

N6650-N6679 Avro 504B   30
80hp Gnome. Built by Parnall. N6650-N6656 to RFC as
B1392-B1394, B1397-B1399, B1400.

N6680-N6749 Beardmore WB.III (SB3D type)   70
Late production to store less engines. N6735, N6736
to Japan.

N6750-N6849 Sopwith 2F1 Camel   100
Bentley BR.1 engines. Shipboard aircraft built by
Beardmore. N6750 to Lettish government and N6803
and N6804 to White Russian forces.

N6900-N6949 Sopwith T1 Cuckoo I   50
Sunbeam Arab engines. Ordered from Pegler in 1917,
but as firm could not deliver until 1919, Blackburn built
N6900-N6929 after their batch given immediately below.
Of these N6910, N6926, N6929 were converted to Mk.II
with Wolseley Viper engines. Pegler built N6930-N6949.

N6950-N6999 Sopwith T1 Cuckoo I   50
Sunbeam Arab engines. Built by Blackburn. N6971,
N6989, N6997, N6999 converted to Mk.II.

N7000-N7099 Sopwith T1 Cuckoo I   50(100)
Sunbeam Arab engines. Ordered from Fairfield
Engineering. N7036-N7049 direct to store. N7050-
N7099 cancelled.

N7100-N7149 Sopwith 2F1 Camel   50
Ordered from Beardmore, but N7140-N7149 sub-let
to Arrol Johnston. N7143 to Lettish government.

N7150-N7199 Sopwith T1 Cuckoo I/II   50
Arab and Viper engines. Built by Blackburn.

N7200-N7349 Sopwith 2F1 Camel   (150)
Bentley BR1 engines. Cancelled orders N7200-N7299
with Fairey, N7300-N7349 with Pegler.

N7350-N7389 Sopwith 2F1 Camel   20(40)
Bentley BR1 engines. Ordered from Arrol Johnston.
Up to N7369 only confirmed built. N7357, N7359,
N7364, N7367 to Canada with 130hp Clerget.

N7400-N7549 Parnall Panther   150
B & C. C/n 5715-5864. N7530 became G-EBCM.

N7550-N7649 Short Shirl   (100)
Cancelled order with Blackburn.

N7650-N7679 Sopwith 2F1 Camel   (30)
Cancelled order with Arrol Johnston.

N7680-N7841 Parnall Panther   (162)
Cancelled order with B & C.

N7850-N7979 Sopwith 2F1 Camel   (130)
Cancelled order with Sage & Co.

N7980-N8079 Sopwith T1 Cuckoo I/II/III   32(100)
Ordered from Blackburn. Delivery up to N8011 only
confirmed. N7990 was single Mk.III with R-R Falcon.

N8130-N8179 Sopwith 2F1 Camel   30(50)
Ordered from Hooper. Delivery up to N8159 only
confirmed. N8136, N8137 to Lettish government with
BR1 engines. N8153, N8156 to Canada with 130hp
Clergets of which the latter is extant.

N8180-N8229 Sopwith 2F1 Camel   25(50)
Ordered from Clayton & Shuttleworth. Delivery up to
N8204 only confirmed. N8185, N8187, N8189 to
Lettish government, N8204 to Canada.

N9000-N9199 Short 184   200
260hp Sunbeam Maori. Built by Robey (N9000-N9059),
Brush (N9060-N9099), J. S. White (N9100-N9139),
Robey (N9140-N9169) and Supermarine (N9170-N9199).
N9135 was first 184 to have Manitou engine fitted.
N9012, N9013, N9078, N9081, N9085 to White Russian
forces. N9128 free issue to Chile. N9127, N9129,
N9130, N9132, N9134, N9190-N9192 to Estonia.
N9096, N9118 became G-EBBM, 'EBBN.

N9230-N9259 Fairey IIIB/C   30
C/n F.307-F.336 built as IIIB converted to IIIC for
North Russian Expedition. N9253, N9256 became
G-EBDI, 'EARS.

N9260-N9289 Short 184   30
275hp Sunbeam Maori III. Built by Brush. N9264-
N9266, N9268 free issue to Chile.

N9290-N9349 Short 184   28(60)
Ordered from Robey. Up to N9317 only confirmed
delivered.

N9350-N9399 Short 184   (50)
Cancelled order with Brush.

N9400-N9449 Short 184   (50)
Cancelled order with J. S. White.

N9450-N9499 Fairey IIID   50
Rolls-Royce Eagle. C/n F.344-F.393. N9455, N9456,
N9467, N9478, N9479, N9485, N9491, N9497,
N9498 DC.

N9500-N9535 Westland Walrus   36
DH.9A development for fleet work.

N9536-N9561 Blackburn T.2 Dart   26
First postwar torpedo bomber to go into production.

N9562-N9566 Supermarine Seagull II   5
First postwar flying boat for the RAF.

N9567-N9578 Fairey IIID   12
Napier Lion II engines. C/n F.421-F.432.

N9579-N9590 Blackburn TSR Blackburn   12
N9589 DC.

N9591-N9602 Avro 555 Bison I   12
Lion II engine. Some conversions to IA. N9594 converted
to Avro 555B amphibian.

N9603-N9607 Supermarine Seagull I   5
N9605 Mk.IV became G-AAIZ.

N9608-N9610 Parnall Plover   3
N9608, N9609 landplane, N9610 floatplane version.

N9611-N9619 Fairey Flycatcher   9
C/n F.430-F.438.

N9620-N9629 Blackburn T.2 Dart   10
Ordered in 1923.

N9630-N9641 Fairey IIID   12
C/n F.445-F.456. N9630-N9635 with R-R Eagle, rest
with Napier Lion engines.

N9642-N9654 Supermarine Seagull III   13
N9653, N9654 became G-EBXH, 'EBXI.

N9655-N9680 Fairey Flycatcher   26
C/n F.451-F.476.

N9681-N9686 Blackburn TSR Blackburn I   6
N9686 converted to Mk.II.

N9687-N9696 Blackburn T.2 Dart   10
N9697 Fairey Flycatcher   1
C/n F.477.

N9698-N9708 Parnall Plover   11
N9705 became G-EBON.

N9709-N9713 English Electric P.5 Kingston   5
N9709 Mk.I, N9712 Mk.II, N9713 Mk.III; N9710
became Cork I.

N9714-N9723 Blackburn T.2 Dart   10
N9724-N9729 Handley Page HP.19/25 Hanley/Hendon   6
To Spec 3/20, built as Hanley converted to Hendon.

N9730-N9791 Fairey IIID   62
Napier Lion II engines. C/n F.552-F.571, F.614-F.655.

N9792-N9823 Blackburn T.2 Dart   32
Ordered August 1924.

N9824-N9835 Blackburn TSR Blackburn I   12
Some conversions to Mk.II. N9828 trials as amphibian.

N9836-N9853 Avro 555A Bison II   18
N9852 DC.

N9854-N9895 Fairey Flycatcher   42
C/n F.578-F.613, F.658-F.663.

N9896-N9901 Supermarine Southampton I   6
N9896 converted to Mk.III prototype.

Serial Nos	Aircraft Type and Remarks	Quantity
N9902-N9965	**Fairey Flycatcher** C/n F.670-F.693, F.697-F.736. N9906 Southampton I/III compromised this batch.	64
N9966-N9977	**Avro 555A Bison II**	12
N9978-N9989	**Blackburn TSR Blackburn II** N9989 DC.	12
N9990-N9999	**Blackburn T.2 Dart**	10

'N' Is Used Again (Second series)

N1000 to N9999

The fact that the RNAS and later the RAF had used an 'N' prefix in the 'twenties did not alter the decision to use 'N' again in the RAF alphabetical allocations and N1000 followed immediately on from L9999, the prefix 'M' having been used as a suffix to instructional airframe numbers. While black-out blocks continued for security reasons for British production, allocations for aircraft purchased in the USA were numbered consecutively.

Serial Nos	Aircraft Type and Remarks	Quantity
N1000-N1186	**Bristol 152 Beaufort I** Continuation from batch at end of 'L' series. N1000-N1047, N1074-N1118, N1145-N1186. N1183 not delivered being destroyed in an enemy attack on the factory. N1004, N1005, N1008, N1010, N1031, N1032, N1046, N1076, N1111, N1145 to SAAF 1941-42. N1006, N1007, N1021, N1026, N1027, N1029, N1030, N1045, N1078, N1107 to RCAF 1941. N1175, N1176 became 3409M, 4188M.	135
N1190-N1194	**Airspeed AS.10 Oxford I** Advanced trainers.	5
N1200-N1320	**Westland Lysander II** N1200-N1227, N1240-N1276, N1289-N1320. Conversions to TT and N1289, N1320 to Mk.III. N1208, N1245, N1300 to Free French Air Force. N1220, N1247, N1266, N1297, N1302 became 3925M, 3939M, 3927M, 3926M, 3889M.	97
N1323-N1324	**Airspeed AS.39** Fleet shadower prototype to Spec S23/37. N1324 not completed.	1(2)
N1330-N1339	**Avro 652A Anson I** N1330-N1336 direct to Australia for RAAF.	10
N1345-N1528	**Armstrong Whitworth AW.38 Whitley V** N1345-N1394, N1405-N1444, N1459-N1508, N1521-N1528. N1346, N1349, N1381, N1407, N1409, N1444, N1466, N1471, N1503 became 3469M, 3053M, 3393M, 3650M, 3392M, 3054M, 3418M, 3057M, 3067M.	148
N1531	**General Aircraft Monospar ST.25** Tricycle undercarriage prototype.	1
N1535-N1812	**Boulton Paul P.82 Defiant I** N1535-N1582, N1610-N1653, N1671-N1706, N1725-N1773, N1788-N1812. N1551 converted to Mk.II, N1550, N1764 to Mk.III. Conversions to TT: N1537, N1538, N1541, N1542, N1544, N1545, N1548, N1549, N1553, N1558, N1559, N1562, N1563, N1571, N1577, N1579, N1610, N1614, N1617, N1622, N1624, N1631-N1634, N1639, N1640, N1642, N1643, N1648, N1672, N1674, N1683, N1689, N1691, N1693, N1696, N1697, N1699, N1700, N1701, N1726, N1728, N1730, N1733, N1736, N1742, N1744, N1747, N1751, N1756, N1758, N1764, N1771, N1772, N1789, N1796, N1807, N1812 of which several went to FAA. N1611, N1616, N1621, N1681, N1703, N1743, N1797, N1801-N1803 became 3260M, 3006M, 2730M, 2981M, 2733M, 2975M, 2999M, 2732M, 3007M, 2976M.	202
N1818-N1847	**DH.82B Queen Bee** All used by Anti-Aircraft Co-operation Units.	30
N1854-N2016	**Fairey Fulmar I** Rolls-Royce Merlin VIII. C/n F.3707-F.3833 built at Stockport, assembled at Ringway. N1854-N1893, N1910-N1959, N1980-N2016. N1854 converted to Mk.II, became G-AIBE. Main deliveries to FAA, but N1883, N1931, N1957, N1987, N1993, N1999, N2004 used by RAF. N1891 became 3859M.	127
N2020-N2258	**Fairey Battle I** C/n F.3075-F.3257, F.3452-F.3457 built at Stockport, assembled at Ringway. N2020-N2066, N2082-N2131, N2147-N2190, N2211-N2258. N2042 had fixed u/c and with N2184 became Hercules test-beds. N2111-N2117, N2120-N2123, N2130, N2131, N2149, N2153-N2155, N2211-N2218, N2220-N2222, N2224 sold direct to Turkish Air Force. 99 shipped to SAAF, RAAF & RCAF unders EATS mainly after some RAF service. N2219 shipped to Poland. N2031, N2059, N2095, N2098, N2101, N2108, N2109, N2129, N2174 became 2481M, 1791M, 3309M, 1882M, 2555M, 1868M, 3316M, 1887M, 3946M.	189
N2259	**Miles M.14A Magister** C/n 628. Replacement for L6917. Became G-AJHB and to Argentine Air Force.	1
N2265-N2314	**Gloster Gladiator II** N2265 temporarily fitted with arrestor hooks. N2278, N2280, N2283, N2285-N2290, N2292-N2294 to SAAF 1941. Nineteen aircraft to Royal Navy.	50
N2318-N2729	**Hawker Hurricane I** Rolls-Royce Merlin III. N2318-N2367, N2380-N2409, N2422-N2441, N2453-N2502, N2520-N2559, N2582-N2631, N2645-N2674, N2700-N2729. Up to N2422 with fabric covered wings and from N2423 metal covered wings. N2322-N2324, N2327, N2347, N2348, N2358, N2395 to Finnish, N2387 to Turkish and N2718, N2719 to Yugoslav air forces. N2351, N2352, N2367, N2399, N2429, N2467, N2469, N2488, N2489, N2590, N2591, N2618, N2630, N2631, N2647, N2648, N2660, N2671 converted to Sea Hurricane. Renumbering on conversion to Mk.II: N2465, N2479, N2544, N2592, N2607, N2665 became BV162, BV168, DG616, BV172, DG633, DR367. N2328, N2341, N2343, N2354, N2398, N2399, N2435, N2455, N2493, N2554, N2591, N2597, N2660, N2669, N2671 became 3590M, 3588M, 2836M, 2646M, 4759M, 4661M, 4577M, 4693M, 4516M, 2835M, 4725M, 3577M, 4560M, 2876M, 4664M.	300
N2735-N2859	**Vickers Wellington IC** Built at Chester. N2735-N2784, N2800-N2829, N2840-N2859. N2755, N2801, N2856, N2857 converted to Mk.XVI. N2735, N2736, N2741-N2743, N2748, N2751, N2753, N2763, N2768, N2804, N2807, N2841, N2842 became 4417M, 4566M, 3180M, 3267M, 3190M, 3325M, 4229M, 3249M, 3261M, 2987M, 3328M, 3069M, 3308M, 3186M.	100
N2865-N3019	**Vickers Wellington IA** Built at Weybridge. N2865-N2914, N2935-N2964, N2980-N3019. N2874-N2879, N2937-N2942 originally built as NZ306-NZ317 for RNZAF but reverted to RAF. N2871, N2877, N2880, N2887, N2944, N2947, N2954, N2955, N2958 converted to Mk.XV and N2990 to Mk.XVI. N2874, N2952, N3001, N3009, N3011 became 4232M, 3110M, 3290M, 3332M, 3109M.	120
N3023-N3299	**Supermarine Spitfire I** N3023-N3072, N3091-N3130, N3160-N3203, N3221-N3250, N3264-N3299. N3297 prototype Mk.III and test-bed for Merlin 20, 45, 60, 61. Conversions: N3044, N3053, N3059, N3098, N3111, N3121, N3124, N3270, N3281, N3292 to Mk.VA. N3113 to PR.IV and N3117, N3241 to PR.V. N3032, N3034, N3072, N3122, N3160, N3169, N3199, N3236, N3288, N3297 became 3184M, 3247M, 3258M, 3077M, 3088M, 2843M, 3167M, 2826M, 3534M, 3396M. N3246, N3281 to Royal Navy.	200
N3300	**Miles M.9 Kestrel Trainer** Prototype Miles Master.	1
N3306-N3520	**Boulton Paul P.82 Defiant I** N3306-N3340, N3364-N3405, N3421-N3460, N3477-N3520. N3514 non-standard, less turret for trials. Conversions to TT: N3312, N3315, N3321-N3324, N3326, N3329, N3335, N3338, N3367, N3370, N3372, N3379, N3384, N3396, N3397, N3403, N3421, N3423, N3425, N3430, N3431, N3433-N3436, N3438, N3440,	161

N3441, N3450, N3454, N3456, N3480, N3487-N3489,
N3491, N3497, N3498, N3502, N3508, N3511, N3519.
N3307, N3337, N3368, N3377, N3394, N3445, N3479
became 2731M, 2977M, 2734M, 2729M, 2982M, 2740M,
3000M. Some transfers to Royal Navy.

N3522-N3631 Bristol 142L Blenheim IV 100
Built by Avro. N3522-N3545, N3551-N3575, N3578-
N3604, N3608-N3631. N3544, N3600 sold to Portugal
1943. N3582, N3622-N3624 to Free French Air Force.
N3523, N3527 to Royal Navy 1944. N3566, N3603
became 2120M, 4442M.

N3635-N3769 Short S.29 Stirling I 100
C/n 902-1001. N3635-N3684, N3700-N3729, N3750-
N3769 of which N3645, N3647-N3651 were destroyed
at Rochester works by enemy action. N3640, N3657
converted to Mk. II and reverted to Mk. I. N3711 built as
Mk. III. N3636-N3639, N3641, N3642, N3652, N3669,
N3674, N3683, N3700, N3760 became 3056M, 3361M,
3013M, 3389M, 3010M, 3012M, 3444M, 3637M, 4671M,
4668M-4670M.

N3773-N3991 Miles M.14A Magister 204
C/n 821-1024. N3773-N3817, N3820-N3869, N3875-
N3914, N3918-N3945, N3951-N3991. N3862-N3866,
N3875-N3879, N3885-N3889, N3895-N3899, N3912-
N3914 offset to REAF. N3901 to Irish Air Corps 1940.
N3804, N3891, N3963, N3964 to Turkey 1943. N3793
to Thai Navy and N3814, N3880, N3978 to Argentine
AF postwar. N3902, N3904, N3927, N3937, N3945,
N3987 became 5364M, 4675M, 5366M, 2212M, 4527M,
4551M. N3775, N3777, N3788, N3795, N3816, N3822,
N3830, N3850, N3851, N3882, N3890, N3926, N3933,
N3954, N3955, N3962, N3963, N3967, N3988 became G-AKPE,
'AJHE, 'ANLT, 'AIUC, 'AKXM, 'AHYK, 'AJHC, 'AJGN,
'AKMK, 'AKOL, 'AKRW, 'ALOE, 'ALHB, 'AKKV,
'AIUG, 'AIUE, 'AJHH, 'AKUA. N3848, N3925, N3940,
N3969 became F-BDPF, 'BDPC, 'BDPM, 'BDPB. N3821,
LV-XSG, ZK-ANK, LV-XPW, LV-XPN.

N3994-N4147 Fairey Fulmar I/II 123
Rolls-Royce Merlin VIII/XXX. C/n F.3834-F.3956.
N3994-N4016 Mk. I, N4017-N4043, N4060-N4100,
N4116-N4147 Mk. II. Delivered to Royal Navy but
N3995-N3997, N3999, N4009, N4014, N4041, N4087
served for a period in RAF.

N4152-N4425 Fairey Albacore I 200
C/n F.3518-F.3706, F.3957-F.3967. N4152-N4200,
N4219-N4268, N4281-N4330, N4347-N4391, N4420-
N4425. To Royal Navy but N4179, N4196-N4198,
N4241, N4247, N4287, N4348, N4380, N4388, N4422
served for a period in RAF.

N4557 Miles M.14A Magister 1
Replacement for L6914.

N4560-N4853 Airspeed AS.10 Oxford I/II 200
N4560-N4609, N4630-N4659, N4681-N4700 (100)
Mk. I, N4720-N4739, N4754-N4803, N4824-N4853
(100) Mk. II. N4648-N4650, N4652-N4654, N4656-
N4658, N4681, N4682, N4685, N4687 direct to RNZAF
and N4651, N4555, N4659, N4683, N4684, N4686,
N4688-N4699, N4700 to SRAF in 1940. N4565,
N4646, N4764, N4796, N4850 became 3658M, 4345M,
3733M, 3152M, 2837M. N4791, N4841 to Royal Navy
1943. Postwar: N4771 to Belgian AF, N4792 to Royal
Danish AF, N4602 to Royal Norwegian AF.

N4856-N5385 Avro 652A Anson I 500
N4856-N4899, N4901-N4948, N4953-N4989, N4995-
N5044, N5047-N5094, N5096-N5125, N5130-N5178,
N5182-N5220, N5225-N5274, N5279-N5318, N5320-
N5359, N5361-N5385. Direct offsets: N4863-N4867 to
Irish Air Corps; N4868, N4870, N4873, N4876, N4879,
N4883, N4887, N4891, N4895, N4899, N4904, N4908,
N4912, N4916, N4918, N4920, N4921, N4926, N4931,
N4936, N4941, N4946, N4955, N4960, N4965, N4970,
N4977, N4984, N4996, N5003 (30) to RAAF; N5150,
N5155, N5160, N5165, N5170, N5175, N5185, N5190,
N5200, N5205, N5210, N5215 (12) for R Hellenic AF.
Shipped out 1940-42 under EATS were 109 to RCAF,
48 to SAAF and 3 to SRAF. N5033, N5089, N5103,
N5240, N5254 became 4548M, 4484M, 4349M, 6557M,
4420M. N5080, N5235 went to RN 1944-46. Postwar
disposals: N4882, N5314 to French AF; N5058, N5218

to Belgian AF and N5366 to R Norwegian AF. N4877
became G-AMDA and is preserved.

N5389-N5438 Miles M.14A Magister I 50
C/n 1025-1074. N5389-N5393, N5400-N5404 direct
to Irish Air Corps, N5395, N5411, N5413, N5425
became 5965M, 4550M, 5359M, 1529M. N5399, N5429,
N5436 to Turkish AF 1943. N5406 postwar to Argentina.

N5444-N5493 DH.82A Tiger Moth II 50
C/n 3707-3720, 3726-3745, 3751-3765, 3777. To
elementary and reserve training schools late 1938. N5446
to Royal Navy 1941. N5455, N5461, N5468 became
5426M, 5356M, 4439M. N5481 to SRAF and N5486 to
SAAF, 1943. Postwar: N5491 to R Netherlands AF.

N5500-N5574 Gloster Sea Gladiator 60
N5500-N5549, N5565-N5574 to Royal Navy. N5513
became Gladiator II

N5575-N5924 Gloster Gladiator II 240
N5575-N5594, N5620-N5649, N5680-N5729, N5750-
N5789, N5810-N5859, N5875-N5924. Direct offsets:
N5584, N5586, N5587, N5683, N5685-N5689, N5691,
N5692, N5694, N5696, N5700, N5704, N5706-N5713,
N5715, N5718, N5721, N5722, N5724, N5726-N5729
to Finnish AF; N5835-N5849 to Portuguese AF; N5919-
N5924 to R Norwegian AF. A number served in RAAF
and SAAF squadrons in the Middle East. N5755, N5758,
N5760, N5762, N5767, N5771, N5875-N5892 to REAF
some of which were repossessed. N5780, N5825, N5827,
N5828, N5830, N5857 to R Iraqi AF 1942-44. N5638
to Royal Navy 1942.

N6000-N6129 Short S.29 Stirling I Series 1 100
Built by Short Bros & Harland, c/ns SH.231-SH.330.
N6000-N6049, N6085-N6104, N6120-N6129 at Belfast
and N6065-N6084 at Aldergrove. N6025-N6028, N6031
were destroyed in the factory by enemy action. N6000,
N6006, N6101 became 3768M, 4165M, 3495M.

N6133-N6138 Short S.35 Sunderland 3
C/n 897-899. N6133, N6135, N6138 built at Rochester.

N6140-N6242 Bristol Blenheim IV 100
C/n 9240-9339. N6140-N6174, N6176-N6220, N6223-
N6242. N6143, N6156 to Royal Navy 1942-44. N6152,
N6209 became 1649M, 1636M.

N6246 DH.86B 1
C/n 2343 ex- G-ADYG. VIP version.

N6250-N6439 Airspeed AS.10 Oxford I/II 140
N6250-N6270 Mk. I less turrets; N6271-N6299, N6320-
N6340 Mk. I standard; N6341-N6349, N6365-N6384,
N6400-N6439 Mk. II. N6327 experimentally fitted with
twin fins. N6280, N6285, N6291, N6298, N6325, N6331,
N6346, N6348, N6377, N6406, N6413, N6420, N6427,
N6439 direct to RCAF. N6253, N6257, N6276, N6332,
N6340, N6341, N6371, N6405, N6412, N6419, N6426
became 3807M, 3806M, 3834M, 5486M, 5329M, 3825M,
3846M, 3804M, 3618M, 3805M, 5511M. Midwar
N6328, N6376, N6410 transferred to USAAF in UK
and N6344 to Royal Navy. Postwar N6418 to R Nor AF.

N6443-N6988 DH.82A Tiger Moth II 400
N6443-N6490, N6519-N6556, N6576-N6625, N6630-
N6674, N6706-N6755, N6770-N6812, N6834-N6882,
N6900-N6949, N6962-N6988. N6640, N6722 converted
to Queen Bee. Direct offsets: N6882-N6901, N6903,
N6905, N6906 to RAAF, N6979 to SRAF plus N6981,
N6988 later. N6966 to Indian government 1940. N6474,
N6521, N6553-N6556, N6576, N6581, N6582, N6596,
N6597, N6604, N6605, N6609, N6672, N6752, N6869,
N6870, N6876, N6902, N6904, N6918, N6923, N6976,
N6980 to SAAF 1940-43. N6479, N6480, N6535,
N6539, N6551, N6612, N6668, N6720, N6725, N6733,
N6804, N6854, N6872 became 6939M, 4205M, 5431M,
7152M, 3403M, 4699M, 6872M, 7014M, 6439M, 3402M,
7040M, 7002M, 5433M. N6488, N6545, N6771, N6795,
N6842, N6868, N6967 to Royal Navy 1945-46. Postwar
disposals: N6445, N6839 R Netherlands AF; N6972 to
R Norwegian AF as 6317M; N6945 to RPAF; N6741,
N6802, N6973 as 6473M to Burmese AF joining N6917,
N6950, N6951 supplied in 1940. Many were sold for
civilian use, including 96 to the UK register.

N7000-N7199 North American NA-16 Harvard I 200
Purchased from America. 124 reshipped to SRAF under
EATS. N7020 retained in the USA. N7070, N7092,
N7096, N7129 became 2123M, 2056M, 2124M, 2203M.

N7205-N7404 Lockheed 414 Hudson I 200
N7344-N7350, N7352, N7354-N7356, N7360, N7370, N7371, N7373, N7375, N7380-N7391 direct to RCAF. N7220 converted to transport and delivered to Dutch government postwar. N7364 became G-AGAR for use by Sidney Cotton. N7208, N7230, N7251, N7259, N7267, N7276, N7297, N7320, N7339, N7393 became 4587M, 3076M, 4266M, 3652M, 4768M, 4799M, 3467M, 2176M, 2168M, 3468M.

N7408-N9017 Miles M.9A Master I 500
Kestrel XXX engines. N7408-N7457, N7470-N7515, N7534-N7582, N7597-N7641, N7672-N7721, N7748-N7782 of which N7412 was prototype fighter conversion and N7780-N7782 were similarly converted; N7801-N7822 6-gun trainer version; N7823-N7846, N7867-N7902, N7921-N7969, N7985-N8022, N8041-N8081, N9003-N9017 Mk.I. N7422 Mk.II prototype and N7447 converted to Mk.II. N7994 prototype Mk.III became 3128M. N7716 not delivered, used by makers for TT trials. N8009 sold to Eire after internment. N7444, N7473, N7475, N7497, N7505, N7507, N7514, N7547, N7548, N7550, N7561, N7568, N7572, N7614, N7631, N7674, N7675, N7696, N7707, N7775, N7776, N7801, N7832, N7838, N7841, N7846, N7878, N7888, N7947, N8004, N8011, N8015, N8019, N8045, N8050, N8053-N8058, N8063, N8077, N8079-N8081 transferred to Royal Navy 1940-44. N7410, N7425, N7431, N7455, N7478, N7499, N7503, N7534, N7535, N7541, N7573, N7599, N7603, N7605, N7623, N7682, N7687 became 2551M, 3812M, 3810M, 3755M, 3818M, 3757M, 3823M, 3868M, 4089M, 3820M, 3765M, 3870M, 3648M, 4601M, 3822M, 3869M, 3821M and N7701, N7751, N7768, N7781, N7803, N7804, N7809-N7811, N7814, N7815, N7817, N7820, N7821, N7829, N7838, N8012, N8051, N9004, N9005 became 3811M, 3756M, 4334M, 4128M, 4158M, 4159M, 4164M, 4160M, 4161M, 4157M, 3460M, 4117M, 4164M, 4162M, 4335M, 3646M, 3661M, 3160M, 3831M, 3819M.

N9020-N9050 Short S.25 Sunderland I 18
C/n S.1004-S.1021, N9020-N9030, N9044-N9050 delivered in 1939.

N9055-N9106 Handley Page HP.53 Hereford/HP.52 Hampden 50
Short & Harland c/ns SH.181-SH.230. N9055-N9081, N9084-N9106 ordered and built as Herefords but N9062, N9064, N9065, N9070, N9080, N9086, N9090, N9096, N9101, N9105, N9106 converted to Hampden I and N9064, N9096, N9106 later to Hampden TB.I. N9055, N9057, N9058, N9068, N9075, N9079, N9089, N9093, N9102, N9104 became 2804M, 2192M, 2805M, 2913M, 2830M, 2914M, 3019M, 2754M, 2767M, 2781M.

N9107-N9108 Airspeed AS.6 Envoy 2
G-AFJD, 'AFJE acquired for Communications Flight, Delhi.

N9114-N9523 DH.82A Tiger Moth II 300
N9114-N9163, N9172-N9215, N9238-N9279, N9300-N9349, N9367-N9410, N9427-N9464, N9492-N9523. Shipped under EATS mainly direct from production: N9129, N9130, N9135, N9136, N9139, N9140, N9173, N9257-N9261, N9263, N9264, N9266, N9269, N9270, N9376 to RAAF; N9142, N9144, N9163, N9172, N9183, N9185, N9245-N9247, N9249, N9254, N9268, N9271, N9273, N9338, N9342, N9405, N9409, N9410, N9427, N9428, N9456-N9459 to RNZAF; N9131-N9133, N9137, N9141, N9143, N9146, N9162, N9262, N9265, N9267, N9308, N9315, N9325, N9329, N9332, N9339-N9341, N9343, N9344, N9379, N9393, N9398, N9400, N9401, N9403, N9404, N9454, N9511, N9522, N9523 to SAAF; N9114, N9118, N9120, N9123, N9248, N9493, N9397, N9513, N9515 to SRAF. N9201, N9335, N9377, N9378, N9507 transferred to Royal Navy. N9174, N9190, N9211, N9239, N9278, N9305, N9374, N9385 became 6619M, 5283M, 5982M, 5436M, 6878M, 3803M, 7041M, 7038M. Postwar disposals: N9302 to RIAF, N9192, N9194, N9391 to R Netherlands AF and N9188, N9203, N9496, N9498 to Burmese AF. Others sold for civil registration.

N9526-N9999 Avro 652A Anson I 350
N9526-N9575, N9587-N9621, N9640-N9689, N9713-N9752, N9765-N9790, N9815-N9858, N9870-N9919, N9930-N9956, N9972-N9999. Deliveries to EATS some

direct from production included 123 to RCAF, 40 to SAAF, 5 to RAAF and 3 to SRAF. N9648, N9657, N9666 were sold direct to REAF and N9947-N9952 to Turkish AF. Transfers: N9608, N9828, N9908 to Royal Navy and N9610 to USAAF in UK. N9612, N9781, N9847 became 6446M, 3385M, 4317M. N9531 became G-AHXS.

The 'P' Series

P1000 to P9999

The letter 'O' was not used and P1000 followed on from N9999 in 1938. Again an exception to the 'blackout blocks', which included P1000-P1004 not used, was made for aircraft bought in America.

Serial Nos	Aircraft Type and Remarks	Quantity
P1005-P1139	**Airspeed AS.10 Oxford II**	25(100)
	P1070-P1094 (25) only built by Percival; P1005-P1054, P1095-P1099, P1120-P1139 cancelled. P1073, P1074 became 3735M, 3736M. P1077 transferred to USAAF in the UK in 1944.	
P1145-P1356	**Handley Page HP.52 Hampden I**	200
	P1145-P1189, P1194-P1230, P1233-P1261, P1265-P1305, P1309-P1356. Converted to TB.I: P1145-P1147, P1150, P1151, P1157, P1158, P1160, P1164, P1166, P1169, P1177, P1188, P1189, P1207, P1208, P1214, P1215, P1219, P1229, P1236-P1238, P1243, P1245, P1246, P1249, P1250, P1257, P1258, P1273, P1282, P1284, P1286, P1287, P1296, P1312, P1314, P1335, P1344-P1346, P1352, P1356. To RCAF 1943: P1167, P1200, P1230, P1311. P1279, P1280, P1324, P1327 became 1857M, 2108M, 2261M, 2214M.	
P1360-P1659	**Armstrong Whitworth AW.41 Albemarle**	200
	P1360, P1361 prototypes to AM Spec B18/38 built by Armstrong Whitworth, remainder built by A.W. Hawkesley Ltd. P1362-P1369 GT.I Srs I, P1370, P1371 ST.I Srs I, P1372, P1373 GT.I Srs I, P1374 ST.I Srs II, P1375, P1376 GT.I Srs I, P1377 ST.I Srs I, P1378 GT.I Srs I, P1379 ST.I Srs II, P1380-P1384 GT.I Srs I, P1385 ST.I Srs II, P1386-P1394 GT.I Srs I, P1395 ST.I Srs II, P1396 GT.I Srs I, P1397 ST.I Srs II, P1398-P1401 GT.I Srs I, P1402 GT.I Srs II, P1403 ST.I Srs II, P1404, P1405 GT.I Srs II, P1406 Mk.IV prototype, P1407-P1409, P1430-P1432 GT.I Srs II, P1433 ST.I Srs II, P1434-P1446 GT.I Srs II, P1447, P1448 ST.I Srs I, P1449-P1451 GT.I Srs II, P1452 ST.I Srs II, P1453 GT.I Srs II, P1454 ST.I Srs II loaned to BOAC, P1455-P1471 GT.I Srs II, P1472, P1473 ST.I Srs II, P1474 GT.I Srs II, P1475 ST.I Srs II, P1476-P1478 GT.I Srs II, P1479, P1480 ST.I Srs II, P1501 GT.I Srs II, P1502-P1510 ST.I Srs III, P1511-P1518 GT.I Srs II, P1519, P1520 ST.I Srs III, P1521-P1529, P1550-P1553 GT.I Srs III, P1554-P1556 ST.I Srs III, P1557 GT.I Srs III, P1558-P1569, P1590-P1609, P1630-P1659 ST.I Srs III. P1477, P1562, P1567, P1590, P1595, P1636-P1638, P1642, P1647 to USSR; P1455, P1645 similarly sent but lost en route. P1361, P1363, P1452 became 3370M, 4450M, 4804M.	
P1665-P1745	**Westland Lysander I/II**	70
	P1665-P1699 Mk.I, P1711-P1745 Mk.II. P1666, P1668, P1680-P1683, P1695, P1716, P1718, P1719, P1728, P1741, P1743, P1744 converted to TT.III. P1723 had mock-up of Boulton Paul 'A' Mk.III turret. P1713, P1735, P1736, P1738 to Free French Air Force, P1728 to RCAF. P1684, P1687, P1695, P1729 became 3939M, 2234M, 3951M, 3973M.	
P1749-P1754	**Percival Vega Gull III**	6
	All to No.24 Sqn 1938 and destroyed by end of 1940.	

P1758-P1759 General Aircraft GAL.38 **1(2)**
To Spec S23/37. P1758 not delivered, P1759 not built.

P1764-P1765 DH.89A Dragon Rapide **2**
Two Gipsy VI. C/n 6421, 6422. Delivered to No.24
Squadron.

P1767 & P1770 Fairey Barracuda prototypes **2**
C/n F.4468, F.4469 to Spec S24/37. P1770/G.

P1774-P1785 Folland 43/37 engine testbeds **12**
Known installations: P1774 Sabres, Centaurus IV; P1775
Hercules VIII, Centaurus IV; P1776 Sabre I, Centaurus I:
P1777 Sabre I, Centaurus I; P1778 Centaurus I, Griffon
and DH propeller tests; P1779 Hercules XI, various
Sabres; P1780 Hercules XI, Sabre I, V, VIII; P1782-
P1785 Hercules XI.

P1800-P2059 Airspeed AS.10 Oxford I/II **200**
P1800-P1849, P1860-P1863 Mk.II; P1864 Mk.III
converted to Mk.V; P1865-P1899, P1920-P1969,
P1980-P2009, P2030-P2044 Mk.I; P2045-P2059 Mk.II.
P1805, P1812, P1819, P1826, P1833, P1840, P1846,
P1863, P1870, P1877, P1884 direct to RCAF. P1944,
P1953, P1963, P1983, P1989-P1992, P1996-P1999,
P2000, P2001, P2003, P2004-P2009, P2030-P2059
direct to RNZAF becoming NZ255-NZ258, NZ261-
NZ270, NZ259, NZ271-NZ280, NZ620, NZ281-NZ290,
NZ1201-NZ1215. P1984, P1993, P2002 became 801-803
of Iranian AF. P1825 to Royal Navy. P1835, P1865,
P1876, P1882, P1936, P1994 became 4115M, 3612M,
4347M, 4346M, 3734M, 3616M. Postwar P1966 went
to Belgian AF, P1957 to R Hellenic AF and P1894 to
R Netherlands AF.

P2062-P2145 Handley Page HP.52 Hampden I **75**
Pegasus XVIII engines. Built by English Electric Co.
P2062-P2100, P2110-P2145. P2064, P2065, P2073-
P2075, P2078, P2080, P2084, P2095, P2113, P2119,
P2126, P2133 converted to TB.I. P2067, P2133 to
RCAF 1943. P2073, P2117, P2131 became 4348M,
2270M, 2177M.

P2150 Miles M.14A Magister I **1**
Replacement.

P2155-P2369 Fairey Battle **150**
C/n F.4068-F.4217. P2155-P2204, P2233-P2278, P2300-
P2336, P2353-P2369. Offsets and subsequent deliveries:
P2155, P2156, P2164, P2165, P2170-P2173, P2185-
P2188, P2196-P2199, P2233-P2242, P2252, P2257,
P2259, P2262, P2301-P2304, P2306, P2308, P2309,
P2311, P2312, P2318-P2320, P2325, P2329, P2331,
P2358, P2361, P2366-P2369 RCAF; P2157, P2166-
P2169, P2245, P2263, P2264, P2276, P2300, P2305,
P2317, P2354, P2363-P2365 RAAF; P2174, P2177-
P2179, P2181, P2307, P2321-P2323 SAAF. P2353 to
Belgian AF after forced landing. P2159, P2243, P2270,
P2272 became 2556M, 2483M, 2143M, 2159M.

P2374-P2510 Miles M.14A Magister I **100**
C/n 1611-1710. P2374-P2410, P2426-P2470, P2493-
P2510. P2384, P2405, P2407 became 4513M, 4111M,
5355M. Postwar P2406, P2426, P2503 to Argentine AF,
others to civil register.

P2515-P2532 Vickers Wellington IA **18**
Conversions: P2518 DW.I, P2522 DW.I then Mk.IX,
P2519, P2521, P2528 Mk.XV. P2517 became 2794M.

P2535-P3264 Hawker Hurricane I **500**
R-R Merlin III engines. Built by Gloster. P2535-P2584,
P2614-P2653, P2672-P2701, P2713-P2732, P2751-
P2770, P2792-P2836, P2854-P2888, P2900-P2924,
P2946-P2995, P3020-P3069, P3080-P3124, P3140-
P3179, P3200-P3234, P3250-P3264. Up to P2681 with
2-blade Watts propeller, from P2682 3-blade Rotols.
First 100 had TR9D rest TR1133. Transfers to Royal
Navy mainly for Sea Hurricane conversion, some of
which reverted to Hurricanes: P2717, P2731, P2826,
P2857, P2878, P2886, P2921, P2948, P2953, P2963,
P2972, P2986, P2994, P3020, P3042, P3056, P3061,
P3090, P3092, P3104, P3111, P3149, P3152, P3165,
P3168, P3206, P3229. To Mk.II and renumbered:
P2674, P2682, P2823, P2829, P2835, P2863, P2904,
P2908, P2975, P3023, P3057, P3068, P3103, P3106,
P3121, P3207, P3216, P3223, P3256 became BV171,
DG641, BV161, DR355, DR353, DR368, DR357,
DR369, DR372, DR342, BV169, DG615, DG340,
DR370, DR350, DG631, BV174, DG614, DR365.

P2544, P2679, P2717, P2722, P2814, P2859, P2911,
P2913, P2979, P3020, P3111, P3119 became 2636M,
3314M, 5054M, 3085M, 3954M, 4685M, 3192M, 3838M,
3087M, 4505M, 4503M, 3585M. P3036, P3114, P3233,
P3250-P3254, P3257-P3259, P3262 to SAAF and P2993
to Free French Air Force. P2617 currently preserved.

P3265-P3984 Hawker Hurricane I **500**
B = Brooklands built, L = Langley built. P3265-P3279,
P3300-P3324, P3345-P3364, P3380-P3399, B; P3400-
P3419, L; P3420-P3429, P3448-P3487, B; P3488-P3492
P3515-P3554, P3574-P3578, L; P3579-P3619, B; P3620-
P3623, L; P3640-P3644, B; P3645-P3684, P3700-P3709,
L; P3710-P3739, P3755-P3774, B; P3775-P3789, P3802-
P3836, L; P3854-P3903, B; P3920-P3944, P3960-P3984,
L. Metal covered wings except P3714-P3717, P3737-
P3739, P3757-P3761, P3767, P3768, P3770-P3774,
P3858-P3869, P3872-P3875, P3882-P3889, P3897-
P3903 with fabric covered wings. Transfers to Royal
Navy mainly for conversion to Sea Hurricane: P3301,
P3320, P3362, P3394, P3398, P3460, P3466, P3467,
P3530, P3544, P3597, P3620, P3654, P3675, P3701,
P3706, P3710, P3719, P3773, P3776, P3784, P3805,
P3814, P3829, P3870, P3877, P3883, P3924-P3926,
P3934, P3975, P3979. Converted to Mk.II: P3216,
P3307, P3351, P3402, P3412, P3449, P3521, P3539,
P3642, P3551, P3670, P3714, P3717, P3756, P3759,
P3811, P3928 became BV174, DR364, DR393, BV160,
DG613, DR362, BV167, DG634, BV166, DR343,
DG646, DR341, DR348, DG612, DR349, DG644,
DR363. P3416 to Irish Air Corps. P3269, P3345, P3357,
P3384, P3410, P3465, P3517, P3544, P3583, P3592,
P3597, P3613, P3656, P3701, P3810, P3814, P3829,
P3835, P3884, P3983 became 3388M, 4861M, 3254M,
3228M, 2749M, 3213M, 2121M, 3583M, 2850M, 3214M,
5044M, 3591M, 4012M, 4576M, 3257M, 4559M, 4561M,
2694M, 4262M, 2747M. P3757 to USAAF in UK.

P3991-P4279 Fairey Swordfish **200**
C/n F.4218-F.4417. P3991-P4039, P4061-P4095,
P4123-P4169, P4191-P4232, P4253-P4279 built for
the Royal Navy. P4016, P4019, P4021, P4026, P4027,
P4028, P4030, P4068 to RAF in Singapore.

P4285-P4418 Handley Page HP.52 Hampden I **120**
P4285-P4324, P4335-P4384, P4389-P4418. Converted
to TB.I: P4304, P4306, P4312, P4315, P4347, P4369,
P4373, P4395, P4401, P4418. P4337, P4349, P4369
became 2196M, 2157M, 2140M.

P4420-P4673 Avro 652A Anson **(200)**
Cancelled. P4420-P4469, P4478-P4500, P4521-P4561,
P4575-P4613, P4627-P4673.

P4677-P4822 DH.82B Queen Bee **110**
C/n 5291-5400. P4677-P4716, P4747-P4781, P4788-
P4822.

P4825-P4927 Bristol 142 Blenheim IV **70**
P4825-P4864, P4898-P4927. P4910, P4911, P4915,
P4916, P4921, P4922 direct to R Hellenic AF. P4829,
P4831, P4847 became 4172M, 3992M, 3980M.

P4930-P5112 Armstrong Whitworth AW.38 Whitley I **164**
P4930-P4974, P4980-P5029, P5040-P5065, P5070-
P5112. P5088 became 2332M.

P5116-P5165 Lockheed Hudson I **50**
P5165 crashed on delivery. P5163, P5164 direct to SAAF.
P5123 to Irish Air Corps after forced landing. P5145
trials aircraft and P5124, P5158 became 4555M, 2429M,
4466M.

P5170-P5209 Hawker Hurricane I/X **40**
Canadian built Mk.I re-designated Mk.X. P5178 to the
Irish Air Corps after forced landing. P5180, P5182,
P5187, P5203, P5206, P5209 to Royal Navy for Sea
Hurricane conversion. P5175, P5190, P5195, P5199,
P5204 converted to Mk.II and renumbered BV159,
DG620, DG623, DG632, BV170. P5170, P5183,
P5191, P5207 became 5045M, 2807M, 3252M, 3272M.

P5212 & P5216 Hawker Typhoon IA/IB **2**
Prototypes to Spec F18/37.

P5219 & P5224 Hawker Tornado **2**
Prototypes to Spec F18/37.

P5228-P5294 Fairey Battle I **50**
C/n F.4418-F.4467. P5228-P5252, P5270-P5294. 40 to
RAAF, RCAF or SAAF under EATS mostly direct from
production.

P5298-P5436 **Handley Page HP.52 Hampden** 80
Built by Canadian Car & Foundry Co, P5298-P5337 by
Quebec Group, P5338-P5346, P5386-P5400, P5421-
P5436 by Ontario Group. Assembled by 7 AAU Hooton
Park. P5301, P5302, P5304, P5309, P5311, P5315,
P5320, P5323, P5327, P5331, P5335, P5341, P5343,
P5387, P5389, P5390, P5394 converted to TB.I. P5298,
P5336, P5337, P5399, P5400, P5421-P5436 to RCAF.
P5311 became 3075M.

P5441-P5565 **Airspeed AS.30 Queen Wasp** 5(65)
P5441-P5445 only completed; P5446-P5450 partly built;
P5451-P5455, P5496-P5525, P5546-P5565 cancelled.

P5571-P5620 **Lockheed 2B14** (50)
Order cancelled.

P5625-P5629 **Airspeed AS.6J Envoy III** 5
Delivered in 1939. P5626 became G-AHAC.

P5634-P5640 **Percival P.16e Petrel** 7
Also known as Q6. P5638 to Royal Navy 1943. P5634,
P5637 became G-AHTB, 'AHOM.

P5646-P5720 **Supermarine Walrus I** 50
P5646-P5670, P5696-P5720 to Royal Navy.

P5723-P5726 **Curtiss Condor** 4
G-AEWD, 'AEZE, 'AEWE, 'AEWF impressed September
1939, scrapped November 1939.

P5731-P5775 **DH.82B Queen Bee** 28
C/n 5401-5428. P5731-P5749, P5767-P5775.

P5778 **Airspeed AS.6 Envoy** 1
C/n 33 Ex- G-ADBA.

P5783-P5982 **North American NA-16 Harvard I** 200
Up to P5915 shipped to UK of which 89 went later to
SRAF and from P5916 shipped direct to SRAF except
P5921 to SAAF.

P5986-P5993 **Percival P.10 Vega Gull III** 8
P5986, P5987 direct to Royal Navy, rest to RAF.
P5992 to Air Attache, Lisbon as G-AFVI.

P5998-P6322 **Percival P.28 Proctor I/IA** 222
P5998 Mk.I became P.29 light anti-invasion bomber;
P5999-P6037, P6050-P6079, P6101-P6113 Mk.IA;
P6114-P6130 Mk.I, P6131-P6145, P6166, P6167 Mk.IA;
P6168-P6200, P6226-P6275, P6301-P6322 Mk.I. Note
Mk.IA for Royal Navy. P6168, P6169, P6265, P6319,
P6321 to USAAF 1944. P6236, P6239, P6261, P6270
became 4811M, 4800M, 4496M, 4786M. P6240 to Czech
Air Attache. Many postwar to civil register.

P6326 **Miles M.15** 1
Trainer prototype to T1/37, was registered U-0234.

P6330 **Waco ZVN** 1
Acquired for tricycle undercarriage tests.

P6343-P6466 **Miles M.14A Magister** 100
C/n 1711-1810. P6343-P6382, P6396-P6424, P6436-
P6466. Direct offsets: P6418 REAF, P6414, P6422,
P6440 to IAC as Nos.76, 77, 74. P6413, P6415, P6424,
P6436, P6437 modified as light bombers in 1940. P6346
& P6452 to Turkish AF 1943. P6345, P6370, P6378
became 5363M, 4047M, 4774M. P6380 first civilianised
Miles Hawk III as G-AGVW and others to civil register.

P6480-P6769 **Fairey Battle I** 200
C/n F.3968-F.4067, F.4470-F.4569. P6480-P6509,
P6523-P6572, P6596-P6645, P6663-P6692, P6718-
P6737, P6750-P6769. Last 100 from P6616 built as
trainers. P6480, P6481, P6483-P6509, P6523-P6569,
P6596, P6599, P6602, P6620, P6622, P6631, P6633,
P6639, P6642, P6663-P6665, P6670, P6672, P6677,
P6684, P6689, P6691, P6692, P6720, P6724, P6729-
P6732, P6734, P6737, P6750, P6760-P6762 to EATS
countries. P6613, P6615 went direct to RHAF. P6616,
P6623, P6640, P6673, P6678, P6680, P6687, P6726,
P6727, P6735, P6763 became 3312M, 3557M, 3317M,
2545M, 3310M, 2934M, 2933M, 2144M, 3910M, 3311M,
3559M.

P6785-P6788 **DH.87B Hornet Moth floatplane** 4
Gipsy Major I engines. C/n 8126, 8135, 8134, 8061
purchased in Canada.

P6795-P6880 **Airspeed AS.10 Oxford II** 75
Intermediate trainers. Built by de Havilland. P6795-
P6819, P6831-P6880. P6831-P6843, P6845, P6847,
P6849, P6852, P6854-P6859, P6866, P6866-
P6868, P6873, P6877, P6879 to SRAF, remainder from
P6844 onwards to RNZAF. P6795, P6819 to USAAF
1944. P6816 became 2839M.

P6885-P6961 **Bristol 142L Blenheim IV** 62
C/n 9410-9471. P6885-P6934, P6950-P6961. P6891,
P6892, P6897, P6898, P6903, P6904 direct to RHAF.
P6907, P6921 became 2541M, 3438M. P6960 to Royal
Navy in 1944.

P6966-P7269 **Westland Whirlwind I** 114(200)
P6966-P7015, P7035-P7064, P7089-P7122 (114) built.
P7123-P7128, P7158-P7177, P7192-P7221, P7240-
P7269 cancelled. P6994 to USAAF 1942. P6967 became
G-AGOI.

P7280-P8799 **Supermarine Spitfire II** 1000
Mk.II as per original order. First Spitfires built at Castle
Bromwich, evolving as 750 Mk.IIA, 170 Mk.IIB, 80
Mk.VA/VB. P7280-P7329, P7350-P7389, P7420-P7449,
P7490-P7509, P7520-P7569, P7590-P7629, P7660-
P7699, P7730-P7759, P7770-P7789, P7810-P7859,
P7880-P7929, P7960-P7999, P8010-P8049, P8070-
P8099, P8130-P8149, P8160-P8209, P8230-P8279,
P8310-P8349, P8360-P8399, P8420-P8449, P8460-
P8479, P8500-P8549, P8560-P8609, P8640-P8679,
P8690-P8698; up to this point all Mk.IIA/IIB except for
P8532, P8537, P8539, P8542, P8560, P8561, P8564,
P8578, P8581, P8585, P8600, P8603, P8604, P8606,
P8607, P8609, P8640 built as Mk.V. Later P7287,
P7297, P7299, P7308, P7316, P7324, P7447, P7498,
P7532, P7619, P7629, P7672, P7686, P7692, P7757,
P7789, P7846, P7849, P7906, P7909, P7920, P7964,
P7965, P7973, P7986, P8017, P8036, P8038, P8073,
P8086, P8095, P8098, P8099, P8167, P8195, P8236,
P8237, P8239, P8246, P8259, P8262, P8324, P8339,
P8436, P8438, P8517, P8545, P8549, P8645 were
converted to Mk.V. Remainder built as follows: P8699-
P8700 Mk.VB, P8701, P8702 Mk.II, P8703 Mk.VB,
P8704-P8706 Mk.II, P8707-P8724 Mk.VB, P8725-
P8729 Mk.II, P8740-P8759, P8780-P8799 Mk.VB.
P7505, P8784 converted to PR.XIII. 52 Mk.IIs converted
to ASR.IIC. 14 of various marks were loaned to USAAF
and 8 transferred to Royal Navy of which P7909, P8708
became Seafire IBs. P8332 to RCAF 1942. P7288, P7914,
P7964, P8090, P8091, P8657, P8700 became 4409M,
4366M, 5262M, 4256M, 4936M, 4431M, 5517M and
P8727 became G-AHZI. P8755, P8783 to Russia 1942
and P8788, P8791 to Portugal 1947. P7350 preserved in
the UK and P7973 in Australia.

P8809-P8818 **Hawker Hurricane I** 10
Built at Brooklands. P8809, P8810, P8816-P8818 with
fabric covered wings, remainder metal wings. P8815 and
P8817 direct to SAAF.

P8822-P9046 **Airspeed AS.10 Oxford I/II** 150
P8822-P8830 Mk.I, P8831-P8854 Mk.II, P8855-P8868,
P8891-P8916 Mk.I, P8917-P8931, P8964-P8994 Mk.II;
P8995-P8998, P9020-P9046 Mk.I. P8832, P8833 fitted
as air ambulances. P8835-P8868, P8891-P8897, P8901-
P8904, P8907-P8909, P8912-P8916 to RNZAF plus
P9045, P9046 despatched but lost at sea. P9024 became
3152M. P8917, P8931, P8977, P8992 to USAAF 1943-
44. P8928 transferred to Royal Navy 1944. P8925,
P9026 to R Danish AF postwar.

P9051-P9199 **Westland Lysander II** 100
P9051-P9080, P9095-P9140, P9176-P9199. P9105
fitted with Blackburn-Steiger high-lift wing and became
3924M. P9109-P9119, P9122, P9123, P9125, P9126,
P9128, P9129, P9130, P9133, P9136 converted to Mk.III.
P9060, P9061, P9065, P9099, P9100, P9110, P9111,
P9113, P9115, P9117, P9122, P9125, P9128, P9187
converted to TT. P9059, P9078, P9102, P9103, P9134,
P9181, P9184, P9197 to Free French Air Force 1940-42.
P9122 to USAAF 1943. P9060, P9065, P9077, P9079,
P9096, P9108, P9187 became 3952M, 3945M, 4004M,
3935M, 3934M, 3943M, 3888M.

P9205-P9300 **Vickers Wellington IA/IC** 82
Built at Weybridge. P9205-P9236 Mk.IA; P9237-P9250,
P9265-P9300 Mk.IC. P9223 converted as DW.I, P9238
Mk.III prototype, P9214, P9231 converted to Mk.XV.
P9237, P9239, P9289 converted to Mk.XVI. P9206,
P9211, P9224, P9233, P9238, P9239, P9271, P9290,
P9296 became 2449M, 3404M, 3645M, 3440M, 3410M,
3103M, 3255M, 3322M, 3321M.

P9305-P9584 **Supermarine Spitfire I** 183(200)
P9305-P9339, P9360-P9399, P9420-P9469, P9490-

P9519, P9540-P9567 built, P9568-P9584 being
cancelled. P9566, P9567 to Turkey direct. Conversions
to Mk.VA: P9367, P9397, P9448, P9540, P9550, P9556,
P9563. Conversions to PR to various standards: P9308,
P9310, P9328, P9385, P9505, P9518, P9551, P9552.
P9325, P9368, P9433, P9556 transferred to Royal Navy.
P9544 to Portugal 1943. P9319, P9332, P9363, P9376,
P9390, P9399, P9460, P9504, P9507 became 3143M,
3595M, 3371M, 4606M, 2111M, 2137M, 3593M, 2728M,
2119M. P9306 preserved in the USA and P9444 in UK.

P9588-P9589	**DH.89A Dominie**	2
	C/n 6455, 6466 used by No.2 Electrical & Wireless School	
P9594	**Martin Baker MB.2**	1
	PV fighter G-AEZD to RAF March 1939.	
P9600-P9624	**Short S.25 Sunderland I**	12
	C/n S.1028-S.1039. P9600-P9606, P9620-P9624. P9623 to Portugal 1941.	
P9630	**Consolidated 28-5**	1
	Delivered July 1939 and sunk on tests February 1940.	
P9639	**Cierva C.40A**	1
P9642-P9986	**Fairey Barracuda I/II**	250
	C/n F.4570-F.4819 built at Heaton Chapel. P9642-P9666 (25) Mk.I; P9667-P9691, P9709-P9748, P9787-P9836, P9847-P9891, P9909-P9943, P9957-P9986 (225) Mk.II. Conversions: P9642 fitted with Merlin 32 became Mk.II. P9655 used to test ASV for Mk.III, P9795/G had underwing containers for agent-dropping, P9976 prototype Mk.V.	
P9990-P9999	**Airspeed Oxford I**	10
	Diverted before delivery to EATS.	

Start of 1939-45 War Orders

R1000 to R9999

After the 'P' series, 'Q' was not used to avoid confusion with 'O', also
omitted, and serialling continued from R1000. War was declared while
this series was being allocated.

Serial Nos.	Aircraft Type and Remarks	Quantity
R1000-R1806	**Vickers Wellington IC/IV**	550
	Built at Chester. R1000-R1049, R1060-R1099, R1135-R1184, R1210-R1254, R1265-R1299, R1320-R1349, R1365-R1414, R1435-R1474, R1490-R1539, R1585-R1629, R1640-R1669, R1695-R1729, R1757-R1806 built as Mk.IC except R1220, R1390, R1490, R1510, R1515, R1520, R1525, R1530, R1535, R1585, R1590, R1610, R1615, R1620, R1625, R1650, R1655, R1695, R1705, R1715, R1725, R1765, R1775, R1785, R1795 built as Mk.IV. R1032, R1089, R1144, R1172, R1409, R1452, R1521, R1531, R1600, R1605, R1649, R1659, R1700, R1710, R1711, R1720 converted to Mk.XVI. R1381-R1389 were tropicalised. R1000, R1023, R1034, R1070, R1074, R1077, R1079, R1083, R1087, R1091, R1147, R1150, R1151, R1252-R1254, R1270, R1338, R1402, R1490, R1497, R1498, R1525, R1595, R1620, R1650, R1656, R1657, R1660, R1663, R1776 became 3737M, 3453M, 3055M, 3269M, 3360M, 3679M, 4807M, 3327M, 3346M, 3685M, 2853M, 3266M, 3239M, 3684M, 2829M, 3657M, 3326M, 3681M, 3390M, 4745M, 4261M, 3357M, 4592M, 3080M, 4583M, 3667M, 3081M, 3465M, 4195M, 4415M, 3972M.	
R1810 & R1815	**Supermarine 322 'Dumbo'**	2
	Merlin 30/32 engine. Prototypes to Spec S24/37, compromised numbers below.	
R1810-R1984	**Miles M.14A Magister**	145
	C/n 1811-1955. R1810-R1859, R1875-R1924, R1940-	

R1984 delivered to home stations except R1880-R1886,
R1940-R1949, R1971-R1974 direct to Middle East.
R1823, R1843, R1849, R1855, R1908, R1980 became
4514M, 2517M, 4096M, 4483M, 4676M, 4318M. R1907
and R1915 to Turkey 1943. Postwar 20 to civil register.

R1987-R2047	**Westland Lysander II**	47
	R1987-R2010, R2025-R2047. R1990, R1998, R2001, R2003 converted to TT.II. R2005, R2036, R2039, R2040, R2043, R2045, R2046 to Free French Air Force. R2003, R2010 became 3936M, 3930M. R2047 to Canada as pattern aircraft, becoming RCAF 700.	
R2052-R2479	**Bristol 156 Beaufighter I/II**	300
	R2052-R2055 prototypes. R2056, R2057 Mk.IF, R2058 prototype Mk.II, R2059, R2060 Mk.IF, R2061, R2062 further Mk.II prototypes; R2063-R2101, R2120-R2159, R2180-R2209, R2240-R2269 Mk.IF; R2270-R2284, R2300-R2349, R2370-R2404, R2430-R2479 Mk.IIF. R2124 destroyed in air raid before delivery. Conversions: R2134 TT, R2268 non-standard silhouette, R2274 Mk.V. Transfers to Royal Navy in 1943: R2284, R2311, R2329, R2336, R2389, R2438, R2462. R2058, R2060, R2061, R2066, R2077, R2078, R2125, R2142, R2145, R2158, R2185, R2189, R2190, R2194, R2202, R2244, R2253, R2308, R2321, R2322, R2328, R2331, R2342, R2345, R2386, R2395, R2436, R2450, R2459 became 3344M, 3401M, 3599M, 3432M, 3442M, 4521M, 4402M, 3155M, 3156M, 2552M, 4035M, 4600M, 2769M, 2552M, 4599M, 3859M, 4570M, 3861M, 4806M, 3960M, 3683M, 4171M, 3860M, 3350M, 4190M, 3788M, 4021M, 3351M, 3789M.	
R2485-R2487	**DH.89 Dragon Rapide**	3
	Two Gipsy VI. C/n 6446-6448 acquired to Spec T29/38 for radio training.	
R2492 & R2496	**Martin Baker MB.3/MB.5**	2
	Prototype. R2492 MB.3 first flew 3.8.42; R2496 first flew 23.5.44.	
R2510-R2560	**DH.95 Hertfordshire**	1(31)
	Two Perseus XIIC. R2510 prototype only completed. R2511-R2529, R2550-R2560 cancelled.	
R2572-R2652	**Westland Lysander I**	68(70)
	R2572-R2600, R2612-R2652 of which R2573, R2574 were not produced. R2572, R2575, R2576, R2578, R2581, R2582, R2588, R2589, R2591, R2593, R2594, R2597, R2598, R2620, R2632, R2638 converted to TT.I and R2651, R2652 to TT.III. R2650 direct to the REAF. R2577, R2579, R2580, R2583, R2584, R2588, R2592-R2597, R2599, R2615-R2620, R2622, R2623, R2626, R2627, R2629, R2635, R2637 became 3203M, 3205M, 3233M, 3918M, 3204M, 3942M, 3217M, 3916M, 3913M, 3232M, 3070M, 3886M, 3265M, 3919M, 3923M, 3245M, 3246M, 3192M, 3921M, 3941M, 3176M, 3940M, 3922M, 3177M, 3917M, 3189M.	
R2676	**Stearman-Hammond Model Y**	1
	Purchased from KLM for evaluation.	
R2680-R2689	**Hawker Hurricane I**	10
	R2680, R2681 built at Brooklands with fabric-covered wings, R2682-R2689 Langley with metal-covered wings. R2683 converted to Mk.II renumbered BV163.	
R2699-R2703	**Vickers Wellington I**	5
	R2701 converted to DW.I. R2700, R2702, R2703 became 2776M, 3135M, 3292M.	
R2764-R2766	**DH.95 Flamingo**	3
	C/n 95003, 95004, 95008. Impressed. R2766 ex-G-AGCC for Kings Flight, to Royal Navy 1945.	
R2770-R3144	**Bristol 142L Blenheim IV**	30(230)
	R2770-R2799 only built by Avro. R2800-R2805, R2825-R2864, R2877-R2926, R2939-R2963, R2995-R3040, R3096-R3123, R3140-R3144 cancelled. R2775, R2781 to Portuguese AF 1943. R2782 to Royal Navy 1944. R2778 became 4027M.	
R3150-R3299	**Vickers Wellington IC**	100
	Built at Weybridge. R3150-R3179, R3195-R3239, R3275-R3299. Conversions: R3221 Mk.II, R3298, R3299 Mk.V, R3217, R3225, R3234, R3237 to Mk.XVI. R3156, R3161, R3166, R3173, R3195, R3204, R3207, R3212, R3214, R3224, R3226, R3228, R3231, R3233, R3283, R3284, R3287, R3290, R3294, R3299 became 2185M, 3867M, 3154M, 2648M, 3163M, 3207M, 3345M, 4428M, 3473M, 2988M, 3179M, 3173M, 3104M, 3304M, 3185M, 3990M, 3235M, 3219M, 3329M, 3504M.	

R3303-R3587	**Avro 652A Anson I**	**200**

R3303-R3351, R3368-R3413, R3429-R3476, R3512-R3561, R3581-R3587. 132 to EATS (RAAF, RCAF, SAAF) mainly direct. R3467 to Royal Navy 1945.

R3590-R3919	**Bristol 142L Blenheim IV**	**250**

Built by Rootes. R3590-R3639, R3660-R3709, R3730-R3779, R3800-R3849, R3870-R3919. R3877 to Free French AF. R3623, R3830 to Portuguese AF and R3601, R3695, R3871, R3888 to Royal Navy.

R3922-R4054	**Fairey Battle I**	**100**

Built by Austin. R3922-R3971, R3990-R4019, R4035-R4054 all direct to RAAF, RCAF or SAAF, under EATS.

R4059	**Lockheed Hudson I**	**1**

Supplied in lieu of N7260 which crashed before delivery.

R4062-R4067	**Airspeed AS.10 Oxford I**	**6**

R4062-R4065 to RNZAF, R4066, R4067 to SRAF direct.

R4071	**Miles M.3 Falcon**	**1**

Ex-PH-EAO for spoiler tests. Became G-AGZX.

R4074-R4232	**Hawker Hurricane I**	**100**

Built by Gloster. R4074-R4123, R4171-R4200, R4213-R4232. R4077, R4078, R4089, R4095, R4105, R4177, R4178, R4226 to Royal Navy for conversion to Sea Hurricane. R4082, R4083, R4104 direct to SAAF. R4089, R4119, R4222 became 4504M, 3452M, 2872M. R4081, R4091, R4218 converted to Mk.II and re-numbered DR358, DR373 and BV155.

R4236-R4237	**Vickers 432**	**(2)**

Ordered to Spec F22/39. Not built. Replaced by DZ217 and DZ223.

R4243-R4521	**Westland Whirlwind**	**(200)**

Cancelled. R4243-R4283, R4296-R4325, R4345-R4384, R4400-R4445, R4460-R4479, R4499-R4521.

R4525-R4744	**Avro 679 Manchester**	**(150)**

Ordered from Fairey. Cancelled. R4525-R4554, R4572-R4611, R4630-R4649, R4670-R4694, R4710-R4744.

R4748-R5265	**DH.82A Tiger Moth II**	**400**

R4748-R4797, R4810-R4859, R4875-R4924, R4940-R4989, R5005-R5044, R5057-R5088, R5100-R5149, R5170-R5219, R5236-R5265. R4835-R4844, R4879-R4893, R5181-R5186, R5256-R5265 to RAAF; R4755, R4768, R4963, R5100, R5105, R5191 to SAAF; R4761, R4781, R4786-R4797, R4810-R4831, R4908-R4917, R4966, R5044, R5217 to SRAF. R4977-R4989, R5005-R5011, R5067-R5076 to RNZAF. R4852, R4898, R4918, R5142, R5144, R5149, R5197, R5198, R5214 transferred to Royal Navy. R4752, R4763, R4766, R4924, R4941, R4945, R5019, R5022, R5037, R5114, R5133, R5199, R5245 became 6049M, 6083M, 5902M, 6488M, 6727M, 6864M, 7042M, 5435M, 6832M, 7043M, 6726M, 5428M, 4934M. Postwar many to civil register and air forces as follows: R4771 Belgian AF; R5138 Burmese AF; R5171 R Hellenic AF; R4769, R4875, R4946, R4949, R5063, R5242 R Netherlands AF.

R5269	**Weir W-6 helicopter**	**1**

Built by G & J Weir for research.

R5273-R5477	**Avro 679 Manchester**	**(150)**

Ordered from Armstrong Whitworth. Cancelled. R5273-R5320, R5339-R5380, R5397-R5426, R5448-R5477.

R5482-R5763	**Avro 683 Lancaster I**	**200**

Four R-R Merlin XX initially. R5482-R5517, R5537-R5576, R5603-R5640, R5658-R5703, R5724-R5763. R5727 became CF-CMS. R5500, R5503, R5504, R5511, R5538, R5559, R5560, R5606, R5609, R5631, R5635, R5668, R5747, R5751 became 4902M, 5452M, 3881M, 3606M, 3481M, 3605M, 3471M, 4130M, 5288M, 5052M, 3508M, 4901M, 4371M, 5257M.

R5768-R5917	**Avro 679/683 Manchester/Lancaster**	**100**

Built by Metropolitan-Vickers. R5768-R5797, R5829-R5841 Manchester I; R5842-R5868, R5888-R5917 Lancaster I. R5771, R5773-R5776, R5784, R5788, R5790, R5791, R5797, R5829, R5832, R5854, R5865, R5910, R5912 became 3746M, 3892M, 3890M, 4281M, 3745M, 3984M, 3983M, 3774M, 4001M, 3778M, 3777M, 3744M, 4864M, 4950M, 4848M, 4949M. R5868 is preserved by the RAF Museum.

R5921-R5934	**DH.89 Dominie I**	**14**

C/ns 6457-6461, 6463-6471. R5921, R5922, R5924, R5926, R5930-R5934 became G-AJKX, 'AKNV, 'AKFO, 'AGFU, 'AIUO, 'AKOO, 'AKNW, 'AKNY, 'AKSH.

R5938-R6403	**Airspeed AS.10 Oxford I/II**	**350**

R5938-R5979, R5991-R6038, R6050-R6059, R6070-R6114, R6129-R6163, R6177-R6196 (200) Mk.I built by Airspeed. R6211-R6235 Mk.II: R6236-R6248, R6263-R6299, R6317-R6341 Mk.I; R6342-R6358, R6371-R6403 Mk.II (150) built by de Havilland at Hatfield. 104 shipped direct under EATS to RAAF, RNZAF, SAAF and SRAF. R5944, R5953, R5961, R6083, R6248, R6268, R6279, R6345 became 2388M, 3959M, 4197M, 6600M, 7282M, 4344M, 5487M, 5087M. Wartime transfers: R6180, R6230, R6237, R6371 to Royal Navy; R6113, R6142, R6358, R6397, R6371 to R6401 to USN. Postwar sales: R6023, R6106, R6133 to Belgian AF; R6161 Burmese AF; R6091 R Danish AF; R5974 R Hellenic AF; R6269 R Netherlands AF; R6386 R Norwegian AF and others to civil registrations.

R6416-R6539	**Airspeed AS.10 Oxford**	**(100)**

Ordered from Phillips & Powis. Cancelled. R6416-R6439, R6453-R6478, R6490-R6539.

R6543-R6591	**Supermarine Walrus**	**25**

R6543-R6557 Supermarine-built. R6582-R6591 Saro-built. To Royal Navy except R6543, R6546-R6549, R6552, R6584, R6588, R6590 transferred to RAF for ASR duties.

R6595-R7350	**Supermarine Spitfire I/V**	**450**

R6595-R6644, R6683-R6722, R6751-R6780, R6799-R6818, R6829-R6840, R6879-R6928, R6957-R6996, R7015-R7044, R7055-R7074, R7114-R7163, R7192-R7218 built as Mk.I of which R6602, R6620, R6720, R6722, R6759, R6761, R6770, R6776, R6801, R6809, R6817, R6833, R6882, R6887-R6890, R6897, R6904, R6908, R6911, R6913, R6917, R6919, R6923, R6924, R6957, R6960, R6992, R7022, R7060, R7127, R7158, R7161, R7192, R7194-R7196, R7205, R7207-R7209, R7213, R7217, R7218 were converted to Mk.V. R7219-R7231, R7250-R7279, R7290-R7309, R7333-R7350 built as Mk.V except for R7250-R7252, R7257 built as Mk.I. Converted for PR: R6598, R6804, R6805, R6894, R6900, R6902, R6903, R6905, R6906, R6910, R6964, R6968, R7020, R7028-R7044, R7055, R7056, R7059, R7070, R7114, R7116, R7118, R7120, R7128, R7130, R7139, R7142, R7143, R7146, R7147, R7197, R7198, R7211, R7308, R7335. Transfers to Royal Navy: R6620, R6629, R6704, R6716, R6722, R6759, R6835, R6881, R6887, R6970, R6972, R6977, R6996, R7119, R7125, R7136, R7145, R7160, R7193, R7200, R7207, R7271, R7301, R7305, R7335. R6636, R6697, R6720, R6754, R6774, R6818, R6889, R6914, R6973, R7058, R7118, R7120, R7220, R7224 became 2139M, 2842M, 5425M, 2419M, 3597M, 2481M, 3650M, 4525M, 2683M, 2877M, 4519M, 3566M, 5586M, 4406M. Wartime transfers to Portuguese AF: R6626, R6920, R6987, R7027, R7071, R7146, R7159. R6626, R6924 converted to Mk.II and R7308, R7335 to PR.XIII. R7143 to RCAF and R7347 to USA. R6915 preserved by the Imperial War Museum.

R7356-R7480	**Fairey Battle (T)**	**100**

C/n F.4820-F.4919. R7356-R7385, R7399-R7448, R7461-R7480. 62 to RCAF, 4 to SAAF and 3 to RAAF. R7375, R7378 became 2485M, 3909M.

R7485-R7573	**Percival P.28/P.34 Proctor I/III**	**50**

Built by F. Hills & Sons. R7485-R7499, R7520-R7529 Mk.I, R7530-R7539, R7559-R7573 Mk.III. Wartime transfers to USAAF. R7533, R7561, R7563. R7538 to RNZAF 1944. Postwar at least 24 to civil register. R7487 became 4809M.

R7576-R7923	**Hawker Typhoon IA/IB**	**247(250)**

Built by Gloster. R7576-R7599, R7613-R7655, R7672-R7721, R7738-R7775, R7792-R7829, R7845-R7890, R7913-R7923. R7693, R7852, R7918 not assembled, parts used as spares and R7625 crashed before delivery. R7576, R7581-R7584, R7586, R7587, R7594, R7599 became 4638M, 3514M, 4633M, 4637M, 3517M, 3521M, 3518M, 3527M, 3511M. R7613, R7615, R7616, R7623, R7626, R7631, R7635, R7636, R7638, R7639, R7641, R7673, R7685, R7699 became 3516M, 4175M, 3520M, 3519M, 3515M, 4639M, 3512M, 3513M, 4568M, 3700M, 3523M, 4632M, 4567M, 4250M. R7700, R7701, R7704, R7709, R7716, R7721, R7754, R7755, R7758, R7760, R7762, R7764-R7769, R7772, R7774, R7775, R7792-R7794, R7797, R7798 became 4645M, 3524M,

5198M, 4286M, 4289M, 3525M, 3723M, 3726M, 3724M, 4272M, 3722M, 4274M, 3728M, 4270M, 4276M, 3727M, 3725M, 3729M, 3710M, 3529M, 3528M, 3716M, 3714M, 3522M, 3711M. R7801, R7802, R7804-R7808, R7826-R7828, R7851, R7860, R7870, R7871, R7874, R7875, R7877, R7878, R7889, R7890, R7916, R7920 became 3706M, 3531M, 3530M, 3713M, 3718M, 3712M, 3719M, 4644M, 3526M, 4287M, 4338M, 4284M, 3707M, 4273M, 3715M, 3717M, 4339M, 3721M, 4869M, 3720M, 4283M, 4275M.

R7936-R8197	**Hawker Tornado**	2(200)

R7936, R7938 prototypes only built, R7936 by A. V. Roe. R7937, R7939-R7975, R7992-R8036, R8048-R8091, R8106-R8150, R8172-R8197 cancelled.

R8198-R8231	**Hawker Typhoon IA/IB**	15

Built at Langley. R8198-R8200, R8220, R8221 Mk.IA, R8222-R8231 Mk.IB. R8222 became 4400M.

R8630-R8981	**Hawker Typhoon IA/IB**	250

Built by Gloster. R8630-R8663, R8680-R8722, R8737-R8781, R8799-R8845, R8861-R8900, R8923-R8947, R8966-R8981 built as Mk.IB except for R8640, R8652, R8661, R8709, R8720, R8746 Mk.IA. R8631, R8640, R8645, R8646, R8648, R8649, R8657, R8659, R8662, R8685, R8689, R8695 became 4336M, 4271M, 4268M, 4277M, 3709M, 3708M, 4269M, 4249M, 3705M, 4643M, 4642M, 4252M. R8707, R8708, R8714-R8716, R8737, R8738, R8740, R8747, R8748, R8764-R8766, R8775, R8780 became 3701M, 4337M, 4288M, 4341M, 3875M, 4110M, 3874M, 4285M, 3873M, 4253M, 3698M, 3692M, 3695M, 4251M, 3702M. R8805, R8806, R8808, R8817, R8818, R8831, R8870, R8887, R8925, R8926, R8939, R8969 became 3704M, 3696M, 3699M, 3703M, 3693M, 3694M, 3697M, 4640M, 3486M, 5870M, 4641M, 5871M.

R8987	**Lockheed 12A**	1

C/n 1206 G-AEMZ impressed for RAE November 1939.

R8991-R9135	**Westland Lysander III**	100

R8991-R9030, R9056-R9079, R9100-R9135. R9003, R9005, R9007-R9009, R9012, R9013, R9016-R9019, R9021-R9026, R9028-R9030, R9057, R9059, R9061, R9062, R9064-R9071, R9073-R9075, R9078, R9103-R9105, R9107-R9109, R9111-R9114, R9116, R9119, R9121-R9126, R9129, R9131, R9133, R9135 converted to TT.III. R8991-R8999 direct to Finland and R9000 direct to REAF. R9117 converted to LR. Transfers: R9011 to USAAF 1943, R9122 to Royal Navy 1942. R9108 became 2943M.

R9138	**Parnall 382 Heck**	1

G-AFKF impressed. Became 3600M.

R9141-R9358	**Short S.29 Stirling I (Series I/II)**	150

C/n S.1040-S.1139: R9141-R9170, R9184-R9203, R9241-R9290 Series I built at Rochester; c/n SH.331-SH.344, SH.396, SH.345-SH.379; R9295-R9334, R9349-R9358. R9188, R9309 converted to Mk.III. R9188, R9203 became 3970M and 4240M.

R9363-R9540	**Handley Page HP.59 Halifax II**	100

R9363-R9392, R9418-R9457, R9482-R9498, R9528-R9540. R9534 became Mk.III prototype and later 4813M. R9535-R9538 to English Electric and R9539, R9540 to London Passenger Transport Board as pattern aircraft. R9366, R9375, R9381, R9428, R9430, R9432, R9436, R9443, R9490 became 3413M, 4751M, 4351M, 4867M, 4126M, 3956M, 4204M, 4167M, 4455M.

R9545-R9564	**DH.89 Dominie**	20

C/n 6473-6492. R9549 to SAAF 1943, R9563 direct to Royal Navy. Postwar R9546, R9548, R9550, R9552, R9554, R9556, R9559, R9562, R9564 became G-AKOK, 'AKVU, 'AHPT, 'AKRO, 'AKTZ, 'ALAS, 'AKED, 'AKUB, 'AKSF, 'AKOB.

R9567-R9969	**Avro 652A Anson I**	300

R9567-R9611, R9627-R9670, R9685-R9725, R9739-R9781, R9798-R9846, R9864-R9899, R9928-R9969. 130 to RCAF, 30 to SAAF, 8 to RAAF. R9578, R9592 became 4183M, 4939M. Postwar disposals: R9605 Belgian AF, R9717, R9757 French AF, R9707 R Hellenic AF, R9694 R Netherlands AF. R9595 became G-AIXV.

R9974-R9988	**Airspeed AS.10 Oxford I**	15+

Batch continues in the 'T' serial series. R9978 became 5488M.

The 'S' Series

S1000 to S1865

By 1925 the first 'N' series had reached 9999 and the allocations for fleet aircraft then continued in the 'S' series at S1000. The choice of 'S' at that time was its significance as implying 'Sea' as the series was for shipboard aircraft or aircraft equipped for flying over the sea. But by the time the series reached S1865 in 1930, a decision was taken to abandon the series and allot all numbers in the 'K' series then current. Thus chronologically the series is out of phase but has been included here in its alphabetical sequence for reference purposes.

Serial Nos	Aircraft Type and Remarks	Quantity
S1000-S1035	**Fairey IIID Mk.II**	36
	C/n F.737-F.772. Ordered March 1925 with interchange-able wheel/float undercarriage.	
S1036-S1045	**Supermarine Southampton I**	10
	Ordered July 1925. S1043 became Mk.II.	
S1046-S1057	**Blackburn TSR Blackburn I**	12
	TSR = Torpedo Spotter Reconnaissance.	
S1058-S1059	**Supermarine Southampton III**	2
S1060-S1073	**Fairey Flycatcher**	14
	C/n F.798-F.811.	
S1074-S1108	**Fairey IIID Mk.II**	35
	C/n F.812-F.846. S1076 became G-EBPZ.	
S1109-S1114	**Avro 555A Bison II**	6
S1115-S1120	**Blackburn T.2 Dart**	6
S1121-S1128	**Supermarine Southampton II**	8
	Two Napier Lion engines. S1124 became Mk.IV proto-type Scapa with Kestrel engines.	
S1129-S1138	**Blackburn T.2 Dart**	10
	Convertible wheel/float undercarriage.	
S1139-S1148	**Fairey IIIF Mk.I**	10
	C/n F.880-F.889. S1140, S1143, S1144, S1146 rebuilt.	
S1149-S1153	**Supermarine Southampton II**	5
	Two Napier Lion VA engines. All to No.205 Squadron. S1153 became RAAF A11-1.	
S1154-S1158	**Blackburn TSR Blackburn II**	5
S1159-S1162	**Supermarine Southampton II**	4
	S1159 became RAAF A11-2. S1160 converted to Mk.III.	
S1163-S1167	**Avro 555A Bison II**	5
S1168-S1207	**Fairey IIIF Mk.II**	40
	Napier Lion VA engine. C/n F.892-F.931 wood/metal construction. S1172, S1174, S1179, S1181, S1204 rebuilt. S1178, S1197, S1199, S1203 rebuilt as Gordons. S1169, S1184, S1189, S1196 converted to Mk.III and S1205 to Mk.IVA and later Gordon. S1185, S1189 sold to R Hellenic AF. S1203, S1205 became 727M, 1315M.	
S1208-S1227	**Fairey IIIF Mk.II**	20
	Napier Lion XI engines. C/n F.932-F.951 all-metal version. S1211, S1217 converted to Mk.III.	
S1228-S1235	**Supermarine Southampton II**	8
	S1235 temporarily became G-AASH.	
S1236-S1247	**Hawker Horsley**	12
	S1247 experimentally fitted with floats.	
S1248-S1249	**Supermarine Southampton II**	2
	Numbers also issued to Horsley.	
S1250-S1262	**Fairey IIIF Mk.II**	13
	C/n F.956-F.968 all-metal construction. S1262 to the Irish Air Corps.	
S1263-S1264	**Blackburn RB1 Iris III/V**	2
	S1263 with three Rolls-Royce Buzzard IIMS, S1264 with three Rolls-Royce Condor IIIB became Mk.V.	
S1265-S1272	**Blackburn T.5A Ripon II**	8
	Napier Lion XI engines. S1266, S1269 converted to Baffin of which S1266 went to RNZAF. S1272 converted to Mk.III (Type T.5E).	
S1273-S1297	**Fairey Flycatcher**	25
	C/n F.1097-F.1121. S1288 to High Speed Flight. S1284 to Argentina.	
S1298-S1302	**Supermarine Southampton II**	5
S1303-S1356	**Fairey IIIF Mk.III**	54
	Napier Lion XIA engines. C/n F.1043-F.1096. S1317	

which became 1028M and CD77 had previously been involved in swept wing version experiments. S1325 became Mk.VI prototype Seal with c/n F.1316 on rebuilding.

Serial Nos	Aircraft Type and Remarks	Quantity
S1357-S1369	**Blackburn T.5A Ripon II**	13
	Napier Lion XI engines. S1358, S1359, S1364, S1366, S1368 converted to Baffin. S1358, S1364, S1368 to the RNZAF.	
S1370-S1408	**Fairey IIIF Mk.IIIM**	39
	Napier Lion XIA. C/n F.1232-F.1270. S1377 to R Hellenic AF. S1393 became 2190M.	
S1409-S1419	**Fairey Flycatcher**	11
	C/n F.1274-F.1284. Ordered March 1920.	
S1420-S1423	**Supermarine Southampton**	4
S1424-S1432	**Blackburn T.5B Ripon IIA**	9
	Napier Lion XIA; Production to Spec 2/29. S1425-S1428, S1430-S1432 converted to Baffin. S1425, S1426, S1430, S1431 to RNZAF.	
S1433-S1435	**Short S.8/8 Rangoon**	3
	C/n S.757, S.755, S.756. S1433 became G-AEIM.	
S1436-S1453	**Hawker Horsley II**	18
	S1436 Merlin C and S1452 Condor III engine testbeds.	
S1454-S1463	**Fairey IIIF (DC)**	10
	Napier Lion IIIA. C/n F.1285-F.1294. All-metal. Ordered September 1929.	
S1464	**Supermarine Southampton II**	1
S1465-S1473	**Blackburn T.5B Ripon IIA**	9
	S1470, S1473 converted to Baffin.	
S1474-S1552	**Fairey IIIF Mk.IIIB**	79
	Napier Lion XIA. C/n F.1317-F.1395. S1504 stainless steel wings. S1536 radio-controlled 'Fairey Queen'.	
S1553-S1574	**Blackburn Ripon/Baffin**	22
	Ordered as Ripon, all converted to Baffin. S1553, S1554, S1558, S1561, S1563, S1570, S1571, S1573 to RNZAF.	
S1575	**Saro A.17 Cutty Sark**	1
S1576	**Parnall Prawn**	1
	65hp Ricardo-Burt engine.	
S1577-S1588	**Hawker Nimrod**	12
	Interchangeable wheel/float undercarriage.	
S1589	**Short Sarafand**	1
	C/n S.763 prototype to Spec R6/28.	
S1590	**Fairey Flycatcher**	1
S1591	**Armstrong Whitworth XVI**	1
	C/n 698 prototype to Spec N21/26.	
S1592	**Fairey Firefly III**	1
	C/n F.1137. G-ABFH High Speed Flight trainer.	
S1593	**Blackburn Iris III**	1
	Zephyrus with 37mm nose gun. Converted to Mk.V and became testbed for Napier Culverin engines (licence built Junkers Jumo IVc).	
S1594	**Hawker Nimrod**	1
	Not confirmed.	
S1595-S1596	**Supermarine S.6B**	2
	Final Schneider Trophy entry aircraft. Both preserved.	
S1597-S1613	**Hawker Horsley II**	17
	Mainly shipped to Far East.	
S1614-S1639	**Hawker Nimrod I**	26
	Interchangeable wheel/float undercarriage.	
S1638	**Supermarine Southampton**	1
	Compromised number above.	
S1640	**Blackburn B 3**	1
	To Spec M1/30.	
S1641	**Vickers 207**	1
	To Spec M1/30.	
S1642	**Handley Page HP.46**	1
	To Spec M1/30.	
S1643-S1647	**Supermarine Southampton**	5
S1648	**Supermarine Southampton IV/Scapa**	1
	Prototype Mk.IV to Spec R20/31 renamed Scapa.	
S1649-S1674	**Blackburn Ripon II/Baffin**	26
	Ripons all converted to Baffin. S1649, S1650, S1653-S1655, S1657, S1670, S1672, S1674 to RNZAF.	
S1675-S1676	**DH.82 Tiger Moth**	2
	Floatplanes to AM Spec T6/33.	
S1677-S1704	**Hawker Osprey I/III**	28
	S1699-S1701 Mk.III built of stainless steel, S1702-S1704 standard Mk.III, remainder Mk.I.	
S1705	**Gloster TSR.38 (FS36)**	1
	To Spec S9/30.	
S1706	**Fairey S9/30**	1
	Rolls-Royce Kestrel IIMS. C/n F.1754. Basic Fairey IIIF with single pontoon float.	
S1707-S1715	**Vickers Vildebeest I**	9
	S1713 converted to Mk.III, S1714, S1715 to Vincent standard. S1707, S1710, S1711, S1715 became 1623M, 1187M, 720M, 1121M.	
S1716-S1778	**Reservation**	(63)
S1779-S1865	**Fairey III/IIIB**	87
	Napier Lion XIA. C/n F.1526-F.1612. S1779-S1836 Mk.IIIB, S1837-S1844 Mk.III, S1845-S1851 Mk.III(DC), S1852-S1865 Mk.IIIB. S1835 centre-float trials. S1805 to RNZAF. S1786, S1817 to R Hellenic AF. S1800, S1826, S1835, S1851, S1859 became 1829M, 1827M, 739M, 1507M, 1826M.	

The 'T' Series

T1000 to T9999

After R9999 was reached in 1939, 'S' was ignored as some aircraft in the abandoned 'S' series were still in use, so that the follow-on was from T1000.

Serial Nos	Aircraft Type and Remarks	Quantity
T1001-T1404	**Airspeed AS.10 Oxford I/II**	285
	Airspeed (Portsmouth) built; batch of 300 included R9974-R9988. T1001-T1028, T1041-T1047 Mk.I; T1048-T1082, T1097-T1111 Mk.II, T1112-T1141, T1167-T1180 Mk.I; T1181-T1215, T1243-T1263 Mk.II; T1264-T1288, T1308-T1332 Mk.I; T1333-T1348, T1404 Mk.II. T1373 converted to Mk.V. Under EATS 25 to SAAF, 22 to RCAF, 17 to SRAF, 7 to RAAF and 4 to RNZAF. Wartime transfers: T1098, T1103, T1107, T1248, T1258, T1345, T1346, T1395 to Royal Navy; T1066, T1070, T1072, T1077-T1079, T1105, T1109, T1187, T1195, T1203, T1211-T1213, T1215, T1244, T1254, T1255, T1259, T1263, T1340, T1371, T1377, T1383, T1388, T1389, T1393 to USAAF; T1379 to BOAC for crew training. T1006, T1016, T1017, T1049, T1213, T1252, T1267, T1341, T1392, T1396 became 3611M, 5481M provisionally, 4906M, 4839M, 4833M, 3864M, 4841M, 6922M, 3617M, 3613M. Postwar disposals: T1204 Belgian AF; T1101, T1386 Burmese AF; T1205, T1342, T1348 R Danish AF; T1260 R Hellenic AF; T1322, T1325 R Norwegian AF.	
T1419	**Cierva C.40**	1
	Used for autogyro training.	
T1422-T1771	**Westland Lysander III**	250
	T1422-T1470, T1501-T1535, T1548-T1590, T1610-T1655, T1670-T1709, T1735-T1771. Most converted to TT.III. T1688, T1771 special LR version. Transfers: T1441, T1443, T1570, T1576, T1708, T1740 to Royal Navy; T1469, T1517, T1524, T1552, T1574, T1616, T1682, T1693, T1695 to USAAF. T1431 to 2465M.	
T1775-T1776	**DH.85 Leopard Moth**	2
	VT-AEP, VT-AJC impressed in India.	
T1777-T1783	**DH.82 Tiger Moth**	5
	T1777-T1779, T1782, T1783 impressed in India.	
T1788	**Comper CF.1**	1
	Built at Heston. Not flown. Serial erroneously applied to Fane F1/40 2-seat AOP G-AGDJ.	
T1793-T2444	**Bristol Blenheim IV**	400
	Built by Rootes. T1793-T1832, T1848-T1897, T1921-T1960, T1985-T2004, T2031-T2080, T2112-T2141, T2161-T2190, T2216-T2255, T2273-T2292, T2318-T2357, T2381-T2400, T2425-T2444. T1800, T1948, T1952, T2131, T2284, T2287, T2425, T2438 became 4124M, 4140M, 2363M, 3977M, 4006M, 2538M, 4015M, 4008M. Wartime transfers: T1876, T2004, T2129, T2224, T2322, T2325, T2351, T2444 to Royal Navy. T1817, T1819, T1855, T1857, T1867, T1975, T1935, T2077,	

T2079, T2340 to Free French AF; T2431, T2434 to Portuguese AF; T1996 to Turkish AF.

T2449 & T2453 Airspeed AS.45 Cambridge 2
Trainer prototypes to Spec T4/39.

T2458-T3000 Vickers Wellington IC 300
T2458-T2477, T2501-T2520, T2541-T2580, T2606-T2625, T2701-T2750, T2801-T2850, T2873-T2922, T2951-T3000.Conversions: T2545 Mk.II; T2919, T2977, T2979, T2982, T2988, T2998 Mk.VIII; T2510, T2511, T2709, T2724, T2823, T2850, T2969 Mk.XVI. T2459-T2461, T2469, T2502, T2579, T2611, T2747, T2808, T2845, T2994 became 2765M, 3324M, 3330M, 3323M, 4009M, 3162M, 4488M, 3303M, 3994M, 3562M, 4226M.

T3009-T3447 Bristol Beaufighter I/II 300
T3009-T3055, T3070-T3107, T3137-T3183, T3210-T3227 Mk.IIF; T3228-T3250, T3270-T3272, T3290-T3333, T3348-T3355 Mk.IC; T3356-T3389, T3410-T3447 Mk.IIF. 73 transferred to Royal Navy. T3227 converted to Mk.I and T3177 used as Griffon IIB testbed. T3013, T3030, T3033, T3034, T3042, T3150, T3177, T3244, T3297, T3363, T3413, T3420, T3421, T3427, T3432, T3437 became 3607M, 3633M, 4678M, 3862M, 3639M, 3793M, 4539M, 3863M, 2599M, 3470M, 3313M, 3790M, 4264M, 4245M, 4248M, 4247M.

T3450-T3907 Bristol 156 Beaufighter (300)
Cancelled order with Vickers Armstrong. T3450-T3493, T3510-T3550, T3583-T3622, T3639-T3685, T3701-T3733, T3743-T3799, T3822-T3866, T3891-T3907.

T3911-T4121 Boulton Paul P.82 Defiant I 150
T3911-T3960, T3980-T4010, T4030-T4076, T4100-T4121. T4106 shipped to USA. Conversions to TT.III: T3917, T3919, T3923, T3925, T3935, T3942, T3947, T3948, T3950, T3951, T3960, T3982-T3984, T3986-T3990, T3992, T3994, T3997, T4000-T4002, T4005-T4007, T4009, T4033, T4035, T4036, T4043, T4046, T4047, T4050, T4060, T4062, T4064-T4066, T4068, T4070, T4072, T4076, T4103, T4109, T4111, T4112, T4114, T4120, T4121. Many transferred to Royal Navy. T3993, T4014, became 2983M, 3008M.

T4130-T4339 Armstrong Whitworth AW.38 Whitley V 150
T4130-T4179, T4200-T4239, T4260-T4299, T4320-T4339. T4149 used in RATO trials. T4210, T4271, T4284, T4288, T4293 became 3058M, 3391M, 4657M, 2579M, 2435M.

T4623-T5352 Bristol 156 Beaufighter 500
T4623-T4646 Mk.IF, T4647-T4670, T4700-T4734, T4751-T4800, T4823-T4846, T4862-T4899, T4915-T4947, T4970-T5007, T5027-T5055, T5070-T5099 Mk.IC; T5100-T5114, T5130-T5175, T5195-T5220, T5250-T5299, T5315-T5352 Mk.VIC. Direct offset to Australia for renumbering in RAAF A19 series: T4920-T4931, T4943-T4947, T4970-T4978, T4991-T4999, T5000-T5004, T5047-T5055, T5070-T5077, T5081-T5084, T5086, T5089-T5095, T5097-T5099, T5200-T5205, T5254, T5255, T5257, T5263, T5264, T5270, T5295, T5296, T5327-T5331, T5336-T5344, plus T5262 which was lost en route. T4628, T4634, T4642, T4790, T4797, T4844, T5298 became 3479M, 3417M, 4461M, 4553M, 4588M, 4586M, 4552M.

T5357 DH.95 Flamingo 1
C/n 95001 ex-G-AFUE to No.24 Squadron.

T5360-T8264 DH.82A Tiger Moth 2000
Early aircraft built by de Havilland, remainder by Morris Motors. T5360-T5384, T5409-T5433, T5454-T5508, T5520-T5564, T5595-T5639, T5669-T5718, T5749-T5788, T5807-T5856, T5877-T5921, T5952-T5986, T6020-T6069, T6094-T6138, T6158-T6202, T6225-T6274, T6286-T6320, T6362-T6406, T6427-T6471, T6485-T6534, T6547-T6596, T6612-T6656, T6671-T6720, T6734-T6778, T6797-T6831, T6854-T6878, T6897-T6921, T6942-T6991, T7011-T7055, T7085-T7129, T7142-T7191, T7208-T7247, T7259-T7308, T7325-T7369, T7384-T7418, T7436-T7485, T7509-T7553, T7583-T7627, T7651-T7700, T7723-T7757, T7777-T7821, T7840-T7884, T7899-T7948, T7960-T8009, T8022-T8066, T8096-T8145, T8166-T8210, T8230-T8264. Conversions to Queen Bee: T6104, T6863, T6867, T7239. Quantities to EATS: 246 to SAAF plus 75 sunk en route, 234 SRAF plus 17 sunk en route, 24 RAAF, 24 Kenya all of which were sunk,

34 RNZAF. 39 were transferred to Royal Navy plus T6099, T7363, T7291 acquired postwar as XL714, XL716, XL717. T5375, T5427, T5428, T5492, T5494, T5536, T5542, T5696, T5700, T5702, T5822, T5836, T5879, T5887, T5957, T5985 became 6868M, 6728M, 6861M, 4104M, 4048M, 4579M, 6919M, 6983M, 6724M, 6924M, 6611M, 5984M, 6854M, 5447M, 4509M, 6856M, T6044, T6067, T6096, T6125, T6240, T6257, T6286, T6305, T6317, T6371, T6391, T6442, T6497 became 4760M, 6898M, 4691M, 4097M, 4467M, 6725M, 5449M, 4468M, 5821M, 4680M, 6897M, 5448M, 6720M. T6612, T6617, T6684, T6688, T6777, T6854, T6865, T6873, T6969, T7024, T7052, T7118, T7164, T7184, T7214, T7244, T7301, T7304, T7395 became 6957M, 2770M, 5901M, 6575M, 6440M, 4074M, 5450M, 4692M, 4682M, 5282M, 6721M, 5281M, 6803M, 4359M, 5427M, 6814M, 6722M, 4724M, 6801M. T7402, T7466, T7682, T7686, T7724, T7731, T7735, T7810, T7910, T7930, T7931, T7965, T8175, T8181, T8192 became 4763M, 4683M, 5987M, 4764M, 4523M, 6875M, 4071M, 6723M, 4065M, 5429M, 5432M, 5434M, 4474M, 5903M, 5280M. T6856 to USAAF 1943. Postwar foreign air force sales: T7338 IEAF; T7390 FAF; T6314, T6776, T6990, T7840, T8198 R Hellenic AF; T7691 RPAF; T5814, T5820, T5835, T6110, T6190, T6911, T6955, T6961, T6964, T7014, T7037, T7262, T7306, T7405, T7409, T7443, T7472, T7602 R Netherlands AF; T5620, T5671, T5986 to MAAF. 368 went to civil registrations postwar.

T8268-T9037 Miles M.9A/M.19 Master I/II 499(500)
T8268-T8292, T8317-T8351, T8364-T8412, T8429-T8469, T8482-T8507, T8538-T8581, T8600-T8640, T8656-T8694, T8736-T8784, T8815-T8855, T8876-T8885 (400) Mk.I. T8886 Mk.IV not completed. T8887-T8923, T8948-T8967, T8996-T9037 Mk.II. T8887-T8894, T8896-T8923, T8948-T8967, T8996-T9037 shipped direct to SAAF. T8278, T8281, T8286, T8290-T8292, T8323, T8328, T8350, T8366, T8459, T8492, T8543, T8603, T8615, T8632, T8677, T8781 transferred to RN. T8271, T8276, T8279, T8319, T8433, T8462, T8495, T8507, T8544, T8549, T8601, T8820, T8842 became 3643M, 3663M, 3837M, 3673M, 3670M, 4463M, 3544M, 3671M, 4163M, 3662M, 4482M, 3347M, 3675M.

T9040-T9078 Short S.25 Sunderland I 20
C/n S.1140-S.1159. T9040-T9050, T9070-T9078. T9042 prototype Mk.III.

T9083-T9115 Short S.25 Sunderland II 15
Built by Blackburn. T9083-T9090, T9109-T9115. T9114 became 4446M.

T9120 Taylorcraft Plus D 1
Acquired for AOP evaluation. Became G-AHAF.

T9131-T9260 Fairey Albacore 100
C/n F.4920-F.5019. T9131-T9175, T9191-T9215, T9231-T9260 for Royal Navy.

T9264 General Aircraft Monospar ST-25 1
F-AQOM ex- G-AEPG impressed. Was originally W7977.

T9266-T9465 Lockheed Hudson I/II/III 200
T9266-T9365 Mk.I, T9366-T9385 Mk.II, T9386-T9465 Mk.III. T9305-T9307 sunk en route and T9446, T9449, T9450 crashed before delivery. T9367, T9370, T9386, T9437 retained in Canada. T9275, T9313, T9363, T9461 became 4822M, 4465M, 3653M, 3623M.

T9519-T9538 Hawker Hurricane I 20
Built by Canadian Car & Foundry Co. T9528 converted to Sea Hurricane. T9531 to SRAF.

T9540-T9657 Bristol 152 Beaufort V 100
Australian-built. T9540-T9569, T9583-T9618, T9624-T9657. Seven produced for RAF offset to RAAF.

T9669-T9982 Miles M.14A Magister I 220
C/n 1956-2175. T9669-T9708, T9729-T9768, T9799-T9848, T9869-T9918, T9943-T9982 part of 300 ordered with numbers continued in 'V' series. Wartime delivery to Turkish AF: T9737, T9763, T9806, T9829, T9842, T9875, T9879-T9882, T9890, T9891, T9897-T9899, T9900-T9906, T9909, T9914, T9917, T9918, T9944, T9945, T9948-T9954, T9960-T9962, T9964, T9969-T9972, T9974, T9975, T9980-T9982. Postwar sales: T9690, T9946, T9959 Argentine AF; T9800 to Belgian AF. T9681, T9836, T9894, T9913, T9979 became 4549M, 4475M, 4512M, 4769M, 6543M. At least 30 postwar to civil registers.

The 'V' & 'W' Series

V1000 to W9999

'U' was not used, since in manuscript it could easily be confused with 'V', so 'V' followed on from 'T' and 'W' on from 'V'. Large blocks in the series suggest changing policies with cancelled orders replaced by others. Although allotted 1939-40, some aircraft did not appear until 1942 when role prefix letters applied to mark numbers.

Serial Nos	Aircraft Type and Remarks	Quantity
V1003-V1102	**Miles M.14A Magister** C/n 2176-2255. V1003-V1042, V1063-V1102 of order for 300 started at end of 'T' series. V1003-V1007, V1009-V1011, V1019, V1021, V1024, V1030-V1038, V1068, V1077-V1080, V1095, V1096 to Turkish AF. V1025 crashed before delivery. V1017, V1087, V1092, V1099 became 4123M, 4367M, 4556M, 5365M. Postwar V1063 to Argentine AF and at least 4 to civil register.	80
V1106-V1183	**Boulton Paul P.82 Defiant I** V1106-V1141, V1170-V1183. V1106-V1108, V1110-V1112, V1114, V1115, V1119, V1120, V1123, V1124, V1126, V1127, V1129, V1132, V1133, V1135, V1136, V1139, V1170, V1181 converted to TT.III mainly for the Royal Navy. V1172 became 2998M.	50
V1186-V1187	**Cierva C.30A** Avro-built G-ACWR, 'ACWO impressed.	2
V1201-V1594	**Fairey Battle TT.I** Rolls-Royce Merlin III. V1201-V1250, V1265-V1280 built by Austin. V1281-V1294, V1305-V1354, V1375-V1394, V1407-V1456, V1470-V1499, V1511-V1560, V1575-V1594 cancelled. Majority built for EATS: 23 to RAAF, 21 to SAAF plus one sunk en route, 4 to SRAF. V1222 sold to Eire after forced landing. V1204 became 3908M.	66(300)
V1598-V2831	**Armstrong Whitworth AW.41 Albemarle** Ordered from A. W. Hawkesley. V1598 ST.I Srs III to Russia 1943; V1599 GT.I long range version; V1600 GT.II; V1601-V1647, V1694-V1723, V1738-V1759 ST.II Srs I; V1760 GT.IV Srs I; V1761-V1787, V1809-V1828, V1841, V1842 ST.V Srs I; V1843-V1885, V1917-V1941, V1962-V2011, V2025-V2039 ST.VI Srs I; V2040-V2054, V2067, V2068 GT.VI Srs II. V2069-V2116, V2155-V2179, V2193-V2242, V2271-V2300, V2314-V2353, V2377-V2404, V2440-V2464, V2503-V2542, V2573-V2622, V2636-V2665, V2681-V2720, V2749-V2749, V2798, V2812-V2831 cancelled.	302(780)
V3137-V3138	**Short S.30M Empire 'C' Class** C/n S.880, S.881. G-AFCU Cabot & G-AFCV Caribou impressed.	2
V3142	**Boulton Paul P.92/2** Half scale model of P.92 project to Spec F11/37 built by Heston Aircraft.	1
V3145-V3862	**Airspeed AS.10 Oxford I/II** Built by de Havilland. V3145-V3194, V3208-V3247, V3267-V3296, V3310-V3359, V3375-V3404, V3418-V3442, V3456-V3480 (250) Mk.I; V3501-V3540, V3555-V3604, V3623-V3647, V3665-V3694, V3719-V3748, V3768-V3792, V3813-V3862 (250) Mk.II. V3636 converted to Mk.V. Quantities to EATS: 58 to SRAF, 24 RCAF, 22 SAAF plus 3 lost en route, 10 RAAF, 6 RNZAF. Wartime transfers: V3390, V3589, V3634, V3816 to Royal Navy; V3521, V3559, V3587, V3599, V3628, V3641, V3668, V3673, V3681, V3684, V3687, V3730, V3780, V3784, V3790, V3830, V3831, V3850 to USAAF. V3213, V3226, V3346, V3472, V3501, V3507, V3516, V3573, V3593, V3595, V3676, V3680, V3682, V3719, V3737, V3813, V3825, V3861 became 4198M, 3833M, 4179M, 6112M, 4061M, 6111M, 4121M, 4896M, 3839M, 3852M, 3659M, 5530M, 4977M, 5445M, 5457M, 3099M, 3615M, 5997M. Postwar disposals: V3575, V3775 Belgian AF; V7346, V3824 Burmese AF; V3331, V3505 R Danish AF; V3418, V3691, V3742, V3745, V3820 R Hellenic AF; V3325,	500
	V3694, V3740 R Norwegian AF; others to civil register.	
V3865-V4283	**Airspeed AS.10 Oxford I** Built by Standard Motors. V3865-V3914, V3933-V3957, V3972-V3996, V4016-V4065, V4079-V4103, V4124-V4173, V4192-V4241, V4259-V4283. V3883 to RCAF on winterisation trials. Wartime transfers: V4026, V4042, V4146, V4201, V4231, V4268, V4269 to Royal Navy; V4173, V4226 to USAAF. V3911, V3944, V4050, V4054, V4087, V4167, V4238 became 5709M, 6187M, 5489M, 5490M, 5483M, 3844M, 6539M. Postwar disposals: V4232, V4236 R Danish AF; V3991, V3994, V4065 R Hellenic AF; V3945, V4023 to R Norwegian AF plus a few to civil use including V3907 to KLM.	300
V4288-V4719	**Fairey Swordfish** Built by Blackburn. V4288-V4337, V4360-V4399, V4411-V4455, V4481-V4525, V4551-V4600, V4621-V4655, V4685-V4719. For Royal Navy.	300
V4724-V4725	**DH.89 Rapide** G-AFNC, 'AFND impressed September 1939.	2
V4730	**DH.60M Moth** VT-ACM impressed in India.	1
V4731	**DH.87 Hornet Moth** VT-AIT impressed in India.	1
V4732	**Lockheed 12A** VT-AJN impressed in India.	1
V4733	**DH.82 Tiger Moth** VT-ALF impressed in India.	1
V4734	**DH.90 Dragonfly** VT-AHY impressed in India.	1
V4738	**DH.60X Moth** G-AABH impressed.	1
V4739	**Miles Whitney Straight** G-AFCN impressed.	1
V4742-V5006	**DH.82B Queen Bee** V4742-V4772, V4787-V4805 built by de Havilland. V4806-V4827, V4852-V4876, V4889-V4909, V4926-V4945, V4995-V5006 cancelled. V4760 to USA 1941.	50(175)
V5010-V5361	**Airspeed AS.30 Queen Wasp** Cancelled. V5010-V5057, V5073-V5112, V5131-V5180, V5206-V5240, V5262-V5306, V5322-V5361.	(258)
V5370-V6529	**Bristol 142L Blenheim IV** Built by Rootes. V5370-V5399, V5420-V5469, V5490-V5539, V5560-V5599, V5620-V5659, V5680-V5699, V5720-V5769, V5790-V5829, V5850-V5899, V5920-V5969, V5990-V6039, V6060-V6099, V6120-V6149, V6170-V6199, V6220-V6269, V6290-V6339, V6360-V6399, V6420-V6469, V6490-V6529. 20 transferred to Royal Navy and V5429, V5434, V5501, V5729, V5883, V6395 released to Portugal in 1943. V5427, V5563, V5695, V5735, V5753, V5964, V6019, V6121, V6178, V6194 became 3968M, 3987M, 4068M, 3982M, 3166M, 3988M, 3998M, 4018M, 3884M, 3996M.	800
V6533-V7195	**Hawker Hurricane I** Built by Gloster. V6533-V6582, V6600-V6649, V6665-V6704, V6722-V6761, V6776-V6825, V6840-V6889, V6913-V6962, V6979-V7028, V7042-V7081, V7099-V7138, V7156-V7195. V6536, V6538, V6546, V6582, V6602, V6739, V6755, V6785, V6790, V6853, V6861, V6914, V6915, V6929, V6934, V6936, V6942, V6950, V6959, V6999, V7006, V7018, V7021, V7054, V7061, V7169 converted to Mk.II and renumbered (see ranges BV155-BV174, DG612-DG651, DR339-DR393 for new identities). V6534, V6545, V6558, V6579, V6609, V6675, V6740, V6779, V6808, V6809, V6818, V6822, V6850, V6867, V6880, V6888, V6889 became 2751M, 4747M, 2798M, 4578M, 2916M, 4687M, 3574M, 4662M, 3730M, 4707M, 2816M, 4558M, 4574M, 5038M, 2628M, 2333M, 2473M and V6920, V6930, V6933, V6945, V6949, V6981, V6984, V6990, V7002, V7028, V7042, V7047, V7055, V7068, V7099, V7108, V7111, V7118, V7157, V7166 became 2690M, 2750M, 4536M, 4319M, 4320M, 3627M, 4517M, 4350M, 4506M, 2752M, 2744M, 2570M, 4663M, 4500M, 3315M, 2745M, 2757M, 2743M, 4499M, 5034M. Transfers to Royal Navy mainly for Sea Hurricane conversion: V6541, V6545, V6555, V6556, V6564, V6577, V6579, V6604, V6649, V6666, V6695, V6700, V6727, V6731, V6751, V6756, V6759, V6760, V6779, V6794, V6801, V6815, V6817, V6843, V6854, V6858, V6867, V6881, V6883, V6886, V6923, V6924, V6927, V6933, V6944, V6952, V7001, V7027, V7046,	500

V7049, V7050, V7063, V7070, V7077, V7100, V7113, V7125, V7129, V7130, V7133, V7157, V7161, V7182, V7189, V7191, V7194, V7195. V6844 loaned to the USAAF and V6881 shipped to Russia. V6576, V6613, V7173 to Irish Air Corps 1943-44.

V7200-V8127   **Hawker Hurricane I**   **494(691)**
Rolls-Royce Merlin III. Brooklands and Langley-built. V7200-V7209, V7221-V7235 with fabric covered wings, remainder metal covered V7236-V7260, V7276-V7318, V7337-V7386, V7400-V7446, V7461-V7510, V7533-V7572, V7588-V7627, V7644-V7690, V7705-V7737, V7741-V7780, V7795-V7838, V7851-V7862. V7863-V7900, V7917-V7956, V7970-V8000, V8023-V8068, V8088-V8127 cancelled. V7246, V7252, V7292, V7377, V7379, V7421, V7441, V7499, V7508, V7600, V7623, V7653, V7750 became 5035M, 4686M, 2376M, 4562M, 4756M, 4726M, 2233M, 2616M, 5744M, 3584M, 4757M, 5036M, 2748M. Shipments: V7276-V7283 to the SAAF, V7402 RCAF and V7476 SAAF. Several of batch served in SAAF units under the RAF in the Middle East. Transfers to Royal Navy mainly for Sea Hurricane conversion: V7208, V7229, V7241, V7244, V7252, V7285, V7301, V7311, V7339, V7349, V7352, V7379, V7386, V7402, V7416, V7421, V7433, V7438, V7439, V7498, V7501-V7506, V7568, V7588, V7600, V7603, V7618, V7623, V7646, V7647, V7650, V7665, V7675, V7681, V7685, V7745, V7824. Renumbering on conversion to Mk.II: V7234, V7258, V7286, V7302, V7351, V7657, V7684 (for new identities see BV, DG, DR batches given in remarks for V6533-V7195). V7411, V7435, V7463, V7540 to Irish Air Corps.

V8131-V8901   **Bristol 156 Beaufighter I/II/VI**   **600**
V8131-V8170, V8184-V8218 (75) Mk.IIF; V8219-V8233, V8246-V8289, V8307-V8356, V8370-V8385, (125) Mk.IF; V8386-V8419, V8433-V8472, V8489-V8528, V8545-V8594, V8608-V8657, V8671-V8720, V8733-V8778, V8799-V8848, V8862-V8901 (400) Mk.VIF. Wartime transfers: V8134, V8156, V8161, V8167, V8169, V8185, V8190, V8201, V8209 to Royal Navy; V8280, V8315, V8321, V8375, V8376, V8390, V8404, V8412, V8466, V8472, V8492, V8500, V8504, V8505, V8516, V8578, V8579, V8625, V8635, V8637, V8638, V8647, V8683, V8684, V8686, V8693, V8694, V8703, V8708, V8743, V8746, V8753, V8757, V8760, V8763, V8765, V8768, V8770, V8772, V8775, V8801, V8806, V8809, V8810, V8811, V8813, V8814, V8817-V8819, V8823, V8827, V8828, V8831, V8834, V8873, V8883, V8891 to USAAF. V8149, V8151, V8188, V8204, V8214, V8248, V8262, V8276, V8286, V8327, V8433, V8441, V8449, V8520, V8545, V8608, V8655, V8713, V8742, V8830, V8869, V8894 became 3791M, 3792M, 4679M, 4460M, 5560M, 3878M, 3857M, 3879M, 3880M, 3855M, 5617M, 5696M, 5626M, 5619M, 5615M, 5573M, 3754M, 5623M, 5630M, 5686M, 5625M, 4705M. V8510 shipped to Canada. V8569/G postwar to French AF.

V8914   **Blackburn B.20**   **1**
Experimental retractable hull flying boat to Spec R1/36.

V8920-V8969   **Westland Lysander**   **(50)**
Cancelled project for Westland-assembled, Canadian built.

V8975-V9254   **Lockheed Hudson III**   **200**
V8975-V8999, V9020-V9065 short range version; V9066-V9069, V9090-V9129, V9150-V9199 long range version; V9220-V9254 short-range version. V9069, V9171, V9223 retained in Canada, V9043, V9045, V9100, V9103 not delivered, V9061, V9181, V9182, V9184 lost on delivery and V9235-V9252 diverted to the RNZAF. V9152 became G-AGDK in 1941. V9068 postwar to the R Netherlands AF.

V9280-V9974   **Westland Lysander IIIA**   **447(500)**
V9280-V9329, V9347-V9386, V9401-V9450, V9472-V9521, V9538-V9557, V9570-V9619, V9642-V9681, V9704-V9750 (347) Mk.IIIA of which 123 were converted to TT.IIIA. V9751-V9753, V9775-V9824, V9844-V9868, V9885-V9906 (100) built as TT.IIIA. V9907-V9914, V9930-V9974 (53) cancelled. Wartime transfers: 40 to Royal Navy, 100 to RCAF, 10 to USAAF. V9309, V9321, V9363, V9439, V9555, V9594, V9705, V9729 released to Portuguese AF. V9445 became 4003M.

V9976-V9994   **Handley Page HP.59 Halifax II**   **200**
&   Built by English Electric. V9976-V9994, W1002-W1021,
W1002-W1276   W1035-W1067, W1090-W1117, W1141-W1190, W1211-W1253, W1270-W1276. V9977 first bomber with H2S. V9991, W1008 became 3781M, 4593M.

W1280-W1498   **Avro 679 Manchester**   **(150)**
Ordered from Armstrong Whitworth. Cancelled. W1280-W1299, W1319-W1350, W1374-W1410, W1426-W1475, W1488-W1498.

W1505-W2665   **Avro 652 Anson I**   **1000**
W1505-W1524, W1529-W1540, W1544-W1570, W1576-W1618, W1627-W1676, W1690-W1736, W1751-W1800, W1814-W1863, W1875-W1924, W1932-W1971, W1986-W2025, W2031-W2072, W2078-W2099, W2109-W2158, W2163-W2212, W2216-W2245, W2252-W2291, W2298-W2347, W2355-W2398, W2403-W2452, W2457-W2496, W2499-W2548, W2554-W2592, W2598-W2646, W2651-W2665. Only 62 delivered to RAF and 6 of those later shipped under EATS to where 938 had been delivered direct from production, mainly RCAF and RAAF with a few to SAAF. Of those remaining in UK, wartime transfers were: W1706 Royal Navy, W1891 Free French AF, W2656 USAAF. Postwar W1731, W2628 became G-ALXH and 'AITK.

W2670-W3101   **Supermarine Walrus I/II**   **200**
Built by Saro. W2670-W2689, W2700-W2729, W2731-W2760, W2766-W2798, W3005-W3051, W3062-W3101, Mk.I except for W3010, W3047, W3051, W3076, W3078 Mk.II. Mainly for Royal Navy, 77 were for varying periods transferred to RAF. Five to RNZAF. W2688, W3070 became G-AHTO, 'AHFM.

W3109-W3970   **Supermarine Spitfire VA/VB**   **450**
W3109-W3114 Mk.VA, W3115-W3117 Mk.VB, W3118-W3121 Mk.VA, W3122-W3138, W3168-W3187, W3207-W3216, W3226-W3265, W3305-W3334, W3364-W3383, W3403-W3412, W3422-W3461, W3501-W3530, W3560-W3579, W3599-W3608, W3618-W3657, W3697-W3726, W3756-W3775, W3795-W3804, W3814-W3853, W3893-W3902, W3931-W3970 Mk.VB except for W3123, W3130, W3136, W3138, W3169, W3184, W3185, W3213, W3216, W3364, W3366, W3369, W3379 Mk.VA. W3237 converted to Mk.III was first aircraft with extended wings. W3112, W3135, W3831 converted to PR.XIII. W3760 experimental floatplane. W3122, W3127, W3229, W3250, W3318, W3322, W3328, W3428, W3445, W3530, W3656, W3707, W3764, W3795, W3798, W3815, became 3457M, 5537M, 5939M, 5572M, 5938M, 3405M, 5584M, 5571M, 5383M, 5393M, 4871M, 5842M, 5932M, 3386M, 3655M, 4263M, 5388M. W3212, W3371 W3372 renumbered as NX883, PA119, NX980 on conversion to Seafire IB. W3119 shipped to USA as sample and W3818, W3936 to Russia. W3136, W3229, W3230, W3235, W3251, W3370, W3437, W3457, W3522, W3602, W3618, W3646, W3756, W3769, W3775, W3796, W3831, W3846, W3933, W3938, W3941, W3953 to Royal Navy of which several were fitted with arrestor hooks. Postwar disposals: W3229, W3322, W3328, W3426, W3619, W3899, W3931, W3957 to French AF; W3128, W3180, W3248, W3430, W3431, W3518, W3519, W3641, W3648, W3803, W3902, W3950, W3951 to Portuguese AF.

W3976-W4037   **Short S.25 Sunderland II/III**   **50**
C/n S.1160-S.1209. W3976-W3998 Mk.II; W3999-W4004, W4017-W4037 Mk.III. W3980, W3983, W3991 became 4908M, 4603M, 5016M. W4037 rebuilt as c/n SH.62C Sandringham 6 LN-LAI. Built at Rochester.

W4041 & W4046   **Gloster E28/29 'Weaver'**   **2**
W4041/G W1 later W1A engine, was first British jet aircraft, first flew 15.5.41. W4046/G W2B engine.

W4050-W4099   **DH.98 Mosquito**   **50**
W4050 ex-E0234 first prototype to Spec B1/40 first flew 25.11.40, W4051 prototype PR version, W4052 prototype F.II, W4053 F.II converted to T.III, W4054-W4056 PR.I, W4057 B.IV converted to T.III, W4058-W4063 PR.I, W4064-W4072 B.IV/PR.IV, W4073-W4099 Mk.II of which W4073, W4075, W4077 were converted to T.III and W4089 for PR work. W4078, W4082, W4094, W4098 became 4880M, 4108M, 3872M, 4107M.

W4102-W4700   **Avro 683 Lancaster B.I**   **207(454)**
Rolls-Royce Merlin 20. W4102-W4140, W4154-W4201, W4230-W4279, W4301-W4340, W4355-W4384 built at

Manchester. W4114 became prototype Mk.III. W4113, W4128, W4161, W4164, W4181, W4231, W4241, W4253, W4264, W4309, W4358, W4380 became 4969M, 3609M, 4451M, 4443M, 4915M, 5451M, 5287M, 4914M, 5289M, 4904M, 4968M, 4886M. W4385-W4400, W4414-W4403, W4481-W4524, W4537-W4585, W4600-W4641, W4655-W4700 cancelled.

W4761-W5012 Avro 683 Lancaster I/III   200
Rolls-Royce Merlin 20/28. Built by Metropolitan Vickers. W4761-W4800, W4815-W4864, W4879-W4905, W4918-W4967, W4980-W4982 (170) Mk.I of which W4926 was converted to Mk.III; W4983-W5012 built as Mk.III. W4783 became RAAF A66-2. W4779, W4845, W4887, W4899, W4940, W4941, W4964 became 4903M, 5291M, 4352M, 4945M, 4874M, 4971M, 4922M.

W5014-W5015 DH.82 Tiger Moth   2
Impressment of G-AFZF, 'ADJE. W5015 became 2487M.

W5017-W5315 Blackburn Botha I   138(270)
Built at Brough. W5017-W5056, W5065-W5114, W5118-W5157, W5162-W5169. W5170-W5211, W5216-W5235, W5239-W5288, W5296-W5315 cancelled. W5132 became 4184M.

W5352-W5735 Vickers Wellington II/IC   300
W5352-W5401, W5414-W5463, W5476-W5500, W5513-W5537, W5550-W5598, W5611 (200) Mk.II; W5612-W5631, W5644-W5690, W5703-W5735 (100) Mk.IC. W5352 was T2545 rebuilt and modified. Conversions: W5623 Mk.III; W5615, W5619, W5631, W5645, W5647, W5649, W5653, W5655, W5657, W5659, W5661, W5662, W5671, W5674, W5676, W5678, W5725, W5728, W5730-W5735 Mk.VIII; W5686, W5709 Mk.XVI. W5389/G had G-AB jet and W5518/G W2/700 jet in tail. W5363, W5725, W5727 became 4170M, 3439M, 3333M.

W5740-W5741 Taylorcraft Plus D   2
G-AFZH, 'AFZI impressed. W5740 became G-AHEI.

W5746-W5782 DH.87B Hornet Moth   23
Impressed originally for Coastal Command patrols. W5746-W5755 ex-G-ADKA, 'ADKH, 'ADKJ-'ADKM, 'ADKR, 'AEKS, 'ADKW, 'ADMM, W5770-W5782 ex-G-ADMN, 'ADMS, 'ADNB, 'ADNC, 'AEPV, 'AESE, 'AETC, 'AEWY, 'AEZT, 'AFDT, 'AFDY, 'AFEE, 'AFMP. W5771 became 2821M.

W5783 DH.85 Leopard Moth   1
G-AFDV impressed.

W5784 DH.87 Hornet Moth   1
G-AFRE impressed.

W5791 Stinson SR-9D Reliant   1
G-AFBI c/n 5400 impressed.

W5795-W5824 Vickers Wellington V/VI   21(30)
W5795 Mk.VI prototype; W5796 Mk.V; W5797 Rolls-Royce test bed, became 3499M; W5798-W5815 Mk.VIA. W5816-W5824 Mk.V cancelled. W5802 became 5750M.

W5830 DH.87 Hornet Moth   1
G-ADKE impressed.

W5836-W5995 Fairey Swordfish II   100
Built by Blackburn for Royal Navy. W5836-W5865, W5886-W5925, W5966-W5995. W5856 to Royal Canadian Navy.

W6000-W6080 Short S.25 Sunderland II/III   50
W6000-W6004 (5) Mk.II; W6005-W6016, W6026-W6033 Mk.III (20) built by Blackburn at Dumbarton. W6050-W6064 (15) Mk.II, W6065-W6068, W6075-W6080 (10) Mk.III built by Short & Harland c/n SH.51-SH.75. W6050, W6056, W6058, W6064 became 4446M, 4782M, 4789M, 4881M.

W6085 Percival Q.6   1
G-AFKC impressed in Middle East.

W6089-W6410 Bristol 156 Beaufighter   (250)
Cancelled order with Boulton Paul. W6089-W6126, W6140-W6185, W6200-W6249, W6265-W6300, W6316-W6360, W6376-W6410.

W6415 DH.60G Gipsy Moth   1
G-ABOU impressed; became 2062M.

W6416 DH.80A Puss Moth   1
G-ABKG impressed; became 2068M.

W6417-W6420 DH.82 Tiger Moth   4
G-AFWC-'AFWF impressed. W6420 to Royal Navy.

W6421-W6422 DH.87 Hornet Moth   2
G-ADKB, 'ADKN impressed.

W6423-W6457 DH.89 Dragon Rapide   6
Impressments W6423-W6425 G-ADNH, 'AEAM, 'AEAJ, W6455-W6457 G-AENN, 'AEOV, 'AFSO all to No.24 Squadron.

W6458-W6460 DH.94 Moth Minor   3
G-AFPC, 'AFPD, 'AFPS impressed.

W6461-W6463 Miles M.17 Monarch   3
G-AFCR, 'AFJZ, 'AFRZ impressed. W6463 became G-AIDE.

W6464 Percival P.10 Vega Gull   1
G-AEYC impressed.

W6467-W6543 Bristol 152 Beaufort I   66
W6467-W6506, W6518-W6543. W6473, W6484 to RCAF. W6523 became 3149M.

W6546-W6657 Airspeed AS.10 Oxford II   100
Built by Percival. W6546-W6595, W6608-W6657. Wartime transfers: W6565, W6591 to Royal Navy; W6554, W6556, W6570, W6588, W6594, W6627, W6646, W6650, W6652 USAAF. W6549, W6580, W6586, W6612 became 3835M, 4060M, 4840M, 3614M. Postwar disposals: W6578, W6638 Burmese AF; W6561 Ceylon Government; W6579, W6613 R Norwegian AF and W6562 became G-AIUU.

W6667-W6670 Hawker Hurricane I   4
Built by Hawker at Langley.

W6675-W7241 Westland Lysander IIIA   17(500)
W6939-W6945, W6951-W6960 built by Westland at Doncaster. W6951 to Royal Navy. W6675-W6724, W6733-W6782, W6788-W6817, W6824-W6863, W6889-W6888, W6896-W6938, W6961-W6990, W6999-W7048, W7053-W7082, W7091-W7140, W7145-W7184, W7192-W7241 cancelled.

W7247-W7409 Blackburn Botha   (150)
Cancelled order. W7247-W7296, W7300-W7339, W7343-W7362, W7368-W7379, W7382-W7409.

W7419 Short S.16 Scion   1
C/n S.778 G-ACUZ impressed.

W7422 Miles M.11A Whitney Straight   1
G-AEUY impressed for Air Attache, Paris.

W7426-W7639 Short S.29 Stirling I   150
Built by Austin Motors. W7426-W7475, W7500-W7539, W7560-W7589, W7610-W7639. W7460, W7468, W7522, W7575 became 4777M, 4532M, 4937M, 4843M.

W7646 General Aircraft GAL.33 Cagnet   1
Ex-T-46 for trials.

W7650-W7939 Handley Page HP.59 Halifax II   200
W7650-W7679, W7695-W7720, W7745-W7784, W7801-W7826, W7844-W7887, W7906-W7939.

W7945 DH.60X Moth   1
G-AAPW impressed.

W7946-W7949 DH.60 Moth   4
G-ABER, 'AAJP, 'ABAI, 'ACRR (DH.60G, DH.60X, DH.60X, DH.60GIII) impressed. W7947 became 2819M.

W7950-W7956 DH.82 Tiger Moth   7
G-AFSL, 'AFSP, 'AFNR, 'AFSR, 'AFSG, 'AFGT, 'AFST impressed. W7950 became 7044M. W7951 and W7956 to Royal Navy.

W7970 DH.82A Tiger Moth   1
G-AFSU impressed, became G-ANCZ.

W7971-W7975 DH.94 Moth Minor   5
G-AFPB, 'AFNI, 'AFOX, 'AFOY, AFOZ impressed. W7971 became 2609M.

W7976 DH.60GIII Moth Major   1
G-ADAN impressed.

W7977 General Aircraft Monospar ST-25   (1)
Became T9264.

W7978-W7984 Stinson SR7-10 Reliant   7
G-AFRS, 'AEFY, 'AEVX, 'AFHB, 'AEXW, 'AFTM, 'AEVY impressed.

W7990-W8129 Westland Lysander   (100)
Cancelled. W7990-W7999, W8020-W8069, W8090-W8129 to have been built in Canada.

W8131-W8250 Brewster 339 Buffalo   120
Mainly shipped direct from USA to Singapore. W8131 ex-NX147B of US civil register. W8132, W8133 became 3133M and 3134M.

W8252-W8401 Douglas Boston III   150
Conversions from bomber to intruder: W8256, W8258, W8259, W8261-W8264, W8266-W8268, W8278, W8281, W8283, W8284, W8290, W8292, W8298, W8303-W8305,

W8314, W8317, W8318, W8321, W8325, W8326, W8332, W8333, W8335, W8338, W8340, W8342, W8344, W8345, W8349-W8351, W8356, W8358-W8360, W8365, W8370, W8374, W8380, W8385, W8386, W8390, W8394, W8395, W8399. Fitted with Turbinlite: W8253-W8255, W8257, W8260, W8265, W8274-W8277, W8279, W8280, W8282, W8294, W8296, W8299, W8300, W8306-W8310, W8312, W8313, W8322-W8324, W8327, W8328, W8336, W8339, W8341, W8343, W8346, W8352, W8353, W8357, W8362, W8364, W8366, W8369, W8379, W8392, W8393, W8398, W8400, W8401. Conversions to Havoc NF.II: W8274, W8277, W8309, W8317, W8328, W8341, W8352, W8366, W8300, W8309, W8328, W8341, W8352, W8364, W8369, W8392, W8393, W8396 to Royal Navy 1944. W8381 became 2828M. W8301, W8311 not delivered and W8252, W8270, W8316 lost on delivery.

W8405-W8434	**Consolidated Catalina I**	30

W8431, W8432 direct to RCAF. W8410 became 4889M.

W8437-W9099	**Miles Master II/III**	500

Built by Phillips & Powis at South Marston. W8437-W8486, W8500-W8539, W8560-W8599, W8620-W8669, W8690-W8739, W8760-W8799, W8815-W8864, W8880-W8909, W8925-W8974, W8990-W9003 (414) Mk.III; W9004-W9039, W9050-W9099 (86) Mk.II. W8449, W8532, W8653, W8654, W8774, W8884, W8905, W8928, W8946, W8955, W8956, W9088 became 4357M, 4358M, 4491M, 4545M, 4091M, 4542M, 3991M, 4897M, 4493M, 4492M, 4544M, 5475M. Wartime transfers: W9018, W9026, W9035, W9064 to Royal Navy; W8853, W8896, W8937, W8938, W8958, W8959, W9071 to USAAF. Wartime direct offsets: W8626, W8627, W8882, W8892, W8893, W8900, W8907, W8943, W8948, W8950, W9019 to Portuguese AF; W9004-W9012, W9050-W9054 to SAAF. W9020, W9087 to Turkish AF 1945.

W9104-W9106	**Lockheed 10A Electra**	3

G-AFEB, 'AEPN, 'AEPO impressed.

W9110-W9359	**Hawker Hurricane I**	200

Built by Gloster. W9110-W9159, W9170-W9209, W9215-W9244, W9260-W9279, W9290-W9329, W9340-W9359. W9127, W9134, W9137, W9152, W9182, W9208, W9221, W9318 became 4533M, 4749M, 2746M, 2849M, 5207M, 5039M, 4502M, 4748M. W9181, W9191, W9265 became DG635, DR345, DR356 on conversion to Mk.II. Wartime transfers: W9124, W9128, W9129, W9134, W9141, W9182, W9188, W9192, W9208, W9209, W9215, W9216, W9219, W9220-W9224, W9237, W9272, W9276, W9277, W9279, W9311-W9313, W9315, W9316, W9318, W9319 to Royal Navy for conversion to Sea Hurricane. W9157 to REAF.

W9365	**DH.89 Dragon Rapide**	1

G-ADNI impressed for Royal Navy.

W9367	**DH.60X Moth**	1

G-ABBD impressed for Royal Navy.

W9368	**DH.60M Moth**	1

G-AFWJ (ex-K1860) impressed for Royal Navy.

W9369	**DH.80A Puss Moth**	1

G-ABIZ impressed for Royal Navy.

W9370-W9371	**DH.85 Leopard Moth**	2

G-ACLK, 'ADHB impressed for Royal Navy.

W9372	**DH.87B Hornet Moth**	1

G-ADKV impressed for Royal Navy.

W9373	**Miles M.3B Falcon Six**	1

G-AEKK impressed for Royal Navy.

W9374	**Percival Q.6**	1

G-AFFE impressed for Royal Navy.

W9375-W9378	**Percival P.10 Vega Gull**	4

G-AFIT, 'AELS, 'AFBW, 'AETF impressed for Royal Navy.

W9379-W9391	**DH.87 Hornet Moth**	13

G-AFDU, 'AFDW, 'AEZH, 'AFDF, 'AEKY, 'AEZY, 'ADND, 'ADKU, 'ADIR, 'ADLY, 'ADMJ, 'AFDG, 'ADIS impressed for the RAF.

W9396-W9975	**Blackburn Botha**	(350)

Cancelled. W9396-W9415, W9434-W9463, W9496-W9545, W9558-W9597, W9646-W9665, W9702-W9741, W9748-W9772, W9821-W9855, W9880-W9899, W9936-W9975 with X1000-X1029 to complete 350 as contracted.

The Licensed Series

X1 to X25

It was made unlawful in 1917, under the Defence Regulations, to construct an aeroplane without official authority, to prevent material wastage on aircraft unlikely to be accepted. The present policy for the service to notify industry of their requirements and invite tenders was then instituted. If a firm wished to venture privately on a promising project, licence to construct could be granted and the aircraft numbered in a special 'X' for experimental series. Full documentation for the series has not been traced. The series was abandoned in 1918 and aircraft were renumbered in the general series.

Serial Nos	Aircraft Type and Remarks	Quantity
X1	**Glendower**	(1)
	Not confirmed but firm made licence application.	
X2-X4	**Sopwith 2FR2 Bulldog**	3
	X2 single-bay wings; X3 Mk.I & X4 Mk.II became H4422 and H4423.	
X7-X8	**Sopwith 2B2 Rhino**	2
	Licence No.14.	
X11	**Sopwith 3F2 Hippo**	1
	Licence No.14; renumbered H4420.	
X12-X13	**Nieuport Fighter**	(2)
	Bentley B.R.2 engine. Not adopted.	
X14	**Saunders T1**	1
	Licence No.17. 'T' for H. H. Thomas designer.	
X15-X17	**Austin AFT3 Osprey**	1(3)
	Licence No.17, X15 only completed. Work abandoned on X16, X17 in March 1918.	
X18	**Sopwith 3F2 Hippo**	1
	Licence withdrawn early 1918. Renumbered H4421.	
X19-X20	**Armstrong Whitworth FM.4 Armadillo**	1(2)
	Licence No.18. 'FM' for designer F. Murphy.	
X21-X24	**Siddeley Sinai**	(4)
	X21, X22 renumbered J6858, J6859. X23, X24 cancelled.	
X25	**Boulton & Paul P.6**	1
	Used by Boulton & Paul sales department 1919.	

The 'X' & 'Z' Series

X1000 to Z9999

'X' having been used only for the brief 'X' series in 1917-18, was a logical follow-on at X1000 from W9999. 'Y' was not used so that 'Z' followed 'X'.

Serial Nos	Aircraft Type and Remarks	Quantity
X1000-X1029	**Blackburn Botha**	(30)
	Included in series starting W9396-W9975.	
X1032-X1034	**Percival P.10 Vega Gull**	3
	G-AEXU, 'AERL, 'AFAV impressed for RAF in the Middle East.	
X1038-X1040	**Airspeed AS.10 Oxford I**	3
	Replacements for P1984, P1993, P2002. All shipped to Southern Rhodesian AF.	
X1045-X1046	**Supermarine Walrus**	2
	Built on contract for experimental aircraft by Saro.	
X1050	**Stinson 105 Voyager**	1
	C/n 7504 on loan. Became G-AGZW, later SE-BYI.	
X1085-X1086	**Percival P.10 Vega Gull**	2
	Impressed. Became SE-ALA, SE-ALZ.	
X2865-X2867	**DH.83 Fox Moth**	3
	G-ACDZ, 'ACEX, 'ABVK impressed.	

X2891	**Heston 1 Phoenix Srs.II**	1
	C/n 1/5 G-AESV impressed.	
X2893-X3154	**Handley Page HP.52 Hampden I**	150
	Built by English Electric. X2893-X2922, X2959-X3008, X3021-X3030, X3047-X3066, X3115-X3154. X3115 Mk.II prototype. X2898, X2903-X2905, X2912, X2961, X2976, X3022, X3026, X3053, X3055, X3061, X3116, X3131, X3137, X3140, X3142, X3145, X3149, X3150 converted to TB.I. X3137, X3149 to RCAF.	
X3160-X4003	**Vickers Wellington IC/III**	500
	Pegasus XVIII/Hercules III/XXI engines. Vickers built at Blackpool. X3160-X3179, X3192-X3221 (50) Mk.IC; X3222-X3226, X3275-X3289, X3304-X3313, X3330-X3374, X3387-X3426, X3445-X3489, X3538-X3567, X3584-X3608, X3633-X3677, X3694-X3728, X3741-X3765, X3784-X3823, X3866-X3890, X3923-X3967, X3984-X4003 (450) Mk.III. X3374, X3595 Mk.X prototypes; X3193, X3935 converted to Mk.XVI. X3286 became glider tug. X3479 adapted for carriage of Smith Gun. X3161, X3176, X3207, X3217, X3277, X3413, X3481, X3483, X3677, X3742, X3752, X3764, X3820, X3821, X3927, X3930, X3948, X3950, X3951 became 3950M, 3478M, 3630M, 3770M, 4828M, 4894M, 4781M, 3488M, 4793M, 4820M, 3601M, 4783M, 4791M, 4808M, 4779M, 4986M, 4825M, 5031M, 4805M.	
X4009-X4997	**Supermarine Spitfire I**	500
	X4009-X4038, X4051-X4070, X4101-X4110, X4159-X4188, X4231-X4280, X4317-X4331 Mk.I; X4332-X4335 Mk.I PR Type C of which X4333, X4334 became PR.V; X4336-X4356, X4381, X4382 Mk.I; X4383-X4386 Mk.I PR Type C; X4387-X4390, X4409-X4428, X4471-X4490 Mk.I; X4491-X4497 Mk.I PR Type C1; X4498-X4505, X4538 PR Type C; X4539-X4562, X4585-X4624, X4641-X4685, X4708-X4722, X4765-X4789, X4815-X4859, X4896-X4945, X4988-X4997 Mk.I. X4708 crashed before delivery. Conversions: X4067, X4622, X4776 Mk.II; X4021, X4028, X4062, X4172, X4173, X4238, X4257, X4258, X4272, X4279, X4280, X4331, X4342, X4353, X4389, X4421, X4476, X4485, X4488, X4604, X4606, X4615, X4660, X4663-X4672, X4709, X4721, X4766, X4784, X4786, X4839, X4846, X4902, X4908, X4922, X4930, X4931, X4937, X4941, X4989, X4997 Mk.V; X4942 Mk.VI; X4021, X4615, X4660, X4766 Mk.XIII. Many to Royal Navy of which X4717, X4989 became Seafire IB and others variously modified for PR work. X4012, X4025, X4033, X4103, X4166, X4175, X4236, X4343, X4355, X4474, X4484, X4603, X4608, X4641, X4661, X4676, X4718, X4779, X4847, X4915, X4916, X4921, X4933, X4934, X4942, X4992 became 3307M, 2655M, 2685M, 2684M, 2827M, 4408M, 2358M, 2635M, 2844M, 3598M, 4524M, 2558M, 2910M, 3466M, 2845M, 2847M, 4437M, 3144M, 2846M, 2842M, 2825M, 4750M, 3596M, 2627M, 4264M, 2631M. Wartime transfers: X4555 to RCAF; X4339, X4589, X4617, X4855, X4857, X4920 Portuguese AF.	
X5000	**Ford 5AT Trimotor**	1
	C/n 5AT-107 G-ACAE ex-NC440H impressed.	
X5006-X5007	**British Aircraft Swallow II**	2
	G-AEIH, 'AEHK impressed.	
X5008	**British Klemm L.25C Swallow**	1
	G-ACWA impressed.	
X5009	**Klemm L25**	1
	Salmson engine. G-AAZH impressed.	
X5010-X5011	**British Klemm L.25C Swallow**	2
	G-ACOW, 'ACRD impressed.	
X5017-X5043	**DH.60 Moth/Gipsy Moth**	27
	Impressments. X5017 DH.60A G-ABOE became 4028M; X5018, X5019 DH.60X/G G-AAMS, 'AAAO; X5020 DH.60X G-AAPH; X5021-X5025 DH.60G G-AAEX, 'ABOY, 'AAVY, 'ABDU, 'AAEH of which X5024 and X5025 became 2603M and 2997M; X5026 DH.60M G-ABPJ; X5027 DH.60G. G-AALW became 4029M; X5028 DH.60G G-AADH; X5029 DH.60A G-ABUB; X5030 DH.60 G-AAIW; X5031-X5037 DH.60A G-AABK, 'AALV, ABDK, 'AABJ, 'AAKO, 'ABJI, 'AAIA; X5038 DH.60X G-AAAA; X5039-X5041 DH.60G G-ABCS, 'AAJW, 'AALN; X5042 DH.60A G-AFKY; X5043 DH.60M G-AASZ.	
X5044	**DH.80A Puss Moth**	1
	G-ABVX impressed.	
X5045	**DH.82 Tiger Moth**	1
	G-ADJH impressed.	
X5046-X5104	**DH.60 Moth/Gipsy Moth**	12
	Impressments. X5046-X5048 DH.60G G-AARA, 'AAKU, 'ABCT; X5049 DH.60A G-AFPY; X5050 DH.60X G-ADIL; X5051 DH.60M G-AFMY; X5052-X5055 DH.60G G-ABXZ, 'AAFO, 'AFTG, 'AAJS; X5056 DH.60 G-AFDZ; X5104 DH.60M G-AALG once used by Prince of Wales. X5049, X5055, X5056, X5104 became 2601M, 2605M-2607M.	
X5105-X5110	**DH.82 Tiger Moth**	6
	G-AEWG, 'AFSH-'AFSJ, 'AFSM, 'AFSN impressed.	
X5111-X5114	**DH.60 Moth/Gipsy Moth**	4
	X5111-X5113 DH.60 G-ABJH, 'ABGM, 'ABLT; X5114 DH.60G III G-ACCW impressed, became 3124M.	
X5115-X5117	**DH.94 Moth Minor**	3
	G-AFOC, 'AFPI, 'AFOB impressed.	
X5118-X5119	**DH.60 Moth/Gipsy Moth**	2
	Impressments. X5118 DH.60 G-ABAL, X5119 DH.60M G-AARU became 4030M.	
X5120-X5123	**DH.94 Moth Minor**	4
	G-AFOD, 'AFOE, 'AFPR, 'AFRY impressed.	
X5124	**DH.60G III Moth**	1
	G-ADAT impressed, became 2756M.	
X5125	**Miles M.2H Hawk Major**	1
	G-ADIT impressed, became 3017M.	
X5126-X5132	**DH.60 Moth/Gipsy Moth**	7
	Impressments. X5126, X5127 DH.60M G-AAYG, 'AASL; X5128 DH.60X G-EBRI; X5129 DH.60G G-ABRO; X5130 DH.60M G-ABHN; X5131, X5132 DH.60G III G-ACGX, 'ACBX.	
X5133	**DH.94 Moth Minor**	1
	G-AFPH impressed.	
X5139-X5319	**Short S.29 Stirling II**	(140)
	Cancelled order placed in Canada. X5139-X5183, X5200-X5249, X5275-X5319.	
X5324	**Stinson 105 Voyager**	1
	Imported from the USA.	
X5330-X6517	**Vickers Wellington**	(750)
	Cancelled Vickers Armstrong order. X5330-X5359, X5372-X5421, X5446-X5490, X5523-X5547, X5596-X5630, X5657-X5701, X5726-X5775, X5810-X5844, X5859-X5903, X5920-X5964, X5985-X6004, X6023-X6062, X6079-X6128, X6153-X6202, X6245-X6294, X6311-X6355, X6380-X6419, X6468-X6517.	
X6520-X7317	**Airspeed AS.10 Oxford I/II**	500
	Built at Christchurch. X6520-X6564, X6589-X6622, X6643-X6692, X6726-X6750, X6764-X6813, X6835-X6879 (250) Mk.I; X6880-X6884, X6932-X6981, X7031-X7075, X7107-X7156, X7176-X7200, X7231-X7265, X7278-X7317 (250) Mk.II. Half retained for UK training and rest shipped under EATS to Commonwealth Air Forces. X6537, X6692 converted to Mk.V. Wartime transfers: X6783, X6838, X6865, X6934, X7058, X7177, X7179 to Royal Navy; X6933, X6939, X6977, X7071, X7176, X7181, X7186, X7193 to the USAAF. Postwar disposals: X7262 R Norwegian AF; X6951 Belgian AF; X6769 Danish AF; X6765, X6784 R Netherlands AF; X7135 Burmese AF. X6646, X6743, X6778, X6786, X6799, X6941, X7125, X7289 became 4842M, 5297M, 5330M, 5508M, 6579M, 4222M, 5477M, 5893M.	
X7320-X7525	**DH.89A Dominie**	149
	First ten aircraft with Gipsy VI, remainder with Gipsy III engines. Built by de Havilland with c/ns 6493-6583, 6585-6642. X7320-X7354, X7368-X7417, X7437-X7456, X7482-X7525 for the RAF except X7332, X7341, X7348, X7350, X7394, X7397, X7400, X7414, X7437, X7448, X7452, X7453, X7482, X7486-X7489, X7494, X7496-X7499, X7506-X7508, X7516 direct or transferred to Royal Navy and X7346, X7403, X7522, X7523 loaned to the USAAF. X7334, X7335, X7337, X7339, X7404, X7509-X7511, X7520 to the SAAF. X7387, X7388 became G-AGDG and 'AGDH on delivery and over 70 others went to civil registration postwar.	
X7533-X7534	**Taylorcraft Plus D**	2
	G-AFGM and 'AFWO impressed.	
X7540-X8269	**Bristol 156 Beaufighter I/VIC/VIF**	500
	X7540, X7541 Mk.IF, X7542, X7543 Mk.VIF/C prototype; X7544-X7589, X7610-X7649, X7670-	

X7719, X7740-X7779, X7800-X7849, X7870-X7879
Mk.I; X7880-X7899, X7920-X7924 Mk.VIF; X7925
Mk.VIC; X7926-X7936 Mk.VIF; X7937-X7939 Mk.VIC;
X7940-X7969, X8000-X8029 Mk.VIF; X8030-X8039,
X8060-X8094 Mk.VIC; X8095 Mk.X prototype; X8096-
X8099 Mk.VIC; X8100-X8109, X8130-X8169, X8190-
X8229, X8250-X8269 Mk.VIF. Built at Old Mixon
Shadow Factory, Weston-super-Mare, except X7925,
X7928-X7936, X8030-X8039, X8061-X8099 at Filton.
X7579 first ASV radar experiments at TRE 1941;
X8065 first torpedo carrying Beaufighter by TDU,
March 1942. X7618 to Royal Navy and X7610, X7636,
X7689, X7883, X7929, X8014, X8105, X8168 to the
USAAF plus X7718 shipped to America. X7543, X7552,
X7577, X7611, X7636, X7641, X7643, X7679, X7683,
X7686, X7688, X7745, X7754, X7811, X7829, X7935,
X8027, X8204, X8227 became 4755M, 3854M, 4405M,
4404M, 5340M, 4597M, 4598M, 3856M, 4489M, 4290M,
3858M, 4120M, 4571M, 4572M, 4291M, 4291M, 4403M, 5580M
and 5581M (to French AF), 5616M.

X8273-X8275	**Short S.26 'G' Class**	3
	G-AFCK, 'AFCJ, 'AFCI *Golden Horn, Golden Fleece, Golden Hind* impressed.	
X8505-X8511	**DH.89 Rapide**	7
	Impressments: G-AEXP, 'AFEO, 'AEXO, 'AFAH, 'ACTT, 'AEPW, 'ADBV.	
X8518-X8522	**Stinson Reliant (Model designations below)**	5
	Impressments: X8518, X8519 SR-5 G-ACSV, 'ADDG; X8520 SR-8D G-AEJI; X8521 SR-9D G-AEYZ; X8522 Junior Reliant G-AFUW.	
X8525-X8817	**Fairey Fulmar II**	200
	C/n F.5020-F.5219. X8525-X8574, X8611-X8655, X8680-X8714, X8729-X8778, X8798-X8817. First 22 delivered packed for shipping. Delivered to Royal Navy but X8693, X8701, X8743, X8773 used for a period by RAF.	
X8825-X8912	**Percival P.30 Proctor IIA**	(50)
	Cancelled. X8825-X8859, X8898-X8912 intended for the Royal Navy.	
X8916-X8939	**Bristol 152 Beaufort I**	24
	C/n 9538-9561. X8931 DC.	
X8940-X9290	**Fairey Albacore**	250
	C/n F.5220-F.5469. X8940-X8984, X9010-X9059, X9073-X9117, X9137-X9186, X9214-X9233, X9251-X9290 for Royal Navy. X8947, X8952 to RCN.	
X9294-X9295	**DH.85 Leopard Moth**	2
	G-ACKR and 'ACUK impressed.	
X9296	**DH.60M Moth**	1
	G-ABNR impressed.	
X9297-X9298	**DH.94 Moth Minor**	2
	G-AFPN and 'AFOU impressed.	
X9299	**DH.83 Fox Moth**	1
	G-ACIG impressed. Became 2614M.	
X9300-X9301	**Miles M.3A Falcon Major**	2
	G-ADHI and 'AEFB impressed.	
X9302-X9303	**DH.60 Gipsy Moth**	2
	G-ACMB and 'ABBJ impressed.	
X9304-X9305	**DH.83 Fox Moth**	2
	G-ABUT and 'ACFF impressed.	
X9306	**Miles M.17 Monarch**	1
	G-AFJU impressed.	
X9310	**DH.87B Hornet Moth**	1
	G-ADMR impressed.	
X9315	**Percival P.10 Vega Gull**	1
	G-AFEH impressed.	
X9316	**Lockheed 12A**	1
	G-AEOI impressed.	
X9317	**DH.95 Flamingo**	1
	G-AFUF impressed.	
X9318	**DH.82A Tiger Moth**	1
	G-AFSS impressed.	
X9319	**DH.87B Hornet Moth**	1
	G-AEET impressed.	
X9320	**DH.89 Rapide**	1
	G-ACYM impressed.	
X9321-X9326	**DH.87B Hornet Moth**	6
	G-ADKD, 'ADKP, 'ADML, 'AFBH, 'ADNE, 'ADOT impressed.	
X9327	**DH.90 Dragonfly**	1
	G-ADXM impressed.	

X9328-X9329	**Percival P.16A Q.6**	2
	G-AEYE and 'AFHG impressed.	
X9330-X9331	**GAL Monospar ST-25 Universal**	2
	G-AFSB and 'AFSA impressed.	
X9332	**Percival P.10 Vega Gull**	1
	G-AFAU impressed; became G-AIIT.	
X9333-X9335	**GAL Monospar ST-25 Universal**	3
	G-AFIP, 'AFIV, 'AFWP impressed.	
X9336	**Percival P.16A Q.6**	1
	G-AFGX impressed.	
X9337	**DH.90 Dragonfly**	1
	G-AFVJ impressed.	
X9338	**Heston Phoenix Srs.II**	1
	G-AEYX impressed.	
X9339-X9340	**Percival P.10 Vega Gull**	2
	G-AEZK and 'AFBC impressed.	
X9341	**GAL Monospar ST-12**	1
	G-ADLL impressed.	
X9342-X9347	**Airspeed AS.5 Courier**	6
	Impressed. AS.5B G-ACLF, AS.5A G-ADAY, 'ACLR, 'ACZL, AS.5B G-ACNZ, AS.5A G-ACVF.	
X9348	**GAL Monospar ST-25 Jubilee**	1
	G-ADPK impressed. Later became DR848.	
X9349	**Percival P.10 Vega Gull**	1
	G-AELW impressed.	
X9363	**Percival P.16A Q.6**	1
	G-AFKG impressed.	
X9364	**Short S.16 Scion II**	1
	G-ADDN impressed; became 2723M.	
X9365	**GAL Monospar ST-25 Jubilee**	1
	G-ADVH impressed.	
X9366	**Short S.16 Scion II**	1
	G-ADDR impressed; became 2724M.	
X9367	**GAL Monospar ST-4 Mk.II**	1
	G-ADJP impressed.	
X9368	**Percival P.10 Vega Gull**	1
	G-AFEM impressed.	
X9369	**GAL Monospar ST-25 Jubilee**	1
	G-ADPL impressed.	
X9370	**Airspeed AS.6J Envoy III**	1
	G-AFWZ (ex-VT-AIC) impressed.	
X9371	**Percival P.10 Vega Gull**	1
	G-AEMB impressed.	
X9372	**GAL Monospar ST-25 Universal**	1
	G-AEPA impressed.	
X9373	**GAL Monospar ST-25 Jubilee**	1
	G-ADYN impressed.	
X9374	**Short S.16 Scion II**	1
	G-ADDP impressed.	
X9375	**Short S.16 Scion I**	1
	G-ACJI impressed; became 2725M.	
X9376	**GAL Monospar ST-4 II**	1
	G-ACCO impressed; became DR849.	
X9377	**GAL Monospar ST-25 Universal**	1
	G-AEGY impressed.	
X9378	**DH.80A Puss Moth**	1
	G-ABRR impressed.	
X9379	**DH.84 Dragon**	1
	G-ACHV impressed; became 2369M.	
X9380-X9385	**DH.85 Leopard Moth**	6
	G-ACLM, 'ACMN, 'ACPK, 'ADCO, 'ACSH, 'ADWY impressed. X9382, X9385 became 2778M, 2991M.	
X9386-X9388	**DH.89 Rapide**	3
	Impressments: G-ADDE, 'AEMH to RAF; 'AFEP to RN.	
X9389-X9390	**DH.90 Dragonfly**	2
	G-AEDV and 'AEFN impressed.	
X9391-X9392	**Percival P.10 Vega Gull**	2
	G-AEXV and 'AFEK impressed.	
X9393	**Heston Phoenix Series II**	1
	G-AEMT impressed.	
X9394	**Airspeed AS.5A Courier**	1
	G-ACLT impressed.	
X9395-X9399	**DH.84 Dragon**	5
	G-ACIU, 'ACMJ, 'ACLE, 'ACAO, 'ACPX impressed.	
X9400-X9405	**DH.80A Puss Moth**	6
	G-ABLB, 'AAZX, 'AAZV,'ABKD, 'AAXO, 'ABHB impressed. X9400, X9401, X9404 became 2306M, 2304M, 2305M.	
X9406-X9407	**Percival P.16A Q.6**	2
	G-AFIX and 'AFFD impressed.	

X9427	Airspeed AS.5 Courier	1
	G-ABXN impressed.	
X9430	Short S.16 Scion II	1
	G-ADDX impressed.	
X9431	Spartan Cruiser II	1
	G-ACYL impressed.	
X9432	Spartan Cruiser III	1
	G-ADEL impressed.	
X9433	Spartan Cruiser II	1
	G-ACSM impressed.	
X9434	GAL Monospar ST-4	1
	G-ABVP impressed.	
X9435-X9436	Percival P.10 Vega Gull	2
	G-AEWS and 'AEZL impressed.	
X9437	Airspeed AS.5 Courier	1
	G-ADAX impressed.	
X9438	DH.60M Moth	1
	G-AFZB (ex-K1845) impressed for Royal Navy.	
X9439	DH.80A Puss Moth	1
	G-ABSO impressed.	
X9440	DH.84 Dragon II	1
	G-ADCP impressed.	
X9441-X9442	DH.86B/DH.86A	2
	G-AEJM and 'ADMY impressed. X9442 to Royal Navy.	
X9443-X9447	DH.87 Hornet Moth	5
	G-ADJX, 'ADJZ, 'ADKC, 'AFEC, 'AFEF impressed.	
X9448	DH.89A Rapide	1
	G-ADAL impressed.	
X9449-X9450	DH.89 Rapide	2
	G-ADWZ and 'AEML impressed.	
X9451	DH.89A Rapide	1
	G-AFEZ impressed for Royal Navy.	
X9452	DH.90 Dragonfly	1
	Prototype G-ADNA impressed.	
X9453	GAL Monospar ST-10	1
	Prototype G-ACTS impressed; later to Royal Navy.	
X9454	Percival P.16A Q.6	1
	G-AFMT impressed.	
X9455	Percival P.10 Vega Gull	1
	G-AEJJ impressed.	
X9456	Short S.16 Scion II	1
	G-ADDV impressed; became 2726M.	
X9457	DH.89A Rapide	1
	G-ADFX impressed.	
X9458	DH.87B Hornet Moth	1
	G-ADKS impressed.	
X9460-X9593	Supermarine Walrus II	100
	Built by Saro. X9460-X9484, X9498-X9532, X9554-X9558 Mk.I; X9559-X9593 Mk.II. X9512, X9567 became NZ158, NZ155 of RNZAF. To Royal Navy but 43 transferred to RAF. X9580 became 6225M.	
X9596	Stinson SR-8 Reliant	1
	G-AELU impressed.	
X9600-X9993 & Z1040-Z1751	Vickers Wellington IC/IV/III	710
	Built by Vickers at Chester. X9600-X9644, X9658-X9707, X9733-X9767, X9785-X9834, X9871-X9890, X9905-X9954, X9974-X9993, Z1040-Z1054, Z1066-Z1115, Z1139-Z1181 Mk.IC; Z1182, Z1183, Z1202-Z1221, Z1243-Z1292, Z1311-Z1345, Z1375-Z1424, Z1459-Z1496 Mk.IV; Z1562-Z1578, Z1592-Z1626, Z1648-Z1697, Z1717-Z1751 Mk.III. X9663, X9678, Z1071, Z1102, Z1150, Z1171, Z1181 converted to Mk.XVI. X9602, X9604, X9605, X9611, X9791, X9927 became 2986M, 3501M, 3680M, 3771M, 3849M, 4233M and Z1050, Z1260, Z1263, Z1268, Z1275, Z1280, Z1289, Z1322, Z1382, Z1390, Z1398, Z1407, Z1492, Z1626, Z1653, Z1672, Z1677, Z1688, Z1740 became 4584M, 4589M, 4605M, 4590M, 3904M, 4677M, 4563M, 4591M, 4582M, 4564M, 4522M, 4580M, 4581M, 4792M, 4778M, 4821M, 4797M, 4830M, 5220M.	
Z1755-Z1823	Supermarine Walrus II	50
	Built by Saro. Z1755-Z1784, Z1804-Z1823 for Royal Navy were transferred to RAF and Z1768, Z1771, Z1814 went to RCAF in 1945.	
Z1826-Z2126	Fairey Firefly I	200
	Z1826-Z1829 prototypes. Z1830-Z1845, Z1865-Z1914, Z1942-Z1986, Z2011-Z2060, Z2092-Z2126 Mk.I. Conversions: Z1831/G Mk.II prototype; Z1826 FR.1 prototype; Z1835 Mk.III prototype; Z1875 NF.II prototype; Z1901 FR.IA; Z2118 Mk.IV prototype;	

	Z1893, Z1909, Z1953, Z1980, Z2020, Z2021, Z2025, Z2027, Z2054, Z2058, Z2111, Z2119 T.I.	
Z2003	Aeronca Chief	1
	VT-ALN impressed in India.	
Z2134-Z2153	Consolidated 28 Catalina	20
	Z2134, Z2136-Z2140 to RCAF. Z2152 to BOAC.	
Z2155-Z2304	Douglas Boston III	150
	Conversions: Z2155, Z2165, Z2171, Z2173, Z2186, Z2188, Z2192, Z2207, Z2210, Z2226, Z2240, Z2241, Z2243, Z2290, Z2299 Intruder version; Z2160, Z2169, Z2184, Z2185, Z2189, Z2214, Z2246, Z2270, Z2280 fitted with Turbinlites. Z2169, Z2184, Z2270 to Royal Navy. Z2268, Z2272 not delivered. Z2262 became 4058M.	
Z2308-Z4018	Hawker Hurricane IIA/IIB/IIC	1000
	Built at Kingston, Brooklands and Langley plants. Z2308-Z2357, Z2382-Z2426, Z2446-Z2465, Z2479-Z2528, Z2560-Z2594, Z2624-Z2643, Z2661-Z2705, Z2741-Z2775, Z2791-Z2840, Z2882-Z2931, Z2959-Z2993, Z3017-Z3036, Z3050-Z3099, Z3143-Z3187, Z3221-Z3270, Z3310-Z3359, Z3385-Z3404, Z3421-Z3470, Z3489-Z3523, Z3554-Z3598, Z3642-Z3691, Z3740-Z3784, Z3826-Z3845, Z3885-Z3919, Z3969-Z4018. Z2340 broken up for spares before delivery. Z2320/G, Z2326, Z2885, Z3092/G, Z3564, Z3919 used for various armament trials. Z3687 used for Armstrong Whitworth wing tests. Z2320, Z2465, Z2515 became 4173M, 6513M, 6512M. Large number shipped to Russia. Z3148, Z3265, Z3426, Z3892 to Portugal and Z3070, Z3359, Z3501, Z3595 to French AF; Z3514 to Turkey.	
Z4022-Z4652	Hawker Hurricane I	400
	Built by Gloster. Z4022-Z4071, Z4085-Z4119, Z4161-Z4205, Z4223-Z4272, Z4308-Z4327, Z4347-Z4391, Z4415-Z4434, Z4482-Z4516, Z4532-Z4581, Z4603-Z4652. Z4489 converted to Mk.II. Z4039, Z4051, Z4053, Z4055-Z4057, Z4094, Z4365, Z4500, Z4504, Z4532, Z4550, Z4553, Z4568, Z4569, Z4581, Z4605, Z4624, Z4638, Z4646, Z4649 to Royal Navy, Z4037 to Irish Air Corps, Z4373 to R Egyptian AF, Z4631 to USAAF. Z4059, Z4062 became 3602M, 4025M.	
Z4686-Z5693	Hawker Hurricane I/IIA/IIB	600
	Built by Gloster. Z4686-Z4720, Z4760-Z4809, Z4832-Z4876, Z4920-Z4939 (150) Mk.I of which Z4686, Z4778, Z4835, Z4846, Z4847, Z4849, Z4851-Z4854, Z4865-Z4867, Z4873, Z4874, Z4876, Z4920-Z4922, Z4924-Z4927, Z4929, Z4933-Z4939 went to Royal Navy. Z4940-Z4969, Z4987-Z4989 (33) Mk.IIA of which Z4941 was converted to IIB; Z4990-Z5006, Z5038-Z5087, Z5117-Z5161, Z5202-Z5236, Z5252-Z5271, Z5302-Z5351, Z5376-Z5395, Z5434-Z5483, Z5529-Z5563, Z5580-Z5629, Z5649-Z5693 (417) Mk.IIB. Large number shipped to Russia. Z4790, Z4809, Z4848, Z4851, Z4927 became 4695M, 4383M, 2862M, 4684M, 4535M.	
Z5721-Z6455	Bristol 142L Blenheim IV	420
	Built by Avro. Z5721-Z5770, Z5794-Z5818, Z5860-Z5909, Z5947-Z5991, Z6021-Z6050, Z6070-Z6104, Z6144-Z6193, Z6239-Z6283, Z6333-Z6382, Z6416-Z6455. Wartime transfers: 20 to Royal Navy; 6 to the Portuguese AF and 5 to Free French AF. Z5756, Z5802, Z5880, Z5952, Z5963, Z5971, Z6169, Z6246 became 3784M, 3997M, 4067M, 3978M, 3979M, 4019M, 3430M, 4066M.	
Z6461-Z6980	Armstrong Whitworth AW.38 Whitley V/VII	300
	Z6461-Z6510, Z6552-Z6586, Z6624-Z6673, Z6720-Z6764, Z6793-Z6842, Z6862-Z6881, Z6931-Z6959 (279) Mk.V; Z6960-Z6969 (10) Mk.VII; Z6970-Z6980 (11) Mk.V. Z6660 loaned to BOAC as G-AGDW.	
Z6983-Z7162	Hawker Hurricane I	100
	Built by Canadian Car & Foundry Corporation. Z6983-Z7017, Z7049-Z7093, Z7143-Z7162. Some to Royal Navy for Sea Hurricane: Z6987, Z6995, Z6997, Z7008, Z7015, Z7016, Z7050, Z7055, Z7057, Z7061, Z7064, Z7065, Z7067-Z7069, Z7071, Z7073, Z7078-Z7080, Z7082-Z7091, Z7093, Z7144, Z7145, Z7147-Z7149, Z7151-Z7155, Z7160-Z7162. Z7078, Z7079, Z7085, Z7086, Z7091, Z7144, Z7145, Z7147, Z7156 became 4537M, 4737M, 4660M, 4688M, 4665M, 4746M, 5042M, 4507M, 3603M.	
Z7187	Short S.22 Scion Senior	1
	Ex-G-ADIP/VT-AHI/VQ-PAD impressed in India.	

Z7188	DH.89A Dragon Rapide	(1)
	Ex-G-AFEN/VQ-PAC impressed in India. Later HK864.	
Z7189-Z7190	Short Scion Junior	2
	VQ-PAA and VQ-PAB impressed.	
Z7193-Z7256	Percival P.30 Proctor II	50

Z7193-Z7222, Z7237-Z7256 of which Z7253-Z7256 compromised numbers below and were renumbered BT278-BT281. Delivery for RAF except Z7239-Z7249, Z7251 fitted out for Royal Navy. Conversions to Mk.III: Z7193, Z7194, Z7196, Z7197, Z7201, Z7203, Z7206, Z7209, Z7212-Z7214, Z7216, Z7218, Z7222, Z7237, Z7238, Z7248, Z7252. Z7195, Z7198 transferred to USAAF and Z7237 became 7033M.

Z7253-Z7266	DH.89/DH.89A Rapide	14

Impressments: G-AFLY, 'AFLZ, 'AFMA, 'AFMF, 'AFME, 'AFMH, 'AFMG, 'AFMI, 'AFMJ, 'ADAI DH.89A, G-ADIM DH.89, G-ADAG, 'ADBW DH.89A, G-ACZE DH.89. Z7258, Z7261 fitted out as ambulances.

Z7271-Z8323	Bristol 142L Blenheim IV	430(600)

Built by Rootes. Z7271-Z7320, Z7340-Z7374, Z7406-Z7455, Z7483-Z7522, Z7577-Z7596, Z7610-Z7654, Z7678-Z7712, Z7754-Z7803, Z7841-Z7860, Z7879-Z7928, Z7958-Z7992 built. Z7993-Z8002, Z8050-Z8099, Z8143-Z8167, Z8202-Z8236, Z8274-Z8323 cancelled. Wartime transfers: Z7373, Z7779, Z7842, Z7885, Z7970 to Free French AF; Z7492 to Portuguese AF plus Z7585, Z7678 interned; Z7986 to Turkish AF; Z7351, Z7354, Z7414, Z7761, Z7961 to Royal Navy.

Z8328-Z9114	Vickers Wellington IC/II/VIII	450

Z8328-Z8377, Z8397-Z8441, Z8489-Z8538, Z8567-Z8601, Z8643-Z8646 (200) Mk.II; Z8702, Z8703 Mk.VIII, Z8704 Mk.IC, Z8705-Z8708 Mk.VIII, Z8709 Mk.IC, Z8710-Z8713 Mk.VIII, Z8714 Mk.IC, Z8715 Mk.IC, Z8716 Mk.IC, Z8717 Mk.VIII, Z8718 Mk.IC, Z8719 Mk.VIII, Z8720 Mk.IC, Z8721 Mk.VIII, Z8722 Mk.IC, Z8723 Mk.VIII, Z8724 Mk.IC, Z8725 Mk.VIII, Z8726 Mk.IC, Z8727 Mk.VIII; Z8728-Z8736, Z8761-Z8810, Z8827-Z8871, Z8891-Z8901 Mk.IC, Z8902 Mk.VIII, Z8903-Z8910, Z8942-Z8991, Z9016-Z9045, Z9095-Z9114 Mk.IC. Z8709, Z8829, Z8831, Z8850, Z8893, Z8982 converted to Mk.XVI. Z8570 fitted with Rover-built W2B booster unit. Z8416 used in Vickers 'S' gun tests. Z8771, Z8772 to USA, the latter as DW.1. Z8437, Z8440, Z8726, Z8827, Z8899, Z8954, Z9112 became 4057M, 4169M, 2787M, 4010M, 3492M, 3692M, 4194M.

Z9119-Z9529	Armstrong Whitworth AW.38 Whitley V/VII	250

Z9119 Mk.V, Z9120-Z9124 Mk.VII, Z9125-Z9134 Mk.V, Z9135-Z9139 Mk.VII; Z9140-Z9168, Z9188, Z9189 Mk.V, Z9190-Z9199 Mk.VII, Z9200-Z9232, Z9274-Z9323, Z9361-Z9363 Mk.V; Z9364-Z9383 Mk.VII; Z9384-Z9390, Z9419-Z9443, Z9461-Z9490, Z9510-Z9515 Mk.V, Z9516-Z9529 Mk.VII. Z9208, Z9216 loaned to BOAC as G-AGDU, 'AGDV. Z9480 became 3451M. Z9367, Z9371, Z9373, Z9379, Z9519 transferred to Royal Navy.

Z9533-Z9978	Bristol 142L Blenheim IV	200(280)

Ordered from Avro. Z9533-Z9552, Z9572-Z9621, Z9647-Z9681, Z9706-Z9755, Z9792-Z9836 built. Z9886-Z9935, Z9949-Z9978 cancelled. Additional 120 of order also cancelled. See 'AA' series below.

Start of the Double Letter Series

AA100 to AE479

When Z9999 was reached in 1940, the allocating authority in the newly-formed Ministry of Aircraft Production had the option of starting again at A1000 or using a new series as a follow-on; the latter course was chosen, and a system evolved using two initial letters in alphabetical sequence, 'AA', 'AB' et seq to 'AZ' and then 'BA', 'BB' et seq to 'BZ'. This was put into effect with the exception of certain letters, or combinations of letters, which for various reasons were not used. Since an additional letter was introduced, the number range was reduced from 1000-9999 to 100-999. Black-out blocks continued, with certain exceptions for which explanations are given under the appropriate headings. 'AC' was not used to avoid confusion with 'AG'.

Unlike the 1914-18 War, when captured enemy aircraft had a separate series, airworthy captured German and Italian aircraft were allotted numbers in the normal sequence and the first of these occurs in this series.

Serial Nos	Aircraft Type and Remarks	Quantity
AA100-AA273	Bristol 142L Blenheim IV	(120)

Avro order cancelled. AA100-AA144, AA178-AA202, AA224-AA273.

AA281-AA713	Boulton Paul P.82 Defiant I/II	270(300)

AA281-AA330, AA350-AA362 Mk.I of which AA282, AA286, AA288-AA292, AA294, AA296, AA298, AA300, AA301, AA306, AA308, AA310, AA311, AA313, AA314, AA316, AA317, AA320-AA324, AA326-AA330, AA354, AA358, AA361 were converted to TT.III mainly for Royal Navy; AA363-AA369 Mk.I converted to Mk.II on production line; AA370-AA384, AA398-AA447, AA469-AA513, AA531-AA550, AA566-AA595, AA614-AA633, AA651-AA670 Mk.II of which many were converted to TT.II and 40 were transferred to the Royal Navy. AA671-AA673, AA687-AA713 cancelled.

AA718-AB536	Supermarine Spitfire V	500

AA718-AA767 Mk.VB of which AA739 was converted to PR.XIII. AA781-AA815 PR.IV; AA833-AA882, AA902-AA946, AA963-AA982 Mk.VB except AA873 Mk.IX and AA874, AA875, AA878, AA963, AA968, AA976, AA977, AA980 Mk.VC; AB118-AB123 Mk.IV, AB124 Mk.VB, AB125-AB129 Mk.IV, AB130 Mk.VA, AB131, AB132 Mk.IV, AB133-AB138 Mk.VB, AB139 Mk.VC; AB140-AB152, AB167-AB216, AB240-AB284 Mk.VB except AB167, AB169, AB174, AB179, AB182, AB188, AB191, AB202, AB204, AB208, AB210-AB212, AB214, AB216, AB248, AB254 Mk.VC, AB176, AB200, AB211 Mk.VI and AB179, AB196, AB197 converted to Mk.IX (AB197 being the prototype conversion); AB300-AB319 Mk.IV; AB320-AB349 Mk.VB tropicalised; AB363-AB382 Mk.VB except for AB365, AB367, AB368, AB371, AB372, AB374, AB377, AB380, AB381 Mk.VC of which AB372 was converted to Mk.IX; AB401-AB416 Mk.VB, AB417 Mk.VC, AB418-AB420 Mk.VB, AB421-AB430 Mk.IV/V PR versions, AB450 Mk.VII prototype, AB451 Mk.VB, AB452, AB453 Mk.VC, AB454 Mk.VB, AB455 Mk.VC, AB456-AB460 Mk.V converted to Mk.IX, AB461-AB469 Mk.VC, AB487 Mk.VB, AB488-AB536 Mk.VC except AB490-AB492, AB494, AB500, AB502 Mk.VB and AB498, AB503, AB506, AB513, AB516, AB523, AB527-AB530, AB533, AB534 Mk.VI, AB505, AB507, AB508, AB511, AB522, AB525 built or converted to Mk.IX. Conversions to Seafire: AA750, AA866, AA872, AA904, AA905, AA932, AA971, AB181, AB190, AB201, AB205, AB261, AB376, AB379, AB404-AB410, AB413-AB416, AB492, AB494 mostly renumbered in the MB, NX and PA ranges. A few transferred to USAAF, French AF and AA908 shipped to Russia. AA728, AA729, AA862, AB487 supplied to Portugal. AA751, AA839, AA849,

AA860, AA927, AA929, AA931, AA969, AB139,
AB140, AB192, AB193, AB202, AB265, AB276, AB278,
AB488, AB499, AB510 became 5583M, 5348M, 5387M,
5028M, 3779M, 5382M, 5336M, 5596M, 5589M, 5590M,
4462M, 5543M, 5597M, 5541M, 5551M, 4407M, 4237M,
4243M, 3649M.

AB639-AB773 Airspeed AS.10 Oxford II 100
Built by Percival. AB639-AB668, AB685-AB729, AB749-
AB773. AB650, AB652, AB660, AB706, AB711,
AB717, AB720, AB752, AB762, AB768, AB770 trans-
ferred to USAAF and AB697 to Royal Navy. AB640,
AB686, AB699, AB765 became 6200M, 5458M, 3157M,
5503M. Postwar AB663 to R Norwegian AF and AB712
to R Hellenic AF.

AB779-AD584 Supermarine Spitfire VB 500
Built at Castle Bromwich. AB779-AB828, AB841-AB875,
AB892-AB941, AB960-AB994, AD111-AD140, AD176-
AD210, AD225-AD274, AD288-AD332, AD348-AD397,
AD411-AD430, AD449-AD478, AD498-AD517, AD535-
AD584. AB786 converted to Mk.IX and AD354, AD501
to PR.XIII. Seafire conversions: AB809, AB817, AB847,
AB902, AB908, AB919, AB928, AB933, AB940, AB967,
AB968, AD120, AD135, AD184, AD187, AD226,
AD241, AD252, AD271, AD274, AD357, AD358,
AD364, AD365, AD368, AD371, AD382, AD387,
AD393, AD394, AD397, AD421, AD426, AD510,
AD517, AD552, AD566, AD567, AD578-AD580,
AD582 most of which were renumbered in MB, NX and
PA series. Transfers: 4 to USAAF, 5 to French AF, 13
to Russia and 10 to Portugal. AB815, AB871, AB904,
AB920, AB971, AD248, AD288, AD299, AD318,
AD376, AD425, AD453, AD508, AD573 became 2697M,
4353M, 5349M, 3656M, 5719M, 5591M, 5599M, 5717M,
5683M, 2799M, 5544M, 4122M, 5594M, 5555M and
AB910 became G-AISU.

AD589-AD653 Vickers Wellington IC 50
AD589-AD608, AD624-AD653. AD646 first TB
conversion.

AD657& AD661 Bristol 160 Bisley (renamed Blenheim V) 2
Prototype c/n 9874, 9875 to Spec B6/40.

AD665-AD714 Armstrong Whitworth AW.38 Whitley V 50
Delivered early 1942.

AD719-AE442 Handley Page HP.52 Hampden I 425
Built by English Electric. AD719-AD768, AD782-AD806,
AD824-AD873, AD895-AD939, AD959-AD988, AE115-
AE159, AE184-AE203, AE218-AE267, AE286-AE320,
AE352-AE401, AE418-AE442. AD724, AD743, AD754,
AD764, AD767, AD792-AD795, AD799, AD801, AD836,
AD838, AD852, AD855, AD857, AD865, AD870, AD906,
AD908, AD920, AD927-AD929, AD963, AD964, AD976,
AD977, AD979, AD982, AD987, AE115, AE116, AE122,
AE125, AE130, AE135, AE145, AE156, AE192, AE194,
AE195, AE198, AE199, AE201, AE228, AE231, AE235,
AE241, AE242, AE245, AE258, AE261, AE287, AE289,
AE293, AE296, AE307, AE309, AE310, AE314, AE356,
AE360, AE361, AE363, AE364, AE366, AE368, AE370-
AE373, AE375, AE378, AE384, AE386, AE388, AE395,
AE401, AE418, AE422, AE423, AE435, AE436 con-
verted to TB.I

AE444 DH.95 Flamingo 1
C/n 95005 G-AGAZ *King of the Air* acquired for RAF.

AE449-AE453 Bristol 142L Blenheim IV 5
Avro-built replacement order.

AE457-AE472 Douglas Boston I 16
Ex-Belgian contract. Some converted to Havoc and
trainers. AE461 to USAAF, AE471 to Royal Navy.
AE462, AE463, AE466, AE468 became 2663M-
2666M.

AE479 Messerschmitt Bf 109E-3 1
C/n 1304 captured by French. To UK May 1940.
To USA in May 1942.

British Purchasing Mission

AE485 to AP384

With the fall of France and the almost desperate situation in the UK, the
British Purchasing Commission in the USA took immediate steps to place
large orders and to take over aircraft contracts by the Belgians, French
and Dutch. Since the USA was officially neutral, with a German Embassy
functioning, there was little chance of keeping orders secret and therefore
blackout blocks were dispensed with and aircraft numbered consecutively.

This series, in the double letter allocation, set the style for subsequent
series, the letters 'I' and 'AO' not being used in case they should be confused with figures. The sequence was therefore: 'AE', 'AF', 'AG', 'AH',
'AJ', 'AK', 'AL', 'AM', 'AN', 'AP'.

Serial Nos	Aircraft Type and Remarks	Quantity
AE485-AE657	**Lockheed Hudson III/IV/V** AE485-AE608 Mk.III, AE609-AE638 Mk.IV, AE639-AE657 Mk.V long range. AE490, AE494-AE504 direct to New Zealand and AE561 to RCAF. AE520, AE567, AE570-AE572, AE584, AE590, AE595-AE599 not delivered. AE536 became 2917M.	173
AE658-AE957	**Lockheed Ventura I/II** C/n 4001-4300. AE658-AE845 Mk.I, AE846-AE957 Mk.II. 16 crashed en route before delivery. 42 held in Canada for RCAF, 82 diverted to SAAF.	300
AE958-AE977	**Hawker Hurricane I (redesignated Mk.X)** Built by Canadian Car & Foundry Corporation. AE971-AE974 sunk en route. AE963 became DR366. AE958-AE962, AE965-AE969, AE975, AE977 became Sea Hurricane IB.	20
AE978-AF744	**Lockheed 322 Lightning I/II** AE978-AF220 Mk.I, AF221-AF744 Mk.II. Only a few Mk.I delivered, rest reverted to USAAF.	667
AF745-AF944	**Vultee V-72 Vengeance II** Built by Northrop. AF745, AF746 were non-standard. AF758, AF778, AF797, AF800, AF814, AF820, AF828, AF840, AF849, AF859, AF860, AF862, AF869, AF874, AF878, AF888, AF912, AF918, AF931 shipped direct to Australia. Remainder diverted to USAAC.	200
AF945-AG344	**Hawker Hurricane I (redesignated Mk.X)** Built by Canadian Car & Foundry Corporation. 7 lost at sea en route. AG287, AG293-AG296, AG299, AG300, AG302, AG304-AG319, AG323, AG325-AG327, AG330-AG332 retained in Canada for RCAF. AG122, AG298, AG301, AG320-AG322, AG324, AG328, AG329, AG331, AG333-AG336, AG339, AG340, AG343, AG344 converted to Mk.IIB and AG292, AG341 to Mk.IIC mainly for Russia. AF945-AF947, AF949-AF955, AF962, AF963, AF965-AF967, AF969, AF971, AF973, AF974, AF976, AF981, AF982 converted to Sea Hurricane. AF945, AF950, AF957, AF981, AG212, AG290 became 4758M, 4694M, 3082M, 4696M, 4515M, 4518M.	300
AG345-AG664	**North American NA-73 Mustang I** 21 lost at sea during deliveries. 10 re-shipped to Russia, AG357 experimentally fitted for RP. AG360, AG387, AG411, AG431, AG491, AG645 became 3089M, 3052M, 2978M, 4225M, 3458M, 4236M.	320
AG665-AG684	**Hawker Hurricane I** Rolls-Royce Merlin 28. Built by Canadian Car & Foundry Corporation. Basic Mk.I but fitted with Mk.IIB 12-gun wings (one apart from possibly two with IIC wings). 3 to Royal Navy and all but one of remainder shipped to Russia.	20
AG685-AH184	**Martin Baltimore I/II/III** AG685-AG734 Mk.I, AG735-AG834 Mk.II; AG835-AG999, AH100-AH184 Mk.III. AG710 not delivered; AG750 retained in Canada. AG685, AG686, AG775, AG791, AG844, AG845, AG849, AG855, AG859, AG867, AG868, AG872, AG874, AG883, AG888-AG891, AG895, AG897, AG908, AG969-AG973, AG985-AG990, AG993, AG996, AG997 (35) lost at sea en route. Many shipped direct to Middle East and served in SAAF units.	400

AG691, AG705, AG928, AH112, AH147, AH172 became 3429M, 4389M, 4216M, 4219M, 4215M, 4220M. Postwar AG953 to French AF.

AH185-AH204 **North American NA-66 Harvard II** 20
USAAC AT-6. Delivered to Southern Rhodesia.

AH205-AH429 **Martin 167 Maryland I/II** 225
AH205-AH279 Mk.I direct to SAAF, AH280-AH429 (c/n 1827-1976) Mk.II mainly delivered direct to Takoradi. AH301-AH311, AH313-AH331, AH371-AH380, AH386-AH395, AH406-AH429 renumbered in SAAF 1600-1699 allocation.

AH430-AH529 **Douglas Boston II** 100
AH430 crashed in USA before delivery. AH431, AH432, AH434, AH436, AH437, AH445-AH447, AH450-AH453, AH455, AH458, AH460, AH462, AH470-AH473, AH478, AH479, AH481, AH483, AH487, AH490, AH491, AH497, AH500, AH502, AH503, AH505, AH509, AH510, AH512, AH518, AH520, AH523-AH525, AH528, AH529 converted to Havoc, some of which had Turbinlites at one period. Turbinlites were fitted to AH431, AH432, AH434-AH436, AH446-AH450, AH452, AH453, AH456-AH458, AH460, AH466, AH468, AH470, AH472, AH473, AH476-AH485, AH489-AH491, AH493, AH497, AH503. 10 transferred to the USAAF. AH437, AH461, AH470, AH474, AH477-AH479, AH487, AH489, AH497, AH498, AH506, AH509, AH512, AH524, AH526 became 3433M, 3422M, 3549M, 3450M, 4365M, 3567M, 3885M, 3668M, 3547M, 3548M, 4434M, 2678M, 3434M, 4363M, 3291M, 3399M.

AH530-AH569 **Consolidated 28 Catalina I** 40
AH534 to RAAF and AH543 interned in Portugal, AH563 to BOAC as G-AGDA. AH538 allotted 5251M.

AH570-AH739 **Bell 14 Airacobra I (basic USAAF P-39D)** 170
About 80 used by RAF, remainder taken over by USAAF or shipped to Russia either after RAF service or direct. Known Russia shipments: AH570, AH571, AH575, AH577, AH586, AH599, AH604-AH608, AH610-AH613, AH615-AH620, AH622-AH628, AH630-AH636, AH638-AH647, AH649, AH650, AH652-AH655, AH658-AH660, AH662-AH671, AH672-AH674, AH694, AH695, AH697, AH699, AH700, AH702-AH712, AH714-AH731, AH733, AH734, AH739 some of which were lost en route. AH578, AH629 became 2808M, 2796M.

AH740 **Douglas Boston III** 1
Replacement aircraft.

AH741-AH999 **Curtiss Tomahawk I/IIA/IIB** 259
AH741-AH880 Mk.I, AH881-AH990 Mk.IIA, AH991-AH999 Mk.IIB. AH936, AH952, AH965-AH971, AH974-AH985, AH987, AH989-AH994, AH997 shipped to Russia. AH750, AH751, AH755, AH760, AH762, AH765, AH767, AH772, AH778, AH779, AH787, AH791, AH800, AH803-AH805, AH808, AH813, AH815, AH819-AH821, AH823, AH826, AH831, AH834, AH835, AH837, AH839, AH841, AH843, AH846, AH854, AH878, AH883, AH886, AH887, AH890, AH894, AH916, AH917, AH927, AH943, AH951 became 3463M, 2809M, 4295M, 2930M, 4296M, 2924M, 2810M, 3153M, 2920M, 2918M, 4298M, 4297M, 4300M, 4299M, 2861M, 2925M, 4307M, 3373M, 2926M, 2929M, 2931M, 2923M, 2928M, 2919M, 4301M-4303M, 2860M, 4304M, 2812M, 2859M, 4305M, 2811M, 2927M, 2932M, 2596M, 4306M, 2858M, 3288M, 2672M, 2671M, 2922M, 2921M, 3476M.

AJ100-AJ153 **Grumman Martlet III (renamed Wildcat III)** 54
Main deliveries direct to India for Royal Navy. AJ107, AJ109-AJ111 lost at sea en route.

AJ154-AJ162 **Consolidated 28 Catalina I** 9
AJ159 became 3664M.

AJ163-AJ537 **Lockheed Ventura II** 375
C/n 4301-4675. AJ235-AJ442 to USAAF, AJ511-AJ537 to USN. With offsets to RCAF and SAAF, and ferrying losses, only 41 served in RAF units.

AJ538-AJ987 **North American NA-66 Harvard II** 450
AJ602-AJ642, AJ663-AJ682, AJ703-AJ722, AJ738-AJ752 shipped direct to Southern Rhodesia. AJ855-AJ892 became 3698-NZ1005 to RNZAF. With offsets to RCAF & SAAF, only 50 reached RAF service.

AJ988-AJ999 **Handley Page HP.52 Hampden I** 12
Built by Canadian Associated Aircraft. Mainly to 32 OTU.

AK100-AK570 **Curtiss Tomahawk IIB** 471
AK210-AK224, AK226-AK241 lost at sea en route. 125 shipped to Russia and 9 transferred to REAF and 1 to Turkish AF. 36 diverted to China for American Volunteer Group. AK104, AK106, AK107, AK117, AK127, AK154, AK176, AK192 became 2674M, 3035M, 4377M, 3532M, 3464M, 2676M, 2675M, 4435M.

AK571-AL230 **Curtiss Kittyhawk I** 560
72 diverted to RCAF and 21 transferred to Turkish AF. AK572, AK573, AK579, AK580, AK597, AK722, AK751, AK764, AL229, AL230 became 3411M, 4101M, 4099M, 4102M, 4398M, 4397M, 3891M, 4100M, 4098M, 4180M.

AL231-AL262 **Grumman Martlet I** 32
AL231-AL235 to Canada, remainder mainly diverted to Donibristle for Royal Navy.

AL263-AL502 **Douglas Boston III** 240
Bomber version in main. AL265, AL267, AL281, AL282, AL287, AL292, AL294, AL295, AL297, AL298, AL300, AL303-AL316, AL318-AL320 were shipped direct from USA to Russia. Many to USAAF. Only 36 aircraft reached the RAF.

AL503-AL667 **Consolidated 32 Liberator II (BII/CII versions)** 165
AL604-AL609, AL611-AL613, AL615, AL617, AL618, AL621-AL623, AL626, AL628, AL631-AL634, AL637, AL639-AL641 retained by USAAF. AL507, AL512, AL514, AL516, AL522, AL524, AL528, AL529, AL541, AL547, AL552, AL557, AL571, AL592, AL603, AL619 used by BOAC as freighters as G-AHYC, 'AGEL, 'AGJP, 'AHZP, 'AHYD, 'AGTJ, 'AGEM, 'AHYE, 'AGTI, 'AGKU, 'AHZR, 'AGZI, 'AGZH, 'AHYF, 'AHYG, 'AGKT. AL504 converted to single fin VIP version for Prime Minister. AL525 became 4218M.

AL668-AL907 **Douglas Boston III** 240
Built by Boeing Aircraft. AL750, AL774, AL778, AL780 converted to Havoc II. 74 to USAAF. 40 shipped to Russia.

AL908-AL957 **Vought Sikorsky V-156-BI Chesapeake I** 50
Main deliveries to Lee-on-Solent for Royal Navy.

AL958-AM257 **North American NA-83 Mustang I** 200
AL975/G Mk.III prototype, AM106/G various armament experiments. AL963, AM121, AM203, AM208 Mk.X experimental aircraft. AL967 became 4228M.

AM258 **Consolidated 28 Catalina** 1
Ex-NC-777 Guba. Number allocated in error. Became SM706.

AM258-AM263 **Consolidated 32 Liberator (Type LB-30A)** 6
AM259, AM262, AM263 temporarily registered as G-AGCD, 'AGHG, 'AGDS.

AM264-AM269 **Consolidated 28 Catalina II** 6
AM264 became 3435M.

AM270-AM369 **Hawker Hurricane X** 100
Rolls-Royce Merlin 28. Built by Canadian Car & Foundry Corporation. In main, shipped to Russia.

AM370-AM519 **Curtiss Tomahawk IIB** 150
Over 60 were delivered direct to American Volunteer Group in China.

AM518-AM537 **Boeing Fortress I** (20)
Numbers marked in error initially on AN518-AN537.

AM520-AM909 **Lockheed Hudson V** 390
From AM703 long range version. AM589-AM594 shipped direct to Auckland to become RNZAF NZ2001-NZ2006 and 18 transferred to USAAF in UK. AM707 loaned to BOAC as G-AGCE. AM580, AM838 became 5779M and 3151M.

AM910-AM929 **Consolidated Liberator I (B-24A)** 20
AM918, AM920 loaned to BOAC as G-AGDR, 'AHYB.

AM930-AM953 **Lockheed Hudson III** 24
Mainly shipped direct to Far East.

AM954-AM999 **Grumman Martlet II** 46
Later redesignated Wildcat II. AM954-AM963 delivered with non-folding wings later replaced by standard wings except for AM954 lost in transit.

AN100-AN167 **Handley Page HP.52 Hampden I** 68
Built by Canadian Associated Aircraft. AN123, AN125, AN127, AN137, AN146, AN148, AN149, AN151-AN161, AN163, AN164, AN166, AN167 converted to TB.I. 35 retained in Canada.

AN168-AN217 **Brewster 339 Buffalo I** 50
Mainly delivered direct to Singapore.

AN218-AN517	**Curtiss Tomahawk IIB** AN469-AN517 shipped direct to Russia and 146 from the UK to Russia. Transfers included 8 to REAF and 24 to the Turkish AF.	300
AN518-AN537	**Boeing Fortress I (B-17C)** Initially incorrectly given AM prefix. Delivered for No.90 Squadron. AN524, AN526 became 3355M, 4449M.	20
AN538-AP137	**Vultee V-72 Vengeance I/II** AN538-AN837 Mk.II, AN838-AP137 Mk.I. AN838, AN993 retained in USA and AN670 crashed before delivery. AN869-AN871, AN873, AN877, AN879, AN971, AN973, AN974 sunk en route to India. AN853-AN857, AN872, AN874-AN876, AN878, AN892, AN894, AN896-AN898 shipped from Los Angeles to Sydney for RAAF.	500
AP138-AP163	**Hawker Hurricane** Built by Canadian Car & Foundry Corporation. Retained in Canada except AP138 lost en route to Russia.	26
AP164-AP263	**North American NA-73 Mustang I** For RAF Army Co-operation Command. AP221, AP225 became 4447M, 4418M.	100
AP264-AP384	**Bell 14 Airacobra I** Taken over by USAAF less 12 lost at sea in transit, and 20 shipped to Russia.	121

A 1940 'Medley'

AP387 to AZ999

The upheaval of events in 1940 is reflected in the allocations that follow. Into this series which includes wartime production orders placed on the home industry, came aircraft hastily impressed, escapees from countries overrun by the Nazis and enrolled into RAF/RN service, captured enemy aircraft and aircraft in transit or ordered by France and Belgium being diverted to the RAF.

Letter combinations not used in this range, were 'AQ' and 'AU' and 'AY' but there was a reversion to black-out blocks.

Serial Nos	Aircraft Type and Remarks	Quantity
AP387-AP500	**Airspeed AS.10 Oxford II** Built by Percival. AP387-AP436, AP451-AP500 of which AP408-AP436, AP451-AP456, AP485-AP496 were shipped for EATS. AP474 taken for BOAC crew training. AP397, AP483 became 4866M, 6084M.	100
AP506-AP510	**Cierva C.30A** G-ACWM, 'ACWP, PH-HHH, G-ACWS, 'ACYE impressed.	5
AP516-AP648	**Hawker Hurricane IIB** Built by Austin Motors. AP516-AP550, AP564-AP613, AP629-AP648. All except AP516, AP524, AP530 shipped to Russia.	105
AP654-AP657	**Airspeed AS.10 Oxford** All to Blind Approach Training Flights.	4
AP670-AR207	**Hawker Hurricane IIB** Built by Austin Motors. AP670-AP714, AP732-AP781, AP801-AP825, AP849-AP898, AP912-AP936 only built. AP937-AP956, AR113-AR162, AR178-AR207 cancelled. Up to AP849 shipped to Russia. From AP880 delivered to India with from AP920 going to India or the Middle East.	195(295)
AR212-AR621	**Supermarine Spitfire I/V** Built by Westland. AR212-AR217 Mk.IB, AR218 Mk.IA, AR219-AR225 Mk.IB, AR226-AR261 Mk.IA; AR274-AR298, AR318-AR347, AR404-AR406, AR422-AR461 Mk.VB; AR462-AR471, AR488-AR532, AR546-AR570, AR592-AR621 Mk.VC. Conversions: AR231 to Mk.VA; AR234, AR235, AR239, AR241, AR242, AR244, AR245, AR257-AR261 to PR.VII; AR319 to PR.XIII; AR384, AR442-AR446, AR457-AR461 to Seafire IB. AR340, AR373, AR399, AR406, AR436, AR451,	300

	AR491, AR493, AR519, AR570, AR604, AR605, AR614 became 4430M, 5588M, 5720M, 5394M, 5334M, 5592M, 5268M, 4697M, 5523M, 5357M, 5399M, 4244M, 5378M and AR213, AR501 became G-AIST, G-AWII. Ten shipped direct to Australia.	
AR625	**Fairey Battle** Rebuilt fuselage of K9192 with parts of K9437 and N2026.	1
AR630-AR694	**Curtiss Mohawk III/IV** Ex-French contract. AR642, AR643, AR652, AR666, AR668, AR673, AR679, AR680 to Portuguese Air Force and AR648, AR657, AR659, AR660, AR683, AR684, AR686, AR688, AR689, AR692-AR694 to SAAF, others shipped to India. AR631, AR670 became 2667M, 2788M.	65
AR702-AR751	**Martin 167 Maryland I** First 35 had no provision for British equipment. AR720, AR736, AR740 to Royal Navy and AR716 to Free French AF. AR708, AR742, AR745-AR747 lost at sea en route.	50
AR756-AS396	**Airspeed AS.10 Oxford I/II** Built by de Havilland. AR756-AR790, AR804-AR853, AR870-AR889, AR909-AR953, AR968-AR982, AS144-AS153 (175) Mk.I; AS154-AS188, AS201-AS230, AS254-AS278, AS297-AS331, AS347-AS396 (175) Mk.II except AR953 and AS376 Mk.V. Only 10 retained in UK rest shipped out to EATS countries, some being lost at sea.	350
AS410-AS437	**Brewster 339 Buffalo** Deliveries to RAF and Royal Navy. AS410, AS411, AS414, AS429, AS430 became 3132M, 2856M, 2855M, 2857M, 2859M and AS417, AS426, AS427 became A37, A39, A38.	28
AS440-AS462	**Northrop 8-A5 Nomad I** Surplus USAAC A-17A shipped to SAAF, but 8 were lost at sea.	23
AS467-AS471	**Curtiss Cleveland I** Surplus USN SBC-4 Helldivers. AS467, AS469, AS470 became 2668M, 2669M, 2785M.	5
AS474-AS942	**Airspeed AS.10 Oxford I/II** Built at Portsmouth. AS474-AS523, AS537-AS571, AS591-AS640, AS665-AS704 (175) Mk.I; AS705-AS709, AS726-AS745, AS764-AS813, AS828-AS877, AS893-AS942 (175) Mk.II. AS592 Mk.V prototype and AS506, AS772 also converted to Mk.V. 304 a/c shipped to Commonwealth countries under EATS; of those retained, AS732 was transferred to USAAF and postwar sales were: AS727, AS729 R Hellenic AF; AS728, AS896, AS900 to R Norwegian AF; AS732 to R Danish AF.	350
AS958-AS976	**Northrop 8-A5 Nomad I** All to SAAF except 6 lost at sea.	19
AS981-AS983	**Handley Page HP.42** G-AAUC, 'AAUE, 'AAXF *Horsa, Hadrian & Helena* impressed.	3
AS987-AS990	**Hawker Hurricane I** Replacement order.	4
AT109-AT434	**Handley Page HP.52 Hampden I** Built by English Electric. AT109-AT158, AT172-AT196, AT216-AT260 built, rest cancelled. AT109, AT111, AT114, AT117, AT125, AT135, AT138, AT140, AT150, AT152, AT153, AT172, AT180, AT184, AT193, AT195, AT222, AT232-AT234, AT238, AT241, AT243, AT244, AT246, AT248-AT260 converted to TB.I.	120(250)
AT439-AV502	**Airspeed AS.10 Oxford I** Built by de Havilland. AT439-AT488, AT502-AT536, AT576-AT625, AT641-AT685, AT723-AT742, AT760-AT799 built. AT800-AT809, AT845-AT889, AT909-AT928, AT962-AT996, AV118-AV167, AV199-AV218, AV242-AV276, AV306-AV355, AV384-AV425, AV453-AV502 cancelled of which from AT914 were planned as Mk.III. AT440 was converted to Mk.III. 129 shipped to EATS countries. AT665 transferred to Royal Navy in 1943 and AT481, AT775 sold postwar to R Danish AF. AT683, AT684, AT787 became 5493M, 5482M, 4063M.	240(600)
AV508-AV944	**Boulton Paul P.82 Defiant II** Cancelled. AV508-AV557, AV571-AV605, AV633-AV682, AV698-AV742, AV768-AV787, AV805-AV839, AV863-AV892, AV910-AV944.	(300)
AV951-AV952	**DH.87A/DH.87B Hornet Moth** G-ADKI, 'ADSK impressed.	2

AV958-AV965	**Fokker T.8W**	8
	Dutch Navy escapees to UK in May 1940 ex- R-1, R-3, R-6, R-7 to R-11.	
AV968	**Airspeed AS.4 Ferry**	1
	Prototype G-ABSI impressed; became 2758M.	
AV969	**DH.87B Hornet Moth**	1
	G-ADMO impressed.	
AV970-AV971	**Miles M.11A/M.11B Whitney Straight**	2
	G-AEWK, 'AERC impressed.	
AV972	**DH.87B Hornet Moth**	1
	G-AEKP impressed.	
AV973	**Miles M.3B Falcon Six**	1
	G-AFBF impressed.	
AV974	**Short S.16 Scion I**	1
	G-ACUY impressed.	
AV975	**DH.85 Leopard Moth**	1
	G-ACKN impressed.	
AV976	**DH.90 Dragonfly**	1
	G-AESW impressed.	
AV977	**DH.94 Moth Minor**	1
	G-AFOT impressed.	
AV978	**Miles M.14A Hawk Trainer III**	1
	G-AFET impressed.	
AV979	**GAL Monospar ST-6**	1
	G-ACGI impressed.	
AV980	**Avro Tutor**	(1)
	G-AFZW (ex- K3237) impressed; became 2427M.	
AV981	**Short S.16 Scion I**	1
	G-ACUW impressed.	
AV982	**DH.84 Dragon II**	1
	G-AECZ impressed.	
AV983-AV986	**DH.85 Leopard Moth**	4
	G-ADBH, 'ACSU, 'AEFR, 'ACRV impressed.	
AV987	**DH.90 Dragonfly**	1
	G-AEDH impressed.	
AV988-AV989	**DH.85 Leopard Moth**	2
	G-ACPG, 'ADAP impressed.	
AV990	**Short S.16/1 Scion II**	1
	G-AEJN impressed; became 2722M.	
AV991	**DH.60G Gipsy Moth**	1
	G-AACY impressed.	
AV992-AV994	**DH.90 Dragonfly**	3
	G-AEDJ, 'AFRF, 'AFRI impressed.	
AV995	**DH.60M Moth**	1
	G-AACU impressed. Now preserved in Montevideo.	
AV996	**DH.60X Moth**	1
	G-AAPG impressed.	
AV997 & AW110	**DH.60M Moth**	2
	G-AARH, 'AASR impressed.	
AW111	**DH.60G Gipsy Moth**	1
	G-ABXR impressed.	
AW112-AW113	**DH.94 Moth Minor**	2
	G-AFNG, 'AFNJ impressed.	
AW114	**DH.87B Hornet Moth**	1
	G-AEIY impressed.	
AW115-AW116	**DH.89/DH.89A Rapide**	2
	G-ACTU, 'ADDD impressed.	
AW117	**DH.85 Leopard Moth**	1
	G-ACSJ impressed.	
AW118	**DH.87B Hornet Moth**	1
	G-AELO impressed for Royal Navy but taken on RAF charge. Extant.	
AW119	**DH.60G Gipsy Moth**	1
	G-ABJN impressed.	
AW120-AW123	**DH.85 Leopard Moth**	4
	G-ACKS, 'ACLZ, 'AEZI, 'ACPF impressed. AW122 became 2992M.	
AW124	**DH.83 Fox Moth**	1
	G-ACEA impressed.	
AW125	**DH.85 Leopard Moth**	1
	G-ACTL impressed.	
AW126	**DH.60G Gipsy Moth**	1
	G-AAET impressed.	
AW127	**DH.60G Moth**	1
	G-AAIV impressed.	
AW128-AW136	**DH.60G Gipsy Moth**	9
	G-AASY, 'ABAE, 'ABBA, 'ABBX, 'ABJT, 'ABPD, 'ABRD, 'ABTS, 'ACJG impressed. AW128 became 4490M.	

AW143	**British Aircraft Eagle**	1
	VT-AKP impressed in India.	
AW144	**DH.60M Moth**	1
	Impressed in India.	
AW145	**DH.60G Moth**	1
	G-AFLV impressed.	
AW146	**DH.60X Moth**	1
	G-EBTZ impressed; became 2833M.	
AW147	**DH.60 Cirrus Moth**	1
	G-EBRY impressed; became 4076M.	
AW148	**DH.60M Moth**	1
	G-AAKP impressed; became 3759M.	
AW149	**DH.60G Gipsy Moth**	1
	G-ABOG impressed.	
AW150	**Miles M.2 Hawk**	1
	G-ADGI impressed; became 2625M.	
AW151	**DH.94 Moth Minor**	1
	G-AFMZ impressed.	
AW152	**Miles M.2 Hawk**	1
	G-ACTO impressed; became 2626M.	
AW153	**DH.60X Moth**	1
	G-EBTD impressed.	
AW154	**DH.84 Dragon I**	1
	G-ACCZ impressed; became 2820M.	
AW155	**DH.89A Rapide**	1
	G-ADAK impressed.	
AW156	**DH.85 Leopard Moth**	1
	G-AFZG impressed.	
AW157-AW159	**DH.60X Moth**	3
	G-EBXT, 'EBZC, 'EBZL impressed. AW159 became 2704M.	
AW160	**DH.60G Gipsy Moth**	1
	G-AAIE impressed.	
AW161-AW162	**DH.60GIII Moth Major**	2
	G-ACPT, 'ADFK impressed.	
AW163	**DH.84 Dragon I**	1
	G-AEKZ impressed.	
AW164	**DH.90 Dragonfly**	1
	G-AEDK impressed.	
AW165-AW166	**DH.85 Leopard Moth**	2
	G-ACLL, 'ACLY impressed.	
AW167	**Messerschmitt Bf 108 Taifun**	1
	D-IJHW seized; postwar falsely marked G-AFZO.	
AW168-AW169	**DH.85 Leopard Moth**	2
	G-ACRC, 'ACKM impressed.	
AW170-AW171	**DH.84 Dragon**	2
	G-ACDN, 'ACET impressed. AW171 became 2779M.	
AW172-AW173	**DH.84 Dragon II**	2
	G-ACKU, 'AEMI impressed.	
AW177	**Heinkel He 111H-1**	1
	C/n 6853 shot down near Dalkeith and repaired.	
AW180-AW181	**DH.60GIII Moth Major**	2
	VT-AFP, VT-AFL impressed in the Far East.	
AW183	**British Aircraft Eagle**	1
	VT-AKP impressed in the Far East.	
AW187-AW384	**Bristol 152 Beaufort I/II**	150
	Built at Filton. AW187-AW221, AW234-AW243 (45) Mk.I. AW244-AW253, AW271-AW315, AW335-AW384 (105) Mk.II. AW372 converted to the only Mk.IV. AW246, AW276 became 5064M, 5065M.	
AW392-AW414	**Douglas Havoc I/Boston II**	23
	Deliveries to Europe diverted to the UK. Variously converted AW393, AW395, AW400, AW401, AW405 AW407, AW411, AW412 fitted with Turbinlites. AW394, AW400, AW403 transferred to USAAF. AW393, AW399, AW401, AW405, AW414 became 3551M, 4356M, 3552M, 3480M, 3957M.	
AW420-AW438	**Northrop 8-A5 Nomad I**	19
	Surplus USAAF A-17s, mainly to SAAF. AW421 became 2670M.	
AW443-AX656	**Avro 652A Anson I/IV**	750
	533 Mk.I and 217 Mk.IV built by Avro Newton Heath plant as follows: AW443-AW454 Mk.I, AW455-AW482 Mk.IV, AW483-AW488 Mk.I; AW489-AW492, AW506-AW515 Mk.IV; AW516-AW521 Mk.I, AW522-AW540, AW586,AW 587 Mk.I, AW588 Mk.I, AW589-AW594 Mk.I, AW595-AW613 Mk.IV, AW614 Mk.I, AW615, AW616 Mk.IV, AW617-AW621 Mk.I, AW622-AW635, AW653-AW657 Mk.IV, AW658-AW683 Mk.I, AW684-AW697, AW739-AW750 Mk.IV, AW751 Mk.I,	

	AW752-AW758, AW778-AW795 Mk.IV, AW796-AW801 Mk.I, AW802-AW812, AW833-AW843 Mk.IV; AW844-AW882, AW897-AW918 Mk.I; AW919 Mk.IV, AW920 Mk.I, AW921-AW923 Mk.I, AW924 Mk.I, AW925-AW927 Mk.IV, AW928 Mk.I, AW929-AW938 Mk.IV, AW939-AW941, AW963-AW968 Mk.I, AW969 Mk.IV, AW970 Mk.I, AW971, AW972 Mk.IV, AW973, AW974 Mk.I, AW975-AW977 Mk.IV, AW978 Mk.I, AW979-AW981 Mk.IV, AW982 Mk.I, AX100-AX104 Mk.IV, AX105 Mk.I, AX106 Mk.IV, AX107-AX127 Mk.I, AX128-AX136 Mk.IV; AX137-AX149, AX163-AX187, AX218-AX267, AX280-AX324, AX343-AX372, AX396-AX445, AX466-AX515, AX535-AX584, AX607-AX656 Mk.I. Majority shipped overseas for EATS and some lost at sea en route. AW911 and AX358 to USAAF in UK. AX474 postwar to R Hellenic AF and AX499 to French Air Force.	
AX659-AX660	Short S.23 Empire 'C'	2
	C/ns S.841, S.846 G-AETY, 'AEUD *Clio* & *Cordelia* impressed.	
AX666	Spartan 7W Executive	1
	YI-SOF impressed; became 2526M.	
AX670-AX671	Martin 167 Maryland	2
	Ex-French.	
AX672-AX673	Potez 63-11	2
	French AF 607, 699. Escaped from French territory in 1940, taken on charge by RAF in Middle East.	
AX674-AX675	Morane 406	2
	French AF 826, 827, details as AX672, AX673.	
AX676	Caudron Simoun	1
	Ex-French, details as AX672, AX673.	
AX677	Marcel Bloch 81	1
	Ex-French AF 4, details as AX672, AX673.	
AX678-AX679	Potez 29	2
	Ex-French AF 54, 99, details as AX672, AX673.	
AX680	Potez 63-11	1
	Ex-French AF 395, details as AX672, AX673.	
AX681-AX682	Lockheed 14	2
	C/n 1417, 1496 ex-NC2333 and NC17398 acquired in the Middle East.	
AX683	Bristol Blenheim I	(1)
	Ex-L1431 from the SAAF.	
AX684	Morane 406	1
	French AF 819 escapee.	
AX685-AX687	Lockheed 18	3
	Acquired in Middle East. Ex-SAAF 231-233.	
AX688	Lockheed 14	1
	Acquired in Middle East and crashed on ferry flight.	
AX689-AX690	Martin 167 Maryland	2
	French AF escapees.	
AX691	Potez 63-11	1
	French AF escapees.	
AX692-AX693	Martin 167 Maryland	2
	French AF escapees.	
AX694	Loire N30	1
	Presumed French AF escapee.	
AX695	Waco ZGC-7	1
	Bought in Egypt for Long Range Desert Group.	
AX696	Martin 167 Maryland	1
	French AF escapee, to the SAAF.	
AX697	Waco YKC	1
	As AX695 above.	
AX698	Percival P.3 Gull Six	1
	G-ADKX impressed.	
AX699-AX701	Lockheed 10A Electra	3
	Taken on charge in Middle East. Ex YU-SAV, YU-SDA and YU-SBB.	
AX702-AX705	Savoia SM.79K	4
	Yugoslav escapees to Middle East. Ex-YU-3712 to YU-3714 and YU-3702.	
AX706-AX707	Dornier Do17Ka	2
	Yugoslav escapees to Middle East. Ex-YU-3363 and YU-3348.	
AX708-AX715	Dornier Do22Kj	8
	Yugoslav escapees to Middle East. Ex-YU-302, YU-306 to YU-309, YU-311 to YU-313.	
AX716	Rogojarski Sim XIV-H Srs 2	1
	Yugoslav escapee to Middle East.	
AX717-AX723	Lockheed 18-08 Lodestar	7
	Purchased from USA for use in the Middle East.	

	Registered G-AGCV, 'AGCR, 'AGCW, 'AGCU, 'AGCP, 'AGCT, 'AGCS for BOAC. See HK974-HK975.	
AX725-AX747	Grumman Martlet I	23
	Delivered to Middle East for Royal Navy.	
AX748-AX752	Avro 652A Anson	5
	Ex-R Hellenic AF N51, N52, N55, N56, N61.	
AX753-AX754	Grumman Martlet I	2
	Believed lost as sea.	
AX755	Douglas DC-2	1
	Acquired in Middle East. Ex-NC14268.	
AX756-AX759	Lockheed 18-08 Lodestar	4
	AX756 ex-NC25630 and G-AGCN, AX757 to Free French AF, AX758, AX759 to BOAC.	
AX760	DH.86B	1
	G-ADFF impressed.	
AX761	Grumman Martlet I	1
	Re-designated Wildcat.	
AX762	DH.86B	1
	G-ADUE impressed.	
AX763-AX765	Lockheed 18-08 Lodestar	3
	Impressed in Middle East.	
AX766	Lockheed 10 Electra	1
	Acquired in Middle East.	
AX767-AX769	Douglas DC-2	3
	Taken on charge in Middle East. Ex-VT-ARA, NC14966, NC14277.	
AX772 & AX774	Messerschmitt Bf110C-5	2
	Captured German aircraft.	
AX775-AX776	Caudron Goeland	2
	Escapees from French AF to Britain.	
AX777	Caudron Simoun	1
	Details as AX775, AX776.	
AX781-AX783	DH.82A Tiger Moth	3
	G-AELB, 'AELC, 'AFMC impressed. AX781 became 2661M.	
AX784	DH.60G Gipsy Moth	1
	G-ABPC impressed.	
AX785-AX788	DH.82A Tiger Moth	4
	G-AFMD, 'AEXG, 'AFGJ, 'AFJH impressed.	
AX789	DH.60G Gipsy Moth	1
	G-AAKI impressed; became 2482M.	
AX790	DH.94 Moth Minor	1
	G-AFPK impressed, became 2610M.	
AX791	DH.82 Tiger Moth	1
	G-AFJG impressed; became G-AMLB.	
AX792	DH.60G Gipsy Moth	1
	G-ABES impressed.	
AX793	DH.60X Moth	1
	G-EBST impressed.	
AX794	DH.60M Moth	1
	G-ADEZ impressed.	
AX795	DH.86B	1
	G-ADYI impressed.	
AX797	DH.90 Dragonfly	1
	VT-AHW impressed in India.	
AX798	DH.82A Tiger Moth	1
	VT-AIF impressed in India.	
AX799	Curtiss Hawk IV	1
	Taken on charge in India.	
AX800	DH.86	1
	VT-AKZ impressed in India.	
AX801-AX802	DH.85 Leopard Moth	2
	Impressed in India.	
AX803	Lockheed 12A	1
	VT-AJS impressed in India.	
AX804-AX805	DH.85 Leopard Moth	2
	Impressed for AHQ India. AX805 ex-VT-AHK.	
AX806	DH.89 Rapide	1
	VT-AIZ impressed in India.	
AX811-AX820	Brewster 339 Buffalo I	10
	Mainly for Royal Navy.	
AX824-AX829	Grumman Martlet I	6
	Assembled by Scottish Aviation.	
AX834	Miles M.20	1
	Ex-U.9. 12-gun fighter prototype utilising standard Master parts.	
AX840-AX844	DH.86/DH.86B	5
	G-ACYG, 'ACZO, 'AENR, 'ACZP, 'ACZR impressed for RN. All DH.86 except for AX842 DH.86B. Original allocation BD104-BD106 cancelled.	

AX848-AX851	**Douglas Boston I**	4
	Ex-French contract. AX848, AX851 converted to Havoc I.	
AX854	**Avro 504N**	1
	G-ACZC impressed; became 2453M.	
AX855	**DH.90 Dragonfly**	1
	G-AECX impressed.	
AX856	**DH.82A Tiger Moth**	1
	G-AFSX impressed.	
AX857	**DH.87B Hornet Moth**	1
	G-ADJV impressed.	
AX858	**DH.85 Leopard Moth**	1
	G-ACGS impressed.	
AX859	**DH.83 Fox Moth**	1
	G-ACFC impressed; became 2583M.	
AX860	**Percival P.14A Q.6**	1
	G-AFVC ex-F-AQOK impressed. To Royal Navy.	
AX861-AX862	**DH.85 Leopard Moth**	2
	G-ACNN, 'ACLW impressed.	
AX863	**DH.84 Dragon I**	1
	G-ACKB impressed.	
AX864	**Short S.16 Scion II**	1
	G-ADDO impressed.	
AX865	**DH.85 Leopard Moth**	1
	G-ACUO impressed.	
AX866	**Percival P.3 Gull Six**	1
	G-ADPR impressed.	
AX867	**DH.84 Dragon**	1
	G-ACEK impressed.	
AX868-AX870	**DH.80A Puss Moth**	3
	G-ACTV, 'ABDG, 'AAZO impressed.	
AX871	**Avro 504N**	1
	G-ADBM (ex-K1055) impressed.	
AX872	**DH.80A Puss Moth**	1
	G-ABGS impressed.	
AX873	**DH.85 Leopard Moth**	1
	G-ACRW impressed and restored.	
AX874-AX875	**Avro 504N**	2
	G-ADBP, 'ADET (ex-K2353, J8533) impressed.	
AX880-AX898	**Curtiss Mohawk I/II**	19
	Ex-French contract shipped to India, Portugal and South Africa.	
AX900	**Lockheed 10A**	1
	Impressed in Middle East. Also number of a Curtiss Tomahawk.	
AX903-AX904	**DH.91 Albatross**	(2)
	K8618, K8619 originally allotted. Ex-G-AEVV, 'AEVW.	
AX910-AX918	**Douglas Boston I/Havoc I**	9
	Ex-French Boston order. All converted to Havoc I. AX913 fitted with Turbinlite and Long Aerial Mine and later transferred to USAAF.	
AX919	**Junkers Ju 88A-1**	1
	Enemy aircraft c/n 7036 landed near Bexhill 28.7.40.	
AX920-AX975	**Douglas Boston I**	56
	AX921, AX923, AX924, AX930, AX936, AX974, AX975 converted to Havoc I. AX922 trainer version transferred to USAAF. AX924, AX930 fitted with Turbinlites. AX928 became 3550M.	
AZ104-AZ856	**Miles M.19 Master II**	525
	AZ104-AZ143, AZ156-AZ185, AZ202-AZ226, AZ245-AZ289, AZ306-AZ340, AZ359-AZ383, AZ408-AZ457, AZ470-AZ504, AZ519-AZ563, AZ582-AZ621, AZ638-AZ672, AZ693-AZ742, AZ773-AZ817, AZ832-AZ856. 252 shipped direct to SAAF. Small numbers to French AF, Irish Air Corps, Royal Navy, Turkish AF and the USAAF. AZ104, AZ499, AZ785, AZ847-AZ853 became 3127M, 5587M, 6240M, 5548M, 5549M.	
AZ861-AZ999	See next section.	

British and American Production Geared

BA100 to BZ999

Orders for aircraft at this critical stage continued to be placed with British and American firms for operational and training aircraft needed in the years ahead for which Winston Churchill had offered no prospect but blood, toil, tears and sweat. Into this range came more orders diverted from French and Belgian orders and further impressments of civil aircraft. For the first time gliders appear, whereas hitherto the serialling system had been confined to powered aircraft.

Orders placed in America from BW100 were again serial numbered consecutively in contrast to British orders with black-out blocks. The sequence set by AA100 to AZ999 was followed, i.e. 100 to 999 using 'BA', 'BB', 'BD', 'BE', 'BF', 'BG', 'BH', 'BJ', 'BK', 'BL', 'BM', 'BN', 'BP', 'BR', 'BS', 'BT', 'BV', 'BW', 'BX' and 'BZ' as prefixes.

Serial Nos.	Aircraft Type and Remarks	Quantity
BA100-BB184	**Bristol Blenheim V**	780
(including	Built by Rootes. AZ861-AZ905, AZ922-AZ971, AZ984-	
AZ numbers	AZ999, BA100-BA118, BA133-BA172, BA191-BA215,	
allotted)	BA228-BA262, BA287-BA336, BA365-BA409, BA424-	
	BA458, BA471-BA505, BA522-BA546, BA575-BA624,	
	BA647-BA691, BA708-BA757, BA780-BA829, BA844-	
	BA888, BA907-BA951, BA978-BA999, BB100-BB102,	
	BB135-BB184. Transfers to other forces: BA306, BA326,	
	BA394, BA525, BA596, BA849 to Free French AF;	
	AZ986, AZ987, BA826 to Portugese AF; BA137, BA292,	
	BA395, BA495, BA591, BA613, BA614, BA713, BA854,	
	BA855, BA887, BA910, BA922, BA925 to Turkish AF.	
	BA106, BA746, BA856 became 4387M, 4444M, 4386M.	
BB189-BB446	**Handley Page HP.59 Halifax II**	200
	Built by LAP. BB189-BB223, BB236-BB285, BB300-	
	BB344, BB357-BB391, BB412-BB446. BB193, BB258,	
	BB270 became 4472M, 4912M, 4911M.	
BB450	**Brewster Buffalo**	1
	Delivered to Royal Navy in September 1940.	
BB455-BB656	**Vickers Wellington IC/VIII**	50(150)
	50 built at Weybridge. BB455-BB484, BB497-BB516 as	
	Mk.IC except BB461, BB466, BB471, BB476, BB481,	
	BB503, BB513 Mk.VIII. BB517-BB541, BB566-BB600,	
	BB617-BB656 cancelled in July 1941.	
BB661-BB671	**Miles M.14 Hawk Trainer II/III**	11
	Impressments. BB661, BB662 Mk.III ex-G-AFBS, 'AFDB,	
	BB663, BB664 Mk.III ex-G-AFTR, 'AFTS, BB665-	
	BB667 Mk.III ex-G-AFWY, 'AFXA, 'AFXB, BB668-	
	BB671 reserved for Mk.III ex-G-AFYV to G-AFYY but	
	not taken up. BB662 became 4557M.	
BB672-BB868	**DH.82A Tiger Moth**	123
	Impressment of aircraft at civilian-operated Elementary	
	Flying Training Schools in 1940. Previous identities as	
	follows: BB672-BB682 G-ADOF to G-ADOP, BB683-	
	BB690 G-ADOR, 'ADVN, 'ADVP, 'ADXK, 'ADXN,	
	'ADXO, 'ADXP, 'ADXR, BB691, BB692 G-AEEA,	
	'AEUV, BB693-BB701 G-ADGU, 'ADGV, 'ADGG,	
	'ADGH, 'ADGT, 'ADGX, 'ADGY, 'ADGZ, 'ADII, BB702-	
	BB706 G-AEBY, 'AEBZ, 'ADGF, 'ADGS, 'ADGW of	
	which BB704 became 6805M, BB723 G-ABRC, BB724-	
	BB730 G-ACDA, 'ACDB, 'ACDC, 'ACDE, ' ACDG,	
	'ACDJ, 'ACDK, BB731-BB738 G-ADCG, 'ADCH,	
	'ADHT, 'ADHU, 'ADHV, ADXB, 'ADXD, 'ADXJ,	
	BB739-BB742 G-AEVB, 'AFGY, 'ACDF, 'ACDI, BB743-	
	BB756 G-ADHR, 'ADHS, 'ADHY, 'ADHZ, 'ADIA,	
	'ADIB, 'ADKG, 'ADLV, 'ADLW, 'ADLZ, 'ADMA,	
	'ADSH, 'ADXE, 'ADXI, BB757-BB760 G-AELP, 'AEMF,	
	'AFGZ, 'AFJK, BB788 G-ADIJ, BB789 G-ADIH became	
	3654M, BB790-BB792 G-ACEZ, 'ADJF, 'ABUL, BB793-	
	BB808 G-ADHX, 'ADWC, 'ADVY, 'ADVZ, 'ADWA,	
	'ADWB, 'ADVX, 'ADWE, 'ADWF, 'ADWK, 'ADWJ,	
	'ADWL, 'ADWM, 'ADWP, 'ADWO, 'ADWN, BB809	

G-ADYB became 4690M, BB810-BB812 G-ADYA,
'ADHN, 'ADUC, BB813, BB814 G-AFFA, 'AFWI,
BB815-BB819 G-ADJC, 'ADJD, 'ADJG, 'ADJI, 'ADJJ,
BB851-BB863 G-ADPA, 'ADPC, 'ADPF, 'ADPG, 'ADPH,
'ADOW to 'ADOZ, 'ADXT, 'ADXU, 'ADXV, 'ADXX,
BB864 G-AECH became 4546M, BB865-BB868 G-AECI,
'AECJ, 'AFAR, 'AFAS.

BB890-BB912	Douglas Boston I	23

BB891-BB895, BB897-BB904, BB907-BB909, BB911,
BB912 converted to Havoc. BB897, BB899, BB907-
BB909 fitted with Turbinlites. BB891, BB896 trans-
ferred to USAAF. BB902 trainer version. BB906 to
Royal Navy. BB892, BB897, BB903 became 3003M,
3475M, 4476M.

BB918-BB979	Curtiss Mohawk IV	26

BB918-BB937, BB974-BB979 shipped to India, South
Africa and Portugal.

BD110-BD127	Douglas Boston I	18

All converted to Havoc. BD110, BD111, BD120 fitted
with Turbinlites. BD115, BD116 converted to trainers.
BD121, BD122 to Royal Navy. BD112, BD126 became
4238M, 3398M.

BD130-BD137	North American NA-66 Harvard II	8

BD130 to UK, BD131-BD134 to SRAF, BD135-BD137
to USAAF.

BD140	DH.85 Leopard Moth	1

G-ACTG impressed; became 2619M.

BD141	Miles M.2H Hawk Major	1

G-ADCY surveyed but not acquired.

BD142	DH.82A Tiger Moth	1

G-AFHT impressed for RN, became G-AMRD.

BD143	DH.89A Rapide	1

G-AEPE impressed.

BD144	DH.85 Leopard Moth	1

G-ACHB impressed. Later 2818M.

BD145	Miles M.11A Whitney Straight	1

G-AFAB impressed.

BD146-BD148	DH.85 Leopard Moth	3

G-ACTJ, 'ACSF, 'ACMA impressed.

BD149	DH.90 Dragonfly	1

G-AFTF (ex-VH-UXA) impressed.

BD150	GAL Monospar ST-12	1

G-ADBN impressed.

BD151-BD156	DH.82A Tiger Moth	6

G-AFHI, 'AEZC, 'ABTB, 'AFCA, 'ADNV, 'AESD
impressed. BD154-BD156 became 2490M, 2489M and
2486M.

BD161	DH.82A Tiger Moth	1

G-AESA impressed; became 2488M.

BD162	DH.60G Gipsy Moth	1

G-ABLZ impressed.

BD163	DH.60X Moth	1

G-ABAO impressed.

BD164	DH.60G Gipsy Moth	1

G-AAJJ impressed.

BD165	Percival P.3 Gull Six	1

G-ADSM surveyed but not acquired.

BD166	DH.60G Gipsy Moth	1

G-AAWR impressed.

BD167	DH.85 Leopard Moth	1

G-ACHC impressed.

BD168	Miles M.11A Whitney Straight	1

G-AFJJ impressed.

BD169	DH.85 Leopard Moth	1

G-ACKL impressed.

BD170-BD171	DH.82A Tiger Moth	2

G-AFJM, 'AFJN impressed.

BD172-BD173	DH.85 Leopard Moth	2

G-ACOO, 'ACXH impressed. BD173 became 2993M.

BD174-BD179	DH.60GIII Moth	6

G-ACDV, 'ACIB, 'ACJB, 'ABZS, 'ABZU, 'ABZV
impressed.

BD180	Miles M.2P Hawk Major	1

G-ADDK impressed.

BD181	DH.80A Puss Moth	1

G-ABDL impressed.

BD182	DH.94 Moth Minor	1

G-AFPG impressed; became 2630M.

BD183	Miles M.11A Whitney Straight	1

G-AFJX impressed.

BD189-BD693	Armstrong Whitworth AW.38 Whitley V/VII	300

BD189-BD238, BD252-BD296, BD346-BD395, BD411-
BD422 Mk.V (BD360-BD362, BD382-BD390 loaned to
BOAC as G-AGCF to 'AGCK, 'AGDX to 'AGDZ, 'AGEA
to 'AGEC; BD423-BD434 Mk.VII; BD435-BD445,
BD493-BD512, BD530-BD560 Mk.V; BD561-BD574,
BD620-BD625 Mk.VII; BD626-BD639, BD659-BD674
Mk.V; BD675-BD693 Mk.VII. BD423, BD425, BD429,
BD430, BD431, BD566, BD625 transferred late in
service to Royal Navy. BD440, BD551 became 4292M,
4293M.

BD696-BE716	Hawker Hurricane IIB/IIC	600

Rolls-Royce Merlin XX. BD696-BD745, BD759-BD765
Mk.IIB, BD766-BD770 Mk.IIC, BD771-BD778 Mk.IIB,
BD779 Mk.IIC, BD780-BD786 Mk.IIB, built at Brook-
lands. BD787, BD788 Mk.IIC; BD789-BD793, BD818-
BD825 Mk.IIB, BD826 Mk.IIC, BD827-BD830 Mk.IIB,
BD831-BD833 Mk.IIC; BD834-BD837 Mk.IIB, BD855
Mk.IIC, BD856 Mk.IIB, BD857-BD861 Mk.IIC, BD862-
BD865 Mk.IIB, BD866-BD868 Mk.IIC, BD869-BD871
Mk.IIB, BD872 Mk.IIC, BD873, BD874 Mk.IIB, BD875
Mk.IIC, BD876-BD899 Mk.IIC, BD914-BD933 Mk.IIB; BD934-
BD956 Mk.IIC, BD957 Mk.IIB, BD958-BD960 Mk.IIC,
BD961 Mk.IIB, BD962 Mk.IIC, BD963 Mk.IIB built at
Langley. BD980-BD983 Mk.IIC, BD984 Mk.IIC con-
verted to Mk.IIB; BD985, BD986, BE105-BE117,
BE130-BE133 Mk.IIB, BE134 Mk.IIC, BE135-BE149
Mk.IIB, built at Brooklands. BE150-BE152 Mk.IIC;
BE153-BE174, BE193-BE227 Mk.IIB, built at Langley.
BE228-BE242, BE274-BE308, BE323-BE334 Mk.IIB;
BE335-BE337 Mk.IIC, BE338 Mk.IIC converted to
Mk.IIB, BE339-BE344 Mk.IIC, BE345, BE346 Mk.IIB,
BE347-BE351 Mk.IIC, BE352 Mk.IIB, built at Brook-
lands. BE353-BE361 Mk.IIC, BE362-BE368 Mk.IIB,
BE369-BE372 Mk.IIC, BE394 Mk.IIB, BE395, BE396
Mk.IIC, BE397, BE398 Mk.IIB, BE399 Mk.IIC, BE400,
BE401 Mk.IIB, BE402 Mk.IIC, BE403-BE405 Mk.IIB,
BE406-BE410 Mk.IIC, BE411-BE428 Mk.IIB, BE468,
BE469 Mk.IIC, BE470-BE479 Mk.IIB, BE480-BE482
Mk.IIC, BE483-BE492 Mk.IIB, BE493-BE497 Mk.IIC,
BE498, BE499 Mk.IIB, BE500, BE501 Mk.IIC, BE502-
BE509 Mk.IIB, BE510-BE517, BE546, BE547 Mk.IIC,
BE548-BE552 Mk.IIB, BE553-BE557 Mk.IIC, BE558-
BE560 built at Langley. BE561-BE563 Mk.IIB, BE564-
BE576 Mk.IIC, BE577-BE579 Mk.IIB, BE580-BE582
Mk.IIC, BE583-BE585 Mk.IIB, BE586 Mk.IIC, BE587-
BE590, BE632, BE633 Mk.IIB, BE634-BE636 Mk.IIC,
BE637-BE641 Mk.IIB, built at Brooklands. BE642-
BE649 Mk.IIC, BE650, BE651, BE667-BE701 Mk.IIB;
BE702-BE716 Mk.IIC built at Langley. Numbers
tropicalised and fitted as bombers. Many shipped to
Russia. BD866, BD982 became 3622M, 4223M.

BE720-BF303	Bristol Blenheim	(375)

Ordered from Avro. Cancelled. BE720-BE769, BE782-
BE816, BE834-BE883, BE897-BE941, BE955-BE994,
BF109-BF138, BF152-BF186, BF199-BF248, BF264-
BF303.

BF274	Supermarine Spitfire IX	1

Prototype. Compromised allocation above.

BF309-BF580	Short S.29 Stirling I/III/IV	200

Built by Short & Harland at Belfast. BF309-BF358,
BF372-BF416, BF434-BF454 (116) Mk.I; BF455-
BF483, BF500-BF534, BF561-BF580 (84) Mk.III.
BF464, BF468, BF532, BF575, BF580 converted to
Mk.IV. BF311, BF324, BF344, BF345, BF388, BF436
became 3893M, 4531M, 4374M, 3767M, 3766M, 4037M.

BF584-BF777	Fairey Albacore I	150

C/n F.5670-F.5819. BF584-BF618, BF631-BF680,
BF695-BF739, BF758-BF777.

BF782-BG668	Airspeed AS.10 Oxford I/II	600

BF782-BF831, BF845-BF889, BF904-BF953, BF967-
BF999, BG100, BG101, BG113-BG132, BG149-BG183,
BG196-BG245, BG260-BG274 (300) Mk.I; BG275-
BG304, BG318-BG337, BG349-BG398, BG415-BG459,
BG473-BG522, BG541-BG545 (200) Mk.II; BG546-
BG575, BG588-BG637, BG649-BG668 (100) Mk.I all
built at Portsmouth. BF807, BF825, BF858, BF859
BF861, BF967, BG100, BG115, BG118, BG171, BG213,
BG263, BG301, BG423, BG444, BG445, BG509, BG521,
BG610 converted to Mk.V. Bulk shipped to EATS chiefly

to SAAF and SRAF. BF938, BG173, BG175, BG179, BG180, BG203, BG235, BG261, BG393 became 5529M, 6508M, 5444M, 5494M, 5491M, 5527M, 5531M, 6537M, 5504M.

BG674-BH723 Hawker Hurricane IIB (450)720
Built by Gloster. BG674-BG723, BG737-BG771, BG783-BG832, BG844-BG888, BG901-BG920, BG933-BG977, BG990-BG999, BH115-BH154, BH167-BH201, BH215-BH264, BH277-BH296, BH312-BH361. BH374-BH408, BH422-BH471, BH489-BH508, BH524-BH568, BH575-BH614, BH630-BH664, BH679-BH723 cancelled. BH253 to SAAF. BH292, BH296 to Russia among others. BH120 became 4211M.

BH727 DH Fighter Trainer (1)
Project to Spec T24/40. Cancelled.

BH732-BJ408 Hawker Hurricane I (440)
Ordered from Canadian Car & Foundry Co as BH732-BH781, BH797-BH841, BH855-BH904, BH921-BH955, BH968-BH997, BJ112-BJ136, BJ150-BJ199, BJ213-BJ257, BJ274-BJ323, BJ332-BJ351, BJ369-BJ408. Re-allotted numbers in allocation to British Purchasing Commission in USA as: AE958-AE977, AF945-AF999, AG100-AG344, AG665-AG684, AM270-AM369.

BJ400-BJ419 North American NA-66 Harvard II 20
BJ400-BJ408 to SRAF late 1940, of remainder record only of BJ410, BJ412-BJ415 delivered.

BJ421-BJ428 Martin 167 Maryland I 8
Ex-French contract to Middle East via UK and Takoradi. BJ422, BJ424, BJ426 lost en route.

BJ434-BJ453 Curtiss Mohawk IV 20
Ex-French order mainly to India and South Africa.

BJ458-BJ501 Douglas Havoc I 37
Ex-French contract. BJ458-BJ477, BJ485-BJ501. BJ474 converted to Mk.II. Several converted to trainers of which BJ464 was the prototype. BJ460, BJ461, BJ466, BJ469, BJ470 fitted with Turbinlites and BJ490, BJ493 with Long Aerial Mines. BJ461, BJ466, BJ473, BJ488, BJ489 transferred to USAAF. BJ459, BJ489, BJ463-BJ465, BJ475-BJ477, BJ491, BJ493, BJ495 became 2813M, 4308M, 3553M, 2814M, 3002M, 3426M, 2677M, 4355M, 4309M, 3001M, 3002M.

BJ507-BJ527 Grumman Martlet I 21
Ex-USN F4F for Royal Navy.

BJ531-BJ550 Curtiss Mohawk IV 20
Mainly shipped to India, Portugal and South Africa.

BJ554-BJ570 Grumman Martlet I 17
For Royal Navy.

BJ574-BJ588 Curtiss Mohawk III 15
Not delivered to RAF.

BJ575 British Aircraft Swallow II 1
G-AFCB impressed, compromised number above.

BJ581-BK564 Vickers Wellington III 600
Built at Chester. BJ581-BJ625, BJ642-BJ675, BJ688-BJ730, BJ753-BJ801, BJ818-BJ847, BJ876-BJ922, BJ958-BJ991; BK123-BK166, BK179-BK214, BK234-BK281, BK295-BK315, BK330-BK368, BK385-BK408, BK426-BK471, BK489-BK517, BK534-BK564. BJ613, BJ623, BJ665, BJ788, BJ799, BJ822, BJ885, BJ908, BK130, BK209, BK351, BK356, BK448, BK451, BK496 became 4790M, 4803M, 4802M, 4773M, 5032M, 4795M, 4848M, 5066M, 5863M, 4794M, 4796M, 5738M, 4895M, 5739M, 5740M.

BK569-BK588 Curtiss Mohawk III 20
Ex-French order mainly shipped to India and South Africa. BK588 became 2501M.

BK592-BK818 Short S.29 Stirling I/III 150
Built by Austin Motors. BK592-BK628, BK644-BK647 (41) Mk.I, BK648-BK667, BK686-BK727, BK759-BK784, BK798-BK818 (109) Mk.III. BK603, BK608 became 4372M, 3565M.

BK822 DH.95 Flamingo 1
G-AGBY impressed and flown to Middle East.

BK826-BK828 DH.60G Gipsy Moth 3
G-AAAV, 'AAHU, 'ABEO impressed.

BK829 DH.60M Moth 1
G-ABTF impressed.

BK830 DH.87B Hornet Moth 1
G-AEZG impressed.

BK831-BK832 DH.94 Moth Minor 2
G-AFPT, 'AFPU impressed becoming 2611M and 2608M.

BK833 DH.60GIII Moth Major 1
G-ACRI impressed; became 2658M.

BK834-BK836 DH.60G Gipsy Moth 3
G-AAGA, 'AAYL, 'ABFT impressed. BK836 became 4031M.

BK837 DH.87B Hornet Moth 1
G-ADMP impressed.

BK838-BK840 DH.94 Moth Minor 3
G-AFNF, 'AFNH, 'AFPM impressed.

BK841-BK843 DH.60G Gipsy Moth 3
G-ABHM, 'ABJJ, 'AAZE impressed. BK841, BK843 became 2604M, 4032M.

BK844 DH.60X Moth 1
G-AAMV impressed.

BK845 DH.60G Gipsy Moth 1
G-ABFD impressed.

BK846 DH.80A Puss Moth 1
G-ABEI impressed.

BK847 DH.94 Moth Minor 1
G-AFNK impressed.

BK848 DH.60G Gipsy Moth 1
G-ABXB impressed.

BK852-BK853 Curtiss Tomahawk 2
Believed ex-French contract. BK852 became 2673M.

BK867 DH.85 Leopard Moth 1
G-ACKP impressed.

BK868-BK869 Fairchild 24C8 & 24C8-C 2
C/ns 2817, 2718 G-AFKW and 'AECO impressed in October 1940. BK869 became 3129M.

BK870-BK871 DH.80A Puss Moth 2
G-ABYP, 'ABLR impressed.

BK872 Percival P.10 Vega Gull 1
VP-KCH impressed.

BK876-BK879 Curtiss Mohawk I/II 4
BK876, BK878 to SAAF, BK877 to UK, BK879 to India.

BK882-BK883 Douglas Havoc I 2
BK882 had Turbinlite fitted, BK883 intruder version with Long Aerial Mine. BK883 became 4364M.

BK891 British Aircraft Swallow 1
Impressed.

BK892 Avro 504N 1
G-ADEV (ex-H5199) impressed; became 3118M.

BK893-BK897 British Aircraft Swallow II 5
G-AFGC, 'AFGE, 'AEHL, 'AELH, 'AFGD impressed. BK897 converted to glider for towed flight experiments.

BK902-BL216 Supermarine Sea Otter (150)
Ordered from Blackburn. Cancelled. BK902-BK940, BK965-BK985, BL112-BL151, BL167-BL216.

BL220-BL223 Curtiss Mohawk I/II 4
Ex-foreign contract. BL220 to Portugal. BL221-BL223 to South Africa.

BL227-BL228 Douglas Havoc I 2
BL227 to Royal Navy, BL228 converted to trainer.

BL231-BM653 Supermarine Spitfire VB 1000
Originally ordered as Mk.III. Built at Castle Bromwich. BL231-BL267, BL285-BL304, BL311-BL356, BL365-BL391, BL403-BL450, BL461-BL500, BL509-BL551, BL562-BL600, BL613-BL647, BL655-BL699, BL707-BL736, BL748-BL789, BL801-BL833, BL846-BL864, BL887-BL909, BL918-BL941, BL956-BL998, BM113-BM162, BM176-BM211, BM227-BM274, BM289-BM329, BM343-BM386, BM402-BM430, BM447-BM493, BM508-BM543, BM556-BM597, BM624-BM653 of which BL526, BM447, BM591 were converted to Mk.XIII. BL239, BL254, BL260, BL296, BL301, BL321, BL373, BL414, BL420, BL428, BL434, BL443, BL492, BL493, BL495, BL521, BL522, BL527, BL529, BL539, BL546, BL566, BL570, BL586, BL593, BL597, BL635, BL639, BL675, BL676, BL678, BL679, BL687, BL689, BL694, BL695, BL726, BL729, BL730, BL736, BL750, BL757, BL770, BL806, BL846, BL855, BL861, BL894, BL901, BL904, BL930, BL931, BL958, BL983, BL986, BL994, BM314, BM367, BM377, BM402, BM457, BM541, BM559, BM570, BM580, BM596, BM625, BM626, BM631, BM632 renumbered to MB; NX and PA batches on conversion to Seafires. 32 shipped to Russia, 29 to Portugal and 10 transferred to Free French/French AF during war. Some conversions to Mk.IX including BL311, BL477 and to Mk.VC e.g. BM588. BL234,

BL291, BL365, BL380, BL450, BL589, BL614, BL665,
BL712, BL719, BL755, BL826, BL892, BL979 became
3387M, 5389M, 5381M, 4002M, 5390M, 5525M, 4354M,
5595M, 5385M, 5386M, 5570M, 5398M, 5392M, 5376M,
and BM155, BM158, BM192, BM201, BM233, BM246,
BM256, BM322, BM354, BM409, BM411, BM461,
BM525, BM569, BM589, BM597, BM637 became 5347M,
5375M, 5542M, 5395M, 5337M, 5721M, 5384M, 5601M,
5335M, 5539M, 5600M, 5593M, 3689M, 5520M, 5350M,
5718M, 3688M.

BM671-BM877   **Airspeed AS.10 Oxford II**   150
Built by Percival. BM671-BM720, BM737-BM785,
BM801-BM844, BM871-BM877 for RAF except BM825
to Royal Navy. Numbers shipped under EATS. BM877
postwar to R Hellenic AF. BM844 became 5056M.

BM898-BP772   **Hawker Hurricane IIB/IIC/IID**   1250
BM898-BM936, BM947-BM969 Mk.IIB except BM905,
BM907, BM908, BM964-BM966 Mk.IIC; BM970-BM988
Mk.IIC; BM989-BM996, BN103, BN104 Mk.IIB built at
Brooklands. BN105 Mk.IIB, BN106-BN114 Mk.IIB
bombers, BN115-BN142, BN155-BN159 Mk.IIC, BN160-
BN170 Mk.IIB, built at Langley. BN171-BN180 Mk.IIB,
BN181-BN189, BN203-BN207 Mk.IIC; BN208-BN226
Mk.IIB, BN227-BN237 Mk.IIC, built at Brooklands.
BN238-BN242, BN265-BN298, BN311-BN329 Mk.IIB
except BN279, BN280, BN282-BN292 Mk.IIC;
BN330-BN337, BN346-BN380 Mk.IIC except BN353,
BN369 Mk.IIB, built at Langley. BN381-BN389, BN399-
BN415 Mk.IIC except BN388, BN406, BN407 Mk.IIB;
BN416-BN435, BN449-BN462 Mk.IIB, BN463-BN484
Mk.IIC, BN485-BN493 Mk.IIB; BN494-BN497, BN512
Mk.IIC; BN513-BN522 Mk.IIB, built at Brooklands.
BN523-BN536 Mk.IIB, BN537-BN547, BN559-BN567
Mk.IIC, BN568-BN603, BN624-BN653 Mk.IIB except
BN583, BN598, BN599 Mk.IIC built at Langley. BN654,
BN667-BN670 Mk.IIB, BN671-BN676 Mk.IIC, BN677
Mk.IIB, BN678, BN679 Mk.IIC, BN680 Mk.IIB, built at
Brooklands. BN681, BN682 Mk.IIC/IIB Langley-built;
BN683-BN685 Mk.IIC, BN686-BN691 Mk.IIB; BN692-
BN705, BN719 Mk.IIC built at Brooklands except
BN694, BN699, BN702 at Langley. BN720-BN758
Mk.IIB of which all but two went to Russia, built at
Brooklands, BN759, BN773-BN779 Mk.IIB, BN780-
BN788 Mk.IIC, BN789 no delivery record, BN790-
BN794 Mk.IIB, BN795-BN797 Mk.IID; BN798-BN802,
BN818-BN839 Mk.IIB, BN840-BN846, BN859-BN863
Mk.IID, BN864, BN865 Mk.IIC, BN866 Mk.IID, BN867-
BN882, BN896-BN898 Mk.IIC, BN899, BN900 Mk.IIB,
BN901, BN902 Mk.IIC, BN903-BN905 Mk.IIB, BN906-
BN908 Mk.IIC, BN909-BN911 Mk.IIB, built at Langley.
BN912-BN935 Mk.IIB built at Brooklands. BN936-
BN940 Mk.IIB, BN953-BN955 Mk.II, BN956-BN960
Mk.IIC, BN961-BN977 alternate Mk.IIC/IIC, BN978
Mk.IIB, BN979 Mk.IID; BN980-BN992 Mk.IIB except
BN989 Mk.IIC, BP109-BP111 Mk.IIC, BP112, BP113
Mk.IIB, BP114 Mk.IIC, BP115-BP119 Mk.IIB, BP120-
BP125 Mk.IIC, BP126 Mk.IID, BP127-BP130 Mk.IIC,
BP131 Mk.IID, BP132-BP135 Mk.IIB, BP136 Mk.IID,
BP137 BP138, BP139 Mk.IIC, BP140 Mk.IIB,
BP141 Mk.IID, BP154-BP200, BP217-BP229 alternate
Mk.IIB/IIC batches built at Langley. BP240-BP245,
BP259-BP302, BP316-BP336 Mk.IIB except BP280,
BP287, BP327, BP328 Mk.IIC; BP337-BP362, BP378-
BP401 Mk.IIC except BP350, BP351, BP356, BP359,
BP361, BP362, BP378, BP393, BP395, BP400 Mk.IIB;
BP402-BP416, BP420-BP479, BP493-BP526, BP538-
BP566, BP579-BP614, BP628-BP675, BP692-BP711,
BP734-BP772 batches of Mk.IIB/IIC/IID and IIB
bomber built at Brooklands or Langley. BP173 converted
to Mk.IV. Deliveries mainly to Russia, India and the
Middle East.

BP775-BP839   **Fairey Fulmar II**   50
Rolls-Royce Merlin 30. C/n F.5820-F.5869. BP775-
BP796, BP812-BP839 for Royal Navy. BP777 transferred
to the RAF.

BP844-BS724   **Supermarine Spitfire III/IV/V/VI/VII/IX**   908(1220)
BP844-BP854 Mk.VB, BP855-BP864 Mk.VC, BP865-
BP878 Mk.VC tropicalised; BP879-BP892, BP904-
BP937 PR.IV/V some tropicalised; BP950-BP993
Mk.VC tropicalised mainly for Malta; BR106-BR137

Mk.VC tropicalised, BR138 Mk.IX, BR139 Mk.VC,
BR140-BR143 Mk.IX; BR159-BR205, BR226-BR256,
BR282-BR330 alternate batches of Mk.VC and Mk.VI;
BR344-BR393 PR.IV, VC & VI mainly to Malta; BR410-
BR435 PR.IV; BR459-BR499, BR515-BR549 mainly
Mk.VC; BR562-BR605, BR621-BR670 completed
variously Mks.IV, V, VI & IX. BR114 was specially
adapted in Middle East for high altitude interception,
BR202 had enlarged belly tank, BR372 modified by
Heston Aircraft with dive brakes. BR413, BR643
crashed on company test flight. BR683-BR721, BR745-
BR772, BR799-BR831, BR849-BR877, BR890-BR929,
BR954-BR976 (192) cancelled. BR977-BR987, BS104-
BS152 Mk.V/VI/IX. BS157-BS202, BS218-BS255,
BS271-BS319, BS335-BS367, BS383-BS411, BS427-
BS474, BS489-BS515, BS530-BS559 (300) ordered as
Mk.IB, built as Mk.V, but many completed as, or
converted to, Mk.IX. BS573-BS618, BS634-BS659,
BS677-BS724 (120) ordered as Mk.III but all cancelled.
BR623, BR632 became 6018M, 6037M and BS142,
BS152, BS227, BS248, BS249, BS280, BS286, BS315,
BS345, BS349, BS386, BS393, BS439, BS449, BS474,
BS499, BS513, BS533 became 4419M, 5263M, 5322M,
6516M, 6452M, 6021M, 6062M or 6052M, 5941M,
5951M, 6035M, 6517M, 5354M, 5972M, 6035M, 5955M,
5933M, 6043M, 6205M. BS464 is preserved in the
French Musée de l'Air.

BS730-BS747   **Curtiss Mohawk IV**   13
BS730-BS738, BS744-BS747 delivered mainly to India
and South Africa.

BS750   **Airspeed AS.49**   (1)
Fighter trainer project to Spec T24/40. Plans and mock-
up destroyed by bombing.

BS755   **Miles M.11A Whitney Straight**   1
G-AECT impressed but not flown.

BS760-BS777   **Martin 167 Maryland**   18
Ex-French order. BS777 to Free French AF, BS770
converted for target towing.

BS784-BS798   **Curtiss Mohawk IV**   15
Eight to South Africa, six to India, one to Portugal.

BS803   **Stinson SR-10C Reliant**   1
C/n 5901 NC21133 impressed; became VP-KDV.

BS808   **North American NA-66 Harvard II**   1
Origin unknown, shipped to South Rhodesia during
December 1940.

BS814-BS815   **Miles M.11A Whitney Straight**   2
G-AEVF, 'AEVM impressed.

BS816   **DH.84 Dragon**   1
G-ACBW impressed; became 2780M.

BS817   **Fairchild 24C-8F**   1
C/n 3126 G-AEOU impressed, became 2659M.

BS818   **Miles M.11A Whitney Straight**   1
G-AEXJ impressed.

BS827-BS890   **Airspeed AS.49**   (50)
Cancelled order.

BS900-BT272   **DH.82 Tiger Moth**   (200)
Allotted for trainers to have been assembled in Bombay.
BS900-BS936, BS949-BS997, BT111-BT136, BT161-
BT183, BT197-BT241, BT261-BT272.

BT278-BT281   **Percival P.30 Proctor III**   (4)
Renumbered from Z7253-Z7256.

BT286-BT303   **Bristol 156 Beaufighter VIF**   18
Built at Filton. All shipped overseas. BT292, BT300
transferred to the USAAF.

BT308/G   **Avro Manchester III**   1
Lancaster prototype. Later F2/1 jet fitted in tail.

BT312   **DH.95 Flamingo**   1
C/n 95011 G-AFYH impressed. Scrapped in 1954.

BT316-BT437   **Supermarine Sea Otter**   (100)
Ordered from Blackburn. Cancelled. BT316-BT347,
BT357-BT401, BT415-BT437.

BT440-BT442   **Piper J-4A Cub Coupé**   3
G-AFSZ, 'AFVL, 'AFWR impressed.

BT447-BT456   **Grumman Martlet**   10
All lost at sea on delivery.

BT460-BT465   **Douglas Havoc I**   6
BT465 fitted with Long Aerial Mine. BT464 transferred
to USAAF. BT461 became 2815M.

BT470-BT472   **Curtiss Mohawk IV**   3
Presumed ex-French contract. All shipped to India.

BT474	**Fiat CR.42**	1
	Brought down in Suffolk in November 1940 and reconditioned. Currently preserved. Allotted 8468M.	
BT479-BV129	**General Aircraft GAL.48 Hotspur II**	390
	Built by Harris Lebus. BT479-BT513, BT534-BT557, BT561-BT579, BT594-BT640, BT658-BT693, BT715-BT755, BT769-BT799, BT813-BT861, BT877-BT903, BT916-BT948, BT961-BT990, BV112-BV129 of which BT540, BT566, BT602, BT632, BT663, BT735, BT747, BT752, BT777, BT784, BT823, BT850, BT886, BT895, BT897, BT898, BT917, BT946 were converted to Mk.III. BT545, BT554, BT597, BT600, BT721, BT933 became 3503M, 3448M, 3416M, 3500M, 3461M, 3449M.	
BV134-BV151	**General Aircraft GAL.48 Hotspur I**	13
	Built by Slingsby. BV134-BV140, BV146-BV151. BV134, BV135, BV137, BV138, BV139, BV140, BV149, became 2884M, 3140M, 3139M, 2882M, 2979M, 3141M, 3074M.	
BV155-BV174	**Hawker Hurricane IIA**	(20)
	Converted Mk.Is: R4218, V6790, L1581, V6785, P5175, P3402, P2823, N2465, R2683, V7302, V6914, P3642, P3521, N2479, P3057, P5204, P2674, N2592, V7351 and P3216. Several shipped to Russia.	
BV180-BV181	**Piper J-4A Cub Coupé**	2
	G-AFWA and 'AFWB impressed.	
BV184-BV187	**Heinkel He 115A-2/B-1'**	4
	Norwegian escapees to UK in 1940 ex-Nos 56, 58, 62, 64. BV184-BV186 A-2, BV187 B-1.	
BV190-BV199	**General Aircraft GAL.48 Hotspur I**	10
	BV199 became Mk.II prototype. BV192, BV197 became 3320M, 3068M.	
BV200	**General Aircraft GAL.48 Hotspur**	1
	Built by Airspeed.	
BV203	**Douglas Havoc 1**	1
	Origin unknown.	
BV207	**Gotha Go 145B**	1
	Ex-Luftwaffe. Communications aircraft lost way, landed at Lewes. Became 2682M.	
BV208-BV209	**Avro 504N**	2
	G-AEMP, 'ACPV (ex-J9017, K1250) impressed; became 2444M, 2447M.	
BV214-BV531	**Vickers Warwick I**	250
	Built at Weybridge. BV214-BV242 B.I of which BV223, BV225, BV227, BV231-BV241 were converted to B(ASR).I, BV242 to ASR.I and BV216 became B.II prototype. BV243-BV256 used by BOAC as G-AGEX to 'AGFK and returned to RAF as C.I; BV269-BV316 of which BV269-BV281, BV283, BV285, BV287, BV289, BV297, BV299, BV300, BV305, BV310, BV315, BV316 delivered as B(ASR).I, BV282, BV284, BV286, BV288, BV290, BV292, BV294, BV298, BV301-BV304, BV306-BV309, BV311-BV314, BV332-BV370, BV384-BV421, BV436-BV484, BV499-BV531 delivered as ASR.I. BV474 became 4924M.	
BV535-BV658	**Percival P.30 Proctor II**	100
	Built by F. Hills & Son. BV535-BV573, BV586-BV612, BV625-BV658. BV633 became Mk.III. Main deliveries to Royal Navy. Postwar disposals to civil market, e.g. BV644 became G-AIEG.	
BV660-BV981	**Fairey Barracuda II**	250
	Built by Blackburn for Royal Navy. BV660-BV707, BV721-BV766, BV788-BV834, BV847-BV885, BV898-BV922, BV937-BV981.	
BV984-BV991	**Piper J-4A Cub Coupe**	8
	G-AFXU, 'AFXX, 'AFXV, 'AFVG, 'AFVM, 'AFTB, 'AFTC, 'AFVF impressed.	
BV999	**Cierva C.30A**	1
	G-ACXW impressed January 1941.	
BW100-BW183	**Bell 13 Airacobra I**	84
	Delivered but many handed over to USAAF and others shipped to Russia.	
BW184-BW207	**North American NA-66 Harvard II**	24
	British direct purchase contract but not delivered to UK.	
BW208-BW307	**Vultee 48C Vanguard**	100
	USAAF P-66 ordered by Sweden, offered to Britain as advanced trainers but eventually shipped to Chinese Air Force.	
BW361-BW777	**Lockheed Hudson IIIA**	417
	Originally ordered by direct purchase, but delivered under Lend/Lease arrangements resulting in BW361-	

	BW385 offset to USN, BW386-BW398 diverted to China, quantities from BW399 held in Canada and from BW413 supplied to RAAF. BW461-BW613 were taken over by USAAF; BW661-BW681, BW736-BW755 supplied to RAAF and BW756-BW767 became NZ2037-NZ2048 of RNZAF.	
BW778-BW827	**Grumman Goose I**	(50)
	Serials reallotted to FP475-FP524 in Lend/Lease series.	
BW828-BW834	**Pitcairn PA-39**	7
	BW828-BW830 lost at sea en route.	
BW835-BX134	**Hawker Hurricane XA/XIB**	200
	Built by the Canadian Car & Foundry Corporation. BW835-BW884 produced as Sea Hurricane except for BW841, BW880 as Mk.X; BW885-BW999, BX100-BX134 Mk.XIB of which BW886, BW900, BW921 were converted to Mk.XIC. 102 shipped to Russia. BW841 became 4659M.	
BX135-BX434	**Bell 14 Airacobra I**	300
	Majority taken over by USAAF and others shipped to Russia and at least 17 were lost at sea.	
BZ100-BZ195	**Vultee Vigilant IA (USAAF L-1A)**	55(96)
	Ex-USAAF 41-18943 to 41-18997. BZ101, BZ102, BZ110 used as spares; BZ109, BZ111-BZ154 not delivered, BZ155-BZ195 cancelled.	
BZ196-BZ669	**Douglas Boston IIIA/IV/V**	459
	Supplied under Lend/Lease. BZ196-BZ352, BZ355-BZ378, BZ381-BZ399 Mk.IIIA ex-A-20C, BZ400-BZ568 Mk.IV ex-A-20G, BZ580-BZ669 Mk.V ex-A-20H. BZ647 crashed in USA before delivery. BZ588-BZ590, BZ593, BZ597, BZ601, BZ602, BZ663, BZ666, BZ669 held in Canada.	
BZ711-BZ999	**Consolidated 32 Liberator III/V/VI**	289
	Ordered under direct purchase but supplied under Lend/Lease. BZ711-BZ832 mainly delivered as GR.V of which BZ723, BZ743, BZ744, BZ760-BZ762, BZ769, BZ773, BZ781, BZ783, BZ786, BZ792, BZ793, BZ804, BZ806 were converted to C.V; BZ833-BZ860 Mk.III, BZ861-BZ889 GR.V of which BZ869, BZ871 were converted to C.V, BZ890-BZ909 Mk.III, BZ910-BZ921 GR.V, BZ922-BZ929 Mk.III, BZ930 GR.V, BZ931 GR.V converted to C.V, BZ932-BZ936 Mk.III, BZ937-BZ945 GR.V of which BZ940 was converted to C.V, BZ946-BZ959 Mk.III, BZ960 GR.VI converted to B.IV, BZ961 GR.VI, BZ962-BZ965 B.IV, BZ966-BZ969 GR.VI of which BZ968 was converted to C.IV, BZ970 C.IV, BZ971, BZ972 C.VI, BZ973, BZ974 B.VI, BZ975 GR.VI, BZ976-BZ978 B.VI, BZ979 GR.VI converted to C.VI, BZ980 Mk.VI, BZ981 C.VI, BZ982, BZ983 B.VI, BZ984 GR.VI, BZ985 GR.VI converted to C.VI, BZ986 C.VI, BZ987, BZ988 GR.VI, BZ989, BZ990 B.VI, BZ991 GR.VI, BZ992, BZ993 B.VI, BZ994, BZ995 GR.VI, BZ996-BZ998 B.VI, BZ999 GR.VI. BZ725, BZ727-BZ729, BZ732-BZ739, BZ747, BZ755, BZ756 renumbered in RCAF service. BZ768 became 5232M.	

Production, Prototypes and Impressments

DA100 to ES999

The possibility of Lend/Lease caused direct purchase orders to be abandoned and the allocations DA100 to DD599 were not taken up. This time 'H' as a second letter was not used as the combination 'DH' was too familiar as an abbreviation for de Havilland aircraft types.

Serial Nos	Aircraft Type and Remarks	Quantity
DD600-DD800	**DH.98 Mosquito II**	150
	de Havilland (Hatfield) built. DD600-DD644, DD659-DD691, DD712-DD759, DD777-DD800 of which DD715 was converted to Mk.XII, DD664 went to RAAF as A52-1001 and DD723 was special version with Merlin 23 engines. DD670-DD691, DD712-DD714 Mk.II (Special) intruder version. DD612, DD613, DD617, DD659, DD667, DD668, DD670, DD675, DD676, DD678, DD715, DD716, DD730, DD735, DD745, DD746, DD757, DD759 became 3802M, 4109M, 4360M, 5084M, 4412M, 4413M, 4780M, 4849M, 4846M, 3632M, 4960M, 3911M, 5061M, 4227M, 4410M, 4241M, 4242M, 5912M.	
DD804-DD815	**Blackburn Firebrand**	3
	Prototypes. DD804, DD810, DD815 to Spec N11/40. DD810 rebuilt as NV636.	
DD818	**DH.85 Leopard Moth**	1
	VT-AJP impressed to India.	
DD820-DD821	**DH.80A Puss Moth**	2
	G-ABCR, 'ABUX impressed. DD820 transferred to the USAAF.	
DD828-DD867	**Short S.25 Sunderland III**	40
	Built by Blackburn at Dumbarton. DD860 became G-AHEP and DD856, DD861 became 5716M, 4405M.	
DD870-DE126	**Bristol 152 Beaufort I/II**	120
	DD870-DD911, DD927-DD944 (60) Mk.II, DD945-DD959, DD974-DD999, DE108-DE126 (60) Mk.I. DD900 became 3485M.	
DE131-DF214	**DH.82A Tiger Moth II**	750
	Built by Morris Motors. DE131-DE178, DE192-DE224, DE236-DE284, DE297-DE323, DE336-DE379, DE394-DE432, DE445-DE490, DE507-DE535, DE549-DE589, DE603-DE640, DE654-DE697, DE709-DE747, DE764-DE791, DE808-DE856, DE870-DE904, DE919-DE957, DE969-DE999, DF111-DF159, DF173-DF214. DE395 became XL715. Many shipped under EATS and at least 44 were lost at sea. During war DE429, DE774, DE826, and DE932 were transferred to USAAF and others to Free French AF and Yugoslav flying training schools. DE156, DE175, DE219, DE306, DE311, DE322, DE409, DE412, DE447, DE455, DE480, DE512, DE530, DE588 became 7009M, 7145M, 7034M, 7035M, 4547M, 6936M, 4469M, 6792M, 4072M, 6901M, 4569M, 5801M, 4700M, 6806M and DE604, DE606, DE611, DE658, DE661-DE663, DE673, DE739, DE779, DE836, DE854, DE872, DE889, DE902, DE933, DE982, DF187, DF191 became 4762M, 6804M, 4681M, 6808M, 5985M, 4672M, 4765M, 6948M, 7036M, 7037M, 6815M, 6802M, 5430M, 7039M, 4073M, 4075M, 6887M, 6807M, 6923M. Postwar disposals to civil register and various air forces.	
DF220-DF536	**Airspeed AS.10 Oxford I**	250
	Built by Standard Motors. DF220-DF264, DF276-DF314, DF327-DF367, DF390-DF433, DF445-DF489, DF501-DF536. DF342, DF351, DF359, DF361, DF391-DF394, DF413, DF420, DF422, DF423, DF430, DF451, DF453, DF454, DF457, DF458, DF460-DF462, DF483, DF505, DF518 transferred to Royal Navy and DF257, DF292, DF299, DF331, DF335, DF364, DF399, DF507, DF514, DF528, DF530 temporarily to USAAF. DF241, DF244, DF290, DF309, DF343, DF362, DF367, DF409, DF417, DF470 became 6467M, 5512M, 5480M, 5479M, 6110M,	

	5526M, 5513M, 6196M, 5505M, 6266M. Postwar disposals to civil register and foreign air forces.	
DF542-DG197	**Vickers Wellington III**	150(400)
	Built at Blackpool. DF542-DF579, DF594-DF642, DF664-DF709, DF727-DF743 Mk.III except DF609, DF686, DF701, DF730, DF740 built as Mk.X and DF614 converted to Mk.X. DF744-DF776, DF794-DF832, DF857-DF900, DF921-DF956, DF975-DF999, DG112-DG134, DG148-DG197 cancelled. DF545, DF619 became 4785M, 4853M.	
DG200	**Messerschmitt Bf109E-3**	1
	C/n 4101 landed at Manston 27.11.40 after attack by Spitfires. Allotted 8379M; extant.	
DG202-DG213	**Gloster F9/40 'Rampage'**	8(12)
	Jet-engined prototypes as follows: DG202/G Rover W2B, became 5758M; DG202/G Power Jets W2/500, became 5928M; DG204/G Metrovick F2; DG205/G Rover W2B/23; DG206/G, DG207/G Halford H1; DG208/G Rover W2B/23; DG209/G Rover W2B/27; DG210-DG213 cancelled.	
DG219-DG424	**Handley Page HP.59/HP.63 Halifax II/V**	150
	Built by Rootes. DG219-DG230 (12) Mk.II; DG231-DG253, DG270-DG317, DG338-DG363, DG384-DG424 (138) Mk.V. DG220, DG251, DG362 became 3651M, 5204M, 4454M. DG399 to Canada as production model.	
DG430-DG444	**North American NA.66 Harvard II**	13
	DG430-DG439, DG442-DG444 of which DG430 and DG431 went to SRAF, DG432-DG439 were lost at sea, DG442-DG444 became 3101M, 3102M, 3168M.	
DG450-DG454	**Armstrong Whitworth AW.15 Atalanta**	5
	G-ABTL, 'ABTI, 'ABTJ, 'ABPI, 'ABTM impressed in India.	
DG468-DG479	**Douglas DC-2**	12
	VT-AOU, 'AOQ-'AOT, 'AOV-'AOZ and VT-APA and 'APB impressed in India.	
DG483-DG529	**DH.82A Tiger Moth**	39
	DG483-DG487, DG490, DG491, DG493-DG503, DG505, DG506, DG508-DG513, DG515-DG524, DG527-DG529 acquired in India.	
DG530	**DH.82A Tiger Moth**	1
	Impressed in India.	
DG531 & DG534	**DH.60GIII Moth Major**	2
	Impressed in India	
DG536-DG548	**DH.82 Tiger Moth**	9
	DG536, DG538-DG540, DG544-DG548 acquired in India.	
DG554-DG555	**Douglas Havoc I**	2
	Origin unknown. DG554 fitted with Long Aerial Mine.	
DG558 & DG562	**Westland P.14 Welkin**	2
	Prototypes to Spec F4/40. DG558/G first flew 1.11.42.	
DG566	**GAL.42 Cygnet II**	1
	G-AGAL impressed.	
DG570-DG573	**Slingsby Hengist**	4
	Prototypes to Spec X25/40.	
DG576	**Miles M.3 Falcon Six**	1
	C/n 280 G-AECC impressed.	
DG577	**Miles M.2F Hawk Major**	1
	G-ACXT impressed; became 4020M.	
DG578	**Miles M.2 Hawk**	1
	G-ACNX impressed; became 2617M.	
DG579-DG580	**DH.60G Gipsy Moth**	2
	G-AAFI, 'AAHG impressed. DG579, DG580 became 4033M, 2547M.	
DG581	**DH.60M Moth**	1
	G-AAVV impressed; became 2593M.	
DG582	**DH.60G Moth**	1
	G-AFKA impressed; became 2592M.	
DG583-DG586	**DH.60G Gipsy Moth**	4
	G-ABDA, 'AARC, 'ABZE, 'AAJZ impressed. DG583-DG586 became 2595M, 2590M, 2591M, 2594M.	
DG587	**DH.60X Moth**	1
	G-AAAC impressed.	
DG588	**DH.60M Moth**	1
	G-ABAT impressed; became 3769M.	
DG589	**DH.60G Gipsy Moth**	1
	G-AAFS impressed; became 2569M.	
DG590	**Miles M.2H Hawk Major**	1
	G-ADMW impressed; became 8379M, extant.	
DG595	**Avro 683 Lancaster**	1
	Second prototype; First flew 13.5.41.	

DG597-DG609	**Airspeed AS.51 Horsa**	3
	DG597, DG603, DG609 prototypes to Spec X26/40.	
DG612-DG651	**Hawker Hurricane IIA**	40
	Conversions from Mk.I by Rolls-Royce: P3756, P3412, P3223, P3068, N2544, V7234, L1596, V6755, P5190, V7258, L1658, P5195, V6950, L1824, V7061, V6959, L1807, V6934, V6536, P3207, P5199, N2607, P3539, W9181, L1836, L2099, V6602, V6582, L1636, P2682, L1831, V6853, P3811, V7684, P3670, V6929, V6999, L1989, V6861, V7657. DG623, DG627, DG633, DG637-DG651 shipped to Russia and DG636 to Turkey.	
DG655-DG656	**Avro 652 Avalon**	2
	C/n 698, 699 G-ACRM, 'ACRN impressed in February 1941 to the Royal Navy.	
DG657-DG660	**DH.60G Gipsy Moth**	4
	G-AAJL, 'AABI, 'ABBK, 'ABTP impressed. DG657, DG658 became 4077M, 2548M.	
DG661-DG662	**DH.80A Puss Moth**	2
	G-AAXR, 'ABLG impressed. DG661 became 2618M.	
DG663	**Airspeed AS.6J Envoy III**	1
	C/n 32 G-ADAZ impressed.	
DG664	**Miles M.2R Hawk Major**	1
	C/n 211 G-ADLN impressed.	
DG665-DG666	**Miles M.2 Hawk Trainer**	2
	G-ADZA, 'AEAX models M.2W & M.2X impressed; DG665 became 3015M.	
DG667	**Piper J-4A Cub Coupé**	1
	C/n 4-647 G-AFXS impressed.	
DG670	**Hafner ARIII Gyroplane**	1
	G-ADMV first flew 6.2.37 acquired for RAE evaluation.	
DG673-DG686	**Slingsby Hengist I**	14
	Stored at Rawcliff Paper Mills until scrapped October 1946.	
DG689-DJ700	**Avro 652A Anson I/IV**	700
	DG689-DG727 Mk.I built at Yeadon, rest built at Newton Heath as follows: DG728-DG737, DG750-DG787 DG799-DG844, DG857-DG880, DG893-DG942, DG956-DG987, DJ103-DJ127Mk.I; DJ128-DJ133Mk.IV; DJ134-DJ149, DJ162-DJ190, DJ205-DJ248, DJ263-DJ298, DJ314-DJ361, DJ375-DJ417, DJ430-DJ478, DJ492-DJ529, DJ545-DJ589, DJ603-DJ639, DJ656-DJ700 Mk.I. Main deliveries to EATS. DG763, DJ188, DJ577 served with USAAF. Many disposed to civil register. DG771 became 5203M.	
DJ702 & DJ707	**Bristol 160HA Blenheim V**	2
	Prototypes to Spec B6/40 originally named Bisley. DJ707 became 3289M.	
DJ710	**Avro 641 Commodore**	1
	C/n 722 G-ACUG impressed.	
DJ711-DJ712	**DH.80A Puss Moth**	2
	G-AAXY, 'ABIN impressed.	
DJ713-DJ714	**Miles M.11A Whitney Straight**	2
	G-AEUX, 'AEWA impressed.	
DJ715	**Airspeed AS.4 Ferry**	1
	G-ACFB impressed.	
DJ716	**DH.90A Dragonfly**	1
	G-AEWZ impressed.	
DJ972-DJ977	**Short S.29 Stirling I Series II**	6
	Replacement order for aircraft destroyed in factory bombing.	
DJ980-DK271	**Handley Page HP.63 Halifax V**	150
	Built by Fairey Aviation. DJ980-DJ999, DK114-DK151, DK165-DK207, DK223-DK271. DJ988, DJ991, DK118 became 4541M, 4667M, 4127M.	
DK274-DK277	**Douglas Boston I**	4
	Arrived in damaged condition and scrapped.	
DK280	**Messerschmitt Bf 108B-1 Taifun**	1
	G-AFRN impressed.	
DK284-DK339	**DH.98 Mosquito IV Series II**	50
	DK284-DK303, DK308-DK333, DK336-DK339 B.IV version but some converted to PR. DK324 converted to PR.VIII and B.IX. DK287 shipped to Canada and DK296 to Russia. DK290 became 4411M.	
DK346-DK358	**Airspeed AS.51 Horsa**	4
	Prototypes DK346, DK349, DK353, DK358. First three became 4084M, 4085M, 4529M.	
DK363-DK412	**Blackburn B.37 Firebrand I-III**	50
	DK363-DK371 F.I; DK372, DK373 TF.III prototypes, DK374-DK385 TF.II, DK386-DK412 TF.III. For Royal Navy.	
DK414-DK667	**Fairey Firefly I**	132(200)
	Ordered from GAL. DK414-DK462, DK476-DK513, DK526-DK570 (132) built as F.I. DK426, DK428, DK429, DK448, DK453, DK478, DK489, DK495, DK499, DK531, DK540, DK543, DK550 converted to T.I. DK588-DK619, DK633-DK667 cancelled. For Royal Navy.	
DK670-DK792	**Fairey Swordfish II**	100
	Built by Blackburn. DK670-DK719, DK743-DK792 for Royal Navy.	
DK800-DM581	**Miles M.19/M.27 Master II/III**	1100(1200)
	Ordered from three different Phillip & Powis plants as Mk.II and built as follows: DK800-DK843, DK856-DK894, DK909-DK957, DK963-DK994, DL111-DL155, DL169-DL204, DL216-DL256, DL271-DL301 T.II; DL302-DL309, DL324, DL325 GT.II; DL326-DL373, DL395-DL435, DL448-DL493, DL509-DL546 T.II with some conversions to GT.II making 500 built at Reading. DL552-DL585, DL599-DL648, DL666-DL713, DL725-DL753, DL767-DL793 (188) Mk.III; DL794-DL803, DL821-DL866, DL878-DL909, DL935-DL983, DM108-DM140, DM155-DM196 (212) Mk.II making 400 built at South Marston. DM200-DM245, DM258-DM295, DM312-DM361, DM374-DM407, DM423-DM454 Mk.II making 200 built at Doncaster and Sheffield plants. DM455-DM464, DM478-DM526, DM541-DM581 (100) cancelled. DL251, DL252, DL271, DL272, DL275, DL276, DL278-DL280, DL976-DL979, DL983, DM166-DM168, DM170, DM173, DM179, DM180, DM227, DM232-DM235 to R Egyptian AF. DK891 to Portuguese AF; DK949, DL277, DL863, DL891, DL902, DL937, DL940, DM113, DM174, DM231, DM273, DM276, DM335, DM346, DM351, DM376 to Turkish AF. DL131-DL155, DL326-DL336 shipped to South Africa. DL852/G used in rocket firing experiments. DL830 loaned to USAAF. DK967, DL372, DL409, DL431, DL526, DL842, DM204, DM215, DM353, DM387, DM395, DM449 became 5438M, 4079M, 5547M, 5715M, 5330M, 5474M, 5722M, 5437M, 6239M, 5772M, 6194M, 6238M. DM442 became G-AIZN.	
DM594-DN232	**Hawker Tornado**	(395)
	Ordered from Avro. Cancelled. DM594-DM642, DM664-DM709, DM727-DM776, DM794-DM842, DM857-DM900, DM921-DM957, DM975-DM999, DN112-DN134, DN148-DN197, DN210-DN232.	
DN241-DN623	**Hawker Typhoon IB**	300
	Built by Gloster. DN241-DN278, DN293-DN341, DN356-DN389, DN404-DN453, DN467-DN513, DN529-DN562, DN576-DN623. DN323 was tropicalised and DN562 had experimental fin and rudder. DN244, DN255, DN277, DN383, DN384, DN450, DN501-DN503, DN531, DN595, DN604, DN605 became 4340M, 4651M, 4342M, 4648M, 5881M, 5401M, 4655M, 5763M, 4652M, 6124M, 4653M, 4656M, 4654M.	
DN625-DN998	**Fairey Barracuda**	18(250)
	Ordered from Westland. DN625-DN629 Mk.I and DN630-DN642 Mk.II only built. DN643-DN669, DN693-DN730, DN756-DN805, DN839-DN874, DN897-DN935, DN957-DN998 cancelled.	
DP176-DP200	**Short S.25 Sunderland III**	25
	Short-built at Windermere. DP191, DP195, DP198, DP199, DP200 converted to Mk.V. DP191 to RNZAF, DP192 to RAAF.	
DP206 & DP210	**General Aircraft GAL.49 Hamilcar**	2
	Prototypes to Spec X27/40. DP206 first flew 27.3.42. DP210 became 4081M.	
DP226	**General Aircraft GAL.50**	1
	Half-scale model of GAL.49 registered T-0227.	
DP237	**Miles M.11A Whitney Straight**	1
	G-AEYA impressed.	
DP240	**General Aircraft GAL.45 Owlet**	1
	C/n 134 G-AGBK impressed.	
DP244	**DH.60GIII Moth Major**	1
	Impressed in India.	
DP245-DP266	**DH.82A Tiger Moth**	22
	Impressments in India. DP248, DP259 not confirmed.	
DP279-DP841	**Airspeed AS.51 Horsa I**	400
	DP279-DP294, DP303-DP315, DP329-DP353, DP368-DP399, DP412-DP440, DP484-DP506, DP513-DP562, DP567-DP575, DP592-DP631, DP644-DP681, DP689-	

DP713 (300) built by Harris Lebus and group factories.
DP714-DP726, DP739-DP777, DP794-DP841 (100) built
by Austin Motors. DP593-DP598, DP614, DP617,
DP701, DP725 to USAAF. DP281, DP284, DP292,
DP304, DP315, DP331, DP341, DP348, DP352, DP380,
DP393, DP394, DP430, DP437, DP484, DP502, DP505,
DP506, DP524, DP531, DP538, DP549, DP554, DP612,
DP615, DP617, DP622, DP649, DP660, DP666, DP670,
DP676, DP677, DP679, DP680, DP692, DP694, DP708,
DP717, DP723, DP724, DP739, DP741, DP745, DP746,
DP751, DP773, DP794, DP795, DP805, DP810, DP813,
DP816, DP822, DP827, DP832 became 4787M, 4199M,
4511M, 4082M, 4177M, 5214M, 4086M, 4873M, 4207M,
4771M, 4753M, 4083M, 4742M, 5211M, 4928M, 4739M,
4729M, 5086M, 4477M, 4743M, 5080M, 5083M, 4738M,
5078M, 5212M, 5210M, 5092M, 5019M, 5081M, 5079M,
5082M, 4191M, 4733M, 4192M, 5093M, 4731M, 4872M,
5027M, 3331M, 5089M, 4741M, 3397M, 5020M, 4201M,
4478M, 4022M, 4736M, 4208M, 4788M, 4728M, 4940M,
4754M, 4433M, 4448M, 4730M.

DP843	**DH.80A Puss Moth** Reported as impressment.	1
DP845	**Supermarine Spitfire III/IV/XX (in succession)** Prototype to Spec F4/40.	1
DP845	**Miles M.11A Whitney Straight** G-AEVG impressed. Compromised number above.	1
DP846	**DH.80A Puss Moth** G-ABTV impressed.	1
DP847	**British Aircraft Eagle 2** G-ADVT impressed.	1
DP848	**Miles M.2H Hawk Major** G-AENS impressed.	1
DP849-DP850	**DH.80A Puss Moth** G-ABMC, 'ABMP impressed.	2
DP851	**Supermarine Spitfire IV/XX/F21 (in succession)** Compromised number below.	1
DP851	**Miles M.2H Hawk Major** G-AEGP impressed; became 3016M.	1
DP852	**Piper J-4B Cub Coupé** C/n 4-653 G-AFXT impressed.	1
DP853-DP854	**DH.80A Puss Moth** G-AEIV, 'ABMS impressed.	2
DP855	**Miles M.11A Whitney Straight** G-AEVL impressed. Compromised number below, renumbered NF751.	1
DP855-DR335	**Fairey Barracuda II** Built by Boulton Paul. DP855-DP902, DP917-DP955, DP967-DP999, DR113-DR162, DR179-DR224, DR237- DR275, DR291-DR335. DP855/G prototype Mk.III was fitted with H2S. DP872 preserved.	300
DR339-DR394	**Hawker Hurricane IIA** Mk.Is renumbered DR339-DR374, DR391-DR394 on conversion and shipment to USSR, ex-V7169, P3103, P3714, P3023, P3551, L1562, W9191, V7286, V7006, P3717, P3759, P3121, V6915, V6739, P2835, L1684, P2829, W9265, P2904, R4081, L1769, V6936, V7054, P3449, P3928, P3307, P3256, AE963, N2665, P2863, P2920, P3106, V6538, P2975, R4091, V6546, V6942, V7018, P3351, V7021.	40
DR423-DR427	**Harlow PJC-5** Assembled in India.	5
DR471-DR600	**Vickers Wellington VIA/VIG** Built at Weybridge. DR471-DR479 Mk.VIA Vickers Type 442, DR480-DR504, DR519-DR528 Mk.VIG with /G suffix to serials as Vickers Type 449. Rear turret on DR484 deleted. DR529-DR549, DR566-DR600 cancelled.	44(100)
DR606	**DH.60G Gipsy Moth** G-AAYT impressed.	1
DR607-DR608	**DH.80A Puss Moth** G-ABKZ, 'ABIU impressed.	2
DR609	**British Klemm BK.1 Eagle** G-ACPU impressed.	1
DR610	**British Aircraft Eagle 2** G-ADJS impressed became 2680M.	1
DR611-DR612	**Miles M.11A Whitney Straight** G-AETS, 'AEVA impressed. DR617 was incorrectly applied to DR611. DR611 became G-AITM.	2
DR613	**Foster Wikner Warferry** G-AFJB Wicko GM1 impressed under name of Warferry. Currently preserved.	1

DR616	**Miles M.20** Naval prototype to Spec N1/41. Ex- U-0228.	1
DR617	*(See note for DR611 above)*	
DR622-DR624	**Cierva C.30A (Avro 671)** Autogyros G-ACYH, 'ACWH, 'ACWF impressed.	3
DR626	**Bucker Bu 131B Jungmann** C/n 4477 stolen in France and flown to Britain.	1
DR628	**Beech D-17S** C/n 295 USAAC 39-139 allotted for personal use of Prince Bernhardt of the Netherlands. Became G-AMBY.	1
DR629	**Consolidated BT-7** Allocation cancelled.	—
DR630	**DH.80A Puss Moth** Re-allotted as HM534.	(1)
DR633-DR749	**Fairey Fulmar II** C/n F.5870-F.5969. DR633-DR682, DR700-DR749 final Fulmar production for Royal Navy.	100
DR755	**DH.80A Puss Moth** G-AAVB impressed.	1
DR761-DR807	**Curtiss Mohawk** Allotted to Middle East for Mohawks. Not all taken up.	(47)
DR848-DR849	**GAL Monospar ST-25 Jubilee/ST-4** Ex-X9348, X9376; ex-G-ADPK, 'ACCO.	(2)
DR851-DR860	**General Aircraft GAL.49 Hamilcar** DR852, DR855, DR856 became 4311M, 4457M, 4528M. DR854 RATOG trials.	10
DR863-DS169	**Boulton Paul P.82 Defiant TT.1** DR863-DR896, DR914-DR949, DR961-DR991, DS121- DS159 built. DR944 ejection seat experiments. DR963 became TT.2. DS160-DS169 cancelled.	140(150)
DS173-DS175	**Bell 14 Airacobra** USAAF P-39s to UK for evaluation.	3
DS180	**Beechcraft C-17R** C/n 118 G-AESJ impressed.	1
DS183-DS598	*Not allotted, presumed cancelled order*	—
DS601-DS852	**Avro 683 Lancaster II** Built by Armstrong Whitworth. DS601-DS635, DS647- DS692, DS704-DS741, DS757-DS797, DS813-DS852. Up to DS627 had Hercules VI engines, remainder Hercules XVI. DS606, DS611, DS612, DS619, DS727, DS730, DS786 became 3995M, 4947M, 4865M, 4990M, 4972M, 4973M, 4976M.	200
DS858-DT479	**Airspeed AS.10 Oxford I/II** Cancelled order with de Havilland for 200 each Mks.I and II. DS858-DS897, DS915-DS950, DS962-DS989, DT108-DT146, DT161-DT210, DT224-DT265, DT279- DT313, DT325-DT374, DT387-DT418, DT432-DT479.	(400)
DT481-DT808	**Handley Page HP.59 Halifax II** Built by English Electric Co. DT481-DT526, DT539- DT588, DT612-DT649, DT665-DT705, DT720-DT752, DT767-DT808. DT523, DT548 became 4375M, 4863M.	250
DT810 & DT812	**Avro 683 Lancaster II** Prototype Mk.II. Only DT810 built.	1(2)
DT813-DT887	**Fairey Barracuda II** C/n F.5970-F.6019 built at Heaton Chapel. DT813- DT831, DT845-DT865, DT878-DT887 for Royal Navy. DT845 Mk.V prototype.	50
DT926-DV150	**Fairey Firefly I** DT926-DT961, DT974-DT998, DV112-DV150 produced as F.1. Conversions: DT974, DV132 T.I, DV121 TT.I, DV119, DV127 F.R.I, DV976 T.3. For Royal Navy.	100
DV155-DV407	**Avro 683 Lancaster III/I** Built by Metropolitan Vickers. DV155-DV202, DV217- DV247, DV263-DV276 Mk.III, DV277-DV282 Mk.I, DV283-DV290 Mk.III, DV291-DV297 Mk.I, DV298 Mk.III, DV299-DV309 Mk.I, DV310 Mk.III, DV311, DV312, DV324-DV345, DV359-DV382 Mk.I, DV383, DV384 Mk.III, DV385-DV394 Mk.I, DV395 Mk.III, DV396-DV407 Mk.I. DV379 became BOAC test-bed G-AGJI. DV170, DV199 converted to Mk.VI. DV193, DV310, DV326 became 4959M, 5930M, 5055M.	200
DV411-DV953	**Vickers Wellington IC** Built at Chester. DV411-DV458, DV473-DV522, DV536- DV579, DV593-DV624, DV638-DV678, DV694-DV740, DV757-DV786, DV799-DV846, DV874-DV898, DV914- DV953 of which DV491, DV594, DV617, DV704, DV738, DV761, DV762, DV822, DV886, DV920, DV921, DV924, DV942 were converted to Mk.XVI. DV427, DV474, DV760, DV879 became 3948M, 4414M, 3760M, 4206M.	415

DV956-DW113   **Short S.25 Sunderland III**   45
DV956-DV980 built by Short Bros at Rochester; DV985-
DV994, DW104-DW113 built by Short & Harland.
DV961 became 4666M.

DW115-DW502   **Vickers Warwick**   (250)
Order cancelled.

DW506 &   **Vickers Windsor**   2
DW512   Prototypes to Spec B5/41. DW506 Vickers Type 447
(Merlin 65), DW512 Vickers Type 457 (Merlin 82).

DW515-DW796   *Not taken up*   –

DW802-DX157   **Bristol 152 Beaufort I**   200
DW802-DW836, DW851-DW898, DW913-DW962,
DW977-DW999, DX114-DX157. DW893, DW930,
DX125, DX144, DX147, DX153 to Turkish
Air Force.

DX160   **Folland E28/40**   (1)
Torpedo bomber project, not built.

DX161   **Percival P.33**   (1)
Fighter project, not built.

DX166 &   **Short S.35 Shetland**   2
DX171   Prototypes to Spec R14/40. DX171 became G-AGVD
on completion.

DX177   **Focke-Wulf Fw 200A-02**   1
Condor OY-DAM impressed initially as G-AGAY.

DX181-DX243   **Percival P.34 Proctor III**   50
Built by F. Hills & Sons. DX181-DX201, DX215-DX243.
Several postwar to civil register. DX193, DX197, DX221,
DX231, became 6281M, 6914M, 6692M, 6698M.

DX249-DX266   **Bristol 163 Buckingham**   4
Ex-Beaumont project. Prototypes to Spec B2/41 as
revised. C/n 11332-11335. DX249, DX255, DX259,
DX266.

DX278-DX420   **Westland P.14 Welkin I**   98(100)
DX278-DX295, DX308-DX349, DX364-DX389, DX407-
DX420 allotted but DX293, DX386 were cancelled.
DX340 engine test bed. Not all built were flown.

DX437-DX835   **DH.82A Tiger Moth II**   420
Built by de Havilland (Australia). DX437-DX461,
DX474-DX512, DX526-DX557, DX569-DX612 and
other numbers incorporated in RAAF A17 series. 120
delivered to SAAF and 94 to S Rhodesian AF.

DX840-DZ202   *Not taken up*   –

DZ203   **Boeing 247D**   1
C/n 1726. NC13344 impressed.

DZ209   **Bellanca Pacemaker**   1
Sole example of type in UK, G-ABNW (ex-I-AAPI)
impressed for Royal Navy communications.

DZ213   **DH.83 Fox Moth**   1
G-ACIY impressed for Royal Navy.

DZ217 &   **Vickers 432**   1(2)
DZ223   Prototypes to Spec F7/41. DZ223 not completed.

DZ228-DZ761   **DH.98 Mosquito II/IV**   400
DZ228-DZ272, DZ286-DZ310 (70) NF.II; DZ311-
DZ320, DZ340-DZ388, DZ404-DZ442, DZ458-DZ497,
DZ515-DZ559, DZ575-DZ618, DZ630-DZ652 (250)
B.IV except DZ411, DZ419, DZ431, DZ438, DZ459,
DZ466, DZ473, DZ480, DZ487, DZ494, DZ517, DZ523,
DZ527, DZ532, DZ538, DZ544, DZ549, DZ553, DZ557,
DZ576, DZ580, DZ584, DZ588, DZ592, DZ596, DZ600,
DZ604 as PR.IV. DZ653-DZ661, DZ680-DZ727, DZ739-
DZ761 (80) NF.II. Conversions: DZ343, DZ364, DZ404,
DZ244 to PR.VIII; DZ302 to NF.XII; DZ366, DZ385
to NF.XV; DZ540 to PR.XVI prototype. DZ520, DZ524,
DZ529, DZ531, DZ537, DZ539, DZ541-DZ543, DZ546,
DZ552, DZ554-DZ556, DZ559, DZ575, DZ577-DZ579,
DZ581-DZ583, DZ585, DZ586, DZ618, DZ639, DZ648,
DZ651, DZ652 converted for Highball operations.
DZ700, DZ761 to Royal Navy and DZ411 loaned to
BOAC. Various special installations and modifications
to others. DZ366, DZ378, DZ385, DZ418, DZ541,
DZ700 became 4883M, 3509M, 4884M, 5342M, 6500M,
5913M.

DZ765-DZ774   **Short Shetland**   (10)
Cancelled.

DZ779-EA201   **Handley Page Halifax**   (250)
Cancelled order. DZ779-DZ819, DZ837-DZ877, DZ893-
DZ924, DZ937-DZ986, EA104-EA147, EA160-EA201.

EB127-EB276   **Handley Page HP.63 Halifax V**   100
Built by Rootes. EB127-EB160, EB178-EB220, EB239-
EB258, EB274-EB276. EB127 sent to Canada.

EB282-EB410   **Armstrong Whitworth AW.38 Whitley V/VII**   100
EB282 Mk.VII, EB283-EB313 Mk.V, EB327-EB336
Mk.VII, EB337-EB367, EB384-EB391 Mk.V, EB392-
EB401 Mk.VII, EB402-EB410 Mk.V. EB327, EB393
to Royal Navy.

EB414-EB975   **Airspeed AS.10 Oxford I/V**   300
Built at Portsmouth. EB414-EB423 Mk.I all to SAAF,
EB424 Mk.V to S Rhodesian AF; EB425-EB461, EB483-
EB518, EB535-EB584, EB599-EB640, EB654-EB677
Mk.V practically all to Canada as airframes; EB689-
EB703, EB717-EB761, EB777-EB826, EB838-EB870,
EB884-EB930, EB946-EB975 Mk.I distributed to RAF at
home and EATS. EB849, EB884, EB888, EB894, EB915,
EB924, EB953, EB962-EB968 converted to Mk.V.
EB719, EB729, EB751, EB799 became 5506M, 6938M,
5507M, 5514M.

EB978-ED300   **Airspeed AS.10 Oxford II/I**   180
Built by Percival. EB978-EB999, ED108-ED157, ED169-
ED196 (100) Mk.II; ED197-ED204, ED215-ED236,
ED251-ED300 (80) Mk.I. Mainly home deliveries. Several
to civil registration postwar. ED122, ED127, ED130,
ED140, ED286 became 5515M, 5460M, 5891M, 5439M,
6892M.

ED303-EE202   **Avro 683 Lancaster**   620
Built at Manchester. ED303-ED334, ED347-ED396 Mk.I
except for ED362, ED371/G (fitted later with Lincoln
type nose), ED378, ED387, ED388, ED390, ED393,
ED395, ED396 Mk.III; ED408-ED453, ED467-ED504,
ED520-ED569, ED583-ED631, ED645-ED668, ED688-
ED737, ED749-ED786, ED799-ED842, ED856-ED888,
ED904-ED953, ED967-ED999, EE105-EE150, EE166-
EE202 Mk.III except ED409, ED411, ED412, ED414,
ED418-ED420, ED422, ED425, ED430, ED436, ED439,
ED443, ED446, ED447, ED451, ED498, ED521, ED522,
ED525, ED528, ED533, ED537, ED548, ED550, ED552,
ED554, ED567, ED569, ED586, ED588, ED591, ED594,
ED600, ED601, ED604, ED610, ED615, ED622, ED631,
ED650, ED661, ED692, ED703, ED715, ED732, ED735,
ED749, ED751, ED754, ED755, ED757, ED758, ED761-
ED763, ED766, ED769, ED770, ED773, ED774, ED777,
ED778, ED780-ED782 Mk.I. Twenty-three B.IIIs were
modified for No.617 Squadron's dam-busting operations
and given /G serials, being ED765, ED817, ED825,
ED864, ED865, ED886, ED887, ED906, ED909, ED910,
ED915, ED918, ED921, ED924, ED925, ED927, ED929,
ED932, ED934, ED935-ED937. ED324, ED382, ED437,
ED474, ED593, ED704, ED756, ED762, ED869, ED904,
ED909, EE128, EE136, EE176, EE187 became 5290M,
5296M, 5060M, 5454M, 4944M, 4370M, 4946M, 4011M,
4967M, 5455M, 6242M, 5295M, 5918M, 5252M, 6747M.

EE205   **Junkers Ju 88A-5**   1
C/n 3457 landed at Lulsgate Bottom in error and
captured on 23.7.41.

EE210-EE599   **Gloster G.41 Meteor I/III/IV (later F.1, F.3, F.4)**   300
EE210-EE229 F.1; EE230-EE254, EE269-EE318,
EE331-EE369, EE384-EE429, EE444-EE453 F.3 with
Derwent engines except EE230-EE244 Wellands; EE454-
EE493, EE517-EE554, EE568-EE599 F.4; Non-standard
Meteors: EE210/G exchanged with US for an XP-59
Airacomet, EE211/G long chord nacelles, EE212/G
revised empennage, EE215 had reheat on Wellands,
EE219 auxiliary fins on tailplane, EE221/G had
W2/700 jets, EE224 converted to 2-seat, EE227 with
Trent turboprops, EE240/G to USA, EE246, EE338,
EE416 used in ejection seat tests, EE249/G W2/700
jets and pressure cabin, EE311 did winterisation tests in
Canada, EE337 & EE387 deck landing tests, EE360/G
F.4 prototype, EE397 flight refuelling trials, EE445
Griffiths wing, EE454, EE455 modified for World Speed
Record, EE521, EE524 converted to U.15; EE548-
EE550 had modified wings. EE530 became T.7, EE531
folding wing tests. EE395 to RNZAF as NZ6001, EE427
to RAAF as A77-1, EE429 to South Africa, EE384-
EE386, EE388-EE393, EE526, EE527, EE532-EE537,
EE539-EE544, EE546-EE548, EE551-EE554, EE569-
EE572, EE574-EE577, EE580-EE583, EE585-EE589 to
Argentine Air Force. Over 50 aircraft became instruc-
tional airframes in the 'M' series, see Appendix 2 for 'EE'
serials between 5229M and 7248M. EE531 and EE549
preserved in the UK.

EE600-EE867	**Supermarine Spitfire VC**	200

Built by Westland. EE600-EE644, EE657-EE690, EE713-EE753, EE766-EE811, EE834-EE867. EE794 to USAAF. EE600, EE624, EE644 became 4187M, 5540M, 5521M.

EE871-EF323	**Short S.29 Stirling III/IV**	260

Built by Short & Harland. EE871-EE918, EE937-EE975, EF114-EF163, EF177-EF217, EF231-EF277, EF289-EF316 Mk.III of which EE889, EE900, EE960, EE962, EE966, EF141, EF213, EF214, EF234, EF237, EF241-EF244, EF248, EF256, EF260, EF261, EF263-EF265, EF267-EF270, EF272-EF277, EF292, EF293, EF295-EF298, EF303, EF305, EF306, EF309, EF311, EF314, EF316 were converted to Mk.IV and EF317-EF323 were built as Mk.IV. EE899, EE945, EF135, EF297, EF301 became 4836M, 4923M, 4202M, 4775M, 4925M.

EF327-EF518	**Short S.29 Stirling I/III/IV**	150

EF327-EF369, EF384-EF400 Mk.I; EF401-EF412 Mk.III, EF413 Mk.I; EF425-EF470, EF488-EF518 Mk.III. EF404, EF429, EF435, EF446, EF470, EF506 converted to Mk.IV. EF405, EF459 became 4920M, 4917M. EF454 became TS261.

EF523	**Fairchild 24C8-F**	1

G-AFFK impressed.

EF526-EF753	**Supermarine Spitfire VC**	185

Built by Westland. EF526-EF570, EF584-EF616, EF629-EF656, EF671-EF710, EF715-EF753. EF541, EF678, EF731 became 5518M, 4203M, 5803M. EF529 to the USAAF.

EF805-EG704	**Avro 652A Anson I**	600

Built at Yeadon. EF805-EF839, EF858-EF890, EF903-EF941, EF952-EF993, EG104-EG148, EG165-EG195, EG228-EG246, EG251-EG280, EG293-EG335, EG350-EG396, EG412-EG447, EG460-EG507, EG524-EG561, EG583-EG616, EG629-EG655, EE672-EE704. Numbers offset to EATS. Postwar: EF807, EF862, EF880, EG120, EG211, EG230, EG277, EG280, EG355, EG356, EG360, EG363, EG464, EG542, EG590, EG606, EG608, EG650 to French AF; EG208, EG268 to Belgian AF; EF992, EG121, EG234, EG495 to R Hellenic AF; EG140 to R Netherlands AF; EG274, EG276, EG672 to R Norwegian AF. EG389, EG390 became 5634M, 6471M.

EH310-EH872	**Bristol 160 Blenheim V**	160(415)

EH310-EH355, EH417-EH420, EH438-EH474, EH491-EH517 built by Rootes. EH518-EH533, EH550-EH581, EH599-EH634, EH651-EH700, EH718-EH749, EH763-EH796, EH802-EH831, EH848-EH872 cancelled. EH320, EH326, EH341, EH372 to Turkish AF; EH347, EH443, EH458 to USAAF.

EH875-EJ127	**Short S.29 Stirling III**	120

Built by Austin Motors. EH875-EH909, EH921-EH961, EH977-EH996, EJ104-EJ127 of which EH897, EH950, EJ106 were converted to Mk.IV. EH904, EH995, EJ122 became 4445M, 4538M, 5223M.

EJ131-EJ172	**Short S.25 Sunderland III**	35

EJ131-EJ145 built at Rochester, EJ149-EJ158 at Windermere and EJ163-EJ172 at Belfast. EJ152, EJ153, EJ155, EJ167 converted to Mk.V.

EJ175-EJ503	**Hawker Typhoon IB/Tempest**	(270)

Cancelled. EJ175-EJ222, EJ234-EJ283, EJ296-EJ334, EJ347-EJ392, EJ405-EJ454, EJ467-EJ503.

EJ504-EJ896	**Hawker Tempest V**	300

EJ504, EJ518-EJ560, EJ577-EJ611, EJ626-EJ672, EJ685-EJ723, EJ739-EJ788, EJ800-EJ846, EJ859-EJ896. EJ518 used in annular cooling trials. Postwar conversions to TT.5: EJ580, EJ585, EJ598, EJ631, EJ643, EJ660, EJ663, EJ667, EJ669, EJ740, EJ744, EJ753, EJ758, EJ786, EJ801, EJ805, EJ807, EJ839, EJ846, EJ862, EJ875, EJ879, EJ880. EJ841 converted to Mk.VI. EJ520, EJ539, EJ543, EJ586, EJ638, EJ754, EJ760, EJ785 became 5519M, 5563M, 6578M, 5468M, 6477M, 5688M, 5703M, 6648M.

EJ900-EK543	**Hawker Typhoon IB**	400

Built by Gloster. EJ900-EJ934, EJ946-EJ995, EK112-EK154, EK167-EK197, EK208-EK252, EK266-EK301, EK321-EK348, EK364-EK413, EK425-EK456, EK472-EK512, EK535-EK543. EJ906 tropicalised. EJ920, EJ992, EK117, EK146, EK150, EK153, EK154, EK180, EK183, EK219, EK230, EK231, EK251, EK284, EK288, EK326, EK371, EK538 became 6123M, 5876M, 5613M,

4647M, 5611M, 4635M, 5880M, 5557M, 5323M, 5643M, 4646M, 4650M, 4634M, 4636M, 4649M, 5446M, 5609M, 5608M.

EK572-EK596	**Short S.25 Sunderland III**	25

Built by Blackburn. EK579, EK592 converted to Mk.V.

EK601-EK967	**Blackburn Firebrand**	170(250)

EK601-EK638, EK653-EK694, EK719-EK740 (102) Mk.IV; EK741-EK748, EK764-EK799, EK827-EK850 (68) Mk.V. EK851-EK867, EK885-EK913, EK934-EK967 (80) cancelled. EK630 was non-standard.

EK969-EL141	**Bristol 152 Beaufort I**	50

EK969-EK999, EL123-EL141.

EL145-EL534	**Bristol 156 Beaufighter VI**	300

Built at Weston. EL145-EL192, EL213-EL218 Mk.VIF; EL219-EL246, EL259-EL305, EL321-EL370, EL385-EL418, EL431-EL479, EL497-EL534 Mk.VIC. EL241, EL243-EL246, EL259-EL262, EL395, EL396, EL411, EL413, EL435, EL436, EL438, EL443, EL510, EL518, EL520 to RAAF A19 series. EL393 Mk.X prototype. EL290, EL445 became 4401M, 4174M.

EM258-EM716	**Miles M.19 Master II/M.25 Martinet I**	360

Original Master order with Phillips & Powis (Reading). EM258-EM304, EM317-EM355, EM371-EM409 (125) Master II of which EM381, EM385, EM405 went to Turkish AF, EM389 became 5944M and EM300 became G-AIZM. EM410-EM420, EM434-EM481, EM496-EM532, EM545-EM593, EM613-EM662, EM677-EM716 (235) built as Martinet Is of which EM414-EM418, EM449-EM452, EM468-EM472, EM504-EM508, EM525-EM529, EM558-EM562, EM577-EM582, EM618-EM623, EM632-EM638, EM654-EM656, EM658-EM660, EM662, EM677, EM678, EM686-EM695, EM708-EM711, EM714-EM716, were delivered to Royal Navy. EM331, EM444, EM530, EM545 became 6181M, 6941M, 5822M, 5776M. Postwar sales: EM683 to Belgian AF and EM474, EM630, EM648, EM661, EM679, EM712, EM713 to French AF.

EM720-EM989	**DH.82A Tiger Moth II**	222

Built by Morris Motors. EM720-EM756, EM771-EM819, EM835-EM884, EM893-EM931, EM943-EM989. Many shipped overseas including 30 to RIAF, others to EATS and RAF in Middle East. EM968, EM969 went direct to Portugal. EM901, EM920, EM967 became 4090M, 6791M, 6940M.

EM995-EM996	**DH.80A Puss Moth**	2

G-ABLP, 'ABLX impressed.

EM999	**Miles M.11A Whitney Straight**	1

G-AERV impressed. Extant in an Ulster Museum.

EN112-EN759	**Supermarine Spitfire VII/IX/XI/XII etc**	440(500)

EN112-EN121 Mk.IX, EN122-EN148 F.IX, EN149-EN151 PR.XI, EN152 F.IX, EN153 PR.IV, EN154 PR.XI, EN155 PR.IV, EN156, EN171-EN175 Mk.IX, EN176 HF.VI, EN177 Mk.IX, EN178 F.VII, EN179, EN180 F.IX, EN181 Mk.IX, EN182 F.IX, EN183 Mk.IX, EN184 F.IX, EN185-EN188 Mk.IX, EN189 Mk.VI, EN190, EN191 Mk.IX, EN192 F.VII, EN193-EN207 Mk.IX, EN221-EN238 F.XII, EN239-EN258 Mk.IX, EN259 F.IX, EN260 PR.XI, EN261 F.IX, EN262 PR.IV, EN263 PR.XI, EN264 PR.IV, EN265-EN270 F.IX, EN285 F.VII, EN286-EN296 Mk.IX, EN297 F.VII, EN298-EN309 Mk.IX, EN310 F.VII, EN311-EN315 Mk.IX, EN329 F.IX, EN330-EN332 PR.XI, EN333-EN336 F.IX, EN337, EN338 PR.XI, EN339, EN340 F.IX, EN341-EN343 PR.XI, EN344, EN345 F.IX, EN346-EN348 PR.XI, EN349, EN350 F.IX, EN351-EN362 Mk.IX, EN363 F.IX, EN364-EN370 Mk.IX, EN385 PR.XI, EN386-EN389 PR.IV, EN390 Mk.IX, EN391 PR.XI, EN392 Mk.IX, EN393 F.IX, EN394 Mk.IX, EN395, EN396 PR.XI, EN397, EN398 F.IX, EN399 Mk.IX, EN400-EN402 F.IX, EN403, EN404 Mk.IX, EN405 F.IX, EN406 Mk.IX, EN407-EN430 PR.XI, EN444-EN453 Mk.IX, EN454-EN456 F.IX, EN457 F.VII, EN458 F.IX, EN459-EN464 Mk.IX, EN465 F.VII, EN466-EN469 Mk.IX, EN470 F.VII, EN471, EN472 Mk.IX, EN473 F.IX, EN474 Mk.VII direct to USA, EN475, EN476 Mk.IX, EN477 F.VII, EN478 F.IX, EN479-EN483, EN490-EN493 Mk.IX, EN494-EN497 F.VII, EN498 F.IX, EN499 F.VII, EN500-EN502 F.IX, EN503, EN504 PR.XI, EN505, EN506 F.VII, EN507, EN508 PR.XI, EN509 F.VII, EN510 F.IX, EN511, EN512 F.VII, EN513, EN514

F.IX, EN515-EN524 Mk.IX, EN525 F.IX, EN526-
EN528 Mk.IX, EN529 LF.IX, EN530-EN534, EN551-
EN553 Mk.IX, EN554, EN555 LF.IX, EN556 Mk.IX,
EN557 LF.IX, EN558, EN559 Mk.IX, EN560 LF.IX,
EN561-EN563 Mk.IX, EN564-EN566 LF.IX, EN567
Mk.IX, EN568, EN569 LF.IX, EN570 Mk.IX, EN571
F.IX, EN572-EN583 LF.IX, EN601-EN627 F.XII,
EN628-EN637 LF.IX, EN652-EN685 PR.XI. Note
Mk.IX has been given where HF, F or LF version
cannot be ascertained. EN686-EN695, EN710-EN759
cancelled on change of contract to Seafires. see NM910
et seq. Deliveries mainly to Malta and North-West Africa.
EN314 was flown experimentally with jettisonable 200
gallon fuel tank. EN177, EN238, EN363, EN396, EN526
became 5969M, 5670M, 6038M, 5934M, 5802M.

EN763-ER200 | **Supermarine Spitfire VB/VC** | **905**

Built at Castle Bromwich. EN763-EN800, EN821-EN867,
EN887-EN932, EN944-EN981, EP107-EP152, EP164-
EP213, EP226-EP260, EP275-EP316, EP327-EP366,
EP380-EP417, EP431-EP473, EP485-EP523, EP536-
EP579, EP594-EP624, EP636-EP669, EP682-EP729,
EP747-EP795, EP812-EP847, EP869-EP915, EP951-
EP990, ER114-ER146, ER159-ER200. Mainly built as
Mk.VB but EN767, EP365, EP654, EP700, EP847,
ER177, ER188, ER194 known to have been Mk.VC.
Conversions: EP499, EP615, EP891 to Mk.IX, EP751,
EP754 to floatplane, EN902 to PR.XIII and various re-
numberings as Seafires in MB, NX and PA prefixed series.
Main deliveries to Gibraltar, Malta and North Africa.
Large number were fitted with tropical filters. Some
deliveries to French, Italian, Portuguese, Russian and
Turkish forces. EN828, EN862, EN913, EN951, EN964,
EP120, EP169, EP250, EP380, EP500, EP570 became
5391M, 5397M, 5380M, 5516M, 5585M, 5377M, 5396M,
5929M, 5931M, 5705M, 5538M. EN830 was fitted with
a DB605A engine after capture. EP120 is preserved in
the UK as 8070M.

ER206-ES369 | **Supermarine Spitfire VB/VC** | **750**

Built at Castle Bromwich. ER206-ER229, ER245-ER283,
ER299-ER345, ER461-ER510, ER524-ER571, ER583-
ER626, ER634-ER679, ER695-ER744, ER758-ER791,
ER804-ER834, ER846-ER894, ER913-ER948, ER960-
ER998, ES105-ES154, ES168-ES214, ES227-ES264,
ES276-ES318, ES335-ES369 built largely as Mk.VB,
but the following known to be Mk.VC: ER265, ER281,
ER496, ER541, ER610, ER614, ER645, ER654, ER666,
ER719, ER733, ER739, ER740, ER742, ER760, ER762,
ER765, ER769, ER771, ER776, ER781, ER782, ER787,
ER804-ER806, ER850, ER851, ER854, ER860, ER865,
ER866, ER870, ER872, ER877, ER879, ER880, ER884,
ER885, ER887, ER889, ER892, ER913, ER914, ER917-
ER921, ER924, ER927, ER928, ER931-ER937, ER939,
ER940, ER944, ER947, ER948, ER976, ER989,
ER990, ER998, ES108-ES112, ES114-ES121, ES124,
ES127, ES129, ES131, ES132, ES134, ES136, ES138,
ES139, ES148-ES150, ES152-ES154, ES168, ES171,
ES174, ES178, ES182, ES183, ES188, ES195-ES199,
ES200, ES202, ES204-ES208, ES210-ES214, ES229,
ES231-ES233, ES236-ES238, ES241-ES243, ES245,
ES249-ES251, ES253, ES254, ES257-ES260, ES263,
ES277-ES282, ES284, ES285, ES287-ES299, ES300,
ES302-ES318, ES335-ES369. ER713, ES107, ES185,
ES291 converted to Mk.IX. Main deliveries to Gibraltar,
North Africa and Middle East and some to Australia.
Some transfers to Italian and Turkish forces. ES127 was
unofficially modified to 2-seat.

ES372-ES902 | **Airspeed Horsa** | **(400)**

Cancelled order placed with Tata Industries, India.
ES372-ES416, ES434-ES471, ES485-ES534, ES548-
ES589, ES601-ES636, ES649-ES695, ES723-ES766,
ES781-ES830, ES855-ES902.

ES906 | **Messerschmitt Bf109F-2** | **1**

C/n 12764 forced down near Dover 10.7.41.

ES913 | **Wicko GM1 Warferry** | **1**

C/n 8 G-AFKK impressed in May 1941.

ES914-ES915 | **General Aircraft GAL.42 Cygnet II** | **2**

G-AGAU, 'AGBN impressed.

ES916-ES921 | **DH.80A Puss Moth** | **6**

G-AAZW, 'ABIA, 'ABJU, 'ABLY, 'ACYT, 'AEOA
impressed.

ES922 | **Miles M.11A Whitney Straight** | **1**

G-AERS impressed.

ES923 | **Piper J-4A Cub Coupé** | **1**

C/n 4-612 G-AFWS impressed.

ES924 & ES943 | **Wicko GM1 Warferry** | **2**

C/ns 4, 2 G-AFAZ and 'AEZZ impressed.

ES944 | **British Aircraft Eagle II** | **1**

C/n 133 G-AEFZ impressed.

ES945 | **DH.85 Leopard Moth** | **1**

Ex-Belgian to Royal Navy.

ES946 | **Desoutter I** | **1**

C/n D4 G-AAPS impressed.

ES947 | **Wicko GM1 Warferry** | **1**

C/n 7 G-AFKU impressed.

ES948 | **British Aircraft Eagle II** | **1**

C/n 131 G-AEKI impressed.

ES949-ES950 | **British Aircraft IV Double Eagle** | **2**

C/ns 901, 902 G-ADVV and 'AEIN impressed.

ES952 | **British Aircraft Swallow II** | **1**

G-AEDX impressed, became 2786M.

ES953-ES954 | **DH.80A Puss Moth** | **2**

G-ABDM, 'ACIV impressed.

ES955 | **Messerschmitt Bf108B-1** | **1**

C/n 1660 G-AFZO ex-D-IDBT impressed ex-German
Embassy. Restored to G-AFZO and sold in Switzerland.
See also ES995.

ES956-ES960 | **Taylorcraft Plus C & C/2 conversions.** | **5**

G-AFWW, 'AFUY, 'AFWK, 'AFWM, 'AFUZ impressed.
ES956, ES958, ES959 converted to C/2.

ES980-ES995 | **Vickers Wellington IC/VIII** | **16**

Built at Weybridge and flown to Middle East. Mk.IC
except ES986 Mk.VIII.

ES995 | **Number erroneously applied to ES955.**

Lend-Lease Introduced

ET100 to HD776

On 11 March 1941 the Lend/Lease Act was passed by US Congress and
an Aircraft Allocation Committee decided the priorities of issue of aircraft
required by the nations deemed 'vital to the defence of the United States'.
In this British numbering system a large block of numbers starting at
ET100 was reserved for requirements approved by the US Authorities.
As America was not yet at war and Germans could travel quite freely in
the USA, there was no point in using blackout blocks and in this section
there is consecutive numbering. Allocations were made from aircraft
ordered for the US Army Air Force, Navy and Marines so that the
American designation is quoted as well as the British name and mark
number.

Serial Nos	Aircraft Type and Remarks	Quantity
ET100-EV699	**Curtiss Kittyhawk I/IA (P-40D/E)**	**1500**
	Ex-USAAF 41-24776 to '25195, 41-35874 to '36953. Many diversions by shipments direct to Australia and New Zealand and by rail consignments to RCAF; others diverted later to RCAF. At least 34 were lost at sea en route. ET573, EV352 became 4181M, 4380M.	
EV700-EV811	**Fairchild Argus I/II (C-61)**	**87(112)**
	EV700-EV724 not delivered, replaced by HM164-HM188. EV725-EV768 (44) Mk.I Model 24W-41 ex-USAAF 41-38789 to '38832; EV769-EV811 (43) Mk.II Model 24W-41A ex-USAAF 41-38833 to '38863 and 42-13572 to '13583. EV755, EV756, EV758, EV760, EV761, EV766 lost at sea en route. EV778 became 4766M.	
EV812-EW322	**Consolidated 32 Liberator B.VI/GR.VI (B-24)**	**411**
	Note B=B.VI bomber, C=cargo, GR=general reconnais- sance. EV812-EV817-B, EV818, EV819 GR, EV820 B, EV821 GR, EV822 B, EV824 GR, EV825, EV826 B, EV827 GR, EV828 B converted to GR & C, EV829-EV837 GR, EV838, EV839 B, EV840	

GR, EV841 B, EV842 GR, EV843-EV847 B, EV848
GR, EV849-EV852 B, EV853 GR, EV854, EV855 B,
EV856 GR, EV857 B, EV858 GR, EV859, EV860 B,
EV861 GR, EV862 B, EV863 GR, EV864, EV865 B,
EV866 GR, EV867, EV868 B, EV869 GR, EV870 B,
EV871-EV874 GR, EV875, EV876 B, EV877-EV899
GR of which EV879, EV880, EV886, EV888, EV890,
EV896, EV898 were converted to C, EV900-EV918 B,
EV919 GR, EV920-EV928 B, EV929 B converted to
C, EV930-EV932 B, EV933 GR, EV934 B, EV935,
EV936 GR, EV937, EV938 B, EV939 GR, EV940,
EV941 B, EV942 GR, EV943 GR converted to C,
EV944 B converted to C, EV945 GR, EV946 B,
EV947 GR, EV948 GR converted to C, EV949 B,
EV950 GR, EV951, EV952 B, EV953-EV956 GR,
EV957-EV961 B, EV962 B converted to C, EV963-
EV971 B, EV972 GR, EV973-EV979 B, EV980 B lost
en route, EV981-EV984 B, EV985 GR, EV986-EV988
GR converted to C, EV989-EV991 B, EV992 converted
to C, EV993 B, EV994 GR, EV995 GR converted to C,
EV996 GR, EV997, EV998 GR converted to C, EV999
B, EW100 GR converted to C, EW101-EW126 B, EW127-
EW137 GR, EW138-EW146 B, EW147 B converted to C,
EW148 B lost en route, EW149-EW207 B, EW208-EW218
GR, EW219-EW248 B, EW249 B converted to C, EW250
B, EW251, EW252 GR, EW253-EW275 B, EW276 B
converted to C, EW277-EW287 B, EW288-EW322 GR
of which EW290, EW297, EW310 were converted to C.
EW297 became 5737M. EW127-EW137, EW208-EW214,
EW216-EW218, EW251, EW252, EW270, EW281 were
diverted to RCAF.

EW341-EW610	**Fairchild Cornell I (PT-26-FA)**	**270**
	Ex-USAAF 44-19288 to '19557. Deliveries mainly to Canada, South Africa and Southern Rhodesia.	
EW611-EW634	**Consolidated Liberator C.VII (C-87-CF)**	**24**
	Ex-USAAF. EW611 (ex-44-39219) became G-AKAG; EW632 became 4956M.	
EW873-EW972	**Lockheed Hudson VI (A-28A)**	**100**
	Ex-USAAF 42-6582 to '6681. EW892, EW898 crashed in USA before delivery and EW949, EW950, EW952, EW953 were diverted to RNZAF.	
EW973-EW997	**Lockheed Lodestar IA/II**	**25**
	EW973-EW982 Mk.IA of which EW973-EW975 were retained in USA. EW983-EW997 Mk.II. EW976, EW977, EW980, EW982 became G-AGIN, 'AGIM, 'AGIG, 'AGJH.	
EW998	**North American NA-97 Mustang (A-36)**	**1**
	USAAF 42-83685 for evaluation as fighter bomber.	
EW999	**Douglas DC-4 Skymaster I (C-54B)**	**1**
	USAAF 43-17126 given for personal use of the Prime Minister.	
EX100-EZ799	**North American Harvard IIA/III (AT-6B/D) 1259(1600)**	
	EX100-EX846 Mk.IIA, EX847-EZ258 Mk.III, EZ259-EZ458 Mk.IIA. EZ459-EZ799 Mk.III cancelled. Many delivered direct to Middle East and African ports for the SAAF and SRAF. Numbers to Royal Navy including batches EZ400-EZ425, EZ427, EZ428. 94 shipped to RNZAF. EX684, EX697 became 6521M, 6522M. EX976 preserved.	
EZ800-EZ999	**Vultee V72 Vengeance I/IA (A-31)**	**200**
	Ex-USAAF 41-30848 to '31047. EZ800-EZ818 Mk.I, EZ819-EZ999 Mk.IA. EZ880-EZ888, EZ906-EZ974 not delivered and 84 offset to RAAF as A27-16 to A27-99. Of those reaching RAF main deliveries were to India.	
FA100-FA674	**Martin Baltimore IIIA/IV (A-30/A-30A)**	**575**
	Ex-USAAF 41-27682 to '28256. FA100-FA380 (281) Mk.IIIA, FA381-FA674 (294) Mk.IV. FA102-FA104, FA106, FA111, FA117, FA120, FA125, FA128, FA135, FA140, FA155, FA174, FA177, FA198, FA205, FA213, FA214, FA218, FA243, FA330, FA334, FA340, FA354, FA363, FA487 crashed before delivery. Transfers: FA385, FA435, FA466 to Royal Navy; FA415, FA420, FA432, FA439, FA464, FA472, FA503, FA504, FA553, FA560, FA592, FA607, FA640 to Italian AF. Main deliveries to Middle East, some issued to SAAF and R Hellenic AF squadrons under RAF command. FA309, FA373 became 4024M, 4217M.	
FA695-FA713	**Boeing 299P Fortress II (B-17F)**	**19**
	RAF use as GR.II.	

FB100-FB399	**North American NA-104/111 Mustang III**	**300**
	(P-51B/C). FB100-FB124 Mk.III (P-51B), FB125-FB399 Mk.IIIB (P-51C). FB205 crashed before delivery and FB235, FB237, FB238, FB240 were not delivered. Some issued to SAAF squadrons in Italy. FB360 became 5096M.	
FB400-FB522	**Martin Marauder II (B-26C-MO)**	**123**
	Main deliveries to Middle East. Some transferred to the SAAF. FB426, FB456 became 4385M, 4715M.	
FB523-FB845	**Stinson V-77 Reliant I (AT-19)**	**323**
	Main deliveries to Royal Navy. FB682 became G-AIYW.	
FB918-FD417	**Vultee Vengeance III/IV (A-31/A-35)**	**400**
	FB918-FD117 Mk.III, FD118-FD221 Mk.IV Srs I, FD222-FD417 Mk.IV Srs.II. FD122-FD124, FD126, FD128-FD130, FD134, FD137, FD159, FD167, FD180, FD184, FD187, FD188, FD190, FD193-FD196, FD200, FD201, FD204, FD207-FD209, FD212, FD213, FD215, FD217, FD220 retained by USAAF. FD288, FD307, FD339, FD381, FD415 crashed in USA before delivery. Mk.III mainly delivered to India and Mk.IV to UK where many were converted to TT. FD221, FD224, FD246, FD287, FD290, FD303, FD320, FD325, FD327, FD334, FD341, FD351, FD353, FD355, FD358, FD359, FD361, FD372, FD377, FD383, FD392, FD394, FD405 to RN.	
FD418-FD567	**North American NA-91 Mustang 1A (P-51)**	**150**
	Ex-USAAF 41-37320 to '37469. FD418-FD437, FD450-FD464, FD466-FD469, FD510-FD527 retained in USA. FD473 Malcolm hood trials.	
FD568-FD767	**Lockheed Ventura IIA (B-34)**	**200**
	C/n 4676-4875 ex-USAAF 41-38020 to '38219. 23 diverted to RNZAF others retained by USAAF.	
FD768-FD967	**Douglas DC-3 Dakota I/III (C-47/C-47A)**	**200**
	FD768-FD818 Mk.I ex-USAAF (except FD815-FD818 ex-US Navy R4D-1) of which FD769-FD771, FD773, FD777, FD796 became G-AGFX to 'AGFZ, 'AGGB, 'AGGA, 'AGGI of BOAC. FD819-FD967 Mk.III. FD906-FD908, FD956-FD958 diverted direct to SAAF and FD819, FD841, FD879, FD930 to RIAF. FD824, FD825, FD827, FD860-FD862, FD867, FD868, FD901, FD941, FD942 became G-AGHF, 'AGHH, 'AGHE, 'AGHK, 'AGHL, 'AGHP, 'AGHJ, 'AGHN, 'AGHM, 'AGHO, 'AGHU of BOAC. FD879 VIP version for C-in-C, Far East. FD772, FD826 became 5949M, 5351M.	
FD968-FD999	**Boeing-Stearman Kaydet I (PT-27)**	**32**
	For use at Flying Training Schools in Canada and USA.	
FE100-FE266	**DH.82C Tiger Moth**	**167**
	Canadian-built Lend/Lease funded as USAAF 42-964 to '1130 for Canadian training schools.	
FE267-FE999	**North American Harvard IIB (AT-16)**	**733**
	Built by Noorduyn in Canada. Initial deliveries to the RCAF and then main deliveries to India. Disposals to several air forces. FE882, FE883 were given incorrectly to FR882, FR883 Expeditors. FE866 became 6314M. FE992 preserved as G-BDAM.	
FF406-FF412	**Fairey Swordfish III**	**7**
	Origin not known.	
FF419-FG268	**Brewster Bermuda I (A-34/SB2A-1)**	**750**
	FF419-FF868 ex-USAAF A-34; FF869-FF999, FG100-FG268 ex-USN SB2A-1. Many conversions to TT.I of which FF457 was the prototype. Main deliveries to UK but no receipt records after FF633. FF423 became 3456M.	
FG857	**Douglas Dakota I**	**1**
	Origin unknown.	
FH100-FH166	**North American Harvard IIB (AT-16)**	**67**
	Built by Noorduyn in Canada. Ex-USAAF 42-12487 to '12553. Early deliveries to RAF, but later mainly diverted. FH107, FH115 became 4913M, 4927M.	
FH167-FH466	**Lockheed Hudson IIIA (A-29A)**	**300**
	Ex-USAAF 41-36968 to '37267. Diversions: FH169-FH174, FH176-FH199, FH200-FH214 to RAAF; FH175, FH215-FH226, FH320-FH328, FH389, FH391, FH393, FH396, FH401, FH402, FH405, FH408, FH412, FH413, FH415, FH432, FH434-FH441 to RNZAF; FH387, FH409, FH450 to Chinese AF; FH340, FH416 to RCAF. FH246, FH296, FH347, FH368, FH397 were lost before delivery. FH240 became 4257M.	
FH618-FH650	**DH.82C Tiger Moth (PT-24)**	**33**
	Canadian-built Lend/Lease funded USAAF 42-1131 to 42-1163.	

FH651-FH999	**Fairchild Cornell I (PT-26)**	**349**
	Ex-USAAF 42-14299 to '14498, 42-15330 to '15478. FH681, FH779, FH954 crashed before delivery. All to Canada except FH651, FH710-FH714, FH766-FH770.	
FJ100-FJ649	**Cessna Crane IA (AT-17A)**	**550**
	For EATS and renumbered in RCAF.	
FJ650-FJ700	**Fairchild Cornell I (PT-26)**	**51**
	Ex-USAAF 42-15479 to '15529 to Canada for EATS.	
FJ709-FJ712	**Douglas Dakota III (C-47A)**	**4**
FJ741-FK108	**Boeing Stearman Kaydet I (PT-27)**	**268**
	Ex-USAAF 42-15602 to '15869 for RCAF.	
FK109-FK160	**Martin Marauder I (B-26A)**	**52**
	FK109, FK111 to UK, rest direct to Middle East. FK113, FK114, FK125, FK129, FK140, FK146, FK158, lost in transit.	
FK161-FK183	**North American NA-62B Mitchell I (B-25B)**	**23**
	FK161, FK162, FK165 only to UK, FK168 retained in Canada. FK178 crashed before delivery, rest to 111 OTU, Nassau.	
FK184-FK213	**Boeing 299-O Fortress IIA (B-17E)**	**30**
	Mainly used as GR.II.	
FK214-FK245	**Consolidated 32 Liberator III (B-24D)**	**32**
	FK216 to RCAF, FK243 crashed in Canada before delivery. FK214, FK226 became 5256M, 5352M.	
FK246-FK312	**Lockheed Lodestar-II (C-60)**	**67**
	FK246 ex-42-32166 only delivered.	
FK313-FK361	**Fairchild 24W-41 Argus I (C-61)**	**49**
	C/n 322-370 ex-USAAF 42-32117 to '32165.	
FK362-FK380	**Martin Marauder IA (B-26B)**	**19**
	FK368, FK369, FK372, FK379, FK380 crashed before delivery. Rest initially to No.14 Squadron.	
FK381-FK813	**Lockheed Hudson VI/IIIA (A-28A/A-29A)**	**433**
	FK381-FK730 Mk.VI, FK731-FK813 Mk.IIIA ex-USAAF 42-46937 to '47369. FK393, FK404, FK413, FK499, FK533 lost before delivery, FK496 returned to USAAF, FK714 to Portuguese AF.	
FK814-FL163	**Stinson V-77 Reliant I**	**250**
	Ex-USAAF 43-43964 to '44213 mainly for Royal Navy.	
FL164-FL218	**North American NA-82 Mitchell II (B-25C)**	**55**
	FL209 crashed in transit in Canada. Delivered mainly direct to UK.	
FL219-FL448	**Curtiss Kittyhawk IIA (P-40F)**	**230**
	Offset from USAAF 41-13697 to '14599. FL273, FL369-FL448 returned to USAAF and FL230-FL232, FL235, FL236, FL239, FL240 lost at sea before delivery. FL263, FL270, FL276, FL280, FL282, FL305, FL307 to Free French AF. FL219, FL220 became 4333M and 4103M.	
FL449-FL464	**Boeing 299-O Fortress IIA (B-17E)**	**16**
	FL461 not received, otherwise all to GR.II standard.	
FL503-FL652	**Douglas DC-3 Dakota III (C-47A)**	**150**
	Main deliveries to RAF in India. Offsets: SAAF 18, to BOAC 16, RCAF 2, RAAF 1. Various postwar disposals. FL546, FL561, FL584 became 5749M, 6253M, 6410M.	
FL653-FL670	**Beech Traveller I (C-43)**	**18**
	Mainly to Middle East but FL659-FL670 were lost at sea en route.	
FL671-FL709	**North American NA-82 Mitchell II (B-25C)**	**39**
	FL709 became 4023M.	
FL710-FL730	**Curtiss Kittyhawk III (P-40M)**	**21**
	Offset from USAAF 43-5403 to '6002 allocation. Deliveries direct to Middle East autumn 1942.	
FL731-FL850	**Republic Thunderbolt I (P-47B)**	**120**
	Deliveries mainly direct to India. FL738 crashed in the USA.	
FL851-FL874	**North American NA-82 Mitchell II (B-25C)**	**24**
	Not delivered to RAF.	
FL875-FL905	**Curtiss Kittyhawk III (P-40M)**	**31**
	Deliveries to Middle East late 1942.	
FL906-FL995	**Consolidated 32 Liberator III/V**	**90**
	FL906-FL926 GR.III of which FL909, FL915, FL917, FL918, FL920 were temporarily registered G-AGFN, 'AGFO, 'AGFP, 'AGFR, 'AGFS and FL913 became 5249M; FL927/G GR.V became 4815M, FL928-FL936 GR.III, FL937, FL938 GR.V, FL939, FL940 GR.III, FL941 GR.V converted to C.V, FL942 GR.V, FL943 GR.III, FL944 GR.V, FL945 GR.III; FL946-FL991 GR.V of which FL970, FL979 were converted to C.V, FL992 GR.V converted to C.III. FL993-FL995 GR.III. FL934 became 5605M.	
FM100-FM229	**Avro 683 Lancaster X**	**130**
	Ordered from Victory Aircraft, Canada. Numbers converted for various duties postwar in the RCAF. Note this production followed on from KB700-KB999 batch. FM184-FM187 delivered as transports, rest to bomber standard. FM104, FM136, FM159, FM213 preserved in Canada.	
FM230-FM999	**Reservation for Canadian built aircraft**	**2**
	FM300 Lincoln XV and FM400 York only built. FM400 became G-ALBX.	
FN100-FN319	**Grumman Wildcat IV (F3F-4B)**	**220**
	For Royal Navy, Martlet IV renamed. FN109-FN111, FN205-FN207 lost at sea in transit. Main deliveries to UK but FN172-FN188 direct to Mombasa.	
FN320-FN449	**Grumman Hellcat I (F6F-3)**	**130**
	For Royal Navy, originally named Gannet.	
FN450-FN649	**Curtiss Seamew I (SO3C-2C)**	**200**
	For Royal Navy but record of FN453, FN463-FN467, FN472, FN483, FN489, FN573, FN608, FN622, FN631 only delivered.	
FN650-FN749	**Vought-Sikorsky Kingfisher I (OS2U-3)**	**100**
	For Royal Navy ex-US Navy 5811-5840 & 9513-9582. Deliveries in main to Middle East, West Africa and Jamaica.	
FN750-FN949	**Grumman Avenger I (TBF-1)**	**200**
	For Royal Navy ex-USN. Originally named Tarpon.	
FN956-FN999	**Lockheed Ventura V (PV-1)**	**44**
	Built by Vega Aircraft Corporation, ex-USN. FN965, FN967, FN968, FN972-FN974, FN977-FN979, FN987, FN991, FN992, FN995, FN996 retained in Canada or by US Navy.	
FP100-FP325	**Consolidated 28 Catalina IB (PBY-5B)**	**195(226)**
	Delivered to Scottish Aviation, Prestwick, then to Saunders-Roe at Beaumaris, for processing for the RAF. FP128, FP130, FP132, FP137, FP156-FP158, FP166-FP170, FP186-FP190, FP196-FP200, FP206-FP208, FP210, FP216-FP220 not delivered. FP135, FP138 lost in transit. FP221, FP244 became G-AGFL, 'AGFM of BOAC; FP164, FP222 became 3634M, 5023M. FP325 (lost on ops 21.9.42) duplicates Anson serial below.	
FP325-FP454	**Avro 652A Anson**	**130**
	Canadian-built for RCAF under EATS.	
FP455-FP469	**Grumman Widgeon I (J4F-2)**	**15**
	Ex-USN for Royal Navy in West Indies. Originally named Gosling.	
FP470-FP524	**Grumman Goose I/IA (JRF-5/6B)**	**55**
	FP470-FP474 Mk.I, FP475-FP524 (replacing BW778-BW827) Mk.IA. Main deliveries to Royal Navy at Piarco. Majority returned to US Navy postwar.	
FP525-FP536	**Consolidated 28 Catalina IIIA (PBY-5A)**	**12**
	FP534 transferred to US Navy in UK.	
FP537-FP684	**Lockheed Ventura V (PV-1)**	**148**
	90 only delivered and FP645, FP647 crashed before delivery.	
FP685	**Consolidated 32 Liberator II**	**1**
	Temporary loan of USAAF service aircraft.	
FP686	**Vultee V72 Vengeance**	**1**
	Delivered to RAF in India. Origin unknown.	
FP687-FP737	**Avro 652A Anson II**	**51**
	Canadian-built for EATS by National Steel Car and Victory Aircraft.	
FP738-FP747	**Grumman Goose I (JRF-5)**	**10**
	Record of FP740, FP742 only delivered to Miami.	
FP748-FP999	**Avro 652 Anson II**	**252**
	Canadian-built for EATS by de Havilland Canada and MacDonald Bros.	
FR111-FR140	**Curtiss Kittyhawk III (P-40M)**	**30**
	Deliveries to Middle East.	
FR141-FR209	**North American NA-82/96 Mitchell II (B-25C/G)**	**69**
	B-25C except FR208, FR209 B-25G. FR141-FR207 allotted for Dutch units under RAF but FR148 was lost in transit and FR153-FR155 were not delivered. Transfer to R Netherlands AF in 1947 concerned FR146, FR156, FR157, FR159-FR161, FR163, FR167-FR171, FR173, FR175, FR183, FR188, FR189, FR192-FR199, FR200, FR201, FR206. FR208, FR209 used by RAF for experimental work became 4823M, 6891M.	
FR210-FR361	**Curtiss Kittyhawk III (P-40M)**	**152**
	Main deliveries to Middle East.	
FR362-FR384	**North American NA-82 Mitchell II (B-25C)**	**23**
	North American (Inglewood) built. FR369 lost in transit.	

	Deliveries mainly to 111 OTU. FR370, FR373 became 5221M, 4604M.	
FR385-FR392	Curtiss Kittyhawk III (P-40M)	8
	Delivered to Middle East.	
FR393-FR397	North American NA-82 Mitchell II (B-25C)	5
	American (Inglewood) built. FR395 not delivered.	
FR401-FR404	Vultee V-74 Vigilant I (L-1)	4
	Ex-USAAF 40-262 to '265.	
FR405-FR406	Noorduyn Norseman	2
	Canadian aircraft for British use.	
FR408	Bell Kingcobra I (P-63A)	1
	Ex-USAAF 42-68937 to RAE for evaluation.	
FR409-FR411	North American Mustang V/IV/III (P-51F/G/B)	3
	FR409 Mk.V, FR410 Mk.IV, FR411 Mk.III.	
FR412-FR521	Curtiss Kittyhawk III (P-40M)	110
	FR460-FR471 diverted from RAF deliveries.	
FR556-FR778	Waco Hadrian I/II (CG-4A)	223
	FR556-FR580 Mk.I, FR581-FR778 Mk.II. FR580 to Canada. FR568, FR577 became 4200M, 5029M.	
FR779-FR872	Curtiss Kittyhawk III (P-40M)	94
	Mainly direct to Middle East.	
FR879-FR883	Beechcraft Navigator (AT-7B)	5
	FR880 became PB2 (Prince Bernhardt 2), FR881, FR882 to India. See FE882, FE883. For Royal Navy.	
FR884-FR885	Curtiss Kittyhawk IV (P-40N)	2
	Delivered October 1943.	
FR886-FR889	Piper Cub (L-4B)	(4)
	Renumbered HK936-HK939.	
FR890-FR939	North American NA-99 Mustang II (P-51A)	50
	FR901 had special LR tanks by Air Service Training.	
FR940-FR948	Beechcraft Expeditor I (C-45B)	9
	All to 32 Operational Training Unit, Canada.	
FS100-FS499	Curtiss Kittyhawk III/IV/II (P-40)	400
	FS100-FS269 Mk.III diverted to Russia, FS270-FS399 Mk.IV, FS400-FS499 Mk.II.	
FS500-FS660	Fairchild 24W-41A Argus II (UC-61A)	161
	C/n 381-541 ex-USAAF 43-14417 to 14577. FS513 to Yugoslav AF.	
FS661-FT460	North American Harvard IIB (AT-16)	700
	Built by Noorduyn in Canada. Ex-USAAF 43-12502 to '13201. Diversions to RIAF and FT140, FT147, FT227, FT236, FT241, FT243, FT253, FT307 temporarily to USAAF in UK. FS814, FS832, FS890, FS906, FT429 became 5208M, 5015M, 7554M, 6276M, 6530M. FT229 FT323, FT391 still exist as G-AZKI, 'AZSC, 'AZBN.	
FT461-FT535	Beechcraft Traveller I (GB2/UC-43)	75
	For Royal Navy ex-USN and USAAF.	
FT542-FT831	Fairchild M-62A-3 Cornell II (PT-26A)	290
	Fleet (Canadian) built in exchange for 286 PT-27 returned to USAAF. Originally USAAF 42-70957 to '71246.	
FT833-FT838	Sikorsky Hoverfly I (YR-4A/B)	7
	FT833, FT834 ex-YR-4A, FT835-FT839 ex-YR-4B all for Royal Navy.	
FT849-FT954	Curtiss Kittyhawk IV (P-40N)	106
	FT898-FT904 lost at sea in transit.	
FT955-FT974	North American Harvard III (AT-6D)	20
	Ex-USAAF 42-44538 to '44557 to Royal Navy.	
FT975-FT996	Beechcraft Expeditor I/II (C-45B/F)	22
	FT975-FT979 Mk.I, FT980-FT996 Mk.II all to RN.	
FT998-FT999	Consolidated Canso	2
	Built in Canada by Boeing Aircraft.	
FV100-FV899	Fairchild Cornell II (PT-26A)	800
	Built by Fleet in Canada. Deliveries mainly to Canada and India. FV661-FV734 taken over by RCAF.	
FV900-FW280	North American NA-82/87 Mitchell II (B-25D/C)	281
	FV900-FV939 ex-B-25D, FV940-FW280 B-25C. FW220, FW237, FW246, FW251, FW259, FW260, FW272-FW274, FW278-FW280 held for RCAF. FV925, FV931 became 4189M, 4858M.	
FW281-FW880	Martin Baltimore V (A-30A)	600
	FW288, FW323, FW337, FW409, FW511, FW664 crashed before delivery. All to RAF except FW326, FW352, FW356, FW365, FW456, FW527, FW746 later to Royal Navy. Transfers from RAF service to French, Italian and Turkish AFs.	
FW881-FX197	Fairchild Cornell II (PT-26A)	217
	Built by Fleet in Canada. Deliveries mainly to Canada and India.	
FX198-FX497	North American Harvard IIB (AT-16)	300
	Built by Noorduyn in Canada. Delivered from April	

	1944 mainly to UK. FX293, FX306, FX321 became 5770M, 5568M, 5771M.	
FX498-FX847	Curtiss Kittyhawk IV (P-40N)	350
	Late deliveries, many diversions.	
FX848-FZ197	North American Mustang III (P-51B/C)	250
	FX848-FX851, FX856, FX857, FX861, FX863, FX867-FX870, FX875, FX877, FX879, FX883, FX886, FX891, FX894, FX902, FX905-FX907, FX909-FX911, FX913-FX916, FX918, FX927, FX928, FX932, FX948 were handed back to USAAF on arrival in UK. FX992 crashed before delivery.	
FZ198-FZ427	Fairchild Cornell II (PT-26B)	230
	Ex-USAAF 43-36248 to '36447 built by Fleet in Canada mainly delivered to India.	
FZ428-FZ439	Beech Traveller I (C-43)	12
	Ex-USAAF 43-10870 to '10877, '10884 to '10887. FZ429 crashed in USA before delivery.	
FZ440	Bell Kingcobra (P-63A)	1
	USAAF 42-69423 for RAE evaluation.	
FZ441	Noorduyn Norseman (C-64)	1
	Built in Canada.	
FZ442-FZ443	Beech Traveller I (C-43)	2
	Ex-USAAF 43-10874, '10875.	
FZ548-FZ698	Douglas DC-3 Dakota (C-47A)	151
	Douglas Oklahoma and Long Beach-built. Offsets: RCAF 19, BOAC 12, SAAF 10, RAAF 1. Many to RIAF postwar. FZ601, FZ640, FZ660, FZ680 became 6299M, 6297M, 6291M, 6298M.	
FZ699-FZ718	Fairchild Cornell II (PT-26B)	20
	Ex-USAAF 43-36478 to '36497.	
FZ719-FZ828	Fairchild 24W-41A Argus II (UC-61A)	110
	Ex-USAAF 43-14695 to '14804 mainly delivered to Middle East and India.	
GA201-GA203	Bucker Bu 181	3
	Used semi-officially in 1945 on captured aircraft.	
GA831-GA838	Bucker Bu 181	8
	Used semi-officially in 1945 on captured aircraft.	
HB100-HB299	Beechcraft Expeditor I/II (C-45B/F)	200
	HB100-HB206 Mk.I, HB207-HB299 Mk.II. Some conversions to Mk.III for RCAF.	
HB300-HB550	Vultee V-72 Vengeance Mk.IV Srs II (A-35B)	251
	Numbers converted to TT.IV. For RAF and Royal Navy.	
HB551-HB758	Fairchild Argus II/III (UC-61A/K)	208
	C/n 788-996 less 881. HB551-HB643 (93) Mk.II ex-USAAF 43-14824 to '14916, HB644-HB758 (115) Mk.III ex-USAAF 43-14918 to '15032. HB751 currently G-BCBL.	
HB759	Beechcraft Expeditor	1
	No delivery record.	
HB760	Fairchild 24R Argus III (UC-61K)	1
	Ex-US 43-14917.	
HB761-HB820	Boeing 299 Fortress III (B-17G)	60
	HB761-HB790 B-17G-BO, HB791-HB820 B-17G-VE. HB761, HB764, HB766, HB770, HB771, HB781, HB783, HB784, HB794, HB797, HB798, HB804, HB806-HB814 diverted back, or retained by USAAF. HB778/G and HB796/G were specially equipped.	
HB821-HB961	North American NA-104 Mustang III (P-51C)	141
	Delivered from April 1944 except HB920 crashed before delivery. HB838 to USAAF. HB864 became 5062M.	
HB962-HD301	Republic Thunderbolt I/II (P-47D)	240
	HB962-HD181 (120) Mk.I, HD182-HD301 (120) Mk.II. Mainly delivered direct to India, but HD182 to UK.	
HD302-HD400	North American NA-87/108 Mitchell II/III (B-25D/J)	99
	HD302-HD345 Mk.II, HD346-HD400 Mk.III. HD310-HD315, HD317-HD320, HD322-HD326, HD331-HD335, HD337-HD345 retained in USAAF.	
HD402-HD751	Martin M-179 Marauder III (B-26F/G)	350
	HD402-HD601 ex-B-26F, HD602-HD751 ex-B-26G. Mostly delivered to Middle East except HD432, HD512, HD605, HD632, HD654, HD664, HD666 crashed en route.	
HD752-HD776	Beechcraft Expediter (C-45F)	25
	HD752-HD762, HD772-HD776 to Royal Navy.	

Mid-War Production and Acquisition

HD804 to JR999

Concurrent with the Lend/Lease allocation from ET100 was the allocation of numbers for orders placed by the Ministry of Aircraft Production from HD804 onwards. When HZ999 was reached, IA100 to IA999 was omitted and the follow-on started at 'JA'. The omissions in this series were 'JC', 'JE', 'JH', 'JI', 'JJ' and 'JO'. Impressments continued including gliders for the ATC.

Serial Nos	Aircraft Type and Remarks	Quantity
HD804-HD936	**Supermarine Walrus II** HD804-HD837, HD851-HD878, HD899-HD936 for Royal Navy in general but 44 to RAF. Built by Saro. HD909 to Canada.	100
HD942-HF606	**Vickers Wellington IC/III/X/XII/XIV** Built at Chester. HD942-HD991, HE101-HE134, HE146 (85) Mk.IC; HE147-HE184, HE197-HE244, HE258-HE306, HE318-HE353, HE365-HE398, HE410-HE447, HE459-HE508, HE513-HE556, HE568-HE615, HE627-HE667, HE679-HE715, HE727-HE772, HE784-HE833, HE845-HE873, HE898-HE931, HE946-HE995 Mk.X; HF112 Mk.III, HF113-HF120 Mk.XII; HF121-HF155, HF167-HF208, HF220-HF252, HF264-HF312, HF329-HF363, HF381-HF422, HF446-HF451 Mk.XIV; HF452-HF495, HF513-HF545, HF567-HF606 Mk.X. Mk.Xs produced as B.X of which HE214, HE910 converted to T.10 postwar. HE413, HE446 became 6213M, 6113M.	1124
HF609-HF816	**Vickers Wellington III/X/XI** Built at Blackpool. HF609-HF650, HF666-HF703, HF718-HF764, HF791-HF816 Mk.III, except HF614, HF622, HF626, HF630, HF634, HF638, HF642, HF646, HF650, HF669, HF723, HF726, HF729, HF732, HF735, HF739, HF743, HF747, HF751, HF755, HF759, HF763, HF793, HF797, HF808, HF811 Mk.X and HF720, HF803, HF804 Mk.XI. HF627, HF640, HF738 became 4772M, 4826M, 4714M.	153
HF828-HF922	**Vickers Wellington IC/VIII** Built at Weybridge. HF828-HF869, HF881-HF922 Mk.IC, except HF828, HF838, HF850, HF854, HF857, HF860, HF863, HF866, HF869, HF883, HF886, HF889, HF892, HF895, HF901, HF904, HF907, HF910, HF913, HF916, HF919, HF922 Mk.VIII. Variously fitted with Leigh Light and for TB. HF853 became 4168M.	84
HF938-HG633	**Vickers Warwick I/II/III** Built at Weybridge. HF938-HF982 ASR.I; HF983-HF987, HG114-HG123 ASR.VI; HG124-HG134 ASR.I; HG135-HG156, HG169-HG193, HG207-HG214 ASR.VI; HG215-HG256, HG271-HG307, HG320-HG340 C.III; HG341-HG345 GR.II Centaurus test-beds; HG346-HG365, HG384-HG414, HG435-HG459, HG476-HG512 GR.II; HG513-HG525, HG538, HG539 GR(MET).II. HG540-HG585, HG599-HG633 cancelled. HF939, HG137, HG149, HG152 became 5675M, 5774M, 4595M, 5068M.	359(440)
HG641	**Hawker Tornado** Prototype tested with Centaurus IV & IV engines.	1
HG644-HG732	**DH.89 Dominie** Built by Brush. HG644-HG674, HG689-HG732. Offsets: HG644-HG647, HG701-HG704 to Turkey; HG648, HG649, HG654-HG656, HG663, HG665, HG669, HG674 to RNZAF; HG659-HG661, HG666-HG668, HG693 to SRAF. Deliveries to RAF except for HG694, HG697, HG686, HG706, HG706, HG708, HG709, HG713-HG714, HG716, HG717, HG725-HG727 for Royal Navy. HG707, HG710, HG711 sold to Iran, HG695 to SAAF and HG699, HG720 to French AF.	75
HG736-HG989	**Airspeed AS.51 Horsa I** Built by Austin Motors: HG736-HG770, HG784-HG819, HG831-HG880, HG897-HG944, HG959-HG989. HG742, HG758, HG765, HG834 to USAAF. HG794, HG797, HG876, HG944, HG972 became 4702M, 4479M, 4740M, 3999M, 4965M.	200
HH109-HH919	**General Aircraft GAL.48 Hotspur II** Built by Harris Lebus assisted by William Lawrence & Co, Mulliners and Waring & Gillow. HH109-HH153, HH167-HH198, HH223-HH268, HH284-HH333, HH346-HH388, HH401-HH431, HH445-HH493, HH517-HH566, HH579-HH623, HH636-HH674, HH688-HH732, HH751-HH800, HH821-HH853, HH878-HH919. Conversions to Mk.III: HH143, HH175, HH180, HH190, HH228, HH231, HH261, HH294, HH313, HH323, HH326, HH330, HH373, HH406, HH457, HH518, HH526, HH529, HH536, HH555, HH565, HH610, HH620, HH691, HH694, HH698, HH704, HH723, HH724, HH754, HH767, HH773-HH776, HH781, HH783, HH784, HH786, HH789, HH835, HH838, HH889. Diversions to RCAF: HH418, HH419, HH421, HH425, HH427, HH521, HH551-HH553, HH557-HH562, HH564, HH579, HH580, HH646, HH647, HH654, HH667. HH118, HH147, HH242, HH264, HH404, HH412, HH588 became 3096M, 5107M, 3415M, 4000M, 6047M, 4093M, 3491M.	600
HH921-HH975	**General Aircraft GAL.49 Hamilcar I** HH921-HH930 built by GAL; HH931-HH935, HH957-HH975 built by group factories consisting of Birmingham Railway Carriage & Wagon Company, Co-operative Wholesale and AC Motors. HH967 became 5013M.	34
HH979	**Avro 641 Commodore** C/n 729 G-ACZB impressed in August 1941.	1
HH980	**Desoutter I** G-AATK impressed.	1
HH981	**DH.80A Puss Moth** G-ABEH impressed.	1
HH982-HH988	**Taylorcraft Plus C** G-AFVA, 'AFVZ, 'AFVY, 'AFVB, 'AFUD, 'AFTZ, 'AFUX impressed. HH983, HH988 were Plus C/1, all others had been converted to Plus C/2 before impressment. Postwar HH982, HH986, HH987 became G-AHAE, 'AHBO, 'AHLJ.	7
HJ108-HJ628	**DH.98 Mosquito** Ordered from de Havilland Canada and cancelled. HJ108-HJ149, HJ164-HJ201, HJ222-HJ270, HJ284-HJ317, HJ333-HJ378, HJ391-HJ422, HJ447-HJ491, HJ510-HJ557, HJ573-HJ628.	(390)
HJ642-HJ833	**DH.98 Mosquito II/VI** Built at Hatfield. HJ642-HJ661 NF.II, HJ662/G FB.VI prototype, HJ663-HJ682 FB.VI, HJ699-HJ715 NF.II; HJ716-HJ743, HJ755-HJ792, HJ808-HJ833 FB.VI except HJ732 FB.XVIII prototype. HJ667, HJ680, HJ681, HJ718, HJ720, HJ721, HJ723, HJ792 temporarily registered G-AGKO, 'AGGC to 'AGGH, 'AGKR. HJ657, HJ732 became 4495M, 5755M. HJ711 currently preserved.	150
HJ851-HK536	**DH.98 Mosquito II/III/XII/XIII/XVII** Built at Leavesden. HJ851-HJ899 T.III, HJ911-HJ944 NF.II, HJ945, HJ946, NF.XII, HJ958-HJ999 T.III. HK107-HK141, HK159-HK204, HK222-HK236 built as NF.II and delivered to Marshall's, Cambridge, for conversion to NF.XII. HK237-HK265, HK278-HK327, HK344-HK362 NF.XVII, HK363-HK382, HK396-HK437, HK453-HK481, HK499-HK536 NF.XIII of which HK535, HK536 were renumbered SM700, SM701. HJ888, HJ938 became 6954M, 5911M. HK232, HK241, HK301, HK313, HK413 became 5255M, 5694M, 5695M, 5296M, 4857M.	450
HK535-HK806	**Avro 683 Lancaster I** Built by Vickers Armstrong at Castle Bromwich. HK535-HK579, HK593-HK628, HK644-HK666, HK679-HK710, HK728-HK773, HK787-HK806. HK541 fitted with LR saddle tank. HK647, HK710 became 5713M, 6234M and HK557 became G-AKAJ.	200
HK811-HK817	**DH.82 Tiger Moth** Impressed in India.	7
HK818	**DH.60 Gipsy Moth** Impressed in India.	1
HK820-HK821	**Douglas DC-2** Impressed in Middle East.	2
HK822	**Grumman G.21A Goose** G-AFKJ presented. Transferred to RAAF.	1
HK823	**Curtiss Mohawk** Believed ex-French.	1

HK827	Junkers Ju87B-1	1
	Captured in Middle East.	
HK828-HK831	DH.86	4
	SU-ACR, G-ACWD, 'ADUI, 'ADUG impressed in the Middle East.	
HK832	Fairchild 91	1
HK833-HK835	Avro Tutor	3
	Impressed in Middle East.	
HK836	Martin Maryland	1
	Origin unknown.	
HK837	Douglas DC-2	1
	Acquired from the USA.	
HK838	Percival Q.6	1
	C/n Q.37 G-AFMV impressed.	
HK839	DH.60 Moth Major	1
	Impressed in Middle East.	
HK843	DH.86B	1
	G-AEAP impressed in Middle East.	
HK844	DH.86 prototype	1
	G-ACPL impressed in Middle East.	
HK845	Martin 167 Maryland	1
	Ex-Vichy aircraft.	
HK846	Messerschmitt Bf 110	1
	Captured enemy aircraft.	
HK847	Douglas DC-2	1
	Ex-NC14280.	
HK848	Savoia S.79	1
	Captured enemy aircraft.	
HK849	Messerschmitt Bf109F	1
	Ex-enemy aircraft.	
HK850	Convair Catalina	1
	Ex-Russian GST.	
HK851-HK852	Lockheed Lodestar	2
	HK851 ex 41-29635. Temporarily G-AGEH.	
HK853	Avro Tutor	1
	Impressed in Middle East.	
HK854	Supermarine Spitfire I	(1)
	Taken on charge in Middle East.	
HK855	Lockheed 18-07 Lodestar	1
	G-AGIL impressed.	
HK859	Caproni Ca101	1
	Captured Italian aircraft.	
HK860	Saiman C.202	1
	Impressed Italian aircraft.	
HK861	DH.80A Puss Moth	1
	G-ABTD impressed in Middle East.	
HK862	DH.89A Rapide	1
	G-AFFC impressed.	
HK863	Miles Hawk	1
	SU-AAP impressed.	
HK864	DH.89A Rapide	1
	G-AFEN impressed.	
HK866	DH.80A Puss Moth	1
	G-AARF purchased by AHQ Iraq.	
HK867	Douglas DC-2	1
	Impressed in Middle East.	
HK868	Short S.22 Scion Senior	1
	C/n S.834 G-AECU of Iraq Petroleum Transport impressed.	
HK869-HK892	Douglas Boston III (non-standard)	24
	Released by Russian Commission at Abadan for use in Western Desert in exchange for Spitfires.	
HK893	Douglas DC-3 Dakota	1
	Origin unknown.	
HK894-HK903	Douglas Boston III (non-standard)	10
	See HK869-HK892.	
HK904-HK910	DH.60T Moth	7
	Ex-Iraq Air Force.	
HK912	Douglas Boston III	1
	Ex-Russian Commission.	
HK913	Percival Q.6	1
	Ex-Iraqi YI-ROI.	
HK914	Caproni	1
	Presumed captured.	
HK915-HK917	DH.89A Rapide	3
	EP-AAA to EP-AAC impressed.	
HK918	Douglas Boston III	1
	To Royal Navy.	
HK919-HK920	Junkers Ju52/3m	2
	Ex-enemy aircraft.	

HK921-HK924	Douglas Boston III	4
	Ex-Russian Commission.	
HK925-HK930	Vultee Vigilant	6
	Ex-USAAF.	
HK931	Fairey Battle	1
	Believed ex-R Hellenic AF.	
HK934-HK935	Douglas Boston III	2
	Presumed ex-Russian Commission.	
HK936-HK939	Piper Cub	4
	Ex-USAAF L-4B for evaluation. Ex-FR886-FR889.	
HK940	Fiat G.12	1
	Captured Italian aircraft.	
HK944-HK947	North American Mustang	4
	Ex-USAAF 12th AF.	
HK948-HK949	Fairchild Argus	2
	Acquired in Middle East	
HK955-HK956	North American Mustang	2
	Ex-USAAF 12th AF.	
HK959	Junkers Ju88D	1
	C/n 430650 acquired in Cyprus. Preserved in the USA.	
HK960-HK972	Douglas Boston III	13
	Ex-Russian Commission.	
HK973	Lockheed 18-07 Lodestar	1
	G-AGBO impressed.	
HK974-HK975	Lockheed 18-08 Lodestar	(2)
	G-AGCT (ex-AX722), G-AGCW (ex-AX719) impressed.	
HK976	Cant Z.501	1
	Ex-Italian AF 147/11.	
HK977-HK979	Cant Z.506B	3
	Ex-Italian.	
HK980	Lockheed 18-07 Lodestar	1
	G-AGBP impressed.	
HK981	Lockheed 18-08 Lodestar	1
	G-AGCX impressed.	
HK982	Lockheed 14-WF62	1
	G-AFKE transferred to RAF; became VF247.	
HK983	Douglas DC-2	1
	Built from spares for use of Sir Keith Park.	
HK984	Lockheed 14-WF62	1
	Allotted for G-AFMR. Became VF251.	
HK986-HK987	Fieseler Fi156 Storch	2
	Ex-enemy aircraft.	
HK990	Lockheed 18	1
	Impressed.	
HK993	Douglas DC-2	1
	VT-CLE impressed.	
HL429-HL432	Vultee Vigilant (L-1)	4
	Origin unknown.	
HL530-HL531	Piper J-4A Cub	2
	EI-ABZ, G-AFTD impressed.	
HL532-HL536	Taylorcraft Plus C/2	5
	G-AFVW, 'AFTO, 'AFUB, 'AFTN, 'AFTY impressed.	
HL537	DH.80A Puss Moth	1
	G-AAZP impressed.	
HL538	Miles M.2H Hawk Major	1
	G-AEGE impressed.	
HL539	General Aircraft GAL.42 Cygnet II	1
	G-AFVR impressed.	
HL544-HM157	Hawker Hurricane IIB/IIC	388
	HL544-HL591, HL603-HL634, HL654-HL683, HL698-HL747, HL767-HL809, HL828-HL867, HL879-HL913, HL925-HL941, HL953-HL997, HM110-HM157 built as 223 Mk.IIC, 116 Mk.IIB fighters and 49 Mk.IIB bombers. HL545, HL546, HL549-HL559, HL561, HL563, HL660, HL728, HL992 shipped to Russia; HL547, HL679, HL892, HL893 to SAAF and HL625, HL681, HL736 to Turkish AF. HL673, HL677 to Sea Hurricane.	
HM159-HM160	Fokker F.XXII	2
	G-AFXR, 'AFZP impressed.	
HM161	Fokker F.XXXVI	1
	G-AFZR impressed.	
HM164-HM188	Fairchild 24W Argus I (C-61)	25
	C/n 208-232 ex-USAAF 41-38764 to '38788, replacement for EV700-EV724 for RAF and ATA. HM172 loaned back to the USAAF.	
HM279-HM485	Percival P.34 Proctor III	162
	Built by F.Hills & Sons, HM279-HM324, HM337-HM373, HM390-HM433, HM451-HM485. HM337, HM340, HM345, HM352, HM361, HM362, HM368, HM397, HM427, HM452, HM476, HM478, HM480 became 6339M,	

6711M, 7031M, 6909M, 5285M, 6668M, 6691M, 6734M, 6928M, 6280M, 6700M, 6771M, 7032M. Several to the civil register postwar including HM354 currently G-ANPP.

HM494	**Tipsy B.2**	1
	Belgian built. G-AGBM ex- F-0222 impressed.	
HM495	**General Aircraft GAL.42 Cygnet II**	1
	G-AGBA impressed.	
HM496	**Miles M.3A Falcon Major**	1
	G-ADFH impressed.	
HM497	**Wicko GM.1 Warferry**	1
	Impressed. Became G-AGPE.	
HM498	**DH.87 Hornet Moth**	1
	OY-DOK escaped from Denmark.	
HM499	**Wicko GM.1 Warferry**	1
	G-AFVK impressed, became 4962M.	
HM500	**British Aircraft Eagle 2**	1
	G-ADID impressed.	
HM501	**Taylorcraft Plus C/2**	1
	G-AFVX impressed, became 3775M.	
HM502	**Cessna C.34 Airmaster**	1
	G-AEAI impressed.	
HM503	**Miles M.12 Mohawk**	1
	G-AEKW impressed.	
HM504-HM505	**Avro 621 Tutor**	2
	G-ABIR, 'ABIS impressed.	
HM506	**British Aircraft Eagle 2**	1
	G-AEGO impressed.	
HM507-HM508	**Desoutter II/I**	2
	G-AAZI, 'AANB impressed.	
HM509	**Junkers Ju88A-5**	1
	C/n 6073 M2+MK of Luftwaffe landed in error at Chivenor, 26.11.41.	
HM510	**Slingsby T.8 Kirby Tutor**	1
	Impressed for ATC.	
HM511	**Scott Primary**	1
	Impressed for ATC.	
HM512	**Slingsby T.2 Primary**	1
	Impressed for ATC.	
HM513	**Dagling Primary**	1
	Built by R. F. Dagnell, for ATC.	
HM514-HM515	**Slingsby T.2 Primary**	2
	Impressed for ATC.	
HM516	**Scott Nacelled Primary**	1
	Impressed for ATC.	
HM517	**Slingsby T.2 Nacelled Primary**	1
	Impressed for ATC.	
HM518	**Zander & Scott Nacelled Primary**	1
	Impressed for ATC.	
HM519-HM533	**Slingsby gliders**	14
	HM519, HM520, HM528-HM533 T.2 Primary; HM522-HM524, HM527 T.7 Kirby Cadet; HM525, HM526 T.8 Kirby Tutor.	
HM534	**DH.80A Puss Moth**	1
	US Navy 8877 used by US Naval Attache London, acquired by RAF. Became G-AHLO.	
HM535	**Zander & Scott Nacelled Primary**	1
	Impressed for ATC.	
HM536	**Kassel Zogling**	1
	Impressed for ATC.	
HM537	**Nacelled primary glider, type unknown**	1
	Impressed.	
HM538	**Kassel Prufling**	1
	Impressed for ATC.	
HM539	**Slingsby T.7 Kirby Cadet**	1
	Impressed for ATC.	
HM540-HM541	**Primary glider types unknown.**	2
	Impressed for ATC.	
HM542	**Slingsby T.8 Kirby Tutor**	1
	BGA294 impressed for ATC.	
HM543	**Slingsby T.7 Kirby Cadet**	1
	Impressed for ATC.	
HM544	**DH.94 Moth Minor**	1
	G-AFPO impressed.	
HM545	**Miles M.18 Mk.II**	1
	Ex- U-8 and U-0224 acquired by RAF, became G-AHKY.	
HM546-HM559	**Slingsby gliders impressed for ATC**	14
	HM546, HM547, HM549, HM551, HM553, HM555-HM557, HM559 T.2 Primary; HM548, HM554 T.2 Nacelled Primary, HM550, HM552 T.7 Kirby Cadet; HM558 T.8 Kirby Tutor.	
HM560	**Desoutter I**	1
	G-ABMW impressed.	
HM561-HM564	**Slingsby T.2 Primary**	1
	Gliders impressed for ATC.	
HM565	**Piper J-4A Cub Coupé**	1
	G-AFSY impressed.	
HM566-HM568	**Slingsby T.4 Falcon III**	3
	Impressed for ATC.	
HM569	**DH.84 Dragon II**	1
	G-ADOS impressed.	
HM570	**Avro 638 Club Cadet**	1
	G-ACHP impressed.	
HM571	**BAC VII**	1
	Tandem type glider impressed for ATC.	
HM572	**Weltensegler Hols-der-Teufel**	1
	Glider for ATC.	
HM573	**Lockheed 12A**	1
	G-AGDT impressed.	
HM574	**Wicko GM.1 Warferry**	1
	G-AFKS impressed.	
HM575	**Slingsby T.7 Kirby Cadet**	1
	Impressed for ATC.	
HM576	**Slingsby T.1 Falcon I**	1
	Impressed for ATC.	
HM577	**Weltensegler Hols-der-Teufel**	1
	Glider for ATC.	
HM578	**Slingsby T.1 Falcon**	1
	Glider impressed for ATC.	
HM579	**DH.94 Moth Minor**	1
	G-AFRR impressed. Currently flying in California.	
HM580-HM581	**Cierva C.30A**	2
	G-ACUU, 'ACUI impressed.	
HM582	**DH.60X Moth**	1
	G-ACXF impressed.	
HM583	**Miles M.28/1**	1
	Ex- U-0237 impressed. Became G-AJVX.	
HM584-HM585	**DH.94 Moth Minor**	2
	G-AFPL, 'AFTH impressed.	
HM586	**Kassel sailplane**	1
	Impressed for ATC.	
HM587	**Schneider Grunau Baby**	1
	Impressed for ATC.	
HM588-HM589	**Primary gliders**	2
	Impressed for ATC.	
HM590	**Secondary glider**	1
	Impressed for ATC.	
HM591	**Slingsby T.12 Gull I**	1
	Impressed for ATC.	
HM592	**Slingsby T.14 Gull II**	1
	Impressed for ATC.	
HM593	**Stinson SR-8 Reliant**	1
	G-AEOR impressed.	
HM595 & HM599	**Hawker Tempest**	2
	Prototypes to Spec F10/41. HM595 Mk.V/VI became 5940M, HM599 Mk.I became 6442M.	
HM603-HN212	**Airspeed AS.10 Oxford I**	375
	Built by Percival. HM603-HM650, HM666-HM700, HM721-HM767, HM783-HM813, HM827-HM875, HM889-HM918, HM945-HM990, HN111-HN149, HN163-HN212. HM604, HM616, HM647, HM742, HM759, HM796, HM809, HM837, HM906, HM955, HN122, HN146, HN170 became 6535M, 5440M, 5478M, 6884M, 6244M, 6159M, 6895M, 6536M, 5353M, 6470M, 4879M, 5946M, 5441M. Wartime transfers: HM607, HM611, HM613, HM621, HM634, HM688, HM746, HM951, HM989, HN126, HN127 to Royal Navy and HM635, HM788 to USAAF. Postwar transfers: HM856, HN120 to Belgian AF; HM686, HM909, HM957, HM958, HN188, HN193, HN198 to R Danish AF; HN123, HN194, HN195 to R Hellenic AF and HM735, HM754, HM798, HN131, HN182 to R Netherlands AF.	
HN217-HN855	**Airspeed AS.10 Oxford I/V**	450
	Built at Portsmouth. HN217-HN239, HN254-HN284, HN298-HN346, HN363-HN386, HN405-HN441, HN467-HN495, HN513-HN554, HN576-HN614, HN631-HN671, HN689-HN738, HN754-HN790, HN808-HN855 Mk.I except HN217, HN235-HN237, HN306, HN340, HN341, HN343, HN346, HN367, HN384, HN533, HN542, HN549, HN551, HN602, HN605, HN790 Mk.V. A quarter of deliveries shipped to EATS. HN422, HN514,	

HN704, HN706, HN776, HN827, HN849 became 6285M, 5327M, 6286M, 5456M, 6189M, 6267M, 5638M. HN554, HN579 trans to USAAF. Postwar sales: HN526/709 to R Danish AF, HN691/771/826 to R. Netherlands AF.

HN861-HP528   **Miles M.25 Martinet TT.1**   **400**
Built by Phillips & Powis at Reading. HN861-894, HN907-916, HN938-984, HP114-149, HP163-183, HP199-227, HP241-288, HP303-335, HP348-393, HP405-448, HP464-496, HP510-528 of which HN909/945, HP222, HP272/310 were converted to Queen Martinet. HP249, HP255, HP495 became 5796M, 5777M, 6009M.

HP531-HP843   **Commonwealth Aircraft Corp. CA-1 Wirraway**   **(245)**
Reservation. HP531-HP568, HP584-HP627, HP645-673, HP687-HP736, HP749-HP784 and HP796-HP843.

HP848-HR648   **DH.98 Mosquito FB.VI**   **500**
Rolls-Royce Merlin 23/25. Built by Standard Motors. HP848-HP888, HP904-HP942, HP967-HP989, HR113-HR162, HR175-HR220, HR236-HR262, HR279-HR312, HR331-HR375, HR387-HR415, HR432-HR465, HR485-HR527, HR539-HR580, HR603-HR648. HP925, HR113, HR132, HR155, HR175, HR185, HR249, HR252, HR349 became 6030M, 6524M, 5534M, 5956M, 6709M, 5030M, 5796M, 6854M, 6549M.

HR654-HR988   **Handley Page HP.59 Halifax II**   **250**
HR654-HR699, HR711-HR758, HR773-HR819, HR832-HR880, HR905-HR952, HR977-HR988. HR845, HR909 fitted with experimental turrets. HR855 became 4876M.

HS101-HS150   **Airspeed AS.51 Horsa I**   **50**
HS110, HS119, HS138, HS139, HS147 shipped to the USA 1943. See 4510M, 4701M, 5215M.

HS154-HS678   **Fairey Swordfish II**   **400**
Built by Blackburn. HS154-HS196, HS208-HS231, HS254-HS299, HS312-HS346, HS361-HS410, HS424-HS471, HS484-HS519, HS533-HS561, HS579-HS625, HS637-HS678. HS618 became A2001 and is preserved having been painted as W5984 to represent Lt Cdr E. Esmonde's aircraft in which he won the VC. HS504, HS517, HS554 currently preserved.

HT525-HV162   **Airspeed Horsa**   **(400)**
Cancelled order. HT525-HT562, HT577-HT621, HT645-HT694, HT712-HT748, HT769-HT812, HT830-HT878, HT896-HT933, HT948-HT996, HV113-HV162.

HV266 &   **Hawker P.1005**   **(2)**
HV270   Prototypes to Spec B11/40 ordered, but cancelled.

HV275-HW881   **Hawker Hurricane IIB/IIC/IID**   **1000**
HV275-HV317, HV333-HV370, HV396-HV445, HV468-HV516, HV534-HV560, HV577-HV612, HV634-HV674, HV696-HV745, HV768-HV799, HV815-HV858, HV873-HV921, HV943-HV989, HW115-HW146, HW167-HW207, HW229-HW278, HW291-HW323, HW345-HW373, HW399-HW444, HW467-HW501, HW533-HW572, HW596-HW624, HW651-HW686, HW713-HW757, HW779-HW808, HW834-HW881 produced as IIB/IIC fighters or bombers or IIDs except HW683, HW747 built as Mk.IV. Offsets to SAAF, Turkish Air Force and shipments to Russia. HV745, HW683, HW685, HW714-HW718, HW723, HW728, HW729, HW731 became 4094M, 4617M, 5344M, 4611M-4613M, 4610M, 4614M, 4615M, 4609M, 4607M, 4616M.

HX147-HX357   **Handley Page Halifax II/III**   **150**
HX147-HX191, HX222-HX225 Mk.II; HX226-HX247, HX265-HX296, HX311-HX357 Mk.III. HX226, HX227, HX315 became 4961M, 4827M, 4941M.

HX360   **Junkers Ju 88A-5**   **1**
C/n 6214, V4+GS of Luftwaffe landed at Steeple Morden on 16.2.41.

HX364-HX786   **Vickers Wellington IC/VIII**   **300**
Built at Weybridge. HX364-HX403, HX417-HX452, HX466-HX489, HX504-HX538, HX558-HX606, HX625-HX656, HX670-HX690, HX709-HX751, HX767-HX786, produced as Mk.VIII except HX364-HX371, HX373-HX375, HX377, HX378, HX380, HX382, HX384, HX385, HX387, HX389, HX390, HX392, HX393, HX395, HX397, HX399, HX400, HX402, HX417, HX421, HX423, HX425, HX429, HX431, HX433, HX435, HX438, HX440, HX442, HX445, HX446, HX447, HX449, HX451, HX468, HX470, HX472, HX475, HX478, HX480, HX483, HX484, HX486-HX488, HX506, HX508, HX510, HX514, HX516, HX518, HX521, HX523, HX525, HX527, HX529,

HX533, HX536, HX558, HX560, HX564, HX567, HX569, HX571, HX573, HX577, HX580, HX583, HX585, HX589, HX591, HX594, HX597, HX601, HX603, HX606, HX627, HX631, HX633, HX635, HX637, HX639, HX643, HX645, HX648, HX651, HX655, HX670, HX673, HX676, HX680, HX682, HX685, HX688, HX710, HX712, HX714, HX716, HX718, HX722, HX724, HX727, HX730, HX734, HX736, HX739, HX742, HX746, HX748, HX750, HX767, HX773, HX775, HX778, HX781, HX785 Mk.IC. Some fitted with Leigh Lights and others produced as torpedo bombers. Deliveries mainly to the Middle East. HX531, HX629 became 4224M, 4129M.

HX789   **DH.86**   **1**
VT-AKM impressed in India.

HX790-HX791   **DH.89A Rapide**   **2**
VT-AJB, VT-ALO impressed in India.

HX792   **DH.90 Dragonfly**   **1**
VT-AIE loaned to RAF by HEH The Nizam of Hyderabad.

HX793   **Lockheed 18**   **1**
VT-AAM impressed in India.

HX794   **Percival P.3 Gull Six**   **1**
VT-AGY ex-G-ACYS impressed in India.

HX795-HX797   **DH.94 Moth Minor**   **3**
VT-ALI, 'AMD, 'AME impressed in India.

HX798   **Lockheed 12A**   **1**
VT-AMB ex- G-AFXP loaned by the Maharajah of Jaipur.

HX802-HX984   **DH.98 Mosquito FB.VI/FB.XVIII**   **130**
Built at Hatfield. HX802-HX835, HX849-HX869, HX896-HX922, HX937-HX984 FB.VI except HX902-HX904 FB.XVIII. HX849, HX850 not delivered. HX902/G had special equipment.

HZ102-JA645   **Vickers Wellington III/X/XI/XIII**   **850**
Built at Blackpool. HZ102-HZ150, HZ173-HZ209, HZ242-HZ250 produced as Mks.III, X or XI; HZ251-HZ284, HZ299-HZ315, HZ351-HZ378, HZ394-HZ439, HZ467-HZ489, HZ513-HZ550 as Mks.X or XI; HZ551 Mk.XIII; HZ552, HZ570-HZ572 Mk.X; HZ573-HZ578 Mk.XIII; HZ582 Mk.X; HZ583-HZ604, HZ633-HZ660, HZ689-HZ712 Mk.XIII; HZ713-HZ720 Mk.X; HZ721-HZ727, HZ752-HZ770, HZ793-HZ808 Mk.XIII; HZ809-HZ818 Mk.X; HZ819, HZ820, HZ862-HZ897, HZ937-HZ940 Mk.XIII; HZ941-HZ950 Mk.X; HZ951-HZ981, JA104-JA110 Mk.XIII; JA111-JA140 Mk.X; JA141-JA151, JA176-JA184 Mk.XIII; JA185-JA194 Mk.X; JA195-JA210 Mk.XIII; JA258-JA260 Mk.X; JA261-JA273, JA295-JA318, JA337-JA340 Mk.XIII; JA341-JA352 Mk.X; JA353-JA363, JA378-JA426, JA442-JA447 Mk.XIII; JA448-JA481, JA497-JA513 Mk.X; JA514-JA518 Mk.XIII; JA519-JA534 Mk.X; JA535-JA539, JA561-JA585, JA618-JA645 Mk.XII. The Mk.Xs were produced as B.X but postwar HZ472 and JA532 were converted to T.10. HZ107, HZ375, HZ428, HZ762 became 4979M, 4907M, 4966M, 5598M. HZ806 postwar to the French Air Force.

JA672-JB748   **Avro 683 Lancaster III**   **550**
Built at Manchester. JA672-JA718, JA843-JA876, JA892-JA941, JA957-JA981, JB113-JB155, JB174-JB191, JB216-JB243, JB275-JB320, JB344-JB376, JB398-JB424, JB453-JB488, JB526-JB567, JB592-JB614, JB637-JB684, JB699-JB748. Merlin 25 engines fitted in early production, 28 or 38 mid-production and 38 only late production. Conversions: JB127 to Mk.I; JB675, JB713 to Mk.VI. JB683/G and JB720/G were specially equipped. JB240 crashed on delivery. JA677, JA693, JA699, JA938, JA959, JB138, JB404, JB456, JB457, JB555, JB643 became 5294M, 5293M, 4313M, 5603M, 5925M, 5224M, 5292M, 5338M, 5533M, 4970M, 5945M.

JB781-JD476   **Handley Page HP.59 Halifax II**   **350**
Built by English Electric. JB781-JB806, JB834-JB875, JB892-JB931, JB956-JB974, JD105-JD128, JD143-JD180, JD198-JD218, JD244-JD278, JD296-JD333, JD361-JD386, JD405-JD421, JD453-JD476. JD212 used for RP experiments and JD300 fitted with 0.5-in ventral gun position. JB899 became 4910M.

JF274-JG695   **Supermarine Spitfire Mk.VIII (F, LF or HF as given)**   **800**
Built by Vickers Armstrong (Supermarine complex). JF274-JF300 F; JF316-JF321 converted to Mk.XIV; JF322-JF327 F; JF328 HF; JF329-JF364, JF392-JF427,

JF443-JF461 F; JF462 LF; JF463-JF485, JF501, JF502
F; JF503, JF504 LF; JF505-JF513 F; JF514, JF515 LF;
JF516-JF528, JF557-JF592, JF613-JF630, JF658-JF676,
JF692-JF716 F; JF740-JF789, JF805-JF850, JF869-
JF893 LF; JF894-JF899 F; JF900-JF902, JF926-JF967,
JG104-JG124, JG157-JG159 LF; JG160 F; JG161 LF;
JG162 F; JG163-JG165 LF; JG166 F; JG167-JG204,
JG239-JG275, JG312-JG356, JG371-JG387, JG404-
JG432, JG465-JG500, JG527-JG568, JG603-JG624,
JG646-JG695 LF. JF477 crashed on test and was not
delivered. JG204 experimentally fitted with special
wings. Deliveries mainly overseas including Australia
and India. JF275, JF296, JG661-JG663 became 4831M,
5835M, 5832M-5834M. 135 aircraft re-numbered in
RAAF A58 series.

| JG713-JL395 | Supermarine Spitfire VC/IX | 989 |

Built by Vickers Armstrong (Castle Bromwich). JG713-
JG752, JG769-JG810, JG835-JG852, JG864-JG899,
JG912-JG960, JK101-JK145, JK159-JK195, JK214-
JK236, JK249-JK285, JK303-JK346, JK359-JK408,
JK425-JK472, JK506-JK551, JK600-JK620, JK637-
JK678, JK705-JK742, JK756-JK796, JK803-JK842,
JK860-JK892, JK922-JK950, JK967-JK992, JL104-
JL140, JL159-JL188, JL208-JL256, JL301-JL338,
JL346-JL395. Known conversions to F or LF.IX on
production or in service were: JG722, JG739, JK429,
JK463, JK535, JK611, JK620, JK641, JK659, JK668,
JK762, JK769, JK770, JK795, JK796, JK840, JK860,
JK880-JK884, JK949, JK979, JK980, JL106-JL111,
JL134-JL138, JL159, JL163, JL165, JL172, JL177-
JL180, JL217, JL223, JL226-JL230, JL239, JL252-
JL256, JL347, JL349, JL351, JL353, JL354, JL356,
JL359, JL361, JL364, JL366, JL369, JL370, JL372,
JL373, JL375-JL377, JL383-JL385, JL395. JK535 and
JL347 used in contra-rotating propeller experiments.
Deliveries to Gibraltar, North-West Africa and Middle
East. JK163, JK547, JL112, JL373 became 4391M,
4708M, 4390M, 4267M.

| JL421-JM417 | Bristol 156 Beaufighter VIC/X/XI | 546 |

Built at Weston. JL421-JL454, JL502-JL549, JL565-
JL593, JL610-JL659, JL704-JL735, JL756-JL779,
JL812-JL855, JL869-JL875 Mk.VIC of which JL583,
JL593, JL610-JL618, JL629-JL638, JL649-JL658,
JL713-JL722, JL827-JL835 were Interim TF version;
JL876-JL915, JL937-JL948 Mk.XI; JL949-JL957,
JM104 Mk.VI Interim TF; JM105-JM136, JM158-JM185,
JM206-JM250, JM262-JM267 Mk.XI; JM268-JM291,
JM315-JM356, JM379-JM417 Mk.X. 42 of all three
marks, delivered to Australia and renumbered in RAAF
A19 series. JL657, JM209, JM416, JM331, JM335
became 4919M, 5888M, 4213M, 5886M, 5885M.

| JM431-JM593 | Bristol 152 Beaufort I | 111 |

JM431-JM470, JM496-JM517, JM545-JM593. Some
transfers to Royal Navy.

| JM659-JM722 | Short S.25 Sunderland III | 50 |

Built at Rochester. JM659-JM689, JM704-JM722.
JM667, JM714-JM720 converted to Mk.V. JM688,
JM719 converted to Sandringhams G-AJMZ, 'AKCO.
JM660-JM665 and JM722 to BOAC as G-AGER to
'AGEW, 'AGYK. JM667 became 7172M.

| JM738-JN257 | Supermarine Sea Otter I | 250 |

JM738-JM773, JM796-JM837, JM861-JM885, JM905-
JM922, JM943-JM989, JN104-JN142, JN179-JN205,
JN242-JN257. JM984 became 18-8 of the Dutch Navy.
JM836, JM943, JM962 became 6870M, 6464M, 6825M,
and JM739 became G-AKWA.

| JN273-JN682 | Miles M.37 Martinet TT.I | 200 |

Built by Phillips & Powis at Woodley. JN273-JN309,
JN416-JN460, JN485-JN513, JN538-JN555, JN580-
JN601, JN634-JN682. JN668 trainer conversion became
G-AKOS. JN588-JN589 to Royal Navy. JN290 converted
to Queen Martinet. JN489 became 5775M.

| JN703 | Miles M.18 | 1 |

Ex-U-0236.

| JN729-JN877 | Hawker Tempest V Srs I | 100 |

Built at Langley. JN729-JN773, JN792-JN822, JN854-
JN877. Conversions: JN807, JN871 TT.V, JN750 F.VI.
JN734, JN753, JN768, JN798, JN801, JN814, JN856,
JN874 became 6164M, 6163M, 4887M, 5819M, 6643M,
4829M, 6644M, 6645M.

| JN882-JP338 | Handley Page HP.59 Halifax II | 250 |

Built by London Aircraft Production Group. JN882-
JN926, JN941-JN978, JP107-JP137, JP159-JP207,
JP220-JP259, JP275-JP301, JP319-JP338. JP124
became 4982M.

| JP361-JR535 | Hawker Typhoon IB | 600 |

Built by Gloster. JP361-JP408, JP425-JP447, JP480-
JP516, JP532-JP552, JP576-JP614, JP648-JP689,
JP723-JP756, JP784-JP802, JP836-JP861, JP897-
JP941, JP961-JP976, JR125-JR152, JR183-JR223,
JR237-JR266, JR289-JR338, JR360-JR392, JR426-
JR449, JR492-JR535. JR210 had TR210 painted in
error. JP406, JP408, JP734, JP859, JR134, JR193,
JR305, JR432, JR508, JR522 became 5305M, 6125M,
5264M, 5502M, 5883M, 5345M, 5556M, 5652M, 5234M,
5346M.

Second Lend-Lease Allocation

JS100 to KV300

These allocations followed on from HD776 and although up to KV300
was allowed, only up to KP328 had been allotted when the war ended
and Lend/Lease ceased. Allocations included orders placed in Canada. All
batches, as with the previous Lend/Lease allocation, were consecutively
numbered.

Serial Nos	Aircraft Type and Remarks	Quantity
JS100-JS218	Avro 652A Anson	119

JS100-JS132 built by MacDonald Bros Aircraft and
JS133-JS218 built in the Amherst Plant of Canadian
Car & Foundry Corporation.

| JS219-JS468 | Hawker Hurricane XII | 248(250) |

Built by Canadian Car & Foundry Corporation as XIIB
except JS233, JS260, JS261, JS270, JS272, JS274,
JS292, JS297, JS304, JS320, JS324, JS328, JS331,
JS333, JS348, JS353, JS356, JS357, JS409, JS411-
JS416, JS418, JS419, JS423-JS425, JS433, JS435-
JS459, JS461, JS464-JS468 Mk.XIIC and JS372-JS373
not built. Offsets: JS281, JS347, JS385-JS387, JS400,
JS401 to Portugal: JS228, JS404, JS415, JS446 and
others to Russia. JS244 became 4105M. Some shipped
direct to India. JS253, JS328, JS334, JS336 converted
to Sea Hurricane.

| JS469-JS888 | Chance Vought Corsair II/III (F3A-1) | 420 |

Built by Brewster. JS469-JS554 ex-USN 04689-04774;
JS555-JS802 ex-USN 08550-08797 Mk.II; JS803-JS888
ex-USN 11067-11152 Mk.III. All for Royal Navy.

| JS889-JS984 | Lockheed Ventura V (PV-1) | 96 |

Delivered to Middle East. Some served in SAAF units
and JS896, JS909, JS930, JS953, JS956, JS975 were
permanently transferred in 1945. JS900, JS971 crashed
in Brazil during delivery. JS903, JS924, JS921-JS925,
JS938, JS939, JS941, JS942, JS976-JS979 were offset
direct to SAAF.

| JS996 | Grumman Gosling I (J4F-2) | 1 |

Used at Miami.

| JS997-JS999 | Douglas Dauntless I (SBD-5) | 3 |

Designated DB.I. JS997, JS999 to Royal Navy, JS998 to
the RAF.

| JT100-JT704 | Chance Vought Corsair I/II (F4U-1/1D) | 605 |

JT100-JT169 ex-USN 18122-18191 Mk.I, JT170-JT704
Mk.II. Main deliveries to Blackburn Aircraft for modification for Royal Navy.

| JT773 | Grumman Avenger I (TBF-1) | 1 |

Originally named Tarpon I. For Royal Navy.

| JT800-JT898 | Lockheed Ventura V (PV-1) | 99 |

Delivered to Middle East. Some served in SAAF units in

Middle East and JT845, JT846, JT855-JT857, JT862, JT864, JT866, JT870-JT872, JT879, JT880, JT886, JT890, JT895 were permanently transferred in 1945. JT801, JT802, JT822 crashed on delivery flight. JT805-JT808, JT839-JT844, JT848-JT852, JT858-JT861, JT863, JT867-JT869, JT875, JT876, JT881-JT883, JT885 were offset direct to SAAF.

JT923-JT928	**Douglas Dauntless I (SBD-5)**	**6**

Ex-USN 54191-54196. JT923 to RAF later Royal Navy, JT924-JT926 to RAF, JT927, JT928 to Royal Navy.

JT963-JT972	**Chance Vought Corsair III (F3A-1)**	**10**

Built by Brewster ex-USN 11153-11162 for Royal Navy.

JT973-JT999	**Consolidated Liberator C.IX (RY-3)**	**27**

Ex-USN 90021-90047. JT973, JT974, JT979 loaned to RCAF, JT984, JT989 returned to US and JT997 remained in USA.

JV100-JV324	**Grumman Hellcat I/II (F6F-3/5)**	**225**

JV100-JV221 Mk.I, JV222-JV324 Mk.II, all for Royal Navy.

JV325-JV924	**Grumman Wildcat V/VI (F4F-4/FM-2)**	**600**

JV325-JV636 Mk.V built by Grumman, JV637-JV924 Mk.VI built by General Motors. All for Royal Navy.

JV925-JV935	**Consolidated Catalina IVA (PBY-5A)**	**11**

Ex-USN 08532-08534, 08542-08549.

JV936-JV999	**Consolidated Liberator C.IX (RY-3)**	**64**

JV936 ex-USN 90048 only delivered.

JW100-JW125	**Curtiss Helldiver I (SBW-1B)**	**26**

Delivered to Royal Navy but not used operationally. JW119 to RAF.

JW550-JW669	**Curtiss Seamew I (SO3C-2C)**	**120**

For Royal Navy but full delivery not made.

JW700-JW784	**Grumman Hellcat II (F6F-5)**	**85**

For Royal Navy.

JW785-JW836	**Grumman Wildcat VI (FM-2)**	**52**

Built by General Motors. For Royal Navy.

JW857-JW899	**Grumman Hellcat II (F6F-5)**	**43**

Ex-USN 70475-70512, 70688-70692 for Royal Navy.

JX100-JX132	**Martin Mariner I (PBM-3B)**	**33**

JX101, JX120, JX126, JX128, JX130 not delivered. JX103/G trials aircraft.

JX200-JX437	**Consolidated Catalina IVA/IVB (PBY-5A/PB2B-1)**	**238**

JX200-JX269 Mk.IVA built by Consolidated of which JX228, JX230-JX237 were diverted to RNZAF, JX270-JX437 Mk.IVB built by Boeing. JX287 to BOAC as G-AGKS. Postwar disposals: JX276, JX298, JX354, JX359 to Dutch; JX356, JX372, JX378, JX381, JX394, JX395, JX398, JX400, JX410-JX412, JX419 to Norway and JX284, JX319, JX337, JX348, JX353, JX362 to SAAF.

JX470-JX501	**Consolidated Coronado (PB2Y-3B)**	**32**

JX470-JX472, JX486, JX490, JX494-JX496, JX498, JX501 only delivered. Used as trans-Atlantic transports.

JX570-JX662	**Consolidated Catalina IVA/IVB, VI**	**93**

JX570-JX585 ex-USN 08117, 08211-08225 Mk.IVA of which JX575, JX577 became G-AGID, 'AGIE of BOAC and JX582 went postwar to R Norwegian AF; JX586-JX617 Mk.IVBs; JX618-JX662 Mk.VI of which only JX628-JX629, JX632, JX634, JX635 were delivered to the RAF, the majority of the remainder going to RAAF.

JX663-JX669	**Curtiss Seamew I (SO3C-1K)**	**7**

Radio-controlled target drones for Royal Navy.

JX670-JX999	**Grumman Hellcat II (F6F-5/5N)**	**330**

JX965-JX967 delivered as F6F-5N (Royal Navy NF.II), remainder for Royal Navy as F6F-5.

JZ100-JZ746	**Grumman Avenger I/II/III**	**647**

JZ100-JZ300 Mk.I (TBF-1B) built by Grumman; JZ301-JZ634 Mk.II (TBM-1C), JZ635-JZ746 Mk.III (TBM-3) built by General Motors. All for Royal Navy.

JZ771-JZ774	**Curtiss Seamew I (SO3C-1K)**	**4**

For Royal Navy.

JZ775-JZ827	**Grumman Hellcat II (F6F-5)**	**53**

For Royal Navy.

JZ828-JZ859	**Consolidated Catalina VI**	**32**

No RAF delivery record. 14 to RAAF.

JZ860-JZ889	**Grumman Wildcat VI (FM-2)**	**30**

Built by General Motors. Deliveries to Royal Navy in the Far East and Australia.

JZ890-JZ999	**Grumman Hellcat II (F6F-5/5N)**	**110**

For Royal Navy. F6F-5 except JZ890-JZ911, JZ947-JZ959, JZ965-JZ967, JZ995-JZ999 as NF.II (F6F-5N).

KA100-KA102	**DH.98 Mosquito FB.21**	**3**

Canadian-built.

KA103-KA773	**DH.98 Mosquito FB.26/T.29**	**335(671)**

Canadian-built except KA287, KA377, KA431, KA432, KA434, KA438, KA442, KA443, KA445-KA449, KA451-KA773 cancelled. Built as FB.26 except KA117, KA120-KA122, KA137-KA139, KA141, KA149, KA150, KA158, KA166, KA167, KA172-KA174, KA202, KA203, KA206, KA207, KA221, KA232-KA234, KA242, KA243, KA280, KA281, KA290, KA297-KA299, KA300, KA301, KA312-KA314 delivered as T.29. KA153, KA197, KA237, KA259, KA260, KA316, KA317 lost in transit. KA306 became 6078M. KA114 preserved in Canada.

KA873-KA999	**DH.98 Mosquito T.22/FB.24/B.25/T.27**	**125(127)**

Canadian-built as follows: KA873-KA876 T.22, KA877-KA895 T.27, KA896, KA897 T.22, KA898-KA927 T.27, KA928, KA929 FB.24 cancelled. KA930-KA999 B.25 of which most went to Royal Navy. KA958 became 6430M.

KB100-KB699	**DH.98 Mosquito B.VII/B.20/B.25**	**600**

Canadian-built as follows: KB100-KB299 B.20, KB300-KB324 B.VII actually the first Canadian-built batch of which several were retained in Canada; KB325-KB369 B.20, KB370-KB699 B.25. KB113, KB119, KB196, KB216, KB220, KB230, KB296, KB340, KB370, KB381, KB398, KB475, KB479, KB489, KB503-KB505, KB525, KB526, KB540, KB562, KB563, KB575, KB589, KB591, KB593, KB626 were written off before delivery. KB130-KB132, KB138-KB141, KB145-KB152, KB154-KB159, KB171, KB180-KB189, KB306, KB312, KB313, KB315-KB317, KB326, KB328 offset to USAAF. KB100, KB122, KB213, KB265, KB345, KB434, KB464, KB491, KB681, KB685 became 5014M, 5812M, 5811M, 5813M, 5820M, 5095M, 5747M, 6327M, 6498M, 6006M. 41 aircraft to Royal Navy. KB336 preserved in Canada.

KB700-KB999	**Avro 698 Lancaster B.X**	**300**

Built by Victory Aircraft, Canada for use of RCAF squadrons in the UK, but KB702, KB703, KB730 retained in Canada. Many variously modified in RCAF postwar. KB729 became G-AKDO. KB839, KB882, KB889, KB944, KB976, KB994 currently preserved.

KD100-KD107	**Spartan 7-W Executive**	**8**

Used in Canada.

KD108-KD160	**Grumman Hellcat II (F6F-5/5N)**	**53**

KD108-KD117, KD153-KD157 NF.II (F6F-5N) remainder F6F-5. All to Royal Navy.

KD161-KE117	**Chance Vought Corsair IV (FG-1D)**	**857**

Built by Goodyear. Main deliveries to British Pacific Fleet. KD431 preserved in FAA Museum.

KE118-KE265	**Grumman Hellcat II (F6F-5/5N)**	**148**

KE160-KE169, KE215-KE219 NF.II (F6F-5N), remainder F6F-5. All to Royal Navy. KE209 in FAA Museum.

KE266-KE285	**Consolidated Liberator C.IX (RY-3)**	**(20)**

Cancelled.

KE286-KE304	**Curtiss Queen Seamew I (SO3C-1K)**	**(19)**

Cancelled.

KE305-KE309	**North American Harvard III (SNJ-4)**	**5**

Possibly delivered to Royal Navy.

KE310-KE429	**Chance Vought Corsair IV (FG-1)**	**120**

Built by Goodyear. For Royal Navy.

KE430-KE609	**Grumman Avenger III/IV (TBM)**	**110(180)**

KE430-KE539 Mk.III (TBM-2) built by General Motors, KE540-KE609 Mk.IV cancelled. For Royal Navy.

KF100-KG309	**North American Harvard IIB (AT-16)**	**990(1110)**

Up to KG189 built by Noorduyn in Canada. KG190-KG309 cancelled. KF901-KF999 delivered as TT.IIB and in general converted to T.IIB. General deliveries to RAF in UK, Middle East and India. Allocations to Royal Navy included KF544-KF546, KF548-KF559. Some retained in Canada. KF403, KF407, KF410 to RNZAF. KF155, KF209, KF219, KF513 became 5569M, 7716M, 6161M, 7113M.

KG310-KG809	**Douglas DC-3 Dakota III (C-47A)**	**500**

50 offset to BOAC, RAAF, RCAF, SAAF, Russia etc. KG507, KG542, KG723, KG765 to VIP standard. Three crashed before delivery. KG367, KG379, KG393, KG418, KG514, KG527, KG529, KG590, KG610, KG622, KG639, KG649, KG654, KG729, KG745,

KG796 became 6346M, 6357M, 4926M, 5567M, 5742M, 4989M, 6359M, 5566M, 6292M, 6301M, 4981M, 6230M, 5201M, 6300M, 6596M, 5245M. Postwar many to various air forces, particularly RCAF and RIAF, and civil registers.

KG810-KG820 Vultee Vengeance IV Srs II (A-35B)   **11**
For RAF except KG812, KG818 to Royal Navy.

KG821-KH420 Consolidated 32 Liberator VI/VIII (B-24J)   **500**
KG821, KG822 GR.VI, KG823-KG846 B.VI of which KG827 was converted to C.VI, KG847 GR.VI, KG848 B.VIII to C.VIII, KG849-KG870 GR.VI of which KG863-KG866, KG868 conv to C.VI; KG871-KG894 B.VI; KG895-KG918 GR.VI of which KG899-KG902, KG905, KG906, KG908, KG914-KG916, KG918 were conv to C.VI; KG919-KG931 B.VI; KG933, KG934 B.VI; KG936 GR.VI conv to C.VI, KG937-KG942 B.VI; KG943-KG958 B.VIII of which KG950 was conv to C.VIII, KG959 GR.VIII conv to C.VIII, KG960 B.VIII conv to C.VIII; KG961-KG966 GR.VIII; KG967-KG978 B.VI; KG979-KG984 GR.VIII of which KG980, KG983, KG984 were conv to C.VIII; KG985, KG986 GR.VI of which KG985 was conv to C.VI; KG987-KG989 GR.VIII conv to C.VIII; KG990-KG992 GR.VI; KG993-KG999, KH100-KH122 B.VI; KH123, KH124 GR.VI; KH125, KH126 GR.VIII to C.VIII; KH127 GR.VI; KH128-KH133 GR.VIII of which all but KH129 were conv to C.VIII; KH134 GR.VI; KH135, KH136, KH143 GR.VIII; KH146 GR.VIII conv to C.VIII; KH147-KH151 B.VI; KH155-KH176 B.VI; KH177-KH184 GR.VIII of which KH177, KH179, KH181, KH182, KH184 were conv to C.VIII; KH189 GR.VIII; KH198-KH200 GR.VI to C.VI; KH202-KH218 B.VI of which KH208 was conv to C.VI; KH219 GR.VI; KH221 GR.VIII; KH222-KH226 GR.VIII conv to C.VIII; KH227-KH238 B.VIII; KH239-KH258 B.VI; KH259-KH268 GR.VIII of which KH265, KH260, KH265, KH266 were conv to C.VIII; KH269-KH284 B.VI of which KH279 was conv to C.VI; KH285-KH289 B.VI; KH290 GR.VIII; KH291-KH294 GR.VIII conv to C.VIII; KH296 Mk.VI; KH298 GR.VIII conv to C.VIII; KH302 GR.VIII; KH305 GR.VI to C.VI; KH306 GR.VIII; KH308 GR.VIII conv to C.VIII; KH309-KH320 B.VI; KH322 GR.VIII conv to C.VIII; KH323, KH325-KH328 B.VI; KH329-KH341 GR.VIII of which KH333, KH334, KH337, KH340 were conv to C.VIII; KH344 GR.VI to C.VI; KH346, KH347 GR.VIII conv to C.VIII; KH348 GR.VI conv to CV.I, KH349-KH368 B.VI; KH369-KH376 B.VIII; KH377-KH385 GR.VI of which KH377, KH380 were conv to C.VI; KH386 B.VI; KH387, KH388 GR.VIII; KH389-KH408 B.VI; KH409 GR.VI; KH410-KH418 GR.VIII of which KH411, KH412 were conv to C.VIII; KH419, KH420 GR.VI conv to C.VI. No record of mark of numbers omitted. KG880, KG886, KG888, KG891, KG892, KG894, KG920, KG922-KG924, KG929-KG932, KG935, KG978, KH105-KH110, KH171-KH176 were retained in Canada. KH225, KH305 became 6022M, 6025M.

KH421-KH870 North American Mustang II/IV/IVA   **450**
KH421-KH640 Mk.III (P-51B/C), KH641-KH670 Mk.IV (P-51D), KH671-KH870 Mk.IVA (P-51K). KH470, KH687 crashed before delivery.

KH871-KH992 Waco Hadrian II (CG-4A)   **122**
Main deliveries to India. KH944-KH947 to Canada.

KH998-KJ127 Boeing 299 Fortress III (B-17G-VE)   **30**
KH998, KH999, KJ100-KJ127 delivered from October 1944. 12 retained in Canada.

KJ128-KJ367 Republic Thunderbolt II (P-47D-25)   **240**
Main deliveries to RAF in India.

KJ368-KJ467 Stinson Sentinel I/II (L-5/L-5B)   **100**
KJ368-KJ407 Mk.I, KJ408-KJ467 Mk.II mainly delivered to Far East.

KJ468-KJ560 Beechcraft Expeditor II (C-45F)   **93**
Main deliveries to South-East Asia.

KJ561-KJ800 North American NA-108 Mitchell III (B-25J)   **240**
Offsets to RCAF and USAAF. KJ756 crashed before delivery. KJ561 became 5266M.

KJ801-KK220 Douglas DC-3 Dakota IV (C-47B)   **320**
30 offsets and many disposals to foreign air forces and civil registers. KJ806 became 5097M and KJ839 Mamba test-bed. At least four still existing in Greece.

KK221-KK378 Consolidated 32 Liberator VI/VIII (B-24J)   **158**

KK221-KK228 GR.VI of which KK221, KK222, KK224, KK226, KK228 were converted to C.VI; KK229-KK236 B.VI; KK237-KK242 GR.VI held in Canada; KK243-KK247 B.VI; KK248 B.VI conv to C.VI; KK249, KK250 GR.VIII; KK251-KK258 GR.VI of which KK251, KK252, KK254, KK255, KK257 were conv to C.VI; KK259 GR.VIII; KK260 GR.VI conv to C.VI; KK261-KK264 GR.VIII; KK265-KK267 GR.VI conv to C.VI; KK268 GR.VIII; KK269-KK288 B.VI; KK289-KK300 GR.VIII of which KK295 was lost before delivery; KK301-KK320 B.VI; KK321-KK336 GR.VIII of which KK322 was conv to C.VIII; KK337 GR.VI conv to C.VI; KK338, KK339 GR.VIII; KK340-KK342 GR.VI conv to C.VI; KK343-KK362 B.VI; KK363-KK367 GR.VIII; KK368 GR.VI conv to C.VI; KK369, KK370 GR.VIII; KK371-KK378 GR.VI conv to C.VI. KK334/G had special equipment.

KK379-KK568 Fairchild 24R Argus III (UC-61K)   **190**
Ex-USAAF 44-83036 to '83225. Main deliveries to India and Middle East. KK522-KK567 to Canada.

KK569-KK968 Waco Hadrian II (CG-4A/13A)   **400**
KK790, KK791 CG-13A, remainder CG-4A delivered in main to India.

KK969-KL113 Sikorsky Hoverfly I (R-4B)   **45**
KL110 to RCAF. Main deliveries to Royal Navy. KK990 became ground running rig for Percival P.74 project.

KL133-KL161 North American NA-87 Mitchell II (B-25D)   **29**
Delivered to 5 OTU RCAF.

KL162-KL167 Waco CG-13A-FO   **6**
Gliders for evaluation. KL162, KL163 to UK, KL164-KL167 to India. KL162 became 5836M.

KL168-KL347 Republic Thunderbolt II (P-47D-25)   **180**
Delivered to Far East.

KL348-KL689 Consolidated 32 Liberator VI/VIII (B-24J)   **342**
KL348-KL351 GR.VI converted to C.VI; KL352-KL388 B.VI; KL390 GR.VIII; KL391-KL393 B.VI; KL394, KL471, KL472 GR.VIII; KL473 B.VI; KL474 GR.VIII; KL475, KL476 B.VI; KL477 GR.VIII; KL478, KL479 B.VI; KL480/G GR.VIII; KL481-KL489 B.VI of which KL486 was conv to C.VI; KL490 GR.VIII; KL491, KL492 B.VI; KL493 GR.VIII; KL494, KL495 B.VI of which KL494 was conv to C.VI; KL496-KL498 GR.VIII of which KL496 was conv to C.VIII; KL499 B.VI conv to C.VI; KL500 GR.VIII; KL501 B.VI; KL502 GR.VIII; KL503 B.VI conv to C.VI; KL504 B.VI; KL505 GR.VIII; KL507, KL508 B.VI; KL509 GR.VIII; KL510 B.VI; KL511 GR.VIII; KL512, KL513 B.VI; KL514 GR.VIII; KL515, KL516 B.VI; KL517, KL520 GR.VIII; KL521 B.VI; KL522 GR.VIII; KL523-KL531 B.VI of which KL529 was conv to C.VI; KL532, KL533/G GR.VIII; KL534, KL536-KL538, KL540, KL541 B.VI; KL542 GR.VIII; KL543 B.VI; KL544 GR.VIII; KL545-KL549 B.VI of which KL548 was conv to C.VI; KL550, KL551 GR.VIII; KL552 B.VI; KL553, KL554 GR.VIII; KL556, KL557 B.VI; KL558, KL559 GR.VIII; KL560 B.VI; KL561, KL562 GR.VIII; KL563, KL564 B.VI; KL565-KL568 GR.VIII; KL569 B.VI; KL570 GR.VIII; KL571-KL601, KL607 B.VI of which KL576, KL578, KL593-KL595 were conv to C.VI; KL608 B.VIII conv to C.VIII; KL609, KL610 B.VIII; KL611-KL617 B.VI of which KL613, KL617 were conv to C.VI; KL618 B.VIII; KL619-KL630 B.VI of which KL619-KL623, KL625, KL627, KL628, KL630 were conv to C.VI; KL631 B.VIII conv to C.VIII; KL632, KL633 B.VI; KL634 B.VIII conv to C.VIII; KL635-KL639 B.VI of which KL637, KL639 were conv to C.VI; KL640 B.VIII conv to C.VIII; KL641, KL642 B.VI conv to C.VI; KL643 B.VIII conv to C.VI; KL644-KL652 B.VI of which KL645-KL647, KL650-KL652 were conv to C.VI; KL653 B.VIII; KL654, KL655 B.VI; KL656 B.VIII; KL657, KL658 B.VI conv to C.VI; KL659-KL662 B.VIII; KL663-KL667 B.VI conv to C.VI; KL668 B.VIII; KL669, KL670 B.VI conv to C.VI; KL671 B.VIII; KL672, KL673 B.VI conv to C.VI; KL674, KL675 B.VIII; KL676 B.VI conv to C.VI; KL677, KL678 B.VIII; KL679 B.VI conv to C.VI; KL680 B.VIII; KL681-KL683 B.VI conv to C.VI; KL684 B.VIII; KL685-KL689 B.VI conv to C.VI; Numbers not given may be presumed not delivered. KL371, KL386, KL392, KL394, KL476 lost before delivery.

KL690-KL829	Douglas Invader I (A-26)	140
	KL690, KL691 only delivered. Remainder to US Navy from June 1945.	
KL830-KL837	Boeing Fortress III (B-17G)	8
	Some retained in Canada.	
KL838-KL976	Republic Thunderbolt II (P-47D-25)	139
	KL838-KL887 only delivered, mainly to Far East.	
KL977-KL999	Douglas DC-4 Skymaster (C-54D)	22
	KL987 not delivered.	
KM100-KM799	North American Mustang IV/IVA (P-51D/K)	700
	KM100-KM492 Mk.IVA (P-51K), KM493-KM743 Mk.IV (P-51D), KM744-KM799 not delivered.	
KN100-KN199	Beechcraft Expeditor II (C-45F)	50(50)
	KN100-KN149 delivered to RAF in India 1945. KN150-KN199 believed cancelled.	
KN200-KN701	Douglas DC-3 Dakota IV (C-47B)	502
	KN267, KN327, KN483, KN669-KN671 offset to SAAF. All to C.IV standard except KN628, KN647 VIP.IV. KN437, KN465-KN467, KN501-KN505, KN523-KN527, KN537, KN539-KN544, KN548-KN555, KN557, KN559, KN585-KN587 fitted with glider pick up winch. KN489, KN524, KN631 became 6345M, 6348M, 6729M. Many disposals postwar to various air forces and civil registers. KN645 preserved in UK, KN451 in Canada and others in Greece.	
KN702-KN836	Consolidated 32 Liberator VI/VIII (B-24J)	135
	KN702-KN707 B.VI converted to C.VI; KN719-KN743 GR.VIII of which KN719, KN720, KN727, KN734, KN737, KN739, KN743 were conv to C.VIII and KN723 to C(VIP)VIII; KN744-KN752 B.VI of which KN747-KN750 were conv to C.VI; KN753-KN758 GR.VIII of which KN754, KN756-KN758 were conv to C.VIII; KN759, KN760 B.VIII, KN761 GR.VIII conv to C.VIII; KN762 B.VIII; KN763 GR.VIII conv to C.VIII; KN764 B.VIII; KN765 GR.VIII converted to C(VIP).VIII standard for Mr Jinnah; KN766 B.VIII; KN767 GR.VIII; KN768 B.VIII crashed before delivery; KN769 GR.VIII conv to C.VIII; KN770 GR.VIII conv to C.VIII; KN771, KN772 B.VIII; KN773 GR.VIII conv to C.VIII; KN774 B.VIII; KN775 GR.VIII conv to C.VIII; KN776-KN779 GR.VIII; KN780-KN784 B.VIII; KN785-KN789 GR.VIII of which KN786 was conv to C.VIII; KN790, KN791 B.VIII; KN792 GR.VIII conv to C.VIII; KN793, KN794 B.VIII; KN795 GR.VIII conv to C.VIII; KN796 B.VIII; KN797 GR.VIII; KN798 B.VIII; KN799, KN800 GR.VIII; KN801, KN802 B.VIII; KN803-KN805 GR.VIII; KN806-KN808 B.VIII; KN809-KN811 GR.VIII; of which KN810 was conv to C.VIII; KN812 B.VIII; KN813 GR.VIII conv to C.VIII; KN814-KN816 B.VIII. From then on to KN836 odd numbers were GR.VIII and even numbers B.VIII of which KN825, KN828, KN829, KN831, KN833, KN835 were conv to C.VIII and KN826 burnt out at Lydda on its delivery flight. Numbers omitted may be assumed aircraft not delivered.	
KN837-KN986	Sikorsky Hoverfly II (R-6A)	150
	Built by Nash-Kelvinator Corporation. First forty only delivered mainly to RAF but KN855, KN879 to Royal Navy; KN864 to Canada. KN837 became 6831M.	
KN987	North American Mustang IV (P-51H)	1
	For evaluation.	
KP100-KP124	Beechcraft Expeditor II (UC-45F)	25
	To Royal Navy.	
KP125-KP196	Consolidated 32 Liberator VIII (B-24J)	72
	KP125-KP140 (GR version odd numbers, B version even numbers); KP141-KP146 GR.VIII of which KP128, KP129, KP146 were conv to C.VIII; KP147-KP196 not delivered.	
KP208-KP279	Douglas DC-3 Dakota IV (C-47B)	72
	Deliveries to Canada and Far East. Various disposals. KP231 became 6731M. KP208 preserved at Airborne Forces Museum.	
KP308-KP328	North American NA-108 Mitchell III (B-25J)	21
	To USAAF before RAF service.	
KP329-KV300	Reservation for Lend/Lease not taken up	—

Quantity & Quality

KV301 to PZ999

Quantities ordered became larger as the war progressed, culminating in a single order for 2,190 Spitfires, the largest order ever placed. New types were introduced and experimentation led to special modifications. The serial system continued on the general lines set by precedent, but there were a few anomalies. The combination 'NC' was used introducing for the first, and only time, the letter 'C' as a second prefix letter. On the other hand 'MR', 'NW', 'NZ' were not used to avoid confusion with Map Reference and RNZAF aircraft prefixed 'NZ'. To set the scene in time, the allocations below were made from February 1942.

Serial Nos	Aircraft Type and Remarks	Quantity
KV301-KV893	Bristol 163 Buckingham	119(400)
	KV301-KV346, KV358-KV372, KV402-KV450, KV471-KV479 only built (C/n 11905-12023) as B.1 up to KV365 and as C.1 for remainder. Non-standard: KV322 central dorsal fin, KV346 and KV421 TB, KV365, KV369 to proposed C.2 standard. KV480-KV500, KV518-KV535, KV549-KV581, KV600-KV641, KV656-KV692, KV723-KV756, KV769-KV786, KV801-KV845, KV861-KV893 cancelled.	
KV896-KW673	Bristol 156 Beaufighter VIF/X	260(500)
	Built by Rootes. KV896-KV944, KV960-KV981, KW101-KW133, KW147-KW171, KW183-KW203 (150) Mk.VIF; KW204, KW216-KW250, KW263-KW276 TF.X cancelled. KW277-KW298, KW315-KW355, KW370-KW416 (110) TF.X; KW431-KW478, KW491-KW536, KW549-KW576, KW586-KW633, KW654-KW673 cancelled. KW923, KW935, KV941, KV961, KW130 to USAAF in Middle East. KV963, KV978, KW101, KW120, KW282, KW285, KW337 became 4265M, 5627M, 5700M, 5620M, 5884M, 6068M, 6064M.	
KW696-LA144	Hawker Hurricane IIB-IID/IV/V	1500
	Note: (B) = bomber version. KW696 Mk.IID; KW697, KW698 Mk.IIC (B); KW699 Mk.IIB; KW700 Mk.IID; KW701-KW703 Mk.IIB; KW704 Mk.IID; KW705-KW706 Mk.IIB; KW707 Mk.IIC; KW708 Mk.IID; KW709, KW710 Mk.IIB; KW711 Mk.IIC; KW712 Mk.IID; KW713, KW714 Mk.IIB; KW715 Mk.IIC; KW716 Mk.IID; KW717, KW718 Mk.IIC; KW719 Mk.IIC (B); KW720 Mk.IID; KW721, KW722 Mk.IIC; KW723 Mk.IIC (B); KW724 Mk.IID; KW725-KW727 Mk.IIC (B); KW728 Mk.IID; KW729-KW731 Mk.IIC (B); KW745-KW747 Mk.IIC; KW748 Mk.IIB; KW749 Mk.IIC; KW750-KW752 Mk.IIC (B); KW753 Mk.IID; KW754-KW756 Mk.IIC (B); KW757 Mk.IID; KW758-KW760 Mk.IIC (B); KW761 Mk.IID; KW762-KW764 Mk.IIC; KW765 Mk.IID; KW766-KW768 Mk.IIC; KW769 Mk.IID; KW770 Mk.IIC (B); KW771, KW772 Mk.IIB; KW773 Mk.IID; KW774 Mk.IIC (B); KW775 Mk.IIB (B); KW776 Mk.IIC (B); KW777 Mk.IID; KW791 Mk.IIC (B); KW792 Mk.IV; KW793 Mk.IIB; KW794 Mk.IID; KW795 Mk.IIC; KW796, KW797 Mk.IIC (B); KW798 Mk.IID; KW799-KW800 Mk.IV; KW801 Mk.IIC (B); KW802 Mk.IID; KW803 Mk.IIC (B); KW804 Mk.IV; KW805 Mk.IIC (B); KW806 Mk.IID; KW807-KW810 Mk.IV; KW811-KW815 Mk.IIC/B/C/B/C all (B); KW816, KW817 Mk.IV; KW818-KW832, KW846, KW847 Mk.IIC (B); KW848 Mk.IIB (B); KW849-KW858 Mk.IIC (B); KW859-KW881 odd nos Mk.IID, even Mk.IIC (B) except KW872 Mk.IIB; KW893 Mk.IIC (B); KW894'Mk.IID; KW895 Mk.IIC (B); KW896 Mk.IID; KW897 Mk.IV; KW898 Mk.IID; KW899 Mk.IV; KW900-KW907 even nos Mk.IID Mk.IIC (B); KW908-KW911 Mk.IV; KW912-KW917 Mk.IIC (B) except KW914 Mk.IIC; KW918-KW921 Mk.IV; KW922-KW924 Mk.IIC (B); KW925 Mk.IIC; KW926-KW936, KW949-KW982, KX101 Mk.IIC (B); KX102-KX105 Mk.IIC of which KX104 was (B); KX106-KX118 Mk.IIC (B); KX119 Mk.IIC; KX120-KX122 Mk.IID; KX123 Mk.IIC; KX124 Mk.IID; KX125-KX133 Mk.IIC (B); KX134-KX137 Mk.IIC; KX138. KX139 Mk.IIC (B);	

KX140, KX141 Mk.IIC; KX142 Mk.IID; KX143-KX146, KX161-KX164 Mk.IIC (B); KX165-KX172 odd nos Mk.IID, even Mk.IIC (B); KX173-KX177 Mk.IID; KX178-KX180 Mk.IV; KX181 Mk.IID; KX182-KX187 Mk.IIC (B); KX188-KX190 Mk.IV; KX191-KX197 Mk.IIC; KX198-KX200 Mk.IV; KX201, KX202, KX220-KX224 Mk.IIC (B); KX225-KX234 Mk.IID; KX235-KX240 Mk.IID; KX241-KX250 Mk.IID; KX251-KX261, KX280-KX292 Mk.IIC (B); KX293-KX305 Mk.IID; KX306, KX307, KX321-KX369, KX382-KX399, KX401-KX404 Mk.IIC (B) except KX367 Mk.IIC; KX405 Mk.V later Mk.IV; KX406-KX414 Mk.IV; KX415-KX424 Mk.IID; KX425, KX452-KX460 Mk.IIC (B); KX461-KX470 Mk.IID; KX471-KX491, KX521-KX535 Mk.IIC (B); KX536-KX545 Mk.IV; KX546-KX564 Mk.IIC (B); KX565-KX567, KX579-KX585 Mk.IV; KX586-KX621, KX691-KX696 Mk.IIC (B); KX697-KX705 Mk.IV; KX706-KX736, KX749-KX784, KX797-KX799 Mk.IIC (B); KX800-KX809 Mk.IV; KX810-KX819 Mk.IIC (B); KX820-KX829 Mk.IV; KX830-KX838, KX851-KX861 Mk.IIC (B); KX862 Mk.IV; KX863 Mk.IIC (B); KX864-KX866 Mk.IID; KX867-KX875 Mk.IIC (B); KX876-KX885 Mk.IV; KX886-KX892, KX922-KX967, KZ111-KZ156, KZ169-KZ184 Mk.IIC (B) of which KZ134 was converted to Mk.IIB; KZ185-KZ192 Mk.IV; KZ193 Mk.V; KZ194 Mk.IV; KZ195-KZ201, KZ216-KZ218 Mk.IIC (B); KZ219-KZ228 Mk.IV; KZ229-KZ238 Mk.IIC (B); KZ239-KZ248 Mk.IV; KZ249, KZ250, KZ266-KZ299 Mk.IIC (B); KZ300, KZ301, KZ319-KZ326 Mk.IV; KZ327-KZ356, KZ370-KZ373 Mk.IIC (B); KZ374-KZ383 Mk.IV; KZ384-KZ393 Mk.IIC (B); KZ394-KZ404 Mk.IV; KZ405 Mk.IIC (B); KZ406, KZ407 Mk.IV; KZ408-KZ412, KZ424-KZ470, KZ483-KZ526, KZ540-KZ549 Mk.IIC (B); KZ550-KZ559 Mk.IV; KZ560-KZ569 Mk.IIC (B); KZ570-KZ579 Mk.IV; KZ580-KZ582, KZ597-KZ603 Mk.IIC (B); KZ604-KZ613 Mk.IV; KZ614-KZ619 Mk.IIC (B); KZ620, KZ621 Mk.IV; KZ622-KZ632, KZ646-KZ653 Mk.IIC (B); KZ654-KZ663 Mk.IV; KZ664-KZ673 Mk.IIC (B); KZ674-KZ683 Mk.IV; KZ684-KZ688, KZ702-KZ705 Mk.IIC (B); KZ706-KZ715 Mk.IV; KZ716-KZ721 Mk.IIC (B); KZ722, KZ723 Mk.IV; KZ724 Mk.IIC (B); KZ725 Mk.IIC; KZ726 Mk.IV; KZ727-KZ750, KZ766-KZ801, KZ817-KZ862, KZ874-KZ903 Mk.IIC (B) except KZ858 Mk.IIC; KZ904-KZ916 Mk.IV; KZ917-KZ920, KZ933-KZ949, LA101-LA144 Mk.IIC (B). Main deliveries to India and Middle East and offsets to Russia. KX179, KX304, KX539, KX567, KX699, KZ405 became 4621M, 4608M, 4438M, 4618M, 5859M, 5908M.

LA157-LA165 Curtiss Mohawk IV   9
Delivered to India.

LA187-LA582 Supermarine Spitfire F.21/Seafire F.45/46   194(300)
Ordered from Vickers Armstrong at Castle Bromwich. LA187-LA236, LA249-LA284, LA299-LA332 built as F.21; LA188 used for high-speed tests. LA333-LA346, LA368-LA395, LA417-LA457, LA481-LA519, LA536-LA582 cancelled as Spitfires, but LA428-LA462, LA481-LA495 were built as fifty Seafire F.45 and LA541-LA564 were assembled at South Marston as twenty-four Seafire F.46. LA193, LA194, LA198, LA210, LA225, LA226, LA228, LA250, LA263, LA265, LA299, LA305 became 6373M, 6393M, 7118M, 6413M, 6490M, 7119M, 7120M, 6833M, 7121M, 6834M, 6459M, 6368M. LA198, LA226, LA255 and LA564 are preserved.

**LA586 &   Percival P.31 Proctor IV   2
LA589**
Prototypes. Originally named Perceptor. LA589 became G-ANXI.

LA594   Hawker Typhoon   (1)
Centaurus-engined prototype, not completed.

LA602-LA610 Hawker Tempest II/III   3
Prototypes. LA602 became 5076M and LA607 Mk.II preserved. LA610 Mk.III completed as Fury and became G-AKRZ.

LA619-LA623 Lockheed 12A   5
LA632-LA750 General Aircraft GAL.49 Hamilcar I   94
Group built. LA632-LA655, LA669-LA691, LA704-LA750. LA704, LA727 converted to Mk.X. LA633, LA653, LA742 became 6617M, 6243M, 5219M.

LA763-LA951 Armstrong Whitworth AW.38 Whitley V/VII   150
LA763-LA793 Mk.V; LA794-LA798, LA813-LA817 Mk.VII; LA818-LA856, LA868-LA899, LA914-LA951 Mk.V. LA794 to Royal Navy.

LA964-LB251 Vickers Wellington IC/VIII   150
Built at Weybridge. LA964 Mk.VIII; LA965 Mk.IC; LA966, LA967 Mk.VIII; LA968 Mk.IC; LA969-LA972 Mk.VIII; LA973 Mk.IC; LA974-LA977 Mk.VIII; LA978 Mk.IC; LA979-LA983 Mk.VIII; LA984 Mk.IC; LA 985-LA987 Mk.VIII; LA988 Mk.IC; LA989-LA993 Mk.VIII; LA994 Mk.IC; LA995-LA998 Mk.VIII; LB110 Mk.IC; LB111-LB115 Mk.VIII; LB116 Mk.IC; LB117-LB119 Mk.VIII; LB120 Mk.IC; LB121-LB125 Mk.VIII; LB126 Mk.IC; LB127-LB130 Mk.VIII; LB131 Mk.IC; LB132-LB140 Mk.VIII; LB141 Mk.IC; LB142-LB147 Mk.VIII; LB148 Mk.IC; LB149-LB151 Mk.VIII; LB152 Mk.IC; LB153-LB156, LB169-LB173 Mk.VIII; LB174 Mk.IC; LB175-LB197, LB213-LB251 Mk.VIII. All Mk.IC completed as torpedo-bombers except LA973. Mk.VIII fitted with Leigh Light: LA966, LA971, LA976, LA982, LA987, LA992, LA998, LB114, LB124, LB129, LB135, LB140, LB145, LB150, LB153, LB156, LB178, LB186, LB194, LB216, LB220, LB224, LB231, LB236. LA969, LB220 became 4399M, 4456M.

LB263-LB395 Taylorcraft Auster I   100+1
LB263-LB299, LB311-LB352, LB365-LB385 plus LB395 built additional to contract. LB316 became 5222M. LB312 preserved as G-AHXE. 52 to British Civil Register.

LB401-LB538 Airspeed AS.10 Oxford I   100
LB401-LB429, LB442-LB462 (50) built by Standard Motors, LB469-LB492, LB513-LB538 Airspeed-built at Christchurch. LB409, LB457 became 6188M, 5639M.

LB542-LF774 Hawker Hurricane Mk.IIB/C(Bomber)/IV   1961
Note: all Mk.IIs ground attack version. LB542-LB575, LB588-LB624, LB639-LB642 Mk.IIC; LB643-LB652 Mk.IV; LB653-LB681 Mk.IIC; LB682-LB687, LB707-LB710 Mk.IV of which LB707 became 4624M; LB711-LB742 Mk.IIC; LB743, LB744, LB769-LB776 Mk.IV of which LB769-LB771 became 4626M-4628M; LB777-LB801, LB827-LB848 Mk.IIC; LB849-LB853 Mk.IV; LB856-LB862, LB873-LB913, LB927-LB973, LB986-LB992 Mk.IIC; LB993-LB999, LD100-LD102 Mk.IV; LD103-LD131, LD157-LD159 Mk.IIC; LD160-LD169 Mk.IV of which LD161 was converted to Mk.IID; LD170-LD185, LD199-LD215 Mk.IIC; LD216-LD219, LD232-LD237 Mk.IV; LD238-LD266, LD287-LD289 Mk.IIC; LD290-LD294 Mk.IV; LD295-LD315, LD334-LD351, LD369-LD389 Mk.IIC; LD390 Mk.IID; LD391-LD416, LD435-LD441 Mk.IIC; LD442-LD451 Mk.IV but LD447 converted to Mk.IID; LD452-LD464 Mk.IIC; LD465, LD466 Mk.IID; LD467-LD470, LD487-LD490 Mk.IV; LD491-LD508, LD524 Mk.IIC; LD525-LD539, LD557-LD562 Mk.IIC for SAAF; LD563-LD572 Mk.IV; LD573-LD580, LD594-LD604 Mk.IIC to SAAF except LD573, LD598, LD605-LD609 Mk.IV; LD610-LD632 Mk.IIC to SAAF except LD615, LD618, LD621, LD623, LD627, LD631, LD632; LD651-LD695, LD723-LD749, LD772-LD787 Mk.IIC; LD788-LD797 Mk.IV of which LD789 was converted to Mk.IID; LD798-LD809, LD827-LD861 Mk.IIC; LD862-LD868, LD885-LD889 Mk.IV; LD890-LD905, LD931-LD968 Mk.IIC; LD969-LD979 Mk.IV; LD993-LD999; LE121-LE131 Mk.IIC; LE132-LE136 Mk.IV; LE137-LE146, LE163-LE183, LE201-LE214, LE247-LE267 Mk.IIC; LE268-LE273, LE291-LE294 Mk.IV; LE295-LE309, LE334-LE368, LE387-LE392 Mk.IIC; LE393-LE402 Mk.IV; LE403-LE405, LE432-LE449, LE456-LE484, LE499-LE504 Mk.IIC; LE505-LE512 Mk.IV; LE513 Mk.IIC; LE514 Mk.IV; LE515-LE535, LE552-LE566 Mk.IIC; LE567-LE571 Mk.IV; LE572-LE593, LE617-LE652 Mk.IIC; LE653-LE661 Mk.IV; LE662-LE665, LE679-LE713 Mk.IIC; LE737 Mk.IIB; LE738-LE744 Mk.IV; LE745 Mk.IIB; LE746, LE747 Mk.IIC; LE748-LE757 Mk.IV; LE758-LE769, LE784-LE816, LE829-LE833 Mk.IIC except LE785-LE794, LE805 Mk.IIB; LE834-LE843 Mk.IV; LE844-LE867, LE885-LE920 Mk.IIC except LE852 Mk.IIB; LE921-LE925 Mk.IV; LE938-LE966, LE979-LE999, LF101-LF105 Mk.IIC; LF106-LF115 Mk.IV; LF116-LF135, LF153-LF184, LF197-LF237, LF256-LF298, LF313-LF346, LF359-LF405, LF418-LF429

Mk.IIC; LF430-LF435, LF451-LF482, LF494-LF510
of which LF431 became a Mk.IID and LF474-LF480
are type unconfirmed; LF511-LF516, LF529-LF542,
LF559-LF591 Mk.IIC; LF592-LF596 Mk.IV; LF597-
LF601, LF620-LF660, LF674-LF721, LF737-LF774
Mk.IIC. LD621, LE398, LE580, LE747, LF512, LF538,
LF540, LF572, LF575, LF578, LF580, LF581, LF583,
LF590, LF597 became 5409M, 5415M, 5402M, 5496M,
5278M, 5414M, 5315M, 6011M, 6282M, 5235M, 5302M,
6332M, 5321M, 5306M, 5309M and LF626-LF628,
LF635, LF636, LF639, LF642, LF645, LF646, LF653,
LF656, LF659, LF674, LF675, LF680, LF684, LF686,
LF690-LF692, LF695, LF703, LF709, LF711, LF718,
LF719, LF742, LF745, LF755, LF761, LF765, LF773
became 5342M, 5411M, 5314M, 5473M, 5308M, 5313M,
5472M, 5276M, 5470M, 5273M, 5368M, 5275M, 5418M,
5341M, 5410M, 5412M, 5270M, 5372M, 5706M, 5274M,
5332M, 6364M, 5369M, 5403M, 5370M, 5371M, 5037M,
5406M, 5419M, 6363M, 5367M, 5319M. LF738 as
5405M and LF751 as 5466M are preserved at Biggin Hill
and Bentley Priory. LF658 incorrectly marked as LF345
is held in Belgium and LF686 in Washington DC.

LF779-LF882	DH.82B Queen Bee	60(75)

LF779-LF803, LF816-LF839, LF857-LF867 built by
Scottish Aviation. LF868-LF882 cancelled. LF858
preserved.

LF886-LF963	Airspeed AS.58 Horsa II	65

Built by Austin Motors. LF886-LF923, LF937-LF963.
Twenty were transferred to the USAAF. LF919 later
became 4732M.

LG511-LH601	Airspeed AS.51 Horsa I	636(750)

Built by Harris Lebus. LG550, LG662-LG699, LG713-
LG749, LG761-LG798, LG814-LG856, LG868-LG896,
LG911-LG952, LG966-LG999, LH113-LH154, LH167-
LH189, LH202-LH249, LH263-LH301, LH316-LH359,
LH373-LH415, LH429-LH476, LH490-LH536, LH549-
LH583, LH597-LH601. Cancelled were LG511-LG534,
LG547-LG549, LG551-LG593, LG616-LG658. Many
transfers to USAAF. LG673, LG683, LG727, LG746,
LG795, LG842, LG854, LG920, LG928, LG996, LH174,
LH245, LH266, LH297, LH391, LH524 became 4481M,
5209M, 4480M, 4520M, 5217M, 5024M, 4963M, 4859M,
4432M, 5091M, 4734M, 4530M, 5259M, 4673M, 4744M,
4735M.

LH942-LJ334	Airspeed AS.51 Horsa I	220

LH942-LH976, LJ101-LJ144, LJ157-LJ193, LJ206-
LJ241, LJ256-LJ291, LJ303-LJ334. LJ271 converted
to Mk.II. Seventy transferred to USAAF. LH948, LH958,
LJ105, LJ119, LJ126, LJ211, LJ281, LJ323, LJ327,
LJ329 became 5021M, 5025M, 4984M, 5018M, 5216M,
5844M, 6088M, 5026M, 5022M, 4983M.

LJ440-LK670	Short S.29 Stirling III/IV	175

Built at Rochester and Swindon. LJ440-LJ483, LJ501-
LJ544, LJ557-LJ596, LJ611-LJ653, LJ667-LJ670
Mk.III. LJ512 Mk.IV prototype, LJ530 Mk.V prototype.
LJ461, LJ475, LJ502, LJ503, LJ532, LJ563, LJ564,
LJ566, LJ572, LJ575, LJ576, LJ583, LJ588-LJ591,
LJ594, LJ596, LJ612, LJ613, LJ615, LJ616, LJ618,
LJ620, LJ622, LJ627, LJ629, LJ631, LJ633, LJ636,
LJ638, LJ640, LJ643, LJ645, LJ647, LJ650, LJ652,
LJ667-LJ669 built as or converted to Mk.IV. LJ538,
LJ564, LJ626 became 5239M, 4845M, 5240M. LJ575
later became TS266.

LJ810-LK370	Short S.29 Stirling IV	360

Built by Short & Harland at Belfast. LJ810-LJ851,
LJ864-LJ899, LJ913-LJ956, LJ969-LJ999, LK114-
LK156, LK169-LK211, LK226-LK257, LK270-LK313,
LK326-LK370. LJ818, LJ834, LJ866, LJ891, LJ952,
LK340 became 5051M, 4776M, 5246M, 4942M, 5247M,
5826M.

LK375-LK624	Short S.29 Stirling III/IV	200

Built by Austin Motors. LK375-LK411, LK425-LK466,
LK479-LK521, LK535-LK576, LK589-LK624 Mk.III
of which LK389, LK405, LK428, LK431-LK433, LK439,
LK440, LK486, LK498, LK505, LK509, LK510, LK512,
LK513, LK542-LK545, LK548, LK549, LK551, LK553-
LK560, LK562, LK566, LK567, LK573, LK589, LK606
converted to Mk.IV. LK483, LK589, LK603 became
4860M, 5238M, 5237M. LK512, LK562 later TS264,
TS262.

LK626-LK887	Handley Page Halifax III/V	200

Built by Fairey. LK626-LK667, LK680-LK711, LK725-
LK746 Mk.V; LK747-LK766, LK779-LK812, LK826-
LK850, LK863-LK887 Mk.III. LK869 became 4819M.

LK890-LL615	Handley Page Halifax III/V	480

Built by Rootes. LK890-LK932, LK945-LK976, LK988-
LK999, LL112-LL153, LL167-LL198, LL213-LL258,
LL270-LL312, LL325-LL367, LL380-LL423, LL437-
LL469, LL481-LL521, LL534-LL542 Mk.V; LL543-
LL559, LL573-LL615 Mk.III. LL148, LL482, LL547,
LL612 became 4918M, 5218M, 5824M, 4916M.

LL617-LM296	Avro 683 Lancaster I/II	450

Built by Armstrong Whitworth. LL617-LL653, LL666-
LL704, LL716-LL739 (100) Mk.II; LL740-LL758,
LL771-LL813, LL826-LL867, LL880-LL923, LL935-
LL977, LM100-LM142, LM156-LM192, LM205-LM243,
LM257-LM296 (350) Mk.I. LL735 jet engine test bed,
LL780/G armament experiments and LL865 and LL948
converted to Mk.III. LL617, LL666, LL722, LL742,
LM186, LM188, LM287 became 4975M, 5423M, 4974M,
6541M, 5846M, 5724M, 5759M.

LM301-LM756	Avro 683 Lancaster I/III	350

Built at Yeadon. LM301-LM310 Mk.I but LM306,
LM308 converted to Mk.III. LM311-LM346, LM359-
LM395, LM417-LM448, LM450-LM493, LM508-LM552,
LM569-LM599, LM615-LM658, LM671-LM697, LM713-
LM756 Mk.III but LM448, LM483, LM489, LM492,
LM695 converted to Mk.I. LM443, LM483, LM591,
LM657 became 5358M, 4767M, 6260M, 5602M. LM639
became G-AHJV.

LM769-LN153	Vickers Warwick GR.V	109(225)

LM777-LM803, LM817-LM858, LM870-LM909 built at
Weybridge. LM769-LM776, LM910-LM913, LM927-
LM968, LM980-LM997, LN110-LN153 cancelled.
LM781 to SAAF.

LN157-LR210	Vickers Wellington B.X	1382

Built at Chester. LN157-LN189, LN221-LN248, LN261-
LN303, LN317-LN353, LN369-LN409, LN423-LN468,
LN481-LN516, LN529-LN571, LN583-LN622, LN635-
LN676, LN689-LN723, LN736-LN778, LN791-LN823,
LN836-LN879, LN893-LN936, LN948-LN989, LP113-
LP156, LP169-LP213, LP226-LP268, LP281-LP314,
LP328-LP369, LP381-LP415, LP428-LP469, LP483-
LP526, LP539-LP581, LP595-LP628, LP640-LP686,
LP699-LP733, LP748-LP788, LP802-LP849, LP863-
LP889, LP901-LP930, LP943-LP986, LR110-LR142,
LR156-LR164, LR168-LR183, LR195-LR210 B.X of
which LN376, LN608, LN657, LN756, LN819, LN865,
LN988, LP256, LP361, LP431, LP596, LP597, LP705,
LP804, LP806, LP846, LP916-LP918, LP926, LP959,
LP968, LR112, LR158, LR203 were converted to T.10
postwar. LN715, LN718 used as flying test-beds, LP523
11-seat transport. LN391, LN697, LN935, LP264, LP712,
LP771, LP877, LP883, LR156, LR182 became 6115M,
6757M, 6450M, 5995M, 6760M, 6218M, 6759M, 6217M,
6465M, 6874M.

LR227	DH.87B Hornet Moth	1

VT-AKE (ex-G-AEVU) impressed in India.

LR228-LR229	DH.82A Tiger Moth	2

VT-AKW and 'AJV (ex-G-ACGE) impressed in India.

LR230-LR235	Douglas DC-3	6

Ex-US civil aircraft purchased and flown in India.

LR236	DH.82A Tiger Moth	1

VT-AQE impressed in India.

LR241 & LR244	Miles M.25 Martinet	2

Prototypes.

LR248-LR513	DH.98 Mosquito VI/IX	202

Built at Hatfield. LR248-LR276, LR289-LR313,
LR327-LR340, LR343-LR389, LR402-LR404 FB.VI;
LR405-LR446, LR459-LR474 PR.IX, LR475-LR477
B.IX, LR478-LR481 PR.IX, LR495-LR513 B.IX. LR387
converted to TR.33 for Royal Navy. LR294 became
6231M. LR296 to BOAC as G-AGKP. LR480 preserved
at Johannesburg.

LR516-LR585	DH.98 Mosquito T.III	59

Built at Leavesden. LR516-LR541, LR553-LR585.
LR516, LR530, LR534, LR584 loaned to USAAF.
LR523, LR528, LR530, LR540, LR571 became 6550M,
6318M, 5910M, 5957M, 6988M. LR568, LR569,
LR577, LR578 to RAAF.

LR631-LR881	**Supermarine Seafire IIC/III**	**213**
	Built by Westland. LR631-LR667, LR680-LR712, LR725-LR764 Mk.IIC; LR765-LR820, LR835-LR881 Mk.III.	
LR885-LS149	**Bristol 152 Beaufort I/II**	**129**
	LR885-LR908, LR920-LR963, LR976-LR999, LS113-LS128 Mk.I, LS129-LS149 T.II. LR900-LR902, LR927, LR929, LR943, LR944, LR946, LR949-LR952, LR955, LR960, LR961, LR980 to Royal Navy.	
LS151-LS461	**Fairey Swordfish I**	**250**
	Built by Blackburn. LS151-LS193, LS214-LS248, LS261-LS299, LS315-LS358, LS362-LS403, LS415-LS461 to Royal Navy. LS326 preserved.	
LS464-LS974	**Fairey Barracuda II**	**400**
	Built at Heaton Chapel. C/n F.6320-F.6719. LS464-LS506, LS519-LS556, LS568-LS595, LS608-LS653, LS668-LS713, LS726-LS763, LS778-LS820, LS833-LS878, LS891-LS936, LS949-LS974 to Royal Navy.	
LS978-LV332	**Avro 652A Anson I**	**750**
	Built at Yeadon. LS978-LS999, LT112-LT160, LT175-LT210, LT231-LT258, LT271-LT307, LT334-LT378, LT410-LT459, LT472-LT503, LT521-LT549, LT575-LT610, LT641-LT682, LT701-LT745, LT764-LT797, LT823-LT849, LT872-LT899, LT921-LT961, LT978-LT999, LV122-LV167, LV199-LV230, LV252-LV300, LV313-LV332. Various deliveries under EATS including 118 to South Africa, others to India, seventeen to BOAC for ferry flights. LT417, LT490 to Royal Navy. LT154 became 6408M.	
LV336-LV346	**Consolidated 32 Liberator GR.III**	**11**
	Special 1942 delivery for Battle of the Atlantic. Ex-USAAF 41-1107, '1087, '1127, '1096, '1122, '1097, '1114, '1111, '1093, '1124, '1108. LV338, LV345 became 4817M, 4816M.	
LV482-LV623	**Armstrong Whitworth AW.41 Albemarle GT.VI Srs.II**	**100**
	Built by Armstrong Whitworth Hawkesley. LV482-LV501, LV532-LV577, LV590-LV623.	
LV626-LV639	**Avro 685 York**	**4**
	Prototypes. LV626 first flew 5.7.42 originally twin-finned and became the only C.II, then 5554M; LV629 also originally twin-finned became 6554M; LV633 was Winston Churchill's *Ascalon*, LV639 paratroop version became 6227M, later 6466M.	
LV643-LV756	**Supermarine Spitfire LF.VIII**	**70**
	LV643-LV681, LV726-LV756. Main delivery to India.	
LV760-LV762	**Lockheed 12A**	**3**
	Ex-Dutch L2-32, L2-30, L201.	
LV763	**DH.87 Hornet Moth**	**1**
	VT-AIU impressed in Far East.	
LV764	**DH.82A Tiger Moth**	**1**
	Impressed in Far East.	
LV765-LV767	**DH.80A Puss Moth**	**3**
	VT-ABG, 'ABZ, 'ABW impressed in India.	
LV768	**Miles M.2H Hawk Major**	**1**
	VT-AIR (ex-G-ACZJ) impressed in India.	
LV769	**Piper Super Cruiser**	**1**
	VT-AKT impressed in Far East.	
LV771-LX210	**Handley Page HP.61 Halifax B.III/VII**	**240**
	LV771-LV799, LV813-LV842, LV857-LV883, LV898-LV923, LV935-LV973, LV985-LV999, LW113-LW143, LW157-LW179, LW191-LW195 B.III; LW196-LW210 B.VII. Conversions: LV776 to B.V; LV838 prototype B.VI later C.VI. LW133, LW161, LW205 became 5073M, 5075M, 6173M.	
LW223-LW724	**Handley Page HP.61 Halifax B.II/III**	**360**
	Built by English Electric. LW223-LW246, LW259-LW301, LW313-LW345 (100) B.II; LW346-LW348, LW361-LW397, LW412-LW446, LW459-LW481, LW495-LW522, LW537-LW559, LW572-LW598, LW613-LW658, LW671-LW696, LW713-LW724 (260) B.III. LW346, LW385, LW514, LW641, LW646 became 5226M, 6226M, 4935M, 4953M, 4951M.	
LW727-LX152	**Airspeed AS.10/46 Oxford I/V**	**240**
	Built by Percival. LW727-LW759, LW772-LW799, LW813-LW835, LW848-LW879, LW891-LW927 Mk.I; LW928-LW930, LW945-LW947 Mk.V; LW948-LW973, LW985-LW999, LX113-LX152 Mk.I. Some sixty shipped out under EATS. Disposals postwar to R Danish AF and R Hellenic AF. LW906 became 5996M.	
LX156-LX777	**Airspeed AS.10 Oxford I**	**450**
	Built at Portsmouth. LX156-LX199, LX213-LX245, LX258-LX289, LX301-LX333, LX347-LX369, LX382-LX401, LX415-LX448, LX462-LX489, LX502-LX541, LX555-LX582, LX595-LX617, LX629-LX648, LX661-LX699, LX713-LX746, LX759-LX777. Various offsets including LX366-LX369, LX382-LX401, LX415, LX416, LX467-LX470, LX510-LX512, LX561-LX565 direct to Middle East for Turkish AF; LX417-LX422, LX489, LX502-LX506 to Portuguese AF; LX423-LX426, LX534 to Takoradi for Free French AF, others to India and EATS countries. Transfers: LX183, LX241, LX243, LX604, LX665 to Royal Navy and LX447, LX555 to the USAAF. LX274, LX277, LX464, LX465, LX474, LX532, LX724, LX725, LX764 became 6883M, 6197M, 5326M, 5528M, 6284M, 5298M-5300M, 6288M.	
LX779-LZ544	**Bristol Beaufighter TF.X**	**480**
	Built at Weston. LX779-LX827, LX845-LX886, LX898-LX914, LX926-LX959, LX972-LX999, LZ113-LZ158, LZ172-LZ201, LZ215-LZ247, LZ260-LZ297, LZ314-LZ346, LZ359-LZ384, LZ397-LZ419, LZ432-LZ465, LZ479-LZ495, LZ515-LZ544. LX880 prototype Mk.XI. LX988-LX995, LZ195-LZ201, LZ215, LZ321-LZ328 became A19-164 to '187 of the RAAF. LX824, LX846, LX854, LX935, LZ184, LZ411 became 5748M, 5756M, 5887M, 4453M, 6495M, 5674M and LZ185 became G-AJMG.	
LZ548 & LZ551	**DH.100 Vampire**	**2**
	Prototypes to Spec E6/41. LZ548/G first flew 20.9.43. LZ551/G hooked for deck trials is now preserved by the FAA Museum.	
LZ556-LZ804	**Percival P.34 Proctor III**	**200**
	Built by F. Hills & Sons. LZ556-LZ603, LZ621-LZ663, LZ672-LZ717, LZ730-LZ771, LZ784-LZ804. LZ757, LZ758, LZ761, LZ762, LZ767, LZ768 to Royal Navy. LZ557, LZ572, LZ592, LZ594, LZ621, LZ628, LZ630, LZ662, LZ675, LZ693, LZ731, LZ741, LZ784, LZ786, LZ794, LZ795 became 5046M, 6733M, 6772M, 5049M, 6908M, 5244M, 5058M, 6693M, 6774M, 5047M, 6730M, 5243M, 5242M, 5059M, 5048M, 6789M. LZ766 as G-ALCK is currently preserved at Duxford.	
LZ807-MA906	**Supermarine Spitfire V/IX** (role letters not known)	**680**
	Built by Vickers Armstrong at Castle Bromwich. LZ807-LZ815 Mk.VC, LZ816 LF.IXB, LZ817-LZ830 Mk.VC, LZ831-LZ833 Mk.IX, LZ834, LZ835 Mk.VC, LZ836-LZ843 Mk.IX, LZ844-LZ848, LZ861-LZ899 Mk.VC, LZ915-LZ925 Mk.IX, LZ926-LZ956, LZ969-LZ988 Mk.VC, LZ989-LZ998, MA221-MA260 Mk.IX, MA261-MA266 F.VC tropicalised, MA279-MA297 Mk.VC, MA298 LF.IX, MA299-MA315, MA328-MA368 Mk.VC but MA329, MA357 converted to LF.IX, MA369 Mk.IX, MA383-MA397 Mk.VC; MA398-MA428, MA443-MA487, MA501-MA546, MA559-MA601, MA615-MA643 Mk.IX, MA644-MA657, MA670-MA704 Mk.VC of which MA645, MA646, MA648, MA651, MA655, MA657, MA687, MA690 converted to Mk.IX; MA705-MA713, MA726-MA767, MA790-MA819, MA831-MA849 Mk.IX, MA850-MA863, MA877 Mk.VC of which MA860 was converted to Mk.IX, MA878, MA879 Mk.IX, MA880-MA906 Mk.VC. LZ949, LZ952, LZ991, MA369, MA426, MA447, MA453, MA471, MA615, MA617, MA618, MA630, MA632 to Italian AF, LZ861 transferred to the USAAF, others to R Egyptian AF, R Hellenic AF and SAAF. LZ919, LZ921, MA298, MA299, MA303, MA524, MA646, MA742, MA803, MA844 became 5954M, 6042M, 6462M, 6039M, 6034M, 6214M, 6040M, 5968M, 5468M, 5379M. LZ842 preserved at Point Cook, Australia and MA793 as 'PT672' in South Africa.	
MA919	**DH.60T Gipsy Moth**	**1**
	VT-AET impressed in India.	
MA920	**Taylorcraft BL-2**	**1**
	VT-ALW impressed in India.	
MA921	**Piper Cub Cruiser**	**1**
	Impressed in India.	
MA922	**DH.85 Leopard Moth**	**1**
	Ex-Madras Flying Club.	
MA923	**Piper J3 Cub**	**1**
	VT-APV impressed in India.	
MA924	**Taylorcraft BL**	**1**
	VT-ALX impressed in India.	

MA925	**Douglas DC-3**	1
	Impressed in India.	
MA926	**Zlin 212 Tourist**	1
	VT-ALU ex-Bata Shoe Company, Calcutta.	
MA927	**Percival P.3 Gull Six**	1
	VT-ALT (ex-G-ADSG) impressed in India.	
MA928-MA929	**Douglas DC-3**	2
	Impressed in India.	
MA930	**Tipsy Trainer**	1
	VT-AKQ impressed in India.	
MA931	**DH.60M Moth**	1
	VT-ANR (ex-K1227, G-AFKM) impressed in India.	
MA932-MA937	**DH.82 Tiger Moth**	6
	VT-AMS, 'AOF, 'APW, 'APX, 'AOM, 'ALM, impressed in India.	
MA938	**DH.82A Tiger Moth**	1
	VP-CAB impressed in India.	
MA939	**DH.60G Gipsy Moth**	1
	VP-CAC (ex-G-AAYY) impressed in India.	
MA940	**DH.82A Tiger Moth**	1
	VP-CAE impressed in India.	
MA941	**DH.60 Gipsy Moth**	1
	VT-AAB impressed in India.	
MA942	**Percival P.3 Gull Six**	1
	VT-AIV impressed in India.	
MA943	**Douglas DC-3**	1
	Impressed in India.	
MA944	**Miles M.11A Whitney Straight**	1
	VT-AKF acquired in India.	
MA945	**British Aircraft Eagle II**	1
	VT-AKO (ex-G-AFIC) impressed in India.	
MA946	**DH.80A Puss Moth**	1
	VT-ACH impressed in India.	
MA947-MA948	**DH.82 Tiger Moth**	2
	Impressed in India.	
MA949-MA950	**DH.60M/60G Moth**	2
	VT-ACW (ex-G-ABNA), 'AEI impressed in India.	
MA951-MA952	**DH.82 Tiger Moth**	2
	Impressed in India.	
MA953	**DH.60G Gipsy Moth**	1
	VT-APU (ex-G-AAKM) impressed in India.	
MA954-MA955	**DH.83 Fox Moth**	2
	Impressed in India.	
MA956-MA957	**North American Mitchell II (B-25C)**	2
	Ex-Dutch. Both to No.681 (PR) Squadron.	
MA958	**Piper Cub**	1
	Impressed in India.	
MA959	**DH.83 Fox Moth**	1
	VT-AFI impressed in India.	
MA960	**Stinson Reliant**	1
	Impressed in India.	
MA961	**DH.89 Rapide**	1
	Impressed in India.	
MA962	**Percival Gull**	1
	Impressed in India.	
MA963-MA966	**DH.89 Rapide**	4
	Ex-HG653, HG650-HG652 used in India.	
MA970-MB326	**Supermarine Seafire IIC**	200
	MA970-MA999, MB113-MB123, MB132-MB164, MB178-MB222, MB235-MB281, MB293-MB326. MA970 became Mk.III prototype.	
MB328-MB375	**Supermarine Seafire IB**	48
	Air Service Training Ltd conversion of Spitfire VB ex-BL676, BL687, BL678, BL694, AB416, AB410, AB413, AB408, AB376, AB261, AB415, BL679, BL689, AB414, AB379, AB409, AR344, AR445, AR446, AR443, AR459, AR442, AB404-AB407, AB492, AB205, EP148, AR457, AR458, EP141, AR460, AR461, EP142, EP144, EP146, EP147, EP291, EP293-EP296, EP299, EP301, EP302, EP304, EP308.	
MB378-MB758	**Fairey Firefly I**	300
	MB378-MB419, MB433-MB479, MB492-MB536, MB549-MB593, MB613-MB649, MB662-MB703, MB717-MB758 for Royal Navy. Various conversions postwar to T.1, T.2 and T.3 and TT.1. Offsets to RCN and sales to Ethiopia and Sweden. MB750 prototype T.1 became F.1 and G-AHYA and MB649 the prototype NF.4. MB757 was mocked-up as Mk.7.	
MB761-MD403	**Supermarine Spitfire VII/VIII/IX/X/XI/XII**	426
	MB761-MB769 F.VII, MB770-MB793 PR.XI, MB794-	

MB805 F.XII, MB806 F.VII, MB807 F.IX, MB808, MB820-MB828 F.VII, MB829-MB863, MB875-MB882 F or LF.XII, MB883-MB887 F.VII, MB888-MB911 PR.XI, MB912-MB916, MB929-MB935 F.VII, MB936-MB958 PR.XI, MB959-MB976 LF.VIII, MD100-MD146, MD159-MD190 F.VII; MD191-MD199, MD213 PR.X, MD214-MD256, MD269-MD303, MD315-MD356, MD369-MD403 LF.VIII. LF.VIIIs mainly to Australia and India. MD301 crashed on initial test. MB787, MB791, MB798, MB804, MB838, MB844, MB855, MB906, MD142, MD170 became 5935M, 5936M, 5919M-5923M, 5937M, 6278M, 6087M.

MD612-MD807	**Fairey Barracuda II**	150
	Built by Blackburn. MD612-MD656, MD678-MD723, MD736-MD778, MD792-MD807. For Royal Navy.	
MD811-ME293	**Fairey Barracuda III**	300
	Built by Boulton Paul. MD811-MD859, MD876-MD924, MD945-MD992, ME104-ME152, ME166-ME210, ME223-ME270, ME282-ME293. For Royal Navy.	
ME295-ME551	**Avro 583 Lancaster B.I/III**	200
	Built at Yeadon. ME295-ME337, ME350-ME395, ME417-ME458, ME470-ME503, ME517-ME551 Mk.III except for forty-four Mk.I; ME328, ME330, ME350, ME352, ME371-ME375, ME383, ME384, ME419-ME421, ME431-ME440, ME445-ME451, ME455-ME458, ME470, ME475-ME477, ME479, ME480, ME482, ME490, ME495. ME324, ME331, ME370, ME376, ME528, ME531, ME545 became 5794M, 6497M, 5852M, 6496M, 6610M, 6334M, 6295M.	
ME554-ME868	**Avro 683 Lancaster B.I/III**	250
	Built by Metropolitan-Vickers. ME554-ME596, ME613-ME650, ME663-ME704, ME717-ME759, ME773-ME814, ME827-ME868 built as Mk.I but ME567, ME590, ME620-ME623, ME625 were converted to B.III.	
ME870-MF742	**Vickers Wellington X/XIII/XIV**	600
	Built at Blackpool. ME870-ME883 Mk.X; ME884-ME914, ME926-ME950 Mk.XIII; ME951-ME960, ME972-ME999, MF113-MF124 Mk.X; MF125-MF130 Mk.XIII; MF131-MF144 Mk.X; MF145-MF156, MF170-MF192 Mk.XIII; MF193-MF203 Mk.X; MF204-MF213, MF226-MF235 Mk.XIII; MF236-MF249 Mk.X; MF250-MF267, MF279, MF280 Mk.XIII; MF281-MF288 Mk.X; MF289-MF310 Mk.XIII; MF311-MF316 Mk.X; MF317-MF320, MF335-MF345 Mk.XIII; MF346-MF351 Mk.X; MF352-MF366 Mk.XIII; MF367-MF372 Mk.X; MF373-MF377, MF389-MF398 Mk.XIII; MF399-MF404 Mk.X; MF405-MF419 Mk.XIII; MF420-MF424, MF439-MF441 Mk.X; MF442-MF449 Mk.XIII; MF450, MF451 Mk.XIV; MF452-MF459 Mk.X; MF460-MF467 Mk.XIII; MF468-MF479 Mk.X; MF480, MF493-MF499 Mk.XIII; MF500-MF538, MF550-MF572 Mk.X; MF573-MF582 Mk.XIII; MF583-MF596, MF614, MF615 Mk.X; MF616-MF623 Mk.XII; MF624 Mk.X; MF625 Mk.XIII; MF626-MF635 Mk.X; MF636-MF643 Mk.XIII; MF644-MF655 Mk.X; MF656-MF659, MF672-MF675 Mk.XIII; MF676-MF687 Mk.X; MF688-MF694 Mk.XIII; MF695-MF706 Mk.X; MF707-MF713, MF725 Mk.XIII; MF726, MF727 Mk.XV; MF728-MF739 Mk.X; MF740-MF742 Mk.XIII. ME890, ME907, ME940, MF190, MF466, MF643 to R Hellenic AF and MF741, MF742 to French AF in 1946. MF359, MF452, MF634 became 5854M, 6910M, 6907M. Mk.X were built as B.X, but ME964, ME972, ME979, ME997, MF313, MF523, MF535, MF564, MF567, MF626-MF628, MF633, MF634, MF695 were converted to T.10 postwar. ME905 crashed on test and was not delivered. MF628 held by RAF Museum.	
MG102-MH237	**Avro 652A Anson I**	800
	Built at Yeadon. MG102-MG147, MG159-MG199, MG214-MG256, MG270-MG314, MG327-MG368, MG381-MG423, MG436-MG478, MG490-MG536, MG549-MG596, MG613-MG656, MG669-MG701, MG714-MG757, MG770-MG813, MG826-MG874, MG888-MG928, MG962-MG999, MH103-MH135, MH149-MH196, MH210-MH237. Many offset to EATS mainly Australia and South Africa. Conversions: MH192, MH231 to Mk.X; MG198, MG220, MG289, MG366, MG500, MG517, MG684 to Mk.XIII; MG159 to Mk.XIX. MG291, MG496, MG787 became 6427M, 6933M, 6605M. Many disposals to Dutch, French and Greek and other air forces.	

MH298-ML428 **Supermarine Spitfire V/IX** (role letters not known) **2196**
Built by Vickers-Armstrong at Castle Bromwich. MH298-
MH311 Mk.VC; MH312-MH336, MH349-MH390 Mk.IX;
MH413-MH456, MH470-MH496 LF.IX; MH497 F.IX;
MH498-MH512, MH526-MH563 LF.IX; MH564-MH568,
MH581-MH596 Mk.VC; MH597-MH599 Mk.IX; MH600
Mk.VC; MH601-MH604 Mk.IX; MH605 Mk.VC; MH606-
MH626, MH635, MH636 Mk.IX; MH637-MH646 Mk.VC
tropicalised; MH647-MH678, MH691-MH711 Mk.IX;
MH712-MH740, MH750-MH796 LF.IX; MH813-MH856,
MH869-MH912, MH924-MH949 Mk.IX; MH950-MH958
LF.IX; MH970-MH999 Mk.IX; MJ114-MJ128 LF.IX;
MJ129, MJ130 F.IX; MJ131-MJ156, MJ169-MJ203
LF.IX; MJ215-MJ223 Mk.IX; MJ224 F.IX; MJ225
LF.IX; MJ226 F.IX; MJ227 Mk.IX; MJ228-MJ258,
MJ271-MJ305 LF.IX; MJ306-MJ314 F.IX; MJ328-
MJ369, MJ382-MJ428, MJ441-MJ485, MJ498-MJ536,
MJ549-MJ589, MJ602-MJ646, MJ659-MJ698, MJ712-
MJ756, MJ769-MJ801, MJ814-MJ868, MJ870-MJ913,
MJ926-MJ967, MJ979-MJ999 LF.IX of which MJ892
was converted to floatplane; MK112-MK158, MK171-
MK213, MK226-MK268, MK280-MK326, MK339-
MK379, MK392-MK429, MK440-MK486, MK499-
MK534, MK547-MK590, MK602-MK646 LF.IX; MK659-
MK699 mainly HF.IX; MK713-MK756, MK769-MK812,
MK826-MK868, MK881-MK926, MK939-MK969,
MK981-MK999 LF.IX; ML112-ML156 LF & HF.IX;
ML169-ML216 Mk.IX mainly HF; ML229-ML277,
ML291-ML323, ML339-ML381, ML396-ML428 mainly
LF.IX but several were HF.IX. Large number direct to
Mediterranean area and numbers shipped to Russia.
MH599, MH602, MH648, MH720, MH779, MH945,
MH947, MH954, MJ358, MJ441, MJ527, MJ668, MJ673,
MJ778, MJ830, MJ841, MJ849, MJ930, MJ996, MK154,
MK155, MK193, MK194, MK207, MK227, MK302,
MK375, MK413, MK419, MK557, MK569, MK636,
MK679, MK805, MK906, MK957 Mk.IX; ML129, ML134,
ML139, ML180, ML195, ML371, ML410 to Italian
AF during war and many disposals to other forces
postwar. MH315, MH318, MH422, MH450, MH473,
MH478, MH731, MH844, MH940 became 5199M,
6184M, 6454M, 6461M, 6142M, 6383M, 6026M, 5970M,
6144M; MJ202, MJ329, MJ452, MJ526, MJ586, MJ814,
MJ887 became 5691M, 6370M, 6081M, 6079M, 5948M,
6183M, 6455M; MK184, MK285, MK303, MK356,
MK426, MK524, MK572, MK623, MK683, MK732,
MK788, MK835, MK922 became 5967M, 6382M, 6456M,
5690M, 6459M, 6583M, 6379M, 6329M, 6162M, 8633M,
5685M, 5693M, 5971M; ML117, ML169, ML171,
ML185, ML230, ML311, ML345, ML370, ML427
became 5495M, 6389M, 6236M, 6585M, 5200M, 5689M,
6460M, 6414M, 6457M. MH434, MJ627, MJ730, ML407,
ML417 now registered G-ASJV, 'BMSB, 'BLAS, 'LFIX,
'BJSG and MJ230, MK356, ML407, ML417, ML427
also preserved in the UK, MJ783 in Belgium, MJ755 in
Greece, MH350 in Norway, MK297, MK923 in the USA.

ML430-ML722 **Bristol 152 Beaufort T.II** **229**
ML430-ML476, ML489-ML524, ML540-ML586, ML599-
ML635, ML649-ML692, ML705-ML722. ML492, ML495,
ML499, ML500, ML501, ML506, ML515, ML518,
ML542-ML545 offset to Turkish AF. ML556, ML560,
ML562, ML569, ML571, ML576, ML579, ML580,
ML582, ML584, ML600, ML602-ML604, ML608,
ML611, ML614-ML621, ML625, ML629, ML665,
ML667, ML669, ML685, ML688, ML716-ML718,
ML720-ML722 transferred to Royal Navy. ML457,
ML471 became 5916M, 5917M.

ML725-ML884 **Short S.25 Sunderland III/V** **150**
ML725-ML774, ML777-ML795 Mk.III and ML796-
ML801 Mk.V (75) built by Short Bros at Rochester;
ML807-ML831 (25) Mk.III built by Short & Harland at
Belfast; ML835-ML884 (50) Mk.III built by Blackburn
at Dumbarton. Many Mk.IIIs converted to Mk.V.
ML730-ML734 to RAAF, ML792-ML795 to RNZAF,
ML798 to SAAF. Several to BOAC and postwar disposals
to France. ML826 became 6100M. ML796, ML824 are
preserved in the UK.

ML896-MM431 **DH.98 Mosquito VI/IX/XVI/XVIII** **350**
Built at Hatfield. ML896-ML924 B.IX; ML925-ML942,
ML956-ML999, MM112-MM156, MM169-MM205,
MM219-MM226 PR.XVI of which ML935, ML956,
ML974, ML980, ML995, MM112, MM147, MM156,
MM162, MM177, MM193 were converted to TT.39 for
Royal Navy; MM227-MM236 PR.IX; MM237, MM238
B.IX; MM239, MM240 PR.IX; MM241 B.IX; MM242-
MM257 PR.IX; MM258, MM271-MM314, MM327-
MM371, MM384-MM397 PR.XVI of which several were
transferred to the Royal Navy and USAAF; MM398-
MM423 FB.VI; MM424, MM425 Mk.XVIII; MM426-
MM431 FB.VI. ML929, ML970, MM301-MM303,
MM363, MM389, MM406, MM426 became 6351M,
5773M, 6352M, 6235M, 5761M, 6662M, 6143M, 4540M,
6054M.

MM436-MM822 **DH.98 Mosquito XIII/XIX/XXX** **300**
Built at Leavesden. MM436-MM479, MM491-MM534,
MM547-MM590, MM615-MM623 NF.XIII of which
MM439, MM462 went to Royal Navy; MM624-MM656,
MM669-MM685 NF.XIX; MM686-MM710, MM726-
MM769, MM783-MM822 NF.XXX of which MM764,
MM765, MM969, MM821 were transferred to USAAF.
MM617, MM631, MM645, MM676, MM700, MM744,
MM798, MM810 became 6028M, 6157M, 5810M,
6545M, 6387M, 6347M, 6503M, 6119M.

MM838-MM948 **Bristol 156 Beaufighter VIF** **100**
Built at Filton. MM838-MM887, MM899-MM948.
MM844, MM848, MM850, MM853, MM912, MM915,
MM919, MM948 became 5576M, 5577M, 5702M, 5578M,
4706M, 5606M, 5575M, 5574M.

MM951-MP203 **Hawker Typhoon IB** **800**
Built by Gloster. MM951-MM995, MN113-MN156,
MN169-MN213, MN229-MN269, MN282-MN325,
MN339-MN381, MN396-MN436, MN449-MN496,
MN513-MN556, MN569-MN608, MN623-MN667,
MN680-MN720, MN735-MN779, MN791-MN823,
MN851-MN896, MN912-MN956, MN968-MN999,
MP113-MP158, MP172-MP203. MN290 tropicalised.
MN235 to USA March 1944. MN198, MN203,
MN208, MN229, MN243, MN283, MN418, MN450,
MN645, MN736, MN934, MN953, MN956, MN987
became 5582M, 5232M, 5656M, 5552M, 5553M, 5762M,
5647M, 5535M, 5877M, 5467M, 5662M, 5668M, 5657M,
5872M, 5536M. MN235 preserved by RAF Museum.

MP275-MP474 **Airspeed AS.10 Oxford I** **150**
Built by Standard Motors. MP275-MP314, MP338-MP376,
MP391-MP430, MP444-MP474. MP309, MP362, MP449,
MP461 became 6185M, 6287M, 6855M, 5492M.
Deliveries mainly for UK stations. Many postwar dis-
posals to foreign forces and civil registers. MP469 re-
numbered MP496. MP425 currently preserved.

MP469 **DH.98 Mosquito XV** **1**
Special high altitude prototype to Mk.XV standard.
Compromised Oxford MP469 above. Became 4882M.

MP486 **General Aircraft GAL.48 Twin Hotspur** **1**
MP496 **Airspeed AS.10 Oxford** **(1)**
Originally numbered MP469.

MP499 **Focke-Wulf FW190A-3** **1**
Captured enemy aircraft. Landed Pembrey 23.6.42.

MP502-MP825 **Vickers Wellington XI/XII/XIII/XIV/XVII** **250**
MP502 Mk.XI; MP503 Mk.XII; MP504 Mk.XI; MP505-
MP515 Mk.XII; MP516-MP535 Mk.XI of which MP518,
MP520, MP522, MP526, MP531, MP533, MP534 were
converted to Mk.XVII; MP536-MP542 Mk.XII;MP543-
MP547 Mk.XI; MP548 Mk.XI converted to Mk.XVII;
MP549, MP562-MP574 Mk.XI; MP575 Mk.XII; MP576,
MP577 Mk.XI; MP578 Mk.XII; MP579, MP580 Mk.XI;
MP581 Mk.XII and similarly Mk.XI with every third
aircraft Mk.XII to MP601; MP615 Mk.XII; MP616
Mk.XI; MP617-MP637 even numbers Mk.XII, odd
numbers Mk.XI; MP638-MP648 Mk.XI; MP649-MP656,
MP679-MP691 even numbers Mk.XII, odd numbers
Mk.XI; MP691-MP703 Mk.XI; MP704-MP708 Mk.XIII;
MP709-MP724 even numbers Mk.XIV odd numbers
Mk.XIII; MP738 Mk.XIII; MP739 Mk.XIV; MP740 Mk.XII;
MP741-MP746 Mk.XIV; MP742-MP749 Mk.XIII; MP750-MP761
even numbers Mk.XIV, odd numbers Mk.XIII; MP762
Mk.XIII; MP763 Mk.XIV; MP764, MP765 Mk.XIII;
MP766 Mk.XIV; MP767, MP768 Mk.XIII; MP769
Mk.XIV; MP770, MP771 Mk.XIII; MP772 Mk.XIV;
MP773 Mk.XIV; MP774, MP789 Mk.XIV; MP790
Mk.XIII; MP791, MP792 Mk.XIV; MP793 Mk.XIII;

	MP794, MP795 Mk.XIV; MP796 Mk.XIII; MP797-MP799 Mk.XIV; MP800 Mk.XIII; MP801-MP825 Mk.XIV. MP519, MP688 became 5684M and 5261M.	
MP829 &	**Vickers Windsor**	**(2)**
MP832	6th & 7th prototypes cancelled before completion.	
MP838/G	**DH.100 Vampire**	**1**
	Originally named Spider Crab. First armed Vampire.	
MS470-MS496	**Vickers Wellington B.X**	**27**
	Built at Blackpool.	
MS499-MS931	**Miles M.25 Martinet TT.I**	**355**
	MS499-MS535, MS547-MS590, MS602-MS647, MS659-MS705, MS717-MS759, MS771-MS820, MS832-MS876, MS889-MS931 of which MS515, MS723, MS730, MS741, MS847 were converted to Queen Martinet. MS533-MS535, MS732-MS740 direct to Royal Navy. MS908 became 6942M.	
MS934-MT454	**Taylorcraft Auster AOP.III/IV/V**	**330**
	MS934-MS981, MT100-MT145, MT158-MT199, MT213-MT256, MT269-MT314, MT328-MT355 AOP.IV; MT356 AOP.V prototype; MT357-MT367 AOP.V; MT368, MT369, MT382-MT419, MT431-MT453 AOP.III; MT454 Mk.III converted to Mk.IV. MT393, MT407, MT408, MT432, MT445, MT450 offset to the RAAF. MT387, MT391, MT442 to R Netherlands AF and MT405, MT406 to R Hellenic AF. 45 to civil register. MS934, MS953, MS960, MT167, MT176, MT358, MT366 became 6013M, 6152M, 6151M, 6192M, 6434M, 5992M, 6071M.	
MT456-MT500	**DH.98 Mosquito NF.XXX**	**45**
	Built at Leavesden. MT466 converted to NF.36. MT462, MT464, MT465, MT478, MT479 to USAAF; MT477 to Royal Navy. MT477, MT490 became 6116M, 6117M.	
MT502-MV514	**Supermarine Spitfire VIII/XIV**	**700**
	MT502-MT527, MT539-MT581, MT593-MT635, MT648-MT689, MT704-MT748, MT761-MT802 LF.VIII except MT675, MT684, MT748 HF.VIII; MT815 LF.VIII; MT816, MT817 HF.VIII; MT818 LF.VIII; MT819-MT822 LF.VIII; MT823, MT824 LF.VIII; MT825 HF.VIII; MT826-MT828 LF.VIII; MT829-MT831 HF.VIII; MT832 LF.VIII; MT833-MT835 HF.VIII; MT836-MT846 LF.VIII; MT847-MT858 FR.XIV; MT872-MT894 LF.VIII; MT895-MT900 HF.VIII; MT901-MT909 LF.VIII; MT910 HF.VIII; MT911-MT913 LF.VIII; MT914 HF.VIII; MT915, MT925-MT969, MT981-MT999 LF.VIII; MV112-MV117 HF.VIII; MV118 LF.VIII; MV119-MV121 LF.VIII; MV122 LF.VIII; MV123-MV125 HF.VIII; MV126, MV127 LF.VIII; MV128, MV129 HF.VIII; MV130, MV131 LF.VIII; MV132, MV133 HF.VIII; MV134-MV140 LF.VIII; MV141 HF.VIII; MV142, MV143 LF.VIII; MV144-MV156, MV169-MV208 HF.VIII; MV231, MV232 LF.VIII; MV233 LF.VIII; MV234 LF.VIII; MV235 HF.VIII; MV236 LF.VIII; MV237 HF.VIII; MV238 LF.VIII; MV239-MV244 HF.VIII; MV245 LF.VIII; MV246-MV273, MV286-MV320 FR.XIV; MV321-MV325 HF.VIII; MV326-MV329 LF.VIII; MV342 HF.VIII; MV343 LF.VIII; MV344 HF.VIII; MV345 LF.VIII; MV346 HF.VIII; MV347-MV386 F or FR.XIV; MV398-MV441, MV456-MV459 LF.VIII; MV460, MV461 HF.VIII; MV462 LF.VIII; MV463-MV479 HF.VIII; MV480 LF.VIII; MV481, MV482 HF.VIII; MV483 LF.VIII; MV484-MV487, MV500-MV514 HF.VIII. Main deliveries to Australia and India. MT818 converted to 2-seat N-32 later G-AIDN. MT601-MT603 and MT847 became 5829M-5831M and 6960M currently preserved. MT719 registered I-SPIT in Italy. MV154 to G-BKMI, MV259 to G-BGHB and 'SPIT, MV370 to G-FXIV, plus MV262 all preserved in the UK and MV239 in Australia.	
MV521-MV570	**DH.98 Mosquito NF.XXX**	**50**
	Built at Leavesden. MV538, MV545, MV562, MV568 postwar to French AF. MV566 became 5868M.	
MV660-MV990	**Supermarine Seafire**	**(260)**
	Cancelled. MV660-MV707, MV720-MV761, MV774-MV823, MV846-MV885, MV899-MV941, MV954-MV990.	
MV993	**Grumman Goose**	**1**
	Ex-Lend/Lease allocation.	
MW100-MW333	**Avro 685 York C.1**	**200**
	MW100-MW149, MW161-MW210, MW223-MW272,	

	MW284-MW333 built in Special (VIP), First Class Passenger, Passenger-cum-Freighter and LR Freighter versions. Special VIP versions: MW100, MW101 general use; MW102 Lord Louis Mountbatten; MW105 general use; MW107 Field Marshal Slim; MW140 Duke of Gloucester as Governor General of Australia; MW295 *Ascalon II* for Far East Air Force. MW103, MW108, MW113, MW121, MW129 became G-AGJA to 'AGJE of BOAC and MW131, MW161, MW166, MW170, MW176, MW250, MW322 became 5559M, 5733M, 5635M, 6082M, 5558M, 5958M, 6715M.	
MW335-MW373	**Hawker Hurricane IIC (Bomber)**	**39**
	MW352, MW353, MW373 sold to Portugal. MW340, MW341, MW354, MW365 became 5463M, 5311M, 5312M, 5310M.	
MW375-MW732	**Hawker Tempest II**	**50(300)**
	Ordered from Bristol Aircraft at Filton and Banbury. MW375-MW423, MW435 only built. MW376-MW383, MW385-MW393, MW395-MW404, MW411-MW415 sold to IAF. MW409, MW418 became 6223M, 6656M. MW436-MW478, MW491-MW536, MW548-MW589, MW591-MW633, MW645-MW686, MW699-MW732 cancelled.	
MW735-MW856	**Hawker Tempest II**	**100**
	Built at Langley. MW735-MW778, MW790-MW835, MW847-MW856 of which fifty-four went to the IAF. MW735, MW798, MW813 became 5841M, 6388M, 6029M.	
MX450-MX455	**Percival P.31A-C Proctor**	**6**
	Development aircraft.	
MX457	**Stampe SV-4B**	**1**
	Ex-OO-ATD Belgian escapee.	
MX459	**Koolhoven FK.43**	**1**
	Ex-Dutch Army No.965 flown to Britain. Was PH-ASN and became PH-NAU.	
MX463	**DH.60 Moth**	**1**
	Belgian Air Attache's aircraft.	
MX535-MX983	**Fairey Barracuda II**	**300(365)**
	Ordered from Blackburn. MX535-MX578, MX591-MX638, MX652-MX696, MX709-MX753, MX767-MX808, MX820-MX864, MX877-MX907 built. MX908-MX923, MX935-MX983 cancelled. MX613 tests with Uffa Fox airborne lifeboat.	
MX988-MX997	**Bristol 164 Brigand**	**3(4)**
	Prototypes to Spec H7/42. MX988 first flew 4.12.44; MX991, MX994 became 6215M, 6592M; MX997 replaced by TX394.	
MZ100-MZ225	**Taylorcraft Auster AOP.III**	**132**
	MZ100-MZ145, MZ157-MZ198, MZ212-MZ255 of which MZ105, MZ110 were temporarily converted to Mk.II. Disposals to other forces: MZ105, MZ122, MZ123, MZ134, MZ135, MZ137, MZ144, MZ158, MZ162, MZ174, MZ181-MZ183, MZ188, MZ195, MZ197, MZ212, MZ213, MZ218, MZ220, MZ228, MZ230, MZ247, MZ249, MZ251, MZ252 to RAAF 1944-45; MZ133, MZ160, MZ169, MZ187, MZ221, MZ227, MZ233, MZ244, MZ248 to R Hellenic AF; MZ110, MZ125, MZ126, MZ136, MZ138, MZ140, MZ141, MZ143, MZ145, MZ164, MZ167, MZ170, MZ178, MZ179, MZ189, MZ192, MZ194, MZ196, MZ214, MZ216, MZ219, MZ223, MZ224, MZ229, MZ231, MZ236, MZ239, MZ250, MZ253 to R Netherlands AF; MZ232, MZ235 to Czech AF. MX236 as PH-NGH preserved in Holland.	
MZ260-MZ264	**Short S.29 Stirling III**	**5**
	Replacement aircraft built by Short & Harland for N6025-N6028, N6031.	
MZ269	**Short S.45 Seaford (Sunderland IV renamed)**	**2**
MZ271	Prototypes used for research. MZ269 became 6416M.	
MZ282-MZ495	**Handley Page HP.61 Halifax B.III**	**180**
	Built by London Aircraft Production Group. MZ282-MZ321, MZ334-MZ378, MZ390-MZ435, MZ447-MZ495. MZ282, MZ411 became 5074M, 5565M.	
MZ500-MZ939	**Handley Page HP.61 Halifax B.III**	**360**
	Built by English Electric. MZ500-MZ544, MZ556-MZ604, MZ617-MZ660, MZ672-MZ717, MZ730-MZ775, MZ787-MZ831, MZ844-MZ883, MZ895-MZ939. MZ627, MZ650, MZ875 became 5063M, 5818M, 5424M.	
MZ945-NA488	**Handley Page HP.61 Halifax B.III/A.VII**	**340(360)**
	Built by Rootes. MZ945-MZ989, NA102-NA150, NA162-NA205, NA218-NA263, NA275-NA309 B.III; NA310-	

NA320, NA336-NA380, NA392-NA431, NA444-NA468
A.VII. NA469-NA488 cancelled. MZ962, NA124,
NA294, NA341, NA399, NA421, NA428, NA452,
NA458 became 5828M, 5687M, 5998M, 6207M, 6077M,
6182M, 6309M-6311M. NA182 converted to B.VI.

NA492-NA704 Handley Page HP.61 Halifax B.III   **180**
Built by Fairey Aviation. NA492-NA531, NA543-NA587,
NA599-NA644, NA656-NA704. NA684 allotted G-AJPG.
NA553, NA587, NA608, NA635, NA643, NA662
became 5633M, 5225M, 5227M, 6204M or 6329M,
5827M, 5780M.

NA710-NB766 Vickers Wellington X   **263(750)**
Ordered from Chester Plant. NA710-NA754, NA766-
NA811, NA823-NA870, NA893-NA937, NA949-NA997,
NB110-NB139 built. NB140-NB155, NB167-NB213,
NB225-NB269, NB282-NB329, NB341-NB385, NB398-
NB443, NB456-NB502, NB514-NB556, NB569-NB613,
NB625-NB670, NB684-NB714, NB739-NB766 cancelled.
Postwar conversions to T.10: NA714, NA752, NA780,
NA781, NA786, NA788, NA793, NA830, NA831,
NA834-NA836, NA841, NA843, NA846, NA848, NA849,
NA852-NA854, NA859, NA868, NA897, NA904-NA907,
NA915, NA916, NA918-NA921, NA924, NA928,
NA955, NA958, NA964, NA967, NA971, NA975,
NA979, NA987, NA989, NB110, NB113, NB115-NB119.
NA724, NA771, NA786, NA828, NA845, NA846,
NA902, NA911, NA960 became 6559M, 6756M, 6952M,
6876M, 7105M, 6896M, 6211M, 6208M, 5809M.

NB767-NC408 Vickers Wellington XIV   **296(441)**
Ordered from Chester plant. NB767-NB783, NB796-
NB841, NB853-NB896, NB908-NB952, NB964-NB999,
NC112-NC160, NC164-NC209, NC222-NC234 built.
NB784-NB787, NC235-NC248, NC280-NC327, NC339-
NC387, NC399-NC408 cancelled. Deliveries mainly to
Mediterranean and West African areas. NB839 to 5057M.

NC414-ND133 Vickers Wellington X/XII/XIV/XVIII   **500**
Built at Blackpool. NC414-NC418 Mk.XIII; NC419,
NC420 Mk.XIV; NC421-NC432 Mk.X; NC433-NC440
Mk.XIII of which NC434-NC438 went to French AF;
NC441, NC442 Mk.XIV; NC443-NC452 Mk.X; NC453-
NC459, NC471 Mk.XIII; NC472-NC480 Mk.X; NC481-
NC489 Mk.XIII; NC490-NC493 Mk.XIV; NC494-NC502
Mk.X; NC503-NC510 Mk.XIII; NC511-NC513 Mk.XIV;
NC514-NC518, NC529-NC533 Mk.X; NC534-NC541
Mk.XIII; NC542-NC544 Mk.XIV; NC545-NC554 Mk.X;
NC555-NC562 Mk.XIII; NC563-NC571 Mk.X; NC572-
NC576, NC588, NC589 Mk.XIII; NC590, NC591
Mk.XIV; NC592-NC601 Mk.X; NC602-NC609 Mk.XIII;
NC610-NC613 Mk.XIV; NC614-NC621 Mk.X; NC622-
NC625 Mk.XIV; NC626-NC631 Mk.XIII; NC632, NC644-
NC647 Mk.XIV; NC648-NC655 Mk.X; NC656-NC663
Mk.XIII; NC664-NC671 Mk.X; NC672-NC677 Mk.XIV;
NC678-NC692, NC706-NC740 Mk.X; NC741-NC747
Mk.XIII; NC748-NC750, NC766-NC770 Mk.X; NC771-
NC776 Mk.XIV; NC777-NC784 Mk.X; NC785-NC788
Mk.XIV; NC789-NC796 Mk.X; NC797-NC800 Mk.XIV;
NC801-NC813, NC825-NC827 Mk.X; NC828-NC835
Mk.XIV; NC836-NC847 Mk.X; NC848-NC855 Mk.XIV;
NC856-NC867 Mk.X; NC868, NC869 Mk.XVIII; NC870,
NC883-NC889 Mk.XIV; NC890-NC901 Mk.X; NC902-
NC907 Mk.XIV; NC908-NC925 Mk.X; NC926-NC928
Mk.XVIII; NC929, NC942-NC990 Mk.X; ND104-ND128
Mk.XVIII; ND129-ND133 Mk.XIV. Postwar NC426,
NC430, NC497, NC498, NC500, NC502, NC515, NC546,
NC615, NC648, NC719, NC720, NC790, NC793, NC811,
NC812, NC836, NC839, NC845, NC856, NC892, NC898,
NC916, NC918, NC920, NC925, NC929, NC958, NC963,
NC968, NC981, NC987 were converted to T.10. NC496,
NC601, NC668, NC792, NC837, NC838, NC865, NC890,
NC891, NC947 became 6751M, 6219M, 6752M, 5808M,
6754M, 6504M, 6558M, 6749M, 6750M, 6210M.

ND139-ND322 Bristol 156 Beaufighter VI   **150**
Built at Filton. ND139-ND186, ND198-ND243, ND255-
ND299, ND312-ND322. ND146, ND148, ND164,
ND216, ND282, ND291, ND296, ND321 transferred to
USAAF. ND222, ND224, ND225, ND227, ND231,
ND232, ND266, ND272 became 5631M, 5622M, 5628M,
5629M, 5618M, 5621M, 5632M, 5624M.

ND324-NE181 Avro 683 Lancaster III   **600**
Built at Manchester. ND324-ND368, ND380-ND425,
ND438-ND479, ND492-ND538, ND551-ND597, ND613-
ND658, ND671-ND715, ND727-ND768, ND781-ND826,
ND839-ND882, ND895-ND936, ND948-ND996, NE112-
NE151, NE163-NE181. ND418, ND479, ND558, ND673,
ND784 converted to Mk.VI. ND784/G later had Mamba
fitted in nose. NE147/G and ND648 to Flight Refuelling
Ltd the latter becoming G-33-1. ND335, ND348, ND584,
ND616, ND619, ND909, NE122, NE180 became 5793M,
5727M, 5865M, 5532M, 5795M, 5726M, 5895M, 6150M.

NE193-NE832 Bristol 156 Beaufighter TF.X   **500**
Built at Weston. NE193-NE232, NE245-NE260, NE282-
NE326, NE339-NE386, NE398-NE446, NE459-NE502,
NE515-NE559, NE572-NE615, NE627-NE669, NE682-
NE724, NE738-NE779, NE792-NE832. NE229-NE232,
NE245, NE356, NE358-NE361, NE482-NE485, NE487,
NE584-NE586, NE588, NE589 to RAAF. NE423,
NE715, NE798, NE832 became 5743M, 6275M, 6016M,
5757M.

NE858-NF414 Fairey Swordfish II/III   **350**
Built by Blackburn. NE858-NE906, NE920-NE957,
NE970-NE999, NF113-NF161, NF175-NF217, NF230-
NF250 (230) Mk.II; NF251-NF274, NF298-NF347,
NF369-NF414 (120) Mk.III. Mainly for Royal Navy.
NF370, NF389 currently preserved.

NF418-NF665 Supermarine Seafire L.III   **200**
Built by Westland. NF418-NF455, NF480-NF526,
NF531-NF570, NF575-NF607, NF624-NF665. This
included twenty-six with fixed wings as L.IIC (hybrid).
All for Royal Navy. NF576 became 6428M.

NF668-NF739 Hawker Sea Hurricane IIC   **60**
Built at Langley. NF668-NF703, NF716-NF739. NF682,
NF686, NF737 became 6989M, 5373M, 5374M.

NF744 Slingsby T.4 Falcon III   **1**
Glider impressed.

NF745 Grunau Baby   **1**
Glider BGA148 impressed.

NF746 BAC Primary   **1**
Glider impressed, ex-BGA101.

NF747 Miles M.11A Whitney Straight   **1**
G-AFZY impressed.

NF748 Miles M.2F Hawk Major   **1**
G-ACWY impressed.

NF749 Parnall Hendy Heck IIC   **1**
G-AEGH impressed.

NF750 Miles M.2W Hawk Trainer   **1**
G-ADWT impressed.

NF751 Miles M.11A Whitney Straight   **(1)**
DP855 renumbered.

NF752 Miles M.2F Hawk Major   **1**
G-ACYO impressed.

NF753 Lockheed 12A   **1**
Bought in USA.

NF754-NF755 Focke-Wulf FW 190   **2**
Captured in Middle East.

NF756 Henschel Hs 129B-1   **1**
C/n 0297 captured in Western Desert.

NF847-NF896 DH.89A Dominie   **50**
For RAF except NF847-NF850, NF854, NF855, NF861,
NF864, NF866, NF867, NF871-NF873, NF879-NF881
to Royal Navy. Many to civil registers, including NF875
flying recently as G-AGTM. C/n 6718-6767.

NF900 Miles M.33 Monitor   **1**
Prototype to Spec Q9/42, first flew 5.4.44.

NF906-NG503 Avro 683 Lancaster B.I   **400**
Built by Armstrong Whitworth. NF906-NF939, NF952-
NF999, NG113-NG149, NG162-NG206, NG218-NG259,
NG263-NG308, NG321-NG367, NG379-NG421, NG434-
NG469, NG482-NG503. Conversions: NG234 Mk.III,
NG465 Mk.VI. NG465 used by Rolls-Royce with nose
ring for icing tests. NG130, NG340, NG489, NG494
became 6174M, 6421M, 6501M, 6449M.

NG506-NG754 Armstrong Whitworth AW.41 Albemarle   **(200)**
Ordered from Armstrong Whitworth Hawkesley. Can-
celled. NG506-NG548, NG561-NG603, NG617-NG656,
NG669-NG710, NG723-NG754.

NG757-NH611 Supermarine Spitfire LF/HF.IX   **368(600)**
Ordered from Vickers Armstrong at Castle Bromwich.
NG757-NG798, NG810-NG856, NG868-NG913, NG929-

NG968, NG979-NG999, NH112-NH147 cancelled.
NH148-NH158, NH171-NH218, NH220-NH276, NH289-
NH326, NH339-NH381, NH393-NH438, NH450-NH496,
NH513-NH558, NH570-NH611 built as LF.IX except
NH148, NH153, NH181, NH190, NH194, NH236,
NH250, NH256, NH262, NH267, NH271, NH275,
NH293, NH297, NH310, NH313, NH360, NH362,
NH418, NH420, NH422, NH433, NH437, NH450,
NH459, NH478, NH482, NH486, NH488, NH513,
NH518, NH528, NH534, NH536, NH539, NH542,
NH545, NH547, NH572, NH577, NH578, NH582,
NH587, NH611 HF.IX. NH242, NH247, NH297, NH307,
NH319, NH426, NH431, NH468, NH526, NH533,
NH599, NH604 to Italian AF others transferred to the
SAAF and USAAF. NH175, NH343 became 5692M,
6384M. NH238 sold to USA has been re-acquired in UK
as G-MKIX and NH188 preserved after becoming
CF-NUS.

NH614-NH929 Supermarine Spitfire VIII/XIV   225
NH614 HF.VIII, NH615-NH636; NH637-NH661, NH685-
NH720, NH741-NH759, NH775-NH813, NH831-NH875,
NH892-NH929 F or FR.XIV. Main deliveries to Far East.
NH643, NH654, NH655, NH658, NH688, NH694,
NH718, NH720, NH754, NH775, NH780, NH797,
NH807, NH863, NH864, NH892, NH894, NH922 to
Belgian AF postwar. NH689, NH694, NH708, NH784
became 6836M, 6340M, 6840M, 6689M. NH749 now
G-MXIV and NH631 preserved in India.

NJ170-NJ194 Short S.25 Sunderland III   25
Built by Blackburn. Conversions: NJ170-NJ172, NJ176,
NJ177, NJ179, NJ180, NJ182, NJ187, NJ188, NJ190-
NJ194 Mk.V. NJ179 Sandringham Mk.IV, NJ171 and
NJ188 Sandringham Mk.V. NJ180 became 7146M.

NJ200-NJ239 Short S.45 Seaford I   8(40)
NJ200-NJ207 only built by Short at Rochester c/n
S.1292 to S.1299. NJ200 became G-ALIJ but was not
converted for civil use, NJ201 became Seaford G-AGWU
evaluated by BOAC later G-ANAJ, NJ202-NJ207 converted to Solent III G-AKNO, 'AKNP, 'AKNR to 'AKNU
of BOAC. NJ205 later WM759. NJ208-NJ239 cancelled.

NJ253-NJ277 Short S.25 Sunderland III/V   25
Built by Short & Harland. NJ253-NJ258 built as Mk.III
and all but NJ256 converted to Mk.V. NJ259-NJ277
built as Mk.V. NJ255 converted to Sandringham IV,
NJ253, NJ257 converted to Sandringham V. NJ258,
NJ259, NJ262, NJ263, NJ266 to SAAF. NJ269 became
5753M.

NJ280-NJ607 Airspeed AS.10 Oxford I   85(250)
Ordered from Percival. NJ280-NJ322, NJ345-NJ382,
NJ397-NJ400 built. NJ401-NJ443, NJ459-NJ494,
NJ510-NJ558, NJ571-NJ607 cancelled. NJ318 re-
numbered VX587. NJ280 became 6959M. Mainly UK
delivery with postwar disposals to air forces and civil
registers. NJ318 became VX587.

NJ609-NK132 Taylorcraft Auster AOP.III/V   338
NJ609-NJ651, NJ664-NJ703, NJ716-NJ746 (114)
AOP.V; NJ747-NJ758, NJ771-NJ818, NJ830-NJ876,
NJ889-NJ935, NJ947-NJ995, NK112-NK132 (224)
AOP.III. Postwar disposals: NK129 Czech AF; NJ780,
NJ786, NJ790, NJ796, NJ811, NJ836, NJ894, NJ895,
NK125 R Hellenic AF; NJ749, NJ771, NJ783, NJ785,
NJ797, NJ800, NJ832, NJ834, NJ838, NJ859, NJ861,
NJ890, NJ910, NK113, NK123, NK126 RAAF; NJ756,
NJ776, NJ779, NJ799, NJ801, NJ808, NJ809, NJ818,
NJ870, NJ871, NJ896, NJ897, NJ916, NJ918, NJ934,
NJ952, NJ957, NJ961, NJ971, NJ972 to R Netherlands
AF. Many to civil registers postwar including NJ695,
NJ703 currently as G-AJXV, 'AKPI. NJ623, NJ626,
NJ639, NJ647, NJ665, NJ671, NJ674, NJ684, NJ700
became 5993M, 6577M, 6075M, 6073M, 6074M, 6014M,
6435M, 6193M, 5991M.

NK136   Vickers 480 Windsor   1
Third prototype, became 6222M.

NK139-NL251 Avro 652A Anson   800
Built at Yeadon. NK139-NK187, NK199-NK244,
NK260-NK303, NK314-NK351 Mk.I; NK352-NK356,
NK368, NK369 Mk.X; NK370-NK406, NK419-NK425
Mk.I; NK426-NK428 Mk.X; NK429, NK430 Mk.I;
NK431-NK433 Mk.X; NK434-NK437 Mk.I; NK438,
NK439 Mk.X; NK440-NK442 Mk.I; NK443 Mk.X;

NK444, NK445 Mk.I; NK446-NK449 Mk.X; NK450
Mk.I; NK451 Mk.X; NK452-NK462 Mk.I for export;
NK475-NK485 Mk.I; NK486 Mk.XIII; NK487-NK493
Mk.X; NK494-NK499 Mk.I; NK500 Mk.X; NK501-
NK506 Mk.I; NK507 Mk.X; NK508-NK516 Mk.I;
NK528-NK534 Mk.X; NK535-NK568, NK581-NK623,
NK636-NK656 Mk.I; NK657-NK662 Mk.X; NK663
Mk.I; NK664-NK668 Mk.X; NK669-NK679, NK692-
NK694 Mk.I; NK695, NK696 Mk.X; NK697, NK698
Mk.I; NK699, NK700 Mk.X; NK701 Mk.I; NK702,
NK703 Mk.X; NK704 Mk.I; NK705-NK707 Mk.X;
NK708, NK709 Mk.I; NK710 Mk.X; NK711 Mk.I;
NK712 Mk.X; NK713-NK715 Mk.I; NK716 Mk.X;
NK717-NK721 Mk.I; NK722 Mk.X; NK723, NK724
Mk.I; NK725 Mk.X; NK726 Mk.I; NK727, NK728
Mk.X; NK729, NK730 Mk.I; NK731 Mk.X; NK732
Mk.I; NK733, NK734 Mk.X; NK735, NK736 Mk.I;
NK737 Mk.X; NK738, NK750-NK752 Mk.I; NK753
Mk.X prototype; NK754-NK765 Mk.I; NK766-NK772
Mk.X; NK773, NK774 Mk.I; NK775 Mk.X; NK776,
NK777 Mk.I; NK778 Mk.X; NK779, NK780 Mk.I;
NK781 Mk.X; NK782, NK783 Mk.I; NK784 Mk.X;
NK785 Mk.I; NK786, NK787 Mk.X; NK788 Mk.I;
NK789 Mk.X; NK790 Mk.X; NK791 Mk.X; NK792
Mk.I; NK793 Mk.X; NK806-NK818 Mk.I; NK819,
NK820 Mk.X; NK821-NK827 Mk.I; NK828 Mk.X;
NK829-NK831 Mk.I; NK832 Mk.X; NK833-NK837 Mk.I;
NK838-NK840 Mk.I; NK841 Mk.X; NK842-NK846 Mk.I;
NK847 Mk.X; NK848, NK861 Mk.I; NK862 Mk.X;
NK863, NK864 Mk.I; NK865 Mk.X; NK866-NK869
Mk.I; NK870-NK875 Mk.X; NK876-NK906, NK919
Mk.I; NK920, NK921 Mk.X; NK922, NK923 Mk.I;
NK924, NK925 Mk.X; NK926-NK929 Mk.I; NK930-
NK935 Mk.X; NK936-NK939 Mk.I; NK940 Mk.XI;
NK941-NK958, NK976-NK985 Mk.I; NK986-NK999
Mk.XI; NL112-NL116 Mk.XI; NL117-NL124 Mk.I;
NL125 Mk.XI; NL126, NL127 Mk.I; NL128, NL129
Mk.XI; NL130, NL131 Mk.I; NL132, NL133 Mk.XI;
NL134, NL135 Mk.I; NL136, NL137 Mk.XI; NL138,
NL139 Mk.I; NL140, NL141 Mk.XI; NL142, NL143
Mk.I; NL144, NL145 Mk.XI; NL146, NL147 Mk.I;
NL148, NL149 Mk.XI; NL150, NL151 Mk.I; NL152,
NL153 C(VIP).XII; NL154, NL155, NL169, NL170
Mk.I; NL171, NL172 C.XII; NL173, NL174 Mk.I;
NL175, NL176 C.XII; NL177, NL178 Mk.I; NL179,
NL180 C.XII; NL181-NL208, NL220-NL235 Mk.XI;
NL236-NL251 C.XII. NK666, NK668 fitted out as
ambulances. Some transferred to Royal Navy and many
disposals to other air forces and civil register. NK291,
NK705, NK767, NK832, NK841, NK847, NK868,
NK924, NL222 became 6580M, 6321M, 6320M, 6958M,
6650M, 6319M, 6886M, 6581M, 6582M.

NL255   Hawker Hurricane V   1
Prototype.

NL690-NM214 DH.82A Tiger Moth I/II   350
Built by Morris Motors. NL690-NL735, NL748-NL789,
NL802-NL847, NL859-NL899 (175) Mk.II; NL903-
NL948, NL960-NL999, NM112-NM157, NM172-NM214
Mk.I. Many disposals to other air forces and civil registers
particularly France. NL698, NL985, NL998, NM154
became 5800M, 7015M, 6443M, 6877M.

NM217-NM810 Airspeed AS.10 Oxford   450
NM217-NM254, NM270-NM314, NM329-NM370,
NM385-NM429, NM444-NM488, NM509-NM550,
NM571-NM615, NM629-NM676, NM681-NM720,
NM736-NM760, NM776-NM810 built at Portsmouth.
NM532, NM533 were destroyed by fire before delivery.
Some transfers to Royal Navy. Widespread disposal to
foreign governments and civil registers. NM339, NM406,
NM589, NM754, NM790, NM797, NM799, NM808,
became 6920M, 6906M, 5840M, 6921M, 6935M, 6106M,
5853M, 6247M.

NM814-NM906 Supermarine Spitfire FR.XIV   10(70)
Ordered from Vickers Armstrong at Chattis Hill and
NM814-NM823 built. NM824-NM855, NM879-NM906
cancelled.

NM910-NM982 Supermarine Seafire L.II   60
NM910-NM949, NM963-NM982 produced in lieu of
Spitfires ordered as EN686-EN695, EN710-EN759.
For Royal Navy.

NM984-NN330   **Supermarine Seafire L.IIC/III**   **200**
Built by Westland. NM984-NM999, NN112-NN157,
NN169-NN214, NN227-NN270, NN283-NN330 built
as L.III but a few had fixed wings designated L.IIC.
For Royal Navy.

NN333-NN641   **Supermarine Seafire L/FR.III**   **250**
Built by Cunliffe-Owen. NN333-NN367, NN379-NN418,
NN431-NN476, NN488-NN528, NN542-NN586, NN599-
NN641 for Royal Navy.

NN644   **Messerschmitt Bf109F-4**   **1**
C/n 7232 landed near Beachy Head 20.5.42.

NN648-NN655   **Gloster E5/42**   **(3)**
NN648, NN651, NN655 prototypes cancelled.

NN660-NN667   **Supermarine Spiteful**   **3**
Prototypes NN660, NN664, NN667 to AM Spec F1/43.

NN670 &   **Vickers Windsor**   **(2)**
NN673   Fourth & fifth prototypes not completed.

NN694-NN816   **Avro 683 Lancaster B.I**   **100**
Built by Austin Motors. NN694-NN726, NN739-NN786,
NN798-NN816. NN801 B.VII prototype. NN812
became 5909M.

NP156-NP403   **Percival P.31 Proctor IV**   **200**
Built by F. Hills & Sons. NP156-NP198, NP210-NP254,
NP267-NP309, NP323-NP369, NP382-NP403. Disposals
to Belgian, Dutch and French forces and to civil registers.

NP406-NP533   **Miles Monitor TT.II**   **20(106)**
NP406-NP425 only built. NP426-NP448, NP461-NP506,
NP523-NP533 cancelled.

NP490   **DH.94 Moth Minor**   **1**
VP-CAG purchased in Ceylon for naval C-in-C.

NP491   **British Aircraft Swallow**   **1**
VP-CAF purchased in Ceylon for RN communications.

NP664   **Waco CG-4A Hadrian**   **1**
Glider. Origin unknown.

NP671 &   **General Aircraft GAL.55**   **2**
NP674   Training glider prototypes to Spec TX3/43.

NP681-NP927   **Handley Page Halifax B.VI/B.VII**   **200**
NP681-NP723, NP736-NP781, NP793-NP820 B.VII
except NP715, NP752, NP753 B.VI; NP821-NP836,
NP849-NP895, NP908-NP927 B.VI.

NP930-NR290   **Handley Page Halifax B.III**   **200**
Built by English Electric. NP930-NP976, NP988-NP999,
NR113-NR156, NR169-NR211, NR225-NR258, NR271-
NR290. NR115, NR279 became 5228M, 6448M and
NR169 became G-AGXA.

NR293-NR666   **Miles M.25 Martinet TT.I**   **300**
NR293-NR336, NR349-NR390, NR405-NR446, NR460-
NR503, NR516-NR556, NR569-NR616, NR628-NR666.
NR542 not delivered and NR387, NR599 converted to
Queen Martinet. Over half delivered to Royal Navy.
Disposals in particular to Belgian and French AF. NR465,
NR636 became 6912M, 6972M.

NR669-NR853   **DH.89A Dominie I**   **150**
Built by Brush Coachworks and given DH c/ns 6768-6917.
NR669-NR701, NR713-NR756, NR769-NR815, NR828-
NR853. NR739, NR748, NR788 built as Mk.II. NR669,
NR672, NR677, NR740, NR753, NR754, NR781,
NR782 to Royal Navy. Disposals to French and other
governments and to civil registers including several to
BOAC and NR747 currently registered G-AJHO.

NR857-NS204   **Fairey Swordfish III**   **200**
Built by Blackburn. NR857-NR898, NR913-NR958,
NR970-NR999, NS112-NS156, NS168-NS204 mainly
to Royal Navy.

NS487-NS493   **Supermarine Seafire XV**   **3**
Prototypes. NS487, NS490, NS493. NS493 modified
to AV standard.

NS496-NT238   **DH.98 Mosquito FB.VI/PR.XVI**   **500**
Built at Hatfield. NS496-NS538, NS551-NS585 PR.XVI;
NS586 PR.XXXII; NS587 PR.XVI; NS588, NS589
PR.XXXII; NS590-NS596, NS619-NS660, NS673-NS712,
NS725-NS758, NS772-NS816 PR.XVI; NS819-NS859,
NS873-NS914, NS926-NS965, NS977-NS999, NT112-
NT156, NT169-NT207, NT219-NT238 FB.VI except
for NT200, NT224, NT225 FB.XVIII. Transfers to the
Royal Navy and USAAF, offsets to RAAF and disposals
to Czech, French, Israeli, Turkish and Yugoslav forces.
NS551, NS572, NS643, NS682, NS686, NS740, NS803,
NS809, NS929, NS982, NT113, NT137, NT181, NT206
became 5952M, 6353M, 5760M, 6986M, 6233M, 6232M,

6120M, 6690M, 4835M, 6055M, 5077M, 5959M, 6810M,
5637M.

NT241-NT621   **DH.98 Mosquito NF.XXX**   **300**
Built at Leavesden. NT241-NT283, NT295-NT336,
NT349-NT393, NT415-NT458, NT471-NT513, NT526-
NT568, NT582-NT621. Postwar a few disposals to
Belgian and French AF. NT242, NT252, NT316, NT334,
NT350, NT363, NT391, NT422, NT428, NT431, NT434,
NT449, NT471, NT505, NT507, NT511, NT543, NT560,
NT566, NT568, NT592, NT596, NT605, NT616, NT620
became 6665M, 6661M, 6519M, 6602M, 6367M, 6118M,
6256M, 6674M, 6601M, 6447M, 6660M, 6934M, 7100M,
6893M, 6816M, 6485M, 6520M, 5915M, 6463M or
6486M, 6659M, 6017M, 6917M, 6598M, 6918M, 6594M.

NT623-NT872   **Westland Welkin**   **1(200)**
NT623 only built. NT624-NT666, NT680-NT725,
NT738-NT779, NT793-NT823, NT836-NT872 cancelled.

NT888-NV632   **Bristol 156 Beaufighter TF.X**   **500**
Built at Weston. NT888-NT929, NT942-NT971, NT983-
NT999, NV113-NV158, NV171-NV218, NV233-NV276,
NV289-NV333, NV347-NV390, NV413-NV457,
NV470-NV513, NV526-NV572, NV585-NV632. NT928,
NT947, NV177, NV192, NV292, NV297, NV387,
NV423, NV425, NV432, NV441, NV492, NV537,
NV541, NV622 became 6098M, 6097M, 6093M, 6094M,
6089M, 6090M, 5766M, 6091M, 6092M, 6095M, 6069M,
6067M, 6099M, 6096M, 5765M.

NV636   **Blackburn Firebrand TF.2**   **(1)**
Prototype built with airframe of DD810.

NV639-NV793   **Hawker Tempest V Srs.II**   **130**
NV639-NV682, NV695-NV735, NV749-NV793. NV768
used for engine cooling experiments by Napier. NV652,
NV653, NV674, NV675, NV682, NV696, NV732,
NV756, NV774 became 6349M, 5857M, 6475M, 5856M,
5858M, 6474M, 6328M, 5855M, 5754M. Postwar
NV645, NV661, NV664, NV665, NV669, NV671,
NV699, NV704, NV711, NV723, NV725, NV762,
NV778, NV780, NV781, NV793 converted to TT.5.
NV778 became 8386M for RAF Museum preservation.

NV805-NV876   **General Aircraft GAL.49 Hamilcar**   **(60)**
Cancelled order. NV805-NV838, NV851-NV876.

NV917-NX482   **Hawker Tempest V/VI**   **211(369)**
Built at Langley. NV917-NV948, NV960-NV996 (69)
Mk.V of which NV917, NV922, NV923, NV928, NV937,
NV940, NV960, NV962, NV965, NV974, NV975,
NV978, NV992, NV994, NV996 were converted postwar
to TT.5. NV997-NV999, NX113-NX156, NX169-NX209,
NX223-NX268, NX281-NX288 (142) Mk.VI. NX289-
NX325, NX338-NX381, NX394-NX435, NX448-NX482
cancelled. NV918, NV944, NX121, NX176, NX286
became 5704M, 5994M, 6620M, 6653M, 6336M.

NX484-NX545   **Taylorcraft Auster III**   **50**
NX484-NX509, NX522-NX545. NX494, NX498, NX500,
NX501, NX528, NX533, NX535 to RAAF; NX486,
NX534, NX537, NX545 to R Netherlands AF.

NX548-NX794   **Avro 683 Lancaster B.I/VII**   **200**
Built by Austin Motors. NX548-NX589, NX603-NX610
(50) B.I (B.VII interim); NX611-NX648, NX661-NX703,
NX715-NX758, NX770-NX794 (150) B.VII to Far East
standard. NX560, NX579, NX629, NX634, NX687,
NX735, NX737, NX790, NX793 became 5845M, 6305M,
6753M, 6216M, 6816M, 6713M, 6736M, 6786M, 6424M.
Several disposals to France for Aeronavale. NX726
became G-ALVC and NX611 became 8375M preserved
at Scampton. NX622 is preserved in Australia and
NX665 in New Zealand.

NX798 &   **Hawker Fury**   **2**
NX802   Prototypes to Spec F2/43. NX798 sold to Egypt and
NX802 to Pakistan.

NX805-NX876   **General Aircraft GAL.49 Hamilcar**   **60**
Group-built. NX805-NX838, NX851-NX876.

NX879-PA129   **Supermarine Seafire IB**   **(118)**
Conversion of Spitfire airframes by Cunliffe Owen.
NX879-NX928 ex-BL635, BL260, BL521, AD421,
W3212, AD517, BL729, BM596, AB933, BL931, AB902,
AD582, BL593, AB908, BL546, BL929, BL301, BL750,
BL373, BL958, AD387, BM625, BM377, AD358, BL495,
AD579, EN825, BL493, BL414, BL986, EN980, BL420,
BL983, BL597, BL846, AD580, AD567, BL675, AB968,
AB919, AD365, BL855, BL894, AD566, BM420,

continued on page 193

P7308 P7308 was already in service when fighter bands were introduced. With large unit code letters serials had to infringe on both codes and bands.

P7420 Close-up shot of Spitfire serialling using 8-inch letter and digit stencils.

R5700 In Bomber Command the stipulated serial presentation was in dull brick red on the night camouflage surfaces of the bombers.

S1648 The excessive spacing between S16 and 48 of S1648 under the wings is due to the area where bomb carriers could be attached.

SR1143 Re-built in the Middle East as the R inserted in S1143 indicates, this Fairey IIIF has lost its Fairey c/n marking in the process.

S1233 Full serial S1233 for rear hull and rudder positions, but just the large number shown forward as a formation identity number.

AG122 A Canadian-built Hawker Hurricane with serial stencilled over the sky fighter band.

AE979 Conspicuously in white, the serials were marked on the booms of Lockheed Lightnings.

AH573 On the Airacobra the under-surface sky finish was raised at the rear fuselage to make a clear display area for the serial.

AM958 The Americans assumed wrongly that the serial prefix letters AM stood for Air Ministry and so made this Marlet II A.M.958.

T8559 A Miles Master shows its neat black serial presentation on its trainer yellow background.

W4041/G Not surprisingly the 'G' for Guard suffix was applied to Britain's first jet aircraft, W4041/G.

Z7785 Stencilled serials in black on a Blenheim serving overseas.

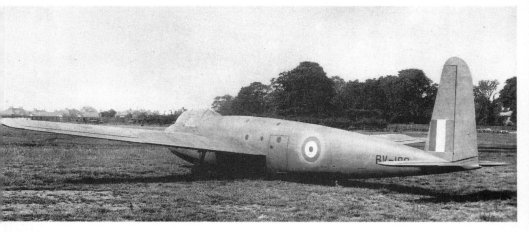

BV100 The first gliders in the BV series came with prefix letters hyphenated to the number.

EE530 The EE series introduced the first production jet-engined aircraft into the serialling system.

EW999 Dual identity for this Skymaster as USAAF 43-17126, taken on RAF charge as EW999.

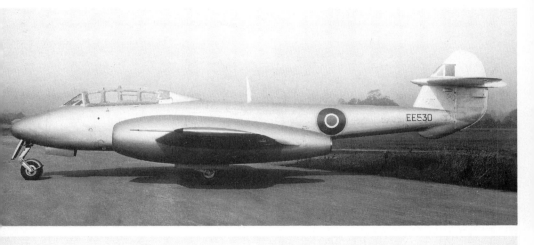

HL864 Whats the quest? It could be the apparant lack of serial, but actually HL864 is marked under the shadow of the tailplane.

FE4xx Serials were marked large on many batches of Harvards so that their serials would also act as 'identity in unit' numbers.

FL503 This SEAC Dakota has had its roundel outlined and serial repainted white.

FK818 A Stinson Reliant snapped on 14th June 1943 displaying its black underwing identity number on its yellow undersurface.

FN106 Many Martlets were delivered with their serials in standard 8-inch characters and were repainted half-size Navy fashion in service.

JK226 A Spitfire in USAAF service retains its original British identity of JK226.

JK608 In Yugoslav service, but with original British serial identities painted small in the fighter band.

JM831 Royal Navy standard presentation style on JM831 marked in 4-inch characters with similar sized ROYAL NAVY marking above.

KH342 KH342/G SNAKE meant that this aircraft was to be guarded (G) and not be diverted in transit through the Middle East to the Far East (Code Snake).

KD300 Navy fashion again in the 4-inch serial marking on this Corsair.

KL887 One of the few Thunderbolts to the reach the UK, the bulk having been shipped direct to the Far East from the USA.

MC561 An MC range of numbers was never officially allotted, but this Tiger Moth has been marked MC561 which, it has been suggested was its Morris Cowley c/n.

PX848 RCAF Lancaster KB848 retains its number identity and its PX code as a prefix, common to all RCAF Lancasters.

NV768 Prototype fighter markings - roundel, prototype P, serial and fighter band.

PK664 Officially ground instructional airframe 7759M, gate guardian at RAF Binbrook PK664 is given its original serial. Photo taken May 1970.

PP375 The re-introduction of underwing serials on operational aircraft postwar made Halifax aircraft much more identifiable.

PS946 Postwar underwing serialling displayed by a Seafire, with serialling cramped between roundel and wheel well.

RA356 Royal Navy standard serial presentation: 4-inch characters and prototype P ring marking.

PR479 British serials were retained by Seafires in RCN service and followed RN pattern as shown by the 4-inch high PR479 in this case.

RA722 Serial numbers at their very largest appeared on postwar Lincolns.

TA379 A clear serial representation on a Mosquito placed centrally over the division between upper and lower surface finishes.

RN784 A Horsa glider shows that aircraft identity markings took precedence over the invasion identity striping.

SR396 Light coloured and small sized serial SR396 on the light PR finish of this Spitfire X.

RB518 The stencilled serial on a Spiteful, the projected Spitfire replacement.

RK558 The underwing serial is barely discernable on this postwar Barracuda. The ruling was that the characters shound be the same height as roundel diameter, but no roundel is displayed.

RN244 On this Spearfish there is no room for the underwing display of prefix letters.

TG/380 Note the addition of a stroke in the form TG/380 on this early 3 Squadron Vampire F.1, at Tangmere, May 1949 (R.Bonser).

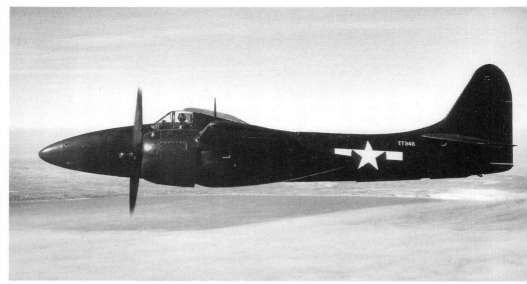

TT346 US Navy markings but the British serial TT346 on this Tigercat sent for Fleet Air Arm trials.

VP422 The Hawker P.1040 prototype displays underwing serials smaller in height than the decreed roundel diameter.

TS475 The black striping on the yellow undersurfaces on target-towing aircraft was broken to allow unimpeded serial number display.

VS837 Brigand T.5 with its large fuselage serial marked over its yellow trainer band.

VW880 A Wyvern S.4 displays its underwing serial matching the roundels in size but out of line with them.

VT103 Meteor F.4 with non-standard small presentation of underwing serial.

VX101 Captured enemy aircraft flown by the RAF or RN for evaluation were allotted serials in the normal series.

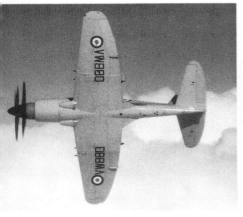

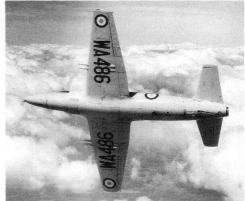

WD918 By marking the underwing serials in a Firefly it was hoped to make them clear irrespective of underwing stores - WD918 is shown.

WA486 Underwing serial display on Attackers were in non-standard 'squashed-up' characters.

VX373 Firefly T.5 VX373 retains its serial in RAN service marked in RN fashion of 4-inch high characters with the letters RAN above.

WD952 Roundels were not applicable to the black undersurfaces of intruder aircraft in order not to compromise camouflage!

VX185 Marked on the nose as 'The Record Breaking Canberra B5' VX185 displays its fuselage serial in 8-inch characters.

VX185 The same Canberra modified as the prototype B(I).8 has its serial three times the height as above.

VX330 The Blackburn-built Handley Page HP.88 in June 1951 had its fuselage roundel as far forward as possible and its fuselage serial as far rearward as possible.

WF331 This Varsity in Training Command finish has its serial adjacent to the roundel.

WF997 The underwing serial presentation on the Balliol was well outboard to avoid marking over the yellow trainer band.

WJ467 Neat and clear, placed between the roundel and trainer band, the underwing serial presentation by a Valetta.

WH904 Unusual here is the phasing in of the fuselage serial with the Dayglo high visibility pattern.

WK379 Sea Venom serial in two parts to avoid figures being covered when underwing stores are carried.

WK131 Serial characters correct to AP.2656A instructions with the 'K' styled as shown and the '3' precisely the same as an eight with part deleted. Cottesmore station badge on fin.

WJ154 Another Firefly shows wide spacing between the initial letter and the rest of the serial.

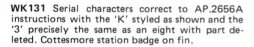

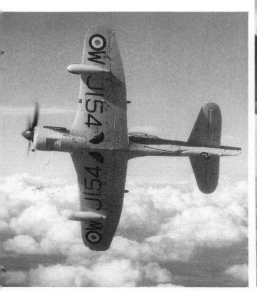

WR784 Venom NF.2 with serial marked over the demarkation between upper and lower surfaces.

WS107 Royal Navy regulation 4-inch fuselage serial presentation.

WT330 A Canberra B.8 shows the clear underwing serial presentation on its black undersurfaces.

WM236 Meteor NF.11 upper surface camouflage raised to contrast the black serial against the lighter undersurface.

WM982 Uniformity of the serials on these Sea Hawks is evident.

WT944 The midnite blue finish of Sky-raider AEW.1s led to their serials being in white in all positions. An 849 Squadron example is featured here.

WT827 This Javelin prototype shows the accomodation of the serial on what was then the newly introduced delta-winged fighter.

WZ722 Austers were finished in overall camouflage which was compromised by the large white serial presentation.

WT314 Back to normal size fuselage serial presentation on Canberras as displayed by a No.213 Squadron aircraft with the unit's Hornet badge.

WV387 On Hunters with swept wings the expedient of displaying prefix letters above the number was adopted.

WZ551 Spaced underwing serial on a Vampire T.11 to take into account the carriage of underwing stores.

XA260 On the Marathon the fuselage serial was placed on the trainer band and underwing it appeared well outboard as shown.

XA891 Underwing serial presentation on the large area available on the delta-winged Avro Vulcan.

XB444 Underwing serial presented well outboard on an Avenger AS.4 supplied under MDAP.

XA539 The Sea Venom's underwing serial presented well forward between roundels and wheel wells.

XA918 An 24-inch high serial presentation on the fuselage of a Handley Page Victor B.1.

XF682 British serial retained on an armed Provost serving with the Sultan of Oman's Air Force.

XD158 With delta-wing fighters like the Javelin with no suitable lateral area on the fuselage, serials were placed on the engine nacelles.

XE169 Standard underwing serial presentation on the unorthodox Short Seamew.

XE796 Air Training Corps gliders are included in the normal military aircraft serialling.

XG308 For the well-swept Lightning wings, the serial was also swept to follow the angle of sweep.

XJ384 It had to happen! The French-built Alouette AH.2s were supplied wrongly painted - their XJ prefixes were later altered to XR (via P.Butler)

XM595 The delta-winged Avro Vulcan lateral serial presentation on the fin (R.Bonser)

XK382 The 'Army' service marking appearing in line with the serial on an Auster AOP.9.

XG589 With RN helicopters the serialling kept to the 4-inch sizing but the wording 'Royal Navy' formerly the same size, was enlarged.

XL513 This Victor displays its fuselage serial in white. Most were eventually repainted in black.

XL571 Hunter T.7 with black under-wing serial over the yellow trainer band and fuselage presentation well to the rear of the band.

XK671 Transport Command trim for Comet C.2 'Aquila' of 216 Squadron. Serial presented large under the wings, fuselage serial in 8-inch characters placed in a break in the cheat line and the number portion repeated on the fin.

XH882 Javelin FAW.9 with white serial forward of wing leading edge at Bruntingthorpe in May 1960. Some of the Javelin squadrons had black serials. (C.J Salter).

XR667 Jet Provost T.4 serials were positioned a little further forward than their T.3 counterparts.

XL500 Gannet AEW.3 reveals where the underwing serial marking was positioned to cope with the wing fold. (C.J.Salter).

XS161 The ribbed construction of the tail boom does not aid the identification of this Royal Navy Hiller HT.2 (via C.J.Salter).

XP357 XP357 with serial position raised and marked in black on a high-visibility finish.

XR456 On United Nations duty, the UN marking replaced the national markings, but not its national identity number.

XV185 Marking the number portion of an RAF Hercules serial large on the nose.

XR143 Ventral view of this Argosy C.1 shows serials displayed underwings, on boom in break of cheat line and the 'last three' on the fin. (C.J. Salter).

XV617 Hovercraft were numbered in the British military aircraft serialling when taken on charge by the Services. The number appears on the prow of this SRN.6.

XX946 A Tornado prototype, known then as the MRCA, bore its serial well forward on the rear fuselage.

XS923 The difference in visibility of black serial numbers on camouflaged and uncamouflaged aircraft is brought out in this photo. The 'lost' serial is XR749.

XV498 The number portion of the Phantom serials - in this case 498 - was presented on the fin in some instances. The fuselage serial has been 'lost' in the camouflage paintwork.

ZA254 Prototype ADV Tornado F.2 reveals its standard-position fuselage serial, and a larger version under the 'taileron' — which wasn't adopted for production examples. (via Paul Jackson)

ZD650 Schleicher ASK.21 - known as the Vanguard TX.1 in 'Air Cadets' service, has a minute fuselage roundel.

A511 Seafire III NN585 ex G4-F of 761 Sqdn at Henstridge, serves to illustrate the Admiralty Instructional Airframes appendix. Photo taken circa 1949 at Ratcliffe, Leics. (via Roy Bonser)

193M This DH.9 is unusual in that it displays its Instructional Airframe number in two differing modes- one prefixed with 'INS' (via Roy Bonser)

7957M Provost T.1 relegated for instructional use, wears its 'M' serial over a red day-glo panel on the rear fuselage. Photo taken Finningley '68.

AIR MIN 11 This Focke-Wulf Ta152H serves to illustrate the appendix dealing with captured enemy aircraft that were used for evaluation.

ZD696 BAe 146 with standard 8-in serial characters barely discernable on the fin below the flash.

ZA101 Demonstrator G-HAWK is carrying a military serial as permit for it being shown armed.

XH200 Latest known serial as we go to press, has been applied over primer. A few days later it was given a two-tone green scheme for its 1st public appearance at the 1987 Paris Air Show. (BAe)

BM580, EN839, AD274, BL254, BM631; NX940-NX967 ex-BM632, BL522, EN763, AB181, BL539, BM559, AA750, AD510, AB817, AD552, BM314, AB928, EN851, EN912, BL736, BL321, AD271, AD368, BL570, BL639, BL901, BM367, EN864, AB809, AB967 and W3646 allocated for conversion but cancelled. AD120, BL757; NX980-NX989 ex-W3372, BL239, AD241, BL930, two not known possibly cancelled, BL434, one unknown; BM541, BL994; PA100-PA129 ex-BL527, BM570, AD397, EN769, BM626, AD393, EN764, AD394, AA932, AD364, BL695, BL492, AD357, BL770, EN790, BL586, BL428, EP166, AD184, W3371, BL296, BL524, EN910, BL861, BM457, BL730, BL806, BL904, AD252, BL566.

PA143-PA152   **Supermarine Seagull**   2(3)
Prototypes to Spec S14/44. PA143 and PA147 built, PA152 not completed.

PA158-PA835   **Avro 683 Lancaster B.I**   235(500)
Ordered from Vickers Armstrong Chester plant. PA158-PA198, PA214-PA239, PA252-PA288, PA303-PA351, PA365-PA396, PA410-PA452, PA473-PA478, PA509 built as B.I and from PA384 modified to Far East standard; some conversions to PR.I later. PA479-PA508, PA510-PA512, PA526-PA563, PA579-PA625, PA646-PA687, PA701-PA737, PA752-PA799, PA816-PA835 cancelled. Disposals to Argentine, Egyptian and French forces. PA252, PA382, PA434, PA478 became 6169M, 6505M, 6493M, 6811M. PA474 preserved.

PA838-PA961   **Supermarine Spitfire PR.XI**   100
PA838-PA871, PA884-PA913, PA926-PA961. Some transferred to USAAF. PA884 became 5679M.

PA964-PD196   **Avro 683 Lancaster/Lancastrian**   757(800)
Built at Manchester. PA964-PA999, PB112-PB158, PB171-PB213, PB226-PB267, PB280-PB308, PB341-PB385, PB397-PB438, PB450-PB490, PB504-PB542, PB554-PB596, PB609-PB653, PB666-PB708, PB721-PB768, PB780-PB823, PB836-PB881, PB893-PB936, PB949-PB994 Mk.III; PB995-PB998, PD112-PD139 Mk.I (Special). PD140-PD146 airframes used for Lancastrians VB873, VD238, VD241, VD253, VF163-VF165; PD159-PD183 airframes used for Lancastrians VF166, VF167, VF152-VF156, VF160-VF162, VF145-VF151, VF137-VF144; PD184-PD192 cancelled; PD193, PD194 completed as Lancastrian VH737, VH742; PD195, PD196 cancelled. PB136, PB142, PB297, PB342, PB420, PB462, PB470, PB480, PB482, PB489, PB529, PB585, PB694, PB855, PB920, PB926, PB986 became 6261M, 5725M, 5849M, 5914M, 6259M, 5815M, 5850M, 6710M, 5723M, 6241M, 7102M, 6167M, 5851M, 5847M, 6386M, 5966M, 6304M

PD198-PD444   **Avro 683 Lancaster B.I**   200
Built by Metropolitan Vickers. PD198-PD239, PD252-PD296, PD309-PD349, PD361-PD404, PD417-PD444. PD328 *Aries*. PD281, PD348, PD418 became 5001M, 5000M, 5736M.

PD446-PD623   **Hawker Typhoon IB**   145
PD446-PD480, PD492-PD536, PD548-PD577, PD589-PD623. PD452, PD512, PD608 became 5641M, 5612M, 5642M.

PD625-PD692   **Gliders (for type see remarks below)**   42
Built up by ATC cadets from spares and acquisitions. PD625-PD635, PD637-PD639, PD643-PD647, PD650-PD652, PD656, PD659-PD662, PD665, PD666, PD679, PD682, PD685, PD686, PD690-PD692 Kirby Cadet type and PD654, PD655, PD658, PD664, PD680, PD681 Dagling type.

PE101-PE248   **Avro 685 York C.1**   8(100)
PE101-PE108 only built; PE109-PE129, PE146-PE191, PE224-PE248 cancelled.

PE510-PE878   **Vickers Windsor I**   (300)
Order reduced to 100, then 40 and finally cancelled. PE510-PE553, PE565-PE606, PE618-PE658, PE671-PE715, PE727-PE769, PE782-PE826, PE839-PE878.

PE882   **Focke Wulf FW 190A-4/U-8**   1
C/n 7155. Captured when landed in error at West Malling on 17.4.43.

PE885-PF367   **Hawker Tempest II**   (300)
Bristol Aeroplane Co order. Cancelled. PE885-PE927, PE939-PE966, PE978-PE999, PF112-PF158, PF171-PF213. PF225-PF266, PF280-PF319, PF333-PF367.

PF370   **Westland Welkin II**   1
Prototype to Spec F9/43. Later became P-17 and WE997.

PF379-PF680   **DH.98 Mosquito B.XVI/PR.XXXIV**   245
Built by Percival. PF379-PF415, PF428-PF469, PF481-PF526, PF538-PF579, PF592-PF619 (195) B.XVI of which PF439, PF445, PF449, PF452, PF481-PF483, PF489, PF560, PF562, PF569, PF576, PF599, PF606, PF609 were converted to TT.39. PF620-PF635, PF647-PF680 (50) PR.XXXIV of which PF652, PF656, PF662, PF669, PF670, PF673, PF678-PF680 were converted to PR.34A. PF388, PF397, PF442, PF484, PF498, PF524, PF547, PF567, PF572, PF594 became 6571M, 5962M, 6587M, 6595M, 6607M, 6608M, 6588M, 6551M, 6237M, 6589M and PF677 was allotted 7147M.

PF690-PF817   **Airspeed AS.51 Horsa I**   100
PF690-PF725, PF739-PF770, PF786-PF817.

PF820-PG422   **Vickers Wellington X/XIV/XVIII**   400
Built at Blackpool. PF820-PF822 Mk.XIV; PF823-PF830 Mk.X; PF831-PF838 Mk.XIV; PF839-PF846 Mk.X; PF847-PF854 Mk.XIV; PF855-PF862 Mk.X; PF863-PF866, PF879-PF882 Mk.XIV; PF883-PF888 Mk.X; PF889-PF893 Mk.XIV; PF894-PF901 Mk.X; PF902-PF911 Mk.XIV; PF912-PF915, PF927-PF930 Mk.X; PF931-PF940 Mk.XIV; PF941-PF948 Mk.X; PF949-PF958 Mk.XIV; PF959-PF966 Mk.X; PF967, PF968, PF979-PF986 Mk.XIV; PF987-PF994 Mk.X; PF995-PF999, PG112-PG116 Mk.XIV; PG117-PG124 Mk.X; PG125-PG134 Mk.XIV; PG135-PG138 Mk.X; PG139-PG148 Mk.XIV; PG149-PG152 Mk.X; PG153-PG157, PG170-PG174 Mk.XIV; PG175-PG182 Mk.X; PG183-PG192 Mk.XIV; PG193-PG196 Mk.X; PG197-PG206 Mk.XIV; PG207-PG210 Mk.X; PG211-PG215, PG227-PG231 Mk.XIV; PG232-PG235 Mk.X; PG236-PG239 Mk.XVIII; PG240-PG245 Mk.XIV; PG246-PG249 Mk.XVIII; PG250-PG253 Mk.X; PG254-PG257 Mk.XVIII; PG258-PG265 Mk.X; PG266-PG269, PG282-PG285 Mk.XIV; PG286-PG297 Mk.X; PG298-PG303 Mk.XIV; PG304-PG326, PG338-PG348 Mk.X; PG349-PG356 Mk.XVIII; PG357-PG366 Mk.X; PG367-PG370 Mk.XVIII; PG371-PG379, PG392-PG394 Mk.X; PG395-PG400 Mk.XVIII; PG401-PG422 Mk.X. Postwar conversion of B.X to T.10 included: PF989-PF991, PG136, PG137, PG152, PG176, PG233, PG262, PG265, PG287, PG292-PG296, PG312, PG314, PG315, PG317, PG318, PG341, PG342, PG357, PG359, PG372, PG373, PG379, PG414, PG416, PG419, PG420. PF915, PF992 became 6871M, 6209M.

PG425-PG610   **Hawker Hurricane IIB/IIC bomber version**   150
PG425-PG456, PG469-PG499, PG512-PG554, PG567-PG610. PG432, PG440, PG445, PG451, PG484, PG486, PG497-PG499, PG516, PG517, PG519, PG539, PG541, PG548, PG551, PG570-PG573, PG604, PG606 became 5498M, 5462M, 5343M, 5420M, 5422M, 5303M, 5417M, 5421M, 5500M, 5499M, 5407M, 5277M, 5708M, 5442M, 5461M, 5465M, 5464M, 5333M, 5707M, 5331M, 5416M, 5408M.

PG614-PG922   **DH.82A Tiger Moth T.II**   110(250)
PG614-PG658, PG671-PG716, PG728-PG746 built by Morris Motors; PG747-PG769, PG782-PG824, PG837-PG871, PG884-PG922 cancelled. 61 to French, 24 to Dutch and 8 to Greek forces from late production.

PG925-PH535   **Airspeed AS.10 Oxford**   400
PG925-PG956, PG968-PG999, PH112-PH157, PH169-PH215, PH227-PH268, PH281-PH327, PH339-PH379, PH391-PH425, PH447-PH489, PH502-PH535 built at Portsmouth. PH528-PH535 were renumbered VB861-VB868. 78 delivered to Royal Navy, a few shipped to New Zealand, Middle and Far East. Disposals to Belgian and Danish forces and to civil registers. PG985, PG988, PH119, PH127, PH299, PH342, PH513, PH521, PH524 became 6191M, 6032M, 5950M, 5484M, 6199M, 6265M, 6888M, 5864M, 6949M.

PH528-PH865   **Avro 652A Anson C.XII/XIX**   268
Built at Yeadon. PH528-PH569, PH582-PH626, PH638-PH679, PH691-PH735, PH747-PH789, PH803-PH840 C.XII of which PH806 became C.XIX prototype; PH841-PH845, PH858-PH865 C.XIX. A few to RN. Disposals to Belgian, Czech and Egyptian forces and civil registers. PH553, PH586, PH644, PH749, PH804, PH834 became 7219M, 7117M, 6999M, 7103M, 7101M, 7110M.

PJ660-PJ872   **Hawker Hurricane XIIA**   150
Built by the Canadian Car & Foundry Corporation.
PJ660-PJ695, PJ711-PJ758, PJ779-PJ813, PJ842-PJ872
to basic Mk.IIC/D standards. Majority shipped to Russia.

PJ876   **Junkers Ju88R-1**   1
C/n 360043. Surrendered enemy aircraft flew to
Dyce 9.5.43. Allotted 8475M. Now preserved.

PJ878-PK237   **Short S.29 Stirling IV/V**   175
Built by Short & Harland. PJ878-PJ923, PJ935-PJ959,
PJ971-PJ999, PK113-PK158, PK171-PK186 Mk.V;
PK225-PK237 Mk.IV. PJ904, PJ958, PK121 became
5745M, 5797M, 5901M and PK148 became G-AKPC.

PK240-PK245   **Supermarine Seafire XV**   3
Prototypes. PK240, PK243, PK245 ordered as
Griffon-engined Seafires.

PK248-PK309   **Airspeed AS.10 Oxford**   50
Built at Portsmouth. PK248-PK269, PK282-PK309.
Some converted postwar to Consuls. PK286 which
became G-AIKR is preserved in Ottawa.

PK312-PL499   **Supermarine Spitfire IX/F.22/F.24**   568(800)
Ordered from Vickers Armstrong at Castle Bromwich.
PK312-PK356, PK369-PK412, PK426-PK435 F.22;
PK436-PK468 cancelled; PK481-PK525, PK539-PK582,
PK594-PK635, PK648-PK677 F.22; PK678-PK689,
PK712-PK726 F.24; PK727-PK754, PK769-PK811,
PK828-PK868, PK883-PK926, PK949-PK990 cancelled.
PK991-PK998, PL123-PL169, PL185-PL227, PL246-
PL288, PL313-PL356, PL369-PL408, PL423-PL466,
PL488-PL499 LF.IX except PL189, PL192, PL194,
PL203, PL209, PL215, PL218, PL222, PL249, PL253,
PL256, PL261, PL263, PL371, PL372, PL374-PL380,
PL384-PL388, PL390, PL392, PL396, PL400, PL432,
PL450, PL452, PL489 HF.IX. Disposals of Mk.IX to
French, Italian and Turkish forces and of F.22s to the
S Rhodesian AF. PK318, PK624, PK664, PK683, PK724,
PL256, PL277, PL371 became 6255M, 8072M, 7759M,
7150M, 7288M, 6371M, 6041M, 5751M, those with
numbers over 7000M being currently preserved in the
UK and PK481 in Australia.

PL758-PM676   **Supermarine Spitfire XI/XIX**   351(600)
Ordered from Vickers Armstrong at Chattis Hill and
Aldermaston. PL758-PL799, PL823-PL866, PL881-
PL925, PL949-PL998, PM123-PM168 Pr.XI; PM184-
PM228, PM245-PM288, PM302-PM347, PM367-PM404,
PM419-PM461 cancelled; PM462 PR.XIX; PM478-
PM495 cancelled; PM496-PM519, PM536-PM581,
PM596-PM637, PM651-PM661 PR.XIX; PM662-PM670
PR.XIX cancelled and PM671-PM676 planned as Spite-
fuls also cancelled. PL837, PM144, PM154, PM610,
PM611, PM633, PM634, PM651 became 5953M, 6248M,
6249M, 6995M, 6996M, 6453M, 6160M, 7758M. PL965,
PL979, PL983, PM627, PM631, PM651 are preserved.

PM679   **Focke Wulf FW 190A-4/U-8**   1
C/n 2596 landed at Manston in error 20.6.43.

PM682-PN164   **Fairey Barracuda III**   300
C/n F.6720-F.7019 built at Heaton Chapel for Royal
Navy. PM682-PM723, PM738-PM780, PM796-PM838,
PM852-PM897, PM913-PM958, PM970-PM999, PN115-
PN164. PM940, PM941, PM944 converted to Mk.V
prototypes.

PN167-PN362   **Handley Page Halifax B.III/A.VII/B.VII**   131(150)
Built by Fairey. PN167-PN207 B.III; PN208, PN223-
PN242 B.VII; PN243-PN267, PN285-PN327, PN343
A.VII; PN344-PN362 not completed. PN315 became
6385M.

PN365-PN619   **Handley Page Halifax B.III**   80(200)
Built by London Aircraft Production Group. PN365-
PN406, PN423-PN460 B.III; PN461-PN470, PN485-
PN527, PN540-PN566, PN580-PN619 cancelled. PN446
became 5731M.

PN623-PN996   **Vickers Warwick V/VI**   127(300)
Built at Weybridge. PN623-PN667, PN681-PN696 can-
celled; PN697-PN725, PN739-PN782, PN796-PN825
GR.V; PN826-PN839, PN853-PN862 ASR.VI; PN863-
PN888, PN910-PN952, PN964-PN996 cancelled.

PN999   **Focke Wulf Fw 190A-4/U-8**   1
C/n 5843 landed in error at Manston 20.5.43. Became
8470M.

PP103-PP132   **Short S.25 Sunderland V**   30
Built at Rochester. PP110, PP124, PP129 became

NZ4105, NZ4113, NZ4110 of the RNZAF. PP104,
PP109, PP125 to the SAAF.

PP135-PP164   **Short S.25 Sunderland III/V**   30
Built by Blackburn. PP135-PP144 as Mk.III of which
PP137, PP141, PP143, PP144 were converted to Mk.V
and PP145-PP164 were built as Mk.V. PP143 became
NZ4119 of RNZAF and PP153, PP156 went to SAAF.
PP145 became 6103M.

PP139   **Supermarine Spitfire F.21**   1
Prototype. Compromised number above.

PP142-PP389   **Handley Page Halifax VI/VII/VIII**   200
PP142-PP164 compromised Sunderland numbers above
and were renumbered TW774-TW796. PP165-PP187,
PP203-PP216 B.VI; PP217-PP243 C.VIII; PP244-PP247
A.VIII; PP259-PP296, PP308-PP338 C.VIII; PP339-
PP350, PP362-PP389 A.VII. PP217-PP220, PP222-
PP224, PP226, PP228-PP231, PP233-PP235, PP237-
PP247, PP259-PP284, PP286-PP296, PP308-PP317,
PP319-PP324, PP326-PP331, PP333-PP338 to British
civil register. PP149, PP227, PP236, PP366 became
6031M, 6010M, 6007M, 6509M.

PP391-PP660   **Fairey Firefly I**   200
C/n F.6120-F.6319. PP391-PP437, PP456-PP497, PP523-
PP567, PP580-PP623, PP639-PP660. PP437, PP458,
PP472, PP474, PP484, PP486, PP487, PP489, PP492-
PP494, PP497, PP526-PP528, PP583, PP590-PP593,
PP601-PP603, PP606, PP607, PP614-PP616, PP619,
PP623 to Royal Netherlands Naval Air Service, others to
the RCN. Many remaining in Royal Naval service variously
converted including PP485, PP523, PP657 to T.3.

PP663-PP918   **Avro 683 Lancaster B.I**   100(200)
Ordered from Vickers Armstrong at Castle Bromwich.
PP663-PP695, PP713-PP758, PP772-PP792 built; PP793-
PP806, PP820-PP866, PP880-PP918 cancelled. PP688-
PP690, PP734. PP739, PP741-PP744, PP746, PP751 to
civil register and PP791 became Rolls-Royce testbed.

PP921-PR334   **Supermarine Seafire L.III**   250
Built by Westland. PP921-PP957, PP969-PP999, PR115-
PR156, PR170-PR215, PR228-PR271, PR285-PR334
for Royal Navy. PP972 has been restored in France.

PR338-PR506   **Supermarine Seafire F.XV**   134
Built by Cunliffe-Owen. PR338-PR379, PR391-PR436,
PR449-PR479, PR492-PR506. Ten disposed of to the
Burmese AF. PR410, PR503 are preserved in Canada.

PR525-PS681   **Hawker Tempest II**   302(800)
Built at Langley. PR525-PR567, PR581-PR623, PR645-
PR689, PR713-PR758, PR771-PR815, PR830-PR876,
PR889-PR921 completed; PR922-PR928, PR941-PR967,
PR979-PR999, PS115-PS117, PS173-PS215, PS229-
PS273, PS287-PS329, PS342-PS387, PS408-PS449,
PS463-PS507, PS520-PS563, PS579-PS625, PS637-
PS681 cancelled. Over thirty disposed to Indian and
Pakistan forces. PR669, PR846 became 5767M, 6625M.

PS684-PS935   **Supermarine Spitfire PR.XIX**   79(200)
PS684-PS725, PS739-PS781, PS795-PS830 ordered as
HF.VIII but cancelled. PS831-PS836, PS849-PS893,
PS908-PS935 built as PR.XIX. PS915 became 7548M
then 7711M for preservation, PS836 preserved in
Thailand and PS890 in the USA.

PS936-PW250   **Supermarine Spitfire/Seafire**   707(1500)
Ordered from Vickers Armstrong at Castle Bromwich as
Spitfire F.22. PS936-PS943 cancelled; PS944-PS957
Seafire F.47; PS958-PS987, PT163-PT203, PT222-
PT229 cancelled; PT335-PT380, PT395-PT436, PT451-
PT498, PT523-PT567, PT582-PT627, PT639-PT683,
PT697-PT738, PT752-PT795, PT818-PT859, PT873-
PT915, PT929-PT970, PT986-PT999, PV115-PV160,
PV174-PV215, PV229-PV270, PV283-PV327, PV341-
PV359 LF.IX except for PT398, PT432, PT434, PT455,
PT460, PT462, PT463, PT465, PT466, PT470, PT473,
PT474, PT480, PT481, PT486, PT488, PT493, PT601,
PT605, PT608, PT612, PT614, PT619, PT627, PT640,
PT650, PT657, PT714, PT733, PT753, PT756, PT760,
PT761, PT764-PT766, PT768, PT781, PT787, PT818,
PT835, PT847, PT876, PT888, PT903-PT905, PT907,
PT910, PT913, PT915, PT929, PT931, PT932, PT941,
PV229, PV232, PV238, PV259 (which reverted), PV261,
PV264, PV269, PV283, PV284, PV286, PV292, PV296,
PV299, PV303, PV304, PV308, PV312, PV318, PV321,
PV324, PV343, PV344, PV346 HF.IX. Many shipped to

Russia, 16 transferred to Italian AF and others to Danish Greek, and Turkish forces. PV360-PV385 and batches between PV399 to PV733 cancelled Spitfires; PV734-PV739, PV752-PV797, PV820-PV865, PV879-PV919, PV934-PV984,PW112-PV122 cancelled Seafires: PW134-PW158, PW173-PW196, PW221-PW250 cancelled Spitfires. PT398, PT640, PT953, PV313 became 6584M, 5746M, 6263M, 6257M. PT462, PV202 recently became G-CTIX, G-TRIX after restoration.

PW255-PW633 Short S.29 Stirling IV   82(280)
PW255-PW266 (12) built by Short Bros; PW276-PW289, PW303-PW347, PW361-PW380 cancelled; PW384-PW425, PW438-PW465 (70) built by Short & Harland. PW466-PW479, PW493-PW525, PW539-PW580, PW592-PW633 cancelled. Last 34 planned as Mk.V. PW256 to 5088M.

PW637-PW897 Airspeed Horsa II   ,206
Built by Harris Lebus. PW637-PW678, PW693-PW735, PW742-PW790, PW812-PW847, PW862-PW897. PW874 became 4985M.

PW925-PW932 Avro 694 Lincoln   3
Prototypes. PW925 became 6141M, PW929 became 5942M. PW932.

PW937 Miles M.28 Mk.III   1
C/n 4684 U-0242 allotted G-AISH.

PW943 Handley Page HP.74 Hermes   1
Prototype flew as G-AGUB, later became VX234.

PW947-PX198 Miles Martinet TT.1   125
PW947-PW988, PX101-PX147, PX163-PX198. PW979 converted to Queen Martinet. Mainly to Royal Navy.

PX203 Cierva W.9   1
Experimental helicopter to Spec E16/43.

PX210-PX530 DH.103 Hornet F.1/III   145(250)
Built at Hatfield. PX210-PX253, PX273-PX288 (60) F.1 of which PX211 was general trials acft, PX212, PX214, converted to Sea Hornet F.20, PX215 used for spares, PX216 F.II prototype, PX222 to Royal Navy, PX227, PX228 to India for tropical trials, PX230 converted to Sea Hornet NF.21, PX239 converted to Sea Hornet F.20 and NF.21, PX249 PR.II prototype. PX289-PX315, PX328-PX369, PX383-PX389 (85) F.III of which PX290 was converted to F.IV. PX399-PX425, PX440-PX487, PX501-PX530 cancelled. PX210, PX231, PX238, PX277 became 6149M, 6612M, 6696M, 6658M.

PZ161-PZ476 DH.98 Mosquito FB.VI/XVIII   250
Built at Hatfield. PZ161-PZ203, PZ217-PZ259, PZ273-PZ316, PZ330-PZ358, PZ371-PZ419, PZ435-PZ476 FB.VI of which PZ251, PZ252, PZ300, PZ301, PZ346, PZ467-PZ470 were completed as FB.XVIII. Deliveries mainly to Coastal and Bomber Commands. PZ196, PZ200, PZ237, PZ254, PZ297, PZ310, PZ313, PZ330, PZ403, PZ413, PZ444, PZ447, PZ474 to RNZAF and PZ467 to USA. PZ194, PZ273, PZ281-PZ283, PZ339, PZ358, PZ373, PZ389 became 6056M, 6057M, 6853M, 5636M, 5604M, 6293M, 6058M, 6678M, 6059M.

PZ479-PZ727 Bristol Beaufighter TF.X   (200)
Cancelled order with Rootes. PZ479-PZ515, PZ528-PZ569, PZ583-PZ626, PZ638-PZ680, PZ694-PZ727.

PZ730-PZ865 Hawker Hurricane IIC   112
Bomber version. Final Hurricane production. PZ730-PZ778, PZ791-PZ835, PZ848-PZ865. PZ865 became G-AMAU Last of the Many and is preserved. PZ777, PZ814, PZ829-PZ831 became 5471M, 5320M, 5316M, 5318M, 5317M.

Victory

RA100 to VN999

The character of serialling reflects the course of the war in its final years. From RA100 reached in July 1943 large orders were placed but, by the time production was being effected, events had overtaken policies and some contracts were modified, cut or cancelled, a trend that was becoming evident at the end of the previous series. 'SA' to 'SK' was reserved for further Lend/Lease deliveries which did not prove necessary. Victory is emphasised by the numbers of captured enemy aircraft taken on charge for evaluation or utilised as transports.

Serial Nos	Aircraft Type & Remarks	Quantity
RA356-RA363	**Fairey Spearfish**	**3**
	Prototypes. C/n 7870-7872. RA356, RA360, RA363 to Spec 05/43 built at Hayes.	
RA365-RA493	**Gloster Meteor F.4**	**100**
	RA365-RA398, RA413-RA457, RA473-RA493. RA382 had lengthened nose as interim T.7, RA418, RA430 FR type nose, RA435 had afterburners, RA490 fitted with F2/4 Beryl engines and F.8 type tail, RA491 Avon and Atar engines fitted. RA367, RA371, RA373, RA375, RA397, RA398, RA415, RA417, RA421, RA430, RA432, RA433, RA438, RA439, RA441, RA442, RA454, RA457, RA473, RA479 converted to U.15. RA370, RA384-RA386, RA388-RA393, RA395, RA396 to Argentine AF. RA416, RA434, RA435, RA445, RA449, RA456, RA476 became 6937M, 7130M, 7131M, 6621M, 7221M, 7222M, 7361M.	
RA500-RA806	**Avro 683 Lancaster/694 Lincoln**	**201(250)**
	Ordered from Metropolitan Vickers. RA500-RA547, RA560-RA607, RA623-RA627 Lancaster B.I; RA628-RA655 Lincoln B.I; RA656-RA658, RA661-RA693, RA709-RA724 Lincoln B.II; RA725-RA749, RA763-RA786 cancelled Lincolns. RA787-RA806 built as Lancaster B.1 of which RA796 and RA801-RA806 were assembled by Vickers Armstrong at Chester. RA638, RA644, RA648 to RAAF RA625, RA788, RA789, RA798 to Argentine AF; RA627, RA787, RA793, RA795-RA797, RA800 to Aeronavale, RA805 to the R Swedish AF. RA626 converted to PR.I. RA630, RA646, RA647, RA649, RA652, RA802 became 6627M, 6632M, 6636M, 6420M, 6631M, 6426M.	
RA809	**Baynes Bat**	**1**
	Experimental carrier wing built by Slingsby.	
RA812-RB140	**Slingsby T.7 Cadet TX.I**	**200**
	Gliders built as follows: RA812-RA841 by S Fox & Son and A Davies Ltd; RA843-RA872 Otley Motors; RA875-RA924 Slingsby Sailplanes; RA928-RA968, RA980-RA999, RB112-RB140 by Papworth Industries except RA939, RA941, RA943, RA945, RA947, RA957, RA995, RA997, RA999, RB113, RB115, RB117, RB119, RB121, RB123, RB125, RB127 by Enham Industries.	
RB140-RB189	**Supermarine Spitfire F.XIV**	**50**
	RB140 compromised a number allotted to previous batch. Postwar RB154, RB156, RB161, RB163, RB166, RB182, RB186 went to Belgian AF. RB151, RB157, RB170, RB171, RB179 became 6841M-6843M, 6837M, 6838M.	
RB192-RB512	**Hawker Typhoon IB**	**255**
	Built by Gloster. RB192-RB235, RB248-RB289, RB303-RB347, RB361-RB408, RB423-RB459, RB474-RB512. RB379 was the only Typhoon shipped to Russia. RB216, RB278, RB282, RB307, RB369, RB377, RB380, RB391, RB425, RB442, RB427, RB442, RB477, RB483, RB495 became 5661M, 5610M, 5654M, 5875M, 5664M, 5665M, 5653M, 5648M, 5651M, 5646M, 5640M, 5655M, 5614M, 5645M.	
RB515-RB987	**Supermarine Spiteful F.XIV**	**17(363)**
	RB515-RB525, RB527-RB531, RB535 only built but not all were test-flown. RB532-RB534, RB536-RB557, RB571-RB615, RB628-RB669, RB683-RB725, RB738-RB783, RB796-RB843, RB857-RB898, RB912-RB953, RB965-RB987 cancelled.	

RD130-RD867 **Bristol 156 Beaufighter TF.X** 500
Built at Weston. RD130-RD176, RD189-RD225, RD239-
RD285, RD298-RD335, RD348-RD396, RD420-RD468,
RD483-RD525, RD538-RD580, RD685-RD728, RD742-
RD789, RD801-RD836, RD849-RD867. Conversions
postwar to TT.10 involved: RD515, RD545, RD546,
RD548, RD564, RD566, RD573, RD577, RD688,
RD693, RD694, RD708, RD710, RD747, RD751,
RD752, RD754, RD758, RD759, RD761, RD763,
RD764, RD767, RD771, RD778-RD781, RD783,
RD788, RD802, RD806, RD807, RD809, RD811,
RD812, RD814, RD815, RD821, RD828, RD831,
RD832, RD849-RD851, RD854, RD855, RD859,
RD860, RD862, RD864, RD867. RD134, RD148,
RD173, RD189, RD197, RD199, RD206, RD209,
RD216, RD220, RD250, RD252, RD253, RD261,
RD319-RD321 to Portuguese and 24 to Turkish AF.
RD135, RD427, RD448 allotted G-AJMB, 'AJMD,
'AJMC. RD254, RD348, RD357, RD466, RD569,
RD750, RD861 became 7931M, 6101M, 6065M, 6207M,
6342M, 6066M, 6682M. RD867 is preserved in Ottawa.

RD869-RD922 **Supermarine Sea Otter ASR.II** 40
RD869-RD898, RD913-RD922.

RE100-RF119 **Avro 683 Lancaster/694 Lincoln** 249(700)
RE100-RE114 cancelled. RE115-RE140, RE153-RE188,
RE200-RE222, RE225, RE226 Lancaster B.III built at
Yeadon of which many were converted to GR or
ASR.III; RE227-RE257 Lincoln B.I built at Chadderton;
RE258-RE268, RE281-RE288 Lincoln B.I built at
Yeadon; RE289-RE325, RE338-RE380, RE393-RE424
Lincoln B.2 built at Chadderton of which RE290 was
converted to Mk.I and RE399 and RE418 became engine
testbeds. RE425-RE435, RE449-RE493, RE518-RE561,
RE575-RE605, RE621-RE670, RE683-RE726, RE740-
RE785, RE798-RE839, RE853-RE895, RE918-RE955,
RE967-RE999, RF111-RF119 cancelled. RE343,
RE349-RE359, RE408-RE410 to Argentine AF of which
RE410 was to *Aries II* standard. RE364, RE367 became
Aries II/III of RAF. RE121, RE219, RE227, RE228,
RE230, RE235, RE236, RE238, RE244, RE252, RE256,
RE262, RE263, RE267, RE284, RE312, RE321, RE342,
RE377, RE414, RE415 became 6586M, 6599M, 6361M,
6279M, 5926M, 6624M, 6623M, 6651M, 6629M, 6630M,
6635M, 6652M, 6634M, 6622M, 6987M, 7018M, 7111M,
6915M, 7025M, 6790M, 7196M.

RF120-RF577 **Avro 683 Lancaster/694 Lincoln** 370
Built by Armstrong Whitworth. RF120-RF161, RF175-
RF197 Lancaster B.I; RF198-RF216, RF229-RF273,
RF286-RF326 Lancaster B.III; RF329-RF332 Lincoln
B.II; RF333, RF334 Lincoln B.I; RF335-RF370, RF383-
RF427, RF440-RF485, RF498-RF539, RF553-RF577
Lincoln B.II. RF187, RF201, RF258, RF268, RF271,
RF301, RF336, RF345, RF363, RF387, RF390, RF393,
RF397, RF398, RF401, RF405, RF409, RF441, RF447,
RF451, RF466, RF482, RF498, RF510, RF564, RF565
became 6294M, 5848M, 6313M, 6206M, 6673M, 6679M,
7160M, 6828M, 7022M, 7019M, 7026M, 6502M, 7023M,
8376M, 7024M, 7028M, 7020M, 6148M, 6830M, 6827M,
6829M, 7027M, 7021M, 7377M, 7600M, 7156M.

RF580-RF966 **DH.98 Mosquito FB.VI** 300
Built by Standard Motors. RF580-RF625, RF639-
RF681, RF695-RF736, RF749-RF793, RF818-RF859,
RF873-RF915, RF928-RF966. RF595, RF597, RF709,
RF719, RF753, RF837, RF849, RF856, RF857, RF882,
RF885, RF903, RF908, RF910, RF935 to RNZAF.
RF777, RF928 to Czech AF and RF929 to French AF.
RF888, RF897, RF930, RF940 became 6274M, 6527M,
6269M, 6270M.

RF969-RG318 **DH.98 Mosquito PR.XVI/PR.34** 200
Built at Hatfield. RF969-RF999, RG113-RG158,
RG171-RG175 (82) PR.XVI of which RF979, RF982,
RF996, RG113, RG145, RG146, RG156, RG157 were
transferred to USAAF in the UK, RF171-RF173 hooked
for Royal Navy and several were shipped for RAAF and
SAAF. RG176-RG215, RG228-RG269, RG283-RG318
(118) PR.34 of which RG176-RG178, RG181, RG189,
RG194, RG195, RG198, RG201, RG202, RG205,
RG207, RG231, RG233, RG236, RG238, RG240,
RG252, RG259, RG262, RG265, RG268, RG300,
RG302, RG314 were converted to PR.34A. RG174,

RG231, RG238, RG267, RG290 became G-AOCM,
'AJZE, 'AJZF, 6372M, 6794M.

RG324 **Armstrong Whitworth AW.52G** 1
Experimental flying wing glider. First flew 2.3.45.

RG327 & **Miles M.38 Messenger** 2
RG333 Prototypes built at Woodley.

RG345-RG879 **Handley Page Halifax B.III/VI/VII** 400
Built by English Electric. RG345-RG390, RG413-RG446
(80) B.III of which some were B(MET).III; RG447-
RG458, RG472-RG479 (20) B.VII; RG480-RG513,
RG527-RG568, RG583-RG625, RG639-RG679, RG693-
RG736, RG749-RG790, RG813-RG853, RG867-RG879
(300) B.VI; Fifty-nine transferred to French AF and
thirty to British civil register. RG364, RG386, RG446,
RG751, RG776, RG778, RG780, RG782, RG820,
RG870-RG872, RG875 became 5750M, 5728M, 5339M,
6415M, 6514M, 6857M, 6858M, 6515M, 6903M, 6699M,
6859M, 6380M, 6354M.

RG882-RH365 **Miles M.25 Martinet/M.50 Queen Martinet** 165(300)
RG882-RG929, RG948-RG997, RH113-RH121 Martinet
TT.1 for RAF and Royal Navy; RH122-RH148, RH162-
RH192 Queen Martinet of which RH169, RH182,
RH185, RH186 went to Royal Navy. RH193-RH205,
RH218-RH259, RH273-RH315, RH329-RH365 can-
celled. RG906 to Irish Air Corps and RG980, RG981 to
Portuguese Air Force.

RH368-RH680 **Miles M.38 Messenger** 21(250)
RH368-RH378 built at Reading; RH379-RH409 can-
celled; RH420-RH429 built at Newtownards. RH430-
RH468, RH483-RH525, RH539-RH580, RH595-RH635,
RH648-RH680 cancelled.

RH742-RH852 **Bristol 164 Brigand I** 80
RH742-RH754 TF/F.1 of which RH745 was non-
standard with triple fins, RH755 TF.1 converted to B.1,
RH756 B.1, RH757, RH758 B.1 to T.4 then T.5, RH759
B.1, RH760 B.1 to T.4, RH761 B.1, RH762 B.2 to T.4
then T.5, RH763 B.1 to MET.3, RH764 B.1, RH765-
RH769 B.1 to T.4, RH770 B.1, RH771 B.1 to T.4,
RH772 B.1, RH773 TF.1, RH774 B.1 to T.4 then T.5,
RH775 B.1 to T.4, RH776, RH777, RH792, RH793
B.1, RH794 B.1 to T.4, RH795 B.1, RH796 TF.1 to B.1,
RH797 B.1 to T.4 then T.5, RH798 B.1, RH799 B.1 to
T.4, RH800 B.1 to T.4 then T.5, RH801 B.1 to T.4,
RH802 B.1 to T.4 then T.5, RH803 B.1, RH804 B.1 to
T.4 then T.5, RH805-RH808 B.1 to T.4, RH809-RH812
B.1, RH813 B.1 to T.4 then T.5, RH814-RH819 B.1,
RH820, RH821 B.1 to Pakistan AF as N-1125, N-1126,
RH822-RH825 B.1, RH826 B.1 to T.4 then T.5, RH827,
RH828 B.1, RH829 B.1 to T.4 then T.5, RH830 B.1,
RH831, RH832 B.1 to T.4 then T.5, RH850-RH852 B.1.

RJ111-RJ231 **Airspeed AS.51 Horsa I** 100
Built at Christchurch. RJ111-RJ143, RJ150-RJ196,
RJ212-RJ231. RJ124 became 4964M.

RJ245-RJ359 **Airspeed AS.51 Horsa I** 100
Built by Harris Lebus. RJ245-RJ287, RJ290-RJ316,
RJ330-RJ359. RJ297 became 5866M.

RJ362/G **Bell 27 Airacomet** 1
USAAF YP-59A 42-108773 for Meteor comparison
trials.

RJ759-RK323 **Fairey Barracuda III** 92(300)
RJ759-RJ799, RJ902-RJ948, RJ963-RJ966 built by
Boulton Paul. RJ967-RJ999, RK111-RK158, RK172-
RK215, RK228-RK269, RK283-RK323 cancelled.

RK328-RK784 **Fairey Barracuda III/V** 190(350)
C/n 7020-7209 built at Heaton Chapel. RK328-RK369,
RK382-RK428, RK441-RK485, RK498-RK523 (160)
Mk.III; RK530-RK542, RK558-RK574 (30) Mk.V.
Batches to RK784 cancelled.

RK787-RK794 **Short Sturgeon** 2(3)
Prototypes. RK787 built at Rochester, first flew 7.6.46,
RK791 shipped to Short & Harland Belfast for com-
pletion, RK794 renumbered VR363.

RK798-RK926 **Supermarine Spitfire IX** 100
Vickers Supermarine built at Castle Bromwich. RK798-
RK819, RK835-RK868, RK883-RK926 LF.IX except
RK860, RK901, RK908, RK911, RK912, RK916,
RK917, RK924 HF.IX. RK905 became 6419M. Wartime
deliveries to Russia and SAAF, postwar sales to Belgian,
Danish and Greek forces.

RK929-RL390 **DH.98 Mosquito NF.30/36** 189(282)
Built at Leavesden. RK929-RK954 NF.30; RK955-
RK960, RK972-RK999, RL113-RL158, RL173-RL215,
RL229-RL268 NF.36 of which RL248 was NF.38
prototype. RL269-RL273, RL288-RL329, RL345-
RL390 cancelled. RK959, RK980, RK987, RK990,
RK997, RL133 became 7029M, 7124M, 7122M, 7125M,
7123M, 7030M.

RL936-RM158 **DH.89A Dominie I/II** 40(100)
Built by Brush Coachworks. de Havilland c/ns 6918-
6957. RL936-RL946 Mk.I; RL947-RL968, RL980-
RL986 Mk.II, RL987-RL999, RM112-RM158 cancelled.

RM160-RM295 **Percival Proctor IV** 50(100)
Built by F. Hills & Sons. RM160-RM197, RM219-RM230
of which RM162, RM163, RM165-RM167, RM174,
RM177, RM178, RM182-RM184 went to French AF
and many others postwar to civil register. RM231-RM257,
RM273-RM295 cancelled.

RM298-RM612 **DH.82A Tiger Moth II** (250)
Cancelled. RM298-RM335, RM348-RM389, RM405-
RM448, RM463-RM507, RM520-RM566, RM579-
RM612.

RM615-RN221 **Supermarine Spitfire XIV/XIX** 406
RM615-RM625 F.XIV; RM626-RM647 PR.XIX; RM648-
RM656, RM670-RM713, RM726-RM770, RM783-
RM825, RM839-RM887, RM901-RM943, RM957-
RM999, RN113-RN160, RN173-RN221 Mk.XIV or
XIVe mainly as F version, but a few FR. Fifty-three
postwar to Belgian AF. RM623, RM638, RM681, RM694,
RM737, RM854, RM856, RM859, RM862, RM884,
RM909, RM929, RN217 became 6839M, 5730M, 6844M,
6640M, 6694M, 6845M, 6846M, 6523M, 6350M, 6847M-
6849M, 6251M. RM689 became G-ALGT. RM797 is
preserved in Australia.

RN228 **Messerschmitt Bf 109G-2/Trop** 1
C/n 10639 captured in Sicily 1943. Became 8478M.

RN236 **Macchi C.202** 1
Captured Italian aircraft.

RN241 & **Fairey Spearfish** 2
RN244 RN241 further prototype built at Heaton Chapel,
RN244 not flown.

RN264-RN306 **Short S.25 Sunderland V** 40
RN264-RN273 (10) built by Short Bros, RN277-RN306
(30) built by Blackburn. RN279, RN305 to SAAF;
RN280, RN286, RN291, RN306 to RNZAF. RN272
became 6534M.

RN309-RN520 **Airspeed AS.58 Horsa II** 175
Built at Christchurch. RN309-RN349, RN362-RN405,
RN418-RN459, RN473-RN520. RN312, RN317,
RN323, RN327, RN330, RN331, RN349, RN362,
RN363, RN512 became 5974M, 6390M, 6391M, 6393M,
6394M, 5823M, 6289M, 6395M, 6392M, 5975M.

RN523-RN941 **Airspeed AS.51 Horsa I** 325
Built by Harris Lebus. RN523-RN568, RN583-RN625,
RN638-RN679, RN693-RN738, RN752-RN795, RN809-
RN865-RN902, RN918-RN941.

RN959-RP299 **Bristol Buckingham/Buckmaster** 100(167)
Order was originally for Buckinghams. RN959-RN999,
RP113-RP121 cancelled. RP122-RP156, RP170-RP215,
RP228-RP246 built as Buckmaster I; RP283-RP299
cancelled. RP151, RP177, RP186, RP242, RP245,
RP246 became 7148M, 6707M, 6708M, 6704M-6706M.

RP312-RR178 **Vickers Wellington X/XVIII** 226(600)
Built at Blackpool. PR312-PR358, RP373-RP415,
RP428-RP469, RP483-RP526, RP538-RP561, RP565-
RP590 B.X except RP330-RP335, RP348-RP351,
RP392-RP395, RP412-RP415, RP428, RP429 B.XVIII.
RP591-RP606, RP619-RP663, RP677-RP718, RP735-
RP778, RP791-RP835, RP848-RP889, RP903-RP947,
RP959-RP999, RR113-RR156, RR169-RR178 can-
celled. B.Xs converted to T.10 postwar concerned:
RP312, RP314, RP316, RP317, RP319-RP323, RP325,
RP328, RP329, RP341, RP352, RP353, RP355, RP375,
RP377, RP382-RP389, RP391. RP468 had tail boom
radar and became G-ALUH. RP322, RP381, RP386,
RP409, RP398, RP246 became 7104M, 6755M, 6882M,
6639M, 6697M, 6669M.

RR181-RR265 **Supermarine Spitfire IX/XVI** 72(73)
Built at Castle Bromwich. RR181-RR205 LF.IX; RR206
HF.IX; RR207, RR208 LF.IX; RR209 HF.IX; RR210,

RR211 LF.IX; RR212, RR213, RR226, RR227 LF.XVI;
RR228 HF.IX; RR229, RR230 LF.XVI; RR231, RR232
HF.IX; RR233 cancelled from contract; RR234 LF.XVI;
RR235 HF.IX; RR236 LF.XVI; RR237 LF.IX; RR238,
RR239 HF.IX; RR240 LF.XVI; RR241 HF.IX, RR242,
RR243 LF.XVI; RR244 HF.IX; RR245 LF.XVI;
RR246 HF.IX; RR247-RR250 LF.XVI; RR251, RR252
HF.IX; RR253 LF.IX; RR254 HF.IX; RR255-RR257
LFXVI; RR258-RR260 HF.IX; RR261 LF.XVI; RR262
HF.IX; RR263 LF.XVI; RR264 HF.IX; RR265 LF.XVI;
RR204, RR235, RR239, RR251 transferred to Italian
AF. RR229, RR245, RR263 became 6180M, 6203M,
7216M. RR232 currently in Australia and RR263 in
France.

RR270-RR319 **DH.98 Mosquito T.III** 50
Built at Leavesden. RR270 became 6033M. RR299
current as G-ASKH.

RR321-RR906 **Airspeed AS.10 Oxford I** 50(450)
RR321-RR367, RR380-RR382 built. RR383-RR425,
RR438-RR480, RR495-RR536, RR549-RR590, RR613-
RR656, RR666-RR708, RR723-RR766, RR779-RR819,
RR835-RR880, RR892-RR906 cancelled. RR333,
RR337 became 6894M, 6268M.

RR915 & **DH.103 Hornet** 2
RR919 Prototypes to Spec F12/43. RR915/G, first flew 28.7.44.
RR919 became 6033M.

RR923-RR995 **General Aircraft GAL.49 Hamilcar I** 60
Group built. RR923-RR959, RR973-RR995 of which
RR948, RR949, RR953, RR956, RR986 were converted
to Mk.X. RR936, RR942, RR948, RR986, RR994
became 6046M, 6788M, 6770M, 6510M, 6444M.

RR997-RR998 **Lockheed Lodestar II** 2
Ex-USAAF 42-56018, '56019 originally allotted FS737
and FS738.

RS102-RS225 **Avro Lancaster B.IV/V** (100)
Cancelled order with Vickers Armstrong at Castle
Bromwich. RS102-RS147, RS159-RS189, RS203-RS225.

RS227-RS497 **Handley Page Halifax** (200)
Cancelled order with Fairey. RS227-RS258, RS273-
RS305, RS318-RS358, RS375-RS418, RS433-RS459,
RS475-RS497.

RS501-RS633 **DH.98 Mosquito FB.VI** 109
Built at Hatfield. RS501-RS535, RS548-RS580, RS593-
RS633. Main delivery to Coastal Command. RS549,
RS551, RS554 became 6687M, 6702M, 6254M. RS504
and RS599 to RNZAF.

RS637-RT123 **DH.98 Mosquito FB.VI/B.35** 75(300)
Ordered from Airspeed. RS637-RS680, RS693-RS698
(50) FB.VI of which RS659 was hooked for Royal Navy
and RS646, RS670, RS693 went to RNZAF. RS699-
RS723 (25) B.35 of which RS701, RS702, RS704,
RS706-RS710, RS712, RS713, RS715, RS713, RS715,
RS717, RS719, RS722 were converted to TT.35. RS713,
RS717 became 6264M, 7126M. RS724, RS725, RS739-
RS779, RS795-RS836, RS849-RS893, RS913-RS948,
RS960-RS999, RT105-RT123 cancelled.

RT140-RT456 **Avro 683 Lancaster B.I** (240)
Cancelled order with Vickers Armstrong at Chester.
RT140-RT183, RT197-RT228, RT245-RT290, RT315-
RT350, RT362-RT403, RT417-RT456.

RT458-RT644 **Taylorcraft Auster AOP.V** 150
RT458-RT499, RT513-RT540, RT553-RT582, RT595-
RT644. Many postwar disposals to civil registers. RT464,
RT515, RT562, RT636 became 6015M, 5988M, 6436M,
5989M.

RT646 **Supermarine Seafang 32** (1)
Prototype. Cancelled.

RT651 & **Blackburn YA-1 Firecrest** 1(2)
RT656 Prototypes to Spec S28/43. RT651 first flew 1.4.47,
RT656 not completed.

RT665 & **Airspeed AS.57 Ambassador** 2
RT668 Serials allotted but not used for G-AGUA, 'AKRD.

RT670-RT750 **Avro 683 Lancaster B.VII** 30(70)
Ordered from Austin Motors, RT670-RT699 built of
which RT673, RT674, RT679, RT682, RT693,
RT697-RT699 were sold to France and RT681 became
6748M. RT700, RT701, RT713-RT750 cancelled.

RT753-RT999 **Handley Page HP.71 Halifax A.VII/IX** 150(200)
RT753-RT757 (5) A.VII; RT758-RT799, RT814-
RT856, RT868-RT908, RT920-RT938 (145) A.IX;

RT939-RT958, RT970-RT999 cancelled. Over fifty of those built were stored and not issued for service. Twenty-five to British civil register and RT788, RT793, RT846, RT852, RT888, RT901, RT907, RT938 to Egyptian AF. RT770, RT777, RT877, RT886, RT934 became 6683M, 6529M, 6431M, 6344M, 6824M.

RV104-RV290   **Handley Page HP.61 Halifax B.III**   (150)
Ordered from LAP. Cancelled. RV104-RV145, RV158-RV198, RV213-RV248, RV260-RV290.

RV295-RV367   **DH.98 Mosquito B.XVI/B.35**   60
Built at Hatfield. RV295-RV326, RV340-RV363 (56) B.XVI of which RV295, RV296, RV303, RV308 went to Royal Navy; RV364-RV367 B.35 of which RV366, RV367 were converted to TT.35. RV312-RV314, RV321 became 6315M, 6438M, 5960M, 6330M.

RV370-RX151   **Supermarine Spitfire**   40(1500)
Ordered from Vickers Armstrong at Castle Bromwich with considerable contract amendments. RV370-RV415, RV428-RV469, RV483-RV526, RV539-RV580, RV593-RV615, RV627-RV653, RV668-RV699, RV713-RV758, RV773-RV815, RV828-RV859, RV873-RV905, RV918-RV959, RV971-RV999, RW113-RW156, RW168-RW209, RW225-RW258, RW273-RW315, RW328-RW343 cancelled. RW344-RW359, RW373-RW396 only built as LF.XVI of which RW349, RW359, RW377, RW378, RW382, RW386, RW388, RW391, RW393, RW394 became 6889M, 6835M, 6555M, 6821M, 7245M renumbered and preserved, 6944M preserved, 6947M preserved, 6552M, 7293M preserved, 7258M and 7280M. Allocations from RW397 to RX181 cancelled.

RX156-RX530   **Supermarine Seafire L.III**   160(300)
Ordered from Westland. RX156-RX194, RX210-RX256, RX268-RX313, RX326-RX353 built. Numbers to RX530 cancelled.

RX534-RZ408   **Airspeed AS.51/AS.58 Horsa I/II**   600
RX534-RX583 (50) Mk.II built at Christchurch. RX595-RX634, RX647-RX688, RX700-RX717 (100) Mk.I; RX718-RX735, RX749-RX779, RX792-RX835, RX848-RX889, RX902-RX937, RX949-RX998, RZ112-RZ156, RZ170-RZ203, RZ215-RZ259, RZ280-RZ325, RZ338-RZ380, RZ393-RZ408 (450) Mk.II built by Harris Lebus. RX535, RX536, RX551, RX562, RX571, RX573, RX578, RX755, RX758, RX770, RX803, RX807, RX857, RX861, RX904, RX910 became 6404M, 6045M, 6402M, 5978M, 5976M, 5680M, 5977M, 6403M, 6405M, 6406M, 6378M, 6432M, 6401M, 6533M, 6407M, 6667M and RZ192, RZ219, RZ290, RZ300, RZ316, RZ351, RZ367 became 6375M, 6374M, 6396M, 6397M, 6376M, 6044M, 6290M.

RZ410-RZ581   **General Aircraft GAL.49 Hamilcar I**   22(100)
RZ410-RZ431 built of which RZ413, RZ430, RZ431 converted to Mk.X and RZ431 became 6768M. Allocations to RZ581 cancelled.

SL541-SM698   **Supermarine Spitfire LF.IX/XVI**   531(800)
SL541-SL571 LF.XVI; SL572 cancelled; SL573-SL579 SL593-SL624 LF.XVI; SL625-SL635, SL648-SL657 LF.IX to Czech AF; SL658, SL659 LF.IX to Saigon for French AF; SL660-SL665 LF.IX of which SL660, SL662, SL664 went to Czechoslovakia and SL661, SL665 Turkey; SL666 LF.XVI; SL667 cancelled; SL668-SL690, SL713-SL745 allotted for LF.XVI but SL677, SL682-SL684, SL686, SL714, SL716, SL722, SL723, SL726, SL729-SL732, SL734-SL744 were cancelled. SL746, SL747, SL759-SL798, SL812-SL857, SL873-SL915, SL928-SL969, SL971-SL999, SM112-SM134 cancelled LF.XVIe. SM135-SM150, SM170-SM177 LF.IX of which SM139, SM144-SM146, SM148 were shipped to Russia and SM171, SM173, SM174 transferred to Italian AF; SM178-SM213, SM226-SM258, SM273-SM316, SM329-SM369, SM383-SM427 LF.XVI; SM441-SM446 LF.IX of which SM445 went to Italian AF; SM447-SM463 LF.IX all shipped to Russia; SM464-SM488, SM503-SM516 LF.XVI; SM517-SM548 LF.IX of which SM524-SM537, SM539-SM548 were shipped to Russia; SM563-SM566 LF.IX to Russia; SM567 LF.XVI to Russia; SM568-SM597, SM610-SM645 LF.IX all to Russia; SM646-SM648, SM663-SM671 LF.XVI; SM672-SM698 cancelled. SL542, SL561, SL565, SL574, SL616, SL674, SL678, SL685, SL719 became 8390M (preserved),

6823M, 6333M, 8391M (preserved), 6885M, 8392M (preserved), 6911M, 6666M, 6676M. SL721 preserved in USA. SM193, SM207, SM243, SM247, SM284, SM301, SM307, SM360, SM385, SM390, SM391, SM394, SM402, SM411, SM418, SM426, SM471, SM479-SM481, SM484, SM507, SM665 became 5979M, 5980M, 5964M, 6323M, 6637M, 6553M, 6175M, 6597M, 6008M, 6201M, 6000M, 6004M, 6248M, 7242M, 6417M, 6570M, 6005M, 6002M, 6003M, 6202M, 5981M, 5999M, 6001M.

SM700-SM701   **DH.98 Mosquito NF.XIII**   (2)
Renumbered from HK535, HK536.

SM706   **Consolidated Catalina**   (1)
AM258 renumbered.

SM801-SM809   **Gloster GA1/2**   2(3)
Prototypes to Spec E1/44. SM801 GA1, SM805 GA1 not built, SM809 GA2 built but damaged in transit and not flown.

SM812-SM997   **Supermarine Spitfire XIV/XVIII**   132(150)
Ordered from Chattis Hill, Eastleigh, Keevil and Winchester plants of Vickers Armstrong. SM812-SM842 F.XIV; SM843-SM845 FR.XVIII; SM858-SM875 cancelled; SM876-SM899, SM913-SM938 FR.XIV; SM939-SM956, SM968-SM997 F.XVIII. SM826, SM899, SM913 became 6626M, 6902M, 6166M and SM832, SM969 allotted G-WWII and G-BRAF.

SN102-SN416   **Hawker Tempest F.V Series II**   201(250)
Ordered from LAP. SN102-SN146, SN159-SN190, SN205-SN238, SN253-SN296, SN310-SN355 built; SN368-SN416 cancelled. SN354 non-standard with two 40mm cannon. Postwar conversions to TT.5: SN127, SN146, SN209, SN215, SN219, SN227, SN232, SN259-SN261, SN271, SN274, SN289, SN290, SN321, SN326, SN327, SN329, SN333, SN340, SN342, SN346, SN354. SN105, SN119, SN126, SN185, SN312, SN331 became 6476M, 6531M, 5301M, 6646M, 6647M, 7277M.

SP136-SP461   **Supermarine Spitfire F.XV/XVII**   70(200)
Built by Cunliffe-Owen. SP136-SP168, SP181-SP197 F.XV; SP323-SP327, SP341-SP355 F.XVII for Royal Navy. SP198-SP223, SP236-SP279, SP293-SP322, SP356-SP380, SP393-SP438, SP453-SP461 cancelled.

SR376-SR389   **Boeing Fortress IIIA**   14
Lend/lease ex-USAAF supplied for 214 Squadron.

SR392   **Miles M.39B 'Libellula'**   1
Tandem wing research aircraft, ex-U-0244.

SR395-SR400   **Supermarine Spitfire PR.X**   6
SR406-SR440   **North American NA-104/NA-111 Mustang III**   35
Ex-USAAF P-51B/C. SR439 not delivered.

SR446-SR645   **Supermarine Seafire XV**   140
SR446-SR493, SR516-SR547, SR568-SR611, SR630-SR645 for Royal Navy. SR451, SR462, SR470, SR471, SR534, SR642 to Burmese Air Force.

SR661 &   **Hawker Sea Fury**   2
SR666   Prototypes to Spec N7/43. SR661 first flew 21.2.45 semi-navalised, SR666 fully navalised. For Royal Navy.

SR707-SR907   **Avro Lancaster B.IV/V (Lincoln)**   (150)
Cancelled order to Vickers Armstrong at Castle Bromwich. SR707-SR749, SR766-SR790, SR814-SR851, SR864-SR907.

SR910-SS338   **Bristol 156 Beaufighter TF.X**   10(250)
SR910-SR919 built at Weston of which SR911-SR914, SR916, SR917, SR919 were converted to TT.10. SR910 became 6947M. Allocations SR920 to SS338 cancelled.

SS341-ST475   **Avro 694 Lincoln (Ordered as Lancaster B.IV/V)**   6(800)
SS341-SS386, SS399-SS435, SS449-SS480, SS493-SS535, SS549-SS589, SS603-SS650, SS664-SS698 cancelled. SS713, SS714 B.I of which SS713 became 6633M; SS715-SS718 B.II built at Yeadon. SS719-SS758, SS773-SS815, SS828-SS869, SS882-SS925, SS937-SS968, SS980-SS999, ST113-ST157, ST171-ST215, ST228-ST269, ST283-ST327, ST339-ST369, ST381-ST425, ST438-ST475 cancelled.

ST477-ST790   **Avro 694 Lincoln (Ordered as Lancaster B.IV)**   (250)
Cancelled order with Metropolitan Vickers. ST477-ST513, ST528-ST569, ST583-ST627, ST641-ST680, ST693-ST735, ST748-ST790.

ST794-SV341   **Handley Page Halifax VI**   25(350)
Ordered from English Electric. ST794-ST818 built as B or GR.VI of which ST796, ST798, ST801-ST804, ST807, ST809-ST813, ST815, ST817, ST818 were converted to MET.VI. ST795, ST797, ST799, ST800 to French AF

and ST801, ST808 to civil register. ST819-ST835, ST848-ST890, ST905-ST946, ST958-ST999, SV113-SV158, SV173-SV215, SV228-SV269, SV280-SV315, SV328-SV341 cancelled.

SV344-SV736   **Handley Page Halifax A.VII**   (300)
Cancelled order with Rootes. SV344-SV388, SV401-SV435, SV448-SV479, SV493-SV535, SV548-SV583, SV595-SV638, SV653-SV695, SV715-SV736.

SV739-SW240   **Miles Monitor**   (300)
Cancelled. SV739-SV768, SV783-SV815, SV828-SV869, SV881-SV923, SV935-SV973, SV985-SV999, SW113-SW158, SW173-SW198, SW215-SW240.

SW243-SW377   **Avro 683 Lancaster B.I/III**   118
SW243-SW279 (37) B.I built by Metropolitan Vickers and assembled by Avro at Woodford. SW244 had LR saddle tank fitted. SW283-SW295 B.III all converted to ASR.III and all but SW290-SW292 subsequently became GR.III; SW295 became 6762M after conversion in 1950; SW296, SW297 B.I; SW298-SW316 B.I(FE) all built by Armstrong Whitworth. SW319-SW345, SW358-SW377 (47) B.III built at Yeadon of which SW319, SW320, SW324-SW327, SW329, SW330, SW334, SW336-SW338, SW344, SW361-SW377 were converted to ASR.III and later most were converted to GR.3. SW342 special test bed with engines in nose and tail. SW328 became 6761M.

SW386-SW772   **Hawker Typhoon IB**   300
Built by Gloster. SW386-SW428, SW443-SW478, SW493-SW537, SW551-SW596, SW620-SW668, SW681-SW716, SW728-SW772. SW398, SW428, SW457, SW500, SW553, SW560, SW620, SW621, SW633, SW641, SW662 became 5644M, 5650M, 5607M, 5882M, 5660M, 5658M, 5905M-5907M, 5649M, 5764M.

SW777   **Supermarine Spitfire**   1
Prototype completed to PR.XIX standard.

SW781-SX546   **Supermarine Seafire F.XV/XVII**   322(500)
Ordered from Westland for Royal Navy. SW781-SW828, SW844-SW875 F.XV with standard fuselages; SW876-SW879, SW896-SW921 F.XV with rear view fuselages. SW922-SW939, SW951-SW985 cancelled. SW986-SW993, SX111-SX139, SX152-SX201, SX220-SX256, SX271-SX316, SX332-SX370, SX386-SX389 F.XVII. SW799, SW817, SW863, SW899 to Burmese AF and SW916, SX300, SX336, SX360 became A2203, A2054, A2055, A2080 Royal Navy instructional airframes. SX390-SX432, SX451-SX490, SX503-SX546 cancelled.

SX549   **Supermarine Spitfire F.21**   (1)
Prototype ordered from Cunliffe-Owen. Cancelled.

SX558-SX921   **Avro 683 Lancaster**   (280)
Cancelled order with Vickers Armstrong Chester plant. SX558-SX589, SX605-SX648, SX663-SX698, SX713-SX759, SX772-SX813, SX828-SX863, SX879-SX921.

SX923-SZ493   **Avro 694 Lincoln B.2**   60(350)
Ordered from Armstrong Whitworth. SX923-SX958, SX970-SX993 built of which three became testbeds: SX971 Derwent under belly, SX973 Proteus and SX974 Nomad installation. SX931, SX933, SX939, SX978, SX986 became 7173M, 7153M, 6943M, 7195M, 7193M. SX994-SX999, SZ113-SZ158, SZ172-SZ215, SZ228-SZ259, SZ275-SZ306, SZ319-SZ363, SZ380-SZ415, SZ429-SZ471, SZ488-SZ493 cancelled.

SZ559-SZ611   **Short S.25 Sunderland GR.V**   28(40)
Ordered from Short & Harland. SZ559-SZ584, SZ598, SZ599 built. SZ561, SZ584 to RNZAF. SZ600-SZ611 cancelled.

SZ958-TA724   **DH.98 Mosquito FB.VI/PR.XVI/NF.XIX/35**   492(500)
Built at Hatfield. SZ958-SZ999, TA113-TA122 (52) FB.VI of which there were disposals to France, Norway and New Zealand. TA123-TA156, TA169-TA198, TA215-TA249, TA263-TA308, TA323-TA357 (180) NF.XIX of which the majority were shipped to the Far East. TA229, TA343 became G-ALGU, 'ALGV. TA369-TA388 (20) FB.VI; TA389-TA413, TA425-TA449 (50) NF.XIX; TA469-TA508, TA523-TA560, TA575-TA603 (107) FB.VI; TA604-TA611 cancelled; TA614-TA616 PR.XVI; TA617, TA618, TA633-TA670, TA685-TA724 (80) B.35 of which TA633, TA634, TA637-TA639, TA641-TA643, TA647, TA649, TA651, TA656, TA657, TA659, TA660, TA662, TA664, TA666-TA669, TA685-TA688, TA691, TA692, TA694, TA695, TA697-TA699,

TA702-TA706, TA711, TA712, TA718-TA724 were converted to TT.35 and TA650, TA710 to PR.35. SZ994, TA373, TA383, TA385, TA479, TA485, TA491, TA577, TA578, TA597 to RNZAF. SZ970, SZ972, SZ973, SZ984 became 6060M, 6677M, 6657M, 6809M and TA243, TA380, TA391, TA399, TA528, TA535, TA582, TA599, TA639, TA722 became 5817M, 6525M, 5894M, 5814M, 6745M, 6526M, 6826M, 6796M, 7806M, 7608M.

TA738-TE578   **Supermarine Spitfire LF/HF.IX/XVI**   1492(1884)
Ordered from Vickers Armstrong at Castle Bromwich. TA738-TA771 LF.IX mostly to Russia; TA772 HF.IX; TA773-TA779 LF.IX; TA780 HF.IX; TA793 LF.IX; TA794-TA796 HF.IX of which TA796 became 6139M; TA797 LF.IX; TA798 HF.IX; TA799 LF.IX; TA800 HF.IX; TA801 LF.IX; TA802 HF.IX; TA803 LF.IX; TA804-TA808 HF.IX; TA809 LF.XVI; TA810-TA813 HF.IX; TA814-TA816 LF.IX; TA817 HF.IX; TA818-TA824 LF.IX; TA825 HF.IX; TA826-TA840, TA854-TA866 LF.IX; TA867-TA888 LF.IX all to Russia; TA905-TA948 LF.IX; TA960-TA999 LF.IX to Russia; TB115-TB125 LF.IX; TB126-TB129 F.IX; TB130-TB132 LF.XVI; TB133-TB135 F.IX; TB136-TB141 LF.XVI; TB142-TB150, TB168-TB193 F.IX mostly to Russia; TB194 cancelled; TB195, TB196 F.IX; TB197 HF.IX; TB213 LF.IX; TB214-TB216 F.IX; TB217-TB236 Mk.IX; TB237 LF.XVI; TB238-TB243 LF.IX; TB244-TB256, TB269-TB308, TB326-TB349, TB352-TB396 LF.XVI; TB413-TB450 LF.IX of which all but TB439 went to Russia; TB464-TB474 LF.IX; TB475, TB476 LF.XVI; TB477-TB491 Mk.IX except TB478, TB480, TB481 LF.XVI; TB492-TB498 LF.IX; TB499, TB500 Mk.IX or XVI; TB501, TB502 LF.XVI; TB503 Mk.IX; TB515 LF.XVI; TB516-TB518 LF.IX; TB519-TB522 LF.XVI; TB523, TB524 LF.IX; TB525, TB526 LF.XVI; TB527 LF.IX; TB528 LF.XVI; TB529-TB531 LF.IX; TB532 HF.XI; TB533-TB536 LF.IX; TB537 HF.IX; TB538 LF.IX; TB539 HF.IX; TB540, TB541 LF.IX; TB542 HF.IX; TB543 LF.IX; TB544-TB546 HF.IX of which TB545 was converted to LF.IX; TB547 Mk.IX; TB548 HF.IX; TB549 LF.XVI; TB563 LF.IX; TB564, TB565 HF.IX; TB566, TB567 LF.IX; TB568-TB570 HF.IX; TB571 LF.IX; TB572-TB574 LF.XVI; TB575 LF.IX; TB576 HF.IX; TB577 HF.IX converted to LF.IX; TB578 LF.XVI; TB579 LF.IX; TB580-TB583 LF.XVI; TB584 HF.IX; TB585 LF.XVI; TB586, TB587 HF.IX; TB588-TB590 LF.XVI; TB591-TB598, TB613-TB637 LF.XVI; TB638 LF.IX; TB639 LF.XVI; TB640-TB659 LF.IX to Russia; TB674 LF.IX; TB675 LF.XVI; TB676-TB712 LF.IX; TB713-TB716 LF.XVI; TB717, TB718 Mk.IX; TB733-TB735 LF.XVI; TB736 LF.IX; TB737-TB739 LF.XVI; TB740 LF.IX; TB741-TB759 LF.XVI; TB771-TB809 LF.IX to Russia; TB824-TB827 LF.IX; TB828, TB829 LF.XVI; TB830 LF.IX; TB831-TB836 LF.XVI; TB837-TB843 LF.IX; TB844-TB847 HF.IX; TB848-TB858 LF.IX; TB859-TB868, TB883-TB900 LF.XVI; TB901-TB904 LF.IX; TB905 LF.XVI; TB906-TB908 LF.IX; TB909 HF.IX; TB910 LF.IX; TB911 LF.XVI; TB912-TB917 LF.IX; TB918 HF.IX; TB919 LF.XVI; TB920 HF.IX; TB921-TB923 LF.XVI; TB924, TB925 HF.IX; TB938-TB959 LF.IX to Russia; TB971-TB980 LF.IX; TB981-TB988 HF.IX; TB989-TB991 LF.XVI; TB992 HF.IX; TB993 LF.XVI; TB994 HF.IX; TB995-TB999 LF.XVI. TB252, TB256, TB308, TB344, TB365, TB382, TB522, TB540, TB542, TB544, TB578, TB592, TB744, TB752, TB903, TB916, TB920 became 7257M and 8073M, 6369M or 6412M, 7559M, 7255M, 6331M, 6362M, 7244M, 6262M, 6063M, 6061M, 6062M, 6177M, 6080M, 6048M, 7256M and 7279M later 8086M, 6178M, 6945M, 6145M. TD113-TD154 LF.XVI; TD155 LF.IX; TD156-TD158 LF.XVI; TD175 LF.IX; TD176, TD177 LF.XVI; TD178-TD183 LF.IX; TD184-TD191 LF.XVI; TD192-TD204 LF.IX; TD205, TD206, HF.IX; TD207-TD213 LF.IX; TD229-TD267, TD280-TD286 LF.XVI; TD287 LF.IX; TD288, TD289 LF.XVI; TD290-TD292 LF.IX; TD293 LF.XVI; TD294-TD304 LF.IX; TD305 HF.IX; TD306-TD309 LF.IX; TD310 HF.IX; TD311, TD312 LF.IX; TD313-TD315 HF.IX; TD316-TD325, TD338-TD351 LF.XVI; TD352, TD353 HF.IX; TD354 LF.IX: TD355, TD356 HF.IX; TD357

LF.IX; TD358, TD359 HF.IX; TD360 LF.IX; TD361-
TD363 HF.IX; TD364, TD365 LF.IX; TD366, TD367
HF.IX; TD368 LF.IX; TD369 LF.XVI; TD370 HF.IX;
TD371 LF.IX; TD372 LF.XVI; TD373, TD374 LF.IX;
TD375-TD377 LF.XVI; TD378, TD379, TD395-TD399
LF.IX; TD400-TD408 LF.XVI. Batches TD409-TD428,
TD443-TD490, TD515-TD546, TD560-TD605, TD618-
TD649, TD660-TD706, TD720-TD766, TD783-TD815,
TD829-TD866, TD884-TD925, TD937-TD951 cancelled.
TD952-TD958, TD970-TD999 LF.IX of which TD952,
TD953, TD955-TD958, TD970-TD980 went to Russia.
TD135, TD143, TD187, TD231, TD236, TD248, TB281,
TD305, TD358, TD377 became 6798M, 6418M, 6224M,
6538M, 6273M, 7246M, 6540M, 6158M, 6146M, 6179M.
TE115 LF.IX; TE116 LF.XVI; TE117, TE118 LF.IX;
TE119, TE120 LF.XVI; TE121-TE158 LF.IX; TE174-
TE196 LF.XVI; TE197 HF.IX; TE198-TE204 LF.XVI;
TE205 HF.IX; TE206-TE210 LF.XVI; TE211-TE213
HF.IX to SAAF; TE214 LF.XVI; TE215 HF.IX; TE228,
TE229 LF.XVI; TE230-TE234 HF.IX; TE235-TE237
LF.XVI; TE238 HF.IX; TE239-TE259, TE273-TE291
LF.XVI; TE292-TE299 HF.IX; TE300 LF.XVI; TE301
HF.IX; TE302 LF.XVI; TE303-TE309 LF.IX; TE310.
TE311 LF.XVI; TE312, TE313 HF.IX; TE314 LF.XVI;
TE315 HF.IX; TE328 LF.XVI; TE329 HF.IX; TE330
LF.XVI; TE331 HF.IX; TE332 LF.XVI; TE333 HF.IX;
TE334, TE335 LF.XVI; TE336, TE337 HF.IX; TE338-
TE342 LF.XVI; TE343 HF.IX; TE344-TE359, TE375-
TE385 LF.XVI; TE386 cancelled;TE387-TE408, TE434-
TE471 LF.XVI; TE472 cancelled; TE473-TE480, TE493,
TE494 LF.IX; TE495-TE535, TE549-TE578 LF.IX of
which all but TE572, TE573 were disposed of to Czech,
French, Russian and Turkish forces. TE184, TE199,
TE207, TE244, TE255, TE288, TE311, TE330, TE338,
TE352, TE356, TE384, TE389, TE392, TE400, TE462,
TE463, TE471, TE476, TE477, TE479, TE623, TE687,
TE696, TE713, TE745, TE759, TE764, TE777, TE851
became 6850M, 6603M, 6272M, 6655M, 6433M, 7287M,
7241M, 7449M, 6642M, 6890M, 7001M, 7207M, 6990M,
7000M later 8074M, 7240M, 7243M, 6822M, 6258M,
8071M, 6820M, 6641M, 6776M-6781M, 6742M, 6782M,
6783M.

| TE580 & TE583 | **Handley Page HP.67 Hastings** | 2 |

Prototypes to Spec C3/44. TE580 first flew 7.5.46.

| TE587-TF206 | **DH.98 Mosquito FB.VI** | 266(400) |

Built by Standard Motors. TE587-TE628, TE640-TE669,
TE683-TE725, TE738-TE780, TE793-TE830, TE848-
TE889, TE905-TE932 of which nineteen went to Royal
Navy and thirty-three to RNZAF. TE933-TE944, TE959-
TE999, TF114-TF150, TF163-TF206 cancelled. TE618,
TE623, TE683, TE687, TE696, TE713, TE745, TE759,
TE764, TE777, TE851 became 6784M, 6776M, 6785M,
6777M-6781M, 6742M, 6782M, 6783M.

| TF209 | **Messerschmitt Me 410A-3** | 1 |

C/n 10259 captured at Monte Corvino, Italy, 27.11.43.

| TF212-TF607 | **Boulton Paul N22/43** | (300) |

Allocation cancelled.

| TF620-TF876 | **Hawker Fury** | (200) |

Allocation cancelled.

| TF895-TG258 | **Hawker Sea Fury FB.10/FB.11** | 100(200) |

To Spec N22/43 for Royal Navy. TF895-TF928, TF940-
TF955 (50) FB.10; TF956-TF973, TF985-TF999, TG113-
TG129 (50) FB.11. TF901, TF909, TF985 and all from
TF993 to RCN. Batches TG130 to TG258 (100) were
cancelled. TF956 preserved.

| TG263-TG271 | **Saro SR/A1** | 3 |

Prototypes TG263, TG267, TG271 to Spec E6/44.

| TG274-TG448 | **DH.100 Vampire F.1** | 120 |

Built by English Electric to an order placed in May 1944.
TG274-TG315, TG328-TG355, TG370-TG389, TG419-
TG448. TG274, TG276 wing tank experiments; TG275
became F.3 prototype; TG276, TG279, TG280 modified
to F.2 standard; TG281 variously modified; TG283 and
TG306 converted to DH.108; TG284 speed tests and
first of twenty-three of order released to French AF;
TG285 to Royal Navy; TG286 converted to F.21 for
Royal Navy; TG314 to Royal Navy; TG328 converted
to F.20 for Royal Navy; TG443 to RNZAF. TG277,
TG278, TG280-TG282, TG289, TG291, TG299, TG300,
TG304, TG308, TG309, TG312, TG329, TG336, TG337,

TG349, TG371, TG373, TG376, TG381, TG382, TG385,
TG387, TG389, TG420, TG429, TG432, TG437, TG440,
TG442, TG445, TG447 became 7004M, 6851M, 6797M,
6355M, 6528M, 7052M, 6613M, 7006M, 7053M, 7054M,
7063M-7065M, 7235M, 7055M, 7066M, 7203M, 7056M,
7067M, 7068M, 7057M, 7047M, 7069M, 7070M, 7058M,
7071M, 7048M, 7072M, 7049M, 7050M, 7073M, 7059M,
7051M.

| TG499-TG755 | **Handley Page HP.67 Hastings C.1** | 100(200) |

TG499-TG535, TG551-TG587, TG601-TG624. Con-
versions: TG503, TG505, TG511, TG517, TG518,
TG521, TG528, TG553 to T.5; TG504, TG505, TG507,
TG510, TG511, TG514, TG516, TG565-TG567, TG572,
TG576, TG616, TG620-TG624 converted to MET.1 but
TG516, TG616, TG620, TG621 reverted to C.1. TG503,
TG511, TG519, TG559, TG573, TG605, TG610 became
8555M, 8554M, 6609M, 7108M, 7594M, 7987M, 7835M.
TG625-TG646, TG659-TG690, TG710-TG755 cancelled.

| TG758-TH182 | **Avro 694 Lincoln** | (250) |

Cancelled order with Austin Motors. TG758-TG799,
TG813-TG856, TG870-TG908, TG921-TG945 plus
batches to TH182.

| TH186-TH446 | **Handley Page HP.61 Halifax B.VI** | (200) |

Cancelled.TH186-TH227, TH241-TH287, TH302-TH338,
TH351-TH392, TH415-TH446.

| TH450-TH974 | **Vickers Wellington B.X** | (376) |

Cancelled order with Vickers (Blackpool). TH450-
TH496, TH521-TH560, TH574-TH598, TH612-TH647,
TH661-TH666, TH719-TH757, TH777-TH815, TH829-
TH869, TH883, TH927, TH937-TH974.

| TH977-TJ158 | **DH.98 Mosquito B.35** | 69 |

Built at Hatfield. TH977-TH999, TJ113-TJ158 ordered
as B.XVI and built as B.35 of which TH977, TH978,
TH980, TH981, TH987, TH989-TH992, TH996, TH998,
TJ113, TJ114, TJ116, TJ119, TJ120, TJ122, TJ125-
TJ128, TJ131, TJ135, TJ136, TJ138, TJ140, TJ147-
TJ149, TJ153-TJ157 were converted to TT.35 and
TJ987, TJ989, TJ124, TJ145 to PR.35. TJ138 became
7607M.

| TJ161 & TJ164 | **Avro 689 Tudor 2** | (2) |

Allocations cancelled.

| TJ167 & TJ170 | **Douglas DC-3 Dakota C.2** | 2 |

TJ167 ex-USAAF 42-6478 became 6252M. TJ170
allotted to Lord Tedder and became G-AJLC.

| TJ175-TJ184 | **Fairey Spearfish** | (3) |

Prototypes. TJ175 not completed, TJ179 and TJ184
not built.

| TJ187-TJ707 | **Taylorcraft Auster AOP.V** | 400 |

TJ187-TJ228, TJ241-TJ276, TJ290-TJ325, TJ338-
TJ380, TJ394-TJ438, TJ451-TJ487, TJ504-TJ546,
TJ563-TJ607, TJ621-TJ657, TJ672-TJ707. TJ207 fitted
with Queen Bee floats; TJ707 became Mk.VI prototype.
TJ651, TJ704 to Royal Navy. Many disposals to civil
registers and other forces including Australian, Burmese
and South African. TJ226, TJ349, TJ396, TJ426, TJ510,
TJ512, TJ529 became 5990M, 6437M, 7129M, 6072M,
5963M, 6303M, 5961M.

| TJ711 | **Slingsby T.12 Kirby Gull** | 1 |

Acquired for the A & AEE.

| TJ714 & TJ717 | **Bristol 166 Buckmaster** | 2 |

Prototypes c/ns 12024, 12025 to Spec T13/43 utilising
two partially completed Buckinghams. TJ714 ff 27.10.44.

| TJ720-TJ909 | **Avro 685 York C.1** | (150) |

Cancelled order. TJ720-TJ762, TJ777-TJ807, TJ820-
TJ866, TJ881-TJ909.

| TJ922-TK288 | **Avro Lancaster B.VI** | (200) |

Allocations cancelled.

| TK292-TK437 | **DH.89A Dominie** | (120) |

Allocations cancelled.

| TK440-TK512 | **Short S.25 Sunderland GR.IV** | (60) |

Allocations cancelled.

| TK517-TK577 | **Fairey Firefly III** | (50) |

Allocations cancelled.

| TK580 | **Saro A.37 Shrimp** | 1 |

G-AFZS research aircraft. Converted from twin to
single fin.

| TK583 | **Bristol Brigand** | (1) |

Cancelled prototype.

| TK586 & TK589 | **North American Mustang F.IV (P-51K)** | |

Trials aircraft.

TK591-TK707	**DH.98 Mosquito B.35**	**54(94)**
	Built at Hatfield. TK591-TK635, TK648-TK656 of which TK591-TK594, TK599, TK603-TK610, TK612, TK613, TK616 were converted to TT.35 and TK615, TK632, TK650 to PR.35. TK624, TK655 became 6429M and G-AOSS. TK657-TK679, TK691-TK707 cancelled.	
TK710	**Schleicher Rhonbussard glider**	**1**
	Acquired for RAE.	
TK714-TK826	**General Aircraft GAL.59 Hamilcar I**	**66(90)**
	TK714-TK750, TK763-TK791 built of which TK722, TK726, TK735-TK738, TK741-TK744, TK746, TK747 were converted to Mk.X. TK738 became 6769M. TK792-TK798, TK810-TK826 cancelled.	
TK828-TL735	**Airspeed AS.58 Horsa II**	**600**
	Built by Harris Lebus. TK828-TK869, TK882-TK913, TK927-TK963, TK978-TK999, TL114-TL157, TL173-TL215, TL229-TL261, TL274-TL312, TL328-TL369, TL384-TL427, TL440-TL481, TL495-TL536, TL549-TL587, TL602-TL643, TL659-TL691, TL712-TL735. TK837, TK887, TK896, TK935, TK982, TK985, TK992, TK998, TL123, TL131, TL146, TL189, TL191, TL194, TL235, TL248, TL251, TL473 became 6670M, 6307M, 6308M, 6741M, 6399M, 6312M, 6400M, 6398M, 6532M, 5896M, 6499M, 6590M, 5843M, 6492M, 6451M, 6740M, 6742M, 6719M.	
TL773-TM251	**Supermarine Spitfire IX**	**(276)**
	Cancelled order with Vickers Armstrong at Castle Bromwich. TL773-TL815, TL829-TL870, TL884-TL916, TL930-TL967, TL979-TL999, TM115-TM136, TM163-TM205, TM218-TM251.	
TM379 & TM383	**Supermarine Seafire**	**2**
	Prototypes TM379 F.45 ex-F.21; TM383 F.45 to F.46.	
TM944-TN247	**Handley Page Halifax**	**(150)**
	Cancelled order with Fairey. TM944-TM983, TN101-TN115, TN130-TN153, TN166, TN213, TN225-TN247.	
TN250-TN462	**Vickers Wellington XIV**	**(150)**
	Cancelled order with Vickers Armstrong at Blackpool. TN250-TN289, TN310-TN324, TN340-TN363, TN380-TN427, TN440-TN462.	
TN466-TN864	**DH.98 Mosquito**	**(300)**
	Cancelled order with Leavesden plant. TN466-TN497, TN513-TN530, TN542-TN590, TN608-TN640, TN652-TN674, TN690-TN736, TN750-TN789, TN802-TN838, TN850-TN864.	
TN866-TP178	**Bristol Beaufighter X**	**(150)**
	Allocation cancelled.	
TP181 & TP187	**Douglas DC-3 Dakota C.IV/GT.IV**	**2**
	TP187 ex-USAAF C-47A 42-92771 glider pick-up aircraft.	
TP190	**Junkers Ju 88G-1**	**1**
	C/n 712273 landed in UK in error 13.7.44. Became Air Min 231.	
TP195-TP811	**Supermarine Spitfire XIV/XVIII**	**(207)473**
	TP195-TP235 FR.XVIII; TP236-TP240, TP256 F/FR.XIV; TP257-TP298, TP313-TP350, TP363-TP408, TP423-TP456 FR.XVIII. TP378, TP408 became 7010M, 6441M. TP457-TP459, TP472-TP507, TP519-TP558, TP573-TP615, TP628-TP659, TP675-TP717, TP730-TP769, TP783-TP811 cancelled.	
TP814	**Messerschmitt Bf109G.6/U-2**	**1**
	C/n 412951. Captured when landed in error at Manston on 21.7.44.	
TP819	**Miles M.17 Monarch**	**1**
	Temporary number of U-0226 later G-AGFW.	
TP823-TR733	**Avro Lancaster IV (Lincoln)**	**(600)**
	Order cancelled.	
TR737-TR860	**DH Mosquito XVI**	**(100)**
	Order cancelled.	
TR864-TS246	**Hawker Typhoon**	**(220)**
	Order cancelled.	
TS261-TS266	**Short S.29 Stirling IV**	**(4)**
	EF454, LK562, LK512, LJ575 renumbered TS261, TS262, TS264, TS266 on conversion.	
TS291-TS358	**Slingsby T.7 Cadet TX.I**	**50**
	TS291-TS311, TS330-TS358.	
TS363 & TS368	**Armstrong Whitworth AW.52**	**2**
	Prototypes to Spec E9/44. TS363 first flew 13.11.47.	
TS371-TS387	**Westland Wyvern I**	**6**
	Prototypes and pre-production aircraft TS371, TS375, TS378, TS380, TS384, TS387 to Spec N11/44.	
TS409-TS416	**Supermarine Attacker**	**3**
	Prototypes TS409, TS413, TS416 to Spec E10/44.	
TS422-TS436	**Douglas DC-3 Dakota C.3**	**12**
	TS422-TS427, TS431-TS436 ex-USAAF.	
TS439	**Heinkel He 177A-5/R6**	**1**
	Ex-enemy aircraft acquired for evaluation.	
TS444 & TS449	**DH.98 Mosquito TR.33**	**2**
	Prototypes built at Leavesden for Royal Navy.	
TS459 & TS463	**Slingsby T.7 Cadet TX.I**	**2**
TS467	**RFD Dagling Glider**	**1**
TS472	**Junkers Ju 88S-1**	**1**
	Found intact at Villacoublay in September 1944.	
TS475-TS504	**Short Sturgeon TT.I**	**23(30)**
	TS475-TS497. Built by Short & Harland. C/ns 1576-1598. Mainly stored except TS475, TS479-TS482 converted to TT.3. TS498-TS504 cancelled.	
TS478	**—**	**1**
	Unofficial serial borne by ex-Luftwaffe Heinkel He 177A-5/R-6.	
TS507-TS515	**General Aircraft GAL.56/61**	**4**
	Tailless research aircraft TS507, TS510, TS513 GAL.56, TS515 GAL.61.	
TS519-TS539	**Convair 32 Liberator IV**	**21**
	TS519, TS520, TS524-TS526, TS528, TS531, TS532, TS535, TS537 delivered as B.IV, rest as C.IV.	
TS543-TS672	**Short S.29 Stirling V**	**(100)**
	Cancelled order. TS543-TS592, TS605-TS620, TS639-TS672.	
TS676-TS783	**Fairey Barracuda**	**(85)**
	Order cancelled.	
TS789-TS863	**Avro 685 York C.1**	**25(60)**
	TS789-TS813 built but transferred to BOAC. TS814-TS822, TS838-TS863 cancelled.	
TS866-TS912	**Avro Tudor I/II/V**	**40**
	TS866-TS875 Mk.I except TS868, TS869 Mk.IVB, TS883 Mk.VII became VX199, TS884-TS892 Mk.II, TS893-TS902 Mk.II becoming G-AJJS to 'AJKB, TS903-TS908 Mk.V becoming G-AKBY to 'AKCD, TS909-TS912 Mk.II becoming G-AKTH to 'AKTK.	
TS915-TT110	**Fairey Spearfish**	**(50)**
	Cancelled order. TS915-TS935, TS963-TS990, TT110.	
TT176 & TT181	**Avro Tudor I/IVC**	**2**
	Ex-G-AGPF, 'AGST. TT176 became VX192, TT181 rebuilt as VX195.	
TT186-TT248	**DH.103 Sea Hornet**	**32**
	TT186-TT213, TT217, TT218 F.20/FR.20 of which TT187 became PR.22 prototype. TT221, TT248 NF.21. All for Royal Navy.	
TT191-TT197	**Vickers Viking**	**(3)**
	Prototypes TT191, TT194, TT197 allotted for aircraft to Spec 17/44 that evolved as civil aircraft.	
TT336-TT343	**Convair 32 Liberator VI (B-24H)**	**3**
	TT336 ex-44-10597 and TT340 ex-42-94797 converted to B.VI, TT343 ex-42-51350 converted to C.IV.	
TT346 & TT349	**Grumman Tigercat (F7F-2N)**	**2**
	USN transfers to Royal Navy for evaluation.	
TT353-TT974	**Airspeed AS.58 Horsa II**	**15(400)**
	TT353-TT367 only built by Harris Lebus. TT368-TT393, TT424-TT469, TT487-TT536, TT568-TT616, TT638-TT669, TT682-TT707, TT747-TT794, TT834-TT872, TT895-TT940, TT952-TT974 cancelled.	
TV100-TV160	**General Aircraft GAL.49 Hamilcar**	**(50)**
	Cancelled order. TV100-TV112, TV124-TV160.	
TV163-TV177	**Percival P.40 Prentice**	**5**
	Prototypes to Spec T23/43. TV163 first flew 31.3.46. TV166, TV168, TV172, TV177 became 6575M, 7106M, 6672M, 6671M.	
TV184-TV482	**DH.98 Mosquito**	**(200)**
	Allocation cancelled.	
TV485-TV950	**Supermarine Seafire F.XVII**	**(300)**
	Allocation cancelled.	
TV954-TW358	**DH.98 Mosquito T.III/Sea Mosquito TR.33**	**100(150)**
	Built at Leavesden. TV954-TV984, TW101-TW119 T.III of which TW101. TV117 became 6953M, 7805M. TW227-TW257, TW277-TW295 TR.33 of which TW230/G was used for Highball trials and TW240 was TR.37 prototype. A further fifty numbers to TW358 were cancelled.	
TW362-TW642	**Taylorcraft Auster AOP.V/VI**	**200**
	TW362-TW402, TW433-TW478, TW496-TW520 AOP.V; TW521, TW522 AOP.V floatplane; TW523-TW540,	

	TW561-TW598, TW613-TW642 AOP.VI. TW461, TW515, TW536, TW575, TW625 became 7114M, 6799M, 7704M, 7434M, 7433M.	
TW647-TW671	Avro 683 Lancaster B.I	25
	Built by Armstrong Whitworth and delivered to await conversion to B.I(FE) of which TW652, TW654, TW658, TW662, TW665, TW671 were converted to PR.I and TW669 to a special photography aircraft. TW648, TW651, TW655 to Aeronavale and TW656 to R Egyptian AF. TW653 became 6506M.	
TW677-TW754	Fairey Firefly I/IV	63
	TW677-TW686 F.I; TW687-TW699, TW715-TW754 FR.IV. TW695 experimental contra-prop version. TW722, TW723, TW733, TW734, TW737, TW744, TW750, TW751, TW753 converted to TT.4.	
TW758-TW769	Convair 32 Liberator B.VI	12
	Delivered to Middle East.	
TW774-TW796	Handley Page Halifax B.VI	(23)
	PP142-PP164 renumbered. Majority to store.	
TW806-TW857	Fairey Barracuda III	(50)
	Cancelled order with Boulton Paul. TW806-TW837, TW840-TW857.	
TW858-TW911	Avro 683 Lancaster B.I	50
	TW858-TW873, TW878-TW911 built by Armstrong Whitworth. To store for conversion to B.I(FE) of which TW859, TW868, TW884, TW899, TW901, TW904, TW905 were converted to PR.I and TW911 became Python testbed. TW890, TW893 to R Egyptian AF. TW896, TW900 became 6638M, 6899M.	
TW915-TW929	Avro 683 Lancaster B.I	15
	Components by Metropolitan Vickers to Vickers Armstrong at Chester for assembly. All except TW923-TW926, TW929 to Armstrong Whitworth for conversion to B.I(FE). TW915, TW918, TW920-TW922, TW927, TW928 to Aeronavale. TW929 became 6425M.	
TW935-TX140	Supermarine Seafire	(100)
	Allocation cancelled.	
TX145-TX150	Gloster GA2/3	2(3)
	Prototypes to Spec E1/44. TX145 GA2 first flew 9.3.48; TX148 GA2; TX150 GA3 not completed.	
TX154-TX257	Avro 652A Anson C.XIX	100
	Built at Yeadon. TX154-TX197, TX201-TX235, TX237-TX257 Srs 1 except TX157, TX223, TX253, TX254, TX256, TX257 Srs 2. TX201, TX202, TX240-TX245, TX247, TX250-TX252, TX255 diverted to civil use. TX157, TX172, TX174 to VIP standard. TX214, TX226 became 7816M, 7865M.	
TX263-TX290	Avro 683/691 Lancaster B.III/Lancastrian C.IV	25
	Ordered from Yeadon. TX263-TX273 Lancaster B.III all of which were converted to ASR.III or GR.III; TX274-TX276, TW280-TW290 Lancastrian C.IV all to civil register.	
TX293	Short S.25 Sunderland GR.V	
	Built at Rochester.	
TX300-TX370	DH.89A Dominie C.II	20(36)
	TX300-TX319 c/ns 6958-6977 only delivered and sold back to de Havilland. TX320-TX339, TX361-TX370 were cancelled.	
TX374	Bristol 164 Brigand TF.1	1
	Fourth prototype in lieu of MX997.	
TX386-TX804	Gloster Meteor III	300
	Cancelled order. TX386-TX428, TX531-TX567, TX572-TX614, TX618-TX645, TX649-TX688, TX693-TX737, TX739-TX776, TX779-TX804.	
TX807-TX870	DH.100 Vampire F.2	1(60)
	TX807 to RAAF as A78-2. TX808-TX848, TX853-TX870 cancelled.	
TX974-TZ240	Supermarine Spitfire XIV/XVIII	157
	TX974-TX998 F.XIV; TZ102-TZ149, TZ152-TZ176, TZ178-TZ199 FR.XIV; TZ200-TZ205, TZ210-TZ240 FR.XVIII. TZ135, TZ148, TZ239 became 6165M, 6562M, 6472M. TX989, TX995, TZ111, TZ127, TZ132, TZ137, TZ154, TZ166, TZ192, TZ193 to Belgian AF.	
TZ245-TZ436	Avro Lincoln B.II	(150)
	Allocations to Metropolitan Vickers. Cancelled.	
TZ483-TZ569	Avro 685 York C.1	(72)
	Cancelled order. TZ483-TZ531, TZ547-TZ569.	
TZ598-TZ738	Supermarine Spitfire PR.XIX	(100)
	Cancelled order. TZ598-TZ637, TZ658-TZ692, TZ714-TZ738.	

TZ747-VA250	Supermarine Spitfire	(260)
	Ordered from Vickers Armstrong at Castle Bromwich but cancelled before deliveries. TZ747-TZ791, TZ815-TZ843, TZ866-TZ898, TZ921-TZ957, TZ969-TZ998, VA123-VA154, VA192-VA195 to have been LF.XVI. VA201-VA250 to have been LF.IX changed to F.22.	
VA278-VA336	Percival Proctor IV	(30)
	Cancelled order with F. Hills and Son. VA278-VA291, VA321-VA336.	
VA359-VA368	Bristol 166 Buckmaster T.I	10
VA386-VA436	Hawker Tempest F.II	(30)
	Ordered from Bristol Aeroplane Co. Cancelled. VA386-VA395, VA417-VA436.	
VA461-VA856	Supermarine Seafire F.XVII/F.XVIII	(250)
	Ordered from Cunliffe Owen. Cancelled. VA461-VA497, VA524-VA558, VA575-VA596, VA613-VA647, VA661-VA694, VA722-VA765, VA783-VA798, VA830-VA856.	
VA701-VA750	Convair 28 Catalina GR.IIA	36(50)
	Canadian Vickers order. Thirty-six built as RCAF Nos 9701-9736. Only twenty-two for RAF: VA703, VA712-VA732 of which VA719, VA721, VA724 were lost on or before delivery flight. Remainder of batch to RCAF.	
VA871-VA948	DH.98 Mosquito T.III	30(50)
	Ordered from Leavesden. VA871-VA894, VA923-VA928 of which VA877-VA881 were delivered to Royal Navy. VA929-VA948 cancelled.	
VA962-VB849	DH.103 Hornet	5(500)
	VA962-VA966 only built as PR.II. VA967-VA997, VB108-VB135, VB154-VB196, VB213-VB257, VB280-VB299, VB324-VB358, VB379-VB394, VB409-VB436, VB452-VB497, VB525-VB558, VB584-VB596, VB621-VB653, VB682-VB699, VB716-VB748, VB764-VB793, VB808-VB849 cancelled.	
VB852	Convair 32 Liberator VI	1
	USAAF 42-50744 converted to C.VI early in 1945.	
VB857	Hawker Fury X	1
	Prototype to Spec N3/43. Built by Boulton Paul and assembled by Hawker at Kingston and retained.	
VB861-VB869	Airspeed AS.10 Oxford T.II	1(9)
	VB861-VB868 ex-PH528-PH535, VB869 built from spares.	
VB873	Avro 691 Lancastrian	1
	Prototype conversion of Lancaster airframe. To G-AGLF.	
VB880-VB889	Short S.25 Sunderland GR.V	10
	Built by Blackburn at Dumbarton. VB880, VB881, VB883 became NZ4111, NZ4112, NZ4107 of RNZAF.	
VB893 & VB895	Supermarine Seafang F.32 (to Spec N5/45)	1(2)
	Prototypes. VB893 not completed; VB895 trials only	
VB904	Convair 32 Liberator C.VI	1
	Ex-USAAF 42-52766.	
VB908-VD154	DH.98 Mosquito PR.34	(100)
	VB908-VB943, VB961-VB997, VD128-VD154 cancelled.	
VD160-VD234	Gliders for Air Training Corps	48(60)
	Slingsby types given by their T-prefix type number. VD160-VD162 T.4 Falcon III; VD163 a primary nacelle; VD164 RFD Dagling; VD165 T.6 Kite; VD166 T.7 Kirby Cadet; VD167 T.8 Kirby Tutor; VD168 Schneider Grunau Baby; VD169 T.8 Kirby Tutor; VD170 T.4 Falcon; VD171 T.7 Kirby Cadet; VD172 Schneider Grunau Baby; VD173, VD174 T.7 Kirby Cadet; VD175 T.4 Falcon; VD176 T.6 Kite; VD177 T.4 Kirby Cadet; VD178 T.8 Kirby Tutor; VD179 T.7 Kirby Cadet; VD180/183 types untraced; VD181 T.8 Kirby Cadet; VD182 Schneider Grunau Baby; VD199 Dart Totternhoe; VD200 T.6 Kite; VD201, VD202 T.4 Falcon III; VD203 T.12 Gull; VD204 Schneider Grunau Baby IIB; VD205 T.4 Falcon; VD206 T.8 Kirby Tutor; VD207 T.9 Kirby Kite; VD208 T.8 Kirby Tutor; VD209 Schneider Grunau Baby; VD210, VD211 T.7 Kirby Cadet; VD212 T.8 Kirby Tutor; VD213 T.6 Kite; VD214 T.7 Kirby Cadet; VD215 Schneider Grunau Baby; VD216 Schleicher Rhonbussard; VD217 T.8 Kirby Tutor ex-BGA368; VD218 T.8 Kirby Tutor; VD219 T.4 Falcon; VD220 type not known; VD221 T.7 Kirby Cadet; VD222 Schneider Grunau Baby; VD223 type not known; VD224 DFS/30 Kranich 2; VD225-VD234 not taken up.	
VD238 & VD241	Avro Lancastrian I	(2)
	Ex-PD141, PD142. Became G-AGLS and G-AGLT. Military marks not taken up.	
VD245 & VD249	Convair 32 Liberator B.VI/C.VI (B-24H/J)	2
	Ex-USAAF 42-52681 and 44-10533.	

Serial	Aircraft	Notes
VD253	**Avro Lancastrian**	(1)
	Ex-PD143. Became G-AGLU instead.	
VD258-VD269	**Fairey O.21/44**	(4)
	Prototypes. VD258, VD261, VD264, VD269 not built.	
VD273-VD278	**Avro 688 Tudor 1**	(6)
	Cancelled.	
VD281-VD352	**Avro 689 Tudor 2**	(49)
	VD281-VD316, VD340-VD352 cancelled BOAC order.	
VD281-VD299	**Avro Lancastrian C.IV**	(19)
	Cancelled.	
VD358 & VD364	**Messerschmitt Bf 109G-14**	2
	Captured enemy aircraft. VD358 c/n 541560.	
VD368-VD487	**DH.98 Mosquito NF.36**	(80)
	Ordered from Leavesden. Cancelled. VD368-VD395, VD421-VD457, VD473-VD487.	
VD490-VE593	**Supermarine Seafire F.45/F.46/F.47**	(600)
	Cancelled order from Castle Bromwich plant. VD490-VD499, VD521-VD568, VD582-VD597, VD618-VD653, VD679-VD696, VD714-VD748, VD763-VD792, VD809-VD856, VD869-VD893, VD925-VD961, VD984-VD999, VE135-VE162, VE176-VE193, VE233-VE259, VE274-VE296, VE328-VE362, VE379-VE391, VE406-VE447, VE462-VE498, VE516-VE542, VE563-VE593.	
VE624-VE996	**Blackburn B.45 Firebrand TF.III**	(250)
	VE624-VE671, VE679-VE695, VE716-VE739, VE752-VE790, VE821-VE868, VE888-VE898, VE912-VE960, VE983-VE996 cancelled.	
VF100-VF133	**Miles M.50 Queen Martinet**	11(34)
	VF100-VF103 to Royal Navy. VF104-VF110 to RAF, VF111-VF133 cancelled.	
VF137-VF167	**Avro 691 Lancastrian C.I**	17(28)
	Order released for civil use. VF137-VF144, VF149-VF151 intended for BOAC but not completed, VF145-VF148 became G-AGMJ to 'AGMM, VF152-VF156, VF160-VF162 became G-AGMA to 'AGMH and VF163-VF167 G-AGLV to 'AGLZ. Originally allotted earlier serials, see notes for PA964-PD196 range.	
VF172	**Blackburn B.48 (SBAC YA-1)**	1
	Experimental aircraft to Spec S28/43 for Royal Navy.	
VF176-VF200	**Slingsby T.7 Cadet TX.1**	25
	Gliders for ATC.	
VF204	**Fiat G.55**	1
	Captured Italian aircraft.	
VF207-VF737	**Airspeed AS.58 Horsa II**	(360)
	Ordered from Harris Lebus. Cancelled. VF207-VF247, VF264-VF301, VF332-VF362, VF378-VF400, VF414-VF439, VF462-VF511, VF531-VF578, VF601-VF648, VF670-VF699, VF713-VF737. A duplication of serial allocations follow due to a clerical error.	
VF241	**Messerschmitt Me 163B-1A**	1
	For evaluation.	
VF247 & VF251	**Lockheed 14/WF42**	(2)
	Ex-HK982, HK984 acquired in the Middle East.	
VF254-VF262	**Blackburn B.48**	(3)
	Further prototypes VF254, VF257, VF262 cancelled before completion.	
VF265-VF348	**DH.100 Vampire F.1/F.3**	68
	Built by English Electric Co. VF265-VF283, VF300-VF314 F.1; VF315-VF348 F.3. VF268, VF269 to Royal Navy plus VF315 as Sea Vampire F.20. VF326, VF328, VF330, VF331, VF334 sold to Norway.	
VF354-VF435	**Supermarine Sea Otter ASR.1**	(50)
	Cancelled order with Saro. VF354-VF374, VF407-VF435.	
VF439-VF478	**Fairey Firefly FR.4**	(40)
	Cancelled order with General Aircraft.	
VF482-VF733	**Taylorcraft Auster AOP.6/T.7**	144(170)
	VF482-VF530, VF547-VF582, VF600-VF648, VF660-VF664 AOP.6; VF665 T.7 prototype became Marshalls MA4; VF666-VF670, VF713-VF733 cancelled. Conversions: VF515 floatplane and VF516, VF543, VF628, VF636 T.10.	
VF737-VG283	**DH.98 Mosquito FB.VI**	(300)
	Ordered from Standard Motors. Cancelled. VF737-VF777, VF790-VF839, VF871-VF900, VF928-VF964, VF993-VF999, VG113-VG156, VG170-VG198, VG209-VG240, VG254-VG283.	
VG286-VG466	**DH.98 Mosquito TR.33**	(120)
	Ordered from Leavesden. Cancelled. VG286-VG310, VG341-VG380, VG399-VG438, VG452-VG466.	
VG471-VG679	**Supermarine Seafang F.31/F.32**	16(150)
	VG471-VG505 not all completed, but VG471-VG480 built as F.31 and VG481, VG482, VG486, VG488-VG490 built as F.32. VG540-VG589, VG602-VG650, VG664-VG679 cancelled.	
VG692-VG760	**DH.100 Vampire F.3**	12(52)
	VG692-VG703 built by English Electric Co. VG701 became F.20 of Royal Navy and VG702, VG703 RAF tropical trials aircraft. VG704-VG732, VG750-VG760 cancelled.	
VG764	**DH.89A Dominie**	(1)
	Ex-NR715 rebuilt to BOAC as G-AGNH.	
VG768-VG908	**Handley Page Halifax A.IX**	(110)
	Ordered from Cricklewood. Cancelled. VG768-VG799, VG821-VG869, VG880-VG908.	
VG913	**Focke-Wulf Fw 190A**	(1)
	Allocation cancelled, duplicated NF755.	
VG916	**Junkers Ju 188**	1
	C/n 190335 deserted to Britain 7.5.45.	
VG919	**Morane MS.500**	1
	French-built Fi 156 Storch c/n 130 acquired.	
VG925-VG952	**Avro 694 Lincoln B.I**	(28)
	Cancelled order with Metropolitan Vickers.	
VG957-VH361	**Fairey Firefly FR.4**	67(200)
	VG957-VG999, VH121-VH144 built as FR.4. VH145-VH148, VH163-VH191 ordered as FR.4 and VH203-VH245, VH270-VH305, VH341-VH361 ordered as NF.IV cancelled. Conversions: VG957, VG959, VG961, VG962, VG965-VG968, VG974, VG977, VG979, VG981, VG982, VG988, VG993 and VH126, VH127, VH132, VH143 to TT.4; VH125, VH130, VH134-VH142 to AS.5, VH130, VH134 to U.9. Transfers to RAN and RCN and sales to India.	
VH367-VH505	**Supermarine Seafire F17/18**	(100)
	Ordered from Westland. Cancelled. VH367-VH398, VH419-VH450, VH470-VH505.	
VH509-VH530	**Captured German aircraft for evaluation**	6
	VH509 Messerschmitt Me 262-2a c/n 500210; VH513 Heinkel He 162A-2 c/n 120098; VH519 Messerschmitt Me 262A-2a/U-1 c/n 110305; VH523, VH526 Heinkel He 162A-2 c/n 120076 and 120221; VH530 Arado AR 234B-2 c/n 140113. Ex-Air Min 52, 67, 50, 59, 58, 54.	
VH534-VH732	**Avro 683 Lancaster B.III**	(150)
	Ordered from Austin. Cancelled. VH534-VH572, VH590-VH636, VH651-VH684, VH703-VH732.	
VH737 & VH742	**Avro 691 Lancastrian C.III**	(2)
	Ex-PD193, PD194, both becoming engine testbeds.	
VH751-VH756	**Fieseler Fi 156 Storch**	6
	Impressed from Luftwaffe.	
VH762	**Messerschmitt Bf 108B**	1
	Operated by No.2 Group Comm Flt.	
VH765-VH896	**Fairey Barracuda**	(100)
	VH765-VH789, VH805-VH843, VH861-VH896 all cancelled.	
VH901-VH977	**Fairey Barracuda TR.5**	(50)
	Ordered from Boulton Paul. Cancelled. VH901-VH934, VH962-VH977.	
VH980-VJ118	**Supermarine Attacker**	(24)
	Order cancelled. VH980-VH985, VH987-VH990, VH995-VH999, VJ110-VJ118.	
VJ120-VJ413	**Waco Hadrian II (CG-4A)**	200
	Ex-USAAF. VG120-VG165, VG198-VG222, VG239-VG284, VG313-VG349, VG368-VG413.	
VJ416 & VJ421	**Lockheed Hudson C.III**	(2)
	Ex-BOAC G-AGDC, 'AGDK, ex-V9061, V9152.	
VJ426-VK874	**Waco Hadrian (CG-4A)**	144(878)
	Ex-USAAF. VJ735-VJ781, VJ821-VJ847, VK873-VK609, VK623-VK655. Others not taken up - see page 228.	
VK877 & VK880	**Arado Ar234B**	2
	VK877 ex-Air Min 26, VK880 ex-Air Min 25.	
VK884	**Junkers Ju 88G-6**	1
	Ex-Air Min 3.	
VK888	**Junkers Ju 88G-7a**	1
	C/n 621642 landed in Eire, May 1945.	
VK893	**Messerschmitt Me 262A-2a**	1
	See Air Min 51. Preserved as 8482M.	
VK895	**Blohm & Voss Bv 138B**	1
	Ex-Air Min S-2. Tested at MAEE.	
VK900 & VK903	**Bristol 170 Freighter**	(2)
	Prototypes registered G-AGPV, 'AGVB before delivery.	

VK907-VL136	Avro 694 Lincoln B.II	(100)
	Allocation cancelled. VK907-VK943, VK958-VK995, VL112-VL134.	
VL140-VL223	DH.100 Vampire F.1	(50)
	Allocation cancelled.	
VL226-VL248	Vickers Viking C.1/C.2	12(20)
	VL226, VL227 C.1A ex-G-AIJE, 'AIKN to which they reverted; VL228 C.2 trials aircraft; VL229 Naiad test-bed; VL230-VL233 C.2; VL237-VL244 cancelled; VL245-VL247 C(VVIP).2; VL248 C.2.	
VL249-VL282	Vickers Valetta C.1	22
	VL249 prototype, VL262 C.2 prototype. VL263-VL282 C.1.	
VL285-VL363	Avro Anson C.19 Srs.II	60
	VL285-VL313, VL333-VL363 of which the last six were diverted direct to civil register. Mainly delivered overseas. VL356 to S Rhodesian AF.	
VL367-VL396	DH.89 Dominie C.II	(30)
	Order cancelled.	
VL401-VL510	Grumman TBM-3 Avenger	(70)
	VL401-VL410, VL432-VL461, VL475-VL494, VL501-VL510 cancelled acquisition from USA.	
VL515-VL518	Scottish Aviation A2/45	2(4)
	VL515, VL516 became G-AKBF, 'ANAZ then Pioneers XE512, XE514. VL517, VL518 cancelled.	
VL522-VL525	Auster N	2(4)
	Prototypes to Spec A2/45. VL522, VL523 later allotted 6818M, 6819M. VL524, VL525 not built.	
VL529-VL532	Heston JC6	2(4)
	Prototypes to Spec A2/45. VL529, VL530 trials aircraft, VL531, VL532 not built.	
VL537-VL610	DH.98 Mosquito B.35	(70)
	Ordered from Hatfield plant. Cancelled. VL537-VL583, VL586-VL599, VL602-VL610.	
VL613-VL723	DH.98 Mosquito PR.34	13(80)
	VL613-VL625 built at Hatfield. VL625 converted to PR.34A. VL626-VL652, VL668-VL697, VL714-VL723 cancelled.	
VL726-VL879	DH.98 Mosquito FB.VI	7(100)
	VL726-VL732 built by Airspeed. VL733-VL755, VL780-VL796, VL813-VL842, VL857-VL879 cancelled.	
VL892-VL954	Boulton Paul P.108 Balliol	3(4)
	Prototypes to Spec T7/45. VL892, VL917, VL935 test aircraft, VL954 cancelled.	
VL958 & VL963	Bristol 171 Mk.I	2
	Prototypes. C/n 12835, 12836. VL958 first flew 27.7.47, VL963 was temporarily G-ALOU.	
VL967-VL986	Avro 691 Lancastrian C.2	15(20)
	Built at Woodford. VL967-VL981 built of which VL967, VL971, VL972, VL977-VL979 went to civil register; VL982-VL986 cancelled.	
VL991	Junkers Ju88G-6	1
	C/n 621965 ex-Air Min 9.	
VL994-VL999	Grumman TBM-3 Avenger	(6)
	Cancelled acquisition from USA.	
VM109-VM118	Slingsby T.24	3
	Glider to Spec TX8/45. VM109, VM113, VM118.	
VM125-VM138	Avro 701 Athena	3(4)
	Prototypes to Spec T7/45. VM125 (first flew 12.6.48) and VM132 Mamba engines; VM129 Dart. VM138 cancelled.	
VM143-VM278	Bucker Bu181 Bestmann	25
	Ex-Luftwaffe aircraft impressed in Germany. VM143, VM148, VM151, VM157, VM162, VM169, VM174, VM179, VM181, VM188, VM193, VM199, VM206, VM215, VM220, VM227, VM231, VM238, VM243, VM252, VM259, VM263, VM269, VM274, VM278.	
VM286	Piper Cub (L-4B)	1
	Ex-USAAF 43-630.	
VM291-VM296	Fieseler Fi156 Storch	6
	Ex-Luftwaffe for 83 Group Communications Squadron. C/ns 779, 1576, 2010, 1665, 5746, 2547.	
VM305-VM458	Avro 652A Anson	95(120)
	VM305 T.20 prototype; VM306 T.22 prototype; VM307-VM342, VM351-VM394, VM406-VM409 C.19; VM410-VM418 T.20. VM355, VM357 direct to S Rhodesian AF. VM419-VM432, VM448-VM458 cancelled.	
VM466	Siebel Si204D-1	1
	Ex-Luftwaffe.	
VM472	Fieseler Fi156 Storch	1
	C/n 5656 ex-Luftwaffe for 21 Army Group HQ.	
VM479	Focke-Achgelis Fa223E (V14)	1
	Ex-Luftwaffe for evaluation.	
VM483	Dornier Do24T	1
	Ex-Luftwaffe for evaluation.	
VM489	Fieseler Fi156 Storch	1
	Ex-Luftwaffe.	
VM495-VM508	Messerschmitt Bf108	3
	VM495, VM502, VM508 ex-Luftwaffe. C/n 3010, 3076, 1105.	
VM515-VM696	Slingsby T.7/T.8 Cadet TX.1/TX.2	115
	Gliders for ATC. VM515-VM559, VM583-VM598, VM630-VM633 (65) TX.1; VM634-VM667, VM681-VM696 (50) TX.2.	
VM701-VM738	Avro 691 Lancastrian C.2	18
	VM701-VM704, VM725-VM738. VM703 Ghost testbed. VM704, VM733 Rolls-Royce testbed. VM737, VM738 to civil register.	
VM743	FGP-227	1
	Ex-Luftwaffe for evaluation. Model of Bv238 flying boat.	
VM748 & VM761	Arado Ar196A	2
	For evaluation. VM748 ex-Air Min 91; VM761 ex-Air Min 92.	
VM768-VM797	Bucker Bu181 Bestmann	30
	Ex-Luftwaffe impressed.	
VM824-VM846	Fieseler Fi156 Storch	23
	Ex-Luftwaffe impressed.	
VM851-VM862	Messerschmitt Bf108	12
	Ex-Luftwaffe impressed.	
VM873-VM897	Impressed ex-Luftwaffe aircraft	8
	VN873, VM874 Fieseler Fi156 Storch; VM879 Bucker Bu181 Bestmann; VM885-VM887 Siebel Si204D; VM892 Junkers Ju52/3m; VM897 Fieseler Fi156 Storch.	
VM900-VM987	Junkers Ju52/3m	60
	VM900-VM932, VM961-VM987 ex-Luftwaffe held for possible use.	
VN101-VN140	Siebel Si204D-1	40
	Ex-Luftwaffe held for possible transport use.	
VN143	Junkers Ju188A-2	1
	Ex-Luftwaffe. Allotted Air Min 113.	
VN148	DFS Grunau Baby	1
	Ex-German glider.	
VN153	Heinkel He162A-2	1
	Ex-Air Min 64.	
VN158 & VN163	Savoia SM.82	2
	Ex-Luftwaffe.	
VN169-VN243	Bucker Bu181 Bestmann	7(60)
	Ex-Luftwaffe. VN169-VN198, VN214-VN243. VN169-VN175 only used, others not taken up. VN176, VN177 reallocated.	
VN176-VN177	Junkers Ju52/3m	2
	Ex-Luftwaffe.	
VN249-VN260	Messerschmitt Bf108	(12)
	Ex-Luftwaffe. Not taken up.	
VN266-VN295	Fieseler Fi156 Storch	2(30)
	Ex-Luftwaffe. VN266 (c/n 5987) and VN267 (5388) only used, others not taken up.	
VN301-VN496	Supermarine Spitfire F.24	54(150)
	Originally ordered as F.22. VN301-VN334, VN477-VN496 built. VN335-VN348, VN364-VN397, VN413-VN439, VN456-VN476 cancelled.	
VN501-VN673	Supermarine Seafire F.46/F.47	(135)
	VN501-VN528, VN542-VN563, VN567-VN598, VN614-VN645, VN653-VN673 cancelled.	
VN679	Heinkel He162A-2	(1)
	C/n 120227 ex-Luftwaffe. Ex-Air Min 65. Serial never used. Preserved at St Athan.	
VN684-VN702	Percival P.40 Prentice	6
	Pre-production. VN684, VN687, VN691, VN695, VN700, VN702 all except VN691 became instructional airframes after service.	
VN709-VN756	Junkers Ju52/3m	40
	Captured Luftwaffe transports held in Germany and UK. VN709-VN731, VN740-VN756. Some used by BEA.	
VN763-VN771	Hawker Tempest VI	(9)
	Cancelled order.	
VN782-VN787	Bucker Bu181 Bestmann	6
	Ex-Luftwaffe.	

Serial Nos	Aircraft Type and Remarks	Quantity
VN799-VN850	English Electric Canberra	4
	Prototypes to Spec B3/45. VN799, VN828, VN850 with Avon engines. VN813 with Nene engines and later Spectre testbed. VN799 first flew 13.5.49.	
VN856 & VN860	E18/45 (DH.108)	(2)
	Not built. Replaced by TG283 and TG306.	
VN865 & VN870	Dornier Do 24T	2
	Ex-Luftwaffe for trials, ex-Air Min 114, 116.	
VN874	Junkers Ju 88A-6/U	1
	Ex-Air Min 112.	
VN877	Fieseler Fi 156 Storch	1
	Ex-Luftwaffe.	
VN881	Blohm & Voss Bv 138B	1
	Ex-Luftwaffe for trials. Possibly ex-Air Min 70.	
VN889	Avro 652A Anson C.19A Srs.1	1
	Possibly became SU-ADN.	
VN895-VN898	Percival P.44 Proctor C.5	4
	For use of British Air Attaches, allotted Rome, The Hague, Brussels and reserve.	
VN907-VN954	Junkers Ju 52/3m	1(40)
	Allocation VN907-VN925, VN934-VN954 of which only VN907 was used.	

Postwar Politics

VP100 to ZZ999

After the war the serialling system continued in exactly the same as hitherto, except that orders were in far smaller quantities and impressment ceased. From 1948, affecting practically all orders after VP100 late 1945, Mark numbers changed from Roman numerals to Arabic letters and role prefix letters were invariably used in the full description.

Apart from straightforward production, the final section includes American aircraft supplied on loan under Mutual Defence Aid Pact and civil aircraft temporarily taken on charge for evaluation or trooping. Also for the first time, hovercraft appear numbered in this series which hitherto had been exclusive to aircraft. Certain missiles might also be included in this series.

Currently allocations have been allotted up to the 'ZH' series, but as by the present rate of allocation it will be many years before ZZ999 is reached, a replacement serialling system has probably not yet been discussed.

Serial Nos	Aircraft Type and Remarks	Quantity
VP102	Douglas DC-2	(1)
	Ex-Luftwaffe (previously KLM). Probably not taken up.	
VP109-VP120	Westland Wyvern TF.2	3
	Prototypes to Spec N12/45. VP109, VP113 Python engine, VP120 Clyde engine.	
VP125-VP174	Slingsby T.24 (to Spec TX8/45)	(40)
	VP125-VP153, VP164-VP174. Allocation cancelled.	
VP178-VP202	DH.98 Mosquito B.35	25
	Built by Airspeed at Christchurch. VP188, VP200 sold before service. VP178, VP181, VP190, VP191, VP197 converted to TT.35 and VP183 to PR.35.	
VP207 & VP213	Hawker Fury	1(2)
	VP207 third prototype built from stock items 1947. VP213 not built.	
VP219-VP248	Airspeed Ambassador	(30)
	Order cancelled.	
VP254-VP294	Avro 696 Shackleton GR.1	29
	VP254-268, VP281-294. VP258/259/293 cnvtd to T.4.	
VP301 & VP312	Avro 688 Tudor 3	2
	Temporary serials for G-AIYA, 'AJKC.	
VP320-VP339	Siebel Si 204D	3(20)
	Ex-Luftwaffe. Only VP320-VP322 taken up.	
VP342-VP355	DH.98 Mosquito T.3	14
	Built at Hatfield. VP353 to French AF, VP355 to RN.	
VP359-VP397	Supermarine Seafire	(30)
	Cancelled allocations.	

Serial Nos	Aircraft Type and Remarks	Quantity
VP401-VP422	Hawker P.1040 Sea Hawk	3
	Prototypes to Spec N7/46. VP401 converted to P.1072, VP413, VP422.	
VP427-VP495	Supermarine Seafire F.47/FR.47	64
	VP427-VP465, VP471-VP495 to RN. FR.47 from VP447.	
VP501	Blohm & Voss Bv 222C	1
	Ex-Luftwaffe for evaluation.	
VP509-VP538	Avro 652A Anson C.19 Srs.II	30
	VP511 diverted before delivery; VP512 was temporarily G-AKFE.	
VP543	Horton Ho IV	1
	Ex-German glider, became BGA647.	
VP546	Fieseler Fi 156C Storch	1
	Ex-Air Min 101, became 7362M.	
VP550	Junkers Ju 352A-1	1
	Ex-Air Min 8.	
VP554	Messerschmitt Me 262A	(1)
	Ex-Air Min 81. Not taken up.	
VP559 & VP582	DFS SG38 Schulgleiter	2
	Ex-German gliders.	
VP587	Schneider Grunau Baby	1
	Ex-German glider.	
VP591	DFS/30 Kranich 2	1
	Ex-German glider.	
VP601-VP620	Gloster E1/44	(20)
	Cancelled.	
VP628-VP669	Taylorcraft Auster AOP.6	(36)
	Cancelled order. VP628-VP646, VP653-VP669.	
VP674-VP874	DH.100 Vampire	(150)
	Cancelled allocations.	
VP901-VP930	Douglas DC-3 Dakota	(30)
	Allocation for ex-Lend/Lease Dakotas in RAF service in India, refurbished for RIAF. 26 confirmed as supplied.	
VP937	Vickers 639 Viking	1
	Temporarily allotment to G-AGRV.	
VP952-VP981	DH.104 Devon C.1	30
	All except VP954, VP964, VP966, VP969, VP970, VP972, VP979 converted to C.2. VP967 later to Royal Navy.	
VP988-VR123	Fairey N16/45	(3)
	Prototypes. VP988, VR104, VR123 cancelled.	
VR131-VR140	Westland Wyvern TF.1	7(10)
	Pre-production to Spec 17/46P. VR131-VR137 for Royal Navy evaluation. VR138-VR140 cancelled.	
VR159	Westland N12/45	(1)
	Prototype cancelled.	
VR164-VR183	Gloster E1/44	(20)
	Order cancelled.	
VR189-VR324	Percival P.40 Prentice T.1	124
	VR189-VR212, VR218-VR253, VR257-VR296, VR301-VR324. Twenty became instructional airframes.	
VR330-VR359	DH.98 Mosquito T.3	20(30)
	Built at Hatfield. All but VR332 sold direct to Belgian, Czech, French or Norwegian forces. VR350-VR359 cancelled.	
VR363 & VR371	Short SA.2 Sturgeon TT.2	2
	Prototypes to Spec Q1/46. VR363 built from RK794 and with VR371 built at Belfast. C/n SH.1560, SH.1561.	
VR380 & VR382	Bristol 170	2
	Prototypes to Spec C9/45. Reverted to G-AGPV, 'AGUT. Used for radar trials.	
VR385-VR541	DH.98 Mosquito T.3/TR.33/NF.36/NF.38	(120)
	Cancelled batches.	
VR546 & VR557	Fairey Gannet	2
	Prototypes, c/n F.8270, F.8271 to Spec GR17/45 originally known as Fairey Q. VR546 first flew 19.9.49.	
VR566-VR582	Avro 701 Athena T.2	15(17)
	VR570 crashed before delivery, VR581, VR582 cancelled.	
VR590-VR606	Boulton Paul P.108 Balliol T.2	17
	VR596 hooked for carrier trials, VR599 became Sea Balliol T.21.	
VR611-VR620	DH.103 Sea Hornet	(10)
	Order cancelled.	
VR625-VR787	DH.98 Mosquito	(100)
	VR625-VR705 NF.36/NF.38; VR713-VR787 T.3 allocation cancelled.	
VR792-VR806	DH.98 Mosquito B.35	15
	Built by Airspeed. VR802, VR806 converted to TT.35 and VR803-VR805 to PR.35.	

VR811-VR830	Auster AOP.6	(20)
	Order cancelled.	
VR836-VR912	DH.103 Sea Hornet F.20	32(51)
	VR836-VR864, VR891-VR893 to Royal Navy. VR894-VR912 cancelled.	
VR918-VR952	Hawker Sea Fury FB.11	35
	To Royal Navy in general, except VR918, VR919 to Royal Canadian Navy.	
VR955	Lockheed 18-56 Lodestar	1
	G-AGCM acquired in 1946.	
VR961-VS165	Supermarine Seafire F.47	12(100)
	VR961-VR972 built at South Marston for Royal Navy. Batches to VS165 cancelled.	
VS172-VS197	DH.98 Sea Mosquito TR.33	?
	Order cancelled.	
VS201-VS220	Gliders acquired, ex-German	4
	VS201 DFS Meise; VS208, VS213 DFS Kranich; VS220 Schneider Grunau Baby.	
VS227-VS236	Airspeed Ayrshire	(10)
	Order cancelled.	
VS241-VS486	Percival P.40 Prentice T.1	125(180)
	Built by Blackburn. VS241-VS290, VS316-VS338, VS352-VS397, VS409-VS414 built; VS415-VS445, VS463-VS486 cancelled. Thirteen became instructional airframes.	
VS491-VS603	Avro 652A Anson T.20/T.21/C.21/T.22	90
	VS491-VS534, VS558-VS561 T.20 mainly to RATG; VS562-VS591 T.21 except VS565, VS566, VS568, VS570-VS572, VS574, VS575, VS578, VS584, VS586, VS588, VS591 C.21; VS592-VS603 T.22.	
VS609-VS804	Percival P.40 Prentice T.1	100(140)
	VS609-VS654, VS681-VS698, VS723-VS758 built; VS759-VS767, VS774-VS804 cancelled.	
VS812-VS877	Bristol 164 Brigand B.1/MET.3	44(52)
	VS812-VS816 B.1 of which VS813 was converted to T.4 and T.5; VS817-VS832 MET.3; VS833-VS839, VS854-VS869 B.1 of which VS833, VS837, VS855, VS858, VS865-VS867 were converted to T.4 and VS833, VS837, VS855, VS865-VS867 were further converted to T.5. VS870-VS877 cancelled.	
VS882-VS952	DH.98 Mosquito B.35	?
	Order cancelled.	
VS968-VS987	Gloster G.41M Meteor PR.10	20
VT102-VT347	Gloster G.41G Meteor F.4	200
	VT102-VT150, VT168-VT199, VT213-VT247, VT256-VT294, VT303-VT347 F.4. Conversions: VT150 Mk.8 (G.41K) prototype, VT347 to PR.5 but crashed on first test; VT104-VT107, VT110, VT112, VT113, VT118, VT130, VT135, VT139, VT142, VT168, VT175, VT177, VT179, VT184, VT187, VT191, VT192, VT196, VT197, VT219, VT220, VT222, VT226, VT230, VT243, VT256, VT259, VT262, VT268, VT270, VT282, VT286, VT289, VT291, VT294, VT310, VT311, VT316, VT319, VT329, VT330, VT332, VT338 to U.15. VT333 to R NethAF.	
VT362-VT504	Fairey Firefly AS.5	117
	C/n F.8272-F.8388. VT362-VT381, VT392-VT441, VT458-VT499 to Royal Navy; VT500-VT504 to RAN. Conversions: VT440 to T.5; VT364, VT370, VT372, VT403, VT413, VT430, VT441, VT461, VT463, VT470, VT481, VT485, VT487, VT493-VT494, VT497 to U.9.	
VT520-VT569	Fairey Firefly	?
	Cancelled order.	
VT581-VT638	DH.98 Mosquito T.3	44(51)
	Built at Hatfield. VT581-VT596, VT604-VT631 of which VT582, VT583, VT595, VT596, VT607, VT611, VT615, VT618, VT619, VT622-VT624, VT626, VT627, VT629-VT631 went direct to Royal Navy and VT585 to French AF; later VT592, VT609 went to Yugoslav AF. VT632-VT638 cancelled.	
VT651-VT707	DH.98 Mosquito NF.38	50
	Built at Hatfield and Chester. VT651-VT683, VT691-VT707 of which twenty-seven supplied to Yugoslav AF.	
VT724-VT749	DH.98 Mosquito TR.37	14(26)
	VT724-VT737 built at Broughton for Royal Navy. VT738-VT749 cancelled.	
VT762	Schneider Grunau Baby glider	1
VT769 & VT784	Boulton Paul P.111	(2)
	Renumbered VT935, VT951.	
VT789	Youngman Baynes High-lift Monoplane (Percival P.46)	1
	Testbed. Wings built by Heston Aircraft Ltd.	
VT793-VT874	DH.100 Vampire F.3	64
	Built by English Electric. VT793-VT835, VT854-VT874 of which VT795, VT805 went direct to Royal Navy and VT806 later to RNZAF. VT832-VT835 sold to Norway. Ten became instructional airframes.	
VT886-VT898	DFS SG.38 Glider	(13)
	Believed not taken up.	
VT916-VT928	Schneider Grunau Baby 2 gliders	10(13)
	VT916-VT925 built, VT926-VT928 cancelled.	
VT935 & VT951	Boulton Paul P.111/P.120	2
	High speed research aircraft to Spec E27/46. VT935 P.111 became P.111A. VT951 P.120. Ex-VT769, VT784 allocation.	
VT976-VT997	Auster AOP.6	22
	All diverted to Belgian Air Force.	
VV106 & VV119	Supermarine 510/535	2
	Research aircraft to Spec E41/46. Became 7175M and 7285M. VV119 originally Type 517.	
VV136-VV232	DH.100 Vampire F.3/FB.5/F.20	64(76)
	VV136-VV153 F.20 for Royal Navy. VV154-VV165 (F.20) cancelled. VV187-VV214 F.3 of which direct sales were VV188, VV212, VV214 Norway, VV213 Sweden and VV209-VV211 India; VV215-VV232 FB.5. All English Electric built.	
VV239-VV381	Avro Anson T.21/T.22	80(91)
	VV239-VV264, VV293-VV333 T.21 of which VV244, VV246, VV248, VV253, VV254, VV261, VV263 cnvtd to C.21; VV358-VV370 T.22; VV371-VV381 canx T.22s.	
VV395	Kirby Cadet	1
	Glider for Royal Navy.	
VV400-VV401	EoN Olympia I sailplane	2
VV405-VV424	DH.104 Devon C.1	(20)
VV430-VV441	DH.103 Sea Hornet NF.21	12
	For Royal Navy.	
VV443-VV736	DH.100 Vampire FB.5	200
	Built by English Electric.VV443-VV490, VV525-VV569, VV600-VV640, VV655-VV700, VV717-VV736. Conversions: VV612, VV613 Venom prototypes, VV675 FB.9. VV548, VV631, VV635 delivered direct to Royal Navy, and VV465 became A78-3 of RAAF. Sales: VV568, VV718, VV720-VV723, VV725-VV736 to France and VV453, VV694 to Lebanon.	
VV740-VW114	Avro 652A Anson C.19/T.20/T.21	92(207)
	VV740-VV789, VV805-VV854 cancelled C.19; VV866, VV867 T.20; VV880-VV919, VV950-VV999 (90) T.21; VW100-VW114 cancelled T.22.	
VW120	DH.108	1
	Research aircraft.	
VW126-VW135	Avro 696 Shackleton	3
	Prototypes to Spec R5/46. VW126 first flew 9.3.49, converted to MR.2, became 7626M; VW131 Napier Nomad testbed; VW135 extended trials.	
VW140-VW206	Vickers Valetta C.1	53
	VW140-VW165, VW180-VW206. VW188 interim T.4.	
VW209	Sikorsky S-51 Dragonfly	1
	Ex-G-AJOP.	
VW214-VW218	Vickers Viking 1A	5
	Temporary serials for G-AGON, 'AGRM, 'AGRN Vickers Type 498 and G-AHPA, 'AHOX Type 614.	
VW224-VW243	Hawker Sea Fury FB.11	20
	For RN. VW225, VW227, VW230, VW231 to RCN.	
VW248 & VW252	Bristol 171 (to Spec A6/47)	(2)
	Prototypes cancelled.	
VW255-VW315	Gloster G41G Meteor F.4	58
	VW255-VW304, VW308-VW315 of which VW263, VW264, VW286, VW288, VW291, VW295, VW296, VW309, VW310, VW313, VW315 went direct to R Neth AF and after service VW258, VW266, VW273, VW275, VW276, VW280, VW285, VW293, VW299, VW303, VW308 were converted to U.15.	
VW360-VW405	Gloster G41L/G41M Meteor FR.9/PR.10	16(42)
	VW360 FR.9 prototype used by Ferranti for radar work; VW361-VW371 FR.9 of which VW366 was sold to Ecuador and VW364 was used for Martin Baker ejection seat tests before becoming 7383M; VW376-VW379 PR.10. VW380-VW405 cancelled PR.5.	
VW410-VW489	Gloster G43 Meteor T.7	70
	VW410-VW459, VW470-VW489. VW443 testbed; VW413 had NF nose fitted. VW436, VW446, VW447 to RN; VW435 sold to Egypt; VW417, VW475 to the Dutch.	

VW495-VW539	Slingsby T.7/T.8 Cadet TX.1/TX.2	42
	Gliders for ATC. VW495-VW524 TX.1; VW528-VW539 TX.2.	
VW541-VW718	Hawker Sea Fury FB.11	128
	VW541-VW590, VW621-VW670, VW691-VW718 for RN. VW552, VW563, VW571, VW584 to RCN. VW643, VW645 to RAN and VW554, VW667 to Burmese AF.	
VW738-VW740	DFS SG.38 Gliders	3
	Built at Fleetlands for R.Navy GSA.	
VW743-VW745	Schneider Granau Baby	3
	Gliders for RN built at Fleetlands Yard.	
VW750-VW776	Hawker Sea Fury	(27)
	Cancelled order.	
VW780-VW791	Gloster G41G Meteor F.4	12
	VW781, VW791 converted to U.15.	
VW796-VW797	Fairey A7/47	(2)
	Prototypes cancelled.	
VW802-VW864	Vickers Valetta C.1	60
	VW802-VW851, VW855-VW864. VW802 became G-APKR.	
VW867-VW886	Westland Wyvern TF.2/S.4	20
	TF.2 except VW880-VW886 completed as S.4 and VW868, VW870, VW871, VW873 converted to S.4. For Royal Navy.	
VW890-VW893	Avro 701 Athena T.2	4
	Prototypes for trials to Spec T14/47.	
VW897-VW900	Boulton Paul P.108 Balliol T.2	4
	Prototypes for trials to Spec T14/47.	
VW905	Bristol Sycamore 2	1
	C/n 12869 ex-G-AJGU for evaluation.	
VW908	Schneider Grunau Baby glider	1
	Glider for ATC.	
VW912	Slingsby T.12 Gull I	1
VW915	BAC VII glider	1
VW918	Dittmar Condor glider	1
VW920	BAC III secondary glider	1
VW925	Slingsby T.8 Tutor	1
	Glider for ATC.	
VW930-VW980	DH.103 Sea Hornet NF.21/PR.22	46
	VW930-VW939 PR.22; VW945-VW980 NF.21 for RN.	
VW985-VX130	Auster AOP.6	40
	VW985-VW999. VX106-VX130. VX123 cnvtd to T.10	
VX101	Messerschmitt Bf 109G/Trop	1
	Ex-enemy aircraft shipped from Middle East to UK in 1944 and given out of sequence number.	
VX133-VX138	Supermarine 508/525/529	3
	Prototypes to Spec N9/47. VX133 Type 508, VX136 Type 529; VX138 Type 525.	
VX141	Vickers 498 Viking 1A	1
	G-AGOM of British European Airways to MoS.	
VX147	Ercoupe 415CD	1
	C/n 4784 ex-NC7465H and G-AKFC for evaluation.	
VX154	Fieseler Fi 156 Storch	1
	Ex-Luftwaffe for evaluation.	
VX158 & VX161	Short SA.4 Sperrin	2
	Prototypes c/n SH.1600, SH.1601. VX158 first flew 10.8.51 later testbed Short PD6.	
VX165-VX185	English Electric Canberra	4
	Prototypes VX165, VX169 B.2; VX181 PR.3 converted to B.5 VX185 B.5 to B.8 prototypes.	
VX190	Brunswick Zaunkönig II	1
	Built at Brunswick Technical College. Tested in UK. Ex-D-YBAR. Became G-ALUA.	
VX192-VX202	Avro 688/689 Tudor	1(4)
	VX192 Mk.1 ex-TT176; VX195 Mk.I ex-TT181 rebuilt as Mk.8; VX199 ex-TS883, G-AGRX Mk.7; VX202 Mk.2 ex-G-AGRY.	
VX206	Bristol 167 Brabazon I	1
	Serial allocated, but first flew 4.9.49 registered G-AGPW.	
VX211 & VX217	Vickers Viscount	2
	VX211, VX217 Vickers Types 630/663 G-AHRF, 'AHRG, the latter for Tay engine trials.	
VX220 & VX224	Armstrong Whitworth AW.55 Apollo	2
	C/n 3137, 3138 G-AIYN, 'AMCH for MoS research.	
VX229 & VX231	Handley Page (Reading) HPR.1 Marathon	2
	G-AILH and 'AHXU for MoS trials.	
VX234	Handley Page HP.74 Hermes	1
	G-AGUB ex-PW943 for MoS use.	
VX238	Vickers 495 Viking 1A	1
	G-AGOL to MoS, became 7215M.	

VX245-VX252	DH.103 Sea Hornet NF.21	8
	For Royal Navy.	
VX259 & VX266	Focke-Achgelis Fa 330	2
	For development of Bevan Bros E1/48 Jet Helicopter.	
VX272 & VX279	Hawker P.1052	2
	Research prototypes to Spec E38/46. VX272 became 7174M, VX279 later Type P.1081.	
VX275	Slingsby T.21B Sedburgh TX.1	1
	Presented to No.123 Gliding School.	
VX280-VX310	Hawker Sea Fury T.20	27
	VX280-VX292, VX297-VX310 for Royal Navy. Later VX280, VX281, VX291, VX300, VX302, VX309 to Germany and VX292 to Burma.	
VX317 & VX323	Bristol Type 174	(2)
	Scale models of Type 172 cancelled.	
VX330	Handley Page HP.88	1
	Supermarine 510 fuselage with scaled Victor wing and tail built by Blackburn.	
VX337	Handley Page HP.88	(1)
	Scale Victor wing for Supermarine. Cancelled.	
VX343	Bristol 167 Brabazon Mk.2	(1)
	Allocation for G-AIML not completed.	
VX350-VX364	Fairey FD.1	1(3)
	Delta-wing research aircraft VX350 c/n F.8477, VX357, VX364 not completed.	
VX371-VX438	Fairey Firefly AS.5	52
	C/n F.8403-F.8454. VX371-VX396, VX413-VX438 for Royal Navy. From VX414 had power-folding wings. VX371-VX390 to RAN. Conversions: VX373 T.5; VX416, VX418, VX421, VX427, VX429 U.9.	
VX442-VX454	Bristol 175 Britannia	3
	Prototypes VX442, VX447 became G-AL IO, 'ALRX for MoS trials. VX454 mock-up only.	
VX461-VX476	DH.100 Vampire FB.5	10
	Built by English Electric at Samlesbury. VX461-VX464, VX471-VX476.	
VX483-VX580	Vickers Valetta C.1/C.2/T.3	63
	VX483-VX485, VX490-VX499, VX506-VX515, VX521-VX530, VX537-VX546, VX555-VX563 C.1; VX564 T.3 prototype to Spec T1/49, VX571-VX590 C.2.	
VX587	Airspeed AS.65 Consul	(1)
	Ex-AKCW converted Oxford NJ318 which became a testbed.	
VX591	Fairey Gyrodyne	1
	C/n F. 8465 FB-1 PV to Spec E4/46 became G-AIKF.	
VX595-VX600	Westland WS-51 Dragonfly HR.1	6
	Initial production for Royal Navy.	
VX608-VX764	Hawker Sea Fury FB.11	112
	VX608-VX643, VX650-VX696, VX707-VX711, VX724-VX730, VX748-VX764 for Royal Navy of which VX675, VX682, VX686, VX688, VX690, VX692, VX695 went to RCN and VX724-VX729, VX749-VX752, VX755-VX764 to RAN.	
VX770 & VX777	Avro 698 Vulcan	2
	Prototypes. VX770 first flew 3.8.52.	
VX784 & VX790	Avro 707/707B	2
	Delta-wing research aircraft. VX784 Type 707 first flew 4.9.49. VX790 Type 707B.	
VX799 & VX808	Avro Vulcan	(2)
	Half scale model cancelled.	
VX818	Hawker Sea Fury T.20	1
	Aircraft ex-Iraqi order. Became Sea Fury T.20 prototype.	
VX828-VX838	Vickers 668 Varsity	3
	Prototypes to Spec T13/48. VX828 first flew 17.7.49, VX835 Eland testbed, VX838.	
VX850	Focke-Achgelis Fa 330	1
	Rotor kite for evaluation.	
VX856	Vickers 618 Viking	1
	G-AJPH Nene testbed for MoS trials.	
VX860-VX916	DH.98 Mosquito NF.38	51
	Built at Broughton. VX860-VX879, VX886-VX916 of which thirty-eight went direct to Yugoslav Air Force.	
VX922-VX942	Auster AOP.6/T.7	12
	VX922-VX925 AOP.6, VX926-VX929, VX934-VX936 T.7, VX942 AOP.6 cnvrtd to T.10.	
VX950-VZ359	DH.100 Vampire FB.5	216
	Built by English Electric at Samlesbury. VX950-VX990, VZ105-VZ155, VZ161-VZ197, VZ206-VZ241, VZ251-VZ290, VZ300-VZ359 of which VX973, VZ142, VZ143 VZ145, VZ146, VZ148 went direct to Royal Navy.	

Direct foreign sales involved VX950-VX952, VX954-
VX972, VZ120, VZ129, VZ130, VZ132-VZ141, VZ144,
VZ152-VZ154, VZ161-VZ169, VZ172, VZ176, VZ191,
VZ196, VZ197, VZ207-VZ209, VZ211, VZ215, VZ217-
VZ221, VZ223, VZ226, VZ257, VZ258, VZ270, VZ282,
VZ284, VZ285 to French AF and VZ252-VZ256 to
Italian AF.

VZ345-VZ372	**Hawker Sea Fury T.20**	**21**

VZ345-VZ355, VZ363-VZ372 for Royal Navy. Numbers
overlapped. Disposals and offsets: VZ345, VZ350,
VZ351, VZ365, VZ373 to West Germany; VZ349,
VZ363 to Cuba; VZ354, VZ368 to Burma.

VZ366	**Avro 689 Tudor 2**	**1**

C/n 1263. G-AGRZ for MoS trials.

VZ386-VZ649	**Gloster Meteor (various marks as detailed)**	**221**

VZ386-VZ419 F.4 of which VZ386, VZ389, VZ401,
VZ403, VZ407, VZ414, VZ415, VZ417 were converted
to U.15. VZ387, VZ388, VZ390, VZ391, VZ393-
VZ399, VZ400, VZ402, VZ408, VZ409 went direct to
R Netherlands AF; VZ420-VZ426 F.4 direct to
R Egyptian AF, VZ427-VZ429, VZ436, VZ437 F.4
making 46 F.4s built by Armstrong Whitworth. VZ438-
VZ485, VZ493-VZ517 (73) F.8 built by Gloster of
which VZ445, VZ485, VZ506, VZ513, VZ514 were
converted to U.16; VZ455, VZ503 converted to U.21.
VZ450, VZ457, VZ459, VZ499 went direct to the
Belgian AF. VZ518-VZ532, VZ540-VZ569 (45) F.8
built by Armstrong Whitworth of which VZ551, VZ554
were converted to U.16 and VZ553, VZ562, VZ566
went direct to Belgian AF. All subsequent Gloster-built
as follows: VZ577-VZ611 (35) FR.9 of which VZ597,
VZ610 were sold to Ecuador; VZ620 PR.10; VZ629-
VZ649 (21) Meteor T.7 of which VZ645-VZ648 went
direct to Royal Navy.

VZ655-VZ715	**DH.103 Sea Hornet FR.20/NF.21/PR.22**	**41**

VZ655-VZ664 PR.22, VZ671-VZ682, VZ690-VZ699,
NF.21, VZ707-VZ715 FR.20.

VZ720	**Avro 689 Tudor 2**	**1**

G-AGSA for MoS trials.

VZ724	**Cierva W.11 Air Horse**	**1**

Experimental helicopter to Spec E19/46. Temporarily
G-ALCV.

VZ728	**Reid & Sigrist RS.4 Bobsleigh**	**1**

Ex-G-AGOS Desford trainer for prone-pilot trials.

VZ739-VZ799	**Westland Wyvern T.3/S.4**	**51**

VZ739 prototype T.3 to Spec T12/48, VZ745-VZ766,
VZ772-VZ799 S.4 for Royal Navy.

VZ808-VZ952	**DH.100 Vampire FB.5**	**63(134)**

Hatfield-built up to VZ840 except VZ839, and remainder
at Broughton. VZ808-VZ852, VZ860-VZ877 of which
VZ823 went to Royal Navy; VZ838, VZ841, VZ843,
VZ852 to RNZAF; VZ873 to Lebanese AF; VZ810,
VZ814, VZ815, VZ817, VZ820 to French AF. VZ878-
VZ904, VZ909-VZ952 cancelled.

VZ960-VZ966	**Westland WS-51 Dragonfly HR.1**	**7**

For Royal Navy, but VZ960 used by the RAF as HC.2.
VZ966 had experimental 4-blade rotor.

WA101-WA460	**DH.100 Vampire FB.5**	**320**

Built by English Electric at Samlesbury. WA101-WA150,
WA159-WA208, WA215-WA264, WA271-WA320,
WA329-WA348, WA355-WA404, WA411-WA460 of
which WA249, WA299, WA306, WA311, WA314,
WA317, WA338, WA342, WA347, WA374-WA376,
WA379, WA383, WA385, WA388, WA392, WA411,
WA428, WA444, WA451, WA452 went to RNZAF and
WA128, WA365 to Lebanese AF after RAF service.

WA469-WA534	**Supermarine Attacker F.1/FB.1**	**60**

WA469-WA498, WA505-WA526 F.1; WA527-WA534
FB.1.

WA546 &	**Gloster Meteor NF.11**	**2**
WA547	Prototypes to Spec F24/48.	
WA555	**Cierva W.11 Air Horse**	**1**

Cunliffe Owen built. G-ALCW stored after crash of
VZ724.

WA560-WA569	**Bristol 164 Brigand B.1/T.4/T.5**	**10**

C/n 12876-12885. WA560 built as B.1 converted to T.4;
WA561-WA569 built as T.4 of which WA561, WA565,
WA566 were converted to T.5.

WA576-WA578	**Bristol 171 Sycamore 3**	**3**

Pre-production ex-G-ALSS to 'ALSU. WA576, WA577

became 7900M, 7718M and WA578 became HC.10
prototype.

WA590-WB181	**Gloster Meteor T.7/F.8/FR.9/PR.10**	**400**

WA590-WA639, WA649-WA698, WA707-WA743 (137)
T.7 of which WA600, WA649, WA650 were delivered to
Royal Navy; WA755-WA794, WA808-WA857, WA867-
WA909, WA920-WA969, WA981-WA999, WB105-WB112
(210) F.8 of which WA756, WA775, WA842, WA982,
WA991 were converted to U.16; WB113-WB125,
WB133-WB143 (24) FR.9, WB153-WB181 (29) PR.10.
Diversions, direct or subsequent: WA592, WA594,
WA623, WA626, WA633, WA674 to R Netherlands AF;
WA680, WA694, WA731, WA732, WA782, WA783,
WA786, WA907, WA909, WA934, WA936-WA939,
WA941, WA942, WA944-WA952, WA954, WA956-
WA958, WA960, WA961, WA964, WA998 mainly direct
to RAAF; WA684, WA688, WA755, WA870, WA876,
WA878, WA881, WA883, WA884, WA887-WA889,
WA892, WA895, WA898, WA900-WA902 direct to
Belgian AF.

WB188-WB202	**Hawker P.1067 Hunter**	**3**

Prototypes to Spec F3/48. WB188, WB195 with Avon
engines, WB202 Sapphire engine and F.2 prototype.

WB210 &	**Vickers 660/671 Valiant**	**2**
WB215	Prototypes to Spec B9/48. WB210 first flew 8.5.51.	
WB220	**Sikorsky S-51**	**1**

G-AJHW for Antarctic exploration.

WB228 &	**Bristol 164 Brigand**	
WB236	Replacements for two Brigands offset to Pakistan AF.	
WB243-WB440	**Fairey Firefly AS.5/AS.6**	**169**

C/n F.8469-F.8637. WB243-WB272, WB281-WB316,
WB330-WB382, WB391-WB424 AS.5; WB425-WB440
AS.6. Conversions: WB271, WB406 to TT.5; WB246,
WB257, WB307, WB331, WB341, WB365, WB373,
WB374, WB391, WB392, WB402, WB410, WB414,
WB416 to U.9. Numbers diverted to RAN.

WB446-WB465	**Avro 652A Anson T.21**	**20**

Built at Woodford. WB450, WB459 converted to C.21.

WB470-WB478	**Bristol 175 Britannia**	**(3)**

WB470, WB473, WB478 cancelled.

WB482-WB484	**Bristol 170 Mk.21E**	**3**

Ex-G-AIMI, 'AIMO, 'AIMR used by the RAAF as
A84-1, A84-2, A84-3.

WB484	**Slingsby T.21B Sedbergh TX.1**	**1**

Local acquisition by gliding school. Duplicated number
above.

WB490-WB494	**Avro 706 Ashton**	**5**

WB490 Mk.I, WB491 Mk.2; WB492, WB493 Mk.3;
WB494 Mk.4.

WB499	**Vickers Viscount 700**	**1**

Allocation for G-AMAV prototype.

WB505-WB523	**Fairey Firefly AS.6**	**14**

C/n F.8638-F.8651. WB505-WB510, WB516-WB523 of
which WB509, WB510, WB518, WB519, WB523 went
to RAN.

WB530-WB535	**DH.104 Devon C.1**	**6**

Built at Chester. All but WB532 ex-G-AMJJ converted
to C.2.

WB543	**Gloster Meteor NF.11**	**1**

Third prototype.

WB549-WB768	**DHC-1 Chipmunk T.10**	**200**

WB549-WB588, WB600-WB635, WB638-WB662,
WB665-WB706, WB709-WB739, WB743-WB768 built at
Hatfield and Chester. WB554, WB565, WB567 to Ghana
AF. A number later transferred to Army Aviation.
Disposal continuing.

WB771 &	**Handley Page HP.80 Victor**	**2**
WB775	Prototypes. WB771 first flew 24.12.52.	
WB781-WB797	**Blackburn B.54/B.88**	**3**

Prototypes to Spec GR17/45. WB781 B.54 (YA7) first
flew 20.9.49; WB788 B.54 (YA8); WB797 B.88 (YB7).

WB802	**Handley Page HP.93 Dufaylite**	**(1)**

Test wing for Miles Messenger. Trials abandoned.

WB810	**Westland WS.51 Dragonfly**	**1**

G-ALIL acquired for MoS evaluation.

WB818-WB862	**Avro 696 Shackleton MR.1A**	**38(39)**

WB818-WB837, WB844-WB861. WB833 converted to
MR.2 and WB819, WB820, WB822, WB826, WB831,
WB832, WB837, WB844, WB847, WB849, WB858 con-
verted to T.4. WB862 cancelled.

WB870-WB912	**DH.103 Hornet F.3**	36
	WB870-WB889, WB897-WB912 mainly delivered to the Far East.	
WB919-WB993	**Slingsby T.21B Sedbergh TX.1**	69
	Gliders mainly for ATC. WB919-WB948, WB955-WB973, WB992 built by Slingsby and WB974-WB991, WB993 assembled by Martin Hearn. WB919 ex-G-ALLH. WB939, WB941 to BGA3220, BGA3219.	
WD111 & WD116	**Heston C.9**	(2)
	Project.	
WD122-WD154	**Avro 694 Lincoln B.2**	21(26)
	Final Lincoln production built by Armstrong Whitworth. WD122-WD133, WD141-WD149. Modifications to B2/4A WD150-WD154 cancelled.	
WD157-WD275	**Vickers Valetta C.1**	15(73)
	WD157-WD171 built. WD162 became G-APIJ. WD172-WD197, WD244-WD275 cancelled.	
WD280	**Avro 707A**	1
	Experimental delta-wing to Spec E10/49.	
WD282-WD397	**DHC-1 Chipmunk T.10**	100
	Built at Hatfield and Chester. WD282-WD310, WD318-WD338, WD344-WD365, WD370-WD397. Several transferred to AAC and WD374 to Royal Navy; various disposals to other forces and civil register.	
WD402-WD458	**Avro 652A Anson T.21/T.22**	25(47)
	WD402-WD418 T.21; WD419-WD422, WD433-WD436 T.22; WD437-WD458 cancelled.	
WD466 & WD472	**Armstrong Whitworth AW.58**	(2)
	Transonic research aircraft project to Spec E16/49.	
WD475-WD576	**Handley Page HP.67 Hastings C.2/C(VIP).4**	26(65)
	WD475-WD499 C.2; WD500 C(VIP).4. WD501-WD505, WD543-WD576 C.2 cancelled.	
WD585-WD800	**Gloster Meteor NF.11**	200
	Built by Armstrong Whitworth. WD585-WD634, WD640-WD689, WD696-WD745, WD751-WD800. Conversions to TT.20 mainly for Royal Navy: WD585, WD589, WD606, WD610, WD612, WD623, WD629, WD630, WD643, WD645-WD647, WD649, WD652, WD657, WD678, WD679, WD702, WD706, WD711, WD767, WD780, WD785. Diversions: WD726-WD733, WD735, WD736 direct to Belgian AF and WD590, WD594, WD596, WD602, WD622, WD661, WD741, WD760, WD763, WD775, WD777 subsequently; WD619, WD628, WD631, WD669, WD674, WD683, WD698, WD701, WD756, WD783 to French AF.	
WD804-WD819	**Gloster GA.5 Javelin**	2(4)
	Prototypes to Spec F4/48. WD804 first flew 26.11.51. WD808 2nd prototype. WD814, WD819 cancelled.	
WD824-WD925	**Fairey Firefly AS.6**	97
	C/n F.8652-F.8748, WD824-WD872, WD878-WD925. Transfers to RAN and RCN including WD824-WD843 direct to RAN.	
WD929-WE195	**English Electric Canberra B.2/PR.3/T.4**	105
	WD929-WD966, WD980-WD999, WE111-WE122 (70) B.2 of which WD944, WD963, WE118 were converted to T.4; WD929, WD961 to U.10, WD955 to T.17 and WE122 for Royal Navy to TT.18; others modified as testbeds as follows: WD930 Avon 26 and 29, WD933 Sapphire Sa6/7, WD943 Avon RA7/14R, WD952 Olympus, WD959 Avon RA7R/14R/24R. WD935, WD939, WD942, WD983 became A84-1, A84-302, A84-2, A84-125 of RAAF. WD932, WD940 became 51-17387 and 51-17352 of USAF. WE120 became 238 of Peru AF. WE135-WE151, WE166-WE175 (27) PR.3 of which WE171, WE172 were sold to Venezuela. WE198-WE195 (8) built as T.4 of which WE190 went to RNZAF and WE193, WE195 were sold to Qatar.	
WE199-WE231	**DH.98 Mosquito PR.34**	(20)
	WE199-WE206, WE220-WE231 cancelled.	
WE235-WE247	**DH.103 Sea Hornet F.20/PR.22**	11
	WE235-WE242 F.20; WE245-WE247 PR.22 for RN.	
WE255-WE483	**DH.112 Venom FB.1**	200
	WE255-WE269 built at Hatfield, WE270-WE274 built at Chester, WE275 built at Hatfield; WE276-WE294, WE303-WE332 built at Chester, WE340-WE389 builder not known and of which WE381 became FB.4 prototype, WE399-WE438, WE444-WE483 were built at Chester except for WE414, WE461-WE463, WE465-WE468 built by Marshalls, WE464 by Fairey and WE469 at Brooklands.	

WE488	**Fairey Gannet**	1
	C/n F.8749, third prototype.	
WE496-WE514	**Handley Page (Reading) HPR.2**	2(3)
	Prototypes WE496, WE505 to Spec T16/48. WE514 cancelled.	
WE522 & WE530	**Percival P.56 Provost**	2
	Prototypes to Spec T16/48.	
WE534-WE622	**Auster T.7**	69(75)
	WE534-WE572, WE587-WE616 built, WE617-WE622 cancelled. WE590 to Hong Kong Auxiliary AF; WE563 became NZ1707 of RNZAF.	
WE625-WE666	**Gloster Meteor F.4**	(42)
	Cancelled.	
WE670	**Avro 706 Ashton Mk.3**	1
	Aircraft variously modified, including fitment of Avon RA14 under fuselage.	
WE673-WE826	**Hawker Sea Fury FB.11/T.20**	104
	WE673-WE694, WE708-WE736 FB.11 for Royal Navy, WE737-WE742, WE767-WE784 FB.11 modified for Pakistan, WE785-WE806 FB.11 and WE820-WE826 T.20 for Royal Navy. Transfers to RAN included WE673, WE674, WE676, WE795-WE797.	
WE830-WE849	**DH.100 Vampire FB.5**	20
	Built by English Electric at Samlesbury.	
WE852-WE976	**Gloster G.41K Meteor F.8**	120
	Built by Gloster and Armstrong Whitworth. WE852-WE891, WE895-WE939, WE942-WE976. Conversions: WE867, WE915, WE934, WE962 to U.16 and WE902, WE960, WE961 to U.21. WE874, WE877, WE880, WE886, WE890, WE896, WE898, WE900, WE903, WE905-WE911, WE918, WE928, WE969, WE971 diverted to RAAF.	
WE979-WE993	**Slingsby T.30B Prefect TX.1**	15
	Gliders mainly for ATC.	
WE997	**Westland Welkin NF.2**	(1)
	PF370 renumbered. Only Welkin NF.2 built.	
WF112-WF114	**Saro Skeeter Mk.3/Mk.4**	3
	WF112, WF113 partly built by Cierva, completed by Saro as Mk.3 and became Mk.3B when modified for Bombardier engines. WF114 Mk.4.	
WF118-WF138	**Percival P.57 Sea Prince T.1/C.1**	19
	WF118-WF133 T.1; WF136-WF138 C.1 for Royal Navy.	
WF143-WF303	**Hawker Sea Hawk F.1/F.2/FB.3**	151
	WF143-WF192, WF196-WF235 F.1; WF240-WF279 F.2; WF280-WF289, WF293-WF303 FB.3. WF143-WF161, WF167-WF177 were built by Hawker, remainder by Armstrong Whitworth. WF284 converted to FGA.4 then FGA.6; WF281, WF286, WF287, WF296, WF297, WF300, WF302 converted to FB.5.	
WF308-WF315	**Westland WS.51 Dragonfly HC.2**	3
	WF308, WF311, WF315 Malayan trials aircraft. WF308 was ex-G-ALMC.	
WF320	**Blackburn GAL.60 Universal**	1
	Beverley prototype. C/n 1000 Universal Freighter ex-G-AMUX.	
WF324-WF429	**Vickers Varsity T.1**	60
	WF324-WF335, WF369-WF394, WF408-WF429, WF416 became VK501 of R Jordanian AF.	
WF434-WF574	**Boeing 345 Washington B.1 (B-29 Superfortress)**	70
	Ex-USAF loaned under MDAP 1950-54. WF434-WF448, WF490-WF514, WF545-WF574.	
WF578-WF586	**DH.100 Vampire FB.5**	5
	Built by English Electric at Samlesbury. WF578, WF579, WF584-WF586.	
WF590-WF627	**Hawker Sea Fury FB.11**	24
	WF590-WF595, WF610-WF627 for Royal Navy. Disposals to RAN, Burma and Cuba.	
WF632 & WF636	**Short SB.3**	2
	Ex S.1599 ex-Sturgeon TT.2 airframe to Spec M6/49 first flew 12.8.50; WF636 not flown.	
WF638-WF883	**Gloster Meteor T.7/F.8**	179
	WF638-WF662, WF677-WF716, WF736-WF760 (90) F.8 of which WF681, WF685, WF706, WF707, WF711, WF741, WF743, WF751, WF755, WF756 were converted to U.16 and WF659 to U.21. WF697-WF694, WF696-WF699, WF701 went to R Netherlands AF and WF652, WF653, WF746, WF750 to RAAF. WF766-WF795, WF813-WF862, WF875-WF883 T.7. Up to and including WF688 built by Armstrong Whitworth, rest by Gloster. WF817, WF818, WF827 direct to Belgian AF.	

WF886-WF928	English Electric Canberra B.2/PR.3	25

WF886-WF892, WF907-WF917 B.2 of which WF890, WF916 were converted to T.17 and WF907 became test-bed for Avon development and Gyron Junior; WF914 went to Venezuelan AF and WF915 to RNZAF. WF922-WF928 PR.3.

WF934 & WF949	Percival P.57 Sea Prince T.1	2

For Royal Navy.

WF954-WF979	DH.103 Hornet F.3/F.4	23

WF954-WF962, WF966, WF967 F.3; WF968-WF979 F.4.

WF984	DH.104 Devon	1

Acquired June 1950 for Empire Test Pilots School.

WF989-WG230	Boulton Paul P.108 Balliol T.2	100

WF989-WF998, WG110-WG159, WG173-WG187, WG206-WG230 of which WG224, WG226, WG227, WG230 became CA310, CA301, CA302, CA311 of R Ceylon AF.

WG236-WG252	DH.110 Sea Vixen	2(5)

Prototypes. WG236 first flew 26.9.51. WG240 became RN instructional airframe. WG247, WG249, WG252 cancelled.

WG256-WG267	Vickers Valetta T.3	12

WG256, WG263, WG267 converted to T.4.

WG271-WG491	DHC-1 Chipmunk T.10	150

WG271-WG289, WG299-WG366, WG348-WG364, WG392-WG432, WG457-WG491 of which WG271-WG286 were shipped to RATG. WG288 to Ghana AF as G151. Numbers later to Army Aviation and civil registers.

WG496-WG499	Slingsby T.21B Sedbergh TX.1	4

ATC gliders. WG496, WG498 to BGA3242, BGA3245.

WG503	Percival P.56 Provost	1

Prototype. Became 7159M.

WG507-WG558	Avro Shackleton MR.1/MR.2	20

WG507-WG511, WG525-WG529 MR.1 of which WG511, WG527 were converted to T.4. WG530-WG533, WG535-WG558 MR.2.

WG564-WG656	Hawker Sea Fury FB.11/T.20	42

WG564-WG575, WG590-WG604, WG621-WG630 FB.11; WG652-WG656 for Royal Navy. WG564-WG575 to RCN, WG627, WG628 to RAN. Disposals to various countries.

WG661-WG754	Westland WS-51 Dragonfly HR.3	34

WG661-WG672, WG705-WG709, WG714, WG718-WG726, WG748-WG754 to Royal Navy except WG725 to RAF becoming 7703M.

WG760-WG765	English Electric P.1A Lightning	3

Prototypes to Spec F23/49. WG760 first flew 4.8.54; WG763 flown; WG765 static test airframe.

WG768	Short SB.5	1

Experimental aircraft c/n SH.1605 for English Electric P.1A data, became 8005M.

WG774 & WG777	Fairey FD.2	2

High speed research aircraft. WG774 held World Speed Record, later re-modelled to BAC.221; WG777 became 7986M.

WG783	Slingsby T.30A Prefect TX.1	1

For Royal Navy.

WG788-WG789	English Electric Canberra B.2	2

Replacement aircraft. WG789 had experimental radar nose.

WG793-WG931	DH.100 Vampire FB.5/FR.9	79

WG793-WG807, WG826-WG847 FB.5; WG848-WG851, WG865-WG902, WG922-WG931 FR.9. Up to WG831 built by de Havilland at Broughton, rest by English Electric at Samlesbury. WG805, WG826, WG846 to the RNZAF.

WG935-WH573	Gloster Meteor T.7/F.8/FR.9/PR.10	390

WG935-WG950, WG961-WG999, WH112-WH136, WH164-WH209, WH215-WH248 T.7; WH249-WH263, WH272-WH330, WH342-WH386, WH395-WH426, WH442-WH484, WH498-WH513 F.8 of which WH258, WH284, WH309, WH315, WH320, WH344, WH349, WH359, WH365, WH369, WH372, WH373, WH376, WH381, WH419, WH420, WH453, WH469, WH499, WH500, WH505, WH506, WH509 were converted to U.16 and WH460 to U.21; WH533-WH557 FR.9; WH569-WH573 PR.10. Offsets and disposals were: WG974, WG977, WH251, WH252, WH254, WH259, WH274, WH405, WH414, WH417, WH418, WH475,

WH479 direct plus WH118, WH474 later to RAAF; WH171, WH174 direct and WG970, WH114 later to Belgian AF; WH540, WH543, WH547, WH549, WH550, WH553-WH555 direct to Ecuador; WH136, WH168 direct and WH228 after RAF service to French AF; WG998, WH125, WH179, WH193, WH196, WH199, WH202, WH203, WH207, WH222, WH233, WH237, WH448 direct and WH116, WH177, WH245, WH247, subsequently to R Netherlands AF. Disposals: WH260, WH503 to Syria and WH371 to Egypt.

WH575	Bristol Freighter Mk.31	1

Ex-G-AINK for winterisation trials in Canada, became ZK-AYG.

WH581-WH623	Hawker Sea Fury FB.11	26

WH581-WH594, WH612-WH623 for Royal Navy of which WH581, WH583, WH586-WH590 went to RAN and WH585, WH613, WH619 to Burma.

WH627-WH632	Fairey Firefly AS.6	6

C/n F.8750-F.8755. For Royal Navy. WH627 and WH632 to Royal Australian Navy.

WH637-WH984	English Electric Canberra B.2/T.4/B.6/PR.7	223

WH637-WH674, WH695-WH742 (86) B.2; WH772 PR.3; WH773-WH780, WH790-WH804 PR.7; WH838-WH850 T.4 built by English Electric Co. WH853-WH887, WH902-WH925, WH944 B.2; WH945-WH984 B.6 built by Short & Harland c/ns SH.1610-SH.1709. Conversions: WH637, WH651, WH658, WH659, WH674, WH706, WH854, WH861 to T.4; WH793 to PR.9; WH652, WH705, WH710, WH729, WH733, WH742, WH860, WH885, WH917 to U.10; WH714, WH724, WH903, WH904 to T.11; WH704, WH720, WH876, WH921 to D.14; WH911, WH947, WH948, WH954-WH961, WH963-WH966, WH968-WH974, WH977, WH981-WH984 to B/E.15; WH646, WH664, WH665, WH740, WH863, WH872, WH874, WH902 to T.17; WH718, WH856, WH887 to TT.18 for RAF and Royal Navy; WH714, WH724, WH903, WH904, WH975 to T.19; WH780, WH797, WH801, WH803 to T.22 for Royal Navy. WH671 became a flying testbed and WH699 became Aries IV. Transfers/sales to other forces; WH702, WH727, WH886, WH913 to Argentina; WH659, WH719, WH726, WH868 to Peru; WH838 to Qatar; WH710 to RAAF as A84-3; WH645, WH666, WH739, WH878 to RNZAF; WH644, WH653, WH658, WH662, WH672, WH674, WH707, WH855, WH867, WH871, WH833 to RRAF; WH711, WH905 to RSAF; WH647, WH649, WH708, WH709, WH712, WH721, WH722, WH730, WH732, WH736, WH737, WH777, WH862, WH877, WH881 to Venezuela; WH638, WH880 to Ethiopia; WH800, WH839, WH845, WH954, WH959, WH961 to IAF; WH666 to Zimbabwe AF.

WH989-WH992	Westland WS-51 Dragonfly HR.3	4

To Royal Navy.

WJ104-WJ216	Fairey Firefly AS.6/T.7/AS.7	72

WJ104-WJ121 AS.6; WJ146-WJ153 AS.7; WJ154-WJ174; WJ187-WJ209 AS.7 completed as T.7; WJ215, WJ216 prototype AS.7s all for Royal Navy. WJ147, WJ149-WJ153 converted to U.8. WJ109, WJ112, WJ113, WJ121 to RAN.

WJ221-WJ301	Hawker Sea Fury FB.11	52

WJ221-WJ248, WJ276-WJ292, WJ294-WJ297, WJ299-WJ301 for Royal Navy. WJ279, WJ284, WJ294, WJ297, WJ299 to RAN; WJ300, WJ301 to RCN; WJ232, WJ280 to Burmese AF.

WJ306	Slingsby T.21B Sedbergh TX.1	1

Glider for ATC. Later BGA3240.

WJ310	DH.104 Dove 1	1

Prototype G-AGPJ for evaluation, later became CR-CAC.

WJ316	Auster Type S	1

Prototype.

WJ320	Bristol 170 Mk.31	1

C/n 12827 Arctic trials aircraft, ex-G-AINL.

WJ324-WJ343	Handley Page HP.94/HP.67 Hastings C.2/C.4	20

WJ324-WJ326 C(VIP).4, WJ327-WJ343 C.2

WJ348-WJ350	Percival P.57 Sea Prince C.2	3

For Royal Navy.

WJ354-WJ455	Auster AOP.6	36(44)

WJ354-WJ378, WJ398-WJ408 built of which WJ368, WJ401, WJ404 were converted to T.10; WJ409-WJ412 AOP.6 and WJ452-WJ455 T.7 cancelled.

WJ461-WJ504   **Vickers Valetta C.1/C.2/T.3**   37
WJ461-WJ487 T.3, WJ491-WJ499 C.1, WJ504 C.2.
WJ464-WJ467, WJ469, WJ471-WJ473, WJ475, WJ477,
WJ482, WJ483, WJ485-WJ487 converted to T.4.

WJ509-WJ561   **Avro 652A Anson T.21/C.21**   28
WJ509-WJ519, WJ545-WJ561 T.21. WJ512, WJ549,
WJ552 later converted to C.21. WJ561 was the last of
the 11,020 Ansons built.

WJ564-WJ707   **English Electric Canberra B.2**   75(100)
WJ564-WJ582, WJ603-WJ649, WJ674-WJ682 built by
Handley Page; WJ683-WJ707 cancelled. WJ622 crashed
on test flight. WJ646 non-standard. Conversions: WJ566,
WJ568, WJ613, WJ617 to T.4; WJ604, WJ621, WJ623,
WJ624, WJ638 to U.10; WJ610 to T.11; WJ565-WJ576,
WJ581, WJ607, WJ625, WJ630, WJ633 T.17; WJ574,
WJ614, WJ629, WJ632, WJ636, WJ639, WJ680, WJ682
TT.18 for Royal Navy and RAF; WJ610 T.19. Transfers:
WJ571, WJ572, WJ578, WJ606, WJ612, WJ613 RRAF,
WJ617 SAAF; WJ570 Venezuelan AF; WJ616 to the
Argentinian AF.

WJ712-WJ881   **English Electric Canberra B.2/T.4/B.6/PR.7**   93
WJ712-WJ734, WJ751-WJ753 (26) B.2 of which WJ715,
WJ717, WJ721 were converted to TT.18; WJ754-WJ784
(31) B.6 of which WJ756, WJ760, WJ762, WJ764, WJ766,
WJ770, WJ771, WJ773, WJ774, WJ776-WJ783 were con-
verted to B/E.16; WJ815-WJ825 (11) PR.7 and WJ857-
WJ881 (25) T.4. Transfers: WJ752, WJ866, WJ874 to
Royal Navy; WJ857 to Ethiopia; WJ763, WJ779, WJ784
to France; WJ712, WJ754, WJ757, WJ860 to Peru;
WJ868 to Qatar; WJ713, WJ714, WJ875 to Argentina;
WJ778, WJ816, WJ859, WJ868 to IAF; WJ864 to SAAF;
WJ869 to Zimbabwe AF.

WJ886-WJ950   **Vickers Varsity T.1**   50
WJ886-WJ921, WJ937-WJ950. WJ900 became 82001 of
the R Swedish AF. WJ945 now preserved in flying
condition as G-BEDV.

WJ954   **Vickers 673 Valiant B.2**   1
Prototype, first flew 4.9.53.

WJ960 &   **Supermarine 541 Swift**   2
WJ965   Prototypes, WJ960 first flew 5.8.51, became also F.4
prototype.

WJ971-WK190   **English Electric Canberra B.2**   75(100)
WJ971-WJ995, WK102-WK146, WK161-WK165 built
by Avro; WK166-WK190 cancelled. Testbeds: WK141
Sapphire 7, Viper 8 & 11; WK163 Scorpion. Conversions:
WJ991 to T.4; WJ987, WK107, WK110 to U.10; WJ975,
WK105 to T.11; WJ984 to B.15; WJ977, WJ981, WJ986,
WJ988, WK102, WK111 to T.17; WK118, WK122-
WK124, WK126, WK127, WK142, WK143 TT.18 for
joint RAF/Royal Navy use; WK106 to T.19. Transfers/
disposals: WK130, WK137, WK138 to FGAF; WJ974,
WJ976, WK112 to Peru; WJ981, WJ986, WJ988 to the
RNZAF on loan; WK108 to RRAF; WJ991 to SAAF;
WK978, WK980 to Venezuelan AF and WJ971 to the
Ethiopian AF.

WK194-WK315   **Supermarine Swift F.1/F.2/F.3/F.4/FR.5**   100
Built at South Marston. WK194-WK213 F.1 of which
WK201 was converted to F.2, WK195 to F.3 and WK198
to F.4; WK214-WK221, WK239-WK246 F.2; WK247-
WK271 F.3; WK272-WK281, WK287-WK315 F.4 of
which all but WK272, WK273, WK275, WK279 were
converted to FR.5. 52 aircraft later became instructional
airframes from 7206M onwards.

WK319-WK342   **Supermarine Attacker FB.2**   24
Built at South Marston for Royal Navy.

WK348-WK373   **Fairey Firefly T.7**   26
C/n F.8828-F.8853 for Royal Navy.

WK376-WK385   **DH.112 Sea Venom FAW.20**   3
Prototypes to Spec N107, WK376, WK379, WK385 of
which WK385 introduced folding wings.

WK389-WK503   **DH.112 Venom FB.1**   85
WK389-WK437, WK468-WK503 built as follows:
WK389, WK390, WK418-WK422, WK492, WK493,
WK496 by Fairey; WK391, WK394, WK411-WK417,
WK426-WK428, WK484-WK488, WK501-WK503 by
Marshalls; WK393, WK394, WK396-WK399, WK400-
WK410, WK429-WK437, WK468-WK483, WK489-
WK491, WK494, WK495, WK497-WK499, WK500 by
de Havilland at Chester; WK395, WK423-WK425 at
Brooklands. WK427 not delivered.

WK506-WK643   **DHC.1 Chipmunk T.10**   100
WK506-WK523, WK547-WK591, WK607-WK643.
Offsets to other air forces, transfers to Royal Navy and
Army Air Corps. Disposals still proceeding.

WK647-WL488   **Gloster Meteor T.7/F.8/FR.9**   480(530)
WK647-WK696, WK783-WK827, WK849-WK893,
WK936-WK955, WK966-WK994, WL104-WL143, WL158-
WL191 F.8 built by Gloster and WK707-WK756, WK906-
WK935 F.8 built by Armstrong Whitworth. Conversions:
WK648, WK675, WK693, WK709, WK716, WK717,
WK721, WK729, WK731, WK737, WK738, WK743-
WK747, WK783, WK784, WK789, WK790, WK793,
WK795, WK799, WK800, WK807, WK812, WK852,
WK855, WK859, WK867, WK870, WK877, WK883,
WK885, WK890, WK911, WK925, WK926, WK932,
WK942, WK949, WK971, WK980, WK989, WK993,
WL110, WL124, WL127, WL134, WL160, WL162,
WL163 to U.16; WK710, WK797, WK879, WL136 to
U.21 and WK654, WK753, WK809, WK814, WK822,
WK824, WK918, WK921, WK947, WK968, WK969,
WL105, WL117, WL159, WL180, WL189 to F(TT).8.
Thirty-one to RAAF, others to Egypt and Syria. WK935
had long nose for prone pilot position and WL375 was
F.8/F.R.9 hybrid. WL192-WL207, WL221-WL234 F.8
cancelled. WL255-WL265 F R.9 built by Gloster of which
WL259 sold to Israel. WL286-WL305 PR.10 cancelled.
WL332-WL381, WL397-WL436, WL453-WL488 T.7
built by Gloster of which WL332-WL334, WL336,
WL337, WL350-WL353 were transferred to Royal
Navy and disposals were to Belgium, Brazil, France,
Holland, Israel and Syria.

WL493-WL616   **DH.100 Vampire FB.9**   82
WL493-WL518, WL547-WL587, WL602-WL616.
WL493 became NZ5771 of RNZAF.

WL621-WL709   **Vickers 668 Varsity T.1**   50(67)
WL621-WL642, WL665-WL692 built at Hurn, WL693-
WL709 cancelled.

WL715-WL734   **Boulton Paul P.108 Sea Balliol T.21**   20
For Royal Navy.

WL737-WL801   **Avro 696 Shackleton MR.2**   40
WL737-WL759, WL785-WL801 of which WL741, WL745,
WL747, WL754, WL756, WL757, WL790, WL793,
WL795 were converted to AEW.2.

WL804-WL874   **DH.112 Venom NF.2**   60
WL804-WL810 built at Hatfield, WL811-WL833, WL845-
WL874 at Chester.

WL876-WL888   **Westland Wyvern S.4**   13
For Royal Navy.

WL892-WM138   **DH.112 Venom FB.1**   (120)
WL892-WL935, WL954-WL999, WM109-WM138 were
ordered from Bristol but cancelled.

WM143-WM403   **Gloster Meteor NF.11/NF.13**   192
Built by Armstrong Whitworth. WM143-WM192,
WM221-WM270, WM292-WM307 NF.11 of which
WM261 became the T.14 prototype; WM308-WM341,
WM362-WM367 NF.13; WM368-WM403 NF.11. Con-
versions to TT.20: WM147, WM148, WM151, WM158-
WM160, WM167, WM223, WM224, WM230, WM234,
WM242, WM245, WM246, WM255, WM260, WM270,
WM292, WM293. Diversions: WM296-WM307, WM364,
WM365, WM368-WM371, WM375-WM383 French AF;
WM309, WM312, WM320, WM334, WM335, WM366 to
Israel; WM325, WM326, WM328, WM338, WM340,
WM362 R Egyptian AF; WM330, WM332, WM333,
WM336, WM337, WM341 Syria; WM384-WM403
R Danish AF.

WM408-WM468   **DH.100 Vampire FB.9**   (50)
WM408-WM429, WM441-WM468 ordered from de
Havilland and cancelled.

WM472-WM495   **Hawker Sea Fury FB.11**   24
WM472-WM478 RCN; WM479-WM482; WM490 RAN;
WM483-WM486 Iraq; WM488 Burma; remainder to RN.

WM500-WM577   **DH.112 Venom FAW.20/FAW.21**   60
WM500-WM523, WM542-WM567 FAW.20; WM568-
WM577 FAW.21 for Royal Navy.

WM583-WM656   **Supermarine Swift F.1**   (50)
WM583-WM596, WM621-WM656 ordered from Vickers
Armstrong at South Marston. Cancelled.

WM659-WM733   **DH.113 Vampire NF.10**   50
WM659-WM677, WM703-WM733 built mainly at Chester

of which WM659-WM662, WM664-WM667, WM675, WM676, WM707-WM710, WM715, WM717, WM719-WM721, WM723-WM725, WM728, WM731, WM733 went to IAF.

WM735-WM756	**Percival P.57 Sea Prince T.1/C.2**	**9**

WM735-WM742 T.1 and WM756 C.2 for Royal Navy.

WM759	**Short S.45 Solent 3**	**(1)**

G-AKNS ex-NJ205 on loan.

WM761-WM899	**Fairey Firefly T.7/U.8**	**101**

C/n F.8854-F.8954. WM761-WM779, WM796-WM809 T.7; WM810-WM823 U.8; WM824-WM832, WM855 T.7; WM856-WM863 U.8; WM864-WM879 T.7; WM880-WM899 U.8 for Royal Navy.

WM901-WN119	**Hawker Sea Hawk F.1/FB.3**	**100**

WM901-WM905 F.1 built by Hawker; WM906-WM945, WM960-WM999, WN105-WN119 FB.3 built by Armstrong Whitworth for Royal Navy. WM906, WM907, WM913, WM926, WM928, WM929, WM931, WM932, WM934, WM936, WM937, WM939, WM940, WM942, WM943, WM961, WM965, WM969, WM972, WM974, WM983, WM984, WM987, WM989, WM992-WM994, WM998, WN107, WN108, WN115-WN117, WN119 converted to FGA.6.

WN124-WN127	**Supermarine Swift FR.5**	**1(4)**

Final production, WN124 only completed.

WN132-WN303	**Boulton Paul P.108 Balliol T.2**	**40(138)**

WN132-WN171 built of which WN132, WN147, WN148, WN155-WN157, WN164 were offset to Ceylon; WN172-WN181, WN196-WN234; WN255-WN303 cancelled.

WN309-WN321	**Gloster G.43 Meteor T.7**	**13**

WN312 to French AF; WN315 to R Netherlands AF; WN320, WN321 to Belgian AF.

WN324-WN336	**Westland Wyvern S.4**	**13**

For Royal Navy.

WN339-WN464	**Fairey Gannet AS.1**	**100**

C/n F.9111-F.9210. Built at Stockport and Hayes. WN339-WN378, WN390-WN429, WN445-WN464. Conversions: WN365 T.2 prototype became XT752, WN372 AS.4 prototype, WN464 to AS.4 then ECM.6. WN456-WN459 to RAN.

WN467	**English Electric Canberra T.4**	**1**

Prototype to Spec T2/49. first flew 6.6.52.

WN470	**Hawker P.1083**	**(1)**

Cancelled at advanced stage. See XF833.

WN474-WN487	**Hawker Sea Fury FB.11**	**10**

WN474-WN479, WN484-WN487 for Royal Navy of which WN474, WN479 went to RCN.

WN492-WN500	**Westland WS.51 Dragonfly HR.3**	**9**

For Royal Navy.

WN506-WN674	**Boulton Paul P.108 Balliol T.2**	**30(120)**

WN506-WN535 built by Blackburn; WN536-WN555, WN573-WN601, WN634-WN674 cancelled.

WN677-WN884	**Hawker Hunter**	**(150)**

WN677-WN726, WN743-WN783, WN806-WN828, WN849-WN884 cancelled.

WN888-WP194	**Hawker Hunter F.2/F.5**	**150**

Built by Armstrong Whitworth. WN888-WN921, WN943-WN953 F.2; WN954-WN992, WP101-WP150, WP179-WP194 F.5.

WP199-WP223	**Vickers Valiant B.1**	**25**

WP199-WP203 pre-production Vickers Type 674, WP204 onwards Vickers Type 706. Conversions: WP199 Pegasus vectored thrust turbofan testbed; WP205 B(PR).1 trials aircraft modified for Blue Streak; WP217, WP219, WP221, WP223 to B(PR).1 standard.

WP227	**DH.112 Venom NF.2**	**1**

Prototype ex-G-5-3 became 7098M.

WP232-WP256	**DH.113 Vampire NF.10**	**25**

Mainly Hatfield-built. WP246, WP249 became ID1605, ID1606 of IAF.

WP262-WP271	**EoN Eton TX.1**	**10**

Primary gliders.

WP275-WP304	**Supermarine Attacker FB.2**	**30**

For Royal Navy.

WP307-WP321	**Percival P.57 Sea Prince T.1**	**15**

C/ns 57-71 for Royal Navy.

WP324-WP333	**Boulton Paul P.108 Sea Balliol T.21**	**10**

For Royal Navy.

WP336-WP346	**Westland Wyvern S.4**	**11**

For Royal Navy.

WP351-WP490	**Fairey Firefly U.8**	**4(105)**

WP351-WP354 only built for Royal Navy. WP355-WP400, WP421-WP453, WP469-WP490 cancelled.

WP493-WP510	**Westland WS.51 Dragonfly HR.3**	**12(18)**

WP493-WP504 built for Royal Navy, WP505-WP510 cancelled.

WP514-WP516	**English Electric Canberra B.2**	**3**

Replacements for exports.

WP520-WP744	**Boulton Paul P.108 Balliol T.2**	**(160)**

WP520-WP555, WP585-WP627, WP648-WP693, WP710-WP744 cancelled.

WP772-WP988	**DHC.1 Chipmunk T.10**	**150**

WP772-WP811, WP828-WP872, WP893-WP930, WP962-WP988. Disposals to Ghana and Jordan and transfers to Royal Navy and Army Air Corps. Sales and disposals continue.

WP990-WR269	**DH.100 Vampire FR.9**	**150**

WP990-WP999, WR102-WR111, WR114-WR158, WR171-WR204 built by de Havilland at Chester; WR205-WR215, WR230-WR269 by Fairey at Stockport.

WR272-WR908	**DH.112 Venom FB.1/NF.2/FB.4**	**270(500)**

WR272-WR321, WR334-WR373 (90) FB.1; WR374-WR383, WR397-WR446, WR460-WR509, WR525-WR564 (150) FB.4; WR565-WR574, WR586-WR635, WR650-WR699, WR715-WR764 FB.4 cancelled; WR779-WR808 (30) NF.2. Assembled as follows: WR272, WR300-WR310, WR316-WR320, WR339-WR343, WR376, WR398, WR399, WR400-WR403, WR497, WR498, WR541-WR564 by Marshalls; WR273-WR275, WR279-WR293, WR296-WR299, WR312-WR315, WR321, WR334-WR336, WR344-WR374, WR377-WR383, WR397, WR404, WR422-WR429, WR439-WR443, WR445, WR446, WR460-WR463, WR471-WR473, WR483-WR492, WR502-WR509, WR530, WR779, WR808 by de Havilland at Chester; WR276-WR278, WR294, WR295, WR311, WR337, WR338, WR375, WR405, WR421, WR438, WR444, WR493-WR496, WR535-WR540 by Fairey; WR406-WR420, WR430-WR437, WR464-WR470, WR474-WR482, WR499, WR500, WR501, WR525-WR529, WR531-WR534 by de Havilland at Hatfield. Some FB.1 disposals to R Iraqi AF and RNZAF. WR809-WR820, WR835-WR880, WR897-WR908 NF.2 cancelled.

WR920-WR943	**Auster AOP.6/T.7**	**(20)**

WR920-WR934 AOP.6; WR939-WR943 T.7 all cancelled.

WR951-WR990	**Avro Shackleton MR.2/MR.3**	**40**

WR951-WR969 MR.2 of which WR966, WR969 were converted to MR.2(T) and WR960, WR963, WR965 to AEW.2; WR970-WR990 MR.3 of which WR973 was non-standard.

WS103-WS211	**Gloster G.43 Meteor T.7**	**30(75)**

WS103-WS117 to Royal Navy. WS111 had FR.9 type nose. WS140, WS141 to Belgium; WS142-WS154 exported. WS155-WS170, WS183-WS211 cancelled.

WS230-WS558	**Gloster Meteor F.8**	**(250)**

WS230-WS279, WS291-WS332, WS349-WS394, WS403-WS451, WS476-WS500, WS521-WS558 cancelled.

WS590-WS848	**Gloster Meteor NF.12/NF.14**	**200**

Built by Armstrong Whitworth. WS590-WS639, WS658-WS700, WS715-WS721 NF.12; WS722-WS760, WS774-WS812, WS827-WS848 NF.14.

WS960-WT122	**English Electric Canberra B.2**	**(50)**

Ordered from Handley Page and cancelled. WS960-WS999, WT113-WT122.

WT097-WT121	**Douglas Skyraider AEW.1**	**(3)**

WT097, WT112, WT121 incorrectly applied to WT943, WT982, WT983.

WT140-WT189	**English Electric Canberra B.2**	**(50)**

Cancelled order placed with Avro.

WT205-WT279	**English Electric Canberra B.6**	**9(50)**

WT205-WT213 built by Short & Harland. C/ns SH.1710; SH.1718. WT214-WT224, WT250-WT279 cancelled. WT205, WT208-WT211, WT213 converted to B.15 of which WT208 went to Peru and WT210 to India.

WT301-WT542	**E.E.Canberra T.4/B.6/B(I).6/PR.7/B(I).8**	**119(190)**

WT301-WT305 B.6; WT306-WT325 B(I).6; WT326-WT348, WT362-WT368 B(I).8; WT369-WT374 B.6 of which WT302, WT303, WT306, WT319, WT369, WT370, WT372-WT374 were converted to B.16 and WT304 had a T.4 type nose. WT375-WT387, WT397-WT422, WT440-

WT469 B.6 cancelled; WT475-WT492 T.4; WT493 and WT494 cancelled; WT503-WT542 PR.7 of which WT528 became *Aries V* and WT510, WT525, WT535 were converted to T.22 for the Royal Navy. Offsets and disposals: WT476 to Argentina; WT338, WT506, WT539, WT541, WT542 to IAF; WT340, WT343, WT344, WT348, WT364, WT368 to Peru; WT485, WT487 to Qatar; WT491, WT492 to RAAF.

WT555-WT811 Hawker Hunter F.1/F.4   **200**
WT555-WT595, WT611-WT660, WT679-WT700 F.1; WT701-WT723, WT734-WT780, WT795-WT811 F.4 of which WT565, WT573 were used as Rolls-Royce testbeds. Conversions for Royal Navy: WT701, WT702, WT722, WT745, WT746, WT755, WT772, WT799 to T.8; WT711-WT713, WT718, WT721, WT744, WT771, WT804, WT806, WT808-WT810 to GA.11; WT723 to PR.11. Disposals India to Peru, Sweden, Switzerland. 52 became instructional airframes in 7000M series.

WT827-WT841 Gloster Javelin   **4**
Prototypes, WT827 first flew 7.3.53, WT830, WT836 further fighter prototypes, WT841 prototype T.3 assembled by Air Service Training.

WT845-WT846 Westland WS-51 Dragonfly HC.4   **2**
WT849 Douglas Skyraider AEW.1   **1**
Supplied under MDAP for Royal Navy.

WT851 Supermarine Attacker FB.2   **1**
Replacement for Royal Navy.

WT854 & Supermarine 544   **2**
WT859
Prototypes to Spec N113D.

WT865-WT919 Slingsby T.31B Cadet TX.3   **40**
WT893-WT877, WT883-WT919 gliders for ATC.

WT923-WT926 Bristol 171 Sycamore HC.11   **4**
For Army communications. Ex-G-ALSV, 'ALSY, 'ALTA, 'ALTC.

WT933 & Bristol 171 Sycamore 3   **2**
WT939
WT933 ex-G-ALSW to Middle East for tropical tests, became 7709M; WT939 ex-G-ALTS to Canada for Arctic trials.

WT943-WV185 Douglas Skyraider AEW.1   **50**
WT943-WT969, WT982-WT987, WV102-WV109, WV177-WV185 supplied under MDAP for Royal Navy.

WV189-WV250 Sikorsky S-55 Whirlwind HAR.21/HAS.22   **25(50)**
Supplied under MDAP for Royal Navy and RAF. WV189-WV198 HAR.21 ex-USN 130182-130191; WV199-WV205, WV218-WV225 HAS.22 ex-USN 133739-133753. WV226-WV250 cancelled.

WV253-WV412 Hawker Hunter F.4   **100**
Built at Kingston. WV253-WV281, WV314-WV334, WV363-WV412 of which WV276 was used for Avon trials. Conversions: WV318, WV372, WV383 to T.7 by ArmstrongWhitworth; WV319, WV322, WV363, WV396, WV397 to T.8; WV256, WV257, WV267, WV374, WV380-WV382 to GA.11 for Royal Navy. Disposals to Abu Dhabi, Jordan and Switzerland.

WV418-WV686 Percival P.56 Provost T.1   **200**
WV418-WV448, WV470-WV514, WV532-WV580, WV601-WV648, WV660-WV686. Offsets: WV645-WV648 to 2 to RRAF 136-139; WV501 and WV678 to Muscat & Oman and WV533 to Sudan.

WV689-WV691 DH.113 Vampire NF.10   **3**
All to IAF as ID607, ID606, ID604.

WV695 Bristol 171 Sycamore 3   **1**
Ex-G-ALSZ became A91-1 of RAAF and then VH-GVR.

WV698-WV766 Percival P.66 Pembroke C.1   **42(53)**
WV698-WV712, WV729-WV753 C.1; WV754, WV755 C(PR).1 of which WV707, WV711 went to SRAF. WV756-WV766 cancelled.

WV781-WV784 Bristol 171 Sycamore HR.12   **4**
C/n 12898-12900, 13062 trials batch for Coastal Command in 1952. WV781, WV783 ex-G-ALTD, 'ALSP became 7839M, 7841M.

WV787 English Electric Canberra B.2 non-standard   **1**
Basic B.2 built for Sapphire trials and much modified.

WV792-WV922 Hawker Sea Hawk FGA.4   **85**
Built by Armstrong Whitworth WV792-WV807, WV824-WV871, WV902-WV922 for Royal Navy of which all but WV800, WV804, WV837, WV843, WV845, WV847-WV850, WV853, WV858, WV862-WV864, WV866, WV867, WV904, WV905, WV910, WV911 were converted to FGA.6.

WV925 Slingsby T.31B Cadet TX.3   **1**
Glider for ATC.

WV928 DH.112 Venom NF.3   **1**
Prototype, became 7189M.

WV933-WV944 Westland WS-51 Dragonfly HR.3   **(12)**
Cancelled order.

WV949-WV952 Supermarine Swift F.1   **(4)**
Cancelled.

WV967-WW128 Fairey Firefly AS.7   **(51)**
Cancelled order, WV967-WV991, WW103-WW128.

WW134 Supermarine Scimitar   **1**
Third prototype.

WW137-WW298 DH.112 Sea Venom FAW.21   **96**
WW137-WW154, WW186-WW225, WW261-WW298 for Royal Navy. WW137, WW138, WW145, WW147, WW151, WW186-WW188, WW199, WW200, WW202, WW205, WW207, WW209, WW210, WW213, WW215, WW217, WW219, WW221, WW263, WW268, WW273, WW276, WW278, WW286, WW289, WW292, WW293, WW296 later converted to FAW.22.

WW303-WW335 Vickers Varsity T.1   **(33)**
Cancelled order.

WW339 Sikorsky S-55   **1**
C/n 55016 G-AMHK for Royal Navy evaluation, later became XA842.

WW342-WW373 Boeing 345 Washington 1 (B-29 Superfortress)   **14(32)**
WW342-WW355 ex-USAF aircraft supplied under MDAP. Returned to USA. WW356-WW373 not delivered.

WW378 Bristol 170 Mk.21E   **1**
Ex-G-AHJN to RAAF as A81-4.

WW381-WW453 Percival P.56 Provost T.1   **55**
WW381-WW398, WW417-WW453. WW382, WW391, WW425 disposed to RMAF.

WW458 & DH.115 Vampire T.11   **2**
WW461
Prototypes, WW458 first flew 1.12.51; WW461 later became T.22.

WW465-WW586 Avro 685 York   **29**
Temporary trooping serials for civil Yorks as follows: WW465-WW468 G-AGNN, 'AGNS, 'AGSO, 'AHFG, WW499-WW504 G-AHFB, 'AHFD, 'AGOB, 'AHFH, 'AGJB, 'AHFA; WW506-WW512 G-AHEY, 'AHFC, 'AGJA, 'AGNP, 'AGNY, 'AGNM, 'AMGK; WW514 G-AGNT; WW540-WW542 G-AGSM, 'AGJA, 'AGOA; WW576-WW582 G-AGNO, 'AGOD, 'AHFE, 'AGOF, 'AGJE, 'AGNL, 'AGNX; WW586 G-AHFB.

WW589-WW598 Hawker Hunter F.4/F.6   **10**
Built at Kingston. WW589-WW591 F.4; WW592-WW598 F.6 of which WW593-WW596 were converted to FR.10. WW591 direct to Denmark and WW597 direct to Jordan. Later disposals to various countries.

WW599-WW665 Hawker Hunter F.1/F.4   **46**
Built at Blackpool. WW599-WW610, WW632-WW645 F.1; WW646-WW665 F.4. Conversions: WW661, WW664 to T.8 and WW654, WW659 to GA.11 for Royal Navy. Disposals to various countries.

WW669-WW710 DH.112 Venom FB.1   **(42)**
Cancelled order with Bristol.

WW715-WX199 DH.112 Venom FB.1   **(300)**
WW715-WW751, WW766-WW815, WW833-WW877, WW895-WW944, WW956-WW990, WX103-WX145, WX160-WX199 cancelled.

WX201-WX487 DH.100 Vampire FB.9   **43(203)**
WX201-WX241, WX259, WX260 built of which WX212, WX219, WX228, WX231-WX233, WX235-WX241 went to SRAF and WX202, WX206, WX208 to Jordan. WX261-WX308, WX327-WX376, WX403-WX435, WX459-WX487 cancelled.

WX493-WX691 Lockheed Neptune MR.1   **52(150)**
Ex-USN supplied under MDAP. WX493-WX529, WX542-WX556 of which WX502, WX512, WX513, WX516, WX522, WX524, WX527, WX549 later went to the Argentine Navy. WX557-WX591, WX616-WX634, WX635-WX691 not delivered.

WX695-WX949 DH.112 Venom NF.3   **123(193)**
WX785-WX810, WX837-WX886, WX903-WX949 built as follows: WX785-WX796, WX798, WX799, WX801-WX804, WX807 built at Christchurch; WX797, WX800, WX805, WX806, WX808, WX810, WX837-WX863, WX867-WX873, WX878-WX883, WX903-WX908, WX913-WX922, WX929-WX949 at

Chester; WX864-WX866, WX874-WX877, WX884-
WX886, WX909-WX912, WX923-WX928 at Hatfield.
WX695-WX740, WX761-WX784 cancelled.

WX953	Westland WS-51 Dragonfly HC.4	1
WX958	DH.104 Dove	1
	Ex-G-ALVT sold to Argentine AF as T-99.	
WX962-WZ151	Gloster G.41L Meteor FR.9	20(82)
	WX962-WX981 only built. WX963, WX967, WX975, WX980 disposed to Israel and WX972 to Syria. WX982-WX994, WZ103-WZ151 cancelled.	
WZ154-WZ267	Gloster Meteor T.7	(91)
	WZ154-WZ203, WZ227-WZ267 cancelled.	
WZ273-WZ302	Supermarine Attacker FB.2	30
	For Royal Navy.	
WZ306 & WZ311	Vickers Viking 1B	2
	G-AJFT, 'AJFS temporarily used for trooping.	
WZ315-WZ348	DH.112 Venom NF.3	6(34)
	WZ315-WZ320 only built, WZ321-WZ348 cancelled.	
WZ353-WZ357	Vickers Viking 1B	5
	G-AJFS, 'AIXS, 'AIXR, 'AKTU, 'AKTV temporarily used for trooping.	
WZ361-WZ405	Vickers Valiant B.1/BK.1	41
	WZ361-WZ375 B.1; WZ376 B(PR)K.1; WZ377-WZ379 B(PR).1; WZ380 B(PR)K.1; WZ381 B(PR).1; WZ382 B(PR)K.1; WZ383, WZ384 B(PR).1; WZ389-WZ405 B(PR)K.1.	
WZ409-WZ411	Percival P.50 Prince	3
	Delivered direct to RAAF as A90-1 to A90-3.	
WZ414-WZ620	DH.115 Vampire T.11	143
	WZ414-WZ430, WZ446-WZ478, WZ493-WZ521, WZ544-WZ593, WZ607-WZ620. Disposals to various air forces.	
WZ627-WZ656	Hawker Sea Fury FB.11	30
	For Royal Navy except WZ633-WZ641 to RCN and WZ642-WZ653 to RAN. Final Sea Fury production.	
WZ662-WZ731	Auster AOP.9	56
	WZ662-WZ679, WZ694-WZ731 for Army Aviation.	
WZ736 & WZ744	Avro 707A/707C	2
	Delta-wing experimental aircraft. WZ736 707A became 7868M; WZ744 707C became 7932M.	
WZ749	Westland WS-51 Dragonfly HC.2	1
	G-ALEG acquired for trials in Malaya.	
WZ753-WZ832	Slingsby T.38 Grasshopper TX.1	65
	WZ753-WZ798, WZ814-WZ832 for ATC.	
WZ838-WZ841	Handley Page HP.81 Hermes 4	4
	G-ALDA to 'ALDC, 'ALDF temporarily used for trooping.	
WZ845-WZ884	DHC-1 Chipmunk T.10	40
	Final Chipmunk production. Some to Army Air Corps.	
WZ889	Blackburn B.101 Universal Freighter 2	1
	C/n 1001. Beverley prototype G-AMVW.	
WZ893-WZ956	DH.112 Sea Venom FAW.53	39(49)
	WZ893-WZ911, WZ927-WZ946 direct to RAN. WZ947-WZ956 cancelled.	
WZ961-WZ962	Heston C.9	(2)
	Scale models ordered from Vickers Armstrong; cancelled.	
WZ966-WZ968	Boeing 345 Washington B.1(B-29 Superfortress)	3
	Ex-USAF 44-62283, 44-62282, 44-62296 supplied under MDAP.	
WZ972-WZ973	Vickers Viking 1A	2
	G-AHOP, 'AHON temporarily used for trooping.	
WZ984-WZ985	Douglas DC-3 Dakota 3	2
	G-AGWS, 'AGZG temporarily used for trooping.	
XA100-XA172	DH.115 Sea Vampire T.22	53
	Built at Christchurch for Royal Navy. XA100-XA131, XA152-XA172. Sales to Chile and RAN.	
XA177	Auster B.4	1
	Ex-G-25-2 and G-AMKL for evaluation.	
XA181 & XA186	Supermarine 545	1(2)
	Prototypes to Spec F105D2. XA181 built at Hursley Park but not flown, XA186 cancelled.	
XA191-XA192	Avro 685 York	2
	G-AMGK, 'AGNM temporarily used for trooping.	
XA197-XA204	Vickers Wild Goose aerodynes	6(8)
	XA197-XA202 built, XA203, XA204 cancelled.	
XA209-XA216	Short Seamew AS.1	3
	Prototypes c/ns SH.1606-SH.1608. XA209 first flew 13.8.53; XA213 flown later; XA216 ground rig only.	
XA219-XA221	Bristol Sycamore HR.50	3
	C/n 13063-13065 basic Sycamore 3 for RAN.	
XA225-XA244	Slingsby T.38 Grasshopper TX.1	20
	Gliders for ATC.	

XA249-XA278	Handley Page (Reading) HPR.5 Marathon T.11	30
	XA249-XA276 ex-G-ALUB, 'ALVW to 'ALVY, 'ALXR, G-AMAX, 'AMAY, 'AMDH, 'AMEK to 'AMEM, 'AMEP, 'AMER', 'AMET to 'AMEW, 'AMGN to 'AMGP, 'AMGR to 'AMGV', 'AMHT, 'AMHU, 'AMHX. XA277, XA278 not taken up by RAF, sold to Japan as JA6009, JA6010.	
XA282-XA313	Slingsby T.31B Cadet TX.3	32
	Gliders for ATC. XA282 preserved. XA308 to BGA3249.	
XA319-XA531	Fairey Gannet AS.1/T.2/AS.4	139(140)
	C/ns F.9211-F.9350. XA319-XA364, XA387-XA409 AS.1; XA410-XA433 AS.4; XA434 AS.1; XA435 AS.4; XA436 AS.1; XA454-XA473 AS.4; XA508-XA530 T.2 built at Stockport and Hayes. XA531 cancelled. XA326-XA334, XA343, XA350, XA351, XA356, XA359, XA389, XA403, XA434, XA436, XA514, XA517 to RAN others to Indonesia. Conversions: XA333 T.2; XA430, XA454, XA466, XA470 COD.4; XA459, XA460 ECM.6; XA470 COD.6.	
XA536	English Electric Canberra B.2	
	Converted to T.11 and T.19, became 8605M.	
XA539	DH.112 Sea Venom FAW.21	1
	For Royal Navy.	
XA544-XA836	Gloster Javelin F(AW)1/2/4/5/6	200
	XA544-XA572, XA618-XA628 F(AW).1; XA629-XA640 F(AW).4; XA641-XA667, XA688-XA719 F(AW).5; XA720-XA737, XA749-XA767 F(AW).4; XA768-XA781, XA799-XA814 F(AW).2; XA815-XA836 F(AW).6 of which XA662-XA667, XA688-XA737, XA749-XA762 were built by Armstrong Whitworth, rest by Gloster.	
XA842	Sikorsky S-55	(1)
	Ex-WW339 for RAE evaluation, became LN-ORK.	
XA847-XA856	English Electric P.1B Lightning	3
	Prototypes. XA847 first flew 4.4.57, XA853, XA856. XA847 became 8371M.	
XA862-XA871	Westland WS-55 Whirlwind HAR.1	10
	For Royal Navy. XA862 ex-G-AMJT.	
XA876	Slingsby T.34A Sky	1
	Glider for Empire Test Pilots School.	
XA879-XA880	DH.104 Devon C.1	2
	C/n 04374 and 04433. XA880 converted to C.2.	
XA885	Supermarine Swift	(1)
	Reconnaissance variant cancelled.	
XA889-XA913	Avro 698 Vulcan B.1	25
	Built at Woodford. XA895, XA900, XA901, XA904, XA906, XA907, XA909-XA913 converted to B.1A and XA903 used as Olympus 593 testbed.	
XA917-XA941	Handley Page HP.80 Victor B.1/B.1A	25
	BK.1 tanker conversions were XA918, XA926, XA928, XA930, XA932, XA936, XA937, XA938, XA939, XA941, later re-designated as K.1s.	
XA947-XA952	Vickers Wild Goose aerodynes	6
XA957-XB241	Supermarine Swift F.2	(140)
	Ordered from Short & Harland. XA957-XA993, XB102-XB151, XB169-XB185, XB206-XB241 cancelled.	
XB246	Douglas DC-3 Dakota 3	1
	Temporary use of G-AMBW for trooping.	
XB251-XB256	Westland WS-51 Dragonfly HR.4	6
	For Far East service.	
XB259-XB291	Blackburn B.101 Beverley C.1	20
	XB259 and XB260 temporarily G-AOAI, 'AOEK and 'paper' c/ns 1002, 1003; XB261-XB269, XB283-XB291.	
XB296-XB449	Grumman Avenger AS.4 (TBM-3E)	100
	Ex-USN supplied under MDAP for Royal Navy. XB296-XB332, XB355-XB404, XB437-XB449. Conversions to AS.5/AS.6 by Scottish Aviation.	
XB474-XB524	Hiller HT.1 (HTE-2)	20
	Ex-USN supplied under MDAP for Royal Navy. XB474-XB481, XB513-XB524.	
XB530-XD210	North American Sabre F.1/F.4	371(421)
	Canadian-built supplied under MDAP. F.1 aircraft were re-designated F.2. XB530-XB532 F.1; XB533-XB551, XB575-XB603, XB608-XB646, XB664-XB713, XB726-XB769, XB790-XB839, XB856-XB905, XB941-XB990, XD102-XD138 F.4 as originally allotted. XD102-XD138 were renumbered XB647-XB650, XB770-XB775, XB851-XB855, XB978-XB999 which caused some duplication. XB901-XB905, XB941-XB990 were re-numbered XB912-XB961, XB973-XB977. XD139-XD144 XD167-XD210 allotted, but immediately cancelled.	

XD143	Supermarine 550 Swift PR.6	(1)
	Part airframe became 7289M.	
XD145-XD153	Saro SR.52	2(3)
	Britain's first mixed power (rocket/turbojet) interceptor. XD145 ff 16.5.57; XD151 completed; XD153 cancelled.	
XD158	Gloster Javelin F.2	1
	Prototype with US radar installed, became 7592M.	
XD163-XD188	Westland WS-55 Whirlwind HAR.4	10
	XD163-XD165, XD182-XD188 of which XD163-XD165, XD182-XD184, XD186 were converted to HAR.10.	
XD196-XD197	Bristol 171 Sycamore HR.13	2
	C/n 13066, 13067 for ASR evaluation.	
XD203 & XD207	Westland WS-55 Whirlwind	(2)
	Development cancelled.	
XD212-XD357	Supermarine Scimitar F.1	76(100)
	XD212-XD250, XD264-XD282, XD316-XD333 built for Royal Navy, XD334-XD357 cancelled.	
XD361	Supermarine Swift F.1	(1)
	Replacement for WK198. Cancelled.	
XD366	Vickers Varsity T.1	1
	Replacement for WJ900	
XD371	Akaflieg München Mü-13A glider	1
	Ex- LG+WZ used by Royal Navy.	
XD375-XD627	DH.115 Vampire T.11	160
	XD375-XD405, XD424-XD463, XD506-XD554, XD588-XD627. Some disposals to other forces.	
XD632	Handley Page HP.81 Hermes 4A	1
	G-AKFP *Hamilcar* used temporarily for trooping.	
XD635-XD637	Vickers 498 Viking 1A	3
	G-AHOT, 'AHOW, 'AHOR used temporarily for trooping.	
XD649	Westland WS-51 Dragonfly IA	1
	G-AKTW for evaluation, became Westland Widgeon G-APPR.	
XD653-XD656	Bristol 171 Sycamore HR.51	4
	For RAN.	
XD662	Vickers 1000	(1)
	Cancelled when partially built.	
XD667-XD670	Avro 685 York	4
	G-AMUN, 'AMUU, 'AMUV, 'AGNU temporarily used for trooping.	
XD674-XD694	Hunting Jet Provost T.1/T.2	10
	Trials batch XD674-XD680, XD692-XD694 of which XD694 built as T.2 prototype.	
XD696 & XD701	Avro 720	(2)
	Prototypes to Spec F137D not completed.	
XD706-XD781	North American Sabre F.4	60
	Canadian-built aircraft supplied under MDAP. XD706-XD736, XD753-XD781.	
XD759	Fairey Jet Gyrodyne	1
	G-AJJP Gyrodyne converted. Compromised number above and renumbered XJ389.	
XD763-XD772	Westland WS-55 Whirlwind HAR.3	(10)
	Compromised numbers above, renumbered XJ393-XJ402.	
XD777-XD806	Westland WS-55 Whirlwind HAR.4	(20)
	XD777-XD784, XD795-XD806 compromised numbers above, renumbered XJ407-XJ414, XJ426-XJ437.	
XD812-XD893	Vickers 758 Valiant BK.1	38(56)
	XD812-XD830, XD857-XD875 built, XD876-XD893 cancelled.	
XD898	Fairey Gannet AS.1	1
	C/n F.9327 replacement for XA531, later to RAN.	
XD903-XE164	Supermarine 549 Swift FR.5	58(113)
	XD903-XD930, XD948-XD977 built at South Marston, XD978-XD988, XE105-XE116, XE133-XE164 cancelled.	
XE169-XE277	Short Seamew AS.1/MR.2	25(60)
	Built by Short & Harland. Planned as 30/30 RAF/Royal Navy. XE169-XE186, XE205-XE211 completed as AS.1 except XE173-XE176, XE180 MR.2. XE212-XE231 not built. XE263-XE277 not built.	
XE280-XE281	Douglas DC-3 Dakota 4	2
	G-AMRA, 'AMZD temporarily used for trooping.	
XE286-XE288	Bristol 173	2(3)
	C/n 13204-13206 built at Weston ex-G-AMYF to 'AMYH. XE286 first flew 9.11.56; XE287 not flown; XE288 not completed.	
XE294-XE299	Vickers Valiant BK.1	(6)
	Order cancelled.	
XE304	Avro York	1
	Trooping serial for G-AMUN. Allocated 27.5.53, but cancelled next day.	

XE306-XE322	Bristol 171 Sycamore HR.14	17
	XE306-XE312, XE313-XE317 originally planned as Sycamore 4 G-AMWK to 'AMWO, XE318-XE322.	
XE327-XE498	Hawker Sea Hawk FGA.4/FGA.6	99(107)
	Built by Armstrong Whitworth. XE327-XE338 FGA.4 of which all but XE329, XE332 were converted to FGA.6, XE339-XE344, XE362-XE411, XE435-XE463, XE489, XE490 built as FGA.6. Disposals to Indian Navy. XE491-XE498 cancelled.	
XE506	Percival Provost T.1	1
	Replacement aircraft for WV437 sold to Malaya.	
XE512-XE515	Scottish Aviation Pioneer CC.1	2(4)
	XE512 ex-VL515, G-AKBF; XE514 ex-VL516, G-ANAZ.	
XE521	Fairey Rotodyne	1
	C/n F.9429 built at Hayes, assembled at White Waltham.	
XE526-XE656	Hawker Hunter F.6	100
	Built at Kingston. XE526-XE561, XE579-XE628, XE643-XE656. Conversions: XE606, XE608, XE627, XE653 to F.6A; XE530, XE532, XE535, XE544, XE546, XE550, XE552, XE581, XE582, XE584, XE592, XE597, XE600, XE601, XE604, XE607, XE609-XE611, XE615-XE618, XE620, XE622-XE624, XE628, XE643, XE645-XE647, XE649-XE652, XE654, XE655 to FGA.9; XE556, XE579, XE580, XE585, XE589, XE596, XE599, XE605, XE614, XE621, XE625, XE626 FR.10; XE531 to T.12. Disposals to various forces.	
XE657-XE718	Hawker Hunter F.4	50
	Built at Blackpool. XE657-XE689, XE702-XE718. Conversions: XE664 to T.8B; XE665 to T.8C; XE668 XE673, XE674, XE680, XE682, XE685, XE689, XE707, XE712, XE716, XE717 GA.11 for Royal Navy. Disposals to various forces.	
XE722-XE754	ML Aviation ML-120D Midget	20
	Pilotless targets. XE722-XE735, XE749-XE754 for Army use at Larkhill.	
XE758-XE812	Slingsby T.8/T.31B Cadet TX.2/TX.3	29(34)
	XE758-XE762 TX.2 being VF181, VM529, VM539, VM589, VM594 rebuilt; XE784-XE812 TX.3 new build. For ATC. XE795 to BGA3251.	
XE816-XE998	DH.115 Vampire T.11	135
	Built at Hatfield, Christchurch and Chester. XE816-XE833, XE848-XE897, XE919-XE961, XE975-XE998. XE816-XE819, XE823-XE826, XE938-XE941 to SRAF.	
XF104-XF253	Supermarine Swift F.4/F.7	12(81)
	XF104-XF109 F.4 cancelled; XF113-XF124 F.7 built; XF125-XF129 F.7 not completed; XF155-XF180, XF196-XF217, XF244-XF253 F.7 cancelled.	
XF259-XF261	Westland WS-51 Dragonfly HC.4	3
XF265-XF269	Bristol 171 Sycamore HR.14	5
	C/n 13225-13229.	
XF273-XF279	Gloster G.43 Meteor T.7	7
	Last production Meteors. All except XF274 disposed of abroad.	
XF284-XF285	Avro 685 York	2
	XF284 ex-MW308, G-AMUL; XF285 ex-MW332, G-AMUM. Temporarily used for trooping.	
XF289-XF370	Hawker Hunter F.4	50
	Built at Blackpool. XF289-XF324, XF357-XF370. Conversions: XF310, XF321 to T.7 for RAF; XF289, XF321, XF322, XF357, XF358 to T.8 and XF291, XF297, XF300, XF301, XF368 GA.11 all for Royal Navy. Disposals to various forces.	
XF373-XF527	Hawker Hunter F.6	100
	Built by Armstrong Whitworth. XF373-XF389, XF414-XF463, XF495-XF527. Conversions: XF382, XF418, XF439, XF515, XF516 to F.6A; XF376, XF388, XF414, XF416, XF419, XF421, XF424, XF430, XF431, XF435, XF437, XF440, XF442, XF445, XF446, XF454-XF456, XF462, XF508, XF511, XF517, XF519, XF523 to FGA.9; XF422, XF426, XF428, XF429, XF432, XF436, XF438, XF441, XF457-XF460 to FR.10. Disposals to other forces.	
XF532	Vickers V.610 Viking 1B	1
	G-AJBU temporarily used for trooping.	
XF537	Avro 689 Tudor 2	1
	G-AGRY temporarily used for trooping.	
XF540-XF614	Hunting-Percival P.56 Provost T.1	50
	XF540-XF565, XF591-XF614. Disposals to Malaya.	
XF619 & XF623	Douglas DC-3	2
	G-AMYX, 'AMYV temporarily contracted for trooping.	

XF629-XF633	**Vickers 610 Viking 1B**	5
	G-AJBO, 'AIVO, 'AHPO, 'AHPM, 'AJCD temporarily contracted for trooping.	
XF638-XF640	**Vickers 639 Viking 1**	3
	G-AHPB, 'AGRP, 'AGRW temporarily contracted for trooping.	
XF645-XF647	**Douglas DC-3 Dakota 4**	3
	G-AMVC, 'AMSF, 'AMVB temporarily contracted for trooping.	
XF650-XF663	**Bristol 170 Freighter**	14
	XF650-XF655 Mk.32; XF656-XF663 Mk.21 of Silver City Airways contracted temporarily for trooping, but only XF662, XF663 believed actually used for G-AIME and G-AIMH.	
XF667	**Douglas DC-3 Dakota 4**	1
	G-AMSH temporarily contracted for trooping.	
XF672-XF673	**Boulton Paul P.108 Balliol T.2**	2
	Replacements for diversions to Ceylon.	
XF678-XF693	**Hunting Percival P.56 Provost T.1**	16
	Replacements for offsets to Rhodesia. XF682, XF683, XF688 to Muscat & Oman AF.	
XF700-XF734	**Avro 716 Shackleton MR.3**	13(17)
	XF700-XF711, XF730 built at Woodford, XF731-XF734 cancelled. Modified progressively to MR.3/2 (Phase 2) standard and then all but XF710 to MR.3/3.	
XF739	**Avro 688 Tudor 1**	1
	G-AGRI temporarily contracted for trooping.	
XF746-XF757	**Douglas DC-3 Dakota 4**	6
	G-AMVL, 'AMYJ, 'AMZG, 'AMZF, 'AMPP, 'AMJU for trooping as XF746-XF749, XF756, XF757.	
XF763-XF765	**Vickers Viking 1**	3
	G-AHPJ, 'AHPC, 'AHOY temporarily contracted for trooping.	
XF766-XF769	**Douglas DC-3 Dakota 4**	4
	G-AMSL, 'AMNL, 'AMSJ, 'AMSK temporarily contracted for trooping.	
XF774 & **XF780**	**Supermarine 550 Swift**	2
	Prototypes. XF774 F.7; XF780 PR.6.	
XF785	**Bristol 173 Mk.I**	1
	C/n 12871 G-ALBN for naval trials.	
XF791-XF792	**Douglas DC-3 Dakota 4**	2
	G-ANAE, 'AMWX temporarily contracted for trooping.	
XF796-XF799	**Hunting Pembroke C(PR).1**	4
	All converted to C.1.	
XF804-XF823	*Numbers reserved but not used*	—
XF828	**DH.110 Sea Vixen 20X**	1
	Pre-production aircraft built at Christchurch, first flew on 20.6.55.	
XF833	**Hawker P.1099**	1
	Prototype Hunter F.6 with parts of WN470 used in manufacture at Kingston.	
XF836-XF914	**Hunting-Percival P.56 Provost T.1**	66
	XF836-XF854, XF868-XF914. Offsets included XF849-XF852, XF870-XF873, XF878-XF881 to RRAF; XF845, XF847, XF848, XF853, XF854 to RMAF and XF868 and XF907 to Muscat & Oman AF.	
XF919	**Avro 685 York**	1
	G-AMUS temporarily contracted for trooping.	
XF923 & **XF926**	**Bristol T.188**	2
	Stainless steel research aircraft c/n 13518, 13519. XF923 first flew 14.4.62; XF926 became 8368M.	
XF929-XF931	**Boulton Paul P.108 Balliol T.2**	3
	Replacements for offsets to Ceylon.	
XF932-XF999	**Hawker Hunter F.4**	55
	Built at Blackpool. XF932-XF953, XF967-XF999. Conversions mainly for Royal Navy: XF978, XF995 to T.8B; XF938, XF939, XF942, XF967, XF983, XF985, XF991, XF992, XF994 to T.8C; XF977 to GA.11 later PR.11. Disposals to other forces.	
XG127-XG298	**Hawker Hunter F.6**	110
	XG127-XG133, XG150-XG172, XG185-XG211, XG225-XG239, XG251-XG274, XG289-XG298 built at Kingston, XG150-XG168 built by Armstrong Whitworth. Conversions: XG152, XG158, XG160, XG172, XG191, XG196, XG197, XG225, XG226 to F.6A; XG128, XG130, XG134-XG136, XG151, XG153-XG156, XG169, XG194, XG195, XG205, XG207, XG228, XG237, XG251-XG256, XG260, XG261, XG264-XG266, XG271-XG273, XG291-XG293, XG296-XG298 to FGA.9; XG127, XG168 to F.R.10. Disposals to other forces.	

XG303	**Saro Skeeter 5**	1
	C/n SR907 G-AMDC for trials. Later modified to Mk.6. Became G-AMTZ.	
XG307-XG337	**English Electric Lightning F.1**	20
	Pre-production batch XG307-XG313, XG325-XG337. XG310 prototype F.3 and XG328-XG331, XG333, XG335-XG337 later to F.3 standard.	
XG341-XG342	**Hawker Hunter F.4**	2
	Built at Blackpool.	
XG349-XG350	**Vickers 610 Viking 1B**	2
	G-AHPM, 'AJCD temporarily contracted for trooping.	
XG354-XG441	**Bristol 173 (type also reported as 191)**	1(28)
	XG354 almost completed and used as ground test rig. Rest, XG355-XG358, XG419-XG441 cancelled.	
XG447-XG476	**Bristol 192 Belvedere HC.1**	26
	C/n 13342-13367 XG447-XG468, XG473-XG476.	
XG480-XG484	**Supermarine Swift F.4**	(5)
	Cancelled.	
XG487-XG492	**ML Aviation ML-120D Midget**	6
	Pilotless target drones.	
XG496	**DH.104 Dove 1B**	1
	G-ANDX acquired by MoA. To Devon C.1 standard and later to C.2.	
XG500-XG549	**Bristol 171 Sycamore HR.14**	36
	XG500-XG523, XG538-XG549 of which XG507, XG547-XG549 were built at Weston and the bulk at Filton.	
XG554	**English Electric Canberra B(I).6**	1
	Replacement.	
XG558-XG563	**Scottish Aviation Prestwick Pioneer CC.1**	6
XG567-XG568	**Vickers 610 Viking 1B**	2
	G-AKBH, 'AIVO temporarily contracted for trooping.	
XG572-XG597	**Westland WS-55 Whirlwind HAR.3/HAS.7**	26
	For Royal Navy. WG572-WG585 HAR.3; WG586 HAS.3 modified to HAS.7; WG587-WG597 built as HAS.7.	
XG603	**DH.114 Heron C.2**	1
	C/n 14058 for British Joint Services Mission, Washington.	
XG606-XG737	**DH.112 Sea Venom FAW.21/FAW.22**	100
	XG606-XG638, XG653-XG680 FAW.21; XG681-XG702, XG721-XG737 FAW.22 for Royal Navy built at Christchurch and Hatfield.	
XG742-XG777	**DH.115 Sea Vampire T.22**	20
	XG742-XG748, XG765-XG777 for Royal Navy built at Christchurch and Hatfield.	
XG783-XG890	**Fairey AS.1/T.2/AS.4/T.5**	59(69)
	Built at Stockport and Hayes for Royal Navy. XG783-XG798, XG825-XG855 AS.4 except XG784, XG785, XG787, XG789, XG791, XG792, XG795, XG796, XG825, XG826 AS.1 for RAN and XG837, XG838, XG841, XG842, XG845, XG847, XG848, XG851, XG854, XG855 cancelled before being built. Conversions: XG786, XG790 to COD.4 and XG787, XG792, XG831, XG832 to AS.6. Diversions: XG829, XG830, XG833-XG836, XG839, XG840, XG843, XG844, XG846, XG849, XG850, XG852, XG853 to Federal German Navy. XG869-XG881 T.2 of which XG873 was converted to T.5, XG882-XG889 built as T.5; XG890 T.2 direct to Federal German Navy.	
XG895-XG896	**Vickers 610 Viking 1B**	2
	G-AJBO, 'AIVH temporarily contracted for trooping.	
XG897-XG898	**Avro 685 York**	2
	G-AMRJ, 'ANRC temporarily contracted for trooping.	
XG900 & **XG905**	**Short SC.1**	2
	VTOL experimental aircraft c/ns SH.1814, SH.1815 to Spec ER143D. XG900 first flew 2.4.57.	
XG912-XG924	**Avro 716 Shackleton MR.3**	(13)
	Cancelled.	
XG929	**Avro 685 York I**	1
	G-ANSY temporarily contracted for trooping.	
XG934-XG992	**Hawker Sea Hawk FGA.4**	(46)
	XG934-XG947, XG961-XG992 ordered from Armstrong Whitworth and cancelled.	
XH116-XH124	**Blackburn Beverley C.1**	9
	XH124 as 8025M preserved at Hendon.	
XH129-XH186	**English Electric Canberra PR.9**	23(52)
	XH129-XH137, XH164-XH177 built by Short & Harland c/ns SH.1719-SH.1741 of which XH132 became the Short SC.9. XH138-XH151, XH158-XH163, XH178-XH186 cancelled.	
XH203-XH244	**English Electric Canberra B(I).8**	25
	XH203-XH209, XH227-XH244. Majority to the IAF.	

XH249	**Fairey Rotodyne Z**	**(1)**
	Not completed.	
XH255-XH260	**Vickers V.1000**	**(6)**
	Jet transport cancelled.	
XH264-XH368	**DH.115 Vampire T.11**	**66**
	XH264-XH278, XH292-XH330, XH357-XH368. Offsets and disposals to Commonwealth and foreign air forces.	
XH375	**DH.114 Heron C.3**	**1**
	C/n 14059 ex-G-5-7 for the Queen's Flight. Became CF-YAP.	
XH379	**Bristol 173 Mk.2**	**1**
	C/n 12872 ex-G-AMJI for naval trials. Later Mk.3.	
XH385	**Bristol 170 Mk.31E**	**1**
	G-AMSA temporarily contracted for trooping.	
XH390-XH447	**Gloster Javelin T.3**	**20**
	XH390-XH397, XH432-XH438, XH443-XH447.	
XH451	**Supermarine 556**	**(1)**
	Two-seat version of the Scimitar. Cancelled.	
XH455 & XH463	**DHC-2 Beaver**	**2**
	G-AMVU Srs 1 and G-ANAR Srs 2 for evaluation.	
XH469	**Scottish Aviation Prestwick Pioneer Srs.2**	**1**
	G-ANRG evaluated in Exercise Battle Royal 1954.	
XH475-XH563	**Avro 698 Vulcan B.1/B.2**	**37**
	XH475-XH483, XH497-XH506, XH532 B.1 all converted to B.1A; XH533-XH539, XH554-XH563 B.2 of which XH534, XH537, XH558, XH560, XH563 were converted to B.2MRR and XH558, XH560, XH561 to K.2.	
XH567-XH584	**English Electric Canberra T.4/B.6**	**6**
	XH567-XH570 B.6 of which XH567 was non-standard, XH568 has nose probe fitted and XH570 was converted to B.16. XH583, XH584 T.4.	
XH587-XH675	**Handley Page HP.80 Victor B.1/B.2**	**33**
	XH587-XH594, XH613-XH621, XH645-XH651, XH667 B.1 of which all but XH617 became B.1A and XH615, XH620, XH646-XH648, XH667 were further converted to B(K).1A then redesignated B.1A (K.2P) and XH587-XH591, XH614, XH616, XH618, XH619, XH621, XH645, XH649-XH651 to K.1A. XH668-XH675 B.2 of which XH669, XH671, XH673, XH675 converted to K.2 and XH672, XH674 to B.2(SR).	
XH682	**Bristol 171 Mk.3**	**1**
	C/n 12886 ex-G-ALSR acquired by MoS.	
XH687-XJ178	**Gloster Javelin FAW.5/6/7/8/9**	**206(219)**
	XH687-XH692 FAW.5 built by Armstrong Whitworth. XH693-XH703 FAW.6; XH704-XH725, XH746-XH758 FAW.7 of which XH707-XH709, XH711-XH713, XH715-XH717, XH719, XH721-XH725, XH746, XH747, XH749, XH751-XH753, XH755-XH758 were converted to FAW.9; XH759-XH772 built as FAW.9; XH773-XH784 FAW.7 of which XH773, XH774, XH776-XH780 were converted to FAW.9; all from XH693 built by Gloster. XH785-XH795, XH833-XH849, XH871-XH899 were ordered as FAW.7 built by Armstrong Whitworth of which XH785, XH787, XH788, XH791-XH795, XH833-XH836, XH839-XH849, XH871-XH899 were converted to, or built as FAW.9. XH900-XH912, XH955-XH965 ordered as FAW.7 of which all from XH903 were built or converted to FAW.9. XH966-XH993, XJ113-XJ130, XJ165 FAW.8, all built by Gloster. XJ166-XJ178 cancelled.	
XJ183-XJ244	**Supermarine Swift F.4**	**(20)**
	XJ183-XJ188, XJ217-XJ226, XJ241-XJ244 cancelled.	
XJ249 & XJ257	**English Electric Canberra B.6**	**2**
	Replacements for WJ779, WJ784 diverted to France.	
XJ264	**Avro 685 York**	**1**
	G-ANVO temporarily contracted for trooping.	
XJ269-XJ288	**Handley Page HP.81 Hermes 4**	**4**
	XJ269, XJ276, XJ281, XJ288 were G-ALDP, 'ALDX, 'ALDK, 'ALDU temporarily contracted for trooping.	
XJ304	**Vickers 610 Viking 1B**	**1**
	G-AJPH temporarily contracted for trooping.	
XJ309	**Handley Page HP.81 Hermes 4**	**1**
	G-ALDI temporarily contracted for trooping.	
XJ314	**Rolls-Royce 'Flying Bedstead'**	**1**
	Thrust measuring rig. Nene 101 VTOL test rig, first flew 9.7.53 tethered, 3.8.54 free.	
XJ319-XJ350	**DH.104 Sea Devon C.20**	**10**
	For Royal Navy. XJ319-XJ324 ex-G-AMXP, 'ANDY, XB-TAN, G-AMYP, 'AMXY, 'AMXZ; XJ347-XJ349 ex-G-AMXT, 'AMXX, 'AMXW.	

XJ355	**Saro Skeeter Mk.6**	**1**
	C/n SR905 G-ANMH AOP prototype acquired in November 1955.	
XJ361-XJ385	**Bristol 171 Sycamore HR.14**	**10**
	XJ361-XJ364, XJ380-XJ385.	
XJ389	**Fairey Jet Gyrodyne**	**(1)**
	Ex-XD759.	
XJ393-XJ437	**Westland WS-55 Whirlwind HAR.1-HAR.5**	**30**
	XJ393-XJ402 HAR.3, originally XD763-XD772, of which XJ396, XJ398 were converted to HAR.5 and later to HAR.10; XJ407-XJ414, XJ426-XJ437 originally numbered XD777-XD784, XD795-XD806 built as HAR.4 except XJ429, XJ430, XJ432-XJ436 HAR.2 of which XJ407, XJ409-XJ412, XJ414, XJ426, XJ428-XJ430, XJ432, XJ433, XJ435, XJ437 were converted to HAR.10.	
XJ440	**Fairey Gannet AEW.3**	**1**
	Prototype c/n F.9431 to Spec AEW154D. Built at Hayes and first flew 20.8.58.	
XJ445	**Westland WS-55 Whirlwind HAR.5**	**1**
	For Royal Navy, ordered as HAR.3, planned as Mk.6, and built as HAR.5.	
XJ450-XJ466	**Scottish Aviation Prestwick Pioneer CC.1**	**4**
	XJ450, XJ451, XJ465, XJ466.	
XJ470	**Bristol 170 Mk.31C**	**1**
	C/n 13217 acquired for A & AEE.	
XJ474-XJ611	**DH.110 Sea Vixen FAW.1/FAW.2**	**78**
	Built at Christchurch for Royal Navy. XJ474-XJ494, XJ513-XJ528, XJ556-XJ586, XJ602-XJ611 FAW.1 of which XJ489-XJ491, XJ491, XJ516-XJ518, XJ521, XJ524, XJ526, XJ558-XJ561, XJ564, XJ565, XJ570-XJ572, XJ574-XJ576, XJ578-XJ582, XJ584, XJ602, XJ604, XJ606-XJ610 were converted to FAW.2	
XJ615 & XJ627	**Hawker P.1101 Hunter T.7**	**2**
	Prototypes to Spec T157D. XJ615 first flew 8.7.55; XJ627 disposed to Chile.	
XJ632-XJ718	**Hawker Hunter F.6**	**45**
	Built at Kingston. XJ632-XJ646, XJ673-XJ695, XJ712-XJ718. Conversions: XJ634, XJ637, XJ639, XJ676 to F.6A; XJ632, XJ635, XJ636, XJ640, XJ642-XJ646, XJ673, XJ674, XJ680, XJ683-XJ692, XJ695 to FGA.9; XJ633, XJ694, XJ714 to FR.10. Majority disposed to other forces.	
XJ723-XJ766	**Westland WS-55 Whirlwind HAR.2/HAR.4**	**19**
	XJ723-XJ730, XJ756-XJ766 HAR.2 except XJ723, XJ724, XJ761 HAR.4 of which XJ723, XJ724, XJ726, XJ727, XJ729, XJ757, XJ758, XJ760, XJ762-XJ764 converted to HAR.10.	
XJ771-XJ776	**DH.115 Vampire T.11**	**6**
	Ex-R Norwegian AF.	
XJ780-XJ825	**Avro 698 Vulcan B.2**	**8**
	XJ780-XJ784, XJ823-XJ825 of which XJ825 was converted to K.2.	
XJ830-XJ831	**Handley Page (Reading) HPR.1 Marathon 1C**	**2**
	For RAE ex-VR-NAS, VR-NAT. Reverted to their original identities G-AMHS, 'AMHV on disposal in 1958.	
XJ836-XJ887	**Gloster P.376 'Thin-wing Javelin'**	**(18)**
	XJ836-XJ842, XJ877-XJ887 ordered to Spec F153D and cancelled.	
XJ895-XJ919	**Bristol 171 Sycamore HR.14**	**9**
	Built at Weston. XJ895-XJ899, XJ915-XJ919.	
XJ924-XJ936	**Fairey Ultra-light helicopter**	**4**
	C/ns F.9423-F.9426. XJ924, XJ928, XJ930, XJ936 to Spec H144T. XJ928, XJ936 became G-AOUJ, 'AOUK.	
XJ941	**Auster J/5G Autocar**	**1**
	G-ANVN to Malaya for pest control trials, became VR-TBR.	
XJ945-XK111	**Hawker Hunter F.6**	**(50)**
	XJ945-XJ958, XJ971-XJ997, XK103-XK111 ordered from Blackpool plant and cancelled.	
XK136-XK355	**Hawker Hunter F.6**	**53(153)**
	Built at Kingston. XK136-XK156 of which XK141, XK149 were converted to F.6A and XK136-XK140, XK142, XK150, XK151 to FGA.9, and XK143-XK147, XK152-XK156 were diverted to Iraq; XK157-XK176, XK213-XK224 were delivered direct to IAF as F.56As; XK225-XK241, XK257-XK306, XK323-XK355 were cancelled.	
XK367-XK370	**Scottish Aviation Prestwick Pioneer CC.1**	**4**
	XK367 used as ambulance.	

XK374-XK421	**Auster AOP.9**	**25**
	XK374-XK382, XK406-XK421 for Army Air Corps.	
XK426	**Rolls-Royce 'Flying Bedstead'**	**1**
	Second prototype thrust measuring rig.	
XK429-XK436	**Bristol T.188**	**(3)**
	XK429, XK434, XK436 cancelled.	
XK440-XK473	**English Electric Canberra PR.9**	**(11)**
	XK440-XK443, XK467-XK473 ordered from Short & Harland, but cancelled.	
XK479-XK482	**Saro Skeeter AOP.10/T.11**	**4**
	XK479 T.11; XK480-XK482 AOP.10 of which XK482 was converted to AOP.12 before delivery.	
XK486-XK536	**Blackburn B.103/NA.39 Buccaneer S.1**	**20**
	Pre-production aircraft XK486-XK491, XK523-XK536 of which XK526, XK527 became S.2 prototypes and XK527 later to S.2D.	
XK542-XK571	**Slingsby T.38 Grasshopper TX.1**	**(10)**
	XK542-XK548, XK569-XK571 cancelled.	
XK577	**Gloster Javelin T.3**	**1**
	Trials aircraft to Spec T118.	
XK582-XK637	**DH.115 Vampire T.11**	**24**
	XK582-XK590, XK623-XK637 built at Chester. XK634 to Austrian AF.	
XK641-XK650	**English Electric Canberra T.4/B.6**	**3**
	XK641 B.6 converted to B.15; XK647, XK650 T.4 both to Indian AF as IQ994, IQ995 to T.45 standard.	
XK655-XK716	**DH.106 Comet C.2/T.2**	**13**
	XK655, XK659, XK663 C.2 ex-G-AMXA, 'AMXC, 'AMXE; XK669, XK670 T.2 ex-G-AMXB, 'AMXF *Taurus* and *Corvus*; XK671, XK695-XK699 C.2 ex-G-AMXG to 'AMXJ, 'AMXL, 'AMXM, *Aquila, Perseus, Orion, Cygnus, Pegasus* and *Sagittarius*; XK715 *Columba*, all built at Hatfield. XK716 *Cepheus* built at Chester. XK655, XK659, XK663, XK695 converted to R.2.	
XK720	**Rolls-Royce VTOL testbed**	**(1)**
	Cancelled.	
XK724-XK768	**Folland Gnat**	**6**
	XK724, XK739-XK741, XK767 for MoS trials, XK768 to Indian AF as IE1059.	
XK773	**Saro W.14 Skeeter Mk.6**	**1**
	C/n 904 ex-G-ANMG for trials in 1955.	
XK776-XK784	**ML Aviation Utility inflatable wing aircraft**	**3**
	XK776 Mk.1; XK781 Mk.2; XK784 prototype.	
XK788-XK824	**Slingsby T.38 Grasshopper TX.1**	**10**
	XK788-XK791, XK819-XK824 for ATC.	
XK831-XK854	**Vickers Swallow research models**	**10**
	XK831-XK835, XK850-XK854.	
XK859-XK885	**Hunting Pembroke C.1**	**6**
	XK859-XK862, XK884, XK885.	
XK889	**Hunting Percival P.74 research helicopter**	**1**
	Not flown.	
XK895-XK897	**DH.104 Sea Devon C.20**	**3**
	C/n 04472-04474 for Royal Navy. XK896, XK897 became G-RNAS, G-AROI.	
XK902-XK903	**Bristol Sycamore HR.14**	**1(2)**
	XK902 to RAN, XK903 incorrectly marked on XL507.	
XK906-XK945	**Westland WS-55 Whirlwind HAS.7**	**20**
	XK906-XK912, XK933-XK945 for Royal Navy.	
XK951-XK959	**English Electric Canberra B(I).8**	**4**
	XK951-XK953, XK959 of which XK951 went to Peru and XK953, XK959 to Indian AF.	
XK964	**Saro W.14 Skeeter Mk.6**	**1**
	C/n 906 ex-G-ANMI.	
XK968-XL113	**Westland WS-55 Whirlwind HAR.2/HAR.4**	**14**
	XK968-XK970, XK986-XK991 HAR.2; XL109-XL113 HAR.4 of which all but XK989 and XL113 were converted to HAR.10.	
XL117-XL152	**Blackburn Beverley C.1**	**8**
	XL117-XL119 renumbered XL130-XL132, XL148-XL152.	
XL158-XL233	**Handley Page HP.80 Victor B.2**	**18**
	XL158-XL165, XL188-XL193, XL230-XL233 of which XL165, XL193, XL230 were converted to B.2(SR) and all others except XL159 to K.2.	
XL237-XL313	**Hawker Sea Hawk FB.50**	**22**
	XL237-XL241, XL269-XL276, XL305-XL313 all for Dutch Navy as 6-50 to 6-71.	
XL317-XL446	**Avro 698 Vulcan B.2**	**24**
	XL317-XL321, XL359-XL361, XL384-XL392, XL425-XL427, XL443-XL446. XL445 converted to K.2.	
XL449-XL503	**Fairey Gannet AEW.3**	**31**
	C/n F.9432-F.9462. XL449-XL456, XL471-XL482, XL493-XL503 for Royal Navy. Built at Hayes.	
XL507	**Bristol 171 Sycamore HR.51**	**1**
	C/n 13407 built at Weston for RAN. Was incorrectly numbered XK903.	
XL511-XL513	**Handley Page HP.80 Victor B.2**	**3**
	All converted to K.2.	
XL517-XL558	**Scottish Aviation Prestwick Pioneer CC.1**	**10**
	XL517 ex-G-AOGK, XL518-XL520, XL553-XL558. XL554 to Oman.	
XL563-XL623	**Hawker Hunter T.7/T.8**	**55**
	XL563-XL587, XL591-XL605, XL609-XL623 T.7 except ten for Royal Navy XL580-XL582, XL584, XL585, XL598, XL599, XL602-XL604 as T.8. All built at Kingston.	
XL628-XL629	**English Electric Lightning T.4**	**2**
	Prototypes. XL628 first flew 6.5.59.	
XL635-XL660	**Bristol 175 Britannia C.1 (Srs 253)**	**10**
	Built by Short & Harland. XL635-XL640 *Bellatrix, Argo, Vega, Sirius, Atria, Antares;* XL657-XL660 *Rigel, Adhara, Polaris, Alphard.* All sold to civil operators.	
XL664-XL706	**Scottish Aviation Prestwick Pioneer CC.1**	**18**
	XL664-XL674, XL700-XL706 of which XL668, XL670-XL674 were offset to R Ceylonese AF.	
XL710	**DHC-3 Otter**	**1**
	For 1956 Commonwealth Trans-Antarctic Expedition, became RNZAF NZ6081.	
XL714-XL717	**DH.82A Tiger Moth**	**(4)**
	Ex-G-AOGR, 'AOIK, 'AOIL, 'AOXG ex-T6099, DE395, T7363, T7291 reconditioned for the Royal Navy.	
XL722	**Sikorsky S-58 (HSS-1)**	**1**
	Purchased as pattern aircraft.	
XL727-XL729	**Westland WS-58 Wessex HAS.1**	**3**
	Pre-production batch for Royal Navy. XL728 later to HC.2 standard.	
XL734-XL814	**Saro Skeeter AOP.12**	**27**
	XL734-XL740, XL762-XL772, XL806-XL814 for the Army Air Corps.	
XL820-XL829	**Bristol 171 Sycamore HR.14**	**10**
	Final Bristol helicopters built at Weston.	
XL833-XL900	**Westland WS-55 Whirlwind HAS.7**	**45**
	XL833-XL854, XL867-XL884, XL896-XL900 of which XL839, XL843, XL873, XL875, XL880, XL896, XL898, XL899, XL900 were converted to HAR.9.	
XL905-XL925	**Saro SR177**	**(9)**
	Order cancelled. XL905-XL907, XL920-XL925.	
XL929-XL956	**Hunting P.66 Pembroke C.1/C(PR).1**	**7**
	XL929-XL931, XL953, XL954 C.1; XL955, XL956 C(PR).1 converted to C.1.	
XL961	**DH.114 Heron 2 Srs.2**	**1**
	G-AMTS for HRH Princess Margaret's East African Tour 1956.	
XL966-XL997	**Scottish Aviation Twin Pioneer CC.1**	**12**
	XL966-XL970, XL991-XL997.	
XM103-XM112	**Blackburn B.101 Beverley C.1**	**10**
	Final Beverley production.	
XM117-XM126	**Hawker Hunter T.7**	**10**
	Diverted to R Netherlands AF as N311 to N320 (T.66).	
XM129	**Hunting Jet Provost T.1**	**1**
	G-AOBU taken on charge temporarily.	
XM134-XM218	**English Electric Lightning F.1/F.1A**	**48(50)**
	XM134-XM147, XM163-XM167 F.1; XM168 cancelled; XM169-XM192, XM213-XM216 F.1A; XM217, XM218 cancelled.	
XM223	**DH.104 Devon C.1**	**1**
	C/n 04498 to RAE, converted to C.2.	
XM228-XM229	**English Electric Canberra T.4**	**(2)**
	Cancelled order.	
XM244-XM279	**English Electric Canberra B(I).8**	**20**
	XM244, XM245, XM262-XM279. XM263, XM273, XM276, XM279 to Peruvian AF.	
XM284-XM291	**Scottish Aviation Twin Pioneer CC.1**	**8**
XM295-XM296	**DH.114 Heron C(VVIP).4**	**2**
	Built at Chester for the Queen's Flight. XM296 later to the Royal Navy as a C.4.	
XM299-XM331	**Westland WS-58 Wessex HAS.1**	**9**
	XM299-XM301, XM326-XM331 of which XM299 was converted to HC.2 and XM327, XM328, XM331 to HAS.3. All for Royal Navy.	

XM336-XM341	**Gloster Javelin T.3**	1(6)
	XM336 only built, rest cancelled.	
XM346-XM480	**Hunting Jet Provost T.3**	100
	XM346-XM387, XM401-XM428, XM451-XM480 of which XM349, XM350, XM352, XM357, XM358, XM365, XM366, XM370-XM372, XM374, XM376, XM378, XM383, XM387, XM401, XM403, XM405, XM412, XM414, XM419, XM424, XM425, XM453, XM455, XM458, XM459, XM461, XM463-XM466, XM470-XM473, XM475, XM478, XM479 were converted to T.3A.	
XM489-XM520	**Bristol 175 Britannia C.1 (Srs 253)**	10
	XM489-XM491, XM496, XM497 *Denebola, Aldebaran, Procyon, Regulus, Schedar* built by Short & Harland; XM498, XM517-XM520 *Hadar, Avoir, Spica, Capella, Arcturus* built by Bristol. All sold to civil contractors.	
XM524-XM565	**Saro Skeeter AOP.12**	20
	XM524-XM530, XM553-XM565 for Army Air Corps.	
XM569-XM657	**Avro 698 Vulcan B.2**	40
	XM569-XM576, XM594-XM612, XM645-XM657 of which XM596 not flown; XM571 converted to K.2.	
XM660-XM687	**Westland WS-55 Whirlwind HAS.7**	15
	XM660-XM669, XM683-XM687 for Royal Navy. XM666 converted to HAR.9.	
XM691-XM709	**Folland Gnat T.1**	14
	XM691-XM698, XM704-XM709 initial T.1 production.	
XM714-XM794	**Handley Page HP.80 Victor B.2**	5(30)
	XM714-XM718 built of which XM715, XM716, XM718 were converted to B.2(SR) and XM715, XM717 to K.2. XM719-XM721, XM745-XM756, XM785-XM794 were cancelled.	
XM797 & XM819	**Edgar Percival EP.9**	2
	For Army Air Corps evaluation. Became G-ARTU and G-ARTV.	
XM823 & XM829	**DH.106 Comet 1XB**	2
	Ex-F-BGNZ, F-BGNY for RAE and A & AEE, became G-APAS and 'AOJU.	
XM832-XM931	**Westland WS-58 Wessex HAS.1**	40
	XM832-XM845, XM868-XM874, XM915-XM931 of which XM833, XM834, XM836-XM838, XM844, XM870-XM872, XM916, XM918-XM920, XM923, XM927 were converted to HAS.3 and XM875 converted for ASR. All for the Royal Navy.	
XM936	**English Electric Canberra B(I).8**	1
	Replacement aircraft. To Peru in 1975.	
XM939-XM963	**Scottish Aviation Twin Pioneer CC.1**	12
	XM939-XM943, XM957-XM963.	
XM966-XN112	**English Electric (later BAC) Lightning T.4**	20(30)
	XM966-XM974, XM987-XM997 of which XM966, XM967 were converted to T.5 and XM989, XM992 to R Saudi AF. XN103-XN112 cancelled.	
XN117	**Hunting (later BAC) Jet Provost T.3**	1
	Ex-G-23-1 for ground attack trials in Aden. Prototype T.3 ex-T.2.	
XN122	**Folland Gnat**	1
	Fighter version for tropical trials in Aden. To Indian AF as IE1064.	
XN126-XN127	**Westland WS-55 Whirlwind HCC.8**	2
	Built for the Queen's Flight, later both converted to HAR.10.	
XN132-XN133	**Sud SE.3130 Alouette II**	2
	Ex-F-WIPG, 'WIPH for Army Air Corps trials, 1958.	
XN137	**Hunting (later BAC) Jet Provost T.3**	1
	Replacement aircraft.	
XN142	**DHC-2 Beaver Srs.2**	(1)
	G-ANAR previously temporarily XH463 for further trials.	
XN146-XN189	**Slingsby T.21B Sedbergh TX.1**	19
	XN146-XN157, XN183-XN189 mainly for ATC.	
XN194-XN253	**Slingsby T.31B Cadet TX.3**	24
	XN194-XN199, XN236-XN253 mainly for ATC.	
XN258-XN314	**Westland WS-55 Whirlwind HAS.7**	25
	XN258-XN264, XN297-XN314 of which XN258, XN298, XN306, XN309-XN311 were converted to HAR.9. All for Royal Navy.	
XN318-XN321	**Scottish Aviation Twin Pioneer CC.2**	4
	For Far East service.	
XN326	**Folland Gnat F.1**	1
	For MoS evaluation, sold to Finland.	
XN332-XN334	**Saro P.531**	3
	Evaluation batch for Royal Navy. XN332 ex-G-APNV.	

XN339-XN355	**Saro Skeeter AOP.12**	17
	For Army Air Corps, final Skeeter production. XN344 to Science Museum.	
XN357-XN387	**Westland WS-55 Whirlwind HAS.7**	15
	XN357-XN362, XN379-XN387 of which XN359, XN384, XN386, XN387 were converted to HAR.9. All to RN.	
XN392-XN404	**Bristol 175 Britannia C.2 (Srs 253)**	3
	XN392, XN398, XN404 *Accrux, Altair, Canopus* ex-G-APPE to 'APPG.	
XN407-XN443	**Auster AOP.9**	15
	XN407-XN412, XN435-XN443 for Army Air Corps.	
XN448-XN450	**Bristol 171 Sycamore HR.51**	3
	All to Royal Australian Navy.	
XN453	**DH.106 Comet 2E**	1
	G-AMXD converted as flying laboratory.	
XN458-XN643	**Hunting (later BAC) Jet Provost T.3**	100
	XN458-XN473, XN492-XN512, XN547-XN559, XN573-XN607, XN629-XN643 of which XN459, XN461, XN462, XN466, XN470-XN473, XN494, XN495, XN497-XN499, XN500-XN502, XN505, XN506, XN508-XN510, XN547, XN548, XN551-XN553, XN574, XN577, XN579, XN581, XN582, XN584-XN586, XN589, XN590, XN593, XN595, XN598, XN605, XN606, XN629, XN634, XN636, XN640, XN641, XN643 were converted to T.3A.	
XN635	**Bristol 171 Sycamore 4**	(1)
	Ex-G-AMWI to HR.51 standard for RAN; XN635 in error and renumbered XR592.	
XN647-XN710	**DH.110 Sea Vixen FAW.1**	40
	XN647-XN658, XN683-XN710 of which all but XN648, XN695, XN698, XN701, XN703, XN704, XN708, XN709 were converted to FAW.2 and XN657 to D.3. For Royal Navy.	
XN714 & XN719	**Hunting H.126**	1(2)
	Jet flap research aircraft to Spec ER189. XN714 first flew 26.3.63; XN719 cancelled.	
XN723-XN803	**English Electric (later BAC) Lightning F.2**	44(50)
	XN723-XN735, XN767-XN797 built of which all but XN723, XN729, XN767-XN770, XN779, XN785, XN794, XN796, XN797 were converted to F.2A. XN729, XN767, XN770, XN796, XN797 to R Saudi AF. 32 to instructional airframes. XN798-XN803 cancelled.	
XN808-XN809	**Government Aircraft Factory (Australia) Jindivik**	2
	Allocation to cover A92-105, A92-106 delivered to Llanbedr.	
XN814-XN858	**Armstrong Whitworth AW.660 Argosy C.1**	20
	XN814-XN821, XN847-XN858 of which XN814, XN816, XN855 were converted to E.1.	
XN862-XN917	**Northrop KD2R-5 Shelduck D.1**	40
	XN862-XN876, XN893-XN917 targets for Royal Navy.	
XN922-XN983	**Blackburn (later Hawker Siddeley) Buccaneer S.1/S.2**	50
	XN922-XN935, XN948-XN973 S.1; XN974-XN983 S.2 for Royal Navy of which XN974, XN982 were converted to S.2A and XN976-XN978, XN981, XN983 to S.2B and there were conversions to S.2C/S.2D for RAF.	
XP103-XP160	**Westland WS-58 Wessex HAS.1**	40
	XP103-XP118, XP137-XP160 for Royal Navy of which XP103-XP105, XP110, XP116, XP118, XP137-XP140, XP142, XP143, XP147, XP150, XP153, XP156 were converted to HAS.3.	
XP165-XP193	**Westland Scout AH.1**	8(9)
	XP165-XP167, XP188-XP193 for Army Air Corps. XP166 ex-G-APVL was non-standard. XP193 cancelled.	
XP197-XP229	**Fairey Gannet AEW.3**	9
	C/n F.9463-F.9471. XP197-XP199, XP224-XP229 for Royal Navy.	
XP232-XP286	**Auster AOP.9**	33
	XP232-XP254, XP277-XP286 for Army Air Corps. XP255 became prototype Beagle-Auster AOP.11 G-ASCC.	
XP289-XP290	**English Electric Canberra T.13**	2
	To RNZAF.	
XP293-XP296	**Scottish Aviation Twin Pioneer CC.2**	3(4)
	XP296 cancelled.	
XP299-XP405	**Westland WS-55 Whirlwind HAR.10**	52
	XP299-XP303, XP327-XP333, XP338-XP363, XP392-XP405. Twenty-two became instructional airframes.	
XP408-XP450	**Armstrong Whitworth AW.660 Argosy C.1**	20
	XP408-XP413, XP437-XP450 of which XP413, XP439, XP448, XP449 converted to E.1; XP411, XP447 were being converted to T.2 when programme was abandoned.	

XP454-XP495	**Slingsby T.38 Grasshopper TX.1** XP454-XP464, XP487-XP495 for ATC.	20
XP500-XP542	**Folland Gnat T.1** XP500-XP516, XP530-XP542. Seventeen became instructional airframes.	30
XP547-XP688	**BAC Jet Provost T.4** XP547-XP589, XP614-XP642, XP661-XP688.	100
XP693-XP765	**BAC Lightning F.3** XP693-XP708, XP735-XP765 of which XP693, XP697 were converted to F.6.	47
XP769-XP827	**DHC-2 Beaver AL.1** XP769-XP780, XP804-XP827 for Army Air Corps.	36
XP831 & XP836	**Hawker P.1127** Prototypes. XP831 first flew tethered 21.10.60, free 19.11.60; became 8406M.	2
XP841	**Handley Page HP.115** Delta-wing experimental to E R197D. First flew 17.8.61.	1
XP846-XP910	**Westland Scout AH.1** XP846-XP857, XP883-XP910 for Army Air Corps.	40
XP915	**DH.106 Comet 3B** Ex-G-ANLO for research.	1
XP918-XP959	**DH.110 Sea Vixen FAW.1/FAW.2** XP918 FAW.1 converted to FAW.2; XP919-XP925, XP953-XP959 built as FAW.2. XP924 converted to D.3.	15
XP966-XP967	**Sud SE.3130 Alouette II** For Army Air Corps evaluation.	2
XP972-XP984	**Hawker P.1127** Development aircraft XP972, XP976, XP980, XP984.	4
XR105-XR143	**Armstrong Whitworth AW.660 Argosy C.1** XR105-XR109, XR133-XR143 of which XR137, XR140, XR143 were converted to E.1 and XR136 to T.2.	16
XR148-XR209	**Northrop KD2R-5 Shelduck D.1** XR148-XR162, XR185-XR209 aerial targets for the RN.	40
XR213-XR216	**DHC-2 Beaver AL.1** For Muscat & Oman AF.	4
XR219-XR227	**TSR-2** Prototype and development aircraft. XR219 first flew 27.9.64; XR220 not flown, became 7933M now at Cosford; XR221 scrapped; XR222 held now at Duxford; XR223-XR227 not completed.	4(9)
XR232	**Sud SE.3130 Alouette AH.2** Ex-F-WEIP purchased.	1
XR236-XR271	**Auster AOP.9** XR236-XR246, XR267-XR271 for Army Air Corps.	16
XR290-XR351	**Beech SD-1 Peeping Tom** Drones for Army. XR290-XR314, XR333-XR351.	44
XR352-XR354	**Northrop KD2R-5 Shelduck D.1** Drones for Royal Navy.	3
XR362-XR371	**Short Belfast C.1** Named in RAF: *Samson, Goliath, Pallus, Hector, Atlas, Heracles, Theseus, Spartacus, Ajax, Enceladus.* Sold to civil operators.	10
XR376-XR387	**Sud SE.3130 Alouette AH.2** For Army Air Corps. Some prefixed in XJ series in error.	12
XR391	**DH.114 Heron C.4** For the Queen's Flight.	1
XR395-XR399	**DH.106 Comet C.4** Built at Chester, all to 216 Squadron. Became G-BDIT to G-BDIX.	5
XR404-XR428	**Northrop KD2R-5 Shelduck D.1** For Army.	25
XR431-XR433	**Fairey Gannet AEW.3** C/n F.9514-F.9516 built at Hayes for Royal Navy.	3
XR436	**Westland P.531 Scout AH.1** Built by Saro. Used by Empire Test Pilots School.	1
XR441-XR445	**DH.114 Sea Heron C.20** Ex-G-AORG, 'AORH, VR-NAQ, 'NCE, 'NCF for R.Navy.	5
XR447-XR450	**Northrop KD2R-5 Shelduck D.1** For Royal Navy.	4
XR453-XR487	**Westland WS-55 Whirlwind HAR.10/HCC.12** XR453-XR458, XR477-XR485 HAR.10; XR486, XR487 HCC.12 for the Queen's Flight.	17
XR493	**Westland P.531** Ex-G-APVM Scout prototype, became 8040M.	1
XR497-XR529	**Westland WS-58 Wessex HC.2** XR497-XR511, XR515-XR529. XR497, XR501, XR504, XR507, XR518, XR520 modified for SAR.	30
XR534-XR574	**Folland Gnat T.1** XR534-XR545, XR567-XR574.	20
XR588	**Westland WS-58 Wessex HC.2**	1

	Prototype. Modified later for SAR.	
XR592	**Bristol 171 Sycamore HR.51** Ex-G-AMWI Mk.4 converted to HR.51 for RAN. Previously XN635.	1
XR595-XR640	**Westland Scout AH.1** XR595-XR604, XR627-XR640. Built as Hayes. C/ns F.9517-F.9540. For Army Air Corps.	24
XR643-XR707	**BAC Jet Provost T.4** XR643-XR681, XR697-XR707.	50
XR711-XR773	**BAC Lightning F.3/F.3A/F.6** XR711-XR722 F.3; XR723-XR728, XR747 built as F.3 and converted to F.6; XR748-XR751 F.3; XR752-XR773 built as F.3A and converted to F.6.	45
XR801-XR802	**Vickers V.744/V.745 Viscount** Ex-G-APKK, 'ARUU for Empire Test Pilots School.	2
XR806-XR810	**Vickers (later BAC) 1106 VC-10 C.1** Named: *George Thompson VC, Donald Garland VC & Thomas Gray VC, Kenneth Campbell VC, Hugh Malcolm VC, David Lord VC.*	5
XR814	**Britten-Norman Cushioncraft CC.2** For evaluation.	1
XR818-XR938	**Northrop Shelduck D.1** XR818-XR842, XR861-XR890, XR894-XR898, XR916-XR923, XR927-XR938 for joint Service use.	80
XR942-XR944	**Beagle-Wallis Wa.116** Gyrocopters G-ARZA to 'ARZC for evaluation.	3
XR948-XS111	**Folland Gnat T.1** XR948-XR955, XR976-XR987, XR991-XR999, XS100-XS111. Twenty became instructional airframes.	41
XS115-XS154	**Westland WS-58 Wessex HAS.1** XS115-XS128, XS149-XS154 of which XS119, XS121, XS122, XS126, XS127, XS149, XS153 were converted to HAS.3. All for Royal Navy.	20
XS159-XS172	**Hiller HT2.1 (UH-12E)** Training helicopters for Royal Navy.	14
XS175-XS231	**BAC Jet Provost T.4** XS175-XS186, XS209-XS231. XS231 prototype T.5, XS230 later converted to T.5.	35
XS235	**DH.106 Comet 4C** Built at Chester. Used for navigational systems trials. Named *Canopus.*	1
XS238	**Beagle Auster AOP.9** Replacement for XP254.	1
XS241	**Westland WS-58 Wessex HU.5** Prototype for Royal Navy.	1
XS246-XS346	**Northrop KD2R-5 Shelduck D.1** XS246-XS257, XS273-XS290, XS294-XS311, XS335-XS346 for joint Service use.	60
XS349	**Hughes 269A** G-ASBL for evaluation, became XS684.	1
XS352-XS408	**Northrop KD2R-5 Shelduck D.1** XS352-XS381, XS398-XS408 for joint Service use.	41
XS412	**Westland WS-55 Whirlwind HAR.10** Replacement for XP392.	1
XS416-XS460	**BAC Lightning T.5** XS416-XS423, XS449-XS460. XS460 exported as T.55.	20
XS463 & XS476	**Westland Wasp HAS.1** Built at Hayes. C/n F.9541, F.9542.	2
XS479-XS523	**Westland WS-58 Wessex HU.5** XS479-XS500, XS506-XS523 for Royal Navy. XS498, XS518 transferred to RAF in 1985 as HU.5Cs.	40
XS527-XS572	**Westland Wasp HAS.1** XS527-XS545, XS562-XS572 for RN. XS528, XS532, XS536, XS543 to RNZN; XS530, XS542, XS564 to Brazil.	30
XS574	**Northrop KD2R-5 Shelduck D.1** Mock-up - unofficial allocation.	1
XS576-XS590	**DH.110 Sea Vixen FAW.2** Final Sea Vixen production for Royal Navy. XS577, XS587 converted to D.3.	15
XS594-XS647	**Avro (later Hawker Siddeley) 780 Andover C.1** XS594-XS613, XS637-XS647 of which XS603, XS605, XS610, XS639-XS641 were converted to E.3/E.3A. XS599, XS600, XS602, XS604, XS608, XS611-XS613, XS638, XS645 to RNZAF as NZ7620-NZ7629.	31
XS650-XS652	**Slingsby T.45 Swallow TX.1** For ATC.	3
XS655	**Westland SRN-3** Hovercraft for evaluation.	1
XS660-XS670	**BAC TSR-2** None completed.	(11)

XS674-XS679	**Westland WS-58 Wessex HC.2**	6
	XS675 modified for SAR.	
XS681-XS683	**Brantly B.2**	3
	XS681 B.2A ex-G-ASHK; XS682 B.2A; XS683 B.2B ex-G-ASHJ for evaluation by Army Air Corps.	
XS684-XS685	**Hughes 269A**	1(2)
	Ex-G-ASBL, 'ASBD for evaluation (see XS349).	
XS688-XS696	**Hawker Kestrel FGA.1**	9
	For tripartite (British, Federal German, US) trials. XS688-XS694 allotted US serials 64-18262 to 18268.	
XS700-XS706	**Hiller HT.2**	7
	Training helicopters for Royal Navy.	
XS709-XS739	**DH.125 Dominie T.1**	20
	XS709-XS714, XS726-XS739.	
XS742-XS784	**Beagle B.206 Basset CC.1**	22
	XS742, XS743 B.206Z1/Z2 for evaluation. XS765-XS784 CC.1. XS770 temporarily used by Queen's Flight.	
XS789-XS794	**Hawker Siddeley 748 Andover CC.2**	6
	XS789, XS790 to VIP standard for the Queen's Flight.	
XS798	**Vickers VA-1**	1
	Hovercraft G-15-252 for evaluation.	
XS802-XS852	**Westland Wasp HAS.1**	(30)
	XS802-XS812, XS834-XS852 cancelled.	
XS856	**Vickers VA-3**	1
	Hovercraft G-15-253 for evaluation.	
XS859	**Slingsby T.45 Swallow**	1
	Presented to ATC, ex-BGA1136.	
XS862-XS889	**Westland WS-58 Wessex HAS.1**	28
	For Royal Navy. XS862 converted to HAS.3. Seventeen became instructional airframes.	
XS893-XS938	**BAC Lightning F.6**	33
	XS893-XS904, XS918-XS938.	
XS941	**Miles M.100 Student 2**	1
	G-APLK for evaluation.	
XS944-XS995	**BAC TSR.2**	(30)
	XS944-XS954, XS977-XS995. Cancelled.	
XT101-XT150	**Agusta-Bell 47G-3B Sioux AH.1**	50
	Italian-built for Army Air Corps.	
XT151-XT250	**Westland-Bell 47G-3 Sioux AH.1**	100
	Built by Westland for Army Air Corps.	
XT255-XT257	**Westland WS-58 Wessex HAS.3**	3
	For Royal Navy.	
XT261-XT266	**Hawker Siddeley HS.681**	(6)
	Cancelled.	
XT269-XT288	**Hawker Siddeley Buccaneer S.2A/S.2C**	20
	For Royal Navy. Transfers to RAF and modifications to S.2B/S.2D.	
XT293-XT410	**Northrop KD2R-5 Shelduck D.1**	85
	XT293-XT323, XT357-XT410.	
XT414-XT443	**Westland Wasp HAS.1**	30
	For Royal Navy. XT417, XT428, XT435 to RNZN. XT419, XT433 to Brazilian Navy.	
XT448-XT487	**Westland WS-58 Wessex HU.5**	40
	For Royal Navy. XT452, XT478 given to Bangladesh. XT463, XT479 transferred to RAF as HU.5Cs.	
XT492-XT493	**Westland SRN-5 Warden**	2
	XT493 converted to SRN-6 Winchester.	
XT498-XT570	**Bell 47G-3 Sioux AH.1**	50
	XT498-XT516, XT540-XT570 built by Westland.	
XT575	**Vickers V.837 Viscount**	1
	Ex-OE-LAG for the RRE.	
XT580-XT589	**Northrop KD2R-5 Shelduck D.1**	10
XT595-XT598	**McDonnell-Douglas Phantom FG.1**	4
	Pre-production F-4K for Royal Navy.	
XT601-XT607	**Westland WS-58 Wessex HC.2**	7
	XT601, XT602, XT604 modified for SAR.	
XT610	**Scottish Aviation Twin Pioneer Srs.3**	1
	Ex-G-APRS. Acquired for Empire Test Pilots School.	
XT614-XT649	**Westland Scout AH.1**	36
	For Army Air Corps.	
XT653	**Slingsby T.45 Swallow TX.1**	1
	Glider presented to the ATC.	
XT657	**Westland SRN-6 Winchester**	1
	Hovercraft for trials.	
XT661	**Vickers V.838 Viscount**	1
	Ex-9G-AAV for the RRE.	
XT667-XT681	**Westland WS-58 Wessex HC.2**	15
	XT670, XT674, XT680 modified for SAR.	
XT685-XT747	**Northrop KD2R-5 Shelduck D.1**	50
	XT685-XT703, XT717-XT747 for Royal Navy.	

XT752	**Fairey Gannet T.5**	(1)
	C/n F.9137 ex-G-APYO, Indonesian AS.14 and WN365.	
XT755-XT774	**Westland Wessex HU.5**	20
	For Royal Navy.	
XT778-XT795	**Westland Wasp HAS.1**	18
	For RN. XT781, XT787 to RNZN. XT792 to Brazil.	
XT798-XT849	**Westland-Bell 47G-3 Sioux AH.1**	49
	XT798-XT820, XT824-XT849 built by Westland.	
XT852-XT928	**MDD Phantom FG.1/FGR.2 (F-4K/F-4M)**	46(60)
	XT852, XT853 FGR.2 (YF-4M); XT857-XT876 FG.1 for RN; XT891-XT914 FGR.2; XT915-XT928 cancelled.	
XT931-XT985	**Northrop KD2R-5 Shelduck D.1**	50
	XT931-XT947, XT953-XT985 for Royal Navy.	
XV101-XV114	**Vickers (later BAC) 1106 VC-10 C.1**	9(14)
	Named: *Lanoe Hawker VC, Guy Gibson VC, Edward Mannock VC, James McCudden VC, Albert Ball VC, Thomas Mottershead VC, James Nicolson VC, William Rhodes-Moorhouse VC, Arthur Scarf VC.* XV110-XV114 cancelled.	
XV118-XV141	**Westland Scout AH.1**	24
	For Army Air Corps.	
XV144	**DH.106 Comet 2E**	1
	Ex-G-AMXK for Blind Landing Experimental Unit.	
XV147-XV148	**Hawker Siddeley HS.801 Nimrod**	2
	Prototypes. Ex-Comet airframes.	
XV152-XV168	**Hawker Siddeley Buccaneer S.2**	17
	Conversions: S.2A to S.2D and transfers from Royal Navy to the RAF.	
XV172	**Britten-Norman Cushioncraft CC.2**	1
	For trials.	
XV176-XV223	**Lockheed Hercules C.1 (C-130K)**	48
	Conversions: XV192, XV201, XV203, XV213 to C.1K; XV179, XV185, XV187, XV191, XV195, XV196, XV200, XV205, XV206, XV210, XV211, XV218 to C.1P; XV208 to W.2; XV176, XV177, XV183, XV184, XV188-XV190, XV197, XV199, XV202, XV204, XV207, XV212, XV214, XV217, XV219-XV221, XV223 to C.3. XV214 first C.3P conversion.	
XV226-XV263	**Hawker Siddeley (later BAe) Nimrod MR.1**	38
	Conversions: XV227-XV232, XV234-XV243, XV247, XV248, XV250-XV257, XV260 to MR.2 and XV259, XV261-XV263 to AEW.3.	
XV268-XV273	**DHC-2 Beaver AL.1**	6
	For Army Air Corps.	
XV276-XV281	**Hawker Siddeley Harrier GR.1**	6
	Pre-production aircraft.	
XV285	**Britten-Norman Cushioncraft CC.2**	1
	For evaluation.	
XV290-XV307	**Lockheed Hercules C.1 (C-130K)**	18
	Conversions: XV296 to C.1K; XV291, XV292, XV298, XV300 to C.1P; XV290, XV294, XV299, XV301-XV303, XV305, XV307 to C.3.	
XV310-XV324	**Westland-Bell 47G-3 Sioux HT.2**	15
	Built by Westland for CFS, some later to Army Air Corps.	
XV328-XV329	**BAC Lightning T.5**	2
	Replacements.	
XV332-XV361	**Hawker Siddeley Buccaneer S.2**	30
	Modifications to S.2A-S.2D; transfers from RN to RAF.	
XV336	**Vickers VA-3 Hovercraft**	(1)
	Ex-G-15-253. C/n 001.	
XV370-XV373	**Sikorsky Sea King HAS.1**	4
	XV370 S-61 SH-3D ex-G-ATYU. XV371-XV373 to WS-61 HAS.1 standard by Westland.	
XV377	**British Hovercraft Corporation SRN-5**	(1)
	Cancelled.	
XV378-XV389	**Northrop KD2R-5 Shelduck D.1**	(12)
	Cancelled.	
XV393-XV610	**McDonnell-Douglas Phantom FG.1/FGR.2**	120(159)
	XV393-XV442, XV460-XV501 (92) FGR.2; XV520-XV551 cancelled; XV565-XV592 FG.1; XV604-XV610 cancelled.	
XV614-XV617	**British Hovercraft Corporation SRN-6 Winchester**	4
	For Joint Service trials.	
XV622-XV639	**Westland Wasp HAS.1**	18
	Built at Hayes. C/ns F.9717-F.9734. XV622 to RNZN. XV633 to Brazilian Navy.	
XV642-XV714	**Westland WS-61 Sea King HAS.1**	56
	XV642-XV677, XV695-XV714 for Royal Navy. Conversions to HAS.2A and AEW.2. XV643, XV647, XV648, XV651-XV655, XV658, XV660, XV661,	

Serial	Description	Qty
	XV663, XV665, XV666, XV668, XV670, XV673, XV675-XV677, XV696, XV699, XV701, XV703, XV706, XV709, XV711-XV713 converted to HAS.5.	
XV719-XV733	Westland WS-58 Wessex HC.2/HCC.4	15
	XV719-XV731 HC.2; XV732, XV733 HCC.4 for the Queen's Flight. XV720, XV724, XV729, XV730 modified for SAR.	
XV738-XV810	Hawker Siddeley Harrier GR.1	60
	XV738-XV762, XV776-XV810 of which majority were converted to GR.1A and then all but XV739, XV743, XV749, XV777, XV780, XV794, XV796, XV798, XV799, XV802, XV803 to GR.3	
XV814	DH.106 Comet 4	1
	Ex-G-APDF for RAE.	
XV818-XV837	Northrop KD2R-5 Shelduck D.1	20
	For Royal Navy.	
XV841-XV855	Boeing Vertol CH-47B Chinook	(15)
	Order cancelled.	
XV859	Westland SRN-6 Winchester	1
	Hovercraft for Royal Navy.	
XV863-XV881	Hawker Siddeley Buccaneer S.2	7(19)
	XV863-XV869 built as S.2B for Royal Navy. Most later converted to S.2D. XV870-XV881 cancelled.	
XV884-XV947	General Dynamics TF/F-111K	(50)
	Cancelled. XV884-XV887 TF-111K; XV902-XV947 F-111K.	
XV951-XV990	Slingsby T.53B Regal TX.1	1(40)
	XV951 only built; XV952-XV990 cancelled.	
XW101-XW170	Northrop KD2R-5 Shelduck D.1	60
	XW101-XW150, XW161-XW170 target drones for the Royal Navy.	
XW174-XW175	Hawker Siddeley Harrier T.2	2
	Prototypes.	
XW179-XW195	Westland-Bell 47G-3 Sioux AH.1	17
	Built by Westland for Army Air Corps. XW179 to the Royal Navy.	
XW198-XW237	Sud SA.330E Puma HC.1	40
	Built by Westland.	
XW241	Sud SA.330E	1
	F-ZJUX for evaluation.	
XW246	British Hovercraft SRN-5 Warden	1
	For evaluation.	
XW249	Cushioncraft CC-7	1
	For evaluation.	
XW255	British Hovercraft BH-7 Wellington	1
	For trials.	
XW260	Hovermarine HM2	1
	For evaluation.	
XW264-XW272	Hawker Siddeley Harrier T.2	9
	Majority converted to T.2A and all except XW264 to T.4.	
XW276	Aerospatiale SA.341	1
	French prototype 03 for trials.	
XW280-XW284	Westland Scout AH.1	5
	For Army Air Corps.	
XW287-XW438	BAC Jet Provost T.5	110
	XW287-XW336, XW351-XW375, XW404-XW438 of which XW288-XW290, XW292, XW294, XW295, XW299, XW301, XW303, XW305, XW308, XW310, XW312-XW323, XW325-XW330, XW332-XW336, XW351, XW353-XW355, XW357-XW375, XW404-XW438 have been converted to T.5A.	
XW444-XW516	Northrop Shelduck D.1	60
	XW444-XW478, XW492-XW516 target drone for the Royal Navy.	
XW525-XW550	Hawker Siddeley Buccaneer S.2B	26
XW555	Hovermarine HM.2	1
	Hovercraft for trials.	
XW560-XW566	SEPECAT Jaguar	3
	British-built prototypes. XW560 S06, XW563 S07, XW566 2-seat B08.	
XW571-XW603	Northrop Shelduck D.1	20
	XW571-XW580, XW594-XW603 for joint Army/Navy use.	
XW608	Hovermarine Hovercat 3	1
	For trials.	
XW612-XW616	Westland Scout AH.1	5
	For Army Air Corps.	
XW620-XW622	Hovermarine Development HD.1/HD.2/HU.4	3
	Hovercraft for evaluation.	
XW626	DH.106 Comet 4c	1
	Ex-G-APDS. Acquired as radar testbed.	
XW630	Hawker Siddeley Harrier GR.1	1
	Replacement aircraft converted to GR.1A and GR.3.	
XW635	Beagle D.5/180 Husky	1
	Ex-G-AWSW presented to ATC.	
XW640	Schleicher Ka.6CR Rhonsegler	1
	BGA1348 used by Empire Test Pilots School.	
XW644-XW655	Hawker Siddeley Harrier Mk.50 (AV-8A)	12
	All delivered to USMC.	
XW660	Hover-Air HA.5 Hoverhawk III	1
	Light hovercraft for RAE.	
XW664-XW666	Hawker Siddeley Nimrod R.1	3
XW670-XW745	Northrop Shelduck D.1	60
	XW670-XW707, XW724-XW745 target drones for RN.	
XW750	Hawker Siddeley 748 Srs.107	1
	G-ASJT for the RAE.	
XW754-XW780	Hawker Siddeley Harrier GR.1/T.2	8(20)
	XW754-XW762 GR.1 re-numbered XW916-XW924, XW763-XW770 GR.1 converted to GR.1A and GR.3, XW778-XW780 re-numbered XW925-XW927.	
XW784	Mitchell-Procter Kittiwake Mk.1	1
	Glider tug built by Royal Navy apprentices at Arboath, became G-BBRN.	
XW788-XW791	Hawker Siddeley 125 CC.1	4
	Built at Chester.	
XW795-XW801	Westland Scout AH.1	5(7)
	XW795-XW799 built at Hayes, c/ns F.9758-F.9762. XW800, XW801 cancelled.	
XW803-XW832	Northrop Shelduck D.1	30
	Target drones for Royal Navy.	
XW835-XW839	Westland WG.13 Lynx	5
	Prototypes. Colour coded: yellow, grey, red, turquoise, orange. XW835 first flew 21.3.71.	
XW842-XW913	Westland Gazelle AH.1/HT.2/HT.3	60
	Mks.1-3 for Army, RN, RAF. XW842-XW844 AH.1; XW845 HT.2; XW846-XW851 AH.1; XW852 HT.3; XW853, XW854 HT.2; XW855 planned as HCC.4 but reverted to HT.3; XW856, XW857 HT.2; XW858 HT.3; XW859-XW861 HT.2; XW862 HT.3; XW863, XW864 HT.2; XW865 AH.1; XW866 HT.3; XW867, XW868 HT.2; XW869 AH.1; XW870 HT.3; XW871, XW884 HT.2; XW885 AH.1; XW886, XW887 HT.2; XW888, XW889 AH.1; XW890, XW891 HT.2; XW892, XW893 AH.1; XW894, XW895 HT.2; XW896, XW897 AH.1; XW898 HT.3; XW899-XW901 AH.1; XW902 HT.2; XW903-XW905 AH.1; XW906 HT.3; XW907 HT.2; XW908, XW909 AH.1; XW910 HT.3; XW911-XW913 AH.1.	
XW916-XW927	Hawker Siddeley Harrier GR.1/T.2	12
	XW916-XW924 (ex-XW754-XW762) GR.1 of which all but XW918 were converted to GR.1A and XW916, XW917, XW919, XW921-XW924 were converted to GR.3, XW925-XW927 (ex-XW778-XW780) T.2 converted to T.4.	
XW930	Hawker Siddeley 125 Srs.1B	1
	G-ATPC for test work.	
XW933-XW934	Hawker Siddeley Harrier T.4	2
XW938	Piper PA-30 Twin Comanche	1
	G-ATMT acquired for College of Aeronautics use.	
XW941-XW980	Northrop Shelduck D.1	40
	Target drones for Royal Navy.	
XW983	Slingsby T.61A Venture T.1	1
	Ex-G-AYUP built by Slingsby for evaluation by ATC.	
XW986-XW989	Hawker Siddeley Buccaneer S.2B	3(4)
	XW986-XW988 for RAE, XW989 cancelled.	
XW990-XW999	Northrop Chukar D.1	10
	For Royal Navy.	
XX101-XX102	British Hovercraft CC-7 Cushioncraft	2
	For Army evaluation.	
XX105	BAC One Eleven Srs.201	1
	Ex-G-ASJD for RAE.	
XX108-XX150	SEPECAT Jaguar GR.1/T.2	30
	XX108-XX122 GR.1, XX136-XX150 T.2.	
XX153	Westland Lynx AH.1	1
	First example for Army Air Corps.	
XX154-XX353	Hawker Siddeley Hawk T.1	176
	XX154, XX156-XX205, XX217-XX266, XX278-XX327, XX329-XX353. Current conversions to T.1A.	
XX367	Bristol 175 Britannia Srs.312F	1
	Ex-EC-BSY for the A & AEE.	
XX370-XX462	Westland Gazelle AH.1/HT.2/HT.3	82
	Mks.1-3 for Army, RN, RAF. XX370-XX373 AH.1; XX374 HT.3; XX375-XX381 AH.1; XX382 HT.3;	

	XX383-XX390 AH.1; XX391 HT.2; XX392-XX395 AH.1; XX396 HT.3; XX397 HT.2; XX398-XX405 AH.1; XX406 HT.3; XX407-XX409 AH.1; XX410 HT.2; XX411-XX414 AH.1; XX415 HT.2; XX416-XX419 AH.1; XX431 HT.2; XX432-XX435 AH.1; XX436 HT.2; XX437-XX440 AH.1; XX441 HT.2; XX442-XX445 AH.1; XX446 HT.2; XX447-XX450 AH.1; XX451 HT.2; XX452-XX462 AH.1.	
XX466-XX467	Hawker Hunter T.1	2
	Ex-Royal Jordanian AF 835, 836.	
XX469	Westland Lynx HAS.2	1
	Development aircraft for Royal Navy.	
XX475-XX500	Scottish Aviation Jetstream T.1/T.2	26
	First seven built for civil operators by Handley Page at Radlett. These and uncompleted airframes and five new, built up by Scottish Aviation. Conversion from T.1 to T.2 of XX475, XX476, XX478-XX481, XX483-XX490 for Royal Navy.	
XX505-XX508	Hawker Siddeley 125 CC.1/CC.2 Srs.400B/600B	4
	XX505, XX506 CC.1; XX507, XX508 CC.2 replaced XX505, XX506 on delivery.	
XX510	Westland Lynx HAS.2	1
	Second development aircraft for Royal Navy.	
XX513-XX716	Scottish Aviation Bulldog T.1	130(132)
	XX513-XX562, XX611-XX640, XX653-XX672, XX685-XX714. XX715-XX716 cancelled.	
XX719-XX847	SEPECAT Jaguar GR.1/T.2	81
	XX719-XX768, XX817-XX827 GR.1; XX828-XX847 T.2. Some aircraft loaned to India. XX765 has special control systems.	
XX850-XX879	Northrop Shelduck D.1	30
	Target drones for Royal Navy.	
XX885-XX901	Hawker Siddeley Buccaneer S.2B	17
XX904-XX911	Westland Lynx	4
	XX904, XX911 development airframes to Aerospatiale becoming F-ZKCU, F-ZKCV; XX907 to Bristol on engine development and XX910 to A & AEE for equipment trials.	
XX914	BAC VC10 Srs.1103	1
	Ex-G-ATDJ for use of RAE. Became 8777M.	
XX915-XX916	SEPECAT Jaguar T.2	2
	Built by SEPECAT, assembled by BAC for use of the Empire Test Pilots School.	
XX919	BAC One-Eleven 402AP	1
	Purchased by Mintech in 1973.	
XX923-XX941	Northrop Shelduck D.1	19
	Target drone for Royal Navy.	
XX944	DH.106 Comet 4	1
	Ex-G-APDP for RAE radio work.	
XX946-XX950	Panavia Tornado (originally known as MRCA)	4
	Prototypes XX946-XX948, XX950. XX946 first flew 30.10.74.	
XX955-XZ120	SEPECAT Jaguar GR.1	45
	XX955-XX979, XZ101-XZ120. XZ101-XZ120 originally allocated XY101-XY120 in error.	
XY101-XY120	SEPECAT Jaguar GR.1	(20)
	Allocated in error, became XZ101-XZ120.	
XY125	Hawker Siddeley AV-8A	1
	For demonstration flights of USMC 158969.	
XY128-XY147	Hawker Siddeley Harrier GR.3/T.4	(15)
	Allocated in error, became XZ128-XZ147.	
XZ128-XZ147	Hawker Siddeley Harrier GR.3/T.4	15
	XZ128-XZ139 GR.3; XZ145-XZ147 T.4. Originally allocated XY128-XY139, XY145-XY147 in error.	
XZ152-XZ164	Northrop Chukar D.1	13
	Target drone for Royal Navy.	
XZ166	Westland Lynx HAS.2	1
	Trials aircraft replacement for Royal Navy.	
XZ170-XZ278	Westland Lynx AH.1/HAS.2/HAS.2(FN)	98
	XZ170-XZ199, XZ203-XZ222 AH.1 for Army Air Corps; XZ227-XZ252, XZ254-XZ257 HAS.2 for Royal Navy; XZ260-XZ267, XZ269-XZ278 HAS.2(FN) for the Aeronavale.	
XZ280-XZ287	BAe Nimrod MR.1/MR.2/AEW.3	8
	XZ280-XZ283 MR.1 converted to AEW.3; XZ284 MR.2; XZ285 MR.1 to AEW.3; XZ286, XZ287 AEW.3.	
XZ290-XZ349	Westland Gazelle AH.1	60
	For Army Air Corps.	
XZ355-XZ400	SEPECAT Jaguar GR.1	44
	XZ355-XZ378, XZ381-XZ400.	
XZ405	Schempp-Hirth Cirrus	1
	BGA1473 for evaluation.	
XZ407	Hawker Siddeley Harrier	(1)
	Allocation for 1974 Farnborough SBAC display, but not taken up.	
XZ410-XZ425	Northrop Shelduck D.1	16
	Target drone for Royal Navy.	
XZ430-XZ432	Hawker Siddeley Buccaneer S.2B	3
	Final procurement.	
XZ438-XZ500	BAe Sea Harrier FRS.1/Harrier T.4	25
	XZ438-XZ440 FRS.1; XZ445 T.4; XZ450-XZ460, XZ491-XZ500 FRS.1.	
XZ505-XZ546	Northrop Shelduck D.1	30
	XZ505-XZ518, XZ531-XZ546 target drones for RN.	
XZ550-XZ564	Slingsby Venture T.2	15
	Powered gliders for ATC.	
XZ570-XZ599	Westland WS-61 Sea King HAS.2/HAR.3	28
	XZ570-XZ582 HAS.2 for Royal Navy, of which all but XZ573, XZ574 converted to HAS.5; XZ585-XZ599 HAR.3.	
XZ605-XZ627	Westland Lynx AH.1/HAS.2/HAS.2(FN)	21
	XZ605-XZ617 AH.1 for Army Air Corps; XZ620-XZ627 for Aeronavale as HAS.2(FN).	
XZ630-XZ631	Panavia Tornado	2
	Pre-production aircraft built by BAC (Warton).	
XZ635	Westland Sea King	1
	Simulator for Royal Navy.	
XZ640-XZ736	Westland Lynx AH.1/HAS.2	67
	XZ640-XZ655, XZ661-XZ681 AH.1 for Army Air Corps; XZ689-XZ700, XZ719-XZ736 HAS.2 for RN.	
XZ741	Westland Commando 2B	1
	Temporary marks for Egyptian aircraft on UK overhaul.	
XZ745-XZ811	Northrop Shelduck D.1	52
	XZ745-XZ774, XZ790-XZ811 target drones for RN.	
XZ815-XZ884	Short MATS-B Mk.1	50
	XZ815-XZ840, XZ861-XZ884 target drones.	
XZ900-XZ909	Beech 1095 (AQM-37B)	(10)
	Reservation for target drones.	
XZ915-XZ922	Westland Sea King HAR.3	8
	For Royal Navy. All except XZ915, XZ917, converted to HAS.5.	
XZ930-XZ942	Westland Gazelle HT.2/HT.3	13
	XZ930-XZ936 HT.3; XZ937-XZ942 HT.2 for RN.	
XZ950-XZ959	Northrop Chukar D.2	10
	Target drones for Royal Navy.	
XZ963-XZ999	BAe Harrier GR.3	24
	XZ963-XZ973, XZ987-XZ999.	
ZA101	BAe Hawk T.50	1
	Civil demonstration aircraft G-HAWK.	
ZA105	Westland Sea King HAR.3	1
ZA110-ZA111	Scottish Aviation Jetstream T.2	2
	Ex-F-BTMI and 9Q-CTC purchased for Royal Navy and modified to T.2.	
ZA117-ZA120	Hawker Siddeley 125 CC.2	(4)
	Cancelled.	
ZA126-ZA137	Westland Sea King HAS.5	12
	For Royal Navy.	
ZA140-ZA150	BAC VC10/Super VC10	9
	Civil VC10 purchased for tanker conversion. ZA140-ZA144 VC10 K.2 ex-A40-VL, 'VG, 'VI, 'VK, 'VC; ZA147-ZA150 K.3 ex-5H-MMT, 5Y-ADA, 5X-UVJ, 5H-MOG.	
ZA155-ZA164	Northrop Chukar D.2	10
	Target drones for Royal Navy.	
ZA166-ZA170	Westland Sea King HAS.5	5
	For Royal Navy.	
ZA174-ZA195	BAe Sea Harrier FRS.1	10
	ZA174-ZA177, ZA190-ZA195 for Royal Navy.	
ZA200-ZA246	Short MATS-B Mk.1A	25
	ZA200-ZA214, ZA237-ZA246 for Army.	
ZA250	BAe Harrier T.52	1
	Demonstrator G-VTOL.	
ZA254-ZA283	Panavia Tornado F.2	3
	Prototypes. ZA254 first flew 28.10.79; ZA267, ZA283.	
ZA290-ZA314	Westland Sea King HC.4	15
	ZA290-ZA299, ZA310-ZA314 for Royal Navy.	
ZA319-ZA494	Panavia Tornado GR.1	91
	ZA319-ZA330, ZA352-ZA362, ZA365-ZA376, ZA392-ZA412, ZA446-ZA475, ZA490-ZA494 of which ZA319, ZA320, ZA323-ZA326, ZA330, ZA352, ZA356-ZA358,	

ZA362, ZA365-ZA368, ZA409-ZA412 built as trainers. ZA365-ZA494 are originally thought to have been allocated in the 'ZB' series.

Serial	Type	Qty
ZA500-ZA538	**Northrop Shelduck D.1**	24
	ZA500-ZA510, ZA526-ZA538.	
ZA540-ZA614	**Panavia Tornado GR.1**	55
	ZA540-ZA564, ZA585-ZA614 GR.1 of which ZA540, ZA541, ZA544, ZA548-ZA549, ZA551, ZA552, ZA555, ZA562, ZA594, ZA595, ZA598, ZA599, ZA602, ZA604, ZA612 were built as trainers.	
ZA620	**Westland Lynx**	1
	Simulator built by Redifon.	
ZA625-ZA666	**Slingsby Venture T.2**	25
	ZA625-ZA634, ZA652-ZA666 motor gliders for use by ATC/CCF.	
ZA670-ZA721	**Boeing Vertol Chinook HC.1**	33
	ZA670-ZA684, ZA704-ZA721.	
ZA726-ZA804	**Westland Gazelle AH.1/HT.3**	29
	ZA726-ZA737, ZA765-ZA777 AH.1 for Army Air Corps; ZA801-ZA804 HT.3.	
ZA806-ZA899	**Short MATS-B Mk.1A**	50
	ZA806-ZA822, ZA837-ZA846, ZA859-ZA874, ZA893-ZA899 target drones for Army.	
ZA903-ZA929	**Northrop Chukar D.2**	15
	Target drones. ZA903-ZA912, ZA925-ZA929.	
ZA934-ZA941	**Westland Puma HC.1**	8
ZA947	**Douglas Dakota C.3**	1
	Ex-RCAF C-47A 661 on MoD charge. Was originally incorrectly serialled as KG661.	
ZB101-ZB499	not allocated.	
ZB500	**Westland Lynx**	1
	Demonstrator G-LYNX. Ex-ZA500 (flown as such).	
ZB503	**Britten-Norman BN-2A Islander**	1
	G-DIVE used for parachute training. Originally ZA503.	
ZB506-ZB507	**Westland Sea King Mk.4X**	2
	For RAE.	
ZB512-ZB516	**Northrop Chukar D.2**	5
ZB520-ZB596	**Short MATS-B Mk.1A**	50
	ZB520-ZB535, ZB548-ZB564, ZB580-ZB596 target drones for the Army.	
ZB600-ZB606	**BAe Harrier T.4/T.4A/T.4N**	7
	ZB600, ZB603 T.4 for RAF; ZB601, ZB602 T.4A for RAF; ZB604-ZB606 T.4N for Royal Navy.	
ZB609	**BAe Hawk T.52**	1
	Allocated to Kenya AF No.1001 for weapons trials in the UK.	
ZB615	**SEPECAT Jaguar T.2**	1
	For RAE.	
ZB618	**BAe Hawk T.53**	1
	Allocated to Indonesia AF LL-5301 for trials in the UK.	
ZB622	**BAe Hawk T.51**	1
	Allocated to Finnish AF HW-302 for trials in UK.	
ZB625-ZB693	**Westland Gazelle AH.1/HT.2/HT.3**	38
	Mks.1-3 to Army, RN, RAF. ZB625-ZB629 HT.3; ZB646-ZB649 HT.2; ZB665-ZB693 AH.1.	
ZB695-ZB709	**Northrop Chukar D.2**	15
	Target drones for Royal Navy.	
ZB715-ZD209	**Short Skeet**	225
	Target drones. ZB715-ZB764, ZB778-ZB827, ZB847-ZB858, ZB870-ZB886, ZB900-ZB907, ZB919-ZB926, ZD115-ZD164, ZD180-ZD209.	
ZD215	**Douglas DC-3 Dakota 4**	1
	RAAF A65-69 for Berlin Airlift Memorial Museum.	
ZD226	**BAe Hawk T.51**	1
	Allocated to Finnish AF HW-305 for trials in the UK.	
ZD230-ZD243	**BAC Super VC10 Srs 1151**	14
	Ex-G-ASGA, 'ASGB, 'ASGD-'ASGM, 'ASGP, 'ASGR.	
ZD249-ZD285	**Westland Lynx AH.1/HAS.3/AH.5**	34
	ZD249-ZD268 HAS.3 for Royal Navy; ZD272-ZD284 AH.1 for Army Air Corps; ZD285 interim Mk.1/5, prototype AH.5 on MoD(PE) charge.	
ZD290-ZD309	**Northrop Chukar D.2**	20
	Target drone for Royal Navy.	
ZD318-ZD319	**BAe Harrier GR.5**	2
	Development batch aircraft, nos DB1 and DB2.	
ZD320-	**BAe Harrier GR.5**	60
	Production aircraft.	
ZD476-ZD480	**Westland Sea King HC.4**	5
	For Royal Navy.	
ZD485-ZD487	**FMA IA.58A Pucara**	3

Serial	Type	Qty
	Ex-Argentine AF A-515, A-533, A-549 captured in the Falklands.	
ZD493	**BAC VC10 Srs.1101**	1
	Ex-G-ARVJ.	
ZD559-ZD567	**Westland Lynx 5X/HAS.3**	5
	ZD559 Lynx 5X for MoD(PE); others HAS.3 of which ZD560 for MoD(PE), ZD565-ZD567 for Royal Navy.	
ZD574-ZD576	**Boeing Vertol Chinook HC.1**	3
ZD578-ZD615	**BAe Sea Harrier FRS.1**	14
	ZD578-ZD582, ZD607-ZD615 for Royal Navy.	
ZD620-ZD621	**BAe 125 CC.3 (Srs.700B)**	2
ZD625-ZD627	**Westland Sea King HC.4**	3
	For Royal Navy.	
ZD643-ZD652	**Schleicher ASK-21 Vanguard TX.1**	10
	Sailplanes for the ATC and CCF Air Cadets. Also BGA2884, BGA2883, BGA2885-BGA2892.	
ZD657-ZD661	**Schleicher ASW-19B Valiant TX.1**	5
	Sailplanes for the ATC and CCF Air Cadets. Also BGA2893-BGA2897.	
ZD667-ZD670	**BAe Harrier GR.3**	4
ZD677-ZD6xx	**Northrop Chukar D.2**	
	Target drones.	
ZD695-ZD696	**BAe 146 Srs.100**	2
	Ex-G-OBAF, 'SCHH.	
ZD703-ZD704	**BAe 125 CC.3 (Srs.700A/700B)**	2
ZD707-ZD941	**Panavia Tornado GR.1/F.2**	71
	ZD707-ZD720, ZD738-ZD749, ZD788-ZD793, ZD808-ZD812, ZD842-ZD851, ZD890-ZD895 GR.1; ZD899-ZD906, ZD932-ZD941 F.2.	
ZD948-ZD953	**Lockheed TriStar Srs.500**	6
	Ex-G-BFCA-'BFCF. ZD948, ZD952 used by RAF unconverted (i.e. as Srs.500); to be 1st and 2nd KC.1s. ZD950, ZD953, ZD951 and ZD949 converted to K.1 (in that order).	
ZD974-ZD975	**Schempp-Hirth Kestrel TX.1**	2
	Sailplanes for the ATC and CCF Air Cadets.	
ZD980-ZD984	**Boeing Vertol Chinook HC.1**	5
ZD990-ZD993	**BAe Harrier T.4/T.4A**	4
ZD996-ZE147	**Panavia Tornado GR.1**	20
	ZD996-ZD998, ZE114-ZE126, ZE144-ZE147 for Saudi Arabia, although ZD996 reported delivered to the RAF.	
ZE154-ZE343	**Panavia Tornado F.3**	72
	ZE154-ZE168, ZE199-ZE210, ZE250-ZE258, ZE287-ZE296, ZE338-ZE343. ZE154 and every third aircraft built as trainer.	
ZE323	**Grob G.103**	1
	Evaluation aircraft. Later ordered as Viking T.1 for ATC/CCF Air Cadets.	
ZE350-ZE364	**McDonnell-Douglas Phantom F-4J(UK)**	15
	Ex-USN F-4J.	
ZE368-ZE370	**Westland Sea King HAR.3**	3
ZE375-ZE383	**Westland Lynx AH.5/AH.7**	9
	For Army Air Corps. ZE375 AH.5, remainder AH.7.	
ZE388	**Westland Lynx Mk.89**	1
	G-BKBL for missile tests.	
ZE395-ZE396	**BAe 125 CC.3**	2
ZE408	**Westland Lynx Mk.89**	1
	Ex-G-BLEM. For Nigerian Navy as 01-F89.	
ZE410-ZE413	**Agusta A.109A**	4
	ZE410, ZE411 captured Argentinian Army AE-334 and AE-331 respectively. For Army Air Corps.	
ZE418-ZE428	**Westland Sea King HC.4/HAS.5**	9
	For RN. ZE418-ZE422 HAS.5; ZE425-ZE428 HC.4.	
ZE432-ZE433	**BAC One Eleven Srs 479F**	2
	For MoD(PE).	
ZE438-ZE441	**BAe Jetstream T.3**	4
	For Royal Navy.	
ZE449	**Sud SA.330 Puma**	1
	Ex-Argentine Coast Guard PA-12.	
ZE452-ZE4xx	**Northrop Chukar**	
	Target drones.	
ZE472	**BAe Hawk T.63**	1
	For Abu Dhabi as 1014.	
ZE477	**Westland Lynx 3**	1
ZE495-ZE686	**Grob G.103 Viking TX.1**	100
	ZE495-ZE504, ZE520-ZE534, ZE550-ZE564, ZE584-ZE595, ZE600-ZE614, ZE625-ZE637, ZE650-ZE659, ZE677-ZE686. For ATC and CCF Air Cadets. Simultaneously BGA3000 to BGA3099.	

ZE690-ZE698	**BAe Sea Harrier FRS.2**	9
	For Royal Navy. May be built as FRS.1.	
ZE700-ZE701	**BAe 146 CC.2**	2
	For the Queen's Flight.	
ZE704-ZE706	**Lockheed TriStar Srs.500**	3
	Ex-Pan Am N508PA, N509PA, N503PA. ZE704, ZE705 used by RAF unconverted; ZE706 prospective 1st K.2.	
ZE728-ZE983	**Panavia Tornado F.3**	92
	ZE728-ZE737, ZE755-ZE764, ZE785-ZE794, ZE808-ZE812, ZE830-ZE839, ZE858-ZE862, ZE882-ZE891, ZE905-ZE914, ZE934-ZE943, ZE960-ZE969, ZE982, ZE983. ZE728 and every seventh aircraft built as trainer.	
ZF107-ZF108	**BAe Hawk T.64**	2
	For Kuwait Air Force as '140' and '142'.	
ZF115-ZF124	**Westland Sea King HC.4**	10
	For Royal Navy. ZF115 non-standard.	
ZF130	**BAe 125 Srs.600B**	1
	Ex-G-BLUW.	
ZF135-ZFxxx	**Shorts Tucano T.1**	130
	ZF135-ZF145 known. Total order stated as 130.	
ZF444	**Britten Norman BN-2T Islander**	1
	Ex-G-WOTG.	
ZF520-ZF522	**Piper PA-31 Navajo Chieftain**	3
	Ex-US civil N35823, N27509, N27728.	
ZF523-ZF524	**Piper PA-31 Navajo Chieftain**	(2)
	Ex-US civil. Not taken up, became G-IMBI and 'BMBC.	
ZF526-ZF527	**Westland Sea King 42B**	2
	For Indian Navy as IN513 and IN514 respectively.	
ZF534	**BAe EAP**	1
	Demonstrator.	
ZF573	**Britten Norman BN-2T Islander**	1
	Dual identity for G-SRAY for Stingray torpedo trials.	
ZF577-ZF598	**BAC Lightning F.53/T.55**	22
	Ex-Saudi Arabia. ZF577-ZF594 F.53; ZF595-ZF598 T.55.	
ZF622	**Piper PA-31 Navajo Chieftain**	1
	Ex-US civil N35487.	
ZF627	**BAe Hawk T.64**	1
	For Swiss evaluation. To Kuwait Air Force as 147.	
ZF641-ZF649	**European Helicopter Industries EH.101**	3
	ZF641, ZF644, ZF649.	
ZF687-ZF798	**Target Technology Limited BTT-3 Banshee**	76
	Target drones. ZF654-ZF663, ZF676-ZF691, ZF704-ZF720, ZF741-ZF751, ZF766-ZF779, ZF791-ZF798. Order for 75 including spare fuselage (ZF681).	
ZG200	**BAe Hawk 200**	1
	Prototype.	
ZG468	**Westland-Sikorsky WS.70 Blackhawk**	1
	Demonstrator for Paris Air Show 1987.	
ZG539-ZG599	**Target Technology Limited BTT-3 Banshee**	32
	Target drones. ZG539-ZG550, ZG580-ZG599.	
ZH200	**BAe Hawk 200**	1
	Pre-production aircraft.	

Additions

Additions

Information additional to that printed on page 203.

VJ426-VK874 Waco Hadrian (CG-4A) **144(878)**
Ex-USAAF. VJ735-VJ781, VJ821-VJ847, VK873-VK609,
VK623-VK655. Others allocated but not taken up:
VJ426-VJ459, VJ481-VJ520, VJ538-VJ559, VJ583-
VJ628, VJ650-VJ687, VJ712-VJ731, VJ850-VJ876,
VJ890-VJ908, VJ912-VJ951, VJ986-VJ999, VK127-
VK159, VK183-VK222, VK261-VK303, VK321-
VK369, VK392-VK431, VK467-VK487, VK491-
VK527, VK555-VK571, VK661-VK693, VK712-
VK747, VK777-VK783, VK786-VK829, VK841-
VK874.

APPENDIX A

How Serials Were Marked

Essentially, the serial number of an aircraft is the key to its identity and the manner of its presentation is thereby a matter of some import. The presentation of aircraft numbers on early aircraft varied greatly. As regards placing the number, the rudder surface was frequently used leading to the numbers being loosely called 'tail numbers'. In general serial numbers were displayed on the rear fuselage, fin or rudder of tractor aircraft and on the nacelle sides of pusher aircraft.

Manufacturers adopted their own style of presentation with size of digits averaging 6 to 8 inches in height, but with Bristol aircraft in particular having larger figures. The quirks of various manufacturers are not detailed here as they are represented in the illustrations.

In November 1915 the RNAS decreed that serials would be 4-inch digits and most Admiralty contractors followed this instruction, but from mid-1917 when the Ministry of Munitions took over aircraft production, there was general RFC/RNAS standardisation on an 8-inch presentation.

With the introduction of camouflage colours, mainly by PC10 doping in 1916, black hitherto invariably used for marking numbers did not show up well. Some manufacturers outlined the numbers thinly in white, while others changed to white paint. At the same time it became usual to mark the serial numbers on the rudder stripes, in addition to, or instead of, the fin or rear fuselage.

In August 1918 Modification Avro 504K/54 introduced the marking of serial numbers under the wing in black figures, 30 inches high using 4 inch strokes, to be effective throughout the RAF from 15 October 1918. The display of serial numbers under the wings in addition to lateral surfaces was extended to all RAF aircraft from 17 March 1927, in similar size to those decreed for Avro 504Ks.

The general introduction of camouflage in 1937 did not affect the regulations for serialling on lateral surfaces, but bombers with black undersurfaces had the numbers painted in white. All undersurfaces serial markings were obliterated on operational aircraft in September 1939 when war was declared, but they continued to be marked on non-operational aircraft.

In September 1940 the Royal Navy regularised Fleet Air Arm aircraft markings, reducing serial number presentation to 4 x 2½ inch characters in 5/8-inch strokes. A special suffix 'G' for 'Guard' was introduced for special prototypes or standard types with secret equipment and a 'SNAKE' suffix was brought in during May 1943 for aircraft bound for India under reinforcement plans that on no account were to be diverted en route to other commands.

Postwar undersurface serials were re-introduced for all classes of aircraft and standardised in April 1946 into three sizes as follows:—

Class of aircraft	Size (length x breadth x thickness)
Single-engined	24 x 15 x 3 inches
Twin-engined	36 x 22 x 4 inches
Multi-engined	48 x 30 x 6 inches

While fuselage serial markings remained at 8-inches for RAF aircraft, a special case was made for bombers in the late 'forties with a 24-inch presentation in 3-inch strokes. Royal Navy aircraft serials remained at 4-inch presentation on fuselage sides with undersurface serial size regulated by height of characters equalling the diameter of the roundel presentation - at least according to the official regulations. In practice there were many anomolies as illustrations show.

Broadly, this is how the situation remained until the late 'fifties/early 'sixties and the widespread re-introduction of camouflage. Some operational aircraft types such as the Canberra PR.7 force of RAF Germany adopted fuselage serials painted in white as an aid to identification by aircraft and groundcrew while underwing serials remained painted in black.

With the end of the 1960s came the need to enhance camouflage as much as possible with the adoption of NATO's 'tone down' policy. As well as camouflaging airfields and installations, aircraft markings were also toned down by re-introduction of red and blue roundels and painting serial numbers black.

Tone-down continued into the early 'seventies. One of the first tasks carried out on Buccaneers newly-delivered from Hawker Siddeley was to repaint the roundels and fuselage serials. This was because new aircraft, delivered to the letter of a production contract, had the standard of markings required at the time of contract placing some years earlier.

The next change to the marking of serial numbers had been put into effect by 1982 — whereby those aircraft carrying underwing serials began, following major overhaul etc, to carry them on only the port wing. This was a first step to reduce the considerable manpower cost of marking, masking and painting serial numbers on newly-painted aircraft. Later, with the adoption of new, overall camouflage schemes, serials were often not marked at all on aircraft undersides.

The Tornado GR.1 posed a special problem — where to apply the serials? With its variable geometry and use of underwing stores pylons the decision was made to apply Tornado's underside serials only on the lower surface of each taileron, although in the time-honoured way, the fuselage serial was painted on the side of the fuselage.

At about the same time as the Tornado GR.1 was coming into service the RAF's air defence aircraft were given an overall light grey camouflage, resulting in the re-appearance of white fuselage serials. As aircraft were repainted in the new scheme, underwing serials disappeared altogether. Although the first VC10 tanker conversion flew in dark green and dark grey camouflage with underwing serials, subsequent aircraft were delivered in hemp camouflage with underwing serials.

When Tornado F.2s came into service in 1985, painted in the standard air defence light grey camouflage, they carried serials in white at the base of the fin only, with no underside serials.

But what does the future hold? Perhaps in deference to the Tornado ADV, or perhaps as an afterthought to its 'designer' colour scheme, the British Aerospace Experimental Aircraft Project (or Programme!) ZF534 also carries its serial at the base of the fin only.

Perhaps the underwing serial has gone forever on operational aircraft.

APPENDIX B

Other Works Detailing Ranges of British Military Serial Numbers

Within a single book it would not be possible to give details of the service and fate of every aircraft and as yet no collection of books gives this fully. Published works that give ranges of serials detailing every single aircraft are as follows:

Serial Range	Publisher	Notes
K1000-K9999	Air-Britain	Every number utilised
L1000-L9999	Air-Britain	From the point black-out blocks were used.
N1000-N9999	Air-Britain	The 2nd N-series of the late 1930s.
P1000-P9999	Air-Britain	RAF aircraft only detailed.
R1000-R9999	Air-Britain	RAF aircraft only detailed.
T1000-T9999	Air-Britain	RAF aircraft only detailed.
V1000-W9999	Air-Britain	RAF aircraft only detailed.
X1000-Z9999	Air-Britain	RAF aircraft only detailed.
AA100-AZ999	Air-Britain	RAF aircraft only detailed.
BA100-BZ999	Air-Britain	RAF aircraft only detailed.
SA100-VZ999	Air-Britain	RAF aircraft only detailed.
WA100-WZ999	Air-Britain	RAF aircraft only detailed.
XA100-XA999	Aviation News	Alan W. Hall (Publications) Ltd.
XB100-XB999	Aviation News	Alan W. Hall (Publications) Ltd.
XD100-XD999	Aviation News	Alan W. Hall (Publications) Ltd.

Various books detail the service and fate of aircraft by type. Air-Britain 'File' series include the Halifax, Lancaster, Stirling, Typhoon, Washington and Whitley with the Hampden in preparation. Several of the above mentioned books are still in print at the time of going to press. Write to Midland Counties Publications (Ref BMAS), 24 The Hollow, Earl Shilton, Leicester, LE9 7NA for availability and/or price details.

APPENDIX C

Instructional Airframe Numbers

RAF Airframes

In 1921 airframes and engines used for instructional purposes on the ground were re-numbered into a simple numerical series for each, with 'M' and 'E' suffix letters respectively to denote the series. The records for the early allocations have not been traced, and little photographic record exists. It is known that a Sopwith Snipe was 16?M and Bristol Fighters were 213M and 540M.

Of all the allocations the M-suffixed series are the most inconsistent, since in many cases they were re-numbered on being transferred to new locations. In not a few cases the numbers allotted were duplicated and in others the allocation was cancelled and the aircraft restored to airworthy status with its original serial number. Also some 'M' numbers were allotted to airframes disposed of as scrap before the new number was marked, but in general the 'M' number replaced the original serial. Where the 'M' number was cancelled this has been indicated by an asterisk.

Given below are the known allocations of 'M' numbers with the serial number of the aircraft to which it was allocated and in most cases applied, or civil registrations, British Gliding Association (BGA) or USAAF number as appropriate.

M-No	Serial	M-No	Serial	M-No	Serial
510M	K3172	662M	K2298*	729M	K3063
565M	J9170	663M	K2299*	730M	K1464
572M	J9614	664M	K2300*	731M	K2553
576M	J9598	665M	K2301*	732M	K2554
586M	K1557	666M	K1230	733M	K2555
592M	J9857	667M	K1237	734M	K2556
593M	K1316	668M	K1591	735M	K1553
595M	K1437	669M	K1592	736M	K1558
596M	J9116	670M	K1593	737M	K3968
597M	K1603	671M	K1594	738M	J9565
598M	K2256	672M	K1596	739M	S1835
599M	K2437	675M	K3282	740M	K2500
600M	K1365*	678M	K1501	741M	K1547
601M	K3674	679M	K1233	742M	K1564
602M	K1735	680M	K1790	743M	K3155
603M	K1737	681M	K1792	744M	K1840
604M	K3665	682M	K1793	747M	K2504
605M	K3664	683M	K1794	748M	K3100
606M	J9936	684M	K1795	749M	K1942
607M	J9945	685M	K1796	750M	J9673
608M	K1427	689M	K1115	751M	K1749
609M	K1430	690M	K1117	752M	K1136
610M	J9942	691M	K1224	753M	K1140
611M	K1443	693M	J9073	755M	K1766
612M	K1733	694M	K1777	757M	K1213
613M	K1734	695M	K2464	770M	K3748
615M	K1338	696M	K3893	771M	K2499
616M	J9946	697M	J9822	772M	K1850
617M	K1386	698M	J9799	773M	K2985
618M	K1826	699M	K1768	774M	K5081
619M	K1405	700M	K1633	775M	K2456
621M	K2990	701M	K1627	776M	K1698
622M	K2833	703M	K2549	778M	K2195
625M	J9861	705M	K1422	780M	K2372
626M	K1955	706M	K1849	781M	K1963
639M	K3218	707M	K1878	782M	K2346
640M	K1541 or K2206	709M	K2454	783M	K2348*
641M	K1514	711M	K1756	787M	K3872*
642M	K1018	712M	K1433	789M	K3872
646M	K2774	713M	K3984	791M	K3173
649M	K3358	714M	K2476	792M	K1111
651M	K2443	715M	K2690	793M	K1568
652M	K2438	716M	K2687	796M	K1570
653M	K2468	720M	S1711	798M	K2516
654M	K2502	721M	K2527	799M	K4798
655M	K1667	722M	K1477	800M	K2034
657M	K3521	723M	K2523	802M	K1471
660M	K2246	724M	K1196	803M	K2368
661M	K2247	725M	K1528	805M	K2497
		727M	S1203	806M	K2503

M-No	Serial	M-No	Serial	M-No	Serial
807M	K1811	905M	K1606	996M	K2243
811M	K2347	906M	K1616	997M	K3766
813M	K1985	907M	K1617	998M	K2075
814M	K2348	909M	K2145	999M	K4327*
815M	K1853	910M	K3172	1000M	K3634
816M	K3899	911M	K3175	1001M	K4537
817M	K1881	912M	K3923	1002M	K1862
818M	K1472	916M	K1954	1003M	K2855
819M	K1479	917M	K1439	1004M	K1806
821M	K2381	918M	K1444	1005M	K3802
826M	K1822	919M	K5891	1006M	K2703
827M	K1731	920M	K1684	1007M	J9138
828M	K1035	921M	K2152	1008M	K2568
829M	K3185	922M	K3640	1009M	K3499
830M	K2239	924M	K2971	1010M	K2153
831M	K3192	925M	K2042	1011M	K2198
832M	K3193	926M	K3806	1012M	K2179
833M	K3190	927M	K5464	1013M	K3511
834M	K3194	928M	K1926	1014M	K3508
835M	K3195	929M	K2033	1015M	K3509
836M	K3196	930M	K1839	1016M	K3510
837M	K3197	931M	K4295	1017M	K2051
838M	K3198	932M	K2442	1018M	K2048
839M	K3200	933M	K2908	1019M	K2043
840M	K3205	934M	K3788	1020M	K3688
841M	K3208	935M	K3790	1021M	K7579
842M	K1832	936M	K2012	1022M	K3780
843M	K3148	937M	K2015	1023M	K7038
844M	K2281	938M	K2897	1024M	K7039
845M	K2282	939M	K4302	1025M	K7043
846M	K2285	941M	K2168	1026M	K2060
847M	K1516	943M	K6012	1027M	K7056
848M	K1534	944M	K3965	1028S	S1317
849M	K2037	945M	K4637	1030M	K5718
850M	K1744	946M	K2069	1031M	K1419
851M	K1745	947M	K2041	1032M	K2427
853M	K1944	948M	K2078	1033M	K7560
855M	K1513	949M	K3775	1034M	K7561
862M	K1597	950M	K3783	1035M	K7568
863M	K1598	951M	K1687	1036M	K7569
864M	K5121	952M	K2144	1037M	K7570
865M	K5122	953M	K2213	1038M	K4538
866M	K5125	954M	K2135	1039M	K7433
867M	K4082	955M	K2165	1040M	K1445
868M	K1843	956M	K2197	1041M	K7746
869M	K1167	957M	K3787	1042M	K7040
870M	J9674	958M	K3776	1043M	K7060
871M	K2685	959M	K6199	1044M	K2055
872M	K2683	960M	K2973	1045M	K1946
873M	K3915	961M	K3805	1046M	K2826
874M	K2892	963M	K4386	1047M	K2016
875M	K2535	964M	K5459	1048M	K2081
876M	K5238	965M	K3914	1049M	K2881
877M	K1434	967M	J9795	1050M	K7872
878M	K2440	968M	K5394	1051M	K3588
879M	K2445	969M	K2817	1052M	K3061
880M	K2450	970M	K3749	1053M	K1971
881M	K1989 or K2373	971M	K3918	1054M	K1972
883M	K3150	972M	K1692	1055M	K2409
884M	K2946*	973M	K2002	1056M	K5711
885M	K3504	974M	K1943	1057M	K2777*
886M	K1218	975M	K4534	1058M	K1969
887M	K2441	976M	K2063	1059M	K2412
888M	K2431	977M	K2224	1060M	K1243
889M	K2429	978M	K2227	1061M	K1799
891M	K3225	979M	K3794	1062M	K3719
892M	K3226	980M	K3782	1063M	K3213
894M	K2831	982M	K5370	1064M	K1980
895M	K1214	983M	K5315	1065M	K7276
896M	K2576	985M	K5986	1066M	K8536
897M	K2575	986M	K2139	1067M	K4544
898M	K2578	987M	K1932	1068M	K1927
899M	K2207	988M	K3232	1069M	K4792
900M	K4281	989M	K3057	1070M	K4214
901M	K2814	990M	K4357	1071M	K8563
902M	K4370	991M	K5714	1072M	K1205
903M	K5617	992M	K2066	1073M	K2969
904M	K5225	993M	K2426	1074M	L5946
905M	K1606	994M	K2686	1075M	K2137
		995M	K2242	1076M	K2170

1077M K2172	1165M K7691	1258M K3753	1347M K3857	1431M L1621	1520M K2761	
1078M K2186	1167M K3934	1259M L2387	1348M K3050	1432M K7874	1521M K2721	
1079M K2205	1168M K3932	1260M L2388	1349M K3018	1433M K5412	1522M K2748	
1081M K8628	1169M K3020	1261M L2389	1350M K3891	1434M K6691	1523M K2641	
1082M K1968	1170M K3141	1262M L2397	1351M K3862	1435M K3036	1524M K2759	
1084M K3673	1172M K5760	1263M L2405	1352M L1447	1436M K3586	1525M J9804	
1085M K1988	1173M K9683	1264M L2407	1353M K9305	1437M K9257	1526M K4990	
1086M K2413	1174M K8323	1265M L2408	1354M K9334	1438M K6280	1527M K5875	
1087M K2414	1175M K4202	1266M L2409	1355M L1455	1439M L1745	1528M K5244	
1088M K2415	1176M K4204	1267M L2402	1356M L2761	1441M L4972	1529M N5425	
1089M K3392	1177M K3701	1268M L2404	1357M K9822	1442M L1809	1532M K3800	
1090M K4786	1178M K2916	1269M L2406	1358M L1634	1444M K5699	1533M J9167	
1091M K4224	1179M K4218	1270M L2411	1359M L1559	1445M K4416	1534M J9787	
1092M K8534	1180M K4292	1271M L2413	1360M L1456	1446M K3342	1535M K2684	
1093M K2945	1181M L1603	1272M L2414	1361M K9820	1447M K3002	1536M K1769	
1096M K4793	1182M K8673	1273M L2415	1362M K9831	1448M K3013	1537M K1764	
1097M K3222	1183M K2910	1274M L2416	1363M L1935	1449M K9241	1538M K5360	
1098M K3577	1184M L1182	1275M L2410	1364M L1648	1450M K9872	1539M K5363	
1099M L8141	1185M K3903	1276M L2394	1365M L1650	1451M K8895	1540M K7817	
1100M K1700	1186M K4203	1277M L2403	1366M K5551	1452M K4243	1541M K4012	
1101M K2605	1187M S1710	1278M L2400	1367M K1436	1453M K7815	1542M K6082	
1102M K2610	1188M L2203	1279M L2395	1368M L1561	1454M L1810	1543M K6076	
1103M K2688	1189M K9261	1280M L2399	1369M K1416	1455M L1165	1544M K6081	
1104M K2689	1190M K2827	1281M L2401	1370M L1625	1456M K8479	1545M K8677	
1105M K2697	1191M L1560	1282M L2396	1371M K5525	1457M K8450	1546M K8247	
1106M J9156*	1193M K6856	1283M L2398	1372M K7042	1458M K8451*	1547M K8249	
1107M K7128	1194M K1830	1284M L2390	1373M L1691	1459M K8452*	1548M K8276	
1108M L7237	1195M K8235	1285M To 2586M	1374M K1746	1460M K5641	1549M K8281	
1109M K2853	1196M K9196	1286M To 2587M	1375M K1747	1461M K5633	1550M K8296	
1110M K7564	1197M K5901	1287M K1899	1376M K2691	1462M K8500	1551M K8279	
1111M K8109	1198M K5345	1288M K1215	1377M K1748	1463M K4304	1552M K8272	
1112M K1648	1199M L5933	1289M K1905	1378M K5434	1464M K3736	1553M K8248	
1113M K7149	1200M L2869	1290M K4086	1379M K5693	1465M K2062	1554M K7842	
1114M K7637	1201M L2870	1291M K8705	1380M L1575	1466M L1672	1555M K7851	
1116M L1150	1203M K2898	1292M K9335	1381M K2813	1467M L1869	1556M K7875	
1117M K6686	1208M K1896	1293M K9315	1382M K9812	1468M L1604	1557M K5308	
1118M K2583	1209M K4935	1294M L2871	1383M L7205	1469M K3873	1558M K5274	
1119M K7682	1211M K5083	1295M K1886	1384M L7050	1470M L1364	1559M K4014	
1120M J9933	1212M K4530	1296M K1902	1387M K4412	1471M K9237	1560M K6056	
1121M S1715	1213M K4708	1297M L1851	1388M L1795	1472M K9260	1561M K6018	
1122M K2010	1214M K4459	1298M K1847	1389M L7215	1474M L1643	1562M K6075	
1123M K2848	1215M L1651	1299M K1888	1390M K1859	1475M K4303	1563M K4298	
1124M L8205	1217M K1249	1303M K2376	1391M K1887	1476M K3849	1564M K5086	
1125M K8128	1218M K2423	1304M K1208	1392M K1833	1478M K7877*	1565M K5087	
1126M K9179	1219M K2411	1305M K1835	1393M K1856	1479M K9845	1566M K5093	
1127M K8475	1220M K2400	1306M K1894	1394M K2906	1480M K3453	1567M K5098	
1128M K2967	1221M K2420	1307M K1897	1395M K4521	1481M K3001	1568M K4794	
1129M K1665	1223M K2408	1308M J9925	1396M K4527	1482M K5607	1569M K7263	
1130M K3230	1224M K2419	1310M K1900	1397M K4503	1483M L1461	1570M K7264	
1131M K2046	1225M K2401	1311M L7698	1398M K2847	1484M K5420	1571M K7266	
1132M K7349	1226M L1677	1314M K1852	1399M K2846	1485M K5353	1572M K7268	
1133M K3692*	1227M K1144	1315M S1205	1400M K2850	1486M L1398	1573M K7269	
1134M K2582	1228M K3648	1316M K1773	1401M K3784	1490M K4240	1574M K7270	
1135M K2258	1229M K5755	1317M K1774	1402M K4542	1491M K8676	1575M K7271	
1136M L1143	1230M K3409	1318M K1166	1403M K2854	1493M L1554	1576M K7277	
1137M K4098	1231M K4446	1319M K1168	1404M K3773	1494M K9798	1577M K7281	
1138M K2998	1232M L1656	1320M K2768	1405M K3976	1495M K2766	1578M K7282	
1139M K7657	1233M L1136	1321M K9236	1406M K3767	1497M K2470	1579M K7285	
1140M K6681	1234M K8215	1322M K9482	1407M K4508	1498M K2995	1580M K1935*	
1141M K1996	1235M K5728	1325M L2192	1408M K3792	1499M K3811	1581M K3751	
1142M K4237	1236M K5247	1326M K9287	1409M K4509	1500M K3841	1582M K1169	
1144M K2387	1237M L1622	1327M K7035	1410M K4531	1501M K3814	1583M K1160	
1145M K2364	1238M K9808	1328M K7045	1411M K5683	1502M To 2566M	1584M J9062	
1146M K2823	1239M L4562	1329M K7046	1412M K3777	1503M K3010	1586M K3896	
1147M K8187	1240M K1884	1330M K7062	1413M K3975	1504M K3810	1587M L6846	
1148M K2136	1241M L2186	1331M K7070	1414M K3799	1505M K8337	1588M K2278	
1149M K2957	1242M L1597	1332M K7071	1415M K4540	1506M K8336	1589M K2300	
1150M K2175	1243M K4498	1333M K7069	1416M K4511	1507M S1851	1590M K2299	
1151M K2223	1244M K5314	1334M K7280	1417M K5713	1508M K2619	1591M K2288	
1152M K2229	1245M K7079	1335M K3819	1418M K5715	1509M K2713	1592M K5414	
1153M K3870	1246M K7121	1336M K8106	1419M K5716	1510M K2769	1593M K1901	
1154M K3574	1247M K1813	1338M L2270	1420M K5720	1511M K1762	1594M K5063	
1155M K7832	1248M K1974	1339M L2272	1421M K5721	1512M K2696	1597M K7981	
1156M K2586	1249M K2349	1340M L2215	1422M K5723	1513M K2754	1598M K6514	
1157M K2585	1250M K2586	1341M L7694	1424M K1754	1514M K1120	1599M K4610	
1158M K2209	1251M K2402	1342M L1199	1425M L4757	1515M K2693	1600M K3316	
1161M K2948	1253M K1892	1343M K6090	1426M L1675	1516M K2614	1602M K7860	
1162M K2952	1254M L8251	1344M K3271	1427M K6828	1517M K2628	1603M K7864	
1163M K2955	1255M K2894*	1345M K7111	1428M K9866	1518M K2714	1604M K7855*	
1164M K2958	1257M L7222	1346M K2999*	1430M L1553	1519M K2751	1605M K7887	

1606M K7855
1607M K7797 and K2467
1608M K3960
1609M K5538
1611M L2010
1612M K9739
1613M K7704
1614M K5085
1615M K5088
1616M K5089
1617M K5092
1618M K5096
1619M K5097
1622M K5317
1623M S1707
1625M L4238
1628M K9837
1629M K3243
1630M K3367
1631M K4438
1632M K9913
1633M K6066
1635M L1241
1636M N6209
1637M L1510
1638M K9806
1640M K7580
1642M K3000
1643M K8280
1644M K8273
1645M J9932
1646M K9855
1647M L4130
1648M L1436
1649M N6152
1650M L1928*
1651M K9373
1652M K2235
1655M K3979
1661M K3695
1673M K8204
1674M K7360*
1675M K8193
1676M K5691
1677M K5717
1678M K5704
1679M To 2370M
1680M K5684
1681M K5709
1682M K4504
1683M K3977
1684M K4510
1685M K8211
1686M K3807
1687M K3795
1688M K8212
1689M K8210
1690M K8206
1691M K8205
1692M K8208
1693M K4532
1694M K4525
1695M K6172
1696M K3961
1697M K8675
1698M K8675
1699M K4830
1701M L6675
1702M K7186
1703M L1602
1704M K8293
1705M K8262
1706M K8304
1707M K8265
1708M K8266
1709M K8267
1710M K8261
1711M K8275
1712M K8252

1713M K8299
1714M K8278
1715M K8226
1716M K8230
1717M K8233
1718M K8288
1719M K2876
1720M K8283
1721M K8284
1722M K8286
1723M K8298
1724M K8287
1725M K8227
1726M K8232
1727M K8269
1728M K8297
1729M K8231
1730M K8229
1731M K8225
1732M K5667
1733M K8237
1734M K8250
1735M K8295
1736M K8306
1737M K8255
1738M K7660*
1739M K1928
1740M K8242
1741M K8259
1742M K8268
1745M K2434
1747M L9683
1748M K8080*
1749M K5604*
1750M K2810
1752M L2374
1753M K2822
1754M L4114*
1755M K7992
1758M K5830
1759M K4499
1760M K4505
1761M K4507
1762M K5632
1763M K4410
1764M K4972
1765M K3761
1766M K3158
1767M K3156
1769M K1999
1770M K5796
1771M K5016
1772M K6430
1774M K7592
1775M K7665
1779M K6509
1780M To 2580M
1781M K7214*
1782M K7692
1783M K7991
1785M K7578
1786M K7583
1787M K7585
1788M K7679
1791M N2059
1792M K7577
1793M K7601
1794M K7581
1795M K7590
1796M K7605
1797M K7586
1798M K7635
1799M K7656
1800M K7677
1801M K7678
1802M K7693
1805M L6594
1809M K3569
1810M K3564
1811M K5077

1812M K4340
1813M K3907
1814M K6034
1819M K6093
1820M K4245
1821M K4274
1822M K4552
1823M K8256
1824M K8290
1825M K9859
1826M S1859
1827M S1826
1829M S1800
1830M K7882
1831M K7648
1832M L4983
1833M K9234
1834M K9235
1835M K9220
1836M K9239
1837M K9313
1838M K9314
1839M K9360
1840M K9361
1841M K9363
1842M K9364
1843M L1867
1845M K5282
1846M K5283
1847M K8291
1848M K3204
1849M K3207
1850M K3263
1851M K4807
1852M K7556
1853M K2857
1856M L2638
1857M P1279
1858M K4242
1859M K4275
1860M K5381
1861M K5438
1862M K5011
1863M K5531
1864M K5557
1865M K6641
1866M K6694
1867M K8906
1868M N2108
1869M To 2554M
1870M K7655
1871M K7624
1872M K7595
1873M K7621
1874M K7669
1875M K7597
1876M K7675
1877M K7650
1878M K7668
1879M K7663
1880M K7674
1881M K7653
1882M N2098
1883M L4177
1884M L1903
1885M L8512
1886M L1420
1887M N2129
1888M L4153
1889M K7202
1890M K7205
1891M K2821*
1892M L1460
1893M L8700
1894M L7628
1895M L8781
1896M To 2395M
1897M To 2394M
1902M K5688
1907M To 2561M

1908M K7324
1909M K8305
1910M K8240
1911M K2879
1912M K8218
1913M K8254
1914M K8264
1915M K8285
1916M K8303
1918M K8239
1919M K8292
1920M K8238
1921M K3467
1923M K2188
1924M K7582
1925M K7629
1926M K8955
1927M K8939
1928M K7215
1929M K5290*
1930M K3344*
1931M K5442
1933M K7662
1934M K7667
1936M K7625
1937M K7641
1938M K7612
1939M K7566
1940M K7880
1941M K8138*
1942M K2600
1943M K6725
1944M K6727
1945M K6536
1948M K8246
1949M K1935
1951M K4879*
1953M K3631
1954M K6529
1955M K7576
1956M K5275
1957M K5321
1958M K5339
1959M K5357
1960M K7806*
1961M K7827
1962M K7841
1963M K5311
1964M K7888
2001M K5300
2003M K6847
2004M K3067
2005M K3248
2006M K3302
2007M K6122
2008M K5727
2009M K3242
2010M K5812
2011M K4991
2012M K6459
2014M K7485
2015M K5600
2016M K5139
2017M K3696
2018M K2052
2019M K6546
2020M K4487
2021M ex-1779M
2022M ex-1758M
2023M K3855*
2024M K3856*
2025M K3139
2026M K3012
2027M K7272
2028M K4513
2029M K4501
2030M K5686
2031M K7274
2032M K7275
2033M K7265

2034M K4390
2035M K7429
2036M K7438
2037M K7464
2038M K4892
2039M K6475
2040M K6772
2043M K6510
2044M K6635
2046M K3272
2047M K3329
2048M K3331
2049M K2567
2050M K7811
2051M K4893
2052M K5811
2053M K5839
2054M K6456
2055M K5024
2056M N7092
2057M L7271
2061M G-EBOI
2062M W6415
2063M G-AAZT
2064M G-ABPB
2065M G-ABNZ
2066M G-ABFV
2067M G-ABFV
2068M To 2582M
2069M G-ABWG
2070M G-ABMO
2071M G-AAGR
2072M G-ACNK
2073M G-ABKB
2074M G-AADF
2075M G-ADEO
2076M G-AAEC
2077M G-EBTY
2078M G-EBXY
2079M G-AAHN
2080M G-AABX
2081M G-EBQN
2082M G-AACE
2083M G-AAWH
2084M K4984
2085M K5123
2086M K5820
2101M K4420
2102M K4414
2103M K3882
2104M K3037
2105M K2990*
2106M K5480
2107M K6627
2108M P1280
2109M K7862
2110M K7811*
2111M P9390
2113M K7425
2114M G-ABMF
2115M K5301
2116M K7798
2117M K7819
2118M K3677
2119M P9507
2120M N3566
2121M P3517
2122M L4609
2123M N7070
2124M N7096
2125M K6299
2126M K4090
2127M K4102
2128M K7873
2129M K7876
2130M K5296
2131M K5309
2132M K5319
2133M K5294
2134M P1261 To 3098M

2135M K3677*
2136M P3057*
2137M P9399
2138M K3388
2139M R6636
2140M P4364
2141M L1785
2142M K6244
2143M P2270
2144M P6726
2145M L4425
2146M K4558
2147M K8177
2148M L4348*
2149M L4214
2150M To 3137M
2151M To 2775M
2152M L4322*
2153M L4346*
2154M L4350
2155M To 2773M
2156M To 3051M
2157M P4349
2158M L3417
2159M P2272
2160M L2020
2161M L9171
2162M L6064
2163M L6007
2164M L6006
2165M L4181
2166M L4206
2167M K8131
2168M N7339
2169M P4337
2170M L4139
2171M L4869
2172M L1791
2173M L5133
2174M K4563
2175M K6156
2176M N7320
2177M P2131
2178M L6596
2179M K3399
2180M L1511
2181M K7183
2182M K7141
2184M ex-1149M
2185M R3156
2186M K2459
2187M K3038
2188M K2444
2189M K6517
2190M S1393
2191M K7304
2192M N9057
2193M K8149
2194M K3043
2195M K2458
2196M K1930
2197M K5708
2198M K5687
2199M K5700
2200M K5696
2201M L5275
2202M K3844
2203M N7129
2204M L5075
2205M K6154
2206M K3791
2207M L4858
2208M K9732
2209M P6603*
2210M L5127
2211M K7557
2212M N3937
2213M K9240
2214M P1327
2215M K7854

2216M K4103	2296M K6729	2376M V7292	2459M K8188	2539M G-ABWW	2623M K2013
2217M L6104	2297M K5907	2378M L4356*	2460M K5900	2540M K3291	2624M K5386
2218M K7383	2298M K4500	2379M L7271*	2461M K2819	2541M P6907	2625M AW150
2219M K7400	2299M K5725	2380M To 2421M	2462M K5071	2542M L9034	2626M AW152
2220M ex-1956M	2300M K2991	2381M L3392	2463M K6020	2543M L4874	2627M X4934
2221M ex-1957M	2301M K4432	2382M K6027	2464M K6033*	2544M L4877	2628M V6880
2222M ex-1958M	2302M K4407	2383M To 2451M	2465M T1431	2545M P6673	2630M BD182
2223M ex-1959M	2303M N3067*	2384M K2988	2466M L1999	2546M K7705	2631M X4992
2224M ex-1960M	2304M K9401	2385M ex-1859M	2467M K6168	2547M DG580	2634M K8771
2225M ex-1961M	2305M X9404	2386M K6155*	2468M K6173	2548M DG658	2635M X4343
2226M ex-1962M	2306M X9400	2387M L9892	2469M K6159	2549M BK833*	2636M P2544
2227M K1442	2307M L1551	2388M R5944	2470M K8837*	2550M R2194	2637M L1750
2228M K4753	2308M K5737*	2389M K3898	2471M K6261	2551M N7410	2638M L1159
2229M L7201	2309M K4437	2390M K2979	2472M K2188*	2552M R2158	2639M K2080*
2230M K7283	2310M K1426	2391M K3051	2473M V6889	2553M K9209	2640M K5329
2231M K8089	2311M K5719	2392M K8194	2474M K7245	2554M K9354	2641M L6625*
2232M K5604	2312M K4763	2393M K4879	2475M ex-671M	2555M N2101	2642M L1310
2233M V7441	2313M K4969	2394M K5704	2476M K7644	2556M P2159	2643M L1552
2234M P1687 and	2314M K5003	2395M K2842	2479M To 2511M	2557M L4242	2644M L1057
K5354	2315M K8121*	2396M W9379	2480M K5732	2558M X4603	2645M K6129
2235M G-ACGV	2316M G-ABPB*	2397M K6304*	2481M N2031 and	2559M T2885*	2646M N2354
2236M L5521*	2317M K8822	2398M K6285	R6818	2560M AK181*	2647M K9851*
2237M K5045	2318M ex-1577M	2399M K6159	2482M AX789	2561M K3087	2648M R3173
2238M To 2338M*	2319M K7803	2400M K8144	2483M P2243	2562M K4771	2649M K7059
2239M K2874	2320M K7804	2401M K8095	2484M K7645	2563M L2426	2650M L1367
2241M K2882	2321M K3858	2402M K8107	2485M R7375	2564M L2427	2651M L4697
2242M K3982	2322M L1188*	2403M K8118	2486M BD156	2565M L7706	2652M L1467
2243M K5686*	2323M K5735	2404M K8120	2487M W5015	2566M K2461	2653M K6058*
2244M K3980	2324M K5710	2405M K8147	2488M BD161	2567M K3391	2654M L1118
2245M K5707	2325M K5694	2406M K9688	2489M BD155	2568M K4799	2655M X4025
2246M K5664	2326M K5698	2407M K8091	2490M BD154	2569M DG589	2656M AB920
2247M K5266	2327M K5733	2408M K9694	2491M L6941	2570M V7047	2657M L4292
2248M K5340	2328M K5731	2409M K9705	2492M K3910	2571M L6431	2658M BK833
2250M K7824	2329M K5695	2410M K9709	2493M K4017	2572M K3874	2659M BS817
2251M K7848	2330M K5706	2411M K9701	2494M K4348	2573M K9833	2660M L7393
2252M K5285	2331M K2977	2412M K9720	2495M K5082	2574M K2771	2661M AX781
2253M K7846	2332M P5088	2413M K9710	2496M K6042*	2575M K8160	2662M BB690*
2254M K5256	2333M V6888	2414M K9700	2497M K6078	2576M L8724	2663M AE462
2255M K7829	2334M K5354	2415M K9786	2498M K6079	2577M L1818	2664M AE463
2256M L6944*	2335M K5367	2416M K8101	2499M K6080	2578M L1883*	2665M AE466
2257M X2963*	2336M K5287	2417M K9722	2500M K8701	2579M T4288	2666M AE468
2258M N9095*	2337M K7821	2418M K9692	2501M K3908 and	2580M K7192	2667M AR631
2259M L6944*	2338M K9717	2419M R6754	BK588	2581M L5297*	2668M AS467
2260M L5715	2339M L7037	2420M K6406	2502M K5073	2582M W6416	2669M AS469
2261M P1324	2340M K5297	2421M L9934	2503M K6013	2583M AX859	2670M AW421
2262M K2982	2341M K5322	2422M K5305	2504M K6048	2585M K7616	2671M AH917
2263M K4421	2342M K5346	2423M K6157	2505M K6039	2586M L2392	2672M AH916
2264M K4426	2343M K5350	2424M K6713	2506M K8680	2587M L2393	2873M BK852
2265M K3033	2344M K7801	2425M L4358	2507M K5702	2588M L7166	2674M AK104
2266M K3880	2345M K4961	2426M L4352	2508M K6206	2589M L3111	2675M AK116
2267M K1446	2346M K5902	2427M AV980	2509M K6204	2590M DG584	2676M AK154
2268M K5898	2347M K5904	2428M K6161	2510M K3764	2591M DG585	2677M BJ476
2269M K8214	2348M K5726	2429M P5124	2511M L6105	2592M DG582	2678M AH506
2270M P2117	2349M K8217	2430M N2173	2512M K6048*	2593M DG581	2679M DR609
2271M K3245	2350M K5740	2431M K9418	2513M K3908*	2594M DG586	2680M DR610
2272M K3327	2351M K5741	2432M K9438	2514M K8680*	2595M DG583	2681M L4398
2273M K3349	2352M K8181	2433M L4965	2515M K5073*	2596M AH886	2682M BV207
2274M K3027	2353M K8184	2434M K9336	2516M K6013*	2597M P4930*	2683M R6973
2275M K3881	2354M K8182	2435M R4293	2517M R1843	2598M K5739	2684M X4103
2276M K2980	2355M To 2459M	2436M L3057	2518M K5362	2599M T3297	2685M X4033
2277M K3040	2356M K9691	2437M L7849	2519M K6186	2600M K7208	2686M L4330
2278M K7652	2357M K9777	2438M K9301	2520M K6188	2601M X5049	2690M V6920
2279M K5025	2358M X4236	2439M K6055	2521M K6170	2603M X5024	2694M P3835
2280M K6119	2359M K6026	2440M K8679	2522M K8758	2604M BK841	2697M AB815
2281M K3330	2360M K5342	2441M K6033	2523M K6191	2605M X5055	2698M K3711
2282M K7191	2361M K6035	2442M K6042	2524M L1627	2606M X5056	2699M L7243
2283M K2994	2362M K6060	2443M K6040	2525M K6934	2607M X5104	2700M K3848*
2284M K3838	2363M T1952	2444M BV208	2526M AX666	2608M BK832	2701M K7251*
2285M K4105	2364M K6015	2445M K2729	2527M K6167	2609M W7971	2702M K4409
2286M V7239*	2365M K6038	2446M K2732	2528M ex-2495M	2610M AX790	2703M K4436
2287M K5738	2366M K6059	2447M BV209	2529M ex-2492M	2611M BK831	2704M AW159
2288M K5734	2367M K8698	2448M R3224	2530M ex-2493M	2613M X9305*	2705M K3210
2289M K8183	2368M K4345	2449M P9206	2531M ex-2494M	2614M X9299	2706M K3442
2290M K5737	2369M K7889	2450M T4293	2532M ex-2496M	2616M V7499	2707M K3382
2291M K5906	2370M K8190	2451M L4221	2533M ex-2505M	2617M DG578	2708M K3474
2292M K8203	2371M To 2565M	2452M K2710	2534M K6078*	2618M DG661	2709M K3365
2293M K5899	2372M K3971*	2453M AX854	2535M K6079*	2619M BD140	2710M K4829
2294M K8198	2373M K7033	2454M K7217	2536M K6080*	2620M K6637	2711M L4032
2295M K8195	2374M K6651	2457M K9921	2537M See 2500M	2621M K5397	2712M L6004
	2375M K6398	2458M J9125	2538M T2287	2622M K5377	2713M L6039

2714M L6063	2806M V7647*	2889M G-ADZN	2970M G-ADAU	3054M N1444	3145M L8373*
2715M L6050	2807M P5183	2890M G-ACEM	2971M G-ADTK	3055M R1034	3146M L1152
2716M L6021	2808M AH578	2891M G-ADLF	2972M G-ADTN	3056M N3636	3147M L4441
2717M L6054	2809M AH751	2892M G-ADFP	2973M G-AEBL	3057M N1471	3148M L9872
2718M L4284	2810M AH767	2893M G-ADFV	2974M L1206	3058M T4210	3149M W6523
2719M L4278	2811M AH854	2894M G-ADFR	2975M N1743	3059M BGA356	3150M AK751*
2720M L4213	2812M AH841	2895M G-ACBH	2976M N1803	3060M BGA375	3151M AM838
2721M L4234	2813M BJ458	2896M G-ADZM	2977M N3337	3061M BGA351	3152M N4796 and P9024
2722M AV990	2814M BT464	2897M G-ADFN	2978M AG411	3062M BGA358	3153M AH772
2723M X9364	2815M BT461	2898M G-AEBE	2979M BV139	3063M L6844	3154M R3166
2724M X9366	2816M V6818	2899M G-ACEO	2980M L6950	3064M HM505	3155M R2142
2725M X9375	2817M Z4036*	2900M G-ACBJ	2981M N1681	3065M HM504	3156M R2145
2726M X9456	2818M BD144	2901M G-AEBK	2982M N3394	3067M N1503	3157M AB699
2727M L1281	2819M W7947	2902M G-ACPZ	2983M T3993	3068M BV197	3158M L6891
2728M P9504	2820M AW154	2903M G-ADFU	2984M L1896	3069M N2807	3159M L6892
2729M N3377	2821M W5771	2904M G-ACES	2985M L4279	3070M R2596	3160M N8051
2730M N1621	2822M K9998	2905M G-ACRA	2986M X9602	3071M L8714	3161M L9604
2731M N3307	2823M L1030	2906M G-ACBK	2987M N2768	3072M AH813	3162M T2579
2732M N1801	2824M X4915	2907M G-ACAH	2988M ex-2448M	3074M BV149	3163M R3195
2733M N1703	2825M X4916	2908M G-ADFT	2990M K7085	3075M P5311	3164M L7848
2734M N3236	2826M N3236	2909M L6727	2991M X9385	3076M N7230	3165M L9955
2736M L4301	2827M X4166	2910M X4608	2992M AW122	3077M N3122	3166M V5753
2737M L6101	2828M W8381	2911M W5655	2993M BD173	3078M L6368	3167M N3199
2738M L7247	2829M R1253	2912M L6100	2995M K3455	3079M T4785*	3168M DG444
2739M ex-2393M	2830M N9075	2913M N9068	2996M K4813	3080M R1595	3169M L1450
2740M N3445	2831M L6082	2914M L6094 and N9079	2997M X5025	3081M R1656	3170M L6842
2741M L1786	2832M L6095	2916M V6609	2998M V1172	3082M AF957	3171M L6976
2743M V7118	2833M AW146	2917M AE536	2999M N1797	3083M K9934	3172M L7022
2744M V7042	2834M L1657	2918M AH779	3000M N3479	3084M L1783	3173M R3228
2745M V7108	2835M N2554	2919M AH826	3001M BJ493	3085M P2722	3174M L1698
2746M W9137	2836M N2343	2920M AH778	3002M BJ495	3086M L1926	3175M L4682
2747M P3983	2837M N4850	2921M AH943	3003M BB892	3087M P2979	3176M R2623
2748M V7750	2838M L4586	2922M AH927	3005M L9486	3088M N3160	3177M R2629
2749M P3410	2839M P6816	2923M AH821	3006M N1616	3089M AG360	3178M L1089
2750M V6930	2841M X4775*	2924M AH765	3007M N1802	3090M BGA264	3179M R3226
2751M V6534	2842M R6697	2825M AH805	3008M T4107	3091M BGA222	3180M N2743
2752M V7028	2843M N3169	2926M AH815	3009M L6962	3092M BGA211	3181M L7019
2753M L6098	2844M X4355	2927M AH878	3010M N3641	3093M K7198	3182M L6964
2754M N9093	2845M X4661	2928M AH823	3012M N3642	3094M K8998*	3184M N3032
2756M X5124	2846M X4847	2929M AH819	3013M N3638	3095M L6038	3185M R3283
2757M V7111	2847M X4676	2930M AH760	3014M K7051	3096M HH118	3186M N2842
2758M AV968	2848M V7064*	2931M AH820	3015M DG665	3097M ex-1857M	3187M L1372
2759M L2422*	2849M W9152	2932M AH883	3016M DP851	3098M P1261	3188M L4674
2765M T2459	2850M P3588	2933M P6687	3017M X5125	3099M V3813	3189M R2637
2767M N9102	2851M K8716	2934M P6680	3018M L6034	3100M V3595*	3190M N2743
2768M K9918	2852M K7143	2936M L6106	3019M N9089	3101M DG442	3191M ex-2524M
2769M R2190	2853M R1147	2937M L4212	3020M L6022	3102M DG443	3192M P2911
2770M T6617	2855M AS414	2938M G-AEBG	3021M L6044	3103M P9239	3193M L2098
2771M L4377	2856M AS411	2939M G-ACCN	3022M L6051	3104M R3231	3194M L2018
2772M L4307	2857M AS429	2940M G-ADTX	3023M L6002	3105M L4293	3195M L8372
2773M L4225	2858M AH890	2941M G-ADTY	3024M L6009	3106M L6957*	3196M L6993
2774M L4295	2859M AH843 and AS430	2942M G-ADTV	3025M L6045	3107M L7535	3197M L6997
2775M L4269	2860M AH837	2943M G-ADTG	3026M L6046	3108M P9233	3198M L6983
2776M R2700	2861M AH804	2944M G-ADTT	3027M L6091	3109M N3011	3199M L6956
2777M L4865	2862M Z4848	2945M G-ACCI	3028M L6015	3117M L7772	3200M K9829
2778M X9382	2863M L7999	2946M G-ACCJ	3029M L6042	3118M BK892	3201M L1090
2779M AW171	2864M L8002	2947M G-ADTU	3030M L6028	3119M L4218	3202M L1697
2780M BS816	2865M K6651*	2948M G-ADTS	3031M L6032	3120M L8971	3203M R2577
2781M N9104	2866M K6794*	2949M G-ADTP	3032M L6060	3121M K7236	3204M R2584
2782M L4033	2867M K9795	2950M G-ADTF	3033M L6068	3122M L4229	3205M R2579
2783M K8310	2868M K9839	2951M G-AENL	3034M L9526	3123M L4351	3206M L1017
2784M K7300	2869M L7183	2952M G-ACCK	3035M AK106	3124M X5114	3207M R3204
2785M AS470	2870M L7189	2953M G-ACNF	3036M K3045*	3125M K8853	3208M L1273
2786M ES952	2871M K9750	2954M G-ADAV	3037M L4311	3127M AZ104	3210M L6951
2787M Z8726	2872M R4222	2955M G-ADTW	3038M L4329	3128M N7994	3211M L7024
2788M AR670	2873M L4879	2956M G-ADCX	3039M L4327	3129M BK869	3212M L7014
2791M N7569*	2874M L4882	2957M G-ABWS	3040M L4277	3130M L6025	3213M P3465
2792M L4373	2875M L4272	2958M G-ABXU	3041M L4342	3132M AS410	3214M P3592
2794M P2517	2876M N2669	2959M G-AEAR	3042M L4389	3133M W8132	3215M K9881
2795M L4251	2877M R7058*	2960M G-ADTJ	3043M L4309	3134M W8133	3216M L7862
2796M AH629	2878M To 4463M	2961M G-ADTL	3044M L4249	3135M R2702	3217M R2592
2797M L1731	2879M K7179	2962M G-ACRZ	3045M L4353	3136M L4359	3218M L1419
2798M V6558	2880M L1480	2963M L6099	3046M L4337	3137M L4386	3219M R3290
2799M AD376	2882M BV138	2964M L6077	3047M L4317	3138M L4325	3220M L4705
2800M L6003	2884M BV134	2965M N9084*	3048M L4271	3139M BV137	3221M L4704
2801M L6017	2885M G-ACLD	2966M N9092*	3049M L4341	3140M BV135	3222M L1659
2802M L6043	2886M G-ACZH	2967M L6092	3050M L4365	3141M BV140	3223M L1012
2803M L6048	2887M G-AEBJ	2968M L6026	3051M L4287	3142M K8983	3224M L7887
2804M N9055	2888M G-ADLG	2969M L6065	3052M AG387	3143M P9319	3225M L6778
2805M N9058			3053M N1349	3144M X4779	

3226M L7036	3308M N2841	3389M N3639	3473M R3214	3556M L5299	3638M K7886	
3227M L7012	3309M N2095	3390M R1402	3474M L7245	3557M P6623	3639M T3042	
3228M P3384	3310M P6678	3391M T4271	3475M BB897	3558M L5423	3641M L8340	
3229M K9843	3311M P6735	3392M N1409	3476M L8548	3559M P6763	3643M T8271	
3230M L1092	3312M P6616	3393M N1381	3477M L4250	3560M L5141	3644M T8495	
3231M L1474	3313M T3413	3394M L6532	3478M X3176	3561M L7847	3645M P9224	
3232M R2595	3314M P2679	3395M L6194	3479M T4628	3562M T2845	3646M N7938	
3233M R2580	3315M V7099	3396M N3297	3480M AW405	3563M L8694	3648M N7603	
3234M L4706	3316M N2109	3397M DP739	3481M R5538	3564M L6736	3649M AB510	
3235M R3287	3317M P6640	3398M BD126	3483M K7151	3565M BK608	3650M N1407 and R6889	
3236M L1011	3318M K5291	3399M AH526	3484M L1478	3566M R7120	3651M DG220	
3238M RCAF315	3319M K5336	3400M K7169	3485M DD900	3567M AH478*	3652M N7259	
3239M R1151	3320M BV192	3401M R2060	3486M R8925	3569M L8521	3653M T9363	
3240M L6979	3321M P9296	3402M N6733	3487M K5280	3570M K7064	3654M BB783	
3241M K7034	3322M P9290	3403M N6551	3488M X3483	3571M K7124	3655M W3795	
3242M L1008	3323M T2469	3404M P9211	3489M L9524	3572M K6118	3656M R1254	
3243M L1457	3324M T2460	3405M W3318	3490M K8929	3573M L2046	3658M N4565	
3244M L1873	3325M N2748	3406M K5153	3491M HH588	3574M V6740	3659M V3676	
3245M R2617	3326M R1270	3407M K7233	3492M Z8899	3575M L2084	3660M L6364	
3246M R2618	3327M R1083	3408M K5289	3493M USAAF C-47	3576M L1798	3661M N8012	
3247M N3034	3328M N2804	3409M N1175	3495M N6101	3577M N2597	3662M T8549	
3248M L1048	3329M R3294	3410M P9238	3496M L4989*	3578M RCAF313	3663M T8276	
3249M N2754	3330M T2461	3411M AK572	3497M P6967	3579M L1814	3664M AJ159	
3250M L1266	3331M DP717	3412M G-AESL	3498M L1473	3580M RCAF1357	3665M K5099	
3251M L6988	3332M N3009	3413M R9366	3499M W5797	3581M L2067	3666M DP600*	
3252M P5191	3333M W5727	3414M EN833*	3500M BT600	3582M L2101	3667M R1650	
3253M L1015	3334M K7219*	3415M HH242	3501M X9604	3583M P3544	3668M AH487	
3254M P3357	3335M K7224	3416M BT597	3502M L7885	3584M V7600	3669M L7804	
3255M P9271	3336M K7256	3417M T4634	3503M BT545	3585M P3119	3670M T8433	
3256M L8719	3337M K7248	3418M N1466	3504M R3299	3586M L1701	3671M T8507	
3257M P3810	3338M K9009	3419M L4247	3505M L6678	3587M L1660	3672M L1969	
3258M N3072	3339M K7249	3420M L4245	3506M L9504	3588M N2341	3673M T8319	
3259M L1068	3340M K8949	3421M L4273	3507M L1473*	3589M L1683	3674M K7554	
3260M N1611	3341M K9011	3422M L7246	3508M R5635	3590M N2328	3675M T8842	
3261M N2763	3342M K8954	3423M L1269	3509M DZ378	3591M P3613	3676M L9520	
3262M L7030	3343M K8959	3424M L1400	3511M R7599	3592M L2102	3677M L9505	
3263M T7000	3344M R2058	3425M L8659	3512M R7635	3593M P9460	3678M L9488	
3264M L3122	3345M R3207	3426M BJ475	3513M R7636	3594M K9789	3679M R1077	
3265M R2599	3346M R1087	3429M AG691	3514M R7581	3595M P9332	3680M X9605	
3266M R1150	3347M T8820	3430M Z6169	3515M R7626	3596M X4933	3681M R1338	
3267M N2742	3348M K7122	3431M L9306	3516M R7613	3597M R6674	3682M Z8954	
3268M L7892	3349M R2345	3432M R2066	3517M R7584	3598M X4474	3683M R2328	
3269M R1070	3350M R2450	3433M AH437	3518M R7587	3599M R2061	3684M R1252	
3270M ex-2765M	3351M K6098	3434M AH509	3519M R7623	3600M R9138	3685M R1091	
3271M L6791	3352M K8169	3435M AM264	3520M R7616	3601M X3752	3686M L1451	
3272M P5207	3353M L8373	3436M L9036	3521M R7586	3602M Z4059	3687M L1361	
3273M L1548	3354M L1833	3437M L9037	3522M R7797	3603M Z7156	3688M BM637	
3274M L1957	3355M AN524	3438M P6923	3523M R7641	3604M*	3689M BM525	
3275M K9983	3356M L2412	3439M W5725	3524M R7701	3605M R5559	3690M L9523	
3276M K9955	3357M R1498	3440M P9233	3525M R7721	3606M R5511	3691M L9563	
3277M K9800	3358M L7889	3441M L1780	3526M R7827	3607M T3013	3692M R8765	
3278M L7033	3359M N1891	3442M R2077	3527M R7792	3608M K6054	3693M R8818	
3279M L6987	3360M R1074	3443M L7605	3528M R7792	3609M W4128	3694M R8831	
3280M L6990	3361M N3637	3444M N3652	3529M R7775	3610M L7577	3695M R8766	
3281M L6989	3362M L9485	3445M K8962	3530M R7804	3611M T1006	3696M R8806	
3282M L7008	3363M L6260	3446M K8979	3531M R7802	3612M P1865	3697M R8870	
3283M L4692	3364M L6159	3447M ex-3097M	3532M AK117	3613M T1396	3698M R8764	
3284M L6984	3365M L6152	3448M BT554	3533M L4934	3614M W6612	3699M R8808	
3285M L1784	3366M L6206	3449M BT553*	3534M L6626	3615M V3825	3700M R7639	
3286M AM264*	3367M L6204	3450M AH474	3535M L4931	3616M P1994	3701M R8707	
3287M K7223	3368M L1727	3451M Z9480	3536M K7115	3617M T1392	3702M R8780	
3288M AH894	3369M L1952	3452M R4119	3537M L1320	3618M N6412	3703M R8817	
3289M DJ707	3370M P1361	3453M R1023	3538M L1186	3619M K5279	3704M R8805	
3290M N3001	3371M P9363	3454M L9580	3539M L6797	3620M K7879	3765M R8662	
3291M AH524	3372M L2160	3455M L9534	3540M L1344	3621M K6160	3706M R7801	
3292M R2703	3373M AH813	3456M FF423	3541M L8669	3622M BD866	3707M R7870	
3293M K8951	3374M L6110	3457M W3122	3542M L1167	3623M T9461	3708M R8649	
3294M K8992	3375M L6254	3458M AG491	3543M L4332	3624M L7464	3709M R8648	
3295M K7214	3376M L6240	3459M ex-2355M	3544M Sailplane	3625M K8696*	3710M R7774	
3296M K9049	3377M L6232*	3460M N7815	3545M N3288	3626M P3456*	3711M R7798	
3297M K7213	3378M L6198	3461M BT721	3546M X4381	3627M V6981	3712M R7807	
3298M K7235	3379M L6133	3463M AH750	3547M AH489	3628M L4370	3713M R7805	
3299M L7244	3380M L6267	3464M AK127	3548M AH497	3630M X3207	3714M R7794	
3300M K9023	3381M K7193	3465M R1657	3549M AH470	3631M K9310*	3715M R7874	
3301M L7254	3382M K7201	3466M X4641	3550M AX928	3632M DD675	3716M R7793	
3302M K9023	3383M R1527*	3467M N7297	3551M AW393	3633M T3030	3717M R7875	
3303M T2747	3384M BGA119	3468M N7393	3552M AW401	3634M FP164	3718M R7806	
3304M R3233	3385M N9781	3469M N1346	3553M BJ463	3635M K8133	3719M R7808	
3305M L4334	3386M W3764	3470M T3363	3554M K6050	3636M G-AEXH	3720M R7890	
3306M L4368	3387M BL234	3471M R5560	3555M K7709	3637M N3669		
3307M X4012	3388M P3269					

Appendix C

3721M R7878	3805M N6419	3890M R5774	3981M L9478	4069M T5289*	4179M V3346
3722M R7762	3806M N6257	3891M AK751	3982M V5735	4070M K4586	4180M AL230
3723M R7754	3807M N6253	3892M R5773	3983M R5788	4071M T7735	4181M ET573
3724M R7758	3808M L4548	3893M BF311	3984M R5784	4072M DE447	4182M DE518*
3725M R7769	3809M L4598*	3904M Z1275	3985M L7492	4073M DE902	4183M R9578
3726M R7755	3810M N7431	3905M L6481	3986M L4902	4074M T6854	4184M W5132
3727M R7768	3811M N7701	3906M L5707	3987M V5563	4075M DE933	4185M L9515
3728M R7765	3812M N7425	3907M L5769	3988M V5964	4076M AW147	4187M EE600
3729M R7772	3813M L4634	3908M V1204	3989M L4781	4077M DG657	4188M N1176
3730M V6808	3814M L4585	3909M R7378	3990M R3284	4079M DL372	4189M FV925
3732M L7468	3815M LA559*	3910M P6727	3991M W8905	4080M DL462*	4190M R2386
3733M N4764	3817M L6673	3911M DD716	3992M P4831	4081M DP210	4191M DP676
3734M P1936	3818M N7478	3912M R2619	3993M L1230	4082M DP304	4192M DP679
3735M P1073	3819M N9005	3913M R2594	3994M T2808	4083M DP394	4193M K6115
3736M P1074	3820M N7541	3914M L4691	3995M DS606	4084M DK346	4194M Z9112
3737M R1000	3821M N7687	3915M L4701	3996M V6194	4085M DK349	4195M R1660
3738M L1288	3822M N7623	3916M R2593	3997M Z5802	4086M DP341	4196M DV705*
3739M L6322	3823M N7503	3917M R2635	3998M V6019	4088M JS322*	4197M R5961
3741M L7425	3824M L4623*	3918M R2583	3999M HG944	4089M N7535	4198M V3213
3742M L7455	3825M N6341	3919M R2615	4000M HH264	4090M EM901	4199M DP284
3743M L7283	3827M L4545	3920M R2581	4001M R5791	4091M W8774	4200M FR568
3744M R5832	3838M L4555	3921M R2620	4002M BL380	4093M HH412	4201M DP745
3745M R5776	3829M L4561	3922M R2627	4003M V9445	4094M HV745	4202M EF135
3746M R5771	3830M L4551	3923M R2616	4004M P9077	4095M R2192*	4203M EF678
3747M L7376	3831M N9004	3924M P9105	4005M ex-3372M	4096M R1849	4204M R9436
3748M L7419	3832M L4606	3925M N1220	4006M T2284	4097M T6125	4205M N6480
3749M L7483	3833M V3226	3926M N1297	4007M L9209	4098M AL229	4206M DV760
3750M L7488	3834M N6276	3927M N1266	4008M T2438	4099M AK579	4207M DP352
3751M L7325	3835M W6549	3928M L6850	4009M T2502	4100M AK764	4208M DP794
3752M L7378	3837M T8279	3929M P1684	4010M Z8827	4101M AK573	4209M T5032*
3753M L7382	3838M P2913	3930M R2010	4011M ED762	4102M AK580	4211M BH120
3754M V8655	3839M V3593	3931M L4805	4012M P3656	4103M FL220	4212M LZ936*
3755M N7455	3840M L4543	3932M L4792	4013M L1225	4104M T5492	4213M JM416
3756M N7751	3841M L9680	3933M L6873	4014M L6640	4105M JS244	4215M AH147
3757M N7499	3842M L4564*	3934M P9096	4015M T2425	4107M W4098	4216M AG928
3758M L1277	3843M L4572	3935M P9079	4016M T1948	4108M W4082	4217M FA373
3759M AW148	3844M V4167	3936M R2003	4017M L8614	4109M DD613	4218M AL525
3760M DV474	3846M N6371	3937M L4753	4018M V6121	4110M R8737	4219M AH112
3761M L9511	3847M L4615	3938M L4790	4019M Z5971	4111M P2405	4220M AH172
3762M L7397	3848M L4591*	3939M N1247	4020M DG577	4112M K8953	4221M L7434
3763M L7293	3849M X9791	3940M R2626	4021M R2436	4113M K8980	4222M X6941
3765M N7573	3850M L9564	3941M R2622	4022M DP751	4114M K7218	4223M BD982
3766M BF388	3851M L4586	3942M R2588	4023M FL709	4115M P1835	4224M HX531
3767M BF345	3852M V3595	3943M P9108	4024M FA309	4116M L7806	4225M AG431
3768M N6000	3853M ex-3034M	3944M L6866	4025M Z4062	4117M N7817	4226M T2994
3769M DG588	3854M X7552	3945M P9065	4026M K7105	4118M L7307	4227M DD735
3770M X3217	3855M V8327	3946M N2174	4027M R2778	4120M X7745	4228M AL967
3771M X9611	3856M X7679	3947M L5559	4028M X5017	4121M V3516	4229M N2751
3772M L7431	3857M V8262	3948M DV879	4029M X5027	4122M AD453	4232M N2874
3773M L7293	3858M X7688	3949M L4460*	4030M X5119	4123M V1017	4233M X9927
3774M R5790	3859M R2244	3950M X3161	4031M BK836	4124M T1800	4234M Z1050
3775M HM501	3860M R2342	3951M P1695	4032M BK843	4125M L1253	4235M DV759
3776M L7484	3861M R2308	3952M P9060	4033M DG579	4126M R9430	4236M AG645
3777M R5829	3862M T3034	3953M L9532	4034M L6811	4127M DK118	4237M AB488
3778M R5797	3863M T3244	3954M P2814	4035M R2185	4128M N7781	4238M BD112
3779M AA927	3864M T1252	3956M R9432	4036M T4647*	4129M HX629	4239M R9203
3781M V9991	3865M L9573	3957M AW414	4037M BF436	4130M R5606	4240M DD746
3782M L1121	3866M L9607	3958M L9639	4038M K5065	4156M N7820	4241M DD757
3783M L6737	3867M R3161	3959M R5953	4039M K5067	4157M N7814	4242M AB499
3784M Z5756	3868M N7534	3960M R2322	4040M L1276	4158M N7803	4244M AR605
3785M L1430	3869M N7682	3961M L5705	4041M L6787	4159M N7804	4245M T3427
3786M L1231	3870M N7599	3962M L5631	4042M L6775	4160M N7810	4246M T3421
3787M L1311	3872M W4094	3963M L6711	4043M L8601	4161M N7811	4247M T3437
3788M R2395	3873M R8747	3964M L6644	4044M L6749	4162M N7821	4248M T3432
3789M R2459	3874M R8738	3965M L6619	4045M L8480	4163M T8544	4249M R8659
3790M T3420	3875M R8716	3966M L6759	4046M L9606	4164M N7809	4250M R7699
3791M V8149	3876M L1049	3967M L8515	4047M P6370	4165M N6006	4251M R8775
3792M V8151	3877M L6893	3968M V6427	4048M T5494	4166M L7569	4252M R8696
3793M T3150	3878M V8248	3969M L4995	4056M L7797	4167M R9443	4253M R8748
3794M L6168	3879M V8276	3970M R9188	4057M Z8437	4168M HF853	4254M DL542*
3795M L6483	3880M V8286	3971M DV782*	4058M R6096*	4169M Z8440	4255M DL461*
3796M L6477	3881M R5504	3972M R1776	4060M W6580	4170M W5363	4256M P8090
3797M L6474	3882M L9528	3973M P1729	4061M V3501	4171M R2331	4257M FH240*
3798M L6476	3883M L4890	3974M L4800	4062M L9692	4172M P4829	4258M BL494*
3799M L6200	3884M V6178	3975M L1522	4063M AT787	4173M Z2320	4259M EN789*
3800M L6428*	3885M AH479	3976M AH951	4064M L9520	4174M EL445	4260M K6237
3801M L6472	3886M R2797	3977M T2131	4065M T7910	4175M R7615	4261M R1497
3802M DD612	3887M L4733	3978M Z5952	4066M Z6246	4176M R2307*	4262M P3884
3803M N9305	3888M P9187	3979M Z5963	4067M Z5880	4177M DP315	4263M W3798
3804M N6405	3889M N1302	3980M P4847	4068M V5695	4178M BP852*	4264M X4942

4265M KV963	4357M W8449	4447M AP221	4532M W7468	4617M HW683	4699M N6612
4266M N7251	4358M W8532	4448M DP827	4533M W9127	4618M KX567	4700M DE530
4267M JL373	4359M T7184	4449M AN526	4534M L1568	4621M KX179	4701M HS118
4268M R8645	4360M DD617	4450M P1363	4535M Z4927	4622M KX877*	4702M HG794
4269M R8657	4362M BL775*	4451M W4161	4536M V6933	4623M LB682*	4703M DP822
4270M R7766	4363M AH512	4452M K6942	4537M Z7078	4624M LB707	4705M V9894
4271M R8640	4364M BK883	4453M LX935	4538M EH995	4625M LB774*	4706M MM912
4272M R7760	4365M AH477	4454M DG362	4539M T3177	4626M LB769	4707M V6809
4273M R7871	4366M AH477	4455M R9490	4540M MM406	4627M LB770	4708M JK547
4274M R7764	4367M V1087	4456M LB220	4541M DJ988	4628M LB771	4714M HF738
4275M R7920	4368M BL523*	4457M DR855	4542M W8884	4629M LB773*	4715M FB738
4276M R7767	4370M ED704	4458M L3283	4543M DL614*	4630M LB775*	4723M L2657
4277M R8646	4371M R5747	4459M L3407	4544M W8956	4631M LB776*	4724M T7304
4278M L7461	4372M BK603	4460M V8204	4545M W8654	4632M R7673	4725M N2591
4279M L7305	4374M BF344	4461M T4642	4546M BB864·	4633M R7582	4726M V7421
4280M L7458	4375M DT523	4462M AB192	4547M DE311	4634M EK251	4727M ex-3275M
4281M R5775	4376M R9422*	4463M T8462	4548M N5033	4635M EK153	4728M DP805
4282M L7430*	4377M AK107	4464M L6922	4549M T9681	4636M EK284	4729M DP505
4283M R7916	4380M EV352	4465M T9313	4550M N5411	4637M R7583	4730M DP832
4284M R7860	4381M HX650*	4466M P5158	4551M N3987	4638M R7576	4731M DP692
4285M R8740	4382M BP983	4467M T6240	4552M T5298	4639M R7631	4732M LF919
4286M R7709	4383M Z4809	4468M T6305	4553M T4790	4640M R8887	4733M DP677
4287M R7828	4384M K9876	4469M DE409	4555M P5145	4641M R8939	4734M LH174
4288M R8714	4385M FB426	4472M BB193	4556M V1092	4642M R8689	4735M LH524
4289M R7716	4386M BA856	4474M T8175	4557M BB662	4643M R8685	4736M DP773
4290M X7686	4387M BA106	4475M T9836	4558M V6822	4644M R7826	4737M Z7079
4291M X7829	4389M AG705	4476M BB903	4559M P3814	4645M R7700	4738M DP554
4292M BD440	4390M JL112	4477M DP524	4560M N2660	4646M EK230	4739M DP502
4293M BD551	4391M JK163	4478M DP746	4561M P3829	4647M EK146	4740M HG876
4294M BF382*	4393M LB180	4479M HG797	4562M V7377	4648M DN383	4741M DP724
4295M AH755	4397M AK722	4480M LG727	4563M Z1289	4649M EK288	4742M DP430
4296M AH762	4398M AK597	4481M LG673	4564M Z1390	4650M EK231	4743M DP531
4297M AH791	4399M LA969	4482M T8601	4565M L7890	4651M DN255	4744M LH391
4298M AH787	4400M R8222	4483M R1855	4566M N2736	4652M DN503	4745M R1490
4299M AH803	4401M EL290	4484M N5089	4567M R7685	4653M DN595	4746M Z7144
4300M AH800	4402M R2125	4485M K6171	4568M R7638	4654M DN605	4747M V6545
4301M AH831	4403M X7835	4486M DG930	4569M DE480	4655M DN501	4748M W9318
4302M AH834	4404M X7611	4487M T2611	4570M R2253	4656M DN604	4749M W9134
4303M AH835	4405M X7577	4489M X7683	4571M X7774	4657M T4284	4750M X4921
4304M AH839	4406M R7224	4490M AW128	4572M X7811	4658M DL617*	4751M R9375
4305M AH846	4407M AB278	4491M W8653	4574M V6850	4659M BW841	4752M HR939*
4306M AH887	4408M X4175	4492M W8955	4576M P3701	4660M Z7085	4753M DP393
4307M AH808	4409M P7288	4493M W8946	4577M N2435	4661M N2399	4754M DP813
4308M BJ459	4410M DD745	4494M W8951	4578M V6579	4662M V6779	4755M X7543
4309M BJ491	4411M DK290	4495M HJ657	4579M T5536	4663M V7055	4756M B7379
4310M L7923	4412M DD667	4496M P6261	4580M Z1407	4664M N2671	4757M V7623
4311M DR852	4413M DD668	4497M L8230	4581M Z1492	4665M Z7091	4758M AF945
4312M K8826*	4414M DV427	4499M V7157	4582M Z1382	4666M DV961	4759M N2398
4313M JA699	4415M R1663	4500M V7068	4583M R1620	4667M DJ991	4760M T6044
4314M L1255	4416M DV706	4501M L1663	4585M T4797	4668M N3683	4761M DE257
4317M N9847	4417M N2735	4502M W9221	4586M T4844	4669M N3700	4762M DE604
4318M R1980	4418M AP225	4503M P3111	4587M N7208	4670M N3760	4763M T7402
4319M V6945	4419M BS142	4504M R4089	4588M T4797	4671M N3674	4764M T7686
4320M V6949	4420M N5254	4505M P3020	4589M Z1260	4672M DE662	4765M DE663
4321M L1910	4421M K8776	4506M V7002	4590M Z1268	4673M LH297	4766M EV778
4322M AH461	4422M K6243	4507M Z7147	4591M Z1322	4674M L3430	4767M LM483
4333M FL219	4423M DJ656	4508M K6182	4592M R1525	4675M N3904	4768M N7267
4334M N7768	4424M K6269	4509M T5957	4593M W1008	4676M R1908	4769M T9913
4335M N7829	4426M K8838	4510M HS149	4594M ex-4472M	4677M Z1280	4770M L8337
4336M R8631	4427M K8765	4511M DP292	4595M HG149	4678M T3033	4771M DP380
4337M R8708	4428M R3212	4512M T9894	4597M X7641	4679M V8188	4772M HF627
4338M R7851	4429M K8715	4513M P2384	4598M X7643	4680M T6371	4773M BJ788
4339M R7877	4430M AR340	4514M R1823	4599M R2202	4681M DE611	4774M P6378
4340M DN244	4431M P8657	4515M AG212	4600M R2189	4682M T6969	4775M EF297
4341M R8715	4432M LG928	4516M N2493	4601M N7605	4683M T7466	4776M LJ834
4342M DN277	4433M DP816	4517M V6984	4602M LR273	4684M Z4851	4777M W7460
4343M L2006	4434M AH498	4518M AG290	4603M W3983	4685M P2859	4778M Z1653
4344M R6268	4435M AK192	4519M R7118	4604M FR373	4686M V7252	4779M X3927
4345M N4646	4436M R9390*	4520M LG748	4605M Z1263	4687M V6675	4780M DD670
4346M P1882	4437M X4718	4521M R2078	4606M P9376	4688M Z7086	4781M X3481
4347M P1876	4438M KX539	4522M Z1398	4607M HW729	4689M BB741*	4782M W6056
4348M P2073	4439M N5468	4523M T7724	4608M KX304	4690M BB809	4783M X3764
4349M N5103	4440M L3421	4524M X4484	4609M HW728	4691M T6096	4784M DP343*
4350M V6990	4441M L3355	4525M R6914	4610M HW717	4692M T6873	4785M DF545
4351M R9381	4442M N3603	4526M L8132	4611M HW714	4693M N2455	4786M P6270
4352M W4887	4443M W4164	4527M N3945	4612M HW715	4694M AF950	4787M DP281
4353M AB871	4444M BA746	4528M DR856	4613M HW716	4695M Z4790	4788M DP795
4354M BL614	4445M EH904	4529M DK353	4614M HW718	4696M AF981	4789M DP747
4355M BJ477	4446M T9114 and	4530M LH245	4615M HW723	4697M AR493	4790M BJ613
4356M AW399*	W6050	4531M BF324	4616M HW731	4698M K4264	4791M X3820

No.	Serial		No.	Serial
4792M	Z1626		4881M	W6064
4793M	X3677		4882M	MP469
4794M	BK209		4883M	DZ366
4795M	BJ822		4884M	DZ385
4796M	BK351		4885M	HE219
4797M	Z1677		4886M	W4380
4798M	W6058		4887M	JN768
4799M	N7276		4889M	W8410
4800M	P6239		4891M	L2163*
4801M	P6378*		4894M	X3413
4802M	BJ665		4895M	BK448
4803M	BJ623		4896M	V3573
4804M	P1452		4897M	W8928
4805M	X3951		4898M	HE558
4806M	R2321		4899M	HE241
4807M	R1079		4900M	HE575
4808M	X3821		4901M	R5668
4809M	R7487		4902M	R5500
4811M	P6238		4903M	W4779
4812M	L4563		4904M	W4309
4813M	R9534		4906M	T1017
4814M	HF647*		4907M	HZ375
4815M	FL927		4908M	W3980
4816M	LV345		4909M	W6055*
4817M	LV338		4910M	JB899
4818M	R3155*		4911M	BB270
4819M	LK869		4912M	BB258
4820M	X3742		4913M	FH107
4821M	Z1672		4914M	W4253
4822M	T9275		4915M	W4181
4823M	FR208		4916M	LL612
4824M	N1428*		4917M	EF459
4825M	X3948		4918M	LL148
4826M	HF640		4919M	JL657
4827M	HX227		4920M	EF405
4828M	X3277		4922M	W4964
4829M	JN814		4923M	EE945
4830M	Z1688		4924M	BV474
4831M	JF275		4925M	EF301
4833M	T1213		4926M	KG393
4835M	NS926		4927M	FH115
4836M	EE899		4928M	DP484
4838M	42-24122 USAAF C-47		4933M	43-40438 USAAF CG-4
4839M	T1049		4934M	R5245
4840M	W6586		4935M	LW514
4841M	T1267		4936M	P8091
4842M	X6646		4937M	W7522
4843M	W7575		4938M	DZ352*
4844M	42-24068 USAAF C-47		4939M	R9592
4845M	LJ564		4940M	DP810
4846M	DD676		4941M	HX315
4847M	HE577		4942M	LJ891
4848M	BJ885		4943M	K7032
4849M	DD675		4944M	ED593
4850M	HP855		4945M	W4899
4851M	L4566		4946M	ED756
4853M	DF619		4947M	DS611
4855M	ex-2457M		4948M	R5910
4857M	HK413		4949M	R5912
4858M	FV931		4950M	R5865
4859M	LG920		4951M	LW646
4860M	LK483		4953M	LW641
4861M	P3345		4956M	EW632
4862M	L1600		4957M	AF945*
4863M	DT548		4958M	DS672*
4864M	R5854		4959M	DV193
4865M	DS612		4960M	DD715
4866M	AP397		4961M	HX226
4867M	R9428		4962M	HM499
4868M	K9895		4963M	LG854
4869M	R7889		4964M	RJ124
4871M	W3530		4965M	HG972
4872M	DP694		4966M	HZ428
4873M	DP348		4967M	ED869
4874M	W4940		4968M	W4358
4876M	HN355		4969M	W4113
4879M	HN122		4970M	JB555
4880M	W4078		4971M	W4941
			4972M	DS727

No.	Serial		No.	Serial
4973M	DS730		5075M	LW161
4974M	LL722		5076M	LA602
4975M	LL617		5077M	NT113
4976M	DS786		5078M	DP612
4977M	V3682		5079M	DP666
4979M	HZ107		5080M	DP538
4980M	RJ285*		5081M	DP660
4981M	KG639		5082M	DP670
4982M	JP124		5083M	DP549
4983M	LJ329		5084M	DD659
4984M	LJ105		5085M	ex-4729M
4985M	PW874		5086M	DP506
4986M	X3930		5087M	R6345
4987M	JX603*		5088M	PW256
4988M	MK210*		5089M	DP723
4989M	KG527		5091M	LG996
4990M	DS619		5092M	DP622
4991M	EJ710*		5093M	DP680
4992M	BR442*		5094M	EE225
5000M	PD348		5095M	KB434
5001M	PD281		5096M	FB360
5013M	HH967		5097M	KJ806
5014M	KB100		5198M	R7704
5015M	FS832		5199M	MH315
5016M	W3991		5200M	ML230
5017M	HH147		5201M	KG654
5018M	LJ119		5203M	DG771
5019M	DP649		5204M	DG251
5020M	DP741		5207M	W9182
5021M	LH948		5208M	FS814
5022M	LJ327		5209M	LG683
5023M	FP222		5210M	DP617
5024M	LG842		5211M	DP437
5025M	LH958		5212M	DP615
5026M	LJ323		5213M	LG971
5027M	DP708		5214M	DP331
5028M	AA860		5215M	HS128
5029M	FR577		5216M	LJ126
5030M	HR185		5217M	LG795
5031M	X3950		5218M	LL482
5032M	BJ799		5219M	LL742
5033M	HS127*		5220M	Z1740
5034M	V7166		5221M	FR370
5035M	V7246		5222M	LB316
5036M	V7653		5223M	EJ122
5037M	LF742		5224M	JB138
5038M	V6867		5225M	NA587
5039M	W9208		5226M	LW346
5042M	Z7145		5227M	NA608
5044M	P3597		5228M	NR115
5045M	P5170		5229M	EE234
5046M	LZ557		5230M	RR429*
5047M	LZ693		5231M	LJ183*
5048M	LZ794		5232M	BZ768
5049M	LZ594		5233M	42-56561 USAAF CG-4
5050M	K6987		5234M	JR508
5051M	LJ818		5235M	L'F578
5052M	R5631		5236M	MK573*
5054M	P2717		5238M	LK589
5055M	DV326		5239M	LJ538
5056M	BM844		5240M	LJ626
5057M	NB839		5241M	43-39744 USAAF CG-4
5058M	LZ630		5243M	LZ784
5059M	LZ786		5243M	LZ741
5060M	ED437		5244M	LZ628
5061M	DD730		5245M	KG796
5062M	HB864		5246M	LJ866
5063M	MZ627		5247M	LJ952
5064M	AW246		5248M	P7964*
5065M	AW276		5249M	FL913
5066M	BJ908		5250M	LJ183
5068M	HG152		5251M	AH538*
5070M	43-40372 USAAF CG-4		5252M	EE176
5071M	43-40593 USAAF CG-4		5253M	MN198
5072M	43-41061 USAAF CG-4		5254M	HK213
5073M	LW133		5255M	HK232
5074M	MZ282		5256M	FK214
			5257M	R5751

No.	Serial		No.	Serial
5258M	43-42162 USAAF CG-4		5337M	BM233
5259M	LH266		5338M	JB456
5260M	EE176*		5339M	RG446
5261M	MP688		5340M	X7626
5262M	P7964		5341M	LF675
5263M	BS152		5342M	LF626
5264M	JP734		5343M	PG445
5265M	NS857*		5344M	HW685
5266M	KJ561		5345M	JR193
5267M	NA548*		5346M	JR522
5268M	AR491		5347M	BM155
5269M	LF296*		5348M	AA839
5270M	LF686		5349M	AB904
5271M	LF399*		5350M	BM572
5272M	LF589*		5351M	FD826
5273M	LF653		5352M	FK226
5274M	LF692		5353M	HM906
5275M	LF659		5354M	BS393
5276M	LF645		5355M	P2407
5277M	PG519		5356M	N5461
5278M	LF512		5357M	AR570
5279M	L8168		5358M	LM443
5280M	T8192		5359M	N5413
5281M	T7118		5360M	L6905
5282M	T7024		5361M	P6345
5283M	N9190		5362M	L5816
5284M	K4282		5363M	L5968
5285M	HM361		5364M	N3902
5286M	HK313		5365M	V1099
5287M	W4241		5366M	N3927
5288M	R5609		5367M	LF765
5289M	W4264		5368M	LF656
5290M	ED324		5369M	LF709
5291M	W4845		5370M	LF718
5292M	JB404		5371M	LF719
5293M	JA693		5372M	LF690
5294M	JA677		5373M	NF686
5295M	EE128		5374M	NF737
5296M	ED382		5375M	BM158
5297M	X6743		5376M	BL979
5298M	LX532		5377M	EP120
5299M	LX724		5378M	AR614
5300M	LX725		5379M	MB855
5301M	SN126		5380M	EN913
5302M	LF580		5381M	BL365
5303M	PG486		5382M	AA929
5304M	PF440		5383M	W3423
5305M	JP406		5384M	BM256
5306M	LF590		5385M	BL712
5307M	LF323*		5386M	BL719
5308M	LF636		5387M	AA848
5309M	LF597		5388M	W3815
5310M	MW365		5389M	BL291
5311M	MW341		5390M	BL450
5312M	MW354		5391M	EN828
5313M	LF539		5392M	BL892
5314M	LF628		5393M	N3445
5315M	LF540		5394M	AR406
5316M	PZ829		5395M	BM201
5317M	PZ831		5396M	EP169
5318M	PZ830		5397M	EN862
5319M	LF773		5398M	BL826
5320M	PZ814		5399M	AR604*
5321M	LF583		5400M	EP770*
5322M	BS227		5401M	DN450
5323M	EK183		5402M	LE580
5324M	DZ418		5403M	LF711
5325M	HN144*		5404M	PG520*
5326M	LX464		5405M	LF738
5327M	HN514		5406M	LF745
5328M	MP308*		5407M	PG517
5329M	N6340		5408M	PG606
5330M	K6778		5409M	LD621
5331M	PG573		5410M	LF680
5332M	LF695		5411M	LF627
5333M	PG571		5412M	LF684
5334M	AR436		5413M	HV729*
5335M	BM354		5414M	LF538
5336M	AA931		5415M	LF398
			5416M	PG604

```
5417M PG497    5498M PG432              5581M X8204    5661M RB216    5744M V7508             5825M EE331
5418M LF674    5499M PG516              5582M MN118    5662M MN736    5745M PJ904             5826M LK340
5419M LF755    5500M PG499              5583M AA751    5663M JR379    5746M PT640             5827M NA643
5420M PG451    5501M PG534              5584M W3322    5664M RB369    5747M KB464             5828M MZ962
5421M PG498    5502M JP859              5585M EN964    5665M RB377    5748M LX824             5829M MT601
5422M PG484    5503M AB765              5586M R7220    5666M MP155    5749M FL546             5830M MT602
5423M LL666    5504M BG393              5587M AZ499    5667M MP184    5750M W5802 and RG364   5831M MT603
5424M MZ875    5505M DF417              5588M AR373    5668M MN934    5751M PL371             5832M JG661
5425M R6720    5506M EB719              5589M AB139    5669M JP512    5752M EE217             5833M JG662
5426M N5455    5507M EB751              5590M AB140    5670M EN238    5753M NJ269             5834M JG663
5427M T7214    5508M X6786              5591M AD248    5672M DL222*   5754M NV674             5835M JF296
5428M R5199    5511M N6426              5592M AR451    5673M DK969*   5755M HJ732             5836M KL162
5429M T7930    5512M DF244              5593M BM461    5674M LZ411    5756M LX846             5837M EE210
5430M DE872    5513M DF367              5594M AD508    5675M HF939    5757M NE823             5838M EE251
5431M N6535    5514M EB799              5595M BL665    5676M EE216    5758M DG202             5839M EE402
5432M T7931    5515M ED122              5596M AA969    5677M EE218    5759M LM287             5840M NM589
5433M N6872    5516M EN951              5597M AB202    5678M EE220    5760M NS643             5841M MW735
5434M T7965    5517M P8700              5598M HZ762    5679M PA884    5761M MM303             5842M W3656
5435M R5022    5518M EF541              5599M AD288    5680M RX573    5762M MN243             5843M TL191
5436M N9239    5519M EJ520              5600M BM411    5681M RX554*   5763M DN502             5844M LJ211
5437M DM215    5520M BM569              5601M BM322    5682M V8569*   5764M SW662             5845M NX560
5438M DK967    5521M EE644              5602M LM657    5683M AD318    5765M NV622             5846M LM186
5439M ED140    5522M X4272              5603M JA938    5684M MP519    5766M NV387             5847M PB855
5440M HM616    5523M AR519              5604M PZ283    5685M MK788    5767M PR669             5848M RF201
5441M HN170    5524M BM588              5605M FL934    5686M V8830    5768M FX293             5849M PB297
5442M PG541    5525M BL589              5606M MM915    5687M NA124    5769M FX321             5850M PB470
5443M R7595*   5526M DF362              5607M SW457    5688M EJ754    5770M FX293             5851M PB694
5444M BG175    5527M BG203              5608M EK538    5689M ML311    5771M FX321             5852M ME370
5445M V3719    5528M LX465              5609M EK371    5690M MK356    5772M DM387             5853M NM799
5446M EK326    5529M BF918              5610M RB278    5691M MJ202    5773M ML970             5854M MF359
5447M T5887    5530M V3680              5611M EK150    5692M NH175    5774M HG137             5855M NV756
5448M T6442    5531M BG235              5612M PD512    5693M MK835    5775M JN489             5856M NV675
5449M T6286    5532M ND616              5613M EK117    5694M HK241    5776M EM545             5857M NV653
5450M T6865    5533M JB457              5614M RB483    5695M HK301    5777M HP255             5858M NV682
5451M W4231    5534M HR132              5615M V8545    5696M V8441    5778M Not used AM580     5859M KX699
5452M R5503    5535M MN418              5616M X8227    5697M ND217*   5779M NA662             5860M LE395*
5453M L7582    5536M MN987              5617M V8433    5698M KW107*   5780M NA662             5861M KZ675*
5454M ED474    5537M W3127              5618M ND227    5699M ND199*   5781M EE235             5862M DG208
5455M ED944    5538M EP570              5619M V8520    5700M KW101    5782M EE240             5863M BK130
5456M HN706    5539M BM409              5620M KW120    5701M EL171*   5783M EE241             5865M ND584
5457M V3737    5540M EE624              5621M ND232    5702M MM850    5784M EE243             5866M RJ297
5458M AB686    5541M AB265              5622M ND224    5703M EJ760    5785M EE231             5868M MV566
5459M NM718*   5542M BM192              5623M V8713    5704M NV918    5786M EE236             5869M NT309
5460M ED127    5543M AB193              5624M ND272    5705M EP500    5787M EE239             5870M R8926
5461M PG548    5544M AD425              5625M V8869    5706M LF691    5788M EE244             5871M R8969
5462M PG440    5547M DL409              5626M V8449    5707M PG572    5789M EE232             5872M MN956
5463M MW340    5548M AZ847              5627M KV978    5708M PG539    5790M EE213             5873M JR378
5464M PG570    5549M AZ853              5628M ND225    5709M V3911    5791M EE242             5874M JR314
5465M PG551    5550M DL526              5629M ND231    5710M NS650*   5792M L7566             5875M RB307
5466M LF751    5551M AB276              5630M V8742    5711M EE233    5793M ND335             5876M EJ992
5467M MN645    5552M MN208              5631M ND222    5712M EE237    5794M ME324             5877M MN450
5468M EJ586    5553M MN229              5632M ND266    5713M HK647    5795M ND619             5878M JP506
5469M PG433*   5554M LV626              5633M NA553    5714M DL431    5796M HP249             5879M JP395
5470M LF646    5555M AD573              5634M EG389    5715M DD856    5797M PJ958             5880M EK154
5471M PZ777    5556M JR305              5635M MW166    5716M DD856    5798M EE214             5881M DN384
5472M LF642    5557M EK180              5636M PZ282    5717M AD299    5799M EE219             5882M SW500
5473M LF635    5558M MW176              5637M NT206    5718M BM597    5800M NL698             5883M JR134
5474M DL842    5559M MW131              5638M HN849    5719M AB971    5801M DE512             5884M KW282
5475M W9088    5560M V8214              5639M LB457    5720M AR399    5802M EN526             5885M JM335
5476M X7125    5561M 42-61897 USAAF CG-4 5640M RB441   5721M BM246    5803M EF731             5886M JM331
5477M HM647    5562M 42-74523 USAAF CG-4 5641M PD452   5722M DM204    5804M EE286             5887M LX854
5478M DF309    5563M EJ539              5642M PD608    5723M PB482    5805M EE315             5888M JM209
5479M DF290    5565M MZ411              5643M EK219    5724M LM188    5806M EE317             5889M ML311
5480M T1016    5566M KG590              5644M SW398    5725M PB142    5807M EE318             5890M ED130
5481M AT684    5567M KG418              5645M RB495    5726M ND909    5808M NC792             5891M X7289
5482M V4087    5568M FX306              5646M RB427    5727M ND348    5809M NA960             5892M TA391
5483M PH127    5569M KF155              5647M MN283    5728M RG386    5810M MM645             5893M NE122
5484M L4655    5570M BL755              5648M RB391    5729M RM638    5811M KB213             5894M TL131
5485M N6332    5571M W3328              5649M SW641    5730M RM638    5812M KB122             5895M EE405
5486M R6279    5572M W3329              5650M SW428    5731M PN446    5813M KB265             5896M EE406
5487M R9978    5573M V8608              5651M RB425    5732M MM498*   5814M TA397             5897M NM635*
5488M V4050    5574M MM948              5652M JR432    5733M MW161    5815M PB462             5898M T6684
5489M V4054    5575M MM919              5653M RB380    5734M ex-5730M 5816M EE228             5899M R4766
5490M BG180    5576M MM844              5654M RB282    5735M LP661*   5817M TA243             5900M T8181
5491M MP461    5577M MM848              5655M RB477    5736M PD418    5818M MZ650             5901M PK121
5492M AT683    5578M MM853              5656M MN203    5737M EW297    5819M JN798             5902M SW620
5493M BG179    5579M EJ520              5657M MN953    5738M BK356    5820M KB345             5903M SW621
5494M ML111    5580M X8027              5658M SW560    5739M BK451    5821M T6317             5904M SW633
5495M LE747                            5659M JR327    5740M BK496    5822M EM530             5905M KZ405
5496M LE715                            5660M SW553    5741M NA124    5823M RN331             5906M NN812
                                                      5742M KG514    5824M LL547
                                                      5743M NE423
```

Appendix C

5910M LR530	5991M NJ700	6076M EE413	6159M HM796	6242M ED909	6323M SM247
5911M HJ938	5992M MT358	6077M NA399	6160M PM634	6243M LA653	6325M HJ828*
5912M DD759	5993M NJ623	6078M KA306	6161M KF219	6244M HM759	6326M MK623
5913M DZ700	5994M NV944	6079M MJ526	6162M MK683	6245M LX427	6327M KB491
5914M PB342	5995M LP364	6080M TB592	6163M JN753	6246M LX694	6328M NV732
5915M NT560	5996M LW906	6081M MJ452	6164M JN734	6247M NM808	6329M NA635
5916M ML457	5997M V3861	6082M MW170	6165M TZ135	6248M SM402	6330M RV321
5917M ML471	5998M NA294	6083M R4763	6166M SM913	6249M PM144	6331M TB344
5918M EE136	5999M SM507	6084M AP483	6167M PB585	6250M PM154	6332M LF581
5919M MB798	6000M SM391	6085M NX745*	6169M PA252	6251M RN217	6333M SL565
5920M MB804	6001M SM665	6087M MD170	6172M L5937	6252M TJ167	6334M ME531
5921M MB838	6002M SM479	6088M LJ281	6173M LW205	6253M FL561	6335M MW228*
5922M MB844	6003M SM480	6089M NV292	6174M NG130	6254M RS554	6336M NX286
5923M MB855	6004M SM394	6090M NV297	6175M SM307	6255M PK318	6337M LZ787*
5924M EE407	6005M SM471	6091M NV423	6176M SM276	6256M NT391	6338M HM346
5925M JA959	6006M KB685	6092M NV425	6177M TB578	6257M PV313	6339M HM337
5926M RE230	6007M PP236	6093M NV177	6178M TB903	6258M TE471	6340M NH694
5927M EE211	6008M SM385	6094M NV192	6179M TD377	6259M PB420	6341M EE446
5928M DG203	6009M HP495	6095M NV432	6180M RR229	6260M LM591	6342M RD569
5929M EP250	6010M PP227	6096M NV541	6181M EM331	6261M PB136	6343M HK327
5930M DV310	6011M LF572	6097M NT947	6182M NA421	6262M TB522	6344M RT886
5931M EP380	6012M R4761*	6098M NT928	6183M MJ814	6263M PT953	6345M KN489
5932M W3707	6013M MS934	6099M NV537	6184M MH318	6264M RS713	6346M KG367
5933M BS499	6014M NJ671	6100M ML826	6185M MP309	6265M PH342	6347M to 6571M
5934M EN396	6015M RT464	6101M RD348	6186M HN411*	6266M DF470	6348M KN524
5935M MB787	6016M NE798	6102M LT136	6187M V3944	6267M HN827	6349M NV652
5936M MB791	6017M NT592	6103M PP145	6188M LB409	6268M RR337	6350M RM862
5937M MB906	6018M BR623	6104M HN422*	6189M HN776*	6269M RF930	6351M ML929
5938M W3250	6019M Not used	6105M HN704*	6190M LX261*	6270M RF940	6352M MM301
5939M W3228	6020M BS286	6106M NM797	6191M PG985	6271M EE250	6353M NS572
5940M HM595	6021M BS280	6107M MP362	6192M MT167	6272M TE207	6354M RG875
5941M BS315	6022M KH225	6108M LX769	6193M NJ684	6273M TD236	6355M TG281
5942M PW929	6025M KH305	6109M LX354*	6194M DM395	6274M RF888	6356M EE229
5943M EE215	6026M MH731	6110M DF343	6195M Glider	6275M NE715	6357M KG379
5944M EM389	6027M RD466	6111M V3507	6196M DF469	6276M FS906	6358M ex-6301M
5945M JB643	6028M MM617	6112M V3472	6197M LX277*	6277M EE458	6359M KG529
5946M HN146	6029M MW813	6113M HE446	6198M NH411	6278M MD142	6361M RE227
5947M L8253	6030M HP925	6114M HF684*	6199M PH299	6279M RE228	6362M TB365
5948M MJ586	6031M PP149	6115M LN391	6200M AB640	6280M HM452	6363M LF761
5949M FD772	6032M PG988	6116M MT477	6201M SM390	6281M DX193	6364M LF703
5950M PH119	6033M RR919	6117M MT490	6202M SM481	6282M LF575	6367M NT350
5951M BS345	6034M MA303	6118M NT363	6203M RR245	6283M T5696	6368M to-6411M
5952M NS551	6035M BS449	6119M MM810	6204M NA635	6284M LX474	6369M TB256
5953M PL837	6036M BS347	6120M NS803	6205M BS533	6285M HN422	6370M MJ329
5954M LZ919	6037M BR632	6121M Cancelled	6206M RF268	6286M HN704*	6371M PL256
5955M BS474	6038M EN363	6122M JP796*	6207M NA341	6287M MP362	6372M RG267
5956M HR155	6039M MA299	6123M EJ920	6208M NA911	6288M LX769	6373M LA193
5957M LR540	6040M MA646	6124M DN531	6209M PF992	6289M RN349	6374M RZ219
5958M MW250	6041M PL277	6125M JP408	6210M NC947	6290M RZ367	6375M RZ198
5959M NT137	6042M LZ921	6126M MW774*	6211M NA902	6291M FZ660	6376M RZ316
5960M RV314	6043M BS513	6127M MN256*	6212M TK983*	6292M KG610	6377M RX545*
5961M TJ529	6044M RZ351	6128M PD555*	6213M HE413	6293M PZ339	6378M RX803
5962M PF397	6045M RX536*	6129M SW694*	6214M MA524	6294M RF187	6379M MK572
5963M TJ510	6046M RR936	6130M SW755*	6215M MX991	6295M ME545	6380M RG872
5964M SM243	6047M HH404	6131M SW695*	6216M NX634	6296M RF940*	6381M MM695*
5965M N5395	6048M TB744	6132M RB281*	6217M LP883	6297M FZ640	6382M MK285
5966M PB926	6049M R4752	6133M RB403*	6218M LP771	6298M FZ680	6383M MH478
5967M MK184	6052M ex-6020M	6134M JP515*	6219M NL601	6299M FZ601	6384M NH343
5968M MA742	6054M MM426	6135M MN378*	6220M L6913	6300M KG729	6385M PN315
5969M EN177	6055M NS982	6136M JR130	6221M Magister	6301M KG622	6386M PB920
5970M MH844	6056M PZ194	6137M SW511*	6222M NK136	6303M TJ512	6387M MM700
5971M MK922	6057M PZ373	6138M RB383*	6223M MW409	6304M PB986	6388M MW798
5972M BS439	6058M PZ358	6139M TA796	6224M TD187	6305M NX579	6389M ML169
5973M SM402	6059M PZ389	6140M PT753	6225M X9580	6306M RF940*	6390M RN317
5974M RN312	6060M SZ970	6141M PW925	6226M LW385	6307M TK889*	6391M RN323
5975M RN512	6061M TB542	6142M MH473	6227M LV639	6308M TK896*	6392M RN363
5976M RX571	6062M TB544	6143M MM389	6228M EE579	6309M NA428	6393M RN327
5977M RX578	6063M TB540	6144M MH940	6229M KN447*	6310M NA452	6394M RN330
5978M RX562	6064M KW337	6145M TB920	6230M KG649	6311M NA458	6395M RN362
5979M SM193	6065M RD357	6146M TD358	6231M LR294	6312M TK985	6396M RZ290
5980M SM207	6066M RD750	6148M RF441*	6232M NS740	6313M RF258	6397M RZ300
5981M NM492	6067M NV492	6149M PX210	6233M NS686	6314M FE866	6398M TK998
5982M N9211	6068M KW285	6150M NE180	6234M HK710	6315M RV312	6399M TK982
5983M K2587	6069M NV441	6151M MS960	6235M MM302	6316M MZ269	6400M TK992
5984M T5836	6070M EL181*	6152M MS953	6236M ML171	6317M N6972	6401M RX857
5985M DE661	6071M MT366	6153M Auster*	6237M PF572	6318M LR528	6402M RX551
5986M T7682	6072M TJ426	6154M Auster*	6238M DM449	6319M NK847	6403M RX755
5987M T7682	6073M NJ647	6156M NS640	6239M DM353	6320M NK767	6404M RX535
5988M RT515	6074M NJ665	6157M MM631	6240M AZ785	6321M NK705	6405M RX758
5989M RT636	6075M NJ639	6158M TD305	6241M PB489	6323M SM247	6406M RX770
5990M TJ226					

6407M RX904	6494M RK947*	6574M EE391	6654M HR252	6735M EE454	6816M NX687
6408M LT154	6495M LZ184	6575M T6688	6655M TE244	6736M NX737	6817M EE400
6409M HZ482	6496M ME376	6576M TV166	6656M MW418	6737M L6737*	6818M VL522
6410M FL584	6497M ME331	6577M NJ626	6657M SZ973	6738M TL190*	6819M VL523
6411M LA305	6498M KB681	6578M EJ543	6658M PZ277	6739M TL280*	6820M TE477
6412M TB256	6499M TL146	6579M X6799	6659M NT568	6740M TL248	6821M RW378
6413M LA210	6500M DZ541	6580M NK291	6660M NT434	6741M TK935	6822M TE463
6414M ML370	6501M NG489	6581M NK924	6661M NT252	6742M TE764	6823M SL561
6415M RG751	6502M RF393	6582M NL222	6662M MM363	6743M SL561	6824M RT934
6416M MZ269	6503M MM798	6583M MK524	6663M NK340*	6744M NC894*	6825M JM962
6417M SM418	6504M NC838	6584M PT398	6664M LZ588*	6745M TA528	6826M TA582
6418M TD143	6505M PA382	6585M ML185	6665M NT242	6746M DE241*	6827M RF451
6419M RK905	6506M TW653	6586M RE121	6666M To 6675M	6747M EE187	6828M RF345
6420M RA649	6507M KG796	6587M PF442	6667M RX910	6748M RT681	6829M RF466
6421M NG340	6508M BG173	6588M PF547	6668M HM362	6749M NC890	6830M RF447
6422M To 6449M	6509M PP366	6589M PF594	6669M RP582	6750M NC891	6831M KN837
6423M TD407*	6510M RR986	6590M TL189	6670M TK837	6751M NC496	6832M RS037
6424M NX793	6511M EE361	6591M DG207*	6671M TV177	6752M NC668	6833M LA250
6425M TW929	6512M Z2515	6592M MX994	6672M TV172	6753M NX629	6834M LA265
6426M RA802	6513M Z2465	6593M EE369	6673M RF271	6754M NC837	6835M RW359
6427M MG291	6514M RG776	6594M NT620	6674M NT422	6755M RP381	6836M NH689
6428M NF576	6515M RG782	6595M PF484	6675M SL685	6756M NA771	6837M RB171
6429M TK624	6516M BS248	6596M KG745	6676M SL719	6757M LN697	6838M RB179
6430M KA958	6517M BS386	6597M SM360	6677M SZ972	6758M NC748*	6839M RM623
6431M RT877	6518M DE220*	6598M NT605	6678M PZ373	6759M LP877*	6840M NH708
6432M RX807	6519M NT316	6599M RE219	6679M RF301	6760M LP712	6841M RB151
6433M TE255	6520M NT543	6600M R6083	6680M TZ226*	6761M SW328	6842M RB157
6434M MT176	6521M EX684	6601M NT428	6681M TP201*	6762M SW295	6843M RB170
6435M NJ674	6522M EX697	6602M NT334	6682M RD861	6763M KN250*	6844M RM681
6436M RT562	6523M RM859	6603M TE199	6683M RT770	6764M TK722*	6845M RM854
6437M TJ349	6524M HR113	6604M EE493	6684M EE429	6765M TL723*	6846M RM856
6438M RV313	6525M TA380	6605M MG787	6685M PX216*	6766M TL724	6847M RM884
6439M NO578	6526M TA535	6606M MV307	6686M EE366	6767M TL725	6848M RM909
6440M T6777	6527M RF897	6607M PF498	6687M RS549	6768M RZ431	6849M RM929
6441M TP408	6528M TG282	6608M PF524	6688M DX691*	6769M TK738	6850M TE184
6442M HM599	6529M RT777	6609M TG519	6689M NH784	6770M RR948	6851M TG278
6443M NL998	6530M FT429	6610M To 5698M	6690M NS809	6771M HM478	6852M T5985*
6444M RR994	6531M SN119	6611M T5822	6691M HN368	6772M LZ592	6853M PZ281
6445M NC631	6532M TL123	6612M PX231	6692M DX221	6773M RR992*	6854M T5879
6446M N9612	6533M RX961	6613M TG291	6693M LZ662	6774M LZ675	6855M MP449
6447M NT431	6534M RN272	6614M VN695	6694M RM737	6775M MW322*	6856M T5985
6448M NR279	6535M HM604	6615M VD162	6695M VT827	6776M TE623	6857M RG778
6449M NG494	6536M HM837	6616M VD201	6696M PX238	6777M TE687	6858M RG780
6450M LN935	6537M BG261	6617M LA633	6697M RP498	6778M TE696	6859M RG871
6451M TL235	6538M TD231	6618M ND115	6698M DX231	6779M TE713	6860M VF306
6452M BS249	6539M V4238	6619M N9174	6699M RG870	6780M TE745	6861M T5428
6453M PM633	6540M TD281	6620M NX121*	6700M HM476	6781M TE759	6862M TD319
6454M MH422	6541M LL742	6621M RA445	6701M TE356*	6782M TE777	6863M WA713
6455M MJ887	6542M TL251	6622M RE267	6702M RS551	6783M TE851	6864M R4945
6456M MK303	6543M T9979	6623M RE236	6703M VN684	6784M TE618	6865M VW828
6457M ML427	6544M EE221	6624M RE235	6704M RP242	6785M TE683	6866M EE269
6458M MA803	6545M MM676	6625M PR846	6705M RP245	6786M NX790	6867M EE360
6459M MK426	6546M EE274	6626M SM826	6706M RP246	6787M DE204*	6868M T5375
6460M ML345	6547M EE471*	6627M RA630	6707M RP177	6788M RR942	6869M VF336
6461M MH450	6548M EE484*	6628M ME528	6708M RP186	6789M LZ795	6870M JM836
6462M MA298	6549M HR349	6629M RE244	6709M HR175	6790M RE414	6871M PF915
6463M NT566	6550M LR523	6630M RE252	6710M PB480	6791M EM920	6872M N6668
6464M JM943	6551M PF567	6631M RA652	6711M HM340	6792M DE412	6873M EE520*
6465M LR156	6552M RW391	6632M RA646	6712M EE454	6793M SM406*	6874M LR182
6466M LV639	6553M SM301	6633M SS713	6713M NX735	6794M RG290	6875M T7731
6467M DF241	6554M LV629	6634M RE263	6714M RT483*	6795M VR572	6876M NA828
6468M MP304*	6555M RW377	6635M RE256	6715M MW322	6796M TA592	6877M NM154
6469M PH401*	6556M W1887	6636M RA647	6716M VV191	6797M TG280	6878M N9278
6470M HM955	6557M N5240	6637M SM284	6717M VV191	6798M TD135	6879M RA491*
6471M EG390	6558M NC865	6638M TW896	6718M EE309	6799M TW515	6880M VV954
6472M TZ239	6559M NA724	6639M RP409	6719M TL473	6800M VW458	6881M VF572
6473M N6973*	6560M LN935*	6640M RM694	6720M T6497	6801M T7395	6882M RP386
6474M NV696	6561M PF388	6641M TE479	6721M T7052	6802M DE854	6883M LX274
6475M NV674	6562M TZ148	6642M TE338	6722M T7301	6803M T7164	6884M HM742
6476M SN105	6563M EE468	6643M JN801	6723M T7810	6804M DE606	6885M SL616
6477M EJ638	6564M LA193	6644M JN856	6724M T5700	6805M BB704	6886M NK868
6485M NT511	6565M VR194	6645M JN874	6725M T6257	6806M DE588	6887M DE982
6486M NT566	6566M VN700	6646M SN185	6726M R5133	6807M DF187	6888M PH513
6487M EE336	6567M VR195	6647M SN312	6727M R4941	6808M DE658	6889M RW349
6488M R4924	6568M VN687	6648M EJ785	6728M T5427	6809M SZ984	6890M TE352
6489M LA299	6569M VN702	6649M PB920*	6729M NK631	6810M NT181	6891M FR209
6490M LA255	6570M SM426	6650M NK841	6730M LZ731	6811M PA478	6892M ED286
6491M EE351	6571M MM744	6651M RE238	6731M KP231	6812M VW433	6893M NT505
6492M TL194	6572M EE271	6652M RE262	6732M EE594	6813M VT277	6894M RR333
6493M PA434	6573M EE247	6653M NX176	6733M LZ572	6814M T7277	6895M HM809
				6734M HM397	6815M DE836	

6896M NA846	6976M EE413	7056M TG371	7136M WE273	7216M RR263	7296M XE989
6897M T6391	6977M EE486	7057M TG381	7137M WE270	7217M WK888	7297M WK888
6898M T6067	6978M EE276	7058M TG389	7138M WE276	7218M WE943	7298M WE943
6899M TW901	6979M EE307	7059M TG445	7139M WE263	7219M PH553	7299M WK218
6900M WA692	6980M EE350	7060M VF301	7140M WE274	7220M RH798	7300M WK240
6901M DE455	6981M EE388	7061M VF311	7141M WA820	7221M RA456	7301M WK241
6902M SM899	6982M EE469	7062M VF272	7142M VT697	7222M RA456	7302M WK242
6903M RG820	6983M T5696	7063M TG308	7143M VR605	7223M VT125	7303M WK245
6904M TB753	6984M DE673	7064M TG309	7144M VR592	7224M VT134	7304M WK210
6905M ED233*	6985M TA590	7065M TG312	7145M DE175	7225M VT317	7305M WK211
6906M NM406	6986M NS682	7066M TG337	7146M NJ180	7226M VT318	7306M WK212
6907M MF634	6987M RE284	7067M TG373	7147M PF677	7227M WW435	7307M WK219
6908M LZ621	6988M LR571	7068M TG376	7148M RP151	7228M WE256	7308M WK220
6909M HM352	6989M NF682	7069M TG385	7149M VZ472	7229M KF126	7309M WK244
6910M MF452	6990M TE389	7070M TG387	7150M PK683	7230M WF967	7310M WK197
6911M SL678	6991M VW216	7071M TG420	7151M VT229	7231M VV361	7311M WK201
6912M NR465	6992M VR600	7072M TG432	7152M N6539	7232M VV367	7312M WK205
6913M EE489	6993M L6930	7073M TG443	7153M SX933	7233M VS275	7313M WK206
6914M DX197	6994M LZ596*	7074M VF304	7154M WB188	7234M VS260	7314M WK207
6915M RE342	6995M PM610	7075M VV205	7155M WK580	7235M TG329	7315M WK249
6916M NT507	6996M PM611	7076M VF316	7156M RF565	7236M WN165	7316M WK246
6917M NT596	6997M PF564*	7077M VF319	7157M WE259	7237M WN535	7317M VZ544
6918M NT616	6998M TE242*	7078M VT801	7158M WJ765	7238M WG138	7318M WH366
6919M T5542	6999M PH644	7079M VT821	7159M WG503	7239M WG142	7319M WE949
6920M NM339	7000M TE392	7080M VT854	7160M RF336	7240M TE400	7320M WF742
6921M NM754	7001M TE356	7081M VT859	7161M VR590	7241M TE311	7321M WA963
6922M T1341	7002M N6854	7082M VT810	7162M WE264	7242M SM411	7322M VZ517
6923M DF191	7003M DE156*	7083M VF321	7163M VW454	7243M TE462	7323M VV217
6924M T5702	7004M TG277	7084M VF335	7164M WD127	7244M TB382	7324M WA885
6925M JN543*	7005M WH296	7085M VF342	7165M EE278	7245M RW382	7325M R5868
6926M HP218*	7006M TG299	7086M VG697	7166M EE339	7246M TD248	7326M VN485
6927M NR636	7007M WF324	7087M VT796	7167M EE352	7247M EE419	7327M WK255
6928M HM427	7008M EE549	7088M VT800	7168M EE397	7248M EE424	7328M WK256
6929M LZ586*	7009M DE156	7089M VF332	7169M EE478	7249M VV912	7329M WK257
6930M DX222*	7010M TP378	7090M EE531*	7170M EE479	7250M VS581	7330M WK258
6931M EE254	7011M NP234	7091M DE658*	7171M EE481	7251M VV329	7331M WK259
6932M EE277	7012M VW790	7092M T7164*	7172M JM667	7252M VV320	7332M WK250
6933M MG496	7013M VA882	7093M DE854*	7173M SX931	7253M VS250	7333M WK251
6934M NT449	7014M N6720	7094M VR591	7174M VX272	7254M WH357	7334M WK252
6935M NM790	7015M NL985	7095M VW899	7175M VV106	7255M TB308	7335M WK254
6936M DE322	7016M VS600	7096M VZ454	7176M VZ216	7256M TB752	7336M WK260
6937M RA416	7017M RH810*	7097M VR191	7177M VR230	7257M To 8073M	7337M WK261
6938M EB729	7018M RE312	7098M WP227	7178M VR307	7258M To 7280M	7338M WK247
6939M N6479	7019M RF387	7099M EE597	7179M VS261	7259M WL112	7339M WK262
6940M EM967	7020M RF409	7100M NT471	7180M VS268	7260M VZ552	7340M WK263
6941M EM444	7021M RF498	7101M PH804	7181M VR241	7261M VZ568	7341M WK264
6942M MS908	7022M RF363	7102M PB529	7182M VS245	7262M WA841	7342M WK265
6943M SX939	7023M RF397	7103M PH749	7183M VS263	7263M WA897	7343M WK266
6944M RW386	7024M RF401	7104M RP322	7184M EE248	7264M WA765	7344M WK267
6945M TB916	7025M RE377	7105M NA845	7185M EE359	7265M WH382	7345M WK268
6946M RW388	7026M RF390	7106M TV168	7186M EE389	7266M VZ561	7346M WK269
6947M SR910	7027M RF482	7107M FT303	7187M WE255	7267M VR219	7347M WK270
6948M DE673	7028M RF405	7108M TG559	7188M VR597	7268M VR223	7348M WK271
6949M PH524	7029M RK959	7109M EE470	7189M WV928	7269M VR225	7349M WK194
6950M VZ265	7030M RL133	7110M PH834	7190M WE267	7270M VR237	7350M WK202
6951M VF318*	7031M HM345	7111M RE321	7191M VS368	7271M VR273	7351M WK652
6952M NA786	7032M HM480	7112M EE272	7192M VR224	7272M VR275	7352M WE455
6953M TW101	7033M Z7237	7113M KF513	7193M SX986	7273M VR281	7353M WS831
6954M HJ888	7034M DE219	7114M TW461	7194M WA788	7274M VR283	7354M WE859
6955M TE657*	7035M DE306	7115M WE417	7195M SX978	7275M VR291	7355M VV990
6956M VT726	7036M DE739	7116M KF209	7196M RE415	7276M VR293	7356M VV695
6957M T6612	7037M DE779	7117M PH586	7197M VV199*	7277M SN331	7357M VX953
6958M NK832	7038M N9385	7118M LA198	7198M VT871*	7278M DF308	7358M WE272
6959M NJ280	7039M DE889	7119M LA226	7199M VT856	7279M TB752*	7359M WM185
6960M MT847	7040M N6804	7120M LA228	7200M VT812	7280M RW394*	7360M WM192
6961M EE254	7041M N9374	7121M LA263	7201M VT861*	7281M TB252*	7361M RA476
6962M EE279	7042M R5019	7122M RK987	7202M VT344	7282M R6248	7362M VP546
6963M EE289	7043M R5114	7123M RK997	7203M TG349	7283M VZ515	7363M WE315
6964M EE367	7044M W7950	7124M RK980	7204M VT128	7284M WB195	7364M VS274
6965M EE300	7045M VF274	7125M RK990	7205M WF641	7285M VV119	7365M WG849
6966M EE306	7046M VF307	7126M RS717	7206M WK203	7286M WB706	7366M WH449
6967M EE314	7047M TG382	7127M EE292	7207M TE384	7287M TE288	7367M WH304
6968M EE420	7048M TG429	7128M EE358	7208M VS627	7288M PK724	7368M WZ575
6969M EE447	7049M TG437	7129M TJ396	7209M VZ478	7289M XD143	7369M XD692*
6970M EE459	7050M TG440	7130M RA434	7210M WL125	7290M WW607	7370M WA275
6971M EE354	7051M TG447	7131M RA435	7211M WE266	7291M WE966	7371M VV480
6972M EE356	7052M TG289	7132M VZ117	7212M WW640	7292M WP143	7372M VZ335
6973M EE428	7053M TG300	7133M WE257	7213M VZ480	7293M RW393	7373M WL498
6974M EE464	7054M TG304	7134M WE262	7214M VZ464	7294M WF759	7374M WT577
6975M EE348	7055M TG336	7135M WE278	7215M VX238	7295M WE966	7375M WT637

7376M WK676	7456M WX922	7536M WT685	7616M WW388	7696M WV493	7776M XF306	
7377M RF510	7457M WX847	7537M WT693	7617M WV573	7697M WV495	7777M XF308	
7378M WE855	7458M WX905	7538M WW601	7618M WW442	7698M WV499	7778M XF316	
7379M WD999*	7459M WX801	7539M WW602	7619M XA560	7699M WV541	7779M WV258	
7380M WF907*	7460M WD958*	7540M WW604	7620M WD959	7700M WV544	7780M WV261	
7381M XF611	7461M XE828	7541M WW609	7621M WV686	7701M WV268	7781M WV266	
7382M WK253	7462M WA824	7542M WW899*	7622M WV606	7702M XN133	7782M WV272	
7383M VW364	7463M WF657	7543M WN901	7623M WH735	7703M WG725	7783M WV331	
7384M WD116	7464M XA564	7544M WN904	7624M WZ870	7704M TW536	7784M WW653	
7385M WF421	7465M XA255	7545M WN906	7625M WD356	7705M WL505	7785M XE659	
7386M ex-7380M	7466M XF598	7546M WJ769	7626M VW126	7706M WB584	7786M XE678	
7387M ex-7379M	7467M WP978	7547M WX932	7627M XA563	7707M WP201	7787M XE679	
7388M WK196	7468M VL268	7548M PS915	7628M WH723	7708M G-ALBO	7788M XE704	
7389M WH297	7469M VL269	7549M WX843	7629M XD386	7709M WT933	7789M WT801	
7390M WA981	7470M XA553	7550M WP110	7630M VZ304	7710M WT897	7790M WT716	
7391M WA993*	7471M WP192	7551M XA567	7631M VX185	7711M PS915	7791M WT778	
7392M WE284	7472M XE926	7552M WT836	7632M WP918	7712M WK281	7792M WT797	
7393M WE293	7473M XE946	7553M XK629	7633M WK614	7713M WP203	7793M XG523	
7394M WE332	7474M VL274	7554M FS890	7634M WA450	7714M WK307	7794M XE702	
7395M WE345	7475M VL276	7555M AR614	7635M WS667	7715M XK724	7795M WK712	
7396M WE349	7476M VL277	7556M WK584	7636M WJ878	7716M WS776	7796M WJ676	
7397M WN958	7477M VL256	7557M WZ423	7637M WF887	7717M XA549	7797M XH782	
7398M VR247	7478M WW396*	7558M XA544	7638M WR433	7718M WA577	7798M XH783	
7399M VR262	7479M WD168	7559M TB287	7639M WR493	7719M WK277	7799M XH784	
7400M VS264	7480M VW838	7560M XK630	7640M WR412	7720M XA628	7800M XH901	
7401M VS279	7481M VW850*	7561M WB846	7641M XA634	7721M XA554*	7801M XH902	
7402M VR282	7482M VW163*	7562M WE547	7642M WD171	7722M XA571*	7802M WD996	
7403M VR290	7483M VW190	7563M WN892	7643M WD375*	7723M XA620	7803M XF385	
7404M VS331	7484M XA550	7564M XE982	7644M WD332	7724M XA919	7804M XF946	
7405M VS369	7485M WT830	7565M WX849	7645M WD293	7725M XA755	7805M TW117	
7406M VS624	7486M WN888	7566M WS687	7646M VX461	7726M XM373	7806M TA639	
7407M WN957	7487M WN910	7567M WS603	7647M WG473	7727M WZ494	7807M XE715	
7408M WK308	7488M WT560	7568M WS666	7648M XF785	7728M WZ458	7808M XH790	
7409M VZ851	7489M WT567	7569M WP126	7649M XA706	7729M WB758	7809M XA699	
7410M WT646	7490M WT568	7570M XD674	7650M WP895	7730M VP289	7810M XK991	
7411M WT591*	7491M WT569	7571M WP146*	7651M XD519	7731M WH546	7811M XH900	
7412M WT679*	7492M WT558	7572M WP122*	7652M WZ544	7732M XD393	7812M XA899	
7413M WW603*	7493M WT559	7573M WP150*	7653M WN158	7733M WP841	7813M WS777	
7414M WB914*	7494M WT566	7574M WP179	7654M XF931	7734M XD536	7814M XD511	
7415M XK989	7495M WT592	7575M WL607	7655M WP836	7735M XP812	7815M XD617	
7416M WN907	7496M WT612	7576M WL414	7656M WJ573	7736M WZ559	7816M WG763	
7417M WG981	7497M WT570	7577M VV542	7657M WH695	7737M XD602	7817M TX214	
7418M VL279	7498M WT576	7578M VL278	7658M WH884	7738M XA904	7818M WH226	
7419M WP244	7499M WT555	7579M WG940	7659M WH701	7739M XA801	7819M XP661	
7420M WZ419	7500M WT616	7580M WP147	7660M WA236	7740M XH840	7820M XM527	
7421M WT660	7501M WT578	7581M WP184	7661M XA627	7741M VZ477	7821M XJ428	
7422M WT684	7502M WT583	7582M WP190	7662M XA554	7742M VZ511	7822M XP248	
7423M XD457	7503M WT584	7583M WP185	7663M XA571	7743M XH698*	7823M XP250	
7424M WW643	7504M WT588	7584M WP191	7664M XA624*	7744M XH727*	7824M XE887	
7425M XF902*	7505M WT593	7585M XE822	7665M XA628	7745M XG509	7825M WK991	
7426M WT624	7506M WR595	7586M XA551	7666M XA626	7746M XA892	7826M WZ675	
7427M WK214	7507M WT686	7587M VX546	7667M XA620*	7747M WP854	7827M XA917	
7428M WK198	7508M WT687	7588M VZ183	7668M WV324	7748M XH710	7828M WF908	
7429M WK279	7509M WT692	7589M WD936	7669M WV326	7749M XA821	7829M XH992	
7430M WE901	7510M WT694	7590M WH668	7670M WV327	7750M WL168	7830M XH273	
7431M WZ667	7511M WN894	7591M WN978	7671M WV329	7751M WL131	7831M XH991	
7432M WZ724	7512M WN895	7592M XD158	7672M WV330	7752M XA820	7832M XJ116	
7433M TW624	7513M WN897	7593M WB115	7673M WV332	7753M WP204	7833M XJ117	
7434M TW575	7514M WT636	7594M TG573	7674M WV364	7754M WD303	7834M XH972	
7435M WE539	7515M WT696	7595M VF582	7675M WV369	7755M WG760	7835M TG610	
7436M WZ726	7516M WW632	7596M WT719	7676M WV316	7756M WK818	7836M XJ122*	
7437M WP773	7517M WW634	7597M WD352	7677M WV367	7757M XH795	7837M XJ126*	
7438M WP905	7518M WW637	7598M WA215	7678M WV371	7758M PM651	7838M XM187	
7439M WZ867	7519M WW638	7599M WD707	7679M WV375	7759M PK664	7839M WV781	
7440M WN898	7520M WW641	7600M RF564	7680M WV376	7760M XH298	7840M XK482	
7441M WN948	7521M WW644	7601M WB709	7681M WV377	7761M XH318	7841M WV783	
7442M WT681	7522M WN908	7602M WE600	7682M WV378	7762M XE670	7842M XH986	
7443M WX853	7523M WT613	7603M WS591	7683M WV379	7763M XH358	7843M WE145	
7444M WX866	7524M WT617	7604M XD542	7684M WV265	7764M WD990	7844M XA924	
7445M WK279	7525M WT619	7605M WS692	7685M WV320	7765M XA701*	7845M XN195	
7446M XE923	7526M WT622	7606M WV562	7686M WV323	7766M Not used	7846M WP214	
7447M XD951	7527M WT625	7607M TJ138	7687M WK952	7767M WV398	7847M WV276	
7448M WX412	7528M WT626	7608M TA722	7688M WV421	7768M WV404	7848M XF312	
7449M TE330	7529M WT641	7609M WA697	7689M WW450	7769M WW590	7849M XF319	
7450M XD430	7530M WT648	7610M G-ALYT	7690M WV428	7770M WT746	7850M XA923	
7451M TE476	7531M WT649	7611M WD937*	7691M WV438	7771M XF309	7851M WZ706	
7452M WX792	7532M WT651	7612M WP775	7692M WV444	7772M XF370	7852M XG506	
7453M WX938	7533M WT680	7613M WV512	7693M WV483	7773M XF317	7853M XD164*	
7454M WX857	7534M WT682	7614M WV618	7694M WV486	7774M XF302	7854M XM191	
7455M WZ318	7535M WT683	7615M WV679	7695M WV492	7775M WV386	7855M XK416	

7856M XA898	7936M XF970	8016M XT677	8096M WJ891	8176M WH791*	8354M WF791*
7857M XA905	7937M WS843	8017M XL762	8097M XS213	8177M WM224	8355M KN645
7858M WD159	7938M XH903	8018M XN344	8098M WL682	8178M XM276*	8356M XL835*
7859M XP283	7939M XD596	8019M WZ869	8099M WD355	8179M XN928	8357M WH576
7860M XL738	7940M XL764	8020M WB847	8100M WZ861	8180M XN930	8358M WF414
7861M XM565	7941M XF369	8021M XL824	8101M WH984	8181M XN972	8359M WF825
7862M XR246	7942M XF360	8022M XN341	8102M WT486	8182M XN953	8360M WP863
7863M WZ679	7943M WJ589	8023M XD463	8103M WR985	8183M XN962	8361M WB670
7864M XP244	7944M WV393	8024M XN348	8104M WR979*	8184M WT520	8362M WG477
7865M TX226	7945M XF975	8025M XH124	8105M WL637	8185M WH946	8363M WG463
7866M XH278	7946M XF982	8026M WD849	8106M WR982	8186M WR977	8364M WG464
7867M XH980	7947M XF951	8027M XM555	8107M WR990	8187M WH791	8365M XK421
7868M WZ736	7948M XF972	8028M WB844	8108M WV703	8188M XG327	8366M XG454
7869M WK935	7949M XF974	8029M WF333	8109M WV704	8189M WD646	8367M XG474
7870M XM556	7950M XF998	8030M XS412	8110M WV741	8190M XJ918	8368M XF926
7871M XE890	7951M XD538	8031M XK698	8111M WV742	8191M XK862*	8369M WE139
7872M XD826	7952M WV471	8032M XH837	8112M WV743	8192M XR658	8370M N1671
7873M WZ382	7953M WV677	8033M XD382	8113M WV753	8193M XR707	8371M XA847
7874M XR568	7954M XF608	8034M XL703	8114M WL798	8194M XK862	8372M K8042
7875M VW148	7955M XH767	8035M WV443	8115M WR984	8195M XN848	8373M P2617
7876M VX527	7956M XF950	8036M WV505	8116M WG460	8196M XE920	8374M XR660
7877M XM170	7957M XF545	8037M XF555	8117M WR974	8197M WT346	8375M NX611
7878M XD601	7958M XK716	8038M XF689	8118M WZ549	8198M WT339	8376M RF398
7879M VW837	7959M WS774	8039M XF841	8119M WR971	8199M XM265	8377M R9125
7880M WZ502	7960M WS726	8040M XR493	8120M WR981	8200M WT332	8378M T9707
7881M WD413	7961M WS739	8041M XF690*	8121M XM474	8201M XH209	8379M DG590
7882M XD525	7962M WS744	8042M VM368	8122M XD613	8202M XM244	8380M Z7197
7883M Sioux	7963M WS751	8043M XF836	8123M XJ774*	8203M XD377	8381M P-5 Rotachute
7884M Sioux	7964M WS760	8044M XP286	8124M XD614*	8204M XM271	8382M VR930
7885M WB832	7965M WS792	8045M XH122	8125M XE857	8205M XN819	8383M K9942
7886M XR985	7966M WS797	8046M XL770	8126M WH804	8206M WG419	8384M X4590
7887M XD375	7967M WS788	8047M XH478	8127M WJ724*	8207M WD318	8385M N5912
7888M WZ397	7968M WS802	8048M XH533*	8128M WH775	8208M WG303	8386M NV778
7889M WZ577	7969M WS840	8049M WE168	8129M WH779*	8209M WG418	8387M T6296
7890M XD453	7970M WP907	8050M XG329	8130M WH798*	8210M WG471	8388M XL993
7891M XM693	7971M XK699	8051M XN929	8131M WT507*	8211M WK570	8389M VX573
7892M XH760	7972M XH764	8052M WH166	8132M WT514	8212M WK587	8390M SL542
7893M WZ562	7973M WS807	8053M WK968	8133M WT518*	8213M WK626	8391M SL574
7894M XD818	7974M XH479	8054M XM410	8134M WT521	8214M WP864	8392M SL674
7895M WF784	7975M XH849	8055M XM402	8135M WT523	8215M WP869	8393M XK987
7896M XA900	7976M XK418	8056M XG337	8136M WT524	8216M WP927	8394M WG422
7897M XA901	7977M XN443	8057M XR243	8137M WT527	8217M WZ866	8395M WF408
7898M XP854	7978M XM961	8058M XK419	8138M XN700	8218M WB645*	8396M XK740
7899M XG540	7979M XM529	8059M XN956	8139M XJ582	8219M XR455	8397M XS583*
7900M WA576	7980M XM561	8060M WW397	8140M XJ571	8220M XN847	8398M WR967
7901M WJ484	7981M XL769	8061M WV751	8141M XN688	8221M XP409	8399M WR539
7902M WZ550	7982M XH892	8062M XR669	8142M XJ560	8222M XJ604	8400M XP583
7903M XH757*	7983M XD506	8063M WT536	8143M XN691	8223M XN658	8401M XP686*
7904M XF933	7984M XN597	8064M WV706	8144M XN707	8224M XN699	8402M XN769
7905M XK715	7985M WD490	8065M WT513	8145M XJ526	8225M XN705	8403M XK531
7906M WH132	7986M WG777	8066M WT533	8146M WJ919	8226M XP921	8404M XP548*
7907M XF944	7987M TG605	8067M WH802	8147M XR526	8227M XM264	8405M TG536*
7908M XF973	7988M XL149	8068M WT516	8148M XA165	8228M XP363	8406M XP831
7909M XL826*	7989M WG475	8069M WT314	8149M XD702	8229M XM355	8407M XP535
7910M XJ915*	7990M XD452	8070M EP120	8150M WT345	8230M XM362	8408M XS186
7911M VX578	7991M WL639	8071M TE476	8151M WV795	8231M XM375	8409M XS209
7912M WK131	7992M XM704	8072M PK624	8152M WV794	8232M XM381	8410M XR662
7913M WK132	7993M XH498	8073M TB252	8153M WV903	8233M XM408	8411M XM139
7914M WK134	7994M XH500	8074M TE392	8154M WV908	8234M XN458	8412M XM147
7915M WJ915	7995M XA910	8075M RW382	8155M WV797	8235M XN549	8413M XM192
7916M XL826	7996M XH475	8076M XM386	8156M XE339	8236M XP573	8414M XM173
7917M WA591	7997M XG452	8077M XN594	8157M XE390	8237M XS179	8415M XM181
7918M XD444	7998M XD515	8078M XM351	8158M XE369	8238M XS180	8416M XM183
7919M WJ476	7999M WG257*	8079M XN492	8159M XD528	8239M XS210	8417M XM144
7920M WL360	8000M XL111	8080M XM480	8160M XD622	8240M to 8339M	8418M XM178
7921M XJ757	8001M WV395	8081M XM468	8161M XE993	not used	8419M WA658*
7922M WV494	8002M XF307	8082M XM409	8162M WM913*	8340M XP341	8420M XM214*
7923M XT133	8003M XF323	8083M XM367	8163M XP919	8341M WP963	8421M XM215
7924M WB555	8004M XF366	8084M XM369	8164M WF299	8342M WP848	8422M XM169
7925M WV666	8005M WG768	8085M XM467	8165M WH791*	8343M TG500*	8423M XM189
7926M XK670	8006M XF941	8086M TB752	8166M XP752	8344M WH960	8424M XM180
7927M XK671	8007M XF990	8087M XN925	8167M XH208	8345M XG540	8425M XM182
7928M XE849	8008M XG515	8088M XN602	8168M XF703	8346M XN734	8426M XM216
7929M XH768	8009M XG518	8089M XF706	8169M WH364	8347M XN768	8427M XM172
7930M WH301	8010M XG547	8090M XM698	8170M XM274	8348M XN779	8428M XH593
7931M RD253	8011M XV269	8091M XG336	8171M XJ607	8349M XN794	8429M XH592
7932M WZ744	8012M VS562	8092M WK654	8172M XJ609	8350M WH840	8430M XV312
7933M XR220	8013M WF412	8093M WT512	8173M XN685	8351M XM823	8431M XM685
7934M XE932	8014M WJ462	8094M WT520*	8174M WZ576	8352M XN632	8432M XK937*
7935M XF969	8015M WH965	8095M WH792	8175M XE950	8353M XN633	8433M XM967

8434M XM411
8435M XN512
8436M XN554
8437M XG362
8438M XP761
8439M WZ846
8440M WD935
8441M XR107
8442M XP411
8443M XP302
8444M XP400
8445M XK968
8446M XP748
8447M XP359
8448M XN775
8449M G-ASWJ
8450M WE145*
8451M WJ611
8452M XK885
8453M XP745
8454M XP442
8455M XP444
8456M XM991*
8457M XS871
8458M XP672
8459M XR650
8460M XP680
8461M XF796
8462M XX477
8463M XP355
8464M XJ758
8465M W1048
8466M Catalina
8467M WP912
8468M BT474
8469M Fa 330
8470M PN999
8471M He 111H
8472M VH513
8473M WP190
8474M Ju 87G
8475M PJ876
8476M Ki 100
8477M DG200
8478M RN228
8479M AX772
8480M Me 163B
8481M Me 163B
8482M VK893
8483M Me 410A
8484M Ki46
8485M Baka
8486M Baka
8487M Vampire ex-Swiss
8488M WL627
8489M XN816
8490M WH703
8491M WJ880
8492M WJ872
8493M XR571
8494M XP557
8495M XR672
8496M XN730
8497M XM698
8498M XR670
8499M XP357
8500M XN786
8501M XP640
8502M XP686
8503M XS451
8504M WK106*
8505M XL384
8506M XR704
8507M XS215
8508M XS218
8509M XT141
8510M XP567
8511M WT305
8512M VP973

8513M XN724
8514M XS167
8515M WH869
8516M XR643
8517M XA932
8518M XN731
8519M XN732
8520M XN733
8521M XN773
8522M XN787
8523M XN790
8524M XN791
8525M XN792
8526M XN783
8527M XW789
8528M XM973
8529M XM970
8530M WD948*
8531M XS418
8532M XS423
8533M XS449
8534M XS450
8535M XS454
8536M XN777
8537M XN778
8538M XN781
8539M XN782
8540M XN784
8541M XM968*
8542M XM995
8543M XN788
8544M XN793
8545M XN726*
8546M XN728
8547M XN727*
8548M WT507
8549M WT534
8550M XT595
8551M XN774
8552M XN735
8553M VP978
8554M TG511
8555M TG503
8556M XN855
8557M XP500
8558M XP439
8559M XN467
8560M XR569
8561M XS100
8562M XS110
8563M XW563
8564M XN387
8565M Hunter F.51
8566M XV279
8567M WL738
8568M XP503
8569M XR535
8570M XR954
8571M XR984
8572M XM706
8573M XM708
8574M XM705
8575M XP542
8576M XP502
8577M XP532*
8578M XR534
8579M XR140
8580M XP516
8581M WJ775
8582M XE874
8583M Fi 103
8584M cockpit only
8585M cockpit only
8586M cockpit only
8587M cockpit only
8588M cockpit only
8589M cockpit only
8590M cockpit only
8591M cockpit only
8592M XM969

8593M XM418
8594M XP661
8595M XH278
8596M Horsa
8597M WE145
8598M WP270
8599M Cadet
8600M cockpit
8601M XL450
8602M XR541
8603M XR951
8604M XS104
8605M XA536
8606M XP530
8607M XP538
8608M XP540
8609M XR953
8610M XL502
8611M WF128
8612M XD182
8613M XJ724
8614M XP515
8615M XP532*
8616M XP541
8617M XM709
8618M XP504
8619M XP511
8620M XP534
8621M XR538
8622M XR980
8623M XR998
8624M XS102
8625M XS105
8626M XS109
8627M XP558
8628M XJ380
8629M WL801
8630M WG362
8631M XR854
8632M XP533
8633M MK732
8634M WP314
8635M XP514
8636M XR540
8637M XR991
8638M XS101
8639M XS107
8640M XR977
8641M XR987
8642M XR537
8643M WJ867
8644M XR457
8645M XD163
8646M XK969
8647M XP338
8648M XK526
8649M XR331
8650M XP333
8651M WG556
8652M WH794
8653M XS120
8654M XL898
8655M XN126
8656M XP405
8657M VZ634
8658M XV358
8659M XV340
8660M XW538
8661M XJ727
8662M XR458
8663M XN780
8664M WJ603
8665M WL754
8666M XE793
8667M WP972
8668M WJ821
8669M G-ARRV
8670M XL384
8671M XJ435
8672M XP351

8673M XD165
8674M XP395
8675M WL793
8676M XL577
8677M XJ695
8678M XE656
8679M XF526
8680M XF527
8681M XG164
8682M XP404
8683M WJ870
8684M XJ634
8685M XF516
8686M XG158
8687M XJ639
8688M XP347
8689M WK144
8690M XP403
8691M WT518
8692M WL741
8693M WH863
8694M XH554
8695M WJ817
8696M WH773
8697M WJ825
8698M WL745
8699M ZD232
8700M ZD234
8701M XP352
8702M XG196
8703M VW453
8704M XN643*
8705M XT281
8706M XF383
8707M XF386
8708M XF509
8709M XG209
8710M XG274
8711M XG290
8712M XF439
8713M XG225
8714M XK149
8715M XG264
8716M XV155
8717M XE608
8718M XX396
8719M XT257
8720M XP353
8721M XP354
8722M WJ640
8723M XL567
8724M Harrier cockpit
8725M XL317
8726M XP299
8727M XR486
8728M WT532*
8729M WJ815
8730M XD186
8731M XP361
8732M XJ729
8733M XL318
8734M XM657
8735M WJ681
8736M XF375
8737M XE606*
8738M XJ695
8739M XH170
8740M WE173
8741M XW329
8742M WH856
8743M cockpit
8744M XH563
8745M XL392
8746M XH171
8747M WJ629
8748M XL387
8749M XH537
8750M XL388
8751M XT255

8752M XR509
8753M WL795
8754M XG882
8755M WJ637
8756M XL427
8757M XM656
8758M XH562
8759M XL321
8760M XL386
8761M WJ977
8762M WH740
8763M WH665
8764M XP344
8765M XM647
8766M XJ782
8767M XX635
8768M Pucara
8769M Pucara
8770M XL623
8771M XM602
8772M WR960
8773M XV156
8774M XV338
8775M XV354
8776M XV152
8777M XX914
8778M XM598
8779M XM607
8780M WK102
8781M WE982
8782M XH136
8783M XW272
8784M VP976
8785M XS642
8786M XN495
8787M XD184
8788M XJ437
8789M XK970
8790M XK986
8791M XP329
8792M XP345
8793M XP346
8794M XP398
8795M VP958
8796M XK943
8797M XX947
8798M XG151
8799M WV703
8800M XG226
8801M XS650
8802M XJ608
8803M XJ524
8804M XJ524
8805M XT772
8806M XP140
8807M XL587
8808M XP695
8809M XH561
8810M XJ825
8811M XL445
8812M XM571
8813M VT260
8814M XM927
8815M XX118
8816M XX734
8817M XN652
8818M XK527
8819M XS479
8820M VP952
8821M XX115
8822M WP957
8823M VP965
8824M WP971
8825M WB530
8826M XV638
8827M XX300
8828M XS587
8829M XE653
8830M XF515
8831M XG160

8832M XG172
8833M XL569
8834M XL572
8835M XL576
8836M XL592
8837M XL617
8838M not RAF
8839M XG194
8840M XG252
8841M XE606
8842M XF418
8843M XG152
8844M XJ676
8845M XS572
8846M XE673
8847M XX344
8848M XZ135
8849M XZ989
8850M XV436
8851M XT595
8852M XV337
8853M XT277
8854M XV154
8855M XT284
8856M XT274
8857M XW544
8858M XW541
8859M XW545
8860M XW549
8861M XW528
8862M XN473
8863M XG154
8864M WJ678
8865M XN641
8866M XL609
8867M XK532
8868M ex-8128M
8869M WH957
8870M WH964
8871M WJ565
8872M WF382
8873M XR453
8874M XE597
8875M XE624
8876M
8877M XP159
8878M XR993
8879M XX948
8880M XF435
8881M XG254
8882M G-BDIU
8883M XX946
8884M VX275
8885M XW922
8886M XA243
8887M WK162
8888M XA231
8889M XN239
8890M WT532
8891M XL566
8892M XL618
8893M WT745
8894M XT669
8895M XX746
8896M XX821
8897M XX969
8898M XX119
8899M XX756
8900M XZ368
8901M XZ383
8902M XX739
8903M XX747
8904M XX966
8905M XX975
8906M XX976
8907M XZ371
8908M XZ382
8909M XV784
8910M XL160
8911M XH673

8912M	XL189
8913M	XT857
8914M	WH844
8915M	XH132
8916M	XL163
8917M	XM372
8918M	XX109
8919M	XT486
8920M	XT469
8921M	XT466
8922M	XT467
8923M	XX819
8924M	XP701
8925M	XP706
8926M	XP749
8927M	XP750
8928M	XP751
8929M	XP764
8930M	XR720
8931M	XV779
8932M	XR718

Astute readers may notice that this listing is in some cases at variance with other recently published material on 'M' serials, but is based on many years patient and careful research, and deliberately avoids the inclusion of 'speculative' entries which would give credence with publication, and over the years become 'fact'. In particular, other sources record 'M' serials where the aircraft was known to be flying many years after the M number would have been allocated in sequence. The official records are now less complete than when the author first examined them in the Air Ministry archives before they passed to AHB, and can be shown to contain an alarming number of clerical errors. Thus our cautious attitude, which we commend to readers on this subject.

Catapult Dummies

A special numbering series was introduced in the 'twenties, following the Fleet use of catapults for launching aircraft in place of flying-off ramps. Instructional and test aircraft were needed for unmanned launching to prove both catapult velocity impart and airframe strengthening for the task. Aircraft written off for normal flying had to be used for economy. Whereas M-numbered aircraft were often airframes, the CD — Catapult Dummy series had to have engines to give the right weighting. Aircraft were converted to CD standard by being weighed to represent crew and service equipment, plus compensatory weighting for salvageable instruments removed since the test was normally to destruction.

It is believed some eighty aircraft numbered 1 to 80 bore CD or SCD prefixes. The plain CDs were for the land-based catapults at Farnborough and Leuchars, and the SCDs (Ship Catapult Dummies) for Fleet tests at sea. Known conversions to CDs are:

SCD18 ex-S1462
SCD20 ex-S1371
SCD29 ex-S1789
SCD30 ex-S1831
SCD35 ex-S1388

Admiralty Instructional Airframes

Until the early 'forties the Fleet Air Arm used RAF M-serialled instructional airframes. Around 1942 the Navy introduced its own series from airframes written off from flying in fleet service. The official records of A1 to A750 are thought not to have survived, but known numbers are:

A37 ex-AS417	A455 ex-LS955	A646 ex-SX300
A38 ex-AS427	A502 ex-RX217	A680 ex-DE373
A39 ex-AS426	A505 ex-NN570	A714 ex-DT932
A132 ex-FN174	A506 ex-NN336	A720 ex-BB731
A337 ex-MD612	A509 ex-NF351	A727 ex-SX341
A350 ex-MB364	A511 ex-NN585	A750 ex-NL750

In 1948 a new series for numbering instructional airframes was introduced starting at A2001 and which remains in use. The early numbers, which have not all been traced, concerned the re-numbering of existing airframes in the original A-series.

A2001 HS618	A2240 MB618	A2339 VW209
A2007 TW694	A2241 MB592	A2343 VX665
A2010 MB388	A2243 WF294	A2346 VV215
A2014 Z2013	A2249 VF269	A2347 WM903
A2054 ex-A646	A2255 PP642	A2348 TF947
A2055 SX336	A2256 SW800	A2349 TF908
A2059 PX239	A2257 PP596	A2350 TF946
A2064 Z2048	A2258 VT417	A2351 TF922
A2080 SX360	A2268 PR394	A2352 TF955
A2087 DE627	A2270 TF900	A2354 VV190
A2093 PR377	A2291 VT421	A2355 TF963
A2106 NF630	A2294 TT192	A2356 WE733
A2123 ex-A750	A2295 EE387	A2357 WN487
A2126 ex-A720	A2298 VW874	A2358 TF950
A2127 ex-A680	A2299 TW687	A2359 WE722
A2162 PR364	A2301 TW719	A2360 WA512
A2173 MB415	A2308 VW877	A2361 WA533
A2178 PR463	A2309 VW878	A2362 WA481
A2182 DK538	A2310 VW879	A2363 WA530
A2187 PR406	A2311 VW880	A2364 WA505
A2190 PR433	A2313 TS409	A2365 WA528
A2193 VF315	A2315 NM661	A2366 WA532
A2195 W7951	A2318 WJ216	A2367 WF147
A2203 SW916	A2320 VF317	A2368 WF143
A2209 VW651	A2326 KE442	A2369 WW458
A2210 EK788	A2327 VV613	A2370 WW461
A2218 EK840	A2328 VX394	A2371 WF155
A2227 VR135	A2332 EE545	A2372 WE825
A2235 Z1889	A2336 WF151	A2373 WA496

A2374 WB250	A2462 WF257	A2542 XA862	A2622 XJ602	A2701 XL500
A2375 VT476	A2463 WH990	A2543 XA870	A2623 XN697	A2702 XS545
A2377 WE801	A2464 WW285	A2544 XJ487	A2623 XN697	A2703 XT441
A2378 WD848	A2465 VX596	A2545 WV836	A2624 XN692	A2704 XT438
A2379 VX664	A2466 WN364	A2546 WV870	A2625 XL846	A2705 XS866
A2380 WE734	A2467 WN454	A2547 WV860	A2626 XL847	A2706 XM868
A2381 VR937	A2468 XA871	A2548 WV861	A2627 XN967	A2707 XS122
A2382 VT429	A2469 XG581	A2549 WV909	A2628 XP558	A2708 XR540
A2384 WN495	A2470 WN391	A2550 XA866	A2629 XM667	A2709 XR991
A2385 WH630	A2471 XA342	A2551 XA868	A2630 XL853	A2710 XW839
A2386 WD909	A2472 XA508	A2552 XN932	A2631 XV312	A2711 XW179
A2392 WB313	A2473 WF220	A2553 AN924	A2632 WV903	A2712 XN359
A2394 VX420	A2474 XG871	A2554 WV865	A2633 ex-A2580	A2713 XN386
A2395 MB408	A2475 WM557	A2555 XE330	A2634 WV794	A2714 XL880
A2396 WA469	A2476 WM520	A2556 XE327	A2635 XE339	A2715 XS568
A2397 VN873	A2477 WM513	A2557 WV798	A2636 XE390	A2716 XT780
A2398 WM505	A2478 WM512	A2558 WV831	A2637 WV797	A2717 XS569
A2399 WE279	A2479 WM509	A2559 WV792	A2638 XV317	A2718 XM916
A2400 WZ279	A2480 WM553	A2560 XF363	A2639 ex-A2612	A2719 XP150
A2401 WZ289	A2481 WG240	A2561 XF365	A2640 XP155	A2720 XP142
A2402 WA520	A2482 WM939	A2562 XD226	A2641 XL729	A2721 XZ249
A2403 WB797	A2483 WF259	A2563 WV405	A2642 XL836	A2722 XT757
A2404 WF211	A2484 WM907	A2564 WV411	A2643 XN311	A2723 ZT487
A2405 WF165	A2485 XJ397	A2565 XF303	A2644 XN358	A2724 XV623
A2406 WF201	A2486 WM543	A2566 XF311	A2645 WF225	A2725 XS538
A2407 WA482	A2487 XG584	A2567 XF318	A2646 XK988	A2726 XT786
A2408 WA506	A2488 WW194	A2568 XF947	A2647 XS463	
A2409 WF200	A2489 WM918	A2569 XF976	A2648 XS125	
A2410 WF146	A2490 WM920	A2570 XF984	A2649 XS869	
A2411 WM564	A2491 WW275	A2571 XG577	A2650 XP160	
A2412 WN354	A2492 XG616	A2572 XJ402	A2651 XG596	
A2413 WD910	A2493 WN346	A2573 XD215	A2652 XN261	
A2414 WN341	A2494 WM937	A2574 XD332	A2653 XK943	
A2415 DK531	A2495 WM965	A2575 XG574	A2654 XN302	
A2416 WN462	A2496 XK933	A2576 WV198	A2655 XN953	
A2417 WM569	A2497 WV904	A2577 XB480	A2656 XS476	
A2418 WK320	A2498 XG621	A2578 XJ399	A2657 XX469	
A2419 WN421	A2499 WT859	A2579 XN332	A2658 XP984	
A2420 WF159	A2500 XF828	A2580 XE369	A2659 XV669	
A2421 WN393	A2501 XN307	A2581 XK532	A2660 WV908	
A2422 WN373	A2502 WM936	A2582 XK534	A2661 WV795	
A2423 WA491	A2503 WM994	A2583 XD280	A2662 ex-A2509	
A2424 WF182	A2504 XG622	A2584 XD272	A2663 XN309	
A2425 WF243	A2505 WM943	A2585 XD272	A2664 XV644	
A2426 WF183	A2506 XG655	A2586 XD278	A2665 XL839	
A2427 WF172	A2507 XJ583	A2587 XD275	A2666 XS872	
A2428 WF163	A2508 WW218	A2588 XD243	A2667 XP226	
A2429 WL806	A2509 WF299	A2589 XD271	A2668 WS885	
A2430 WF752	A2510 WM913	A2590 XD324	A2669 XP149	
A2431 WM901	A2511 WM983	A2591 XD276	A2670 XS128	
A2432 WN118	A2512 XG637	A2592 WV828	A2671 XS867	
A2433 WM924	A2513 WW267	A2593 WV825	A2672 XS537	
A2434 WL881	A2514 XL722	A2594 XM920	A2673 WF122	
A2435 WN376	A2515 XE868	A2595 XL868	A2674 WF125	
A2436 WN453	A2516 XM835	A2596 XT448	A2675 XS881	
A2437 WN344	A2517 WM961	A2597 XS509	A2676 XR572	
A2438 VW870	A2518 WW189	A2598 XJ482	A2677 XR993	
A2439 WF219	A2519 XN333	A2599 XJ486	A2678 XR955	
A2440 WF213	A2520 WW270	A2600 XN934	A2679 XP535	
A2441 WF158	A2521 WV841	A2601 XJ477	A2680 XP157	
A2442 XK908	A2522 WM993	A2602 XN925	A2681 XP117	
A2443 WF294	A2523 WM915	A2603 XK911	A2682 XM845	
A2444 VZ777	A2524 WM998	A2604 XN259	A2683 XS878	
A2445 WZ299	A2525 XN334	A2605 XN308	A2684 XP151	
A2446 WP286	A2526 WV911	A2606 XN305	A2685 XS886	
A2447 WM503	A2527 XP107	A2607 XK944	A2686 XS873	
A2448 WW148	A2528 XA363	A2608 XA459	A2687 XS877	
A2449 WW219	A2529 VX133	A2609 XM329	A2688 XP158	
A2450 WN343	A2530 WM969	A2610 XN647	A2689 XM874	
A2451 WF196	A2531 WG718	A2611 XJ575	A2690 XS887	
A2452 WF144	A2532 WV826	A2612 XN650*	A2691 XS868	
A2453 WW223	A2533 XA456	A2613 XN706	A2692 XM917	
A2454 WF277	A2534 XE368	A2614 XN314	A2693 XM843	
A2455 WM514	A2535 XJ484	A2615 XT256	A2694 XS865	
A2456 WW261	A2536 WV914	A2616 XN651	A2695 XS876	
A2457 WW269	A2537 WV190	A2617 XN954	A2696 XS882	
A2458 WM570	A2538 XJ393	A2618 XP116	A2697 XS870	
A2459 XA523	A2539 XG831	A2619 XS695	A2698 XP105	
A2460 WM981	A2540 WN464	A2620 ex-A2612	A2699 XS570	
A2461 WW146	A2541 XA869	A2621 XJ584	A2700 XP980	

*A2612 re-issued to XJ521

RAF Display
Air Park Numbers

From 1920 until 1937 the RAF gave an annual display at Hendon, called an Air Pageant to 1924 and a Display from 1925. From 1923 onwards an Air Park was featured with a static display of new aircraft types which flew past as one of the events programmed. In order that the aircraft types could be recognised by display visitors, they bore large numbers, keyed to the listing in the official programme. As the numbers were officially allotted for identification purposes, and covered some civil aircraft or others not marked in any other way, the listing of these numbers was considered pertinent for inclusion in this work. The numbers are given for each year an Air Park was organised; the numbers concerned varying from year to year. Where the aircraft bore a normal serial, this alone is given as the type is ascertainable from the tabling within the book, in other cases, where known, fuller details are given.

30 June 1923
1 N9549, 2 J6852, 3 F2914, 4 N9900, 5 N9581, 6 N155, 7 Seagull, 8 N163, 9 N162, 10 J6583, 11 J6973, 12 N143, 13 J6907, 14 J6969.

28 June 1924
1 J6969, 2 J6988, 3 J6902, 4 J7005, 5 J7277, 6 J6994, 7 J6993, 8 J7261, 9 J6997 programmed but did not appear, 10 J6862, 11 Handley Page W.8F G-EBIX, 12 J7272, 13 J7323.

27 June 1925
1 Gamecock presumed J7497, 2 J6989, 3 J7295, 4 N187, 5 HP Hendon, 6 N167, 7 J6997, 8 DH.54 Highclere G-EBKI, 9 Vickers Vanguard G-EBCP, 10 J6910.

3 July 1926
1 J8067, 2 N207, 3 N208, 4 Gorcock, 5 J7782, 6 Avro Avenger G-EBND, 7 Fairey Firefly c/n F.572, 8 AW Atlas G-EBLK, 9 Bristol Bloodhound G-EBLG, 10 J7780, 11 Vickers Vespa G-EBLD, 12 Fairey Fox (unmarked), 13 J7511 or J7721, 14 N171, 15 AW Argosy G-EBLF, 16 Cierva I autogyro.

2 July 1927
1 Gamecock (believed unmarked), 2 J8675, 3 J7295, 4 J7745, 5 N172, 6 J8674, 7 J8006, 8 J7939, 9 Fairey III identity not known, 10 no details, 11 Vickers Valiant unmarked, later became G-EBVM, 12 Wapiti identity not known, 13 Bulldog c/n 7155 bearing no markings, 14 HP Hamlet G-EBNS, 15 J9251.

30 June 1928
1 J9251, 2 J8459, 3 J8776, 4 Bulldog unmarked, 5 J9252 by identity but unmarked at that date, 6 Fairey Fox VI no markings, 7 Halton Cherub G-EBOO, 8 DH.71 G-EBQU, 9 J7557, 10 N219, 11 J8906 when registered G-EBYX, 12 N231, 13 J7938, 14 J9126.

1929
New types were not flown and not all in Park had numbers.

28 June 1930
1 Fairey Firefly II G-ABCN, 2 J9051, 3 J9771, 4 J8627, 5 not known, 6 K1102, 7 J9131, 8 Blackburn Lincock I G-EBVO but unmarked at the time.

27 June 1931
1 Hawker Fury unmarked, presumed J9682, 2 J9051, 3 N237, 4 J9125, 5 Fairey Gordon, 6 K2873 when marked provisionally R-3, 7 N229, 8 Avro 626 G-ABJG, 9 Westland Wessex G-ABEG, 10 Vickers Viastra G-AAUB, 11 Vickers 163 O-2, 12 Saro Cloud, 13 not known, 14 K1947, 15 K1908, 16 K1696.

25 June 1932
1 J9122, 2 Hawker Osprey, 3 Bristol Bulldog IIIA R-5, 4 S1577, 5 Westland PV6 P-6, 6 J9832, 7 AW Atlas II G-ABIV, 8 Short Valetta G-AAJY, 9 Bristol 120 R-6, 10 N230, 11 J9950, 12 J9130, 13 K1695, 14 Blackburn CA.15L G-ABKW, 15 Tiger Moth.

24 June 1933
1 Cierva C.30 G-ACFI, 2 K3586, 3 J9125, 4 Bristol Bulldog IV R-7, 5 AW.16 A-2, 6 Vickers TB details not known, 7 S1640, 8 BP P.64 G-ABYK, 9 Vickers Vespa O-5, 10 Fairey IIIF for silence research, 11 J9102, 12 J8003, 13 J9833, 14 Blackburn monoplane G-ABKV, 15 K1991.

30 June 1934
1 K3586, 2 K2890, 3 Hawker PV3 marked IPV-3, 4 K2891, 5 K2434, 6 K3020, 7 Bristol Bulldog IV R-8, 8 K4048, 9 Westland PV7 unmarked, 10 AW.19 A-3, 11 K4295, 12 Fairey G4/31 marked F-1, 13 J9186, 14 K3503, 15 K4230, 16 Saro Cloud.

29 June 1935
1 K5200, 2 K2770, 3 Hawker GP marked IPV-4, 4 not known, 5 K2773, 6 K2771, 7 K4771 but then unnumbered, 8 K3585, 9 K3583, 10 J9833, 11 Supermarine Seagull N-1 (later RAAF A2-1).

27 June 1936
1 K5083, 2 K5054, 3 Vickers Venom marked PVO-10, 4 K4303, 5 K7557, 6 K6127, 7 K4049, 8 K4240, 9 K4586, 10 Miles Nighthawk U-5.

26 June 1937
1 L2387 marked then E-3, 2 Miles Kestrel Trainer unmarked, 3 L4534, 4 K8887, 5 K5099, 6 K5115, 7 not·present, 8 K5178, 9 DH.91 Albatross E-2. That year there was also something of an Old Types Park, as participating and displayed statically were Bristol Fighter F4587, Sopwith Triplane N5912 marked '5', an SE.5A and LVG and a Horace Farman marked '3'. C. G. Grey's caustic comment in The Aeroplane on this array was: 'We are not sure whether intention was to show how much or how little progress we have made since those days'.

Air Ministry Series 1945-46

A total of 4,810 aeroplanes and 291 gliders were recorded in the areas occupied by British troops from 6 June 1944 onward to late May 1945 when the British Zone of Germany was stabilised, The majority of these aircraft were destroyed under Disarmament Plans, but the Air Ministry has compiled a list of aircraft types and quantities, known as 'Category A', required for examination and assessment. The list was amended from time-to-time, but to avoid such aircraft required in the UK being confused with other requirements, for example the French eventually acquired 417 aircraft in our Zone, they were given an Air Ministry identification number prefixed AIR MIN or merely AM to denote the series. As far as can be ascertained these aircraft were as tabled. Where aircraft were required to fly on test a serial in the normal series was allotted as shown in the remarks column. Allocations 1-123 were made for aircraft then on the continent and Nos.200-233 for aircraft taken to Farnborough. The 'Remarks' column may include entries such as 'Held at 6 MU', which indicates its last known location, where it was probably scrapped - and not that it is still held there!

AM No.	Aircraft type	C/n	Code	Remarks
1	Junkers Ju 88G-6	622983	4R+RB	To Central Fighter Est.
2	Junkers Ju 88G-6	620560	4R+CB	To Radio Warfare Establishment
3	Junkers Ju 88G-6	622838	3C+AN	Became VK884
4	Siebel Si 204D-1	322127	BU+PP	Held at RAE
5	Siebel Si 204D-1	321523		Held by 6 MU
6	Junkers Ju 290A-7	110186	A3+OB	Stored at 6 MU
7	Dornier Do 217M	0040	KF+JN	
8	Junkers Ju 352A	100010	KT+VJ	Became VP550
9	Junkers Ju 88G-6	621965	4R+DR	Became VL991
10	Focke Wulf FW 190A/R6	550214	PN+LU	Sent to S.Africa
11	Focke Wulf Ta 152H	150004		Not delivered, replaced.
11	Focke Wulf Ta 152H	150168		Replacement for 150004.
12	Siebel Si 204D	351547		Stored at 6 MU
13	Siebel Si 204D	251922		Allotted to Cranwell
14	Junkers Ju 88G	620788	C9+AA	For radar trials
15	Messerschmitt Bf 110G-4/R8	180560	3C+BA	To CFE
16	Junkers Ju 88G-6	622311	3C-DA	To CFE
17	Arado Ar 232B		A3+RB	Exhibited at RAE
18	Junkers Ju 352A	100015	G6+WX	Limited use at RAE
19	Junkers Ju 352A		G6+YX	Used by RAE
20	Heinkel He 219A-7	290126	D5+BL	Held at 6 MU
21	Heinkel He 219A-7	310109		Stored in MUs
22	Heinkel He 219A-5/R2	310189	D5+CL	Exhibited at RAE
23	Heinkel He 219A	310200	D5+DL	Believed not delivered to UK.
24	Arado Ar 232B-2	140466	8H+HH	Crashed 27.8.45
25	Arado Ar 232B	140009	T9+6L	Became VK880
26	Arado Ar 234B	140476	8H+DH	Became VK877
27	Focke Wulf FW 189A-3	00173	3X+AA	Stored at 6 MU
28	Siebel Si 204D-1	221558	BJ+90	Used by RAE
29	Focke Wulf FW 190S-8	584219	38+	2-seat. To 8470M
30	Messerschmitt Bf 110G-4	730037	D5+DK	Used at RAE
31	Junkers Ju 88G-6	623192	C9+HB	Exhibited at RAE
32	Junkers Ju 88G-6	622960	+VH	Crashed 15.10.45
33	Junkers Ju 88G-6	621186		Stored at 6 MU
34	Messerschmitt Bf 110G-4/R6	730301	D5+RL	Preserved
35	Junkers Ju 188	150245		Shipped to USA
36	Focke Wulf FW 190F-8/U1	580508	55+	2-seat trainer
37	Focke Wulf FW 190S-1	582004	54+	2-seat trainer
38	Messerschmitt Bf 110G-4/R8	180551	D5+DM	Possibly not delivered
39	Messerschmitt Me 410A-1/U2	420439		Possibly not delivered
40	Focke Wulf FW 190F-8/U1	580392	51+	2-seat trainer
41	Junkers Ju 88G-6	622054	7J+OV	Replaced
41	Junkers Ju 88G	622461		Replacement
42	Siebel Si 204D	251147	7J+ZK	Held at RAE
43	Heinkel He 219A-2	310215		Stored at 6 MU
44	Heinkel He 219A-2	310106		Stored at 6 MU
45	Junkers Ju 188A-2	180485		Became VH610
46	Siebel Si 204D			Stored at 6 MU
47	Junkers Ju 88G-6	620968		Stored at 6 MU
48	Junkers Ju 88G-7	622811	3C+MN	Stored at 6 MU
49	Siebel Si 204D-1	251104		Stored at 6 MU
50	Messerschmitt Me 262B-1a	110305	8	Preserved S.Africa
51	Messerschmitt Me 262-2a	112373	X	Allotted XK893
52	Messerschmitt Me 262-2a	500210		Allotted VH509
53	Bucker Bu 180 Student			Held at RAE
54	Arado Ar 234B	140113	F1+AA	Became VH530
55	Siebel Si 204D	321288		Stored at 6 MU
56	Siebel Si 204D	321308	BU+AP	Abandoned
57	Junkers Ju 290A-2	11-157	BK+	Exhibited at RAE
58	Heinkel He 162A	120221		Became VH526
59	Heinkel He 162A-2	120076		VH523 to Canada
60	Heinkel He 162A-2	120074	11	Stored at 6 MU
61	Heinkel He 162A-2	120072		Crashed at Aldershot 9.11.45
62	Heinkel He 162A-2	120086		Preserved in Canada
63	Heinkel He 162A-2	120095		Held in Imperial War Museum
64	Heinkel He 162A-2	120097		Became VN153
65	Heinkel He 162A-2	120227		
66	Heinkel He 162A-2	120091		Exhibited at RAE
67	Heinkel He 162A-2	120098		Became VH513
68	Heinkel He 162A-2	120223		Held at 6 MU
69	Blohm & Voss BV 138			
70	Blohm & Voss BV 138C-1	310081		Held at Felixstowe
71	Blohm & Voss BV 138			
72	Messerschmitt Me 410A-1/U2	420430		Preserved
73	Messerschmitt Me 410A-1	130360		Held at 6 MU
74	Messerschmitt Me 410B-6	410208		Exhibited at RAE
75	Focke Wulf FW 190A-8/R6	733682		Imperial War Museum
76	Ju 88/FW 190 Mistrel			Not delivered
76	Messerschmitt Bf 108B			Number incorrectly marked on AIR MIN 84
77	Focke Wulf FW 190D-9	210596		Shipped to South Africa
78	Not known			
79	Messerschmitt Me 262			No details known
80	Messerschmitt Me 262A	111690	5	
81	Messerschmitt Me 262	500200		Became VP554
82	Not known			
83	Junkers Ju 388K	500006	PE+1F	Exhibited at Farnborough
84	Messerschmitt Bf 108B	1547	GJ+AU	Held at 6 MU
85	Messerschmitt Bf 110G-4/R3	420031		Held at 6 MU
86	Messerschmitt Bf 110G			
87	Messerschmitt Bf 108B			
88	Not known			
89	Messerschmitt Bf 108B			
90	Fieseler Fi 156C Storch			
91	Arado Ar 196A-5			Serialled VM748
92	Arado Ar 196A-5			Serialled VM761
93	Not known			
94	Focke Wulf FW 200C-4/U1	000176	GC+AE	Himmler's personal aircraft
95	Focke Wulf FW 200C			No details known
96	Focke Wulf FW 200C	0111		Given to Denmark
97	Focke Wulf FW 200C	0181		Given to Denmark
98	Not known			
99	Fieseler Fi 156C Storch	475099	VD+TD	Preserved in South Africa
100	Fieseler Fi 156C-7 Storch	2008		Used at RAE
101	Fieseler Fi 156C Storch	475081	RR+KE	Became VP546 and 7362M
102	Junkers Ju 52/3m	6840	D-AKUA	Held by 6 MU
103	Junkers Ju 52/3m	6567	D-AGAC	Held by 6 MU
104	Junkers Ju 52/3m	641038	D-AUAV	Exhibited at RAE
105	Not known			
106	Dornier Do 217M-1	56527	U5+HK	Held at RAE

107 Dornier Do 217M-1	56158	U5+	Held at 4 MU
108 Junkers Ju 188A-1	230776		Exhibited at RAE
109 Junkers Ju 352A-1		G6+RX	
110 Junkers Ju 352A			
111 Focke Wulf FW 190F-8/U			TB version
112 Junkers Ju 88A-6/U	0660	1H+MN	VN874
113 Junkers Ju 188A-2	00327	1H+GT	Became VN143
114 Dornier Do 24T	1135		Serialled VN865
115 Dornier Do 24T-3			
116 Dornier Do 24T			Serialled VN870
117 Focke Wulf FW 58 Weihe	2093	TE+8K	Spraying aircraft
118 Dornier Do 24T			
119 Siebel Si 104A			Landed in Goodwins
120 Arado Ar 96B			To Woodley
121 Bucker Bu 181 Bestmann			
122 Bucker Bu 181C-3 Bestmann	120417		Became G-AKAX
123 Arado Ar 96B			To Woodley
200 Messerschmitt Me 163B			Held at 6 MU
201 Messerschmitt Me 163B			
202 Messerschmitt Me 163B			Held at 6 MU
203 Messerschmitt Me 163B	310061		Allotted to France
204 Messerschmitt Me 163B	191454		To Canada
205 Messerschmitt Me 163B			Held at 6 MU
206 Messerschmitt Me 163B			Held at 6 MU
207 Messerschmitt Me 163B			Held at 6 MU
208 Messerschmitt Me 163B			Held at 6 MU
209 Messerschmitt Me 163B			Held at 6 MU
210 Messerschmitt Me 163B			Preserved Munich
211 Messerschmitt Me 163B	191095		To Canada
212 Messerschmitt Me 163B			Held at 6 MU
213 Messerschmitt Me 163B			Held at 6 MU
214 Messerschmitt Me 163B	191660		Held at Duxford
215 Messerschmitt Me 163B-1a	191659	15	Preserved in UK
216 Messerschmitt Me 163B			Held at 6 MU
217 Messerschmitt Me 163B-1a	191904	25	Held at Colerne
218 Messerschmitt Me 163B-1a			Held at 6 MU
219 Messerschmitt Me 163B			Held at 6 MU
220 Messerschmitt Me 163B	191914		Held at 6 MU
221 Messerschmitt Me 163B			Held at 6 MU
222 Messerschmitt Me 163B	191907		Held at MUs
223 Dornier Do 335A-12	240112		Crashed 18.1.46 at Cove
224 Savoia-Marchetti SM.95	41003		Used at RAE
225 Dornier Do 335A-1			Crashed 13.12.45
226 Arado Ar 234B	140356		Held at 6 MU
227 Arado Ar 234B			Held at 6 MU
228 Arado Ar 234B-2			Held at 6 MU
229 Arado Ar 234B			Held at 6 MU
230 Focke-Wulf FW 190	171747		
231 Junkers Ju 88G-1	712273	4R+UR	Ex-TP190
233 Focke Achgelis Fa 223			Became VM479

In addition a number of ex-Luftwaffe aircraft reached the UK for investigation without a number being allotted. The most comprehensive list of all ex-Luftwaffe aircraft reaching the UK has been published in *The Captive Luftwaffe* by Kenneth S. West (Putnam 1978 - now out of print), whilst the 'Air Min' series was dealt with in greater detail by Phil Butler's *Air Min* (Merseyside Aviation Society 1977 also now out of print). A new and expanded version including aircraft evaluated by the Allies, is in preparation for Midland Counties Publications. Photographs and information (however small) will be welcomed via the publishers.